£33·99

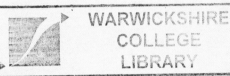
Business
Accounting
and Finance

Business Accounting *and* Finance

Tony Davies

Brian Pain

McGraw-Hill Publishing Company

London · Burr Ridge IL · New York · St Louis · San Francisco · Auckland · Bogotá · Caracas · Lisbon · Madrid · Mexico
Milan · Montreal · New Delhi · Panama · Paris · San Juan · São Paulo · Singapore · Sydney · Tokyo · Toronto

Published by
McGraw-Hill Education Europe
Shoppenhangers Road, Maidenhead, Berkshire, SL6 2QL, England
Website: www.mcgraw-hill.co.uk

Editorial Director	Melissa Rosati
Acquisitions Editor	Andy Goss
Editorial Assistant	Nicola Wimpory
Senior Production Manager	Max Elvey
Senior Marketing Manager	Petra Skytte
New Media Designer/Developer	Doug Greenwood

British Library Cataloguing in Publication Data
A catalogue record for this book is available from the British Library

Library of Congress Cataloguing in Publication Data
The Library of Congress data for this book has been applied for at the Library of Congress

McGraw-Hill

A Division of The McGraw·Hill Companies

Produced for McGraw-Hill by the independent production company Steven Gardiner Ltd
Printed and bound by Mateu Cromo, Madrid
Cover design by Hybert Design

ISBN: 0-07-709825-0

Brief contents

Detailed contents

Preface

Accounting and finance are of critical importance in the support of all business activities. The formal study of accounting and finance is exciting because it introduces a toolkit that allows a better understanding of the performance of businesses, and the decisions and problems they face. These issues are discussed daily by managers and in the media. This new textbook provides you with the toolkit and shows you how to apply it in practice, utilising a comprehensive range of learning features, illustrative examples and assessment material to support and reinforce your study.

This textbook is aimed primarily at students who are not majoring in accounting or finance, but who are undertaking an introductory-level module as part of their degree or diploma course in business management, economics or any other subject. As such, our main objective was to produce a tightly-written, clear and engaging text which distils the core principles of accounting and finance for those students who do not have the luxury of devoting all their time to its study, and so eliminating the need to purchase two or more separate books.

Content and structure

The content and structure of the text have been carefully researched to follow closely the typical requirements of introductory undergraduate and MBA modules. This text assumes no prior knowledge of the subject: we start at square one and take you step-by-step through the concepts and application of techniques, with clear explanations and numerous examples.

The text comprises 15 chapters, and is structured into three parts, these being the main areas of accounting and finance:

- **financial accounting** which is broadly concerned with the recording and analysis of historical financial data, the presentation of information on financial performance, and compliance with legislation, and accounting rules and standards
- **management accounting** which is mainly involved in looking ahead, and includes the roles of costing and pricing of products and services, and support of the planning, control, and decision-making functions
- **business finance** (or financial management) which includes capital investment decision-making, the ways in which a business may be financed, and the management of the assets that the organisation has at its disposal

Each of these areas and their component chapters are outlined in the introductory section to each part of the text.

A further key objective in writing this text was to provide a flexible study resource. There is a linkage between each of the chapters, which follow a structure that has been designed to facilitate effective learning of the subject in a progressive way. However, each chapter may also be used on a stand-alone basis; equally, chapters may be excluded from study if they relate to subjects that are not essential for a specific course. Likewise, basic bookkeeping is a topic that may or may not be a requirement of some modules and so it has been placed in an appendix towards the end of the text. Therefore, the text is intended to be suitable for modules of either one or two semesters' duration.

Just as the principles and practice of genetics or information technology are steadily progressing, so accounting and finance continue to develop, sometimes in exciting ways.

Some of the chapters introduce topics typically not covered in some more traditional and technical introductory accounting texts, including some contemporary issues and areas of growing importance such as corporate governance and activity based costing.

Given that this text has been written primarily for non-specialist students, each chapter aims to help students understand the broader context and relevance of accounting and finance in the business environment, and how accounting statements and financial information can be used to improve the quality of management decision-making. We have therefore provided numerous examples and commentary on company activity within each chapter, including at least one cutting from the press; companies featured include Lastminute.com, Nissan, The Millennium Experience Company, Corus, Marks & Spencer, Thorntons, MG Rover, Sportingbet.com and Iceland. In addition, two of the chapters feature extracts and analysis of the actual Report and Accounts 2000 of Johnson Matthey plc.

Using this book

To support your study and reinforce the topics covered, we have included a comprehensive range of learning features and assessment material in each chapter, including:

- learning objectives
- introduction
- highlighted key terms
- fully-worked examples
- integrated progress checks

- key points summary
- glossary of key terms
- questions
- discussion points
- exercises

Within each chapter we have also included numerous diagrams and charts that illustrate and reinforce important concepts and ideas. The double-page Guided tour that follows on pages xiv–xv summarises the purpose of these learning features and the chapter-end assessment material. To gain maximum benefit from this text and to help you succeed in your study and exams, you are encouraged to familiarise yourself with these elements now, before you start the first chapter.

It is easy, but mistaken, to read on cruise control, highlighting the odd sentence and gliding through the worked examples, progress checks and chapter-end questions and exercises. Active learning needs to be interactive: if you haven't followed a topic or an example, go back and work through it again; try to think of other examples to which particular topics may be applied. The only way to check you have a comprehensive understanding of things is to attempt all the integrated progress checks and worked examples, and the chapter-end assessment material, and then to compare with the text and answers provided. Fully-worked solutions are given immediately after each example, and solutions to 45% of the chapter-end exercises (those with their numbers in colour) are provided in Appendix 4. Additional self-assessment material is available in the student centre of the book's accompanying website (see page xiii).

Case studies

Each of the three main parts of the book concludes with a case study that may be tackled either individually or as a team. The case studies are a little more weighty than the chapter-end exercises; in addition, they integrate many of the topics included in the chapters in each part of the text to which they relate, although not exclusively. Each case study therefore gives you an opportunity to apply the knowledge and techniques gained from each part, and to develop these together with the analytical skills and judgement required to deal with real-life business problems. Additional cases are provided on the accompanying website.

We hope this textbook will enhance your interest, understanding and skills. Above all, relax, learn and enjoy!

Website

www.mcgraw-hill.co.uk/textbooks/davies

The website accompanying this text includes an extensive range of chapter-based student and lecturer resources, and comprises three main sections:

Information centre

- Textbook contents
- Preface
- Guided tour
- Sample chapter
- About the authors
- Author interview
- What the reviewers say

Student centre

- Additional chapter-based exercises
- Solutions to all the additional chapter-based exercises
- Additional part-based case studies
- Self-testing multiple-choice questions (by chapter) with automatic grading
- Revision notes (by chapter)
- Glossary of key terms
- The press room
- Annotated weblinks

Lecturer centre

- Solutions to all chapter-end exercises
- Debriefings to all the part-end case studies
- Additional chapter-based exercises
- Solutions to all the additional chapter-based exercises
- Additional part-based case studies
- Debriefings to all the additional part-based case studies
- PowerPoint lecture slides
- Textbook figures
- PageOut

Remember to check the website frequently throughout your studies, as these resources will be regularly updated.

Guided tour

Learning objectives
Listed at the start of each chapter, these bullet points identify the core learning outcomes you should have acquired after completing each chapter.

Introduction
This section gives you a brief overview of the coverage and purpose of each chapter, and how it links to the previous chapter.

Press cuttings
Included in every chapter, these topical extracts feature real company examples from the press, including commentary that highlights the practical application of accounting and finance in the business environment.

Key terms
These are colour highlighted the first time they are introduced, alerting you to the core concepts and techniques in each chapter. A full explanation is contained in the glossary of key terms section at the end of each chapter.

Examples
The numerous worked examples in each chapter provide an application of the learning points and techniques included within each topic. By following and working through the step-by-step solutions, you have an opportunity to check your knowledge at frequent intervals.

Progress checks
Each topic within each chapter includes one or more of these short questions that enable you to check and apply your understanding of the preceding key topics before you progress to the next one in the chapter.

Summary of key points

Following the final section in each chapter there is a comprehensive summary of the key points in terms of the learning outcomes listed at the start of each chapter. These allow you to check that you understand all the main points covered before moving on to the next chapter.

Glossary of key terms

At the end of each chapter a glossary of key terms in alphabetical order provides full definitions of all main terms that have been introduced throughout each chapter. The numbers of the pages on which key term definitions appear are colour-highlighted in the index.

Exercises

These comprehensive examination-style questions are graded by their level of difficulty, and also indicate the time typically required to complete them. They are designed to assess your knowledge and application of the principles and techniques covered in each chapter. There are typically 6 to 8 exercises at the end of each chapter. Full solutions to the colour-highlighted exercise numbers are provided in Appendix 4 to allow you to self-assess your progress.

Questions

These are short narrative type questions that encourage you to review and check your understanding of all the key topics. There are typically 7 to 10 of these questions at the end of each chapter.

Discussion points

This section typically includes 2 to 4 thought-provoking ideas and questions that encourage you to critically apply your understanding and/or further develop some of the topics introduced in each chapter, either individually or in team discussion.

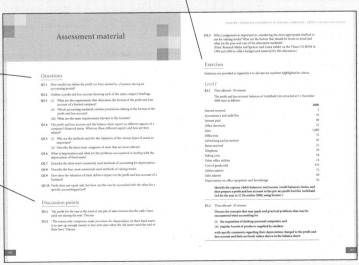

Acknowledgements

Thank you to the following lecturers who were involved in either the initial market research and/or in providing useful review comments and technical checks of the draft chapters during the development phase of this project:

- Graham Ball, Nottingham Trent University
- Zeljko Seviç, Greenwich University
- Cedric McCallum, Abertay University
- Steward Hughes, Coventry University
- Jenny Maynard, Coventry University
- Steve Dungworth, De Montfort University
- Brian Telford, University of Hertfordshire
- Graham Diggle, Oxford Brookes University
- Rona O'Brien, Sheffield Hallam University
- Tariq Bashir, University of East London
- Richard Pike, University of Bradford
- Gary Owen, Greenwich University
- Mark Richer, Wolverhampton University
- Chris Knight, Nottingham Trent University
- Robert Devlin, University of Ulster
- Jon Simon, University of Humberside
- Bruce Bowhill, Portsmouth University
- Chris Simpson, University of Derby
- Mary Canny, Luton University
- Graeme Reid, Hull University
- Pauline Willis, Dublin City University
- Carolyn Isaaks, Nottingham Trent University

Thank you to CIMA (the Chartered Institute of Management Accountants) for their permission to include extracts from their Management Accounting Official Terminology 2000 edition.

Thank you to Johnson Matthey plc for permission to use extracts of their Report and Accounts 2000 as an excellent example of the information provided to shareholders by a major UK plc, and to *Accountancy Age*, the *Daily Telegraph* and *The Times* for their permission to use extracts from their publications.

Thank you to Andy Goss for his support and encouragement in the writing of this book and the development of the website.

1

Underlying principles – the building blocks

LEARNING OBJECTIVES

Completion of this chapter will enable you to:

- outline the uses and purpose of accounting and the practice of accountancy

- explain what is meant by financial accounting, management accounting, and financial management

- identify the wide range of users of financial information

- illustrate the different types of business entity: sole traders, partnerships, private limited companies, public limited companies

- outline the main accounting concepts and accounting standards

- outline accounting processes and systems

- explain the nature and purpose of financial statements

- consider the issues of accountability and financial reporting

Introduction

This chapter explains why accounting and finance are such key elements of business life. Both for aspiring accountants, and those of you who may not continue to study accounting and finance beyond the introductory level, the fundamental principles of accounting and the ways in which accounting is regulated to protect owners of businesses, and the public in general, are important topics. A broad appreciation will be useful not only in dealing with the subsequent text, but also in the context of the day-to-day management of a business.

This chapter will look at why accounting is needed and how it is used. Accounting and finance are wide subjects which often mean many things to many people. They are broadly concerned with the organisation and management of financial resources. Accounting and accountancy are two terms which are sometimes used to mean the same thing, although they more correctly relate separately to the subject and the profession.

Accounting and accountancy are generally concerned with measuring and communicating the financial information provided from accounting systems, and the reporting of financial results to shareholders, lenders, creditors, employees and Government. The owners or shareholders of the wide range of business entities which use accounting may be assumed to have the primary objective of maximisation of the wealth of their business. Directors of the business manage the resources of the business to meet shareholders' objectives.

The framework of accounting operates through basic accounting rules. This chapter will examine these rules embodied in what are termed accounting standards and accounting concepts. We will consider the processes used in accounting and look at an overview of the financial statements used in financial reporting.

We will provide an introduction to the way in which financial reporting is used to keep shareholders informed. The timely and accurate disclosure of truthful information is a fundamental requirement in the preparation of appropriate statements of the financial performance and financial position of the entity. Directors and managers are responsible for running the business and their accountability to shareholders is maintained through their regular reporting on the activities of the business.

Uses and purpose of accounting

The original, basic purposes of **accounting** were to classify and record monetary transactions (see Appendix 1) and present the financial results of the activities of an entity, the scorecard that shows how the business is doing. The accounting profession has evolved and accounting techniques developed for use in a much broader business context. To look at the current nature of accounting and the broad purposes of accounting systems we need to consider the three questions these days generally answered by accounting information:

- how are we doing, and are we doing well or badly?   a scorecard (like scoring a game of cricket, for example)
- which problems should be looked at?   attention-directing
- which is the best alternative for doing a job?   problem solving.

Although accountants and the accounting profession have retained their fundamental roles they have grown into various branches of the profession which have developed their own specialisms and responsibilities.

Accounting is a part of the information system within an organisation (see Appendix 1, which explains double-entry **bookkeeping**, and how data is identified, recorded and presented as information in the ways required by the users of financial information). Accounting also exists as a service function which ensures that the financial information that is presented meets the needs of the users of financial information. To achieve this, accountants must not only ensure that information is accurate, reliable and timely but also that it is relevant for the purpose for which it is being provided, consistent for comparability, and easily understood (see Fig. 1.1).

In order to be useful to the users of financial information, the accounting data from which it is prepared, together with its analysis and presentation must be:

- accurate – free from error of content or principle
- reliable – representing the information that users believe it represents
- timely – available in time to support decision-making
- relevant – applicable to the purpose required, for example a decision regarding a future event or to support an explanation of what has already happened

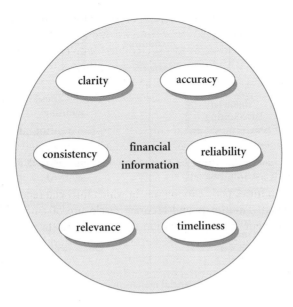

FIGURE 1.1   Features of useful financial information

- consistent – the same methods and standards of measurement of data and presentation of information to allow like-for-like comparison
- clear – capable of being understood by those for whom the information has been prepared.

The provision of a great deal of information, as we shall see as we progress through this book, is mandatory; it is needed to comply with, for example, the requirements of Acts of Parliament, the Inland Revenue, and HM Customs and Excise. However, there is a cost of providing information that has all the features that have been described, which therefore renders it potentially useful information. The benefits from producing information, in addition to mandatory information, should therefore be considered and compared with the cost of producing that information to decide on which information is 'really' required.

Accountants may be employed within accountancy firms, where they may specialise in audit, corporate taxation, personal taxation, VAT, or consultancy (see Fig. 1.2). Accountants may also be employed in commercial and industrial organisations, public services, and not-for-profit organisations, in accounting, financial management and general management. The responsibilities of accountants employed within business and public service organisations tend to be split between the main functions of financial accounting, and management accounting. Responsibilities may also include financial management, treasury management, and corporate finance.

Financial accounting, management accounting, and financial management

Financial accounting

Financial accounting is primarily concerned with the first question raised in the previous section. Taking a car-driving analogy, financial accounting makes greater use of the

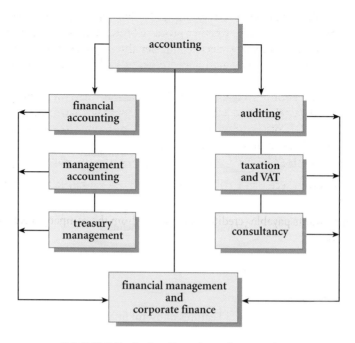

FIGURE 1.2   Branches of accounting

rear-view mirror than the windscreen; financial accounting is primarily concerned with historical information.

Financial accounting is the function responsible in general for the reporting of financial information to the owners of a business, and specifically for preparation of the periodic external reporting of financial information, statutorily required, for shareholders. It also provides similar information as required for Government and other interested third parties, such as potential investors, employees, lenders, suppliers, customers, and financial analysts. Financial accounting is concerned with the three key financial statements: the balance sheet; profit and loss account; cash flow statement. It assists in ensuring that financial statements are included in published reports and accounts in a way that provides ease of analysis and interpretation of company performance.

The role of financial accounting is therefore concerned with maintaining the scorecard for the entity. Financial accounting is concerned with the classification and recording of the monetary transactions of an entity in accordance with established concepts, principles, accounting standards and legal requirements and their presentation, by means of profit and loss accounts, balance sheets and cash flow statements, during and at the end of an accounting period.

Within most companies, the financial accounting role usually involves much more than the preparation of the three main financial statements. A great deal of analysis is required to support such statements and to prepare information both for internal management and towards the annual audit by the company's external auditors. This includes preparation of sales analyses, bank reconciliations, analysis of expenditure, and cash flow.

A typical finance department has the following additional functions within the financial accounting role: control of accounts payable to suppliers (the purchase ledger); control of accounts receivable from customers (the sales ledger), and credit control; control of cash (and possible wider treasury functions) including cash payments, cash receipts, managers' expenses, petty cash, and banking relationships. The financial accounting role also usually includes responsibility for payroll, whether processed internally or by an external agency. However, a number of companies elect to transfer the responsibility for payroll to the personnel, or human resources department, bringing with it the possibility of loss of internal control.

The breadth of functions involved in financial accounting can require the processing of high volumes of data relating to purchase invoices, supplier payments, sales invoices, receipts from customers, other cash transactions, petty cash, employee expense claims, and payroll data. Control and monitoring of these functions therefore additionally requires a large number of reports generated by the accounting systems, for example:

- analysis of accounts receivable (debtors): those who owe money to the company – by age of debt
- analysis of accounts payable (creditors): those to whom the company owes money – by age of invoice
- sales analyses
- cheque payments
- records of fixed assets
- invoice lists.

Management accounting

Past performance is never a totally reliable basis for predicting the future. However, the vast amount of data required for the preparation of financial statements, and maintenance of the further subsidiary accounting functions, provides a fertile database for use in another branch of accounting, namely management accounting.

Management accounting is primarily concerned with the provision of information to managers within the organisation for product costing, planning and control, and decision-making, and is to a lesser extent involved in providing information for external reporting.

The functions of management accounting are wide and varied. As we shall discover in Part II, whereas financial accounting is primarily concerned with past performance, management accounting aims to focus almost entirely on the future. Management accounting is involved with the scorecard role of accounting, but in addition is particularly concerned with the other two areas of accounting, namely problem solving and attention directing. These include cost analysis, decision-making, sales pricing, forecasting and budgeting, all of which will be discussed later in this book.

Financial management

Financial management has its roots in accounting, although it may also be regarded as a branch of applied economics. It is broadly defined as the management of all the processes associated with the efficient acquisition and deployment of both short- and long-term financial resources. Financial management assists an organisation's operations manage-ment to reach its financial objectives. This may include for example, responsibility for corporate finance and treasury management, which is concerned with cash management, and the management of interest rate and foreign currency exchange rate risk.

The management of an organisation generally involves the three overlapping and inter-linking roles of strategic management, risk management, and operations management. Financial management supports these roles to enable management to achieve the financial objectives of the shareholders. Financial management assists in the reporting of financial results to the users of financial information, for example shareholders, lenders, and employees.

The responsibility of the finance department for financial management includes the setting up and running of reporting and control systems, raising and managing funds, the management of relationships with financial institutions, and the use of information and analysis to advise management regarding planning, policy and capital investment. The overriding requirement of financial management is to ensure that the financial objectives of the company are in line with the interests of the shareholders; the underlying fundamental objective of a company is to maximise shareholder wealth.

Financial management, therefore, has its roots in accounting and treasury management. This book will identify the relevant areas within these subjects, which will be covered as deeply as considered necessary to provide a good introduction to financial management.

As management accounting continues to develop its emphasis on decision-making and strategic management, and broaden the range of activities that it supports, the distinction between management accounting and financial management is slowly disappearing.

Example 1.1

A friend of yours is thinking about pursuing a career in accountancy and would like your views on the major differences between financial accounting, management accounting and financial management.

Answer

Financial accounting   The financial accounting function deals with the recording of past and current transactions, usually with the aid of computerised accounting systems. Of the various reports prepared, the majority are for external users, and include the profit and loss account, balance sheet, and the cash flow statement. In a plc, such reports must be prepared at least every six months, and must comply with current legal and reporting requirements.

Management accounting   The management accounting function works alongside the financial accounting function, using a number of the day-to-day outputs from the accounting system, for example the trial balance, to produce many of the routine reports. Management accounting is concerned largely with looking at the future, for example the consideration of 'what if' scenarios during the course of preparation of forecasts and budgets. Management accounting outputs are mainly for internal users, with much confidential reporting, for example to the directors of the company.

Financial management   Financial management may include responsibilities for corporate finance and the treasury function. This includes the management and control of corporate funds, within parameters specified by the board of directors. The role often includes the management of company borrowings, investment of surplus funds, the management of both interest rate and exchange rate risk, and giving advice on economic and market changes and the exploitation of opportunities. The financial management function is not necessarily staffed by accountants. Plcs report on the treasury activities of the company in their periodic reporting and financial review.

The following article which appeared in *Accountancy Age* illustrates some of the important applications of accounting and financial management. These include

- the planning activities, particularly with regard to restructuring of the business
- negotiations with bankers.

Blair talks offer little hope for Corus
By Larry Schlesinger

Talks between prime minister Tony Blair and Welsh Assembly first minister Rhodri Morgan look unlikely to stop Britain's biggest steel maker from closing its Llanwern plant and cutting thousands of jobs.

Morgan was by joined by Welsh secretary Paul Murphy and trade secretary Stephen Byers at 10 Downing Street, where talks continued with Blair on a possible rescue plan to save the Corus' Welsh steel carbon plant.

The closure would force 3,000 workers out of their jobs and would form part of large-scale restructuring plans at Corus to cut massive losses in its steel carbon division.

But reports in today's press suggest Corus is already in advanced talks with its bankers, ABN Amro and Dresdner Bank, to renegotiate its Pounds 1.7bn debt. The move could make funds available to the steel manufacturer to pay off 7,000 workers at its British operations.

Corus' merger with Dutch steelmaker Hoogovens created a complex debt structure and renegotiating its debt would increase its financial flexibility.

In addition, a Corus spokesperson told *AccountancyAge.com*: 'We are currently reviewing all our operations in the UK, and closures and job reductions are still likely to take place'.

The steel industry has plunged into crisis due to a shrinking UK carbon steel manufacturing industry, the euro/sterling exchange rate and the increasing number of imported steel products.

As a result Corus recorded a loss of Pounds 226m in its steel carbon division for the first six months of 2000, despite its stainless steel and aluminium operations making healthy profits. For the nine months to 1 July 2000, the Group made a combined operating loss of Pounds 96m.

Last week, *AccountancyAge.com* reported that the proposed climate change levy would further cripple the competitiveness of the UK's steel industry, with Corus having to pay the lion's share of an annual Pounds 10m tax.

In addition it would have to fund a Pounds 40m upgrade of its operations to meet DTI environmental requirements. Over the next five years, environmental upgrades and taxes could cost Corus as much as Pounds 80m.

Since then, things have gone from bad to worse for the beleaguered conglomerate as unions prepare to mobilise support for a strike and the government demands Corus pay a £800m for an environmental clean-up.

A report in this weekend's *Sunday Business* said the Iron & Steel Trades Confederation, which represents most of the workers at Llanwern and Redcar, a plant on Teeside, was planning a mass meeting this week to discuss strike action at a number of plants. Redcar has been earmarked for large-scale job cuts.

An announcement on restructuring plans is expected by Corus Group chairman Sir Brian Moffat in the next few weeks with analysts remaining divided at the prospects for Corus after its restructuring.

Source: *AccountancyAge.com*, 23 January 2001

- evaluation of the impacts of regulatory changes, for example the climate change levy
- union demands
- costs of compliance with environmental requirements.

Following public criticism and union reaction, in February 2001 the stock market gave a 'thumbs up' to the announcement by Corus of its extensive job and plant cut-back package and balance sheet clean-up. A total of 11,000 redundancies (5,000 from the year 2000, and 6,000 from the 2001 plans) was costing Corus £220m; the plant closures and clean-up costs were going to total around a further £700m.

Progress check 1.1

What are the main differences between financial accounting, management accounting, and financial management?

Accounting and accountancy

A large number of accounting concepts and terms are used throughout this book, the definitions of which may be found in the glossary of key terms at the end of each chapter (or appendix) in which they are first used.

The term 'accounting' may be defined as:

● the classification and recording of monetary transactions

● the presentation and interpretation of the results of those transactions in order to assess performance over a period and the financial position at a given date

● the monetary projection of future activities arising from alternative planned courses of action.

 Accountancy is defined as the practice of accounting. A **qualified accountant** is a member of the accountancy profession, and in the UK is a member of one of the six professional accountancy bodies (see Fig. 1.3). An accountant becomes qualified within each of these institutes through passing a very large number of extremely technically-demanding examinations and completion of a mandatory period of three years' practical training. The examination syllabus of each of the professional bodies tends to be very similar; each body provides additional emphasis on specific areas of accounting.

Chartered management accountants (CIMA) receive their practical training in industrial and commercial environments, and in the public sector, for example the NHS. They are involved in practical accounting work and development of broader experience of strategic and operational management of the business. Certified accountants (ACCA) and

FIGURE 1.3   The professional accounting bodies

chartered accountants (ICAEW, ICAS, ICAI) usually receive training while working in a practising accountant's office which offers services to businesses and the general public, but may also receive training while employed in industrial and commercial organisations. Training focuses initially on auditing, and may then develop to include taxation and general business advice. Many accountants who receive training while specialising in central and local government usually, but not exclusively, qualify for the CIPFA qualification.

A few secondary bodies like AAT provide bookkeeping and accounting training through examination and experience to a high level of competence, but short of that required to become a qualified accountant. In addition, treasury management is served by the Association of Corporate Treasurers (ACT). This qualification has tended to be a second qualification for accountants specialising in corporate funding, cash and working capital management, interest rate and foreign currency exchange rate risk management. In the same way, the Institute of Taxation serves accountants who are tax specialists.

Progress check 1.2

What services does accounting offer and why do businesses need these services?

Example 1.2

Young Gordon Brown decided that he would like to start to train to become an accountant after he finished his degree. Gordon had a vague idea that there are differences between financial accounting and management accounting, and treasury management. He also heard that some accountants are auditors whilst others are employed in the industrial and commercial sectors, and yet others employed in local government. Gordon was not really sure about the direction he would like to follow and so decided to try and put together a list of each of the types of professional accounting bodies and link them with the sort of accounting he may become involved in.

How do you think Gordon's list might have looked?

Answer

Gordon's list may have looked something like:

Chartered Institute of Management Accountants (CIMA)   management accounting and financial accounting roles with a focus on management accounting in the industrial and commercial sectors, and strategic and operational management

Institutes of Chartered Accountants (ICAEW, ICAS, ICAI)   employment within a firm of accountants, carrying out auditing, investigations, taxation and general business advice – possible opportunities to move into an accounting role in industry

Chartered Institute of Public Finance and Accountancy (CIPFA)   accounting role within central government or local government

Association of Chartered Certified Accountants (ACCA)   employment either within a firm of accountants, carrying out auditing etc., or management accounting and financial accounting roles within commerce/industry

Association of Corporate Treasurers (ACT)   commercial accounting roles with almost total emphasis on treasury issues: corporate finance; funding; cash management; working capital management; financial risk management

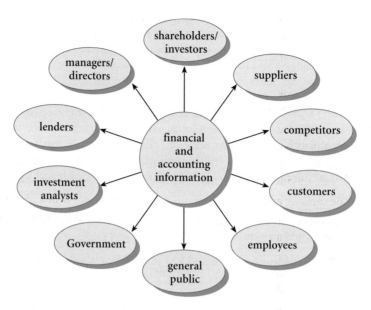

FIGURE 1.4   Users of financial and accounting information

Users of financial information

Financial information is important to a wide range of groups both internal and external to the organisation. Such information is required, for example, by individuals outside the organisation to make decisions about whether or not to invest in one company or another, or by potential suppliers who wish to assess the reliability and financial strength of the organisation. It is also required by managers within the organisation as an aid to decision-making. The main users of financial information are shown in Fig. 1.4.

Progress check 1.3

How many users of financial information can you think of and in what ways do you think they may use this information?

Example 1.3

Kevin Green, a trainee accountant, has recently joined the finance department of a newly formed public limited company. Kevin has been asked to work with the company's auditors who have been commissioned to prepare some alternative formats for the company's annual report.

As part of his preparation for this, Kevin's manager has asked him to prepare a draft report about who is likely to use the information contained in the Annual Report, and how they might use such information.

Answer

Kevin's draft report may include the following:

Competitors   as part of their industry competitive analysis studies to look at market share, and financial strength

Customers to determine the ability to provide regular, reliable supply of goods and services, and to assess customer dependence

Employees to assess the potential for providing continued employment and assess levels of remuneration

General public to assess general employment opportunities, social, political and environmental issues, and to consider potential for investment

Government VAT and corporate taxation, Government statistics, grants and financial assistance, monopolies and mergers

Investment analysts investment potential for individuals and institutions with regard to past and future performance, strength of management, risk versus reward

Lenders the capacity and the ability of the company to service debt and repay capital

Managers/directors to a certain extent an aid to decision-making, but such relevant information should already have been available internally

Shareholders/investors a tool of accountability to maintain a check on how effectively the directors/managers are running the business, to assess the financial strength and future developments

Suppliers to assess the long-term viability and whether the company is able to meet its obligations and pay suppliers on an ongoing basis.

Types of business entity

Business entities are either involved in manufacturing (for example, food and automotive components) or in providing services (for example retailing, hospitals or television broadcasting). Such entities include profit-making and not-for-profit organisations, and charities. The main types of entity, and the environments in which they operate, represented in Fig. 1.5 are explained in the sections that follow.

The variety of business entities can be seen to range from quangos (quasi-autonomous non-government organisations) to partnerships to limited companies. Most of the topics covered in this book apply to any type of business organisation: limited liability companies, both private (Ltd) companies and public (plc) limited companies, sole traders, and partnerships.

Progress check 1.4

What are the different types of business entity? Can you think of some examples of each?

Sole traders and partnerships

A sole trader entity is owned and financed by one individual even though more than one person may work in the business. The individual has complete flexibility regarding:

● the type of (legal) activities in which the business may be engaged
● when to start up or cease the business
● the way in which business is conducted.

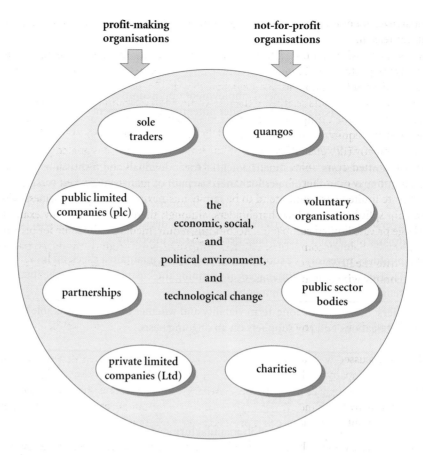

FIGURE 1.5 Types of business entity

Unlike limited companies, sole traders are not required to file a formal report and accounts each year with the **Registrar of Companies**, but they must submit annual accounts for tax purposes to the Inland Revenue. Legally, a sole trader is not separate from the business, unlike the legal position of owners, or shareholders, of limited and unlimited companies who are recognised as separate legal entities from the businesses they own.

Partnerships are similar to sole traders except that the ownership of the business is in the hands of two or more persons. The main differences are in respect of how much each of the partners puts into the business, who is responsible for what, and how the profits are to be shared. These factors are normally set out in formal partnership agreements, and if the partnership agreement is not specific then the provisions of the Partnership Act 1890 apply. Apart from certain professions, the number of persons in a partnership is limited to 20.

Limited companies

A limited company is a legal entity separate from the owners of the business. The owners limit their obligations to the amount of finance they have put into the company by way of the share of the company they have paid for. Normally, the maximum that may be claimed from shareholders is no more than they have paid for their shares, regardless of what happens to the company. Equally, there is no certainty that shareholders may recover their original investment if they wish to dispose of their shares or if the business is wound up, for whatever reason.

A company with unlimited liability does not give the owners, or members, of the company the protection of limited liability. If the business were to fail, the members would be liable, without limitation, for all the debts of the business.

The legal requirements relating to the registration and operation of limited companies is contained within the Companies Act 1985 as amended by the Companies Act 1989. Limited companies are required to be registered with the Registrar of Companies as either a private limited company (designated Ltd) or a public limited company (designated plc).

Public limited companies must have a minimum issued share capital of (currently) £50,000, and may offer their shares for sale to the public, but private limited companies may not. Private limited companies tend to be family businesses and smaller business with the ownership split between a few shareholders, although there have been many examples of very large private limited companies. Accounting requirements are the same for private and public limited liability companies. Limited companies must produce annual accounts that are filed with the Registrar of Companies and are available to the public. Sole traders do not have to comply with any such requirement.

Example 1.4

Ike Andoowit is in the process of planning the setting up of a new residential training centre.

Ike has discussed with a number of his friends the question of registering the business as a limited company, or being a sole trader. Most of Ike's friends have highlighted the advantages of limiting his liability to the original share capital that he would need to put into the company to finance the business. Ike feels a bit uneasy about the whole question and decides to obtain the advice of a professional accountant.

(i)   What advice do you think Ike would have received regarding the main disadvantages of setting up a limited company as opposed to a sole trader?

(ii) Are Ike's friends correct about the advantage of limiting one's liability?

(iii) What other advantages are there?

Answer

Setting up as a sole trader is a lot simpler and easier than setting up a limited company. A limited company is bound by the provisions of the Companies Act 1985 as amended by the Companies Act 1989, and for example, if its annual sales exceed £350,000, has to hold an annual general meeting and is required to have an independent annual audit. A limited company is required to be much more open about its affairs.

The financial structure of a limited company is more complicated than that of a sole trader. There are also additional costs involved in the setting up and administration of a limited company.

Running a business as a limited company lacks flexibility, for example in choosing a business name and the requirement to register the business with the Registrar of Companies.

As Ike's friends have pointed out, the financial obligations of a shareholder in a limited company are generally restricted to the amount he/she has paid for his/her shares. Any finance provided by a bank is likely to require a personal guarantee. In addition, the number of shareholders is potentially unlimited which widens the scope for raising additional capital.

Progress check 1.5

> There are some differences between those businesses that have been established as sole traders and those established as partnerships, and likewise there are differences between private limited companies and public limited companies. What are these differences?

The framework of accounting

Financial accounting, management accounting, corporate finance, treasury management, and financial management all operate within a framework of accounting. This framework is constantly changing and evolving as new problems are encountered, as new practices and techniques are developed, and the objectives of users of financial information are modified and revised.

Many countries have sought to produce a 'conceptual framework'. In the UK this has been titled a Statement of Principles (SOP). The key issues are:

- the definition of a conceptual framework
- the development of a conceptual framework.

The 1975 Corporate Report was the first UK attempt at a conceptual framework. The SOP is a basic structure for determining objectives, in which there is a thread from the theory to the practical application of accounting standards to transactions that are reported in published accounts. The SOP is not an accounting standard, but it is a statement of guidelines; it is, by virtue of the subject, constantly in need of revision.

 The term **true and fair view** was introduced in the Companies Act 1947. It was not defined in that Act and has not been defined since. Some writers have suggested that conceptually it is a dynamic concept but over the years it could be argued that it has failed, and various business scandals and collapses occurred without users being alerted. The concept of true and fair was adopted by the European Community Council in its fourth directive, implemented by the UK in the Companies Act 1981, and subsequently in the implementation of the seventh directive in the 1989 Act (section 226 or 227). Conceptually the directives require additional information where individual provisions are insufficient.

It may be interesting to research the issue of derivatives and decide whether the true and fair view concept was invoked by those companies that used or marketed these financial instruments, and specifically consider the various collapses or public statements regarding losses incurred over the last few years. Before derivatives, the issue which escaped disclosure under true and fair view was leasing.

The framework revolves around accounting and the accountancy profession, which is bounded by rules, or concepts (see Fig. 1.6, in which the five most important concepts are shown shaded) of what data should be included within an accounting system and how that data should be recorded.

We have looked generally at how the finance function is organised within a business. A number of guidelines, or standards, have been developed by the accountancy profession to ensure truth, fairness, and consistency in the preparation and presentation of financial information. Accounting processes are concerned with how data is measured and recorded and how the accounting function ensures the effective operation of accounting and financial systems.

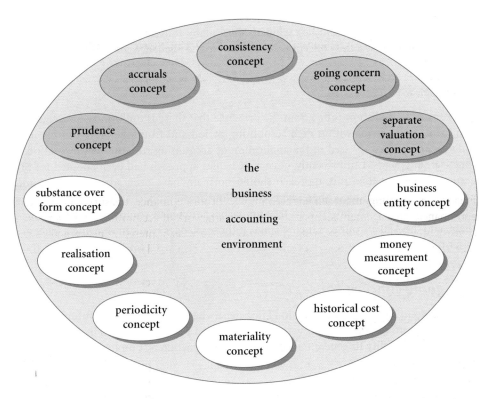

FIGURE 1.6 Accounting concepts

Accounting concepts

Accounting concepts are the principles underpinning the preparation of accounting information. Fundamental accounting concepts are the broad basic assumptions, which underlie the periodic financial accounts of business enterprises. The five most important concepts are as follows:

The prudence concept

The **prudence concept** is based on the principle that revenue and profits are not anticipated, but are included in the profit and loss account only when realised in the form either of cash or of other assets, the ultimate cash realisation of which can be assessed with reasonable certainty; provision is made for all known liabilities and expenses, whether the amount of these is known with certainty or is a best estimate in the light of information available, and for losses arising from specific commitments, rather than just guesses.

The accruals concept

The **accruals concept** (or the matching concept) is based on the principle that revenue and costs are recognised as they are earned or incurred, are matched with one another, and are dealt with in the profit and loss account of the period to which they relate, irrespective of the period of receipt or payment. It would be misleading to report profit as the difference between cash received and cash paid during a period because some trading and commercial activities of the period would be excluded, since many transactions are based on credit. Where a conflict arises, this concept is subservient to the prudence concept.

The consistency concept

 The **consistency concept** is based on the principle that there is uniformity of accounting treatment of like items within each accounting period and from one period to the next. Judgement may be exercised in the application of accounting rules to the preparation of financial statements. Until recently, once a particular approach had been adopted for one accounting period then this approach should normally have been adopted in all future accounting periods, unless there were compelling reasons to change. The **Accounting Standards Board (ASB)** now prefers the approaches adopted by companies to be revised by them, and the ASB encourages their change, if those changes result in showing a truer and fairer picture.

The going concern concept

The drug-testing company Huntingdon Life Sciences has faced threats to its future existence from the actions of animal rights activists. This has led to a re-evaluation by its bankers of the company's ability to generate income in order to pay interest on loans and ultimately repay those loans.

Judgment day for animal testing firm
By Benjamin Wootliff

Huntingdon Life Sciences, the drug testing company targeted by animal rights protesters, will find out today if it has secured a last-minute cash injection to save it from bankruptcy.

HLS has until midnight to secure new financing, or the Royal Bank of Scotland may pull the company's £22.6 million overdraft. Brian Cass, chief executive, said: 'I am confident we will sort out financing. We're in talks with several parties, some of which are North American, about new funds'.

However, the group leading the campaign against HLS, Stop Huntingdon Animal Cruelty, said it would extend its fight to new supporters. Greg Avery, a spokesman for Shac, said: 'They will be ruthlessly pursued – we will financially destroy them'. One potential source of financing is a loan from FHP Realty, a private American property company owned by the HLS chairman Andrew Baker.

Mr Baker made his fortune in the Eighties from his investment in laboratories in California. Mr Cass said the new financing was more likely to involve loans backed by property than the sale of new shares. HLS shares rose 5.25p to 10p after the company said it was still in talks to secure new financing, but later slipped back to close just 1.5p up at 6.25p.

Earlier this week, the shares fell to 1p on fears that Royal Bank of Scotland would force the company into bankruptcy. The bank said that it could not comment on HLS without breaching customer confidentiality. Its branches have received bomb threats as part of the campaign against HLS.

HLS has been the target of animal rights campaigners for several years, but its problems increased after a 1997 Channel 4 documentary showed lab technicians abusing the animals outside the regular experiments. Mr Cass – who joined the company 18 months after the documentary – said: 'After the Channel 4 programme Huntingdon's business went south, with about a third of our clients leaving as they didn't want to be associated with us'.

The business had been slow to recover, with HLS losing money for four out of the past five years.

© *Daily Telegraph*, 19 January 2001

Animal protesters continued to try to put the company out of business through 2001. Together with its largest shareholder, Stephens Group, in April 2001 Huntingdon Life Sciences requested an injunction to prevent four United States anti-vivisectionist groups and individuals from carrying out violent protests, which were a threat to the future survival of their business.

The **going concern concept** assumes that the entity will continue in operational existence for the foreseeable future. This is important because it allows the original, historical costs of assets to continue to be used in the balance sheet on the basis of their being able to generate future income. If the entity was expected to cease functioning then such assets would be worth only their break-up values and therefore usually considerably less.

The separate valuation concept

The **separate valuation concept** relates to the determination of the aggregate amount of any item. The amount of each individual asset or liability that falls to be taken into account shall be determined separately. This is important because material items may reflect different economic circumstances. There must be a review of each material item to comply with the appropriate accounting standards (see the next section, which covers accounting standards):

- FRS 11 (Impairment of Fixed Assets and Goodwill)
- FRS 15 (Tangible Fixed Assets)
- FRS 12 (Provisions, Contingent Liabilities and Contingent Assets).

Note the example of the Millennium Dome 2000 project, which was developed in Greenwich, London, throughout 1999 and 2000 and cost around £800m. At the end of the year 2000 a valuation of the individual elements of the attraction resulted in a total of around £100m.

Further fundamental accounting concepts are:

The business entity concept

The **business entity concept** ensures that financial accounting information relates only to the activities of the business entity and not to the other activities of its owners.

The money measurement concept

The **money measurement concept** enables information relating to transactions to be fairly compared by providing a commonly-accepted unit of converting quantifiable amounts into recognisable measures. Most quantifiable data is capable of being converted, using a common denominator of money, into monetary terms. However, accounting deals only with those items capable of being translated into monetary terms, which imposes a limit on the scope of accounting reporting to such items.

The historical cost concept

The **historical cost concept** relates to the practice of valuing assets with reference to their acquisition cost. Although this basis of valuation may not be as realistic as using say current values, it does provide a consistent basis for comparison and almost eliminates the need for any subjectivity.

The materiality concept

Information is material if its omission or misstatement could influence the economic decisions of users taken on the basis of the financial statements. Materiality depends on the size of the item or error judged in the particular circumstances of its omission or misstatement. Thus, materiality provides a threshold or cut-off point rather than being a primary qualitative characteristic that information must have if it is to be useful. The materiality concept allows a certain amount of judgement in the application of all the other accounting concepts. The level of materiality will depend on the size of the organisation and the type of revenue or cost, or asset or liability being considered.

The periodicity concept

The periodicity concept is the requirement to produce financial statements at set time intervals. This requirement is embodied, in the case of UK corporations, in the Companies Act. Both annual and interim financial statements are required to be produced by public limited companies each year.

The realisation concept

The realisation concept is the principle that increases in value should only be recognised on realisation of assets by arms-length sale to an independent purchaser. This means, for example, that sales revenue from the sale of a product or service is recognised in accounting statements only when it is realised. This does not mean when the cash has been paid over by the customer. It means when the sale takes place, that is when the product or service has been delivered, and ownership transferred, to the customer.

The substance over form concept

Where a conflict exists, the substance over form concept requires the structuring of reports to give precedence to the representation of financial or economic reality over strict adherence to the requirements of the legal reporting structure. An example of this is where a lessee discloses an asset in the balance sheet even though not holding legal title to the asset.

Example 1.5

You are thinking of changing jobs (within marketing) and moving from a local, well-established retailer that has been in business for over 20 years. You have been asked to attend an interview with a new plc that started up around two years ago. The plc is a retailer via the Internet. Your family have suggested that you investigate the company thoroughly before your interview, paying particular attention to its financial resources. There is a chance the plc may not be a going concern if its business plan does not succeed.

What questions should you ask at your interview?

Answer

1. Are any published accounts available for review?
2. What is the share capital of the company (for example, is it £10,000 or £1,000,000)?
3. Is the company profitable?
4. Is the company working within banking facilities?

5. Are any press analyses of the company available?

6. What is the current customer base?

The answers may suggest whether the company can continue trading for the foreseeable future.

Accounting standards

A number of bodies have been established to draft accounting policy, set accounting standards, and to monitor compliance with standards and the provisions of the Companies Act. The Financial Reporting Council (FRC), whose chairman is appointed by the Department of Trade and Industry (DTI) and the Bank of England, develops accounting standards policy and gives guidance on issues of public concern. The ASB, which is comprised of members of the accountancy profession, and on which the Government has an observer status, has responsibility for development, issue, and withdrawal of accounting standards.

The accounting standards are called Financial Reporting Standards (FRS). Up to 1990 the accounting standards were known as Statements of Standard Accounting Practice (SSAPs). Although some SSAPs have now been withdrawn there are, in addition to the new FRSs, a large number of SSAPs that are still in force. A list of all FRSs and SSAPs that are currently in force may be found in Appendix 3 at the end of this book. The website accompanying this book contains the up-to-date position with regard to changes in accounting standards. The ASB is supported by the Urgent Issues Task Force (UITF) whose main role is to assist the ASB in areas where an accounting standard or Companies Act provision exists, but where unsatisfactory or conflicting interpretations have developed or seem likely to develop.

The Financial Reporting Review Panel (FRRP) reviews comments and complaints from users of financial information. It enquires into the annual accounts of companies where it appears that the requirements of the Companies Act, including the requirement that annual accounts shall show a true and fair view, might have been breached. The Stock Exchange rules covering financial disclosure of publicly quoted companies require such companies to comply with accounting standards and reasons for non-compliance must be disclosed.

The International Accounting Standards Committee (IASC), which is supported by each of the accountancy institutes referred to above, fosters the harmonisation of accounting standards internationally. To this end each FRS includes a section explaining its relationship to any relevant International Accounting Standard.

Pressure groups, organisations and individuals may also have influence on the provisions of the Companies Act and FRSs (and SSAPs). These may include some Government departments (for example, Inland Revenue, HM Customs & Excise, Office of Fair Trading) in addition to the DTI and employer organisations such as the Confederation of British Industry (CBI), and professional bodies like the Law Society, Institute of Directors, and Institute of Management.

There are therefore many diverse influences on the form and content of company accounts. In addition to legislation, standards are continually being refined, updated and replaced and further enhanced by various codes of best practice. As a response to this, a UK Generally Accepted Accounting Practices (UK GAAP) was first published in 1989. UK GAAP includes all practices that are considered to be permissible or legitimate, either through support by statute, accounting standard or official pronouncement, or through consistency with the needs of users and of meeting the fundamental requirement to present a true and fair view, or even simply through authoritative support in the accounting literature. UK GAAP is therefore a dynamic concept, which changes in response to changing circumstances.

Within the scope of current legislation, best practice and accounting standards, each company needs to develop its own specific accounting policies. Accounting policies are the specific accounting bases selected and consistently followed by an entity as being, in the opinion of the management, appropriate to its circumstances and best suited to present fairly its results and financial position. Examples are the various alternative methods of valuing stocks of materials, or charging the cost of a machine over its useful life, its depreciation.

Progress check 1.6

What are meant by accounting concepts and accounting standards, and why are they needed? Give some examples.

Accounting processes

Accounting is sometimes referred to as a process of identifying, measuring and communicating economic information to permit informed judgements and decisions by users of the information, and also to provide information which is potentially useful for making economic and social decisions.

Accounting processes follow a system of recording and classification of data, followed by summarisation of financial information for subsequent interpretation and presentation. An accounting system is a series of tasks and records of an entity by which the transactions are processed as a means of maintaining financial records. Such systems identify, assemble, analyse, calculate, classify, record, summarise and report transactions.

Most companies prepare an accounting manual that provides the details and responsibilities for each of the accounting systems. The accounting manual is a collection of accounting instructions governing the responsibilities of persons, and the procedures, forms and records relating to preparation and use of accounting data.

There may be separate accounting manuals for the constituent parts of the accounting system, for example:

- financial accounting manual – general ledger and coding
- management accounting manual – budget and cost accounting
- financial management/treasury manual – bank reconciliations and foreign currency exposure management.

Example 1.6

Some time after Gordon Brown graduated (and after an extended backpacking trip across a few continents) he registered with The Chartered Institute of Management Accountants (CIMA). At the same time Gordon started employment as part of the graduate intake in the finance department of a large engineering group. The auditors came in soon after Gordon started his job and he was intrigued and a little confused at their conversations with some of the senior accountants. They talked about accounting concepts and this standard and that standard, SSAPs and FRSs, all of which meant very little to Gordon. Gordon asked his boss, the Chief Accountant Angela Jones, if she could give him a brief outline of the framework of accounting one evening after work over a drink.

Give a summary of what you think Angela's outline might have been?

Answer

- Accounting is supported by a number of rules, or concepts, that have evolved over many hundreds of years, and by accounting standards to enable consistency in reporting through the preparation of financial statements.
- Accounting concepts relate to the framework within which accountancy operates, ethical considerations and the rules relating to measurement of data.
- A number of concepts relate to the boundaries of the framework: business entity; going concern; periodicity.
- A number of concepts relate to accounting principles or ethics: consistency; prudence; substance over form.
- A number of concepts relate to how data should be measured and recorded: accruals; historical cost; materiality; realisation; separate valuation.
- Accounting standards are formulated by a body comprised of members of the accounting institutes (Accounting Standards Board – ASB) and are guidelines which businesses are recommended to follow in the preparation of their financial statements.
- The original standards were the Statements of Accounting Standards (SSAPs) which have been and continue to be superseded by the Financial Reporting Standards (FRSs).
- The aim of the SSAPs/FRSs is to cover all the issues and problems that are likely to be encountered in the preparation of financial statements and they are the authority to ensure that 'financial statements of a reporting entity give a true and fair view of its state of affairs at the balance sheet date and of its profit or loss for the financial period ending on that date' (as quoted from the ASB foreword to *Accounting Standards*).
- SSAPs were promulgated by the Accounting Standards Committee (ASC).
- FRSs are promulgated by the ASB.

An introduction to financial statements

Companies produce financial statements for each accounting period to provide adequate information about how the company has been doing. There are three key financial statements – balance sheet, profit and loss account (or income statement), and cash flow statement. Companies are also obliged to provide similar financial statements at each year end to provide information for their shareholders, the Inland Revenue, and the Registrar of Companies. This information is frequently used by City analysts, investing institutions and the public in general.

After each year end companies prepare their **annual report and accounts** for their share-holders. Copies of the annual report and accounts are filed with the Registrar of Companies and copies are available to other interested parties such as financial institutions, major suppliers and other investors. In addition to the profit and loss account and cash flow statement for the year and the balance sheet as at the year end date, the annual report and accounts includes Notes to the Accounts, and much more financial and non-financial information such as company policies, financial indicators, corporate governance compliance, directors' remuneration, employee numbers, business analysis, and segmental analysis. The annual report also includes an Operating and Financial Review of the business, a report of the auditors of the company, and the chairman's statement.

The auditors' report states compliance or otherwise with accounting standards and that the accounts are free from material misstatement, that the accounts give a true and fair view prepared on the assumption that the company is a going concern. The chairman's statement offers an opportunity for the chairman of the company to report in unquantified and unaudited terms on the performance of the company during the past financial period and on likely future developments. However, the auditors would object if there was anything in the chairman's statement which was inconsistent with the audited accounts.

Progress check 1.7

What are the financial statements of a business? How are business transactions ultimately reflected in financial statements?

Accountability and financial reporting

When we talk about companies we are generally referring to limited companies, as distinct from sole traders and partnerships (or firms – although this term is frequently wrongly used to refer to companies). As we have discussed, limited liability companies have an identity separate from their owners, the shareholders, and the liability of shareholders is limited to the amount of money they have invested in the company, their shares in the company. Ownership of a business is separated from its stewardship, or management, by the shareholders' assignment to a board of directors the responsibility for running the company. The directors of the company are accountable to the shareholders, and both parties must play their part in making that accountability effective.

The directors of a limited company may comprise one or more professionally qualified accountants (usually including a finance director). The directors of the company necessarily delegate to middle managers and junior managers the responsibility for the day-to-day management of the business. It is certainly likely that this body of managers, who report to the board of directors, will include a further one or more qualified accountants responsible for managing the finance function.

Accountability is maintained by the reporting on the financial performance and the financial position of the business to shareholders on both a yearly and an interim basis. The reporting made in the form of the financial statements includes the balance sheet, profit and loss account, and cash flow statement, which will be considered in detail in Part I of this book.

External auditors are appointed by, and report independently to, the shareholders. They are professionally qualified accountants who are required to provide objective verification to shareholders and other users that the financial statements have been prepared properly and in accordance with legislative and regulatory requirements; that they present the information truthfully and fairly and that they conform to the best accounting practice in their treatment of the various measurements and valuations.

The audit is defined by the Auditing Practices Board (APB) as 'an independent examination of, and expression of an opinion on, the financial statements of the enterprise'. There is a requirement for all companies registered in the UK to have an annual audit, except for those companies which (currently) have an annual turnover of less than £350,000 and a balance sheet total of less than £1.4m.

The financial reporting of the company includes preparation of the financial statements, notes and reports which are audited and given an opinion on by the external auditors. A regulatory framework exists to see fair play, the responsibility for which is held jointly by the

Government, and the private sector, including the accountancy profession and the Stock Exchange.

The Government exercises influence through bodies such as the Department of Trade and Industry (DTI) and through Parliament by the enactment of legislation, for example the Companies Act. Such legal regulation began with the Joint Stock Companies Act of 1844.

Subsequent statutes exerted greater influence on company reporting: the Companies Acts 1948, 1967, and 1981. The provisions included in these Acts were consolidated into the Companies Act 1985, which was then amended in 1989. The Companies Act 1985, as amended in 1989, contains the overall current legal framework.

Progress check 1.8

In what ways may the reliability of financial reporting be ensured?

Example 1.7

Gordon Brown soon settled into his graduate trainee role and pursued his CIMA studies with enthusiasm. Although Gordon was more interested in business planning and getting involved with new development projects, his job and his studies required him to become totally familiar with and able to prepare the financial statements of a company. Gordon was explaining the subject of financial statements and what they involved to a friend of his, Jack, another graduate trainee in human resources. Where? – you've guessed it – over an after-work drink.

How do you think Gordon would have put across the subject of financial statements to Jack, who is very much a non-financial person?

Answer

Apart from small companies who are not required to produce a cash flow statement, all limited companies are required to produce three main financial statements for each accounting period with information about company performance for

- shareholders
- the Inland Revenue
- banks
- City analysts
- investing institutions
- the public in general.

The three key financial statements are the

(a) Balance sheet

(b) Profit and loss account (or income statement)

(c) Cash flow statement

(a) **Balance sheet:** a financial snapshot at a moment in time, or the financial position of the company comparable with pressing the 'pause' button on a video. The video in 'play' mode shows what is happening as time goes on second by second, but when you press 'pause' the video stops on a picture; the picture does not tell you what has happened over the period of time up to the pause (or what is going to happen after the pause). The balance sheet is the consequence of everything that

◀ has happened up to the balance sheet date. It does not explain how the company got to that position.

(b) **Profit and loss account:** this is the video in 'play' mode. It is used to calculate whether or not the company has made a gain or deficit on its operations during the period, through producing and selling its goods or services. Net earnings or net profit is calculated from revenues derived throughout the period between two 'pauses', minus costs incurred from deriving those revenues.

(c) **Cash flow statement:** this is the video again in 'play' mode, but net earnings is not the same as cash flow, since revenues and costs are not necessarily accounted for when cash transfers occur. Sales are accounted for when goods or services are delivered and accepted by the customer but cash may not be received until some time later. The profit and loss account does not reflect non-trading events like an issue of shares or a loan that will increase cash but are not revenues or costs. The cash flow statement summarises cash inflows and cash outflows and calculates the net change in the cash position for the company throughout the period between two 'pauses'.

Summary of key points

● The main branches of accounting within commercial and industrial organisations are financial accounting, management accounting, treasury management, financial management and corporate finance.

● The main branches of accounting which provide services to commercial and industrial organisations are auditing, corporate taxation, personal taxation, VAT, and consultancy.

● Accountancy is the practice of accounting.

● There is a wide range of users of financial information: external to the organisation, for example potential investors, suppliers and financial analysts; internal to the organisation, for example managers, shareholders, employees.

● The large variety of types of business entity includes profit and not-for-profit organisations, both privately and Government owned, involved in providing products and services.

● The framework of accounting is bounded by concepts (or rules) and standards, covering what data should be included within an accounting system and how that data should be recorded.

● Accounting processes follow a system of recording and classifying data, followed by a summarisation of financial information for subsequent interpretation and presentation.

● The three main financial statements that appear within a business's annual report and accounts, together with the chairman's statement, directors' report, and auditors' report, are the balance sheet, profit and loss account, and cash flow statement.

● Accountability is maintained by the reporting to shareholders on a yearly and half-yearly basis of sales and other activities and profits or losses arising from those activities, and the audit function.

Glossary of key terms

accountancy The practice or profession of accounting.

accounting The classification and recording of monetary transactions, the presentation and interpretation of the results of those transactions in order to assess performance over a period and the financial position at a given date, and the monetary projection of future activities arising from alternative planned courses of action.

accounting concepts The principles underpinning the preparation of accounting information. Fundamental accounting concepts are the broad basic assumptions which underlie the periodic financial accounts of business enterprises.

accounting period The time period covered by the accounting statements of an entity.

accounting policies The specific accounting bases selected and consistently followed by an entity as being, in the opinion of the management, appropriate to its circumstances and best suited to present fairly its results and financial position (SSAP 2 and Companies Act).

accounting standard Authoritative statement of how particular types of transaction and other events should be reflected in financial statements. Compliance with accounting standards will normally be necessary for financial statements to give a true and fair view (ASB).

Accounting Standards Board (ASB) A UK standard-setting body set up in 1990 to develop, issue and withdraw accounting standards. Its aims are to 'establish and improve standards of financial accounting and reporting, for the benefit of users, preparers and auditors of financial information'.

accounts payable Also called trade creditors, is the money owed to suppliers for goods and services.

accounts receivable Also called trade debtors, is the money owed to entities by customers.

accruals concept The principle that revenues and costs are recognised as they are earned or incurred, and so matched with each other, and dealt with in the profit and loss account of the period to which they relate, irrespective of the period of receipt or payment. Where a conflict arises, this concept is subservient to the prudence concept.

annual report and accounts A set of statements which may comprise a management report (in the case of companies, a directors' report), an operating and financial review (OFR), and the financial statements of the entity.

audit A systematic examination of the activities and status of an entity, based primarily on investigation and analysis of its systems, controls and records. A statutory annual audit of a company is defined by the ASB as an independent examination of, and expression of an opinion on, the financial statements of the enterprise.

auditor A professionally qualified accountant who is appointed by, and reports independently to, the shareholders, providing an objective verification to shareholders and other users that the financial statements have been prepared properly and in accordance with legislative and regulatory requirements; that they present the information truthfully and fairly, and that they conform to the best accounting practice in their treatment of the various measurements and valuations.

balance sheet A statement of the financial position of an entity at a given date disclosing the assets, liabilities and accumulated funds such as shareholders' contributions and reserves, prepared to give a true and fair view of the financial state of the entity at that date.

bookkeeping Recording of monetary transactions, appropriately classified, in the financial records of an entity, either by manual means or otherwise.

business entity concept The concept that financial accounting information relates only to the activities of the business entity and not to the activities of its owners.

cash flow statement A statement that summarises the inflows and outflows of cash for a period, classified under the following standard headings (FRS 1):

- operating activities
- returns on investment and servicing of finance
- taxation
- investing activities
- liquid funds
- equity dividends
- financing.

consistency concept The principle that there is uniformity of accounting treatment of like items within each accounting period and from one period to the next.

depreciation A measure of the wearing out, consumption or other reduction in the useful economic life of a fixed asset, whether arising from use, effluxion of time or obsolescence through technological or market changes (FRS 11 and FRS 15). Depreciation should be allocated so as to charge a fair proportion of the total cost (or valuation) of the asset to each accounting period expected to benefit from its use.

financial accounting Financial accounting is the function responsible for the periodic external reporting, statutorily required, for shareholders. It also provides such similar information as required for Government and other interested third parties, such as potential investors, employees, lenders, suppliers, customers, and financial analysts.

financial management The management of all the processes associated with the efficient acquisition and deployment of both short and long-term financial resources. Within an organisation financial management assists operations management to reach their financial objectives.

going concern concept The assumption that the entity will continue in operational existence for the forseeable future.

historical cost concept A basis of accounting prescribed by the Companies Act for published accounts that uses a system of accounting in which all values are based on the historical costs incurred.

internal control As defined in the Cadbury Report, it is the whole system of controls, financial or otherwise, established in order to provide reasonable assurance of

(a) effective and efficient operation

(b) internal financial control

(c) compliance with laws and regulations.

limited company A limited liability company is one in which the liability of members for the company's debts is limited to the amount paid and, if any, unpaid on the shares taken up by them.

management accounting The application of the principles of accounting and financial management to create, protect, preserve and increase value so as to deliver that value to the stakeholders of profit and not-for-profit enterprises, both public and private. Management accounting is an integral part of management, requiring the identification, generation, presentation, interpretation and use of information relevant to

- formulating business strategy
- planning and controlling activities
- decision-making
- efficient resource usage
- performance improvement and value enhancement
- safeguarding tangible and intangible assets
- corporate governance and internal control.

materiality concept Information is material if its omission or misstatement could influence the economic decisions of users taken on the basis of the financial statements. Materiality depends on the size of the item or error judged in the particular circumstances of its omission or misstatement. Thus, materiality provides a threshold or cut-off point rather than being a primary qualitative characteristic that information must have if it is to be useful.

money measurement concept Most quantifiable data is capable of being converted, using a common denominator of money, into monetary terms. The money measurement concept holds that accounting deals only with those items capable of being translated into monetary terms, which imposes a limit on the scope of accounting reporting to such items.

periodicity concept The requirement to produce financial statements at set time intervals. This requirement is embodied, in the case of UK corporations, in the Companies Act.

profit and loss account (or income statement) Measures whether or not the company has made a profit or loss on its operations during the period, through producing and selling its goods or services.

prudence concept The principle that revenue and profits are not anticipated, but are included in the profit and loss account only when realised in the form either of cash or of other assets, or the ultimate cash realisation can be assessed with reasonable certainty; provision is made for all known liabilities (expenses and losses) whether the amount of these is known with certainty or is a best estimate in the light of information available.

qualified accountant A member of the accountancy profession, and in the UK a member of one of the six professional accountancy bodies: CIMA; ICAEW; ICAS; ICAI; ACCA; CIPFA.

realisation concept The principle that increases in value should only be recognised on realisation of assets by arms-length sale to an independent purchaser.

Registrar of Companies Government official agency that is responsible for initial registration of new companies and for collecting and arranging public access to the annual reports of all limited companies.

separate valuation concept In determining the aggregate amount of any item, the amount of each individual asset or liability that falls to be taken into account shall be determined separately (Companies Act 1985).

substance over form concept Where a conflict exists, the structuring of reports to give precedence to the representation of financial reality over strict adherence to the requirements of the legal reporting structure.

treasury management The corporate handling of all financial matters, the generation of external and internal funds for business, the management of currencies and cash flows, and the complex strategies, policies and procedures of corporate finance.

true and fair view The requirement for financial statements prepared in compliance with the Companies Act to 'give a true and fair view' overrides any other requirements. Although not precisely defined in the Companies Act this is generally accepted to mean that accounts show a true and fair view if they are unlikely to mislead a user of financial information in giving a false impression of the company.

Assessment material

Questions

Q1.1 (i) How many different types of business entity can you think of?

(ii) In what respect do they differ fundamentally?

Q1.2 (i) Why are accountants required to produce financial information?

(ii) Who do they produce it for and what do they do with it?

Q1.3 Describe the broad regulatory, professional, and operational framework of accounting.

Q1.4 (i) What are accounting concepts?

(ii) What purpose do they serve?

Q1.5 (i)   What is accountancy?

(ii) What is an accountant?

(iii) What do accountants do?

Q1.6 What do accountants mean by SSAPs and FRSs, and what are they for?

Q1.7 (i) What is financial management?

(ii) How does financial management relate to accounting and perhaps other disciplines?

Q1.8 How do financial statements ensure accountability for the reporting of timely and accurate information to shareholders is maintained?

Discussion points

D1.1 The managing director of a large public limited company stated: 'I've built up my business over the past 15 years from a one man band to a large plc. As we grew we seemed to spend more and more money on accountants, financial managers, and auditors. During the next few months we are restructuring to go back to being a private limited company. This will be much simpler and we can save a fortune on accounting and auditing costs.' Discuss.
(Hint: You may wish to research Richard Branson and, for example, Virgin Air on the Internet, to provide some background for this discussion.)

D1.2 The managing director of a growing private limited company stated: 'All these accounting concepts and standards seem like a lot of red tape to me, and we've got financial accountants and management accountants as well as auditors. Surely all I need to know at the end of the day is how much have we made.' Discuss.

Exercises

Exercises E1.1 to E1.8 require an essay-type approach. You should refer to the relevant sections in Chapter 1 to check your solutions.

Level I

E1.1   *Time allowed – 15 minutes*

Discuss the implications of preparation of the profit and loss account if there were no accounting concepts.

E1.2   *Time allowed – 30 minutes*

At a recent meeting of the local branch of the Women's Institute they had a discussion about what sort of organisation they were. The discussion broadened into a general debate about all types of organisation, and someone brought up the term business entity. Although there were many opinions, there was little sound knowledge about what business entities are. Jane Cross said that her husband was an accountant and she was sure he wouldn't mind spending an hour one evening to enlighten them on the subject. Chris Cross fished out his text books to refresh his knowledge of the subject and came up with a schedule of all the different business entities he could think of together with the detail of their defining features and key points of difference and similarity.

Prepare the sort of schedule that Chris might have drafted for his talk and identify the category that the Women's Institute might fall into.

E1.3   *Time allowed – 30 minutes*

Mary Andrews was an accountant but is now semi-retired. She has been asked by her local comprehensive school careers officer to give a talk entitled 'what is an accountant and what is accounting, its use and its purpose?'

Prepare a list of bullet points that covers everything necessary for Mary to give a comprehensive and easy-to-understand presentation to a group of sixth formers at the school.

Level II

E1.4   *Time allowed – 30 minutes*

Accounting standards in general are reasonably clear and unambiguous.

Are there any major areas where accountants may disagree in balance sheet accounting?

E1.5   *Time allowed – 30 minutes*

Financial statements are produced each year by businesses, using prescribed formats.

Should major plcs be allowed to reflect their individuality in their own financial statements?

E1.6 *Time allowed – 45 minutes*

Professionals in the UK, for example, doctors, solicitors, accountants etc., normally work within partnerships. Many tradesmen, such as plumbers, car mechanics, carpenters, and so on, operate as sole traders. Software engineers seem to work for corporations and limited companies.

Consider the size of operation, range of products, financing, the marketplace, and the geographical area served, to discuss why companies like Microsoft and Yahoo should operate in this way.

E1.7 *Time allowed – 60 minutes*

Bill Walsh has just been appointed Finance Director of a medium sized engineering company, Nutsan Ltd, which has a high level of exports and is very sensitive to economic changes throughout the UK and the rest of the world. One of the tasks on Bill's action list is a review of the accounting and finance function.

What are the senior financial roles that Bill would expect to be in place and what are the important functions for which they should be responsible?

E1.8 *Time allowed – 60 minutes*

The Millennium Dome was opened to the general public in the UK for the year 2000 and was planned to close at the end of 2000 for the site to be used for some other purpose. There were problems financing the construction and the general day-to-day operations. There were many crises reported in the press during 2000. A proposed takeover of the site fell through in September 2000, with various reasons given by the potential acquirer.

You are required to research into the Dome using the BBC, *Financial Times* **and the other broadsheets, and the Internet, and summarise the financial aspects of the project that you gather. You should focus on the attitudes expressed by the general public, select committees of MPs, Government ministers, the Opposition, the Dome's management, and consider examples of bias, non-timeliness, and lack of transparency.**

PART I

Financial accounting

Part I is about financial accounting. The first three chapters deal with the three key financial statements: balance sheet; profit and loss account; cash flow statement, and in particular those relating to limited companies. In most respects these also apply to other profit-making and not-for-profit organisations in both the private and public sectors.

Chapter 2 begins with an introduction to the preparation of simple financial statements and then goes on to consider the balance sheet in detail.

Chapter 3 looks in detail at the profit and loss account. It looks at how to recognise that a profit (or loss) has been made and how it is linked with the balance sheet and cash flow.

Chapter 4 deals with the cash flow statement, which shows from where an organisation has received cash during an accounting period and how cash was used.

Chapter 5 is headed *Business performance analysis*. The three financial statements provide information about business performance. Much more may be gleaned about the performance of the business through further analysis of the financial statements, using financial ratios and other techniques, for example trend analysis, industrial and inter-firm analysis. This chapter also introduces non-financial performance measures, including the balanced scorecard.

Chapter 6 looks at the analysis and interpretation of the published accounts of a business. It uses the report and accounts for the year 2000 of Johnson Matthey plc to illustrate the type of financial and non-financial information provided by a major UK public company.

In Chapter 7 we broaden the scope of our study of accounting and finance to provide an introduction to corporate governance, a topic that is becoming increasingly important, as the responsibilities of directors continue to increase. The burden lies with management to run businesses in strict compliance with statutory, regulatory and accounting requirements, so it is crucial that directors are aware of the rules and codes of practice in place to regulate the behaviour of directors of limited companies.

2

Financial statements of limited companies – balance sheet

LEARNING OBJECTIVES

Completion of this chapter will enable you to:

● identify the financial information shown in the financial statements of a company: balance sheet; profit and loss account; cash flow statement

● construct simple financial statements

● outline the structure of the balance sheet of a limited company

● classify the broad balance sheet categories of shareholders' equity; liabilities; assets

● outline the alternative balance sheet formats

● prepare a balance sheet

● evaluate some of the alternative methods of asset valuation

● appreciate the limitations of the conventional balance sheet

Introduction

We talked about business entities in general in Chapter 1. There are a number of differences and similarities between sole traders, partnerships, private and public limited companies. A sole trader business is owned and run by one individual. A partnership is very similar to a sole trader, except that it is owned and managed by two or more individuals who share the profits or losses of the business. The financial accounting and reporting of companies are similar to those of sole traders and partnerships, except that they are more detailed and require a greater disclosure of information. This is to comply with current legislation and the requirements for reporting of financial information to the owners of the business (the shareholders).

Each type of business is required to prepare periodic financial statements in one form or another for internal control purposes, the shareholders and, for example, the Inland Revenue. To provide a comprehensive coverage of financial statements in this chapter, the following two chapters and subsequent chapters about business performance analysis and published reports and accounts, we will therefore consider the accounts and financial statements of limited companies, both private and public.

Before dealing specifically with the balance sheets of limited companies we will look in a little more detail at the subject of financial statements that was introduced in Chapter 1. We will see how these are constructed and interrelated, by working through a comprehensive example that illustrates how transactions are reflected in the profit and loss account, balance sheet and cash flow statement of a business.

This chapter deals with how balance sheets are structured and how the accounts within the balance sheet are categorised. Each of the items within each of the balance sheet categories will be described in detail and form the basis to enable the preparation of a balance sheet of a limited company in the appropriate format.

The chapter closes by illustrating the subjective nature of the balance sheet and considers one of the areas in which this is apparent through looking at examples of the alternative methods for valuation of assets that are available to companies.

Financial statements of limited companies

In Chapter 1 we introduced the topic of the financial statements that businesses need to prepare for each accounting period to provide adequate information about the financial performance and the financial position of the business.

We will now look in more detail at the three key financial statements (see Fig. 2.1): balance sheet, profit and loss account (or income statement), and cash flow statement.

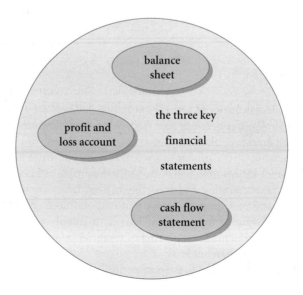

FIGURE 2.1   The three key financial statements

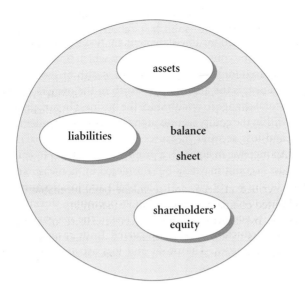

FIGURE 2.2 The main elements of the balance sheet

Balance sheet

The balance sheet summarises the financial position of the business; it is a financial snapshot at a moment in time. It may be compared to looking at a video on television. In 'play' mode the video is showing what is happening as time goes on second by second. If you press 'pause' the video stops on a picture. The picture does not tell you what has happened over the period of time up to the pause (or what is going to happen after the pause). The balance sheet is the financial position of the company at the 'pause' position. It is the consequence of everything that has happened up to that time. It does not explain how the company got to that position, it just shows the results of financial impacts of events and decisions up to the balance sheet date. The year end may be 31 December, but other dates may be chosen. A company's year end date is (normally) the same date each year.

The balance sheet comprises a number of categories, within the three main elements, which are labelled assets, liabilities or shareholders' equity (usually referred to as just equity). The assets are debit balances and the liabilities and shareholders' equity are credit balances. (Note: the concepts of debit and credit, and double-entry bookkeeping are fully covered in Appendix 1.) The balance sheet is always in balance so that

total assets (TA) = equity (E) + total liabilities (TL)

The balance sheet is a summary of the general ledger in which the total assets equal the shareholders' equity plus total liabilities.

If the balance sheet is the financial snapshot at a moment in time – the 'pause' on the video – the two other financial statements are the equivalent of what is going on throughout the accounting period – the 'play' mode on the video.

Profit and loss account

The profit and loss account and income statement are two terms that really mean the same thing. Profit (or loss) may be considered in two ways, which both give the same result.

The profit and loss account shows the change in wealth of the business over a period. The wealth of the business is the amount it is worth to the owners, the shareholders. The accumulation of the total change in wealth since the business began, up to a particular point in time, is reflected within the equity section of the balance sheet under the heading retained profits. The profit and loss account measures the change in the balance sheet from one 'pause' to another. An increase in equity is a profit and a decrease in equity is a loss.

The profit and loss account may also be considered in its measurement of the trading performance of the business (see Fig. 2.3). The profit and loss account calculates whether or not the company has made a profit or loss on its operations during the period, through producing and selling its goods or services. The result, the net earnings or **net profit** (or loss), is derived from deducting expenses incurred from revenues derived throughout the period between two 'pauses'. The profit and loss account is dealt with in detail in Chapter 3.

The total of the expenses (debits) and revenues (credits) accounts within the general ledger comprise the profit and loss account. The total of these may be a net debit or a net credit. A net debit represents a loss and a net credit represents a profit. The net profit or loss is reflected in the balance sheet of the business under the heading retained profits, which is part of 'shareholders' equity'. All the other accounts within the general ledger, other than expenses and revenues, may be summarised into various other non-profit and loss account categories and these represent all the other balances that complete the overall balance sheet of the business.

There are three main points to consider regarding the profit and loss account and how it differs from the cash flow statement. First, revenues (or **sales** or income) and expenses (or costs or expenditure) are not necessarily accounted for when cash transfers occur. Sales are normally accounted for when goods or services are delivered and accepted by the customer. Cash will rarely be received immediately from the customer, except in businesses like high-street retailers and supermarkets; it is normally received weeks or months later.

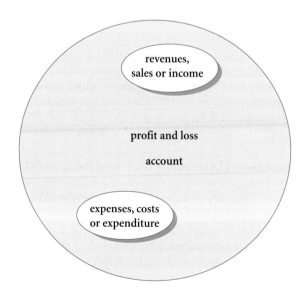

FIGURE 2.3   The main elements of the profit and loss account

Second, the profit and loss account does not take into account all the events that impact on the financial position of the company. For example, an issue of new **shares** in the company, or a loan to the company, will increase cash but they are neither revenue nor expenses.

Third, non-cash flow items, for example depreciation and bad debts, reduce the profit or increase the loss, of the company but do not represent outflows of cash. These topics will be covered in detail in the next chapter.

Therefore it can be seen that net profit is not the same as cash flow. A company may get into financial difficulties if it suffers a severe **cash** shortage even though it may have positive net earnings (profit).

Cash flow statement

Between them, the balance sheet and profit and loss account show a company's financial position at the beginning and at the end of an accounting period and how the profit or loss has been achieved during that period.

The balance sheet and profit and loss account do not show or directly analyse some of the key changes that have taken place in the company's financial position, for example:

- how much **capital expenditure** (for example, equipment, machinery and buildings) has the company made, and how did it fund the expenditure?
- what was the extent of new borrowing and how much **debt** was repaid?
- how much did the company need to fund new **working capital** (which includes, for example, an increase in **debtors** and **stock** requirements as a result of more business activity)?
- how much of the company's funding was met by funds generated from its trading activities, and how much by new external funding (for example, from banks and other lenders, or new shareholders)?

The profit and loss account and the cash flow statement (see Fig. 2.4) are the two 'videos' which are running in parallel between the two 'pauses' – the balance sheets at the start

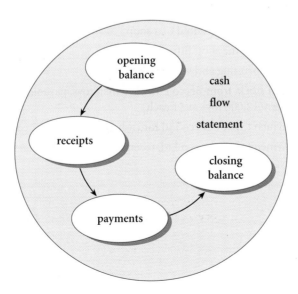

FIGURE 2.4 The main elements of the cash flow statement

and the finish of an accounting period. However, the cash flow statement goes further in answering the questions like those shown above. The aim of the cash flow statement is to summarise the cash inflows and outflows and calculate the net change in the cash position for the company throughout the period between two 'pauses'.

| Progress check 2.1 | Explain the fundamental differences between the types of information presented in each of the three key financial statements. |

Construction and use of financial statements

An example will best illustrate how financial statements may be constructed. We will use the example of Mr Bean's business, Ayco (see also Example A1.1, Appendix 1), to track how some simple transactions are reflected in the profit and loss account, cash flow statement, and balance sheet.

Examples 2.1 to 2.4 will look at the four one-week periods during Ayco's first month of trading and show the profit and loss account reflecting the trading transactions of the business. The result, the change in wealth of the business is shown as the resources held at the end of each period and reflected in the balance sheet. The example will show the cash flow statement as movements in cash and changes to the cash balance, which is reflected in the balance sheet that gives a summary of the financial position of the company at the end of each period.

Example 2.1

Mr Bean decides to set up a wholesale business, Ayco, on 1 January 2000. He has his own cash resources for the purpose of setting up the business and has estimated that an initial £50,000 would be required for this purpose. During the first four-week period in business, January 2000, **Ayco** will enter into the following transactions:

		£
Week 1	Receipt of cheque from Mr Bean	50,000
Week 1	Purchase for cash the freehold of a shop	30,000
Week 1	Purchase for cash the shop fittings	5,000
Week 2	Cash paid for printing and stationery used	200
Week 3	Purchases of stock, from Beeco Ltd, of Aymen toys, payable two months later (12,000 toys at £1 each)	12,000
Week 3	Sales of Aymen toys to Ceeco Ltd for cash (1,000 toys at £2 each)	2,000
Week 4	Sales of Aymen toys to Deeco Ltd, receivable one month later (8,000 toys at £2 each)	16,000

		Week 1 £	Total £
Profit and loss account	Sales	0	0
	Cost of sales	0	0
	Gross profit	0	0
	Expenses	0	0
	Profit/(loss)	0	0
	Cumulative profit/(loss)	0	0
Cash flow statement	Opening balance	0	0
	Cash received ex Mr Bean	50,000	50,000
	Cash received from customers	0	0
	Cash paid for shop freehold	(30,000)	(30,000)
	Cash paid for shop fittings	(5,000)	(5,000)
	Cash paid for stationery	0	0
	Closing balance	15,000	15,000
Balance sheet	Cash closing balance	15,000	15,000
	Freehold shop	30,000	30,000
	Shop fittings	5,000	5,000
	Stocks	0	0
	Debtors	0	0
	Creditors	0	0
	Total wealth	50,000	50,000
	Represented by:		
	Mr Bean's original capital	50,000	50,000
	Profit/(loss) to date	0	0
	Total capital	50,000	50,000

The statement above shows that no trading took place during the first week of January. Mr Bean paid £50,000 of his personal funds into the bank account of Ayco, representing his capital invested in Ayco. The company immediately used £35,000 of this to purchase the freehold of a shop together with shop fittings. We can summarise the financial position at the end of the first week as follows:

There was neither a profit nor a loss.

Cash has been increased by Mr Bean's capital invested, less payments for the shop and fittings, to give a closing cash (bank) balance of £15,000.

The wealth of the business at the end of the first week was Mr Bean's original capital of £50,000. Wealth had not been increased or decreased as there was no profit or loss. The wealth was represented by the shop, its fittings, and the closing bank balance.

Totals for the month to date are of course the same as for week 1.

Example 2.2

Let's look at the subsequent three weeks accounting periods, one week at a time, beginning with week 2.

		Week 1 £	Week 2 £	Total £
Profit and loss account	Sales	0	0	0
	Cost of sales	0	0	0
	Gross profit	0	0	0
	Expenses	0	(200)	(200)
	Profit/(loss)	0	(200)	(200)
	Cumulative profit/(loss)	0	(200)	(200)
Cash flow statement	Opening balance	0	15,000	0
	Cash received ex Mr Bean	50,000	0	50,000
	Cash received from customers	0	0	0
	Cash paid for shop freehold	(30,000)	0	(30,000)
	Cash paid for shop fittings	(5,000)	0	(5,000)
	Cash paid for stationery	0	(200)	(200)
	Closing balance	15,000	14,800	14,800
Balance sheet	Cash closing balance	15,000	14,800	14,800
	Freehold shop	30,000	30,000	30,000
	Shop fittings	5,000	5,000	5,000
	Stocks	0	0	0
	Debtors	0	0	0
	Creditors	0	0	0
	Total wealth	50,000	49,800	49,800
	Represented by:			
	Mr Bean's original capital	50,000	50,000	50,000
	Profit/(loss) to date	0	(200)	(200)
	Total capital	50,000	49,800	49,800

We can summarise the financial position at the end of the second week as follows:

There was still no trading but printing and stationery had been used, and there was a charge for their expense to the profit and loss account, therefore there was a loss for the week. The cumulative two weeks is obtained by adding across each line in the profit and loss account, which is also the sum of the totals, to give a cumulative two-week loss of £200.

Cash was reduced in week 2 by the cash paid for printing and stationery expenses to give a closing balance of £14,800. It can be seen that the two-week cumulative cash position is calculated by starting with the week 1 opening balance and then adding across all the payment and receipt elements. The sum of the total column will give the same closing balance as that shown for week 2.

The wealth of the business at the end of the second week was Mr Bean's original capital reduced by the cumulative loss of £200 to give £49,800. The wealth was represented by the shop, its fittings, and the closing bank balance.

Note that the cumulative balance sheet at the end of week 2 is exactly the same as that shown in the week 2 column and not the totals of each of the elements added across in weeks 1 and 2. This is always true for however many weeks or any other period we may be looking at, which is what we would expect since the balance sheet does show the financial position at a point in time, in this example the position at the end of week 2.

Progress check 2.2

How can a business have made a loss during an accounting period if it hasn't been involved in any trading during the period?

Example 2.3

Let's now look at accounting period week 3.

		Week 1 £	Week 2 £	Week 3 £	Total £
Profit and loss account	Sales	0	0	2,000	2,000
	Cost of sales	0	0	(1,000)	(1,000)
	Gross profit	0	0	1,000	1,000
	Expenses	0	(200)	0	(200)
	Profit/(loss)	0	(200)	1,000	800
	Cumulative profit/(loss)	0	(200)	800	800
Cash flow statement	Opening balance	0	15,000	14,800	0
	Cash received ex Mr Bean	50,000	0	0	50,000
	Cash received from customers	0	0	2,000	2,000
	Cash paid for shop freehold	(30,000)	0	0	(30,000)
	Cash paid for shop fittings	(5,000)	0	0	(5,000)
	Cash paid for stationery	0	(200)	0	(200)
	Closing balance	15,000	14,800	16,800	16,800
Balance sheet	Cash closing balance	15,000	14,800	16,800	16,800
	Freehold shop	30,000	30,000	30,000	30,000
	Shop fittings	5,000	5,000	5,000	5,000
	Stocks	0	0	11,000	11,000
	Debtors	0	0	0	0
	Creditors	0	0	(12,000)	(12,000)
	Total wealth	50,000	49,800	50,800	50,800
	Represented by:				
	Mr Bean's original capital	50,000	50,000	50,000	50,000
	Profit/(loss) to date	0	(200)	800	800
	Total capital	50,000	49,800	50,800	50,800

We can summarise the financial position at the end of the third week as follows:

There was some trading, which gave a profit for the week of £1,000. The cumulative three weeks is obtained by adding across each line in the profit and loss account, which is also the sum of the totals, to give a cumulative three-week profit of £800.

Cash was increased in week 3 by the cash received from customers, and with no cash payments the closing balance was £16,800. It can be seen that the three-week cumulative cash position is calculated by starting with the week 1 opening balance and then adding across all the payment and receipt elements. The sum of the total column will give the same closing balance as that shown for week 3.

The wealth of the business at the end of the third week was Mr Bean's original capital increased by the cumulative profit of £800 to give £50,800. The wealth was represented by the shop, its fittings, the closing bank balance, plus stocks less creditors (two new categories introduced in this example). The first category is stocks. Stocks had been purchased in the month, but had been reduced by the amount used in trading. The second new category is the result of the purchase of stock for £12,000, which had not yet been paid out in cash but nevertheless was a claim against the company. This claim is an amount due to be paid to suppliers, or creditors of the business, and therefore a reduction in the wealth of the company.

The amount of stocks used in trading to provide the sales of £2,000 is called **cost of sales**, which in this example is £1,000. Note again that the cumulative balance sheet at the end of week 3 is exactly the same as that shown in the week 3 column and not the totals added across each of the elements in weeks 1, 2 and 3.

Example 2.4

Let's now look at the final accounting period, week 4.

		Week 1 £	Week 2 £	Week 3 £	Week 4 £	Total £
Profit and loss account	Sales	0	0	2,000	16,000	18,000
	Cost of sales	0	0	(1,000)	(8,000)	(9,000)
	Gross profit	0	0	1,000	8,000	9,000
	Expenses	0	(200)	0	0	(200)
	Profit/(loss)	0	(200)	1,000	8,000	8,800
	Cumulative profit/(loss)	0	(200)	800	8,800	8,800
Cash flow statement	Opening balance	0	15,000	14,800	16,800	0
	Cash received ex Mr Bean	50,000	0	0	0	50,000
	Cash received from customers	0	0	2,000	0	2,000
	Cash paid for shop freehold	(30,000)	0	0	0	(30,000)
	Cash paid for shop fittings	(5,000)	0	0	0	(5,000)
	Cash paid for stationery	0	(200)	0	0	(200)
	Closing balance	15,000	14,800	16,800	16,800	16,800
Balance sheet	Cash closing balance	15,000	14,800	16,800	16,800	16,800
	Freehold shop	30,000	30,000	30,000	30,000	30,000
	Shop fittings	5,000	5,000	5,000	5,000	5,000
	Stocks	0	0	11,000	3,000	3,000
	Debtors	0	0	0	16,000	16,000
	Creditors	0	0	(12,000)	(12,000)	(12,000)
	Total wealth	50,000	49,800	50,800	58,800	58,800

Represented by:

Mr Bean's original capital	50,000	50,000	50,000	50,000	50,000
Profit/(loss) to date	0	(200)	800	8,800	8,800
Total capital	50,000	49,800	50,800	58,800	58,800

We can summarise the final financial position at the end of the fourth week as follows:

There was further trading, which gave a profit for the week of £8,000. The cumulative four weeks is obtained by adding across each line in the profit and loss account, which is also the sum of the totals, to give a cumulative four-week profit of £8,800.

No cash was received or paid during week 4, and so the closing balance remained at £16,800. It can be seen that the four-week cumulative cash position is calculated by starting with the week 1 opening balance and then adding across all the payment and receipt elements. The sum of the total column will give the same closing balance as that shown for week 4.

The wealth of the business at the end of the fourth week was Mr Bean's original capital increased by the cumulative profit of £8,800 to give £58,800. The wealth was represented by the shop, its fittings, closing bank balance, stock, less creditors, and now another additional element: debtors. Sales of £16,000 had been made in the month, none of which had been paid in cash. The amount remaining due from customers, the debtors of the company, at the end of the week was £16,000 which represented an element of the wealth of Ayco. The stock used for those sales had reduced the stock from the end of the previous week £11,000 to £3,000 at the end of week 4.

Note again that the cumulative balance sheet at the end of week 4 is exactly the same as that shown in the week 4 column and not the totals of each of the elements added across in weeks 1, 2, 3 and 4.

Progress check 2.3

Why is there usually a difference between profit and cash in an accounting period?

Examples 2.1 to 2.4 introduced a number of terms relating to financial statements. Whilst they gave an introduction to the principles and put things in context they were by no means exhaustive. In this chapter and the next two, we will consider each of the financial statements in more detail, beginning with the balance sheet.

What does the balance sheet tell us?

In theory the balance sheet of a private limited company or a public limited company should be able to tell us all about the company's financial structure and liquidity – the extent to which its assets and liabilities are held in cash or in a near cash form (for example, bank accounts and deposits). It should also tell us about the assets held by the company, the proportion of **current assets** and the extent to which they may be used to meet current obligations. In later chapters we will look at many of the important ratios used to evaluate the strength of a company's balance sheet. We will also see how the balance sheet tells us about the financial structure of companies and the sources of such financing.

An element of caution should be noted in analysing balance sheet information. The balance sheet is an historical document. It may have looked entirely different six months or a year ago, or even one week ago. There is not always consistency between the information included in one company's balance sheet with that of another company. Two companies even within the same industry are usually very difficult to compare. Added to that, very often different analysts use the same ratios in different ways.

We will look at some of the variety of methods used to value the various items contained in the balance sheet. However, in addition to the wide choice of valuation methods, the information in a typical published balance sheet does not tell us anything about the quality of the assets, their real value in money terms or their value to the business.

'Off balance sheet financing' and 'window dressing' are two terms that often crop up in discussions about the accuracy of balance sheet information. The former relates to the funding of operations in such a way that the relevant assets and liabilities are not disclosed in the balance sheet of the company concerned. The latter is a creative accounting practice in which changes in short-term funding have the effect of disguising or improving the reported liquidity (cash and near cash) position of the reporting organisation.

Structure of the balance sheet

Assets are acquired by a business to generate future benefits, for example from trading or whatever activities the business has been set up to provide. To acquire assets the business must first raise the necessary funds. In doing so the claims or obligations are created in the form of shareholders' equity or liabilities.

Shareholders' equity and both long-term and current liabilities represent claims, or obligations, on the company to provide cash or other benefits to a third party. Equity, or capital, represents a claim by the owners, or shareholders, of the business against the business.

Liabilities represent claims by other than the owners of the business, against the business. These claims arise from transactions relating to the provision of goods or services, or lending money to the business.

An example of a balance sheet format adopted by a limited company, Flatco plc, is shown in Fig. 2.5. It is shown in what is termed an horizontal format in order to illustrate the grouping of the assets categories, the total of which equal the total of the liabilities and equity categories. UK companies invariably adopt the vertical format (see Fig. 2.8), rather than the horizontal format balance sheet, which we shall discuss in a later section of this chapter.

The detail of each of the categories within the balance sheet will be explained in the sections that follow. As we have shown in Fig. 2.5, each balance sheet category, both assets and liabilities, may be described as either financial or operational. Capital and reserves and financial debt are financial resources, whereas fixed assets, stocks, debtors, prepayments, long-term liabilities and short-term liabilities are operational, relating to the manufacturing, commercial and administrative activities of the company. Cash, which is also financial, represents the temporary difference between the financial resources and its uses.

We will now look at each of the balance sheet categories in detail, beginning with shareholders' equity and liabilities.

Flatco plc
Balance sheet as at 31 December 2000

Figures in £000

	Assets			Liabilities		
	Fixed assets			**Capital and reserves (shareholders' equity)**		
operational	Intangible	416		Capital	1,200	financial
operational	Tangible	1,884		Premiums	200	financial
operational	Financial	248		Profit and loss account	1,594	financial
			2,548			2,994
				Long-term liabilities (over 1 year)		
				Financial debt	173	financial
				Creditors	154	operational
				Provisions	222	operational
						549
	Current assets			**Current liabilities (less than 1 year)**		
operational	Stocks	311		Financial debt	50	financial
operational	Debtors	573		Creditors	553	operational
operational	Prepayments	589		Accruals	202	operational
financial	Cash	327				805
			1,800			
			4,348			4,348

FIGURE 2.5   A typical horizontal balance sheet format showing the balancing of assets with liabilities

Capital and reserves or shareholders' equity

Shareholders' equity is usually simply called 'equity'. It represents the total investment of the shareholders in the company, the total wealth. Equity comprises capital, premiums, and retained earnings. The cost of shareholders' equity is generally regarded as the dividends paid to shareholders, the level of which is usually dependent on how well the company has performed during the year.

Capital

The nominal value of a share is the value of each share, decided at the outset by the promoters of the company. The nominal value is the same for each of the shares and may be, for example, 25p, 50p, or £1 (the usual maximum). The initial share capital is the number of shares in the company multiplied by the nominal value of the shares (for example, 2 million shares at 50p per share is £1,000,000, or at £1 per share is £2,000,000). Each share is a title of ownership on the assets of the company. This is an important issue in respect of control and growth of the company.

Example 2.5

Arthur King is setting up a small limited company, Round Table Ltd, for which he needs initial capital of £10,000. Arthur creates 100 shares each having a nominal value of £100. Arthur decides to start off as king of his empire and keep 90% of the shares for himself and so buys 90 shares at £100 each and pays £9,000 out of his personal account into the bank account of the new company, Round Table Ltd. The remaining 10 shares are purchased by ten of Arthur's friends each for £100. Arthur owns 90% of the company, and each friend owns 1% of the company, has 1% of the voting rights at shareholders' meetings and will receive 1% of dividends paid by the company.

Round Table Ltd does well and after some time Arthur considers that he needs additional capital of a further £10,000 to fund its growth. Arthur may issue 100 new shares at £100 each.

Discuss the implications for Arthur if he is unable to afford any additional shares himself and the new shares are sold to new investors. Then the total number of shares becomes 200 of which he will own 90, that is 45%.

Answer

Because Arthur has less than 50% we may say that he therefore loses control of the company. There are two main considerations regarding the issue of shares and control.

The first point is that the founder of a growing business must face a difficult dilemma: growing, but losing control or keeping control but losing growth opportunities. An alternative may be to go to the bank and fund growth with a loan. However, along with this goes a vulnerability to failure at the first cash crisis the company may face.

The second point is that the issue of new shares at the same price as the existing original shares may be considered unfair. When Round Table Ltd was created it was worth only the money that the original shareholders invested in it. The company's credibility has now been built up through successful operations and an understanding of the market. Surely this must have a value so that the new share issue should be made at a higher price? The difference in price between the original nominal value and the price new investors will have to pay is the share premium.

Premiums

The **share premium** may be best illustrated with an example.

Example 2.6

Using the company in Example 2.5, let us assume that for potential investors the value of one share is now £400. This means that 25 shares of £400 would be needed to raise additional capital of £10,000.

Explain how these new shares should appear in the company's balance sheet.

Answer

(i)   These new shares cannot appear in the balance sheet with a nominal value of £400 because it would then mean that legally the shareholders would have voting and dividend rights four times those of the £100 nominal shares.

CHAPTER 2 FINANCIAL STATEMENTS OF LIMITED COMPANIES – BALANCE SHEET

(ii) The capital in the balance sheet will need to be increased by 25 × £100, the nominal value of the shares, that is £2,500.

(iii) A new category, share premiums, is required on the balance sheet.

(iv) Share premiums will have a value of 25 × (£400 − £100), that is £7,500.

Retained earnings

Retained earnings is the final element within the equity of the company. The profit or net earnings generated from the operations of the company belongs to the shareholders of the company. It is the shareholders who decide how much of those earnings are distributed to shareholders as **dividends**, the balance being held and reinvested in the business. The retained earnings of the company are increased by the annual net profit less any dividends payable; they are part of the shareholders' wealth and therefore appear within the equity of the company. Similarly, any losses will reduce the retained earnings of the company.

Liabilities

Current, or short-term, liabilities

Short-term liabilities are items that are expected to become payable within one year from the balance sheet date. These comprise trade **creditors** (or accounts payable) within one year, financial debts, **accruals**, tax, and dividends.

Short-term financial debt

Short-term financial debts are the elements of overdrafts, loans and leases that are payable within one year of the balance sheet date.

Trade creditors or accounts payable

Whereas there is a cost associated with equity and financial debt in the form of dividends and interest payable, creditors are sometimes considered 'free' of such cost. This, however, is not really true. Creditors payable within one year comprise taxes, national insurance, VAT, etc. as well as accounts payable to suppliers of materials, goods and services provided to the company. Accounts payable, for example, are not free debt.

Example 2.7

A supplier may offer to a company payment terms of three months from delivery date.

What is the effect of the company proposing to the supplier payment terms of two months from delivery date, for which the supplier may for example offer 1% or 2% early settlement discount?

Answer

A discount of 1% for settlement one month early is equivalent to over 12% per annum. Consequently, it becomes apparent that the supplier's selling price must have included some allowance for financial charges; accounts payable are therefore not a free debt.

47

Accruals

Accruals are allowances made for costs and expenses incurred and payable within one year of the balance sheet date but for which no invoices have yet been processed through the accounts. This is in line with the matching (or accruals) concept we discussed in Chapter 1. Expense recognition is an important concept. Expenses should be recognised immediately they are known about. Accruals are treated in a similar way to payables but the invoices for these charges have not yet been processed by the entity. They are charges or expenses, which are brought into the period because, although goods (or services) have been provided, they have not yet been included in the supplier's accounts. Some examples are telephone and electricity charges which are incurred but for which invoices may not normally be received until the end of each quarter. On the other hand, revenues or profits should not be recognised until they are earned.

Example 2.8

We know that in the Ayco example the business had used and had been invoiced for and paid for £200 worth of stationery. Assume, for example, that more than £200 worth of stationery had been used in the month of January, say £1,000.

(i) What would be the impact on Ayco if £500 worth of the additional stationery had been used, and an invoice had been received but not processed through the ledgers?

(ii) What would be the impact on Ayco if £300 worth of the additional stationery had been used, and an invoice had not yet been received but was still in the mail?

Answer

Both amounts would have to be charged to printing and stationery expenses for a total of £800. The balancing entries that would have to be made would be to credit a total of £800 to accruals. Ayco knew they had used stationery for which there was a cost even though an invoice may not have been processed.

The net impact of the above on Ayco would have been a reduction in profit, a debit of £800 and an increase in liabilities, a credit of £800 to accruals.

Long-term liabilities

Long-term liabilities are items that are expected to become payable after one year from the balance sheet date. These comprise long-term trade creditors (or accounts payable), financial debt, and provisions.

Long-term financial debt

Long-term financial debts are the elements of loans and leases that are payable after one year of the balance sheet date. To help the company finance its operations it may take on further debt – financial debt for a limited period of time. The company has to pay interest on financial debt, over the period of the loan, regardless of how well or not the company performs, that is, regardless of whether it has made a profit or a loss.

Financial debt, provided by various financial institutions such as banks, may take the form of overdrafts, loans, debentures and leases. Interest rates vary according to the risk of

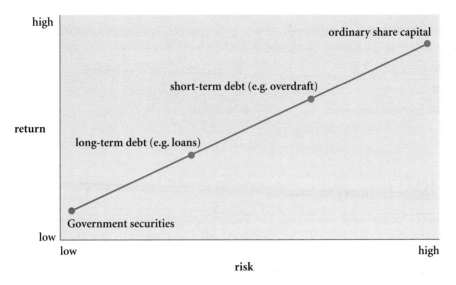

FIGURE 2.6   An illustration of the relationship between risk and return

the investment. The level of interest payable, and thus the choice of which type of debt the company may wish to take on, will be determined by how risky the potential lender regards this particular company.

A banker or investor may wish to invest in Government securities, which are risk free, and receive the low rate of return offered by such investments. For a company, which is not risk free, the investor will expect a higher rate of interest as an incentive or compensation for the risk being taken. The higher the risk of a security, the higher the expected rate of return (see Fig. 2.6).

The difference between the interest rate paid on Government securities and the interest rate that a company pays on loans is called the risk premium. Shareholders' equity is even riskier than shorter-term corporate debt (for example, a loan made to the company). Therefore, the company should not only make a profit but the level of profit should be such that the shareholders get a return in line with their level of risk. This should be the return on Government securities plus a risk premium which is even higher than the risk premium payable on the corporate debt.

Long-term trade creditors or accounts payable

Creditors payable after one year mainly comprise accounts payable to suppliers of goods and services provided to the company that may typically be, for example, relating to capital projects taking place over an extended period.

Provisions

Provisions are amounts charged against profit to provide for an expected liability or loss even though the amount or date of the liability or loss is uncertain. This is in line with the prudence concept we discussed in Chapter 1.

Progress check 2.4

Which of the following do you think may be classified as liabilities or shareholders' equity within a balance sheet, and under which headings should they appear?

- bank overdraft
- computer
- five-year bank loan
- accruals
- amounts owed to suppliers
- ordinary shares
- amounts owed by customers

Assets

We have seen that assets are acquired by a business to generate future benefits, for example from trading or whatever activities the business has been set up to provide. In addition to providing benefits from transactions, accounting assets have a number of other characteristics. Assets must be capable of being measured in monetary units; the business must have exclusive control over such assets.

The assets side of the balance sheet is more homogeneous than the equity and liabilities side of the balance sheet. The liabilities side of the balance sheet generally describes where the financing comes from, whereas the assets side generally represents how the money has been used.

Fixed assets

Fixed assets include land and buildings, equipment, machinery, furniture, fittings, computers, software, and motor vehicles, which the company has purchased to enable it to meet its strategic objectives. They have a very important common feature, namely that they are not renewed within the **operating cycle**, which is normally measured in months, weeks, days, or even hours. The operating cycle is the period of time between the point at which cash starts to be spent on production, and the collection of cash from customers who have been supplied with finished product. Fixed assets last longer, and in most cases much longer, than one year.

A building may have a life of 20 years, whereas a personal computer may have a life of three years, both being longer than the cycle in which raw materials and packaging are renewed, for example. Regardless of this, fixed assets are 'consumed' on a day-to-day basis. The measure of this consumption or wearing out, or other loss of value of these assets, whether arising from use, passage of time or obsolescence through technology or market changes, is called depreciation.

Fixed assets are comprised of tangible fixed assets, intangible fixed assets, and financial assets (or long-term investments).

Tangible fixed assets

These are the assets that one can touch, for example land, buildings, equipment, machinery, computers, fixtures and fittings.

Intangible fixed assets

These are all the other fixed assets, except for investments in **subsidiary companies**, and include software, patents, trademarks, and **goodwill**.

Financial assets

Financial assets include investments in subsidiaries, and other specific items such as loans to subsidiary companies.

Current assets

In addition to the investment in its whole fixed environment (buildings, equipment, machinery, computers, and furniture) the company has to invest additional funds in its operating cycle, which involves the management of its current assets and current liabilities. We will look in detail at the operating cycle in Chapter 15 when we look at the management of working capital.

Stocks

Stocks comprise raw materials, partly completed finished goods, work in progress and finished goods. They may also include sundry other consumable items purchased for use over a period of time such as stationery, replacement parts, and cleaning materials, if these are of any significant value, so that the inclusion of their total cost on acquisition would provide a distortion in the profit and loss account.

Debtors or accounts receivable

Debtors represent money owed to the company by customers.

Cash

Cash includes bank balances and actual cash held.

Prepayments

A prepayment is expenditure on goods (or services) for future benefit, which is to be charged to future operations. Such amounts are similar to debtors and are included in current assets in the balance sheet.

Prepayments include prepaid expenses for services not yet used, for example rent, insurance, subscriptions, or electricity charges in advance, and also accrued income. Accrued income relates to sales of goods or services that have occurred and have been accounted for within the trading period but have not yet been invoiced to the customer. This is in accord with the matching (or accruals) concept discussed in Chapter 1.

Example 2.9

In the Ayco example we may assume, for example, that Ayco had received an invoice in January for £2,000 for advertising to be paid in March, but the advertising was not taking place until February.

An invoice may have been received and processed through the ledgers. What would be the impact on Ayco?

Answer

Payables would be increased by (or credited with) £2,000 and advertising expenses charged with (or debited with) £2,000 in the month of January. However, because the advertising had not yet taken place the charge of £2,000 would be considered as being in advance, or to use its technical term, a prepayment. The payables entry remains as a credit of £2,000, but an additional entry is required to credit advertising expenses with £2,000 and debit prepayments with £2,000.

The net impact of the above on Ayco would have been no change to profit.

Progress check 2.5

(i)   Which of the following items do you think may be classified as assets within a balance sheet?

(ii) Which ones are fixed assets and which ones are current assets?

(iii) In which categories should the assets appear?

- long-term debt
- products for sale to customers
- goodwill
- computer printer
- an invoice not yet received for photocopy expenses already incurred
- materials held to be used in production
- share premium
- water charges paid in advance

Balance sheet formats

The summary balance sheet that we saw in Fig. 2.5 is known as the horizontal format. Although now rarely used in practice within businesses, it was a conventional format in which assets are shown in one column and liabilities (and equity) in the other column. Such a presentation clearly illustrated how total assets equalled the total of liabilities (and equity).

The horizontal balance sheet format can be represented by the equation

$$\text{total assets (TA)} = \text{equity (E)} + \text{total liabilities (TL)}$$
$$\text{TA} = \text{E} + \text{TL}$$

or

$$\text{fixed assets (FA)} + \text{current assets (CA)}$$
$$= \text{equity (E)} + \text{long-term liabilities (LTL)} + \text{current liabilities (CL)}$$
$$\text{FA} + \text{CA} = \text{E} + \text{LTL} + \text{CL}$$

An alternative, more commonly used format is the vertical format. The vertical format simply rearranges the above equation to become

$$\text{FA} + (\text{CA} - \text{CL}) - \text{LTL} = \text{E}$$

Each element in the equation is represented vertically with total assets less total liabilities equal to, or represented by, the equity of the company.

Using the data from Fig. 2.5 the balance sheet for Flatco plc is shown in a vertical format in Fig. 2.7. The vertical format balance sheet has some advantages over the horizontal format. It shows a balance sheet total, that is the equity, or total capital, of the business; it is the total wealth that is represented by the **net assets** of the business. A balance sheet is probably easier to read down the page rather than across, and the vertical format does clearly highlight each of the main sections of the balance sheet.

Flatco plc
Balance sheet as at 31 December 2000

Figures in £000

Fixed assets			
Intangible			416
Tangible			1,884
Financial			248
			2,548
Current assets			
Stocks	311		
Debtors	573		
Prepayments	589		
Cash	327		
		1,800	
Current liabilities (less than 1 year)			
Financial debt	50		
Creditors	553		
Accruals	202		
		805	
Net current assets			995
(working capital)			
Total assets			
less current liabilities			3,543
less			
Long-term liabilities (over 1 year)			
Financial debt	173		
Creditors	154		327
less			
Provisions			222
Net assets			2,994
Capital and reserves			
Capital			1,200
Premiums			200
Profit and loss account			1,594
			2,994

FIGURE 2.7 A vertical format balance sheet

The Companies Act requires comparative figures for the previous year for each line in the balance sheet (not shown in the Flatco plc balance sheet example). These are normally shown in a column to the right of the current year's figures.

In Appendix 1, the concept of the **trial balance**, and its links with the profit and loss account and balance sheet are examined in detail. Example 2.10 uses the trial balance of Perfecto Ltd to identify the various categories of assets, and liabilities and equity (the debits and the credits).

Example 2.10

The balances extracted from the trial balance of Perfecto Ltd at 30 September 2000 are presented in an alphabetical list:

	£000
Accruals	100
Bank and cash balances	157
Creditors due within one year	277
Creditors due after one year	77
Debtors	284
Intangible fixed assets	203
Long-term loans	85
Prepaid expenses and accrued income	295
Profit and loss account year to 30 September 2000 (loss)	54
Provisions	103
Retained earnings at 30 September 1999	709
Share capital	600
Share premium	105
Stocks of finished goods	95
Stocks of materials	37
Tangible fixed assets	902
Work in progress	29

First, identify which are assets (debit balances) and which are liabilities and equity (credit balances). Second, check that the trial balance is actually in balance. Is there any information missing? Prepare a balance sheet for Perfecto Ltd as at 30 September 2000 using a vertical format.

(Hints: Remember that a loss is a debit.
         A provision is similar to an accrual.
         If the total of the debit balances is equal to the total of the credit balances it may be assumed that the information is complete.)

Answer

	Assets (debits) £000	Liabilities and equity (credits) £000
Accruals		100
Bank and cash balances	157	
Creditors due within one year		277
Creditors due after one year		77
Debtors	284	
Intangible fixed assets	203	
Long-term loans		85

Prepaid expenses and accrued income	295	
Profit and loss account year to September 2000 (loss)	54	
Provisions		103
Retained earnings at 31 December 1999		709
Share capital		600
Share premium		105
Stocks of finished goods	95	
Stocks of materials	37	
Tangible fixed assets	902	
Work in progress	29	
Total	2,056	2,056

The total of the assets is £2,056,000, which is equal to the total of the liabilities plus equity. The trial balance is therefore in balance and there doesn't appear to be any information missing. However, errors of omission, for example, or transposed figures, may not be spotted from the information given. There could be equal and opposite debit and credit balances that have been excluded from the list in error.

Given that the data is correct, an accurate balance sheet for Perfecto Ltd as at 30 September 2000 may be prepared.

Perfecto Ltd
Balance sheet as at 30 September 2000

	£000	£000	£000
Fixed assets			
Intangible			203
Tangible			902
			1,105
Current assets			
Stocks	161		
Debtors	284		
Prepayments	295		
Cash	157		
		897	
Current liabilities (less than 1 year)			
Creditors	277		
Accruals	100		
		377	
Net current assets (working capital)			520
Total assets less current liabilities			1,625

less

Long-term liabilities (over 1 year)

Financial debt	85	
Creditors	77	162
less		
Provisions		103
Net assets		1,360
Capital and reserves		
Capital		600
Premiums		105
Profit and loss account		655
		1,360

Progress check 2.6

What does the horizontal format balance sheet tell us? Why is the vertical format balance sheet preferred by most UK companies?

Many of the larger businesses in the UK consist of a number of companies rather than just one company. The control of such companies, or groups of companies, rests with a parent company, which is called the holding company. The other companies within the group are called subsidiaries. The holding company holds the required number of shares in each of the subsidiaries to give it the required control.

Businesses operate in a group structure for a variety of reasons. It may be because they cover different countries, different products, or different market sectors; it may be to provide independence, or separate accountability, or may very often be a result of successive takeovers or mergers of businesses.

The Companies Acts 1985/1989 require group accounts to be prepared for the holding company in addition to the accounts that are required to be prepared for each of the individual companies within the group. These 'consolidated accounts' exclude all transactions between companies within the group, for example inter-company sales and purchases, to avoid double counting of transactions. In most other respects, the group consolidated accounts reflect an amalgamation of each of the components of the balance sheets of all the companies within the group.

Valuation of assets

The question of valuation of assets at a specific balance sheet date arises in respect of choosing the most accurate methods relating to fixed assets, stocks and debtors (and similarly creditors) which support the fundamental requirement to give a true and fair view.

Companies must be very careful to ensure that their assets are valued in a way that realistically reflects their ability to generate future cash flows. This applies to both current assets such as stocks, and fixed assets such as land and buildings. At Marks and Spencer plc, for example, throughout 1999 and 2000 it became apparent that the high levels of stocks of

M&S stunned as trading plunges 14pc
By Kate Rankine, Deputy City Editor

Trading at Marks & Spencer has deteriorated sharply during the past five weeks, suggesting that a recovery remains as elusive as ever.

Luc Vandevelde, M&S's chairman and chief executive, admitted that the sudden downturn came as a surprise to him and the rest of the struggling retailer's board. Total sales of clothes, footwear and gifts plunged by 14.6pc for the five weeks ending November 4, but stripping out the effects of opening new stores, like-for-like sales tumbled by 17.4pc.

Only seven weeks ago, when the company axed Peter Salsbury as chief executive, M&S said that total general merchandise sales were down by 0.3pc for the 26 weeks to September 16, while like-for-like sales fell 2.8pc. Mr Vandevelde said: 'It was a big surprise, not a shock, and it took us a while to figure out why. Clearly we're not satisfied'.

One analyst said: 'There's no sign of a recovery whatsoever. It's just getting worse. The whole thing is a fiasco and they're being hopelessly optimistic'. Mr Vandevelde, who became M&S executive chairman eight months ago, said: 'I'm on record saying that I give myself two years to turn it round. I still think it can be done'.

Mr Vandevelde claimed that the recent sales performance had partly been distorted by a comparison to autumn 1999 when M&S ran extensive promotions, including reducing all menswear by 20pc. However, excluding this impact on the figures, Mr Vandevelde reckoned that general merchandise sales still fell by 5.4pc for the five weeks ending November 4.

He blamed the deterioration in trading on 'major problems' getting supplies of lingerie, knitwear and shoes into its British stores. As a result, total lingerie sales have fallen and Mr Vandevelde admitted that the company has lost market share, although it remains the country's biggest seller of women's underwear. He said the company did not plan to take any legal action against Courtaulds, which was responsible for supplying the underwear to M&S.

However, Mr Vandevelde refused to rule out legal action against Coats Viyella, which he blames for £6m of lost knitwear sales during the past five weeks. Their relationship has become increasingly strained, culminating in Coats's decision two months ago to pull out of making clothes for M&S.

M&S reported yesterday that profits before tax and exceptional items fell to £183m for the six months ending September 30, from £193m for the same period last year. Half-year profits at its troubled UK business plunged by almost 23pc to £125m.

One analyst, who declined to be named, said: 'The current trading figures are absolutely awful. M&S is performing worse than its competitors. Personally I blame that fat bird running around naked on the telly for putting off the customers'.

The company also announced that it is closing six 'satellite' stores out of 19 that were bought from Littlewoods two years ago, but there will be no job losses. Mr Vandevelde said: 'These are our worst-performing stores, but the bulk are in pretty good shape. However, I'd definitely not do the acquisition today'.

M&S shares reversed some of Monday's losses and closed up 10 at 195p yesterday. The interim dividend is maintained at 3.7p.

© *Daily Telegraph*, 8 November 2000

clothing, footwear and gifts held in the group's stores and warehouses were unlikely to realise the expected levels of income from sales, which continued their downward slide over both those years.

Additionally, many of the Littlewoods stores that had been acquired by M&S in 1998 to provide an expansion of sales, actually failed to deliver anywhere near expectation.

Subsequently, M&S's problems continued through 2000 and into 2001. These resulted in further restructuring of the business, proposed closure of its stores in France (which was met with considerable opposition as a result of an inadequate consultation process), and the chairman, Luc Vandevelde's decision to waive payment of his £800,000 bonus for the year.

Differences between the methods chosen to value various assets (and liabilities) at the end of accounting periods may have a significant impact on the results reported in the profit and loss account for those periods. Examples of this may be seen in

● fixed assets and depreciation

● stocks valuations and cost of sales

● valuations of accounts payable and accounts receivable denominated in foreign currencies

● provisions for doubtful debts.

The valuation of assets and liabilities will all be covered in detail in Chapter 3 when we look at the profit and loss account. The rules applicable to the valuation of balance sheet items are laid down in the Companies Act 1985, as amended by the Companies Act 1989. These rules allow companies to prepare their financial statements under the historical cost convention (the gross value of the asset being the purchase price or production cost), or alternative conventions of historical cost modified to include certain assets at a revalued amount or current cost.

Under alternative conventions, the gross value of the asset is either the market value at the most recent valuation date or its current cost: tangible fixed assets should be valued at market value or at current cost; investments (fixed assets) are valued at market value or at any value considered appropriate by the directors; investments (current assets) are valued at current cost; stocks are valued at current cost. If a reduction in value of any fixed assets is expected to be permanent then provision for this must be made. The same applies to investments even if the reduction is not expected to be permanent.

Fixed assets with finite lives are subject to depreciation charges. Current assets must be written down to the amount for which they could be disposed of (their **net realisable value**), if that value is lower than cost or an alternative valuation. It should be noted that provisions for reductions in value no longer considered necessary must be written back to the profit and loss account.

There is an element of choice between alternative valuation methods that may be adopted by businesses. Because of this, difficulties may arise in trying to provide consistent comparisons of the performance of companies even within the same industrial sectors. If changes in accounting policies have been introduced, further inconsistencies arise in trying to provide a realistic comparison of just one company's performance between one accounting period and another.

The Companies Acts 1985/1989, accounting concepts, and the accounting standards (SSAPs and FRSs) lay down certain rules for the valuation of balance sheet items. We will look at some of the most important valuation rules in respect of fixed assets and current assets.

Fixed assets

Capital expenditure on fixed assets is defined in the 1985 Companies Act as those assets intended for use on a continuing basis in the company's activities. As we have already discussed, fixed assets comprise tangible assets, **intangible assets**, and investments (financial assets). Within tangible fixed assets there are various categories of asset: land and buildings (freehold, long leasehold and short leasehold); plant and machinery; fixtures, fittings, tools and equipment; assets in the course of construction.

Capital expenditure relates to acquisition of fixed assets and includes all the costs of putting an asset into service with the company so that the company will benefit from the services of the asset for more than one trading period.

Interest charges incurred in the financing of the production of an asset may be added to and included in the total cost of the asset. Such charges are said to have been capitalised, and if they are included in the total fixed asset cost this must be disclosed in a note to the financial statements.

Which other acquisition costs should be added to the asset price to give the total acquisition cost? The total amount recorded in the accounts of a company, the capitalised cost, for each category of fixed asset, should include various acquisition costs in addition to the purchase price of the asset, as follows:

- land
  - agent's commissions
  - legal fees
  - survey fees
  - draining, clearing, landscaping, demolition costs
- buildings
  - repair, alteration and improvement costs
- other assets
  - freight costs
  - customs duty
  - installation charges
- building construction
  - subcontract work
  - materials costs
  - labour costs
  - direct construction overheads
  - excavation costs
  - construction offices
  - professional fees
- own-built plant and machinery
  - materials costs
  - labour costs
  - production overheads.

Overheads that may be capitalised relate to costs of wages, salaries and expenses not directly incurred in the construction of buildings or machinery, but which nevertheless are necessary costs incurred to enable construction to take place. Examples may be a proportion or the full costs of management and supervision of projects, and a share of electricity or similar charges incurred on such projects.

Example 2.11

You have been asked to decide on which of the following items should be disclosed in the balance sheet and which should be disclosed in the profit and loss account.

		£
1.	Extension to the factory	500,000
2.	New plant	100,000
3.	Architect's fee for supervising the building of the extension	10,000
4.	Haulier's invoice for delivering the plant	5,000
5.	Invoice from decorators for painting the reception area	2,000
6.	Insurance premium for twelve months on new cars	15,000
7.	Invoice from garage for ten new cars	200,000

◀ **Answer**

	£
1. Balance sheet – fixed assets	500,000
2. Balance sheet – fixed assets	100,000
3. Balance sheet – fixed assets	10,000
4. Balance sheet – fixed assets	5,000
5. Profit and loss account – repairs	2,000
6. Profit and loss account – insurance	15,000
7. Balance sheet – fixed assets	200,000

A valuation problem arises with regard to fixed assets because such assets have been 'consumed' over time and will currently be worth less than at the time of acquisition. The total cost of using a fixed asset over its life is generally defined as the original investment less a portion of its cost recovered (its residual value) at the end of the asset's useful life. Depreciation is allocated to charge a fair proportion of the total cost (or valuation) of the asset to each accounting period expected to benefit from its use. The net fixed asset figure reported in each period's balance sheet will reflect the reduction to the historical cost, or revalued amount, of the asset using the depreciation calculated for each period.

Intangible assets include: development costs; concessions, patents, licences, trademarks; goodwill; payments on account. Investments (financial assets) primarily include shares and loans in non-consolidated group companies.

Progress check 2.7	Does it really matter if the year-end balance sheet of a company shows fixed assets at cost, less depreciation, but ignores any change in their value? This should be discussed from the points of view of an investor and a lender as two major users of financial statements.

Brand names

Some organisations have included brand names for products like chocolate bars and beers in their balance sheets as intangible assets, therefore inflating the totals of their balance sheets. Examples of companies that have capitalised brand names have been

● Ranks Hovis McDougall (1991) capitalised non-purchased brand names

● Guinness (1993) capitalised purchased brand names.

Brands purchased by a company may be capitalised, whereas non-purchased brands may not normally be capitalised. The ASB have viewed the inclusion of non-purchased brands as undesirable because of the difficulty in ascertaining historical costs and the inappropriateness of trying to capitalise the earnings or cash flows, which have been generated by the brand names. Capitalisation of purchased brand names is permitted under FRS 10. Purchased brands have proved to be as desirable as traditional tangible fixed assets, and so should be disclosed in the balance sheet.

Goodwill

FRS 10 defines goodwill as the difference between the value of the business as a whole and the aggregate of the fair values of its separable net assets. It can only appear on the balance sheet if a business has been acquired for a value in either cash or shares, so a company may not capitalise internally generated goodwill. FRS 10 requires purchased goodwill to be capitalised, along with all other purchased fixed assets. It may be amortised (depreciated) through the profit and loss account over its useful economic life, or left in the balance sheet at its purchased cost indefinitely, and justified annually.

Research and development costs

Development costs do not include research costs. A development cost is defined in SSAP13 as the cost of scientific or technical knowledge in order to produce new or substantially improved materials, devices, products or services; to install new processes or systems prior to the commencement of commercial production or commercial applications; or to improve substantially those already produced or installed. Development expenditure on new products or services is normally undertaken with an expectation of future commercial benefits, either from increased profits or reduced costs, and so to the extent that such costs are recoverable they may be matched against the future revenues.

Pure research costs are defined in SSAP 13 as the costs of experimental or theoretical work undertaken primarily to acquire new scientific or technical knowledge and understanding, not primarily directed towards any specific practical aim or application. Applied research costs are the costs of original or critical investigation undertaken in order to gain new scientific or technical knowledge and directed towards a specific practical aim or objective. In general, no one particular period rather than any other will be expected to benefit and so these costs should be charged to the profit and loss account as they are incurred.

Stocks

Problems arise in the area of valuation of stocks for three main reasons. First, homogenous items within various stock categories are purchased continuously and consumed continuously in the manufacturing processes. The purchase prices of these homogenous items may vary considerably. How do we know the specific prices of each item as we take them from stock and use them?

The general rule is that stocks must be valued at the lower of purchase cost (or production cost) and their net realisable value. The Companies Acts 1985/1989 allow a number of alternative methods to be used to determine the cost of stock, the most common being FIFO (first in first out, where the oldest items of stock or their costs are assumed to be the first to be used), LIFO (last in first out, where the most recently acquired items of stock or their costs are assumed to be the first to be used), average cost, and market value. LIFO is not permitted in the UK by the accounting standard for Stocks and Long-term Contracts, SSAP 9, and is not acceptable for taxation purposes.

Second, materials may be purchased from a variety of geographical locations. Additional costs such as duty, freight, and insurance may be incurred. How should these be accounted for? The costs of stocks should comprise the expenditure that has been incurred in the normal course of business in bringing the product or service to its present location and condition.

Third, as materials, packaging and other consumable items are used during the production processes to manufacture work in progress, partly finished product and fully finished product, how should costs be correctly apportioned to give a true cost? Which costs should be included and which should be excluded?

Stocks are disclosed as a main heading in the balance sheet and comprise raw materials and consumables, work in progress, finished goods, and long-term contracts. SSAP 9 requires that companies must disclose accounting policies adopted in respect of stocks and work in progress.

Debtors

Debtors, or accounts receivable, are normally paid to the company according to contractual terms of trading agreed at the outset with each customer. However, economic and trading circumstances may have changed. Can the company be sure that it will receive payment in full against all outstanding receivables? If not, what is a more realistic valuation of such debtors?

Accounts receivable may need to be reduced by an assessment of debts that will definitely not be paid (bad debts), or debts that are unlikely ever to be paid (doubtful debts). Bad and doubtful debts and their impact on the profit and loss account will be examined in detail in Chapter 3 which looks at the profit and loss account.

When goods or services are supplied to a customer they are invoiced at the agreed price and on the trading terms that have been contracted. The trading terms may be, for example, 30 days. In this case the sales value will have been taken into the current period profit and loss account but the debt, or the account receivable, will remain unpaid in the sales ledger account until it is settled after 30 days.

Foreign currency transactions

A general factor that may impact on the valuation of all asset types (and liabilities) is foreign currency exchange rate risk. For example, a customer in the USA may insist on being invoiced by the company in US$, say 10,000 US$. At the time of delivery of the goods or services the value of the US$ sale in £ at the exchange rate on the day will be, say, £6,250 (£ = 1.60 US$). The sales invoice may be issued a few days later and the exchange rate may have changed, for example £6,173 (£ = 1.62 US$). The customer may have agreed payment for two months later and the exchange rate may have moved again, say £5,714 (£ = 1.75 US$). What value should have been attributed to the account receivable at the balance sheet date?

The value attributed to a sales invoice is its £ value on the day if invoiced in £ sterling. If a sales invoice is rendered in foreign currency SSAP 20 requires it to be valued at the exchange rate at the date of the transaction, or at an average rate for the period if exchange rates do not fluctuate significantly. If the transaction is to be settled at a contracted exchange rate then the exchange rate specified in the contract should be used. Such a trading transaction is then said to be covered by a matching forward contract.

A foreign exchange forward contract is a contract, for example between a company and a bank, to exchange two currencies at an agreed exchange rate. Note also the foreign exchange forward option contract which extends this idea to allow the bank or the company to call for settlement of the contract, at two days' notice, between any two dates that have been agreed between the bank and the company at the time of agreeing the contract.

UK International Ltd invoiced a customer in the USA for goods to the value of 100,000 US\$ on 31 December 2000. The US\$ cheque sent to UK International by the customer was received on 31 January 2001 and was converted into £ sterling by the bank at 1.45 US\$ to £1. Discuss the two transactions, the invoice and its settlement, and their impact on UK International's profit and loss account and its balance sheet as at 31 December 2000.

At the end of each accounting period, all debtors denominated in foreign currency should be translated, or revalued, using the rates of exchange ruling at the period-end date, or, where appropriate, the rates of exchange fixed under the terms of the relevant transactions. Where there are related or matching forward contracts in respect of trading transactions, the rates of exchange specified in those contracts may be used. A similar treatment applies to all monetary assets and liabilities denominated in a foreign currency, that is, cash and bank balances, loans, and amounts payable and receivable.

An exchange gain or loss will result during an accounting period if a business transaction is settled at an exchange rate which differs from that used when the transaction was initially recorded, or, where appropriate, that used at the last balance sheet date. An exchange gain or loss will also arise on unsettled transactions if the rate of exchange used at the balance sheet date differs from that used previously. Such gains and losses are recognised during each accounting period and included in the profit or loss from ordinary activities.

Summary of key points

- Limited companies are required to prepare periodically three main financial statements: balance sheet; profit and loss account; cash flow statement.

- Financial statements are required for the shareholders and the Registrar of Companies, and are also used by, for example, analysts, potential investors, customers, suppliers.

- Categories within the balance sheet are classified into shareholders' equity, liabilities, and assets.

- The structure of the balance sheet lends itself to two main formats: horizontal format and vertical format, the latter being the most popular and having many advantages.

- Valuation of the various items within the balance sheet is covered by the Companies Act 1985 as amended by the Companies Act 1989, accounting concepts and standards, but nevertheless gives rise to problems and differences in approach.

- Within the rules alternative methods may be used to value the different categories of assets (and liabilities) within the balance sheet.

- There are limitations to the conventional balance sheet arising not only from the fact that it is an historical document, but from inconsistencies in its preparation between companies and industries, the employment of various asset valuation methods, off-balance sheet financing, and window dressing.

Glossary of key terms

accruals Allowances made for costs and expenses payable within one year of the balance sheet date but for which no invoices have yet been received.

amortisation In the same way that depreciation applies to the charging of the cost of tangible fixed assets over their useful economic lives, amortisation is the systematic write-off of the cost of an intangible asset, relating particularly to the passage of time, for example leasehold premises (FRS 11 and FRS 15).

asset A right or other access to future economic benefits controlled by an entity as a result of past transactions or events (FRS 5).

capital expenditure The cost of acquiring, producing or enhancing fixed assets.

cash Cash in hand and deposits repayable on demand with any bank or other financial institution. Cash includes cash in hand and deposits denominated in foreign currency (FRS 1).

consolidated accounts The consolidated financial statements which present financial information for the group as a single economic entity, prepared using a process of adjusting and combining financial information from the individual financial statements of a parent undertaking and its subsidiary undertakings (FRS 2).

cost of sales The sum of direct cost of sales, adjusted for closing stocks, plus manufacturing overhead attributable to the sales. Direct costs include the wages and salaries costs of time worked on products, and the costs of materials used in production. Manufacturing overheads include the wages and salaries costs of employees not directly working on production, and materials and expenses incurred on activities not directly used in production but necessary to carry out production. Examples are cleaning materials and electricity costs.

creative accounting A form of accounting which, while complying with all regulations, nevertheless gives a biased (generally favourable) impression of a company's performance.

creditor A person or an entity to whom money is owed as a consequence of the receipt of goods or services in advance of payment.

current assets Cash or other assets, for example stocks, debtors and short-term investments, held for conversion into cash in the normal course of trading.

current liabilities Liabilities which fall due for payment within one year. They include that part of long-term loans due for repayment within one year.

debenture The written acknowledgement of a debt by a company, usually given under its seal, and normally containing provisions as to payment of interest and the terms of repayment of principal. A debenture may be secured on some or all of the assets of the company or its subsidiaries.

debt One of the alternative sources of capital for a company, also called long-term debt or loans.

debtors Money that is owed to the company by customers, usually called trade debtors.

dividend: An amount payable to shareholders from profits or distributable reserves. Dividends are normally paid in cash, but scrip dividends, paid by the issue of additional shares, are permissible. Listed companies usually declare two dividends each year, an interim dividend based on the mid-year profits, and a final dividend based on annual profit.

equity The total investment of the shareholders in the company, the total wealth. Equity comprises capital, premiums, and retained earnings.

fixed assets Any asset, tangible or intangible, acquired for retention by an entity for the purpose of providing a service to the business, and not held for resale in the normal course of trading. This includes, for example, equipment, machinery, furniture, fittings, computers, software, and motor vehicles, that the company has purchased to enable it to meet its strategic objectives; such items are not renewed within the operating cycle.

general ledger Also called the nominal ledger, contains all accounts relating to assets, expenses, revenue and liabilities.

goodwill The difference between the value of a business as a whole and the aggregate of the fair values of the separable net assets (FRS 10). Goodwill is normally recognised on the purchase of a business, when the price paid for the net assets acquired exceeds their fair values. Where the fair value of the separable net assets exceeds the value of the business as a whole, the difference is termed negative goodwill.

intangible assets Assets, except for investments in subsidiary companies, which do not have a physical identity and include software, patents, trademarks, and goodwill (FRS 10).

liabilities An entity's obligations to transfer economic benefits as a result of past transactions or events (FRS 5).

net assets The excess of the book value of assets over liabilities, including loan capital. This is equivalent to net worth, which is used to describe the paid-up share capital and reserves.

net profit (or profit after tax) Profit before tax less corporation tax.

net realisable value The amount for which an asset could be disposed, less any direct selling costs (SSAP 9).

off balance sheet financing The funding of operations in such a way that the relevant assets and liabilities are not disclosed in the balance sheet of the company concerned.

operating cycle The operating cycle, or working capital cycle, is calculated by deducting creditor days from stock days plus debtor days. It represents the period of time which elapses between the point at which cash begins to be expended on the production of a product and the collection of cash from the customer.

prepayments Prepayments include prepaid expenses for services not yet used, for example rent in advance or electricity charges in advance, and also accrued income. Accrued income relates to sales of goods or services that have occurred and have been included in the profit and loss account for the trading period but have not yet been invoiced to the customer.

provision Amount charged against profit to provide for an expected liability or loss even though the amount or date of the liability or loss is uncertain (FRS 12).

reserves Retained profits or surpluses. In a not-for-profit entity these are described as accumulated funds. Reserves may be distributable or non-distributable.

sales Also called turnover or revenue, sales are amounts derived from the provision of goods or services falling within the company's ordinary activities, after deduction of sales returns, trade discounts, value added tax, and any other taxes based on the amounts so derived (Companies Acts 1985/1989).

sales ledger The sales ledger contains all the personal accounts of each individual customer, and records every transaction with each customer since the start of their relationship with the company.

share A fixed identifiable unit of capital which has a fixed nominal or face value, which may be quite different from the market value of the share.

share capital Capital is the number of existing shares in the company multiplied by the nominal value of the shares.

share premium The difference in price between the original nominal value and the price new investors will have to pay for shares issued by the company.

stocks Stocks, according to SSAP 9, are goods held for future use comprising

- goods or other assets purchased for resale
- consumable stores
- raw materials and components purchased for incorporation into products for sale
- products and services, in intermediate stages of completion (work in progress)
- long-term contracts
- finished goods.

subsidiary companies A subsidiary company, defined by the Companies Act 1985/1989, is a company for which another company – the parent company – is

- directly a member of it and controls the composition of its board of directors; or
- holds or controls, either by itself or in agreement with other shareholders, a majority of the voting rights; or
- has the right to exercise a dominant influence over it.

trial balance The list of account balances in a double-entry accounting system. If the records have been correctly maintained, the sum of the debit balances will equal the sum of the credit balances, although certain errors such as the omission of a transaction or erroneous entries will not be disclosed by a trial balance.

window dressing A creative accounting practice in which changes in short-term funding have the effect of disguising or improving the reported liquidity position of the reporting organisation.

working capital Also called net current assets, is the capital available for conducting day-to-day operations of an organisation; normally the excess of current assets over current liabilities.

Assessment material

Questions

Q2.1 (i) What are the three main financial statements?

(ii) What is their purpose?

Q2.2 Consider two ways of looking at the profit of a business: an increase in the wealth of the company; and the net result of the company's trading operations (sales less expenses). What do these terms mean, and is the result different using the two approaches?

Q2.3 Explain the vertical format structure of the balance sheet for a typical limited company.

Q2.4 Explain what assets, liabilities and shareholders' equity are, and give some examples of each.

Q2.5 Illustrate the difference between current liabilities and long-term liabilities with some examples of each.

Q2.6 (i) What accounting convention is generally used in the valuation of fixed assets?

(ii) What additional costs may sometimes be included and to which assets may these be applied?

Q2.7 Why are current assets and fixed assets shown under different balance sheet classifications?

Q2.8 Describe what are meant by intangible assets and give some examples of their valuation.

Q2.9 What factors influence the accurate valuation of a company's debtors?

Q2.10 Why should a potential investor exercise caution when analysing the balance sheets of potential companies in which to invest?

Discussion points

D2.1 'Surely the purchase of fixed assets is expenditure just like spending on stationery or photocopy expenses so why should it appear as an entry in the balance sheet?' Discuss.

D2.2 'It has often been said that the value of every item in a balance sheet is a matter of opinion and the cash balance is the one and only number that can truly be relied upon.' Discuss.

Exercises

Solutions are provided in Appendix 4 to all exercise numbers highlighted in colour.

Level I

E2.1   *Time allowed – 30 minutes*

The trial balance of Archibald Ltd extracted at 31 December 2000 is as follows:

	£000
Bank overdraft	203
Electricity paid in advance	15
Computer system	104
Share premium account	80
Amount for final payment on factory machine March 2002	84
Trade debtors	370
Goodwill	68
Ten-year lease on factory (fixed asset)	110
Prepaid expenses and accrued income	295
Retained earnings at 31 December 2000	241
Stocks of materials	209
Computer software (fixed asset)	18
Furniture and fixtures	243
Finished product	28
Long-term loan	250
Trade creditors	419
Petty cash	3
Share capital	520
Computer printers	25
Plant and equipment	309

You are required to

(i)   identify the debit and credit balances

(ii) confirm that the trial balance is in balance

(iii) prepare a balance sheet for Archibald Ltd at 31 December 2000 using a vertical format.

E2.2   *Time allowed – 30 minutes*

The balances in the accounts of Vertico Ltd at 31 July 2000 are as follows:

	£000
Accrued expenses	95
Bank overdraft	20
Debtors	275
Plant and equipment	309
Finished product	152
Computer system	104
Petty cash	5
Share capital	675
Trade creditors	293
Final payment on computer system due 1 September 2001	52
Loan for a factory building	239
Buildings	560
Raw materials	195

(i)   **An important number has been omitted. What is that?**

(ii) **Using the data provided and the missing data prepare a balance sheet for Vertico Ltd as at 31 July 2000 in a vertical format.**

E2.3   *Time allowed – 45 minutes*

You are required to prepare a balance sheet for Trainer plc as at 31 December 2000 using the trial balance at 31 December 2000 and the additional information shown below.

Trial balance at 31 December 2000	Debit £000	Credit £000
Bank	73	
Ordinary share capital		320
Land and buildings at cost	320	
Plant and machinery at cost	200	
Cumulative depreciation provision (charge for year 2000 was £20,000)		80
Stocks	100	
Sales		1,000
Cost of sales	600	

Operating expenses	120	
Depreciation	20	
Bad debts written off	2	
Debtors	100	
Accruals		5
Trade creditors		130
	1,535	1,535

Additional information:

The company will be paying £20,000 for corporation taxation on the 2000 profits during 2001.

E2.4 *Time allowed – 45 minutes*

The following information relates to Major plc at 31 December 2000, and the comparative numbers at 31 December 1999.

	1999 £000	2000 £000
Accruals	800	1,000
Bank overdraft		16,200
Cash at bank	600	
Plant and machinery at cost	17,600	23,900
Debentures (interest at 15% per annum)	600	750
Plant and machinery depreciation	9,500	10,750
Proposed dividends	3,000	6,000
Ordinary share capital	5,000	5,000
Preference share capital	1,000	1,000
Prepayments	300	400
Profit and loss account	3,000	10,100
Stocks	5,000	15,000
Taxation	3,200	5,200
Trade creditors	6,000	10,000
Trade debtors	8,600	26,700

Prepare a balance sheet in the format adopted by most of the leading UK plcs showing the previous year comparative figures.

E2.5 *Time allowed – 60 minutes*

From the trial balance of Gremlins plc at 31 March 2000 identify the assets and expenses (debit balances) and income, liabilities and equity (credit balances), confirm that the trial balance is in balance, then prepare a balance sheet for Gremlins Ltd as at 31 March 2000 using a vertical format.

	£000
Depreciation on office equipment and furnishings (administrative expenses)	156
Bank overdraft	609
Accountancy and audit fees	30
Electricity paid in advance	45
Computer system (net book value)	441
Advertising and promotion	135
Share premium account	240
Interest received	15
Plant and equipment (net book value)	927
Amount for final payment on factory machine due March 2002	252
Trade debtors	1,110
Goodwill	204
Twelve-year lease on factory	330
Rents received	63
Prepaid expenses	885
Interest paid	120
Office electricity	66
Retained earnings at 31 March 1999	513
Stocks of materials at 31 March 2000	585
Telephone	87
Distribution costs	162
Other office utilities	72
Cost of goods sold	1,659
Administrative salaries	216
Sales salaries	267
Furniture and fixtures (net book value)	729
Sales	3,267
Office rent	165
Finished product at 31 March 2000	84
Debenture	750
Trade creditors	1,257
Cash	51
Share capital	1,560

Level II

E2.6   *Time allowed – 60 minutes*

You are required to prepare a balance sheet for Optical plc as at 31 December 2000 using the trial balance and the additional information shown below.

Trial balance at 31 December 2000	Debit £000	Credit £000
Share capital (400,000 £1 ordinary shares)		400
Share premium		100
Revaluation reserve		100
Profit and loss account		200
Debentures (interest at 15% per annum)		200
Land at valuation	350	
Buildings at cost	200	
Buildings depreciation provision		24
Plant at cost	450	
Plant depreciation provision		180
Stocks	225	
Trade debtors	200	
Provision for doubtful debts		20
Trade creditors		220
Accruals		11
Prepayments	10	
Bank	20	
	1,455	1,455

Additional information not yet shown in the trial balance:
During the year 2000

1. The company has issued 100,000 £1 ordinary shares at a £1 premium.
2. The company has purchased plant costing £100,000
3. A customer owing £10,000 went into liquidation, with massive debts and few assets.
4. The company re-valued its land at £330,000 and decided to adjust its accounts.
5. £50,000 of debentures were repaid at par.

E2.7   *Time allowed – 60 minutes*

You are required to prepare a balance sheet as at 31 December 2000 from the following summary of Pip Ltd's financial position at 31 December 2000.

Brands worth £10,000 (director's opinion)

Reputation in the local area £10,000 (director's opinion)

Stocks at cost £50,000 and resale value £85,000, with obsolete stocks £5,000 within the £50,000

Bank overdraft facilities £20,000 agreed by the bank manager

Cash in the office £1,000

Cash in the bank number one current account £10,000

Overdraft in the bank number two current account £10,000, per the bank statement

Land and buildings at cost £100,000

Plant and equipment at cost £150,000

Plant and equipment cumulative depreciation £50,000

Plant and equipment market value £110,000

Trade creditors £81,000

Invoices outstanding by all customers £50,000, including an invoice of £5,000 owed by a customer in liquidation (Pip Ltd have been advised by the receiver that 1p in the £1 will be paid to creditors)

Past unspent profits re-invested in the business £110,000

Ordinary shares issued £100,000 (authorised ordinary shares £200,000)

3

Financial statements of limited companies – profit and loss account

CONTENTS

LEARNING OBJECTIVES

Completion of this chapter will enable you to:

● describe what is meant by profit (or loss)

● outline the structure of the profit and loss account (income statement) of a limited company

● classify the categories of income and expenditure that comprise the profit and loss account

● appreciate the alternative profit and loss account formats

● prepare a profit and loss account

● explain the links between the profit and loss account and the balance sheet, particularly with regard to the valuation of fixed assets and depreciation, stock and cost of sales, and debtors and the doubtful debt provision

● explain the links between the profit and loss account and cash flow

● appreciate the subjective aspects of profit measurement

Introduction

In Chapter 2 we looked at how to prepare simple financial statements from transactions carried out by a business during an accounting period. We then looked in a little more detail at the first of these financial statements, namely the balance sheet. This chapter will be concerned with the second of the financial statements, the profit and loss account (or income statement). Although profit and loss accounts are prepared by all forms of business entity, in a similar way to Chapter 2, this chapter deals primarily with the profit and loss accounts of limited companies, both private and public.

This chapter deals with how profit and loss accounts are structured and how the accounts within the profit and loss account are categorised. Each of the items within each of the profit and loss account categories will be described in detail and form the basis to enable the preparation of a profit and loss account of a limited company in the appropriate format.

We will look at the relationship between the profit and loss account and the balance sheet and provide an introduction to the relationship between profit (or loss) and cash flow. Like the balance sheet, the profit and loss account is subjective largely because of the impact on costs of the variety of approaches that may be taken to the valuation of assets and liabilities.

What does the profit and loss account tell us?

The profit and loss account of a private limited company or a public limited company should be able to tell us all about the results of the company's activities over specified accounting periods. The profit and loss account shows us what revenues have been generated and what costs incurred in generating those revenues, and therefore the increase or decrease in wealth of the business during the period.

The same note of caution we mentioned in Chapter 2 that should be exercised in the analysis of balance sheet information, applies to profit and loss account information. The profit and loss account is an historical statement and so it does not tell us anything about the ability of the business to sustain or improve upon its performance over subsequent periods.

There is not always consistency between the information included in one company's profit and loss account and that of another company. As with the balance sheet, the profit and loss accounts of two companies even within the same industry may be very difficult to compare. This will be illustrated in the wide variety of methods of depreciation calculations and stock valuation methods examined in this chapter. In addition, the bases of financial ratios (to be examined in detail in Chapter 5) used by analysts in looking at a company's profit and loss account may often be different.

It is often said of profit and loss statements, as well as balance sheets, that the value of every item included in them is a matter of opinion. This is due not only to the alternative stock valuation and depreciation methods, but because of the subjective assessment of whether the settlement of a customer account is doubtful or not, and the sometimes imprecise evaluation of accruals and provisions.

What is profit?

We saw from the examples in Chapter 2 that profit (or loss) may be considered from two perspectives. We may consider these perspectives to illustrate the links between the profit and loss account and the balance sheet.

The first perspective, which is not suggested as a method for calculating profit in practice, compares the balance sheet of an entity at the start of an accounting period with the balance sheet at the end of the accounting period. We may see from these that the values of each of the components of the balance sheet may have changed. For example, levels of stocks, debtors, creditors, cash, fixed assets, and accruals may have changed during an accounting period. We have seen that the net value of the assets and liabilities in the balance sheet represents the capital, or equity, or the wealth of the business at a point in time. The change in wealth over an accounting period between the beginning and end of the accounting period is the profit or loss for the period reflected in the retained earnings category in the balance sheet.

Profit (or loss) considered in this way can be represented in the equation

$$\text{total assets (TA)} - \text{total liabilities (TL)} = \text{equity (E)} + \text{profit (P)}$$

Example 3.1

Using the opening balance sheet 1 March 2000 below and the further transactions (a) and (b), we are required to

(i) show how the balance sheet will change after these transactions/events have taken place

(ii) discuss which profit the shareholders should consider is potentially distributable as a dividend

Opening balance sheet 1 March 2000	£
Fixed assets	100,000
Current assets	100,000
less	
Current liabilities	(100,000)
	100,000
Shareholders' funds	100,000

During March

(a) The fixed assets were re-valued from £100,000 to £120,000

(b) All the stock of £20,000 was sold for £40,000 cash (that is, not on credit)

Answer

(i)

Closing balance sheet 31 March 2000	£
Fixed assets [100,000 + 20,000]	120,000
Current assets [100,000 − 20,000 + 40,000]	120,000
Current liabilities [no change]	(100,000)
	140,000
Shareholders' funds [100,000 + 20,000 + 20,000]	140,000

(ii)

The revised balance sheet reflects two profits:

● the revaluation surplus of £20,000 is a paper profit, as no cash has been involved it is not prudent to pay a dividend from this profit (and legally it is not permitted)

● the other £20,000 profit is from trading and is a cash profit; it is quite prudent to pay a dividend from this profit

The balance sheets show the categories of assets, liabilities and capital, but it can be seen there must be an analysis of the movements between the balance sheets to appreciate their fundamental nature.

The second perspective, as we discussed in Chapter 2, considers the profit and loss account by summarising all the trading and non-trading transactions that have occurred during an accounting period (see Fig. 3.1). This is the method used in practice to calculate

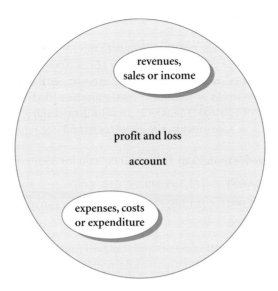

FIGURE 3.1   The main elements of the profit and loss account

the profit or loss for an accounting period. This summary, or profit and loss account, gives the same result as that derived by simply looking at the change in wealth between the beginning and end of the accounting period. It is the same because all the transactions relating to items contained in the profit and loss account are also all reflected in some way within one or more balance sheet categories. For example, sales are reflected in debtors, expenses are reflected in creditors, cost of goods that have been sold came out of stocks.

Profit (or loss) considered in this way can be represented in the equation

$$\text{profit (P)} = \text{total revenue (TR)} - \text{total costs (TC)}$$

Example 3.2

A trading company, Squirrel Ltd, has an accounting period that covers the 12 months to 31 December 2000. During that period the company entered into the following transactions:

Sales of £1,300,000, included a sales invoice for January 2001, amounting to £100,000.

Expenses of £1,000,000, included a payment of £60,000 for rent relating to the six months to 31 March 2001.

The expenses excluded some heating costs relating to the last two weeks of December 2000, for which the estimated cost was around £5,000. The quarterly invoice covering that period was not expected until late March 2001.

We are required to use the above information to discuss why the annual net profit should be revenues less expenses, and why there should be accounting concepts applied to the treatment of those expenses.

Answer

The profit and loss account for a year tries to match revenues and expenses for that year (complying with the matching concept – see Chapter 1). The term net profit means the difference between revenues and expenses. Gross profit is derived from sales less the costs of those sales, and net profit is derived from deducting expenses from gross profit. Net profit

◄ is not the difference between cash receipts and cash payments. Cash inflows and outflows suffer from timing differences.

The reported sales for the year must relate only to the 12 months to 31 December. Sales for Squirrel Ltd for the year 2000 are £1,200,000 (£1,300,000 less £100,000). Using the matching concept, the expenses must also be for 12 months. So, the estimated heating costs of £5,000 for the last two weeks of December 2000 must be added, and the rent relating to January to March 2001 of £30,000 (£60,000/2) must be deducted from the total expenses of £1,000,000. Without these adjustments, the expenses would not represent twelve months' expenses.

Net profit for the twelve months to 31 December 2000 for Squirrel Ltd is therefore

Sales	£1,200,000	[£1,300,000 less £100,000]
less Expenses	£975,000	[£1,000,000 plus £5,000 less £60,000 plus £30,000]
Which equals	£225,000	

There must be an application of concepts and standard practices in arriving at net profit, otherwise users of financial information would not have reasonable confidence in the amounts being shown in the accounts reported by companies, large or small.

In this chapter we will look at the profit and loss account from the second perspective. We will look at how a profit and loss account is constructed and prepared by deducting total costs from total revenues, as the second of the three key financial statements that are required to be prepared by a limited company.

Progress check 3.1

Explain the perspectives from which we may consider the profit (or loss) of a business.

Structure of the profit and loss account

As we have seen previously, the profit and loss account measures whether or not the company has made a profit or loss on its operations during the period, through producing or buying and selling its goods or services. It measures whether total sales or revenues are higher than the total costs (profit), or whether total costs are higher than total sales or revenues (loss).

The total revenue of a business is generated from the provision of goods or services and maybe, for example, in the form of:

● sales (goods)
● interest received (on loans)
● rents (from property)
● subscriptions (to TV channels)
● fees (professions)
● royalties (books, CDs).

The total costs of a business include the expenditure incurred as a result of the generation of revenue. The total costs of a business include, for example:

● costs of goods purchased for resale
● costs of manufacturing goods for sale
● transport and distribution costs
● advertising
● promotion
● insurance
● costs of the 'consumption' of fixed assets over their useful lives (depreciation)
● wages and salaries
● interest paid
● stationery costs
● photocopy costs
● communications costs
● electricity
● water and effluent costs
● travel expenses
● entertaining expenses
● postage.

Each of the above examples of costs (by no means an exhaustive list) incurred in the generation of revenue by a business appears itself as a separate heading, or is grouped within one or other of the other main headings within the profit and loss account. Fig. 3.2 shows each of the levels of profit that are derived after allowing for the various categories of revenues and expenses.

We will look at how a basic profit and loss account is constructed to arrive at the profit on ordinary activities after taxation (or net profit) for the company. Net profit is also

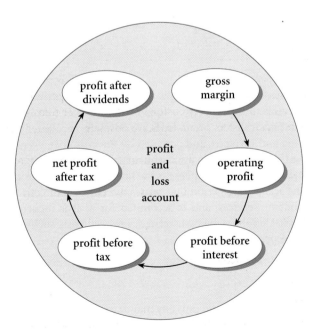

FIGURE 3.2 Levels of profit within the profit and loss account

Flatco plc
Profit and loss account for the year ended 31 December 2000

	£000
Turnover	3,500
Cost of sales	(2,500)
Gross profit	1,000
Distribution costs	(300)
Administrative expenses	(250)
	450
Other operating income	100
Operating profit	550
Income from other investments	100
Profit before interest and tax	650
Net interest	(60)
Profit before tax	590
Tax on profit on ordinary activities	(50)
Net profit (or profit on ordinary activities after tax)	540
Dividends	(70)
Net result (or retained profit for the financial year)	470

FIGURE 3.3 A profit and loss account format

sometimes called net earnings, from which may be deducted dividends payable to ordinary shareholders. The net result is then the retained profit for the financial year.

Fig. 3.3 shows an example of the profit and loss account format adopted by a **public limited company**, Flatco plc.

Each of the categories of revenue and cost within the profit and loss account (see Fig. 3.4) can be examined in a little more detail.

Turnover

The main source of income for a company is its **turnover**, primarily comprised of sales of its products and services to third-party customers. Revenues and costs are not necessarily accounted for when cash transfers occur. Sales are normally accounted for when goods or services are delivered and invoiced, and accepted by the customer, even if payment is not received until some time later, even in a subsequent trading period.

It should be noted that a cost or expense is the financial result of the 'consumption' that occurred during the accounting period that relates directly or indirectly to the production or sales of the goods or services, and is accounted for as it is incurred rather than on a cash payment basis. Costs may be cash-related, invoiced costs such as raw materials or non-cash items like depreciation charges.

Cost of sales (COS)

The sum of direct costs of goods sold plus any manufacturing expenses relating to the sales (or turnover) is termed cost of sales, or production cost of sales, or cost of goods sold. These costs include

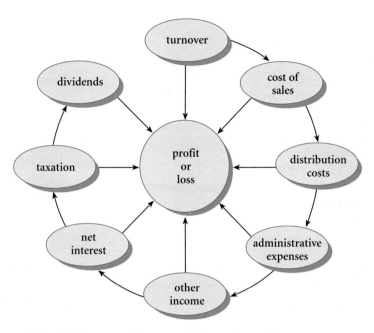

FIGURE 3.4 Elements of the profit and loss account

- costs of raw materials stocks
- costs of inward-bound freight paid by the company
- packaging costs
- direct production salaries and wages
- production expenses, including depreciation of trading-related fixed assets.

Gross margin (or gross profit)

The difference between turnover, or sales, and COS is gross profit or **gross margin**. It needs to be positive and large enough to at least cover all other expenses.

Other operating expenses: distribution costs and administrative expenses

Although not directly related to the production process, but contributing to the activity of the company, are further costs that are termed 'other operating expenses'. These include distribution costs and selling costs, administration costs, and research and development costs (unless they relate to specific projects and the costs may be deferred to future periods).

Distribution costs include the costs of selling and delivering goods and services. Such costs may include

- advertising
- market research
- promotion
- costs of the sales department

- outbound freight costs
- delivery fleet costs
- costs of the warehouse and goods outward department.

Administrative expenses effectively include all costs not included in cost of sales, distribution costs, and financial costs. They may include

- costs of service departments such as
  - finance
  - human resources
  - research and development
  - engineering
- telephone costs
- computer costs
- amortised goodwill.

Distribution costs and administration expenses include all expenses related to the 'normal' operations of the company, except those directly related to manufacturing like the costs of the purchasing department, logistics department, and quality department. They also exclude the share of overhead costs, for example, heating and lighting, business rates, water and effluent costs, relating to manufacturing activities. Administrative expenses exclude financial expenses and revenues, because these are really a function of the financial structure of the company (the extent of its funding by owners' share capital and by lenders' debt, or loans), and any other non-operational expenses and revenues.

Other operating income

Other operating income includes all other revenues that have not been included in other parts of the profit and loss account. It does not include sales of goods or services, reported within turnover, or any sort of interest receivable, reported within the net interest category.

Operating profit (OP)

Operating profit (see Fig. 3.2 and Fig. 3.3), or

$$OP = \text{turnover} - COS - \text{other operating expenses} + \text{other operating income}$$

The operating profit is the net of all operating revenues and costs, regardless of the financial structure of the company and whatever exceptional events occurred during the period that resulted in exceptional costs. Operating profit is not required to be disclosed according to the Companies Act 1985/1989, but its disclosure is one of the specific recommendations within the standard on Reporting Financial Performance, FRS 3. It is therefore an extremely important profit/loss subtotal because it allows inter-firm comparisons of companies operating in the same markets but having different financial policies.

Income from other fixed asset investments

Income from other fixed asset investments specifically excludes interest receivable, but includes dividends receivable from subsidiary or fellow subsidiary companies and from non-related companies

Profit before interest and tax (PBIT)

Profit before interest and tax, or

$$\textbf{PBIT} = \textbf{OP} + \textbf{income from other fixed asset investments}$$

PBIT is a measure of the profitability of the operations of a company regardless of the amount of interest payable and receivable on overdrafts and loans, and regardless of the amount of corporation tax it may have to pay.

Net interest

Net interest is the difference between financial revenues and charges, interest receivable and payable, and includes other financial costs like bank charges, and costs of transferring funds. The overall level of cost (or revenue) will be dependent on the type of company and level of interest rates and debt/equity mix within the funding of the company.

Profit before tax (PBT)

Profit before tax, or

$$\textbf{PBT} = \textbf{PBIT} +/- \textbf{net interest}$$

Tax on profit on ordinary activities

Corporation tax is payable on profits of limited companies. The companies, as entities, are responsible for the tax, rather than individuals as with sole traders and partnerships. Tax is shown in the profit and loss accounts, balance sheets and cash flow statements of limited companies.

The corporation tax shown on the face of the profit and loss account will have been based on a computation carried out prior to the exact amount payable, having been agreed with the Inland Revenue. There may therefore be some differences from year to year between the tax payable numbers reported and tax actually paid.

Profit after tax (PAT)

PAT, or net profit, is the profit on ordinary activities after tax. The final charge that a company has to suffer, provided it has made sufficient profits, is therefore corporate taxation.

$$\textbf{PAT} = \textbf{PBT} - \textbf{corporation tax}$$

Progress check 3.2

What exactly do we mean by cost of sales? What types of expense does cost of sales include and what types of expense does it exclude?

The net profit has resulted from the following processes. The assets, owned by the shareholders, have generated the operating profit. Operating profit has been used to pay interest to bankers and other lenders, and corporation tax to the Inland Revenue. What is left belongs to the owners of the assets, the shareholders. The net profit is the increase in wealth of the company.

The directors propose how much will be distributed to shareholders in dividends, and how much will be held as retained earnings as part of the equity of the company and reinvested in the operations of the company. The shareholders vote on whether to accept or reject the directors' proposal. The net profit is used to provide the shareholders' returns, the dividends they receive from their total investment in the equity of the company. So, not only does the net profit have to be positive, but it has to be high enough to reward the risk the shareholders took in investing in the company.

Dividends

The Companies Acts do not have a specific requirement for dividends to be shown in the profit and loss account, but both the Acts and FRS 3 imply that dividends are usually deducted from the profit or loss for the financial year in arriving at the profit or loss retained for the year. The dividend line in the profit and loss account includes any interim payment that may have been made and any final dividend proposed by the directors to be paid to shareholders later in the year.

Retained profit for the financial year

The **retained profit** for the year is what is left on the profit and loss account after deducting dividends for the year. The balance on the profit and loss account forms part of the capital (or equity, or shareholders' funds) of the company. The company's annual report is required to include a statement that discloses the reconciliation of the movement on shareholders' funds that has taken place between the beginning and the end of the financial year (see Fig. 3.5).

Progress check 3.3

The profit or loss that a business has earned or suffered during an accounting period may be ascertained by deducting the total costs from the total revenues for the period. Identify in which category of the profit and loss account the following items may appear.

- interest received
- share premiums
- interest paid
- depreciation on factory machinery for the year
- CD royalties received
- outward freight costs
- sales of redundant stocks
- travel and subsistence

- accountancy fees
- electricity standing charge
- rents received
- telephone charges
- advertising and promotion
- raw materials purchases
- stocks of work in progress
- sales of finished product

Profit and loss account formats

The 1985 Companies Act, as amended 1989, outlines the permitted formats for published financial statements. There are four alternative formats for the profit and loss account.

In formats 1 and 3, expenses are classified by function, for example, cost of sales, distribution costs, administrative expenses. Both formats require identical information and have much in common with the internal management accounts prepared monthly by most UK companies.

In formats 2 and 4, expenses are classified by type, for example, raw materials and consumables, staff costs, and depreciation. Formats 3 and 4 are rarely used. Format 1 is seen more frequently than format 2, and is the format adopted by most of the larger UK plcs. The profit and loss account in the example adopted by Flatco plc (Fig. 3.2) has been based on format 1.

FRS 3, Reporting Financial Performance, contains supplementary provisions relating to the format of the profit and loss account, in addition to the four alternative formats allowed in the Companies Act. One of the main provisions of FRS 3 relates to the separate identification within the profit and loss account of turnover and operating profit relating to continuing operations and discontinued operations.

The other important provisions of FRS 3 relate to the treatment of

1. **Extraordinary items**
2. **Exceptional items**
3. **Earnings per share**
4. Reconciliation of the movement in shareholders' funds.

1. Extraordinary items

Extraordinary items, defined as material (significant) income or costs which are derived or incurred from events or transactions outside the ordinary activities of the company which were not expected to occur frequently or regularly, were previously required to be disclosed in a separate line on the profit and loss account. A company's ordinary activities have now been defined so broadly that extraordinary items have now effectively disappeared from the face of the profit and loss account.

The costs resulting from the complete destruction of a factory may be sufficiently extraordinary to warrant the appearance of extraordinary items as a separate item on the profit and loss account.

2. Exceptional items

Exceptional items are items of abnormal size and incidence, which are derived from the ordinary activities of the business. FRS 3 requires exceptional items to be included under the statutory format headings to which they relate and disclosed on the face of the profit and loss account if necessary to give a true and fair view.

3. Earnings per share

FRS 3 also refers to earnings per share, which would normally be disclosed after the retained profit for the year (not shown in the Flatco plc example).

4. Reconciliation of the movement in shareholders' funds

The movement in shareholders funds for Flatco plc, disclosed in accordance with the requirements of FRS 3, is shown in Fig. 3.5. The actual report would of course include the previous year 1999 comparative figures.

Fig. 3.6 shows the profit and loss account for Flatco plc restated in line with format 1 and illustrating the provisions of FRS 3. The Companies Act requires comparative figures for the previous year for each line in the profit and loss account (not shown in the example), usually shown in a column to the right of the current year's figures.

Flatco plc
Reconciliation of movement in shareholders' funds
for the year ended 31 December 2000

	£000	£000
Shareholders' funds at start of year		2,524
Profit for the financial year	540	
Dividends	(70)	470
Shareholders' funds at end of year		2,994

FIGURE 3.5   Reconciliation of movement in shareholders' funds

Flatco plc
Profit and loss account for the year ended 31 December 2000

		£000
Turnover		
Continuing operations		3,500
Discontinued operations		–
		3,500
Cost of sales		(2,500)
Gross profit		1,000
Distribution costs	(300)	
Administrative expenses	(155)	
Other operating costs		
Exceptional items: redundancy costs	(95)	(550)
Other operating income		100
Operating profit		
Continuing operations	550	
Discontinued operations	–	550
Income from other investments		100
Profit before interest and tax		650
Net interest		(60)
Profit before tax		590
Tax on profit on ordinary activities		(50)
Profit on ordinary activities after tax		540
Dividends		(70)
Retained profit for the financial year		470

FIGURE 3.6   Format 1 profit and loss account
in compliance with the Companies Acts 1985/89 and FRS 3

Example 3.3

The relevant profit and loss account balances, representing the costs and revenues for the year to date as extracted from the trial balance of Perfecto Ltd at 30 September 2000, are presented in an alphabetical list:

	£000
Advertising and promotion	54
Corporation tax	70
Costs of administration departments	146
Costs of production departments	277
Costs of purchasing and logistics department	77
Depreciation on factory machinery	284
Depreciation on office equipment	35
Direct labour cost of sales	203
Freight out costs	230
Interest paid	20
Interest received	10
Materials cost of sales	611
Rent and utilities (2/3 factory, 1/3 office)	48
Sales	2,279
Warehousing and goods outward costs	84

Prepare a profit and loss account for Perfecto Ltd for the year to 30 September 2000, using format 1, and complying as far as possible with the provisions included in FRS 3.

Answer

Perfecto Ltd
Profit and loss account for the year ended 30 September 2000

Figures in £000

Turnover		2,279
Cost of sales [277 + 77 + 284 + 203 + 611 + 32 (2/3 of 48)]		(1,484)
Gross profit		795
Distribution costs [54 + 230 + 84]	(368)	
Administrative expenses [146 + 35 + 16 (1/3 of 48)]	(197)	
		(565)
Operating profit		230
Net interest		(10)
Profit before tax		220
Tax on profit on ordinary activities		(70)
Profit on ordinary activities after tax		150

The Companies Acts 1985/1989 require group accounts to be prepared for the holding company in addition to the accounts that are required to be prepared for each of the individual companies within the group. Consolidated accounts exclude all transactions between companies within the group, for example, inter-company sales and purchases. In most other respects the group consolidated accounts reflect an amalgamation of each of the components of the profit and loss accounts of all the companies within the group.

Progress check 3.4

> There are four profit and loss account formats that comply with the requirements of the Companies Acts 1985/1989. How do formats 1 and 3 differ from formats 2 and 4? Which format appears to be favoured by the majority of UK companies?

Profit and loss and the balance sheet

The balance sheet and the profit and loss account, whilst they are both historical statements, are not alternatives or competing options. They show different financial information, as we have discussed. The balance sheet shows the financial position at the start and at the end of an accounting period, and the profit and loss account shows what has happened during the period, the financial performance.

The profit and loss account and the balance sheet are linked in two ways:

● the cumulative balance on the profit and loss account is reflected within the equity, or the shareholders' funds category of the balance sheet representing the increase in the wealth of the business

● some of the items contained in the profit and loss account are also all reflected in some way within one or more balance sheet categories.

In Chapter 2 we saw how the balance on the profit and loss account was reflected in retained earnings, within the equity of the company. We will now look at some of the types of adjusting entries used to prepare the profit and loss account, which are also reflected in the balance sheet. Two of these types of adjusting entries, accruals and prepayments, are described in Appendix 1.

In this chapter we will look at some further categories of adjusting entries:

● depreciation, the depreciation provision, and fixed assets

● the cost of sales, and the valuation of stocks

● bad and doubtful debts, and trade debtors.

Example 3.4

Ronly Bonly Jones Ltd, or RBJ, buys and sells giftware. It made a profit of £10,000 during the month of January 2000.

We are required to use the balance sheet as at 1 January 2000 as the starting point and then look at how each of the elements in the profit and loss account for January is reflected in the balance sheet to derive the balance sheet as at 31 January 2000.

The profit and loss account for January 2000 and the balance sheet as at 1 January 2000 are as follows:

Profit and loss account for January 2000   **£000**

Sales   650

Cost of goods sold

Opening stocks	45	
Purchases	424	
	469	
less Closing stocks	79	(390)

Gross profit   260

Depreciation   (5)

Expenses   (245)

Profit for January [650 − 390 − 5 − 245]   10

Additional information

RBJ acquired fixed assets in January for £20,000 cash, and raised additional share capital of £10,000.

Creditors were paid £422,000 in the month and £632,000 was received from customers. The bank account at the end of January 2000 was overdrawn by £39,000.

Balance sheet as at 1 January 2000   **£000**

Fixed assets at cost	130
Depreciation provision	(20)
Stocks	45
Debtors	64
Cash and bank	6
	225
Creditors	(87)
Share capital	(50)
Profit and loss account	(88)
	(225)

Answer

Let's derive the 31 January 2000 balance sheet from the information that has been provided

Figures in £000	Fixed assets	Depn	Stocks	Debtors	Cash	Creditors	Equity	Profit/loss account
1 January 2000	130	(20)	45	64	6	(87)	(50)	(88)
Sales				650				(650)
Cash from customers				(632)	632			0
Purchases			424			(424)		0
Cash to creditors					(422)	422		0
Stock sold			(390)					390
Depreciation		(5)						5
Expenses					(245)			245
Fixed asset additions	20				(20)			0
Issue of shares					10		(10)	0
31 January 2000	150	(25)	79	82	(39)	(89)	(60)	(98)

▶

◀ **Ronly Bonly Jones Ltd**
Balance sheet at 1 January 2000 and at 31 January 2000 is as follows:

	1 January 2000	31 January 2000
	£000	£000
Fixed assets at cost	130	150
Depreciation provision	(20)	(25)
Stocks	45	79
Debtors	64	82
Cash and bank	6	–
	225	286
Creditors	(87)	(89)
Bank overdraft	–	(39)
Share capital	(50)	(60)
Profit and loss account	(88)	(98)
	(225)	(286)

Example 3.4 shows the changes in the balance sheet that have taken place over the month of January. The 31 January balance sheet has been derived from considering each element in the profit and loss account for January and its impact on the balance sheet, and movements between accounts within the balance sheet:

- sales to customers on credit are the starting point for the profit and loss account, which also increase debtors
- cash received from customers increases cash and reduces debtors
- purchases of goods on credit for resale increase stock and increase creditors
- cash paid to creditors reduces cash and reduces creditors
- stock sold reduces stock and is a cost to the profit and loss account
- depreciation of fixed assets increases the depreciation provision and is a cost to the profit and loss account
- payments of expenses reduce cash and are a cost to the profit and loss account
- payments for additions to fixed assets increase fixed assets and reduce cash
- issues of ordinary shares increase equity capital and increase cash.

In Example 3.4, depreciation is a relatively small number. Normally, profit and loss account movements may have significant impacts on the balance sheet in the areas of both stocks and depreciation:

- during the years 1999 and 2000 several major retailers had to announce that their profits would be lower due to their stocks having to be heavily discounted (for example, Marks and Spencer plc)
- depreciation of an automotive assembly line may need to be changed due to a revision in its estimated useful economic life following a reassessment of the life cycle of a vehicle.

Progress check 3.5

Describe the ways in which a company's profit and loss account and its balance sheet are linked.

We have already discussed the links between the various categories in the profit and loss account and those within the balance sheet. Consequently, the ways in which specific balance sheet items are valued have a significant impact on the profit reported for an entity for a particular period. The requirement for the valuation, or revaluation of, for example, assets like machinery, raw materials, and finished product may be a result of their consumption or being used up; it may be because of their deterioration or obsolescence, or significant changes in their market value. For whatever reason, such changes in the valuation of assets must be reflected in the profit and loss account in the period in which they occur. We will focus here on the valuation of the three key areas of

- fixed assets, reflected in the profit and loss account within *depreciation*
- stocks, reflected in the profit and loss account within *cost of sales*
- debtors, reflected in the profit and loss account within *bad and doubtful debts*.

Depreciation

Generally, the total cost of using a fixed asset over its life may be defined as the original investment less a portion of its cost recovered (its residual value) at the end of the asset's useful life. FRS 15 defines depreciation as a measure of the wearing out, consumption or other reduction in the useful economic life of a fixed asset, whether arising from use, effluxion of time or obsolescence through technological or market changes. Depreciation should be allocated so as to charge a fair proportion of the total cost (or valuation) of the asset to each accounting period expected to benefit from its use, with a corresponding entry to credit the cumulative **depreciation provision** account.

Example 3.5

Many companies operate and succeed in one market for many years. One of many business 'facts of life' is that recurring profits can come to an abrupt end, when a successful business model develops a basic flaw. Changes in technology can cause a change in trading or force a complete review of the equipment that has been highly profitable in the past. Photo-Me International, the photo-booth operator, announced a £24.1m non-cash write-down of its old analogue photo-booths in January 2001.

You are required to explain why this type of equipment review might affect the annual profits.

Answer

1. The profit and loss account for a year aims to match incomes and expenses for that year, complying with the matching concept (see Chapter 1).

2. One of the expenses relates to the use of plant and equipment, which normally represents wear and tear, and is called depreciation.

3. The choice of method of depreciating an asset will result in differing amounts of depreciation for the year and so the annual profit and loss account can be quite

different because of this subjective decision (which involves opinions that may vary from manager to manager).

4. The Accounting Standards Board (ASB) introduced FRS 11, Impairment of Fixed Assets and Goodwill, to force companies to formally review the fixed assets for any changes in circumstances (impairment is not recurring, whereas depreciation or wear and tear is recurring).

5. In the Photo-Me circumstances outlined above, the company would have had to acknowledge a change in technology from analogue to digital. The result is that the balance sheet net book values of its fixed assets would no longer be tenable because of their sharp decline. The remaining net book value of the amount that was paid for their original acquisition can no longer be regarded as a fixed asset, for current and future balance sheet purposes, and therefore must be written off against the current profits.

The useful life of an asset is the period of its service relevant to the business entity. With regard to the useful life of the asset, there are a number of problems in dealing with depreciation of fixed assets:

- determining the useful life of the asset
- determining the correct way to spread the total cost of the asset over the useful life
- physical limitations regarding the useful life
  - intensity of use of the asset
  - the actions of the elements
  - adequacy of maintenance
  - the simple passage of time (e.g. legal rights or patents)
- economic limitations in respect of useful life
  - technological developments
  - business growth.

There are five main depreciation methods:

- straight line
- reducing balance
- sum of the digits
- activity rate
- double declining.

We will consider the first three in a little more detail in Example 3.6, being the ones that are most frequently encountered.

Straight-line depreciation is calculated by deducting the residual value from the acquisition cost and dividing the result by the life of the asset.

The reducing balance method is used to derive the rate required (d) to reduce the cost of the asset, period by period, to the residual value by the end of its life. This may be expressed as:

$$d = 1 - \sqrt[life]{\text{residual value/original cost}}$$

The sum of the digits method considers the life of the asset, say for example five years, and allocates the total cost of the asset over that period as follows:

For a five-year life the sum of digits is $5 + 4 + 3 + 2 + 1 = 15$

So each year's depreciation is calculated:
1st year $5/15 \times$ (acquisition cost − residual value)
2nd year $4/15 \times$ (acquisition cost − residual value)
3rd year $3/15 \times$ (acquisition cost − residual value)
4th year $2/15 \times$ (acquisition cost − residual value)
5th year $1/15 \times$ (acquisition cost − residual value)

Example 3.6

Castle Ltd purchases an item of equipment for £16,000 and estimates its residual value, at the end of its useful economic life of five years, at £1,000. At the start of year 1 the net book value (NBV) is the acquisition cost of the asset £16,000.
We are required to calculate the different net book values derived from using each of the three methods:

- straight line
- reducing balance
- sum of the digits

Answer

Straight line divides acquisition cost less residual value by 5 (the number of years economic life).

Reducing balance calculates

$$d = 1 - \sqrt[5]{1{,}000/16{,}000} = 42.57\%$$

Sum of the digits is $(5 + 4 + 3 + 2 + 1) = 15$

Figures in £000

Year	Straight line Start NBV	Straight line Depn	Straight line End NBV	Reducing balance Start NBV	Reducing balance Depn	Reducing balance End NBV	Sum of the digits Start NBV	Sum of the digits Depn	Sum of the digits End NBV
1	16,000	3,000	13,000	16,000	6,810	9,190	16,000	5,000	11,000
2	13,000	3,000	10,000	9,190	3,912	5,278	11,000	4,000	7,000
3	10,000	3,000	7,000	5,278	2,247	3,031	7,000	3,000	4,000
4	7,000	3,000	4,000	3,031	1,290	1,741	4,000	2,000	2,000
5	4,000	3,000	1,000	1,741	741	1,000	2,000	1,000	1,000

The resultant cost of £1,000 in the balance sheet under the fixed assets category at the end of year 5 is the same using each of the methods. This cost is likely to be offset exactly by the proceeds of £1,000 expected to be received on disposal of the asset.

In addition to the methods already discussed, there are many further alternative ways of accounting for depreciation. It is not necessary at this stage to be able to carry out the detailed calculations, but Example 3.7 serves to illustrate some of these alternatives, and the wide variations in yearly depreciation, and therefore net book values, derived from each of them.

Example 3.7

Consider a company van, which cost £20,000 to purchase new. Its residual value is considered to be zero at the end of its useful life of five years. The rate of inflation is 10% and the cost of capital is 15%.

We are required to evaluate the net book value (NBV) at the end of year one using six alternative methods.

Answer

		NBV at end of year 1
1. Straight line depreciation over five years, i.e. 20% per annum using an historical cost of £20,000	£20,000 at 20%	£16,000
2. Constant purchasing power, which means allowing for an inflationary price increase (in this case 10%), and using straight line depreciation at 20% per annum	£20,000 × 1.10 at 20%	£17,600
3. Replacement value for an identical one-year old van based on used van market values		£17,000
4. Replacement cost of a new van less 1 year's depreciation based on an estimated replacement cost of say	£21,600 at 20%	£17,280
5. Net realisable value	net sales proceeds say from a trade auction	£16,000
6. Economic value using estimated net cash flow from using the van for each year 1: £6,000; 2: £6,000; 3: £6,000; 4: £6,000 present values of future cash flows, using a cost of capital of 15% per annum (see the discounted cash flow technique in Chapter 13)		
$6,000/1.15 + 6,000/1.15^2 + 6,000/1.15^3 + 6,000/1.15^4$		£17,130

Whichever method of depreciation is used, it must be consistent from one accounting period to another. The depreciation method adopted must be disclosed within the company's accounting policies that accompany the financial statements and include the depreciation rates applied to each of the categories of fixed asset.

Progress check 3.6

What are the various methods that may be used to depreciate an asset? Describe two of the most commonly used methods.

The amount of depreciation calculated for an accounting period is charged as a cost in the profit and loss account, the depreciation charge. A corresponding amount is also reflected in an account in the balance sheet, the cumulative depreciation provision account, the effect of which is to reduce the original cost of the fixed assets at the end of each accounting period.

The difference between depreciation cost and other costs such as wages is that it is not a cash expense, that is it will generate no cash inflow or outflow. The only cash outflow relating to depreciation took place when the asset was originally purchased. The depreciation is really only the 'memory' of that earlier cash outflow.

Progress check 3.7

Why are assets depreciated and what factors influence the decision as to how they may be depreciated?

Cost of sales

As we saw in Chapter 2, stocks of **raw materials, work in progress, finished product**, and consumable stores, pose problems in their valuation for three main reasons:

- raw materials may be purchased from a variety of geographical locations, and additional costs such as duty, freight, and insurance may be incurred – the costs of stocks should comprise the expenditure that has been incurred in the normal course of business in bringing the product or service to its present location and condition

- packaging and other consumable items, in addition to raw materials, are used during the production processes to manufacture work in progress, partly-finished product and fully-finished product, and such costs must be correctly apportioned to give a true cost – stocks are disclosed as a main heading in the balance sheet and comprise raw materials and consumables, work in progress, finished goods, and long-term contracts

- homogenous items within various stock categories are purchased continuously and consumed continuously in the manufacturing processes and the purchase prices of these homogenous items may vary considerably – stocks must be valued at the lower of purchase cost (or production cost) and their net realisable value

A number of alternative methods may be used to determine the cost of stock:

- **first in first out (FIFO)**
- **last in first out (LIFO)**
- average cost
- market value
- retail method
- specific identification
- next in first out (NIFO)
- base cost.

The choice of method adopted by individual companies depends largely on their particular requirements and will be influenced by a number of factors:

- ease of use
- volumes of stocks
- costs of stocks
- management information requirements.

The first four methods of valuation are among the most commonly known, with FIFO being by far the most popular. FIFO (first in first out, where the oldest items of stock, or their costs, are assumed to be the first to be used) assumes that costs are matched with the physical flow of stock.

LIFO (last in first out, where the most recently acquired items of stock, or their costs, are assumed to be the first to be used) matches current costs with current revenues. LIFO is not permitted in the UK by the accounting standard for Stocks and Long-term Contracts, SSAP 9, and is not acceptable for taxation purposes.

The average cost method smoothes income and stock values and assumes that individual units cannot be tracked through the system. The use of market values begs the questions as to which market value is most appropriate and should replacement or realisable values be used?

Progress check 3.8	
	What factors must be considered regarding the valuation of stocks?

The following example looks at the four main methods of valuation of stocks to enable us to provide a comparison in numerical terms and represent this graphically.

Example 3.8	

A retailing company at 1 January 2000 has 400 units in stock of a product that cost £3 each, and therefore a total cost of £1,200. The company's purchases over January and February are

	Units	Price £	Value £	
January	600	4.00	2,400	
	800	5.00	4,000	Total £6,400
February	200	6.00	1,200	
	1,000	4.00	4,000	Total £5,200

and its sales over the same periods are

	Units	Price £	Value £
January	1,400	12.00	16,800
February	1,400	12.00	16,800

The market value of a unit of each product is

	Price £
January	6.00
February	3.00

Answer

FIFO – first in first out, matching costs with physical stock flows

	Units	£		Units	£
January opening stock	400	1,200	Sales	1,400	16,800
Purchases	1,400	6,400			
	1,800	7,600			
January closing stock	400	2,000			
Cost of goods sold	1,400	5,600			
Gross profit		11,200			
		16,800			16,800
February opening stock	400	2,000	Sales	1,400	16,800
Purchases	1,200	5,200			
	1,600	7,200			
February closing stock	200	800			
Cost of goods sold	1,400	6,400			
Gross profit		10,400			
		16,800			16,800

Note that purchases are always valued at their actual cost regardless of which stock valuation method is used.

There were 400 units in stock at the beginning of January that cost £3 each and then 600 units were purchased at £4 each and then 800 purchased at £5 each. On a FIFO basis it is assumed that the 1,400 units sold in January first used the 400 opening stock and then the 600 units first purchased and then 400 of the 800 units next purchased. The cost of these units was $(400 \times £3) + (600 \times £4) + (400 \times £5) = £5,600$. The 400 units of stock remaining at the end of January (which becomes the opening stock at the beginning of February) are the 400 units left from the purchase of 800 units at £5 each and so are valued at £2,000. Using the same basis, the cost of the 1,400 units sold in February was $(400 \times £5) + (200 \times £6) + (800 \times £4) = £6,400$. The 200 units of stock remaining at the end of February are the 200 units left from the purchase of 1,000 units at £4 each and so are valued at £800.

The result is a gross profit of £11,200 for January and £10,400 for February.

LIFO – last in first out, matching current costs with current revenues

	Units	£		Units	£
January opening stock	400	1,200	Sales	1,400	16,800
Purchases	1,400	6,400			
	1,800	7,600			
January closing stock	400	1,200			
Cost of goods sold	1,400	6,400			
Gross profit		10,400			
		16,800			16,800

	Units	£		Units	£
February opening stock	400	1,200	Sales	1,400	16,800
Purchases	1,200	5,200			
	1,600	6,400			
February closing stock	200	600			
Cost of goods sold	1,400	5,800			
Gross profit		11,000			
		16,800			16,800

There were 400 units in stock at the beginning of January that cost £3 each and then 600 units were purchased at £4 each and then 800 purchased at £5 each. On a LIFO basis it is assumed that the 1,400 units sold in January used the 800 last purchased at £5 each and then the 600 units purchased at £4 each. The cost of these units was (800 × £5) + (600 × £4) = £6,400. The 400 units of stock remaining at the end of January (which becomes the opening stock at the beginning of February) are the 400 units left from opening stock at £3 each and so are valued at £1,200. Using the same basis, the cost of the 1,400 units sold in February was (1,000 × £4) + (200 × £6) + (200 × £3) = £5,800. The 200 units of stock remaining at the end of February are the 200 units left from the opening stock of 400 units at £3 each and so are valued at £600.

The result is a gross profit of £10,400 for January and £11,000 for February.

Average cost – smoothing of revenues and stock values, assuming that individual units purchased cannot be followed through to actual sales so total purchases combined to calculate an average cost per unit

	Units	£		Units	£
January opening stock	400	1,200	Sales	1,400	16,800
Purchases	1,400	6,400			
	1,800	7,600			
January closing stock	400	1,689			
Cost of goods sold	1,400	5,911			
Gross profit		10,889			
		16,800			16,800

$$\text{Average cost per unit for January} = \frac{(1,200 + 6,400)}{(400 + 1,400)} = \frac{7,600}{1,800} = £4.222$$

$$\text{January closing stock} = 400 \times \frac{7,600}{1,800} = £1,689$$

	Units	£		Units	£
February opening stock	400	1,689	Sales	1,400	16,800
Purchases	1,200	5,200			
	1,600	6,889			
February closing stock	200	861			
Cost of goods sold	1,400	6,028			
Gross profit		10,772			
		16,800			16,800

$$\text{Average cost per unit for February} = \frac{(1,689 + 5,200)}{(400 + 1,200)} = \frac{6,889}{1,600} = £4.305$$

$$\text{February closing stock} = 200 \times \frac{6,889}{1,600} = £861$$

The result is a gross profit of £10,889 for January and £10,772 for February.

The lower of FIFO or market value

	Units	£		Units	£
January opening stock	400	1,200	Sales	1,400	16,800
Purchases	1,400	6,400			
	1,800	7,600			
January closing stock	400	2,000			
Cost of goods sold	1,400	5,600			
Gross profit		11,200			
		16,800			16,800
February opening stock	400	2,000	Sales	1,400	16,800
Purchases	1,200	5,200			
	1,600	7,200			
February closing stock	200	600			
Cost of goods sold	1,400	6,600			
Gross profit		10,200			
		16,800			16,800

January closing stock using FIFO is £2,000. Using market value, January closing stock is 400 units at £6 per unit – £2,400. Using the lower value, stock at the end of January is £2,000. February closing stock using FIFO is £800. Using market value, February closing stock is 200 units at £3 per unit – £600. Using the lower value, stock at the end of February is £600.

The result is a gross profit of £11,200 for January and £10,200 for February.

Summary of stock valuation methods

	FIFO £	LIFO £	Average cost £	Lower of cost or market value £
Profit				
January	11,200	10,400	10,889	11,200
February	10,400	11,000	10,772	10,200
Stock valuation				
January	2,000	1,200	1,689	2,000
February	800	600	861	600

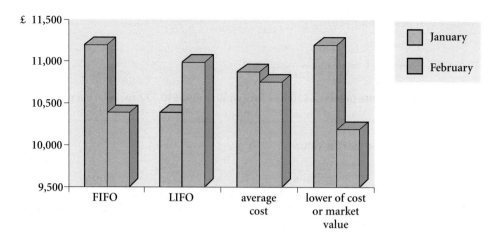

FIGURE 3.7   Profit comparison from use of various stock valuation methods

FIGURE 3.8   Stock value comparison from use of various stock valuation methods

Graphical representations of the summary of stock valuation methods used in Example 3.8 are shown in Fig. 3.7 and Fig. 3.8.

It can be seen from the summary of results in Example 3.8 that wide variations in profit may be reported from period to period. However, over the long run the total result will eventually be the same, as all stocks become used up. It is important to stress that a method may not be chosen to give, for example, a required result for one period. There must be consistency in the use of stock valuation method from one period to the next.

Progress check 3.9

Why does stock valuation cause such problems and why is it so very important?

Bad and doubtful debts

The term provision often means very much the same thing as accrued expenses. The difference is that a provision is normally an amount charged against profit to provide for an expected liability or loss even though the amount or date of the liability or loss is uncertain. However, the word provision is sometimes used in a different context, most commonly the depreciation provision relating to a fixed asset. It is also used in dealing with debtors at the end of an accounting period.

When goods or services are sold to a customer on credit, an invoice is issued to record the transaction and to obtain settlement. The sale is reflected in the profit and loss account within the turnover of the business for the relevant period. The 'other side' of the entry is debited to the sales ledger, appearing as an account receivable from the customer in line with the agreed payment terms. Most customers pay in accordance with their agreed terms, whether it is for example within ten days, one month, or two months of invoice date. Unfortunately, there may sometimes be slow payers; there may be customers, for a variety of reasons, from whom payment will never be received. In the event of an invoice not being settled at all, as soon as this is known with certainty, the debt is deemed to be a **bad debt** and must be written off. The effect of this on the profit and loss account is not to reduce sales. It is a cost charged to the bad debt account. The double entry is to the debtor account to cancel the appropriate account receivable.

At the end of each accounting period debtors who have still not paid, falling outside their normal credit terms, must be reviewed as to the likelihood of their not paying in full or at all. If non-payment is certain then the debt must be written off. If there is uncertainty as to whether or not a debt will be settled then a provision for **doubtful debts** may be made on a specific basis, based on knowledge of particular customers, or on a general basis, say as a percentage of total debtors, based on past trading experience.

An amount in respect of estimated doubtful debts that is charged to an account in the profit and loss account, the bad and doubtful debt account, is also reflected as a credit to an account in the balance sheet, the **doubtful debt provision**. The effect of the provision for doubtful debts is to reduce the value of the debtors in the balance sheet but without permanently eliminating any accounts receivable. Debtors that are deemed to be bad debts are actually written off (charged as a cost to the profit and loss account) and the debts are permanently eliminated from accounts receivable.

Progress check 3.10

What are bad debts and doubtful debts and how are they reflected in the profit and loss account and balance sheet of a business?

Example 3.9

Trade debtors on the books of Sportswear Wholesalers Ltd at 31 January 2000 were £429,378: current month £230,684, month two £93,812, three to six months £64,567, over six months £40,315. On 18 January 2000 one of Sportswear's customers, Road Runner Ltd, had gone into liquidation owing Sportswear £15,342, which had been invoiced over six months previously. Sportswear's policy was to provide for doubtful debts on the basis of three to six months' debts 5%, and over six months' debts 10%.

What entries would appear in Sportwear's cumulative profit and loss account to January 2000 and its balance sheet at 31 January 2000 in respect of bad and doubtful debts? We may assume that no other debts have been written off during the year to date.

◀ **Answer**

Road Runner Ltd has gone into liquidation owing Sportswear £15,342, of which it is assumed there is no chance of any recovery, therefore it must be written off as a bad debt in the profit and loss account in January 2000.

The effect of the bad debt write off is to reduce trade debtors by £15,342, and the debts over six months old will reduce down to £24,973 [£40,315 − £15,342].

The doubtful debt provision at 31 January in line with Sportswear's policy is

5% × £64,567   = £3,228

10% × £24,973 = £2,497

Total   = £5,725 (assuming no opening bad debt provision at 1 January 2000)

Profit and loss account for the year to 31 January 2000:

Bad and doubtful debts

Road Runner Ltd write off 31/01/00	£15,342
Doubtful debt provision at 31/01/00	£5,725
Balance at 31 January 2000	£21,067

Balance sheet as at 31 January 2000:

Trade debtors:

Balance per accounts receivable at 31/01/00	£429,378
Road Runner Ltd write off 31/01/00	£15,342
Balance at 31 January 2000	£414,036

Doubtful debt provision:

Doubtful debt provision at 31/01/00	£5,725
Balance at 31 January 2000	£5,725

Trade debtors in Sportswear's balance sheet as at 31 January 2000 would be **£408,311 [£414,036 − £5,725].**

Such bad and doubtful debt entries would not be individually apparent from inspection of Sportswear Wholesalers Ltd's financial statements. Bad and doubtful debt charges are normally included under the profit and loss account heading *Distribution Costs*, and the corresponding balance sheet entries are reflected within the total *Trade Debtors* heading.

Profit and loss and cash flow

The past few years have seen growing activity in the birth and growth of so-called dot.com companies. Their aim has been to exploit the use of the Internet to provide opportunities to sell products and services in wider markets and on an increasingly global basis. The apparent success of the majority of these businesses has been based on growth of potential in both market share and profitability reflected in the numbers of subscribers attracted to their websites. Actual and potential profitability do not necessarily inevitably result in a healthy cash position. As we can see from Lastminute.com's position early in the year 2000,

Lastminute could be the last word

Has Martha Lane Fox's dream already died? Just a week after the media razzmatazz surrounding the flotation of Lastminute.com, the shares have sunk embarrassingly below the 380p offer price, to 320p yesterday. Ouch!

Critics fear that Lastminute's arrival could mark the top of the market for internet stocks. Lastminute's sales, £409,000 in the quarter ending December 31, are not much more than those of a couple of newsagents. No corner shops would ever get backing to float and, even if they did, the market would never value them at over half a billion pounds.

To add to the problems, investor goodwill is low. Retail investors are deeply disappointed that their allocations amounted to a measly 35 shares. Plus Lastminute's underwriters Morgan Stanley chose to raise the flotation price from an original range of 190p to 230p to a greedy 380p.

However, it is worth remembering the company has growth potential of which few newsagents could ever dream. It has a global first mover advantage. Nobody else – online or otherwise – specialises in clearing last minute services, from flights to theatre tickets.

Plus, Lastminute's international expansion will obviously boost sales and has barely begun. The company has just started to build a presence in France, Sweden and Germany, and with £113m in the bank from the float is ready to do a lot more.

Customer numbers and items sold are growing at 50pc month on month. Supplier numbers have expanded from just over 20 when the company started to over 1,100 by December, just over a year later.

Yet it isn't quite yet time to buy. The market's fury has to subside and the price stabilise – ironically, perhaps down as far as the original price range for the offer. Given there's a lot of good news to come out of this company, that could be a last-minute signal for the speculative to move in.

© *Daily Telegraph*, 22 March 2000

such companies invariably require large amounts of cash for them to continue operating for extended periods prior to achieving profitability and to generate their own cash flows.

Around a year after the flotation of Lastminute.com, and following much cost-cutting and a focus on the UK and France, which were seen as the areas with the highest profit potential, the company announced that it expected to be profitable by the year 2002 without the need to raise extra cash to support it.

In Chapter 2 we discussed how profit and cash flow do not mean the same thing. In fact, the profit earned and the net cash generated during an accounting period are usually very different, and often significantly different. How often do we see cases reported of businesses in serious financial difficulties because of severe cash shortages, even though they may appear to be trading profitably?

There is a relationship between cash and profit and it is possible to identify and quantify the factors within this relationship. The profit or loss made by a business during an accounting period differs from the net cash inflows and outflows during the period because of:

● cash expected to be paid or received relating to transactions during a period may in fact not be paid or received until the following or subsequent periods

● cash may have been paid or received in advance of goods or services being received or provided and invoices being received or issued

● cash may have been paid or received relating to non-manufacturing, non-trading, or non-profit items – for example, cash received for shares in the business, and cash paid out on capital expenditure

● profit will have been calculated to include the impact of non-cash items such as depreciation.

When we look at the cash flow statement in the next chapter we shall see that one of the schedules that is required to be prepared in support of the cash flow statement is in fact a reconciliation of operating profit to net cash flow.

Prior to that, we can consider the following example, which is not in strict compliance with the cash flow reconciliation schedule requirement, but will serve to illustrate how profit and cash flow are linked and how the links may be identified.

Example 3.10

In Example 3.4 we saw that Ronly Bonly Jones Ltd made a profit of £10,000 during the month of January 2000. A summary of its balance sheet at 1 January 2000, and the 31 January 2000 balance sheet that we derived, are as follows:

	1 January 2000 £000	31 January 2000 £000
Fixed assets at cost	130	150
Depreciation provision	(20)	(25)
Stocks	45	79
Debtors	64	82
Cash and bank	6	–
	225	286
Creditors	(87)	(89)
Bank overdraft	–	(39)
Share capital	(50)	(60)
Profit and loss account	(88)	(98)
	(225)	(286)

We are required to provide a reconciliation of Ronly Bonly Jones profit for the month of January with the cash flow for the same period.

Answer

We may reconcile the profit for the month with the cash flow for the month as follows:

	January 2000 £000
Profit for the month	10
Add back non-cash item	
Depreciation for month	5
	15
Cash gained from	
Increase in creditors	2
Additional share capital	10
	27

	£000
Cash reduced by	
Purchase of fixed assets	(20)
Increase in stocks	(34)
Increase in debtors	(18)
	(72)
Cash outflow for month	(45)
Cash and bank 1 January 2000	6
Cash outflow for month	(45)
Cash and bank 31 January 2000	(39)

Example 3.10 shows that despite making a profit of £10,000 during an accounting period the company in fact had a shortfall of cash of £45,000 for the same period. After adjusting profit for the non-cash item of depreciation and adding the increase in share capital it effectively had an increase in funds during the month of £25,000. It then had to finance the purchase of fixed assets of £20,000 and finance an increase in its working capital requirement of £50,000 (stocks £34,000 plus debtors £18,000 less creditors £2,000). This resulted in its cash deficit for the month of £45,000. The company therefore went from having a positive cash balance of £6,000 at the start of the month to an overdraft of £39,000 at the end of the month.

Both the company and its bankers would obviously need to monitor its performance very closely over future months! A company will normally continuously review its cash, overdraft, accounts payable, and accounts receivable position. The bank manager will regularly review a company's balances and require advance notice of potential breaches of its overdraft limits.

Progress check 3.11

In what ways does the profit earned by a business during an accounting period differ from the cash generated during the same period? In what ways is profit and cash affected by the settlement (or not) of their accounts by the customers of the business?

Summary of key points

● Profit and loss account and income statement are two terms usually used to mean the same thing.

● The profit (or loss) of an entity may be considered from two perspectives: by considering the change in wealth between the start and end of an accounting period; by deducting total costs from total revenues (sales) generated during the accounting period.

● Categories within the profit and loss account are classified into turnover, cost of sales, other operating costs, other operating income, net interest, taxation, and dividends.

- There are four alternative profit and loss account formats permitted by the Companies Acts 1985/1989, and in line with the provisions of FRS 3; format 1 is the most widely used by the majority of limited companies.
- The profit and loss account is closely linked with the balance sheet in two ways: they both reflect the change in wealth of the business; most transactions are reflected once in the profit and loss account and once in the balance sheet.
- Valuation of the various items within the balance sheet in accordance with the Companies Acts 1985/1989, accounting concepts and standards, has a significant impact on the level of profit (or loss) earned by a business during an accounting period.
- The profit (or loss) earned during an accounting period is not the same as the cash flow generated during the period, but the links between the two measures may be quantified and reconciled.
- There are limitations to the profit and loss account, which like the balance sheet is an historical document, primarily due to the impact on costs of the employment of alternative methods of valuation of assets and liabilities.

Glossary of key terms

bad debt A debt which is or is considered to be uncollectable and is, therefore, written off either as a charge to the profit and loss account or against an existing doubtful debt provision.

corporation tax Tax chargeable on companies resident in the UK, or trading in the UK through a branch or agency, as well as on certain unincorporated associations (FRS 16).

depreciation provision The amount of depreciation that has cumulatively been charged to the profit and loss account, relating to a fixed asset, from the date of its acquisition. Fixed assets are stated in the balance sheet at their net book value (or written down value) which is usually their historical cost less the cumulative amount of depreciation at the balance sheet date.

doubtful debt A debt for which there is some uncertainty as to whether or not it will be settled, and for which there is a possibility that it may eventually prove to be bad. A doubtful debt provision may be created for such a debt by charging it as an expense to the profit and loss account.

doubtful debt provision An amount charged against profit and deducted from debtors to allow for the estimated non-recovery of a proportion of the debts.

earnings per share (eps) Profit after tax less preference share dividends divided by the number of ordinary shares in issue measures the return per share of earnings available to shareholders.

exceptional items Material items which derive from events or transactions that fall within the ordinary activities of the reporting entity individually or, if a similar type, in aggregate and which need to be disclosed separately by virtue of their size or incidence if the financial statements are to give a true and fair view (FRS 3).

extraordinary items Material items possessing a high degree of abnormality that arise from events or transactions that fall outside the ordinary activities of the reporting entity and which are not expected to recur. They do not include exceptional items, nor do they include prior period items merely because they relate to a prior period (FRS 3).

finished product Finished product or finished goods are manufactured goods ready for sale or despatch.

first in first out (FIFO) Assumes that the oldest items or costs are the first to be used. It is commonly applied to the pricing of issues of materials, based on using first the costs of the oldest materials in stock, irrespective of the sequence in which actual material usage takes place. Closing stocks are therefore valued at relatively current costs.

gross margin (GM) Gross margin (or gross profit) is the difference between sales and the total cost of sales.

last in first out (LIFO) Assumes that the last item of stock received is the first to be used. In the UK it is a little-used method of pricing the issue of material using the purchase price of the latest unit in stock. It is used more often in the USA as a method of valuing stock using indices to charge most recent prices against profits.

non-related company A company in which a business has a long-term investment, but over which it has no control or influence. If control exists then the company is deemed to be a subsidiary.

operating profit Gross profit, or gross margin, plus/less all operating revenues and costs, regardless of the financial structure of the company and whatever exceptional events occurred during the period.

profit before tax (PBT) Operating profit plus or minus net interest.

public limited company A company limited by shares or by guarantee, with a share capital, whose memorandum states that it is public and that it has complied with the registration procedures for such a company. A public company is distinguished from a private company in the following ways: a minimum issued share capital of £50,000; public limited company, or plc, at the end of the name; public company clause in the memorandum; freedom to offer securities to the public.

raw materials Goods purchased for incorporation into products for sale.

retained profits Profits that have not been paid out as dividends to shareholders, but retained for future investment by the company.

turnover Also called sales or revenue, are amounts derived from the provision of goods or services falling within the company's ordinary activities, after deduction of sales returns, trade discounts, value added tax, and any other taxes based on the amounts so derived (Companies Act 1985).

work in progress Products or services in intermediate stages of completion.

Assessment material

Questions

Q3.1   How would you define the profit (or loss) earned by a business during an accounting period?

Q3.2   Outline a profit and loss account showing each of the main category headings.

Q3.3   (i)   What are the requirements that determine the format of the profit and loss account of a limited company?

(ii)   Which accounting standard contains provisions relating to the format of the profit and loss account?

(iii)   What are the main requirements relevant to the formats?

Q3.4   The profit and loss account and the balance sheet report on different aspects of a company's financial status. What are these different aspects and how are they related?

Q3.5   (i)   Why are the methods used for the valuation of the various types of assets so important?

(ii)   Describe the three main categories of asset that are most relevant.

Q3.6   What is depreciation and what are the problems encountered in dealing with the depreciation of fixed assets?

Q3.7   Describe the three most commonly used methods of accounting for depreciation.

Q3.8   Describe the four most commonly used methods of valuing stocks.

Q3.9   How does the valuation of trade debtors impact on the profit and loss account of a business?

Q3.10   Profit does not equal cash, but how can the one be reconciled with the other for a specific accounting period?

Discussion points

D3.1   'My profit for the year is the total of my pile of sales invoices less the cash I have paid out during the year.' Discuss.

D3.2   'The reason why companies make a provision for depreciation on their fixed assets is to save up enough money to buy new ones when the old assets reach the end of their lives.' Discuss.

D3.3 Why is judgement so important in considering the most appropriate method to use for valuing stocks? What are the factors that should be borne in mind and what are the pros and cons of the alternative methods?
(Hint: Research Marks and Spencer and Laura Ashley on the Times CD-ROM in 1999 and 2000 to collect background material for this discussion.)

Exercises

Solutions are provided in Appendix 4 to all exercise numbers highlighted in colour.

Level I

E3.1 *Time allowed – 30 minutes*

The profit and loss account balances of Archibald Ltd extracted at 31 December 2000 were as follows:

	£000
Interest received	5
Accountancy and audit fees	10
Interest paid	40
Office electricity	22
Sales	1,089
Office rent	55
Advertising and promotion	45
Rents received	21
Telephone	29
Selling costs	54
Other office utilities	24
Cost of goods sold	553
Administrative salaries	72
Sales salaries	89
Depreciation on office equipment and furnishings	52

Identify the expense (debit balances) and income (credit balances) items, and then prepare a profit and loss account to the pre-tax profit level for Archibald Ltd for the year to 31 December 2000, using format 1.

E3.2 *Time allowed – 30 minutes*

Discuss the concepts that may apply and practical problems that may be encountered when accounting for

(i) the acquisition of desktop personal computers, and

(ii) popular brands of products supplied by retailers

with specific comments regarding their depreciation charged to the profit and loss account and their net book values shown in the balance sheet.

E3.3   *Time allowed – 30 minutes*

A friend of yours owns a shop selling CDs and posters for the 12 – 14-year-old market. From the following information advise him on the potential problems that may be encountered in the valuation of such items for balance sheet purposes:

(i)   Greatest hits compilation CDs have sold consistently over the months and cost £5,000 with a retail value of £7,000

(ii) Sales of specific group CDs, which ceased recording in the previous year, have now dropped off to zero and cost £500 with a total retail value of £700

(iii) Specific group CDs, which are still constantly recording and selling in the shop every week cost £1,000 with a total retail value of £1,400

(iv) Specific artist posters are currently not selling at all (although CDs are), and cost £50 with a retail value of £100

E3.4   *Time allowed – 30 minutes*

The Partex company began trading in 1996, and all sales are made to customers on credit. The company is in a sector that suffers from a high level of bad debts, and a provision for doubtful debts of 4% of outstanding debtors is made at each year end.
Information relating to 1996, 1997 and 1998 was as follows:

	Year to 31 December		
	1996	**1997**	**1998**
Outstanding debtors at 31 December*	£88,000	£110,000	£94,000
Bad debts to be written off during year	£4,000	£5,000	£4,000

*before bad debts have been written off

You are required to state the amount that will appear

(a) in the balance sheet for debtors, and

(b) in the profit and loss account for bad debts

E3.5   *Time allowed – 45 minutes*

Tartantrips Ltd, a company in Scotland, operates several ferries and has a policy of holding several in reserve, due to the weather patterns and conditions of various contracts with local authorities. A ferry costs £5 million and has an estimated useful life of ten years, at which time its realisable value is expected to be £1 million.

Calculate and discuss three methods of depreciation available to the company

(i)   sum of the digits

(ii) straight line

(iii) reducing balance

E3.6   *Time allowed – 60 minutes*

From the following profit and loss information that has been provided by Lazydays Ltd, for the year ended 31 March 2000 (and the corresponding figures for the year to 31 March 1999), construct a profit and loss account, using the format adopted by the majority of UK plcs, including comparative figures.

	2000 £	1999 £
Administrative expenses	22,000	20,000
Depreciation	5,000	5,000
Closing stock	17,000	15,000
Distribution costs	33,000	30,000
Dividends paid	32,000	30,000
Dividends received from non-related companies	5,000	5,000
Interest paid	10,000	10,000
Interest received	3,000	3,000
Opening stock	15,000	10,000
Purchases	99,000	90,000
Redundancy costs	5,000	
Sales	230,000	200,000
Taxation	25,000	24,000

(a) Depreciation is to be included in the administrative expenses

(b) Redundancy costs are to be regarded as an exceptional item

Level II

E3.7 *Time allowed – 60 minutes*

Llareggyb Ltd started business on 1 January 2000 and its year ended 31 December 2000. Llareggyb entered into the following transactions during the year.

Received funds for share capital of £25,000

Paid suppliers of materials £44,000

Purchased 11,000 units of materials at £8 per unit, one of which was required in one unit of finished goods

Heating and lighting costs paid for cash £16,000

Further heating and lighting costs £2,400 were incurred within the year, but still unpaid at 31 December 2000

Mr D Thomas loaned the company £80,000 on 1 January at 8% per annum

Loan interest was paid to Mr Thomas for January to June 2000

8,000 finished goods units were sold to customers at £40 each

Customers paid £280,000 to Llareggyb for sales of finished goods

Rent on the premises £60,000 was paid for 18 months from 1 January 2000, and business rates for the same period of £9,000 were also paid

Salaries and wages were paid for January to November amounting to £132,000 but the December payroll cost of £15,000 had not been paid

A lorry was purchased for £45,000 on 1 January 2000 and was expected to last for 5 years after which it could be sold for £8,000

The company uses the straight line method of depreciation

Prepare a profit and loss account for Llareggyb Ltd for the year ended 31 December 2000.

PART I FINANCIAL ACCOUNTING

E3.8   *Time allowed – 90 minutes*

From the trial balance of Gremlins plc at 31 March 2000 identify the expenses and assets (debit balances) and income, liabilities and equity (credit balances); confirm that the trial balance is in balance; then prepare a profit and loss account for the period to 31 March 2000 using format 1.

	£000
Depreciation on office equipment and furnishings (administrative expenses)	156
Bank overdraft	609
Accountancy and audit fees	30
Electricity paid in advance	45
Computer system (net book value)	441
Advertising and promotion	135
Share premium account	240
Interest received	15
Plant and equipment (net book value)	927
Amount for final payment on factory machine due March 2002	252
Trade debtors	1,110
Goodwill	204
Twelve-year lease on factory	330
Rents received	63
Prepaid expenses	885
Interest paid	120
Office electricity	66
Retained earnings at 31 March 199	513
Stocks of materials at 31 March 2000	585
Telephone	87
Distribution costs	162
Other office utilities	72
Cost of goods sold	1,659
Administrative salaries	216
Sales salaries	267
Furniture and fixtures (net book value)	729
Sales	3,267
Office rent	165
Finished product at 31 March 2000	84
Debenture	750
Trade creditors	1,257
Cash	51
Share capital	1,560

4

Financial statements of limited companies – cash flow statement

LEARNING OBJECTIVES

Completion of this chapter will enable you to:

● describe what is meant by cash flow

● outline the structure of the cash flow statement of a limited company, and its supporting schedules

● classify the categories of cash inflows and cash outflows that comprise the cash flow statement

● illustrate how both the direct and indirect cash flow approaches are used to derive net cash flows from operating activities

● prepare a cash flow statement

● explain the links between the cash flow statement and the balance sheet

● explain the links between the cash flow statement and the profit and loss account

● consider the merits of cash flow versus profit as a measure of financial performance

CONTENTS

Introduction

Chapters 2 and 3 have been concerned with the first two of the three key financial statements required to be prepared periodically by limited companies: the balance sheet and the profit and loss account. This chapter will be concerned with the third of the financial statements, the cash flow statement. The cash flow statement, in one form or another, is prepared and used as an important management tool by all businesses. However, as in the previous two chapters, this chapter deals primarily with the cash flow statements of limited companies, both private and public.

Chapter 4 looks at how cash flow statements are structured and how each of the different types of cash inflows and cash outflows are categorised. This forms the basis to enable the preparation of a cash flow statement of a limited company, and its supporting schedules, in the appropriate format.

We will look at the relationship between the cash flow statement and the balance sheet and the profit and loss account. In Chapters 2 and 3 we have seen the subjective aspects of both the balance sheet and the profit and loss account. Cash flow is not subjective in any way but is a matter of fact.

What does the cash flow statement tell us?

Cash is a crucial requirement for any business to develop and survive, whether involved in the public services, manufacturing, retailing, or in a major national project like the Millennium Dome 2000 project (see the press cutting below).

The Millennium Dome project demonstrated the need for realistic and timely cash planning both prior to and during its life, through the preparation of regular, clearly understood cash reports. Such cash planning and reporting may have avoided the problems faced by the managers throughout and subsequent to the life of the project.

The definition of cash includes not only cash in hand but also deposits and overdrafts, including those denominated in foreign currencies, **repayable on demand** with any bank or other financial institutions. Deposits repayable on demand include any kind of account where additional funds may be deposited at any time or funds withdrawn at any time without prior notice. All charges and credits on these accounts such as bank interest, bank fees, deposits or withdrawals, other than movements wholly within them, represent cash inflows and outflows of the reporting entity.

Virtually all transactions are conducted ultimately by cash or near cash (for example, bank accounts and credit cards). Sales of goods or services, or any other business assets, whether they are settled immediately or settled at some future date, are settled by cash

Smith issued order to bail out Dome

Culture secretary Chris Smith and eight members of the Millennium Commission ordered a senior civil servant to pay £76m to keep the Millennium Dome afloat after he had told them it was a waste of public money.

The revelation was made in *The Guardian* at the weekend and is based on the National Audit Office inquiry into the controversial project. The NAO told AccountancyAge.com it would be 'inappropriate' to comment on its forthcoming report.

With the Commons Public Accounts Committee set to quiz civil servants about the report on 20 November, the NAO is expected to issue its findings in the first week of November.

According to *The Guardian*, the damning report will say that Smith has twice had to issue a ministerial direction order forcing Commission director Mike

O'Connor to hand out cash to the 'near bankrupt' attraction.

The first order was made last May when Smith, in his capacity as commission chairman, ordered £29m to be given to keep the Dome going. The second undisclosed order for another £47m was made last month after O'Connor made a second objection to spending the cash on the dome, the paper said.

The draft report, according to *The Guardian*, reveals that Smith received unanimous support from his fellow commissioners to demand the money after they had examined whether to close down the Dome.

But they were told that millions of pounds of more cash would be needed to compensate donors, pay out redundancy to staff and meet creditors' bills, the report said.

Source: *AccountancyAge.com*, 16 October 2000

or cash equivalents. Cash is an asset like any other asset, such as fixed asset machinery, or current asset debtors. Cash has the same properties as other assets, but also many more.

Cash is

- a unit of measurement – we evaluate transactions and report financial information in £ sterling or whatever other foreign currency denominated
- a medium of exchange – rather than using the exchange or barter of other assets, cash is used as the accepted medium, having itself a recognisable value
- a store of value – cash may be used for current requirements or held for future use.

The inability of a business to pay its creditors, and other claims on the business, is invariably the reason for that business to fail. Cash, therefore, is a key asset and different from all other assets, which is why the performance of cash as a measure of business performance is so important.

In Chapters 2 and 3 we have discussed how the balance sheet and the profit and loss account do not show or directly deal with some of the key changes that have taken place in the company's financial position. We will see in this chapter how the cash flow statement addresses this shortfall of information provided by the other two key financial statements, by answering questions like:

- how much capital expenditure (for example, machines, and buildings) has the company made, and how did it fund the expenditure?
- what was the extent of new borrowing and how much debt was repaid?
- how much did the company need to fund new **working capital requirements** (for example increases in debtors and stock requirements as a result of more business activity)?
- how much of the company's funding was met by funds generated from its trading activities, and how much met by new external funding (for example, from banks and other lenders, or new shareholders)?

We introduced the VCR analogy in Chapters 2 and 3 with regard to the balance sheet and the profit and loss account. In the same way as profit (or loss), cash represents the dynamic 'video' of changes in the cash position of the business throughout the period between the two 'pauses' – the balance sheets at the start and the finish of an accounting period. The cash flow statement summarises the cash inflows and outflows and calculates the net change in the cash position throughout the period. In this way it provides answers to the questions shown above. Analysis and summary of the cash inflows and outflows of the period answers those questions by illustrating

- changes in the level of cash between the start and end of the period
- how much cash has been generated, and from where
- for what purpose cash has been used.

Structure of the cash flow statement

The basic purpose of a cash flow statement, as we saw in Chapter 2, is to report the cash receipts and cash payments that take place within an accounting period (see Fig. 4.1), and to show how the cash balance has changed from the start of the period to the balance at the end of the period. This can be seen to be objective and clearly avoids the problems of allocation associated with the preparation of a conventional profit and loss account.

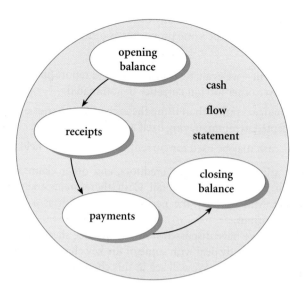

FIGURE 4.1   The main elements of the cash flow statement

However, a more useful presentation would describe

● how the company generated or lost cash
● how the company financed its growth and investments
● the extent to which the company was funded by debt and equity.

The cash flow statement is covered in FRS 1, Cash Flow Statements, and its objective is to ensure that **reporting entities** fall within its scope:

● for companies to report their cash generation and cash absorption for a period by highlighting the significant components of cash flow in a way that facilitates comparison of the cash flow performances of different businesses
● for companies to provide information that assists in the assessment of their liquidity, solvency and financial adaptability.

Statements of Source and Application of Funds, SSAP 10, was the original accounting standard that required companies to provide a statement of source and application of funds. This statement was difficult to understand and did not provide a clear explanation of the cash flows of the company. SSAP 10 was replaced in September 1991 by the ASB with FRS 1, requiring companies to publish a cash flow statement. FRS 1 was subsequently revised in 1996. FRS 1 requires that the company's cash flow statement should list its cash flows for the period, and classified under standard headings. These headings are represented in Fig. 4.2.

Progress check 4.1	**Explain what is meant by a cash flow statement.**

The headings under which cash inflows and outflows for the period are itemised follow a particular order. We will look at explanations of each of the headings and how they are put together to provide an analysis of the cash movements of the business over an accounting period.

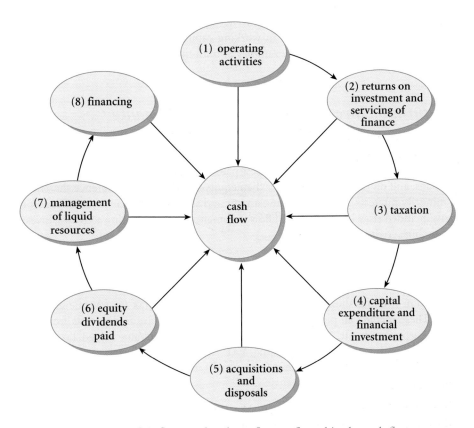

FIGURE 4.2 Cash inflows and cash outflows reflected in the cash flow statement

What are the aims and purposes of the cash flow statement?

1. Operating activities (using either the direct or indirect method)

Net cash flows from operating activities include the cash effects of transactions and other events relating to the operating or trading activities of the business. They are the movements in cash and cash equivalents of the operations that are included in the profit and loss account to derive operating profit. Net cash flows from operating activities include the cash effects only and not all the revenues and costs that together represent the profit and loss account.

Reference to the direct and **indirect method** relates to the choice of two options that are available for a business to derive the net cash flows from operating activities. The **direct method** involves individual identification of each of the cash items during the period that have been included in the profit and loss account. They are:

- cash received from customers in respect of sales
- cash paid to suppliers in respect of purchases
- cash paid to employees
- cash paid for all other expenses.

The indirect method involves use of the net operating profit for the period adjusted for non-cash items and movements in working capital to arrive at net cash flows from operating activities. We will look at examples of both these techniques in a later section of this chapter.

2. Returns on investment and servicing of finance

Returns on investment and servicing of finance are receipts of cash that result from owning an investment, and payments of cash to providers of finance. This includes interest received on long-term and short-term loans, interest paid on overdrafts and long-term and short-term loans, and dividends paid to other than equity shareholders (preference shareholders and minority interests). Returns on investment and servicing of finance excludes all other returns included elsewhere in the cash flow statements under operating activities, investing or financing activities.

3. Taxation

The taxation heading should include all items in respect of tax on revenue and capital profits. These include all payments relating to corporation tax, and receipts from rebate claims, overpayments, etc. Payments and receipts in respect of Value Added Tax (VAT) are not included within the taxation heading. VAT payments and receipts are netted against the cash flows to which they relate, for example, operating activities and fixed assets investments.

4. Capital expenditure and financial investment

Capital expenditure and financial investment includes payments and receipts for the acquisition and disposal of fixed assets. It does not include any income derived from these investments, since these are shown under the heading returns on investment and servicing of finance.

5. Acquisitions and disposals

Cash payments and receipts for acquisitions and disposals relate to the acquisition and sale of investments in subsidiary undertakings, or investment and sales of investments in other undertakings. As with capital expenditure investments, this category does not include any income derived from these investments, which are included under the heading returns on investment and servicing of finance.

6. Equity dividends paid

This heading includes all dividends actually paid in cash during the accounting period to equity (ordinary share) shareholders. It does not include proposed dividends or dividends declared, which will not be paid until a subsequent accounting period.

7. Management of liquid resources

The management of liquid resources is concerned with cash payments and cash receipts from the acquisition and disposal of investments held as a result of short-term cash surpluses. Such investments may include investments in equity shares or short-term Government loans.

8. Financing

Financing cash flow generally includes the receipts and payments of cash relating to the long-term financing of the business. It relates to the financing itself rather than the servicing of such finance through dividends and interest. Financing cash flows include receipts from

● share issues
● debentures
● loans
● notes
● bonds
● other long-term borrowings.

The last two headings may be shown in a single section, provided that a subtotal is given for each heading. Individual categories of inflows and outflows under the standard headings should be disclosed separately either in the cash flow statement or in a note to it unless they are allowed to be shown net. In some circumstances cash inflows and outflows may be shown net if they relate to the management of liquid resources or financing. The requirement to show cash inflows and outflows separately does not apply to cash flows relating to operating activities.

Progress check 4.3

Explain what cash inflows and outflows are reflected within each of the headings in the cash flow statement.

Example 4.1

The following is a list of some of the different types of cash inflows and cash outflows of a typical plc. Within which of the cash flow statement headings would they normally be reported?

● sale of a subsidiary
● dividends paid to ordinary shareholders
● VAT
● interest paid
● purchase of a copyright (intangible fixed asset)
● interest received
● issue of debentures
● corporation tax.

● short-term Government loans (for example Treasury Stock)
● purchase of a building
● income from investments
● receipts from trade debtors
● payments to trade creditors (due within one year)
● purchase of factory machinery

Answer

Net cash flow from operating activities
Receipts from trade debtors
Payments to trade creditors (due within one year)

Returns on investments and servicing of finance
Interest received
Interest paid
Income from investments

◀ **Taxation**
  Corporation tax
  VAT? No, because VAT is netted against the cash flow to which it relates

Capital expenditure and financial investment
  Purchase of a copyright
  Purchase of a building
  Purchase of factory machinery

Acquisitions and disposals
  Sale of a subsidiary

Equity dividends paid
  Dividends paid to ordinary shareholders

Management of liquid resources
  Short-term Government loans

Financing
  Issue of debentures

Progress check 4.4

What questions does the cash flow statement set out to answer and how does it achieve this?

Direct and indirect cash flow

As we touched on earlier, the heading relating to net operating cash flow can be presented by using either the direct method or indirect method. We shall consider both methods in a little more detail, although the indirect method is by far the easiest to use in practice and is the method used by most companies.

Direct method

The direct method involves an analysis of all the cash transactions for the appropriate period to identify all receipts and payments relating to the operating activities for the period. The analysis therefore shows the relevant constituent cash flows, operating cash receipts and cash payments including in particular cash receipts from customers, cash payments to suppliers, and cash payments to and on behalf of employees.

An example of the adoption of the direct method by Flatco plc is illustrated in Fig. 4.3.

The standard FRS 1 makes it mandatory to provide a reconciliation between operating profit and net cash flow from operating activities, even where the direct method is adopted. Because of this, the amount of time, and other resources required to analyse the relevant cash information, the direct method has not been popular with many companies, although it does provide some very useful information.

Indirect method

The indirect method is by far the one most frequently adopted by UK companies. The basis of this approach is that operating revenues and costs are generally associated with cash receipts and cash payments and so profits earned from operating activities during an

Flatco plc
Cash flow statement for the year ended 31 December 2000
Cash flow from operating activities

	£000
Operating activities	
Net cash received from customers	3,472
Cash payments to suppliers	(1,694)
Cash paid to and on behalf of employees	(631)
Other cash payments	(211)
Net cash inflow from operating activities	936

FIGURE 4.3 Cash flow from operating activities – direct method

accounting period will approximate the net cash flows generated during the period. The actual operating cash flow may be determined from adjustment to the operating profit reported in the profit and loss account for non-cash items and changes in working capital during the period:

- stocks
- debtors
- creditors.

Example 4.2

Indirect Ltd earned operating profits of £247,000 during 1999/2000, and its retained profit for the year was also £247,000. Indirect Ltd had acquired fixed assets totalling £290,000 during the year and had made no disposals of fixed assets. Indirect's balance sheets as at 1 July 1999 and 30 June 2000 were as follows:

	1 July 1999 £000	30 June 2000 £000
Fixed assets	385	525
Stocks	157	277
Debtors	224	287
	766	1,089
Creditors due within 1 year	(305)	(312)
Bank overdraft	(153)	(222)
Equity	(308)	(555)
	(766)	(1,089)

We are required to use the indirect method to calculate the net cash flow from operating activities.

◀ **Answer**

Calculation of depreciation	£000
Fixed assets at the start of the year were	385
Additions during the year were	290
Disposals during the year were	zero
	675
Fixed assets at the end of the year were	525
Therefore, depreciation for the year was	150

Indirect Ltd
Cash flow statement for the year ended 30 June 2000

Reconciliation of operating profit to net cash inflow from operating activities

	£000
Operating profit	247
Depreciation charges	150
Increase in stocks [277 − 157]	(120)
Increase in debtors [287 − 224]	(63)
Increase in creditors due within 1 year [312 − 305]	7
Net cash inflow from operating activities	221

The above example shows how the net cash inflow from operating activities of £221,000 was calculated by starting with the operating profit for the year of £247,000 and adjusting for changes in depreciation and working capital over the year.

The only other cash activity during the year appears to be the acquisition of fixed assets totalling £290,000. If we deduct that from the net cash inflow from operating activities of £221,000 we get a net cash outflow of £69,000. This agrees with the movement in the cash and bank balances, which have worsened from an overdraft of £153,000 at the beginning of the year to an overdraft of £222,000 at the end of the year.

Progress check 4.5

Describe the direct and the indirect cash flow methods that may be used to derive net operating cash flow from operating profit, their differences and their purpose.

Cash flow statement formats

There is no statutory requirement for companies to prepare a cash flow statement. FRS 1 requires all reporting entities that prepare financial statements, intended to give a true and fair view of their financial position and profit and loss, to include a cash flow statement as a primary statement within their financial statements, except for small companies which are specifically exempted.

There is one standard format for the cash flow statement prescribed by FRS 1, which includes the headings we have discussed above. The cash flow statement actually comprises a number of statements:

- Reconciliation of operating profit to net operating cash flows (Fig. 4.4)
- Cash flow statement of cash inflows and outflows (Fig. 4.5)
- Reconciliation of net cash flow to movement in **net debt** (Fig. 4.6)
- Note on gross cash flows (Fig. 4.7)
- Note on analysis of changes in net debt (Fig. 4.8).

Figs 4.4 to 4.8 illustrate the format of the cash flow statements and have been prepared from the balance sheet and profit and loss account for Flatco plc included in Chapter 2 and Chapter 3.

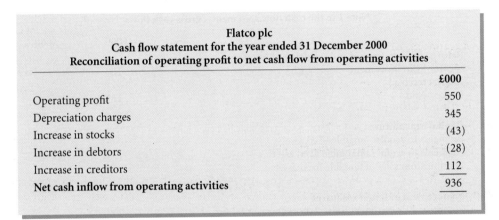

Flatco plc
Cash flow statement for the year ended 31 December 2000
Reconciliation of operating profit to net cash flow from operating activities

	£000
Operating profit	550
Depreciation charges	345
Increase in stocks	(43)
Increase in debtors	(28)
Increase in creditors	112
Net cash inflow from operating activities	936

FIGURE 4.4   Reconciliation of operating profit
to net cash flow from operating activities

Cash flow statement

	£000
Net cash inflow from operating activities	936
Returns on investments and servicing of finance (note 1)	40
Taxation	(44)
Capital expenditure (note 1)	(299)
	633
Equity dividends paid	(67)
	566
Management of liquid resources (note 1)	–
Financing (note 1)	373
Increase in cash	939

FIGURE 4.5   Cash flow statement

123

Reconciliation of net cash flow to movement in net debt/funds (note 2)

	£000
Increase in cash for the period	939
Cash inflow from increase in long-term debt	(173)
Change in net debt	766
Net debt at 1 January 2000	(662)
Net funds at 31 December 2000	104

FIGURE 4.6   Reconciliation of net cash flow to movement in net debt/funds

Note 1 to the cash flow statement – gross cash flows

	£000	£000
Returns on investments and servicing of finance		
Income from investments	100	
Interest received	11	
Interest paid	(71)	
		40
Capital expenditure		
Payments to acquire tangible fixed assets	(286)	
Payments to acquire intangible fixed assets	(34)	
Receipts from sales of tangible fixed assets	21	
		(299)
Management of liquid resources		
Purchase of Government bills (short-term	(200)	
Sale of Government bills investments)	200	
		–
Financing		
Issue of ordinary share capital	200	
Debenture loan	173	
		373

FIGURE 4.7   Note 1 – gross cash flows

Note 2 to the cash flow statement – analysis of change in net debt/funds

	At 1 January 2000 £000	Cash flows £000	At 31 December 2000 £000
Cash in hand and at bank	17	310	327
Overdraft	(679)	629	(50)
Debenture	–	(173)	(173)
Total (debt)/funds	(662)	766	104

FIGURE 4.8   Note 2 – analysis of change in net debt/funds

Example 4.3

The reconciliation of operating profit to net cash flow from operating activities shown below is an extract from the published accounts of Tomkins plc, which is a diversified multinational UK plc with interests in the UK, USA and other parts of the world. Tomkins has been acquisitive in the past, but sold off activities it wished not to develop in the future.

You are required to comment on the working capital movements for the year 2000.

Figures in £m	2000	1999
Operating profit	519.1	495.3
Depreciation	197.9	175.0
Profit/(loss) on sale of fixed assets	(1.0)	(6.1)
(Increase)/decrease in stocks	(64.4)	4.7
(Increase)/decrease in debtors	(73.2)	7.2
Increase/(decrease) in creditors	(0.9)	(89.7)
Other	0.5	1.3
Net cash inflow from operating activities	578.0	587.7

Answer

Operating profits may initially be considered to be on a plateau, but as the group is not solely involved in one industrial sector further analysis is difficult.

The stocks movement of £64.4m is quite significant and the company may be expected to explain what activity or decision brought this about.

The debtors movement of £73.2m is also worthy of separate comment to assist users of the cash flow statement to make their economic judgement.

The creditors movement of £0.9m is most unexpected as many companies would use creditors in part to finance increases in stocks and debtors.

Net cash inflows for the two years are so similar that the company may have set internal targets to ensure sufficient cash flows were achieved, allowing for acquisitions, disposals and trading.

Example 4.4

The extract from a leading UK supermarket retailer's cash flow statement shown below is its net debt note for the year to February 2000.

Figures in £m	Opening balance 1 Mar 1999	Cash flow	Closing balance 28 Feb 2000
Cash at bank	127	(39)	88
Overdrafts	(31)	(4)	(35)
	96	(43)	53
Liquid resources	201	57	258
Short-term loans	(799)	(13)	(812)
Long-term loans	(1,218)	(341)	(1,559)
Net debt	(1,720)	(340)	(2,060)

Discuss each of the elements in the net debt note and comment briefly on the cash flow movements over the year.

Answer

(a) Both cash and overdraft balances have contributed to the increase in net debt. This apparent policy of reducing cash balances and increasing overdrafts may be questioned. The actual policy can be established by looking at the trends over several years and any comments made by the company in its published report and accounts.

(b) The liquid resources were in fact increased, possibly to take advantage of the increase in interest rates being paid in the UK. The company was actually publicly criticised in late 2000 by the UK Government for holding on to suppliers' funds for too long.

(c) The company is obviously using short-term funds to finance the business. The users of financial information usually require information on the timing of repayments of loans (in this case the bulk of the £812 million short-term debt is owed to banks), which plcs are required by the Companies Act to disclose in their published reports and accounts.

(d) All major UK plcs provide an overview of their treasury activities in their published reports and accounts, which links current policies with the components of net debt (for example, banking facilities).

(e) The financial press sometimes comment on net debt movement. This may vary from year to year and from analyst to analyst. A typical comment might be 'the £340 million increase has pushed net borrowings of the company to over £2 billion for the first time'.

The comparative figures for the previous year (not shown in the Flatco plc illustrations, Figs 4.3 to 4.8) are usually reported in columns to the right of the current year's figures. Each of the statements shown in Figs 4.4 to 4.8 is important for the following reasons:

- the reconciliation of operating profit to net cash flow from operating activities (Fig. 4.4) shows how the net cash flow from operating activities is derived from adjusting operating profit for non-cash items and movements in working capital
- the cash flow statement (Fig. 4.5) reports the net cash flow for an accounting period, derived from the net cash flow from operating activities and adjusted for all non-operating categories of cash inflows and outflows
- the reconciliation of net cash flow to movement in net debt (Fig. 4.6) shows how the net cash flow for an accounting period is the difference between the net debt at the beginning of the period and the net debt at the end of the period
- note 1 – gross cash flows (Fig. 4.7) provides more detail with regard to the non-operating cash inflows and outflows used in the cash flow statement (Fig. 4.5)
- note 2 – analysis of changes in net debt (Fig. 4.8) analyses the net debt movement shown in Fig. 4.6 in greater detail to show each of the categories that comprise net debt

The Companies Acts 1985/1989 require group accounts to be prepared for the holding company in addition to the accounts that are required to be prepared for each of the individual companies within the group. These 'consolidated accounts' exclude all transactions between companies within the group, for example, inter-company sales and purchases. Undertakings preparing consolidated financial statements should prepare a consolidated cash flow statement and related notes; they are not then required to prepare an entity cash flow statement.

Progress check 4.6

What are the schedules that are used to support the main cash flow statement and what is their purpose?

Example 4.5

Using the following data, extracted from the financial records of Zap Electronics plc, prepare a cash flow statement in compliance with the provisions of FRS 1, together with the appropriate notes and reconciliations. The data relate to the financial statements prepared for the year ended 31 July 2000.

	£000
Dividends paid on ordinary shares	49
Purchase of Government bills (short-term investments)	200
Issue of ordinary share capital	100
Reduction in stocks	25
Corporation tax paid	120
Interest paid	34
Operating profit	830
Bank and cash balance 31 July 2000	527
Purchase of machinery	459
Sale of Government bills	100
Interest received	18
Purchase of a copyright (intangible fixed asset)	78
Depreciation charge for the year	407
Purchase of a building	430
Sale of a patent (intangible fixed asset)	195
Increase in trade debtors	35
Reduction in trade creditors (due within 1 year)	85
Bank and cash balance 1 August 1999	342

Answer

Zap Electronics plc
Cash flow statement for the year ended 31 July 2000
Reconciliation of operating profit to net cash flow from operating activities

	£000
Operating profit	830
Depreciation charge	407
Reduction in stocks	25
Increase in debtors	(35)
Reduction in creditors	(85)
Net cash inflow from operating activities	1,142

◀

Cash flow statement

	£000
Net cash inflow from operating activities	1,142
Returns on investments and servicing of finance (note 1)	(16)
Taxation	(120)
Capital expenditure (note 1)	(772)
	234
Equity dividends paid	(49)
	185
Management of liquid resources (note 1)	(100)
Financing (note 1)	100
Increase in cash	185

Reconciliation of net cash flow to movement in net debt/net funds (note 2)

	£000
Increase in cash for the period	185
Change in net debt	185
Net funds at 1 August 1999	342
Net funds at 31 July 2000	527

Note 1 to the cash flow statement – gross cash flows

	£000	£000
Returns on investments and servicing of finance		
Interest received	18	
Interest paid	(34)	
		(16)
Capital expenditure		
Payments to acquire intangible fixed assets	(78)	
Payments to acquire tangible fixed assets [430 + 459]	(889)	
Receipts from sales of intangible fixed assets	195	
		(772)
Management of liquid resources		
Purchase of Government bills	(200)	
Sale of Government bills	100	
		(100)
Financing		
Issue of ordinary share capital		100

Note 2 to the cash flow statement – analysis of change in net debt/funds

	At 1 August 1999 £000	Cash flows £000	At 31 July 2000 £000
Bank and cash	342	185	527
Overdraft	–	–	–
	342	185	527

Example 4.6

The profit and loss account for Perfecto Ltd for the year ended 30 September 2000 and its balance sheets as at 30 September 1999 and 30 September 2000 are shown below.

Perfecto Ltd
Profit and loss account for the year ended 30 September 2000

	£000	£000
Turnover		2,279
Cost of sales		(1,484)
Gross profit		795
Distribution costs	(368)	
Administrative expenses	(197)	
		(565)
Operating profit		230
Net interest		(10)
Profit before tax		220
Tax on profit on ordinary activities		(70)
Profit on ordinary activities after tax		150

Perfecto Ltd
Balance sheet as at 30 September 2000

	2000 £000	1999 £000
Fixed assets		
Intangible	203	193
Tangible	902	1,071
	1,105	1,264
Current assets		
Stocks	161	142
Debtors	284	193
Prepayments	295	278
Cash	157	–
	897	613

◀ **Current liabilities (less than 1 year)**

Bank overdraft	–	20
Creditors	187	231
Corporation tax	70	55
Proposed dividend	20	–
Accruals	100	81
	377	387
Net current assets	520	226
Total assets less current liabilities	1,625	1,490
less		
Long-term liabilities (over 1 year)		
Creditors	77	184
Financial debt	85	126
Provisions	103	185
	265	495
Net assets	1,360	995
Capital and reserves		
Capital	600	450
Premiums	105	–
Profit and loss account	655	545
	1,360	995

During the year Perfecto Ltd acquired new plant and machinery for £150,000, bought a patent for £10,000, and made no disposals of either tangible or intangible fixed assets.

Perfecto Ltd paid an interim dividend of £20,000 during the year and declared a final dividend of £20,000. Interest paid was £20,000 and interest received was £10,000. The company paid corporation tax of £55,000 during the year.

We are required to prepare a cash flow statement for the year ended 30 September 2000 complying with FRS 1, including all supporting reconciliations and notes.

Answer

	£000
Fixed assets at the start of the year were	1,264
Additions during the year were	160 [150 + 10]
Disposals during the year were	zero
	1,424
Fixed assets at the end of the year were	1,105
Therefore, depreciation for the year was	319

	30 Sep 1999 £000	30 Sep 2000 £000	Difference £000
Stocks	142	161	19 increase
Debtors and prepayments	471 [193 + 278]	579 [284 + 295]	108 increase
Creditors, accruals, and provisions	681 [231 + 81 + 184 + 185]	467 [187 + 100 + 77 + 103]	214 decrease

Perfecto Ltd
Cash flow statement for the year ended 30 September 2000
Reconciliation of operating profit to net cash flow from operating activities

	£000
Operating profit	230
Depreciation charges	319
Increase in stocks	(19)
Increase in debtors	(108)
Reduction in creditors	(214)
Net cash inflow from operating activities	208

Cash flow statement

	£000
Net cash inflow from operating activities	208
Returns on investments and servicing of finance (note 1)	(10)
Taxation	(55)
Capital expenditure (note 1)	(160)
	(17)
Equity dividends paid	(20)
	(37)
Management of liquid resources (note 1)	–
Financing (note 1)	214
Increase in cash	177

Reconciliation of net cash flow to movement in net debt/funds (note 2)

	£000
Increase in cash for the period	177
Cash outflow from decrease in long-term debt	41
Change in net debt	218
Net debt at 30 September 1999	(146)
Net funds at 30 September 2000	72

▶

◀

Note 1 to the cash flow statement – gross cash flows

	£000	£000
Returns on investments and servicing of finance		
Interest received	10	
Interest paid	(20)	
		(10)
Capital expenditure		
Payments to acquire tangible fixed assets	(150)	
Payments to acquire intangible fixed assets	(10)	
		(160)
Financing		
Issue of ordinary share capital [600 + 105 – 450]	255	
Repayment of loans [126 – 85]	(41)	
		214

Note 2 to the cash flow statement – analysis of change in net debt/funds

	At 30 September 1999 £000	Cash flows £000	At 30 September 2000 £000
Cash	–	157	157
Bank overdraft	(20)	20	–
Long-term debt	(126)	41	(85)
Total (debt)/funds	(146)	218	72

Cash flow links to the balance sheet and profit and loss account

The diagram shown in Fig. 4.9 is a representation of some simple links between cash flow and the profit and loss account, and the relationship with the balance sheet. It shows how for example

● a purchase of fixed assets for cash of 50 has

  – increased fixed assets in the balance sheet from the opening balance of 100 to the closing balance of 150
  – decreased the opening cash balance by 50

● a profit of 100, that has been realised in cash, has

  – increased by 100 the opening cash balance of 100 which, less the outflow of 50 for fixed assets, gives a closing balance of 150
  – increased the profit and loss account from the opening balance of 100 to the closing balance of 200.

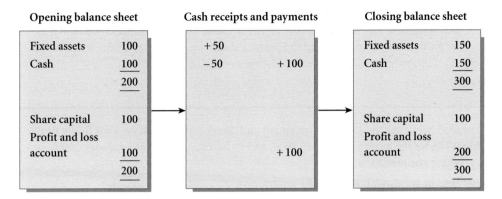

FIGURE 4.9 Some simple links between cash flow and the profit and loss account, and the balance sheet

The effect of the above transactions is

● cash has increased by 50
● fixed assets have been increased by 50
● profit has increased by 100
● the balance sheet is still in balance with increased total assets and total liabilities.

We may see from the more detailed information given as part of cash flow statement reporting how cash flow may be appreciated in the context of the information given by the balance sheet and the profit and loss account. The accounting standard FRS 1 (Cash Flow Statements) requires companies to provide two reconciliations included as part of the cash flow statement reporting, between:

● operating profit and the net cash flow from operating activities

and between:

● the net cash flow during the period and the movement in net debt.

These reconciliations do not form part of the cash flow statement but each are provided in a supporting schedule and in a separate note. The links between cash flow and the profit and loss account may therefore be observed by way of the operating profit, adjusted for non-cash items and the changes in working capital to arrive at net cash flow from operating activities.

Opening and closing balances of cash do not appear on the face of the cash flow statement and so do not provide a direct link with the corresponding numbers reported in the balance sheet. It is for this reason that the increase or decrease in cash that appears in the cash flow statement must be reconciled with the opening and closing balance sheet numbers – the movement in net debt.

Usually this reconciliation is a simple matter of adding the increase or decrease in cash during the accounting period to the opening balance of cash and cash equivalents to agree the closing balance of cash. However, there are some situations when, in addition to the cash flows of the entity, the movement in net debt has to identify specific items, which must be reconciled to the opening and closing balance sheet amounts:

● the acquisition or disposal of subsidiaries (excluding cash balances)
● other non-cash charges
● the recognition of changes in market value and exchange rate movements.

How is the cash flow statement of a business related to its other financial statements, the profit and loss account and the balance sheet?

Example 4.7

Detailed below are the cash flow statement and direct cash flow analysis for Ronly Bonly Jones Ltd for the month of January 2000, and its balance sheet as at 1 January 2000.
We are required to

(i)   Reconcile the cash flow for the month with the profit for the month
(ii) Derive the profit and loss account for the month
(iii) Derive the changes in the balance sheet during the month from the 1 January balance sheet
(iv) Prepare the balance sheet as at 31 January 2000

Figures in £000

Reconciliation of operating profit to net cash flow from operating activities

Operating profit	10
Depreciation charges	5
Increase in stocks	(34)
Increase in debtors	(18)
Increase in creditors	2
Net cash outflow from operating activities	(35)

Cash flow statement

Net cash outflow from operating activities	(35)
Capital expenditure – tangible fixed asset additions	(20)
	(55)
Financing – increase in equity share capital	10
Decrease in cash	(45)

Direct method

Operating activities	
Net cash received from customers	632
Cash payments to suppliers	(422)
Cash paid to and on behalf of employees	(190)
Other cash payments	(55)
Net cash outflow from operating activities	(35)

Balance sheet as at 1 January 2000	**£000**
Fixed assets at cost	130
Depreciation provision	(20)
Stocks	45
Debtors	64
Cash and bank	6
	225
Creditors	(87)
Share capital	(50)
Profit and loss account	(88)
	(225)

Answer

We may reconcile the cash flow for the month with the profit for the month as follows:

	January 2000 **£000**	
Increase in debtors during the month	18	
Cash received from customers	632	
Sales for the month	650	
Increase in stocks during the month	(34)	
Purchases of materials from suppliers	424	[increase in creditors 2 + cash payments to suppliers 422]
Cost of goods sold in the month	390	
Depreciation charge in the month	5	
Cash paid to and on behalf of employees	190	
Other cash payments	55	
Expenses for the month	245	

Therefore the profit and loss account for January 2000 is

	£000
Sales	650
Cost of goods sold	(390)
Depreciation	(5)
Expenses	(245)
Profit for January	10

Let's derive the 31 January 2000 balance sheet from the information that has been provided ▶

◀

Figures in £000	Fixed assets	Depn	Stocks	Debtors	Cash	Creditors	Equity	Profit/loss account
1 January 2000	130	(20)	45	64	6	(87)	(50)	(88)
Sales				650				(650)
Cash from customers				(632)	632			0
Purchases			424			(424)		0
Cash to creditors					(422)	422		0
Stock sold			(390)					390
Depreciation		(5)						5
Expenses					(245)			245
Fixed asset additions	20				(20)			0
Issue of shares					10		(10)	0
31 January 2000	150	(25)	79	82	(39)	(89)	(60)	(98)

Therefore the balance sheets at 1 January 2000 and at 31 January 2000 are as follows:

	1 January 2000 £000	31 January 2000 £000
Fixed assets at cost	130	150
Depreciation provision	(20)	(25)
Stocks	45	79
Debtors	64	82
Cash and bank	6	(39)
	225	247
Creditors	(87)	(89)
Share capital	(50)	(60)
Profit and loss account	(88)	(98)
	(225)	(247)

In Example 4.7, we have

● used the cash flow statement to derive the profit and loss account for the month

and we have then used the

● 1 January balance sheet
● profit and loss account for the month of January
● non-profit and loss items also shown in the January cash flow statement

to derive the balance sheet for 31 January.

In this way, we can see how the balance sheet, profit and loss account and cash flow statement of a business are inextricably linked.

Example 4.8

How may a shareholder in Ronly Bonly Jones Ltd react to the net cash outflow of £45,000 shown in Example 4.7?

(Hint: use the cash flow reconciliation statement.)

Answer

During January 2000 there was a profit before depreciation of £15,000 (£10,000 + £5,000). This, together with the increase in share capital of £10,000, provided a total cash inflow for the month of £25,000. However, there was a net outflow of cash on increased working capital of £50,000 (£34,000 + £18,000 − £2,000) and capital expenditure of £20,000. This all resulted in a net cash outflow of £45,000 (£25,000 − £50,000 − £20,000).

The net cash outflow may be in line with what the company had planned or forecast for January 2000. Alternatively, the outflow may not have been expected. Changes in trading circumstances and/or management decisions may have been the reason for the difference between the actual and expected cash flow for January 2000.

The shareholders of Ronly Bonly Jones Ltd need to be reassured that the current cash position is temporary, and under control, and within the overdraft facility agreed with the company's bankers. The shareholders must also be reassured that the company is not in financial difficulty or that if problems are being experienced then the appropriate remedial actions are in place.

Summary of key points

- Cash flow includes not only cash in hand but also deposits and overdrafts, repayable on demand with any bank or other financial institutions.

- The cash flow statement lists the inflows and outflows of cash for a period classified under the standard headings of: operating activities; returns on investment and servicing of finance; taxation; capital expenditure and financial investment; acquisitions and disposals; equity dividends paid; management of liquid resources; financing.

- The preparation of a cash flow statement is not a legal requirement. However, FRS 1 requires all reporting entities which prepare financial statements intended to give a true and fair view of their financial position and profit and loss to include a cash flow statement as a primary statement within their financial statements, unless specifically exempted.

- There is only one standard format for the cash flow statement prescribed by FRS 1, comprising a main statement of cash inflows and outflows, supported by schedules and notes reconciling net operating cash flow to operating profit and reconciling net cash flow to changes in net debt.

- Net cash flow from operating activities may be derived using the direct method or the indirect method, with both methods giving the same result.

- The cash flow statement is directly related to both the profit and loss account and the balance sheet and the links between them may be quantified and reconciled.

- The preparation of the cash flow statement is a highly objective exercise, in which all the headings and amounts are cash based and therefore easily measured.

- The cash flow generated during an accounting period is a matter of fact and does not rely on judgement or the use of alternative conventions or valuation methods.

Glossary of key terms

direct method A method of calculating cash flow as the net of operating cash receipts and payments that is summarised for inclusion in the cash flow statement. It is a time-consuming process that is not straightforward and is not widely used by UK companies.

financing The section of the cash flow statement that shows the long-term funds raised by or repaid by the company during the year.

indirect method A method of calculating cash flow which uses the starting point of operating profit, since it is the operating activities of sales and costs that normally give rise to the majority of cash inflows and cash outflows of an entity. Operating profit for the period must then be adjusted for depreciation, as well as movements in stock, debtors and creditors over the same period to derive the net cash flow from operating activities.

liquid resources Liquid resources, or liquid assets, are cash, and other assets readily convertible into cash, for example short-term investments.

net debt The total borrowings of the company net of liquid resources. Net debt excludes non-equity shares because, although similar to borrowings, they are not actually liabilities of the entity. Net debt excludes debtors and creditors because, whilst they are short-term claims on and sources of finance to the entity, their main role is as part of the entity's trading activities.

repayable on demand This refers to the definition of cash where there is a loss of interest if cash is withdrawn within 24 hours.

reporting entity A public or private limited company required to file its annual report and accounts with the Registrar of Companies.

working capital requirement Stocks plus debtors plus prepayments less creditors and accruals. This investment in the operating cycle represents the financial resources specifically required for the company to purchase and create stocks and while it waits for payments from its customers.

Assessment material

Questions

Q4.1 (i) How would you define cash generated by a business during an accounting period?

(ii) Which accounting standard deals with cash flow?

Q4.2 Give an example of the main cash flow statement showing each of the main categories.

Q4.3 Give an example of the reconciliations and notes that are prepared in support of the main cash flow statement.

Q4.4 Describe the ways in which both the direct method and the indirect method may be used to derive the net operating cash flow during an accounting period of a business from the operating profit it has earned during that period.

Q4.5 (i) Which reconciliation statement is used to link the cash flow statement to the profit and loss account?

(ii) How does it do that?

Q4.6 (i) Which reconciliation statement is used to link the cash flow statement to the balance sheet?

(ii) What are the links?

Q4.7 Why is cash so important, compared to the other assets used within a business?

Q4.8 (i) What questions does the cash flow statement aim to answer?

(ii) How far does it go towards answering them?

Discussion points

D4.1 Why is the information disclosed in the profit and loss account and the balance sheet not considered sufficient for users of financial information? What was so important about cash flow that is was considered necessary for the Accounting Standards Board to issue FRS 1 (Cash Flow Statements) in 1991, which was subsequently revised in 1996?

D4.2 'Forget your profit and loss accounts and balance sheets, at the end of the day it's the business's healthy bank balance that is the measure of its increase in wealth.' Discuss.

Exercises

Solutions are provided in Appendix 4 to all exercise numbers highlighted in colour.

Level I

E4.1   *Time allowed – 60 minutes*

Candice-Marie James and Flossie Graham obtained a one-year lease on a small shop which cost them £15,000 for the year 2000, and agreed to pay rent of £4,000 per year payable one year in advance. Candyfloss started trading on 1 January 2000 as a florist, and Candice and Flossie bought a second-hand, white delivery van for which they paid £14,500. The business was financed by Candice and Flossie each providing £9,000 from their savings and an interest free loan from Candice's uncle of £3,000. Candice and Flossie thought they were doing OK over their first six months but they weren't sure how to measure this. They decided to try and see how they were doing financially and looked at the transactions for the first six months:

	£
Cash sales of flowers	£76,000
Rent paid	£4,000
Wages paid	£5,000
Payments for other operating expenses	£7,000
Purchases of stocks of flowers for resale	£59,500
Legal expenses paid for the lease acquisition	£1,000

In addition, at 30 June 2000 they owed a further £4,000 for the purchase of flowers and £1,000 for other operating expenses. Customers had purchased flowers on credit and the sum still owed amounted to £8,000. One customer was apparently in financial difficulties and it was likely that the £1,500 owed would not be paid. Stocks of flowers at 30 June 2000 valued at cost were £9,500. They estimated that the van would last four years, at which time they expected to sell it for £2,500, and that depreciation would be spread evenly over that period.

(a) **Prepare a cash flow statement for Candyfloss for the first six months of the year 2000 using the direct method.**

(b) **Prepare a conventional profit and loss account statement for Candyfloss, on an accruals basis.**

(c) **Why is the profit different from the cash flow?**

(d) **Which statement gives the best indication of the first six months performance of Candyfloss?**

E4.2   *Time allowed – 60 minutes*

Using the information from Exercise E4.1 prepare a cash flow statement for Candyfloss for the first six months of the year 2000, using the indirect method.

E4.3 *Time allowed – 60 minutes*

Jaffrey Packaging plc have used the following information in the preparation of their financial statements for the year ended 31 March 2000.

	£000
Dividends paid	25
Issue of a debenture	200
Reduction in stocks	32
Corporation tax paid	73
Interest paid	28
Operating profit for the year	450
Bank and cash balance 31 March 2000	376
Purchase of factory equipment	302
Dividends payable at 31 March 2000	25
Interest received	5
Depreciation charge for the year	195
Purchase of a new large computer system	204
Sale of a patent (intangible fixed asset)	29
Increase in trade debtors	43
Reduction in short-term creditors	62
Bank and cash balance 1 April 1999	202

You are required to prepare a cash flow statement in compliance with the provisions of FRS 1, together with the appropriate supporting schedules and reconciliations.

E4.4 *Time allowed – 60 minutes*

From the profit and loss account for the year ended 31 December 2000 and balance sheets as at 31 December 1999 and 31 December 2000, prepare a complete cash flow statement for Medco Ltd for the year to 31 December 2000.
   During the year 2000 the company

(i)   **acquired new fixed assets that cost £12,500**

(ii) **issued new share capital for £5,000**

(iii) **sold fixed assets for £2,000 that had originally cost £3,000 and had a net book value of £2,500**

(iv) **depreciated its fixed assets by £2,000**

Figures in £	2000
Profit and loss account	
Operating profit	2,500
Interest	(100)
Net profit pre-tax	2,400
Tax	(500)

Net profit post tax	1,900	
Interim dividend	(300)	
Final dividend	(600)	
Retained net profit	1,000	

Balance sheet as at 31 December	**2000**	1999
Fixed assets	28,000	20,000
Current assets		
Stocks	6,000	5,000
Debtors	4,000	3,000
Investments	5,100	3,000
Cash and bank	2,150	5,000
Creditors due in less than one year		
Overdraft	(6,000)	(2,000)
Trade creditors	(4,000)	(6,000)
Taxation	(500)	(400)
Dividend (proposed)	(600)	(450)
Creditors due in over one year		
Loan	(2,000)	(1,000)
	32,150	26,150
Ordinary shares	14,000	10,000
Share premium	6,000	5,000
Profit and loss account	12,150	11,150
	32,150	26,150

Level II

E4.5   *Time allowed – 90 minutes*

Llareggyb Ltd started business on 1 January 2000 and its year ended 31 December 2000. Llareggyb made the following transactions during the year.

Received funds for share capital of £25,000

Paid suppliers of materials £44,000

Purchased 11,000 units of materials at £8 per unit, one of which was required in one unit of finished goods

Heating and lighting costs paid for cash £16,000

Further heating and lighting costs £2,400 were incurred within the year, but unpaid at 31 December 2000

Mr D Thomas loaned the company £80,000 on 1 January 2000 at 8% per annum

Loan interest was paid to Mr Thomas for January to June 2000

8,000 finished goods units were sold to customers at £40 each

Customers paid £280,000 to Llareggyb for sales of finished goods

Rent on the premises £60,000 was paid for 18 months from 1 January 2000, and business rates of £9,000 for the same period were also paid

Salaries and wages were paid for January to November amounting to £132,000 but the December payroll cost of £15,000 had not been paid

A lorry was purchased for £45,000 on 1 January 2000 and was expected to last for 5 years after which it could be sold for £8,000. The company uses the straight line method of depreciation.

You are required to

(i) prepare a balance sheet for Llareggyb Ltd as at 31 December 2000.

(ii) prepare a cash flow statement for Llareggyb Ltd for the year ended 31 December 2000.

(Note: you may use the profit or loss figure calculated in Exercise E3.7 to complete this exercise)

E4.6   *Time allowed – 90 minutes*

From its profit and loss account for the year ended 31 December 2000 and balance sheets as at 31 December 1999 and 31 December 2000, prepare a complete cash flow statement for Littleco Ltd for the year to 31 December 2000.
   During the year 2000 Littleco Ltd:

(i) acquired new fixed assets that cost £10,000

(ii) issued new share capital for £5,000

(iii) depreciated its fixed assets by £2,000

Figures in £	2000	
Profit and loss account		
Operating profit	2,100	
Interest	(100)	
Net profit pre-tax	2,000	
Tax	(500)	
Net profit post tax	1,500	
Dividend	(500)	
Retained net profit	1,000	

Balance sheet as at 31 December	2000	1999
Fixed assets	28,000	20,000
Current assets		
Stocks	3,000	5,000
Debtors	5,000	3,000
Cash and bank	2,150	2,000
Creditors		
Overdraft	(6,000)	(2,000)
Trade creditors	(4,000)	(6,000)
Taxation	(500)	(400)
Dividend (proposed)	(500)	(450)
	27,150	21,150
Ordinary shares	15,000	10,000
Profit and loss account	12,150	11,150
	27,150	21,150

E4.7   *Time allowed – 90 minutes*

Sparklers plc have completed the preparation of their profit and loss account for the year ended 31 October 2000 and their balance sheet as at 31 October 2000. During the year Sparklers sold for £2m some fixed assets that had originally cost £11m. The cumulative depreciation on those assets at 31 October 1999 was £7.6m.

You have been asked to prepare a full cash flow statement for the same period in compliance with the provisions contained in FRS 1. The directors are concerned about the large bank overdraft at 31 October 2000 which they believe is due mainly to the increase in trade debtors as a result of apparently poor credit control. What is your assessment of the reasons for the increased overdraft?

Sparklers plc
Profit and loss account for the year ended 31 October 2000

Figures in £m	2000	1999
Operating profit	41.28	18.80
Interest paid	(0.56)	–
Interest received	0.08	0.20
Profit before tax	40.80	19.00
Tax on profit on ordinary activities	(10.40)	(6.40)
Profit after tax	30.40	12.60
Dividends		
Preference paid	(0.20)	(0.20)
Ordinary: interim paid	(4.00)	(2.00)
final proposed	(12.00)	(6.00)
Retained profit for the financial year	14.20	4.40

Sparklers plc
Balance sheet as at 31 October 2000

	2000 £m	1999 £m
Fixed assets		
Tangible at cost	47.80	35.20
Depreciation	(21.50)	(19.00)
	26.30	16.20
Current assets		
Stocks	30.00	10.00
Debtors	53.40	17.20
Prepayments	0.80	0.60
Cash and bank	–	1.20
	84.20	29.00

Current liabilities (less than 1 year)

Overdraft	32.40	–
Creditors	20.00	12.00
Accruals	2.00	1.60
Dividends	12.00	6.00
Taxation	10.40	6.40
	76.80	26.00
Net current assets	7.40	3.00
Total assets less current liabilities	33.70	19.20
less		
Long-term liabilities (over 1 year)		
Debenture	1.50	1.20
Net assets	32.20	18.00
Capital and reserves		
£1 ordinary shares	10.00	10.00
£1 preferences shares 10%	2.00	2.00
Profit and loss account	20.20	6.00
	32.20	18.00

E4.8 *Time allowed – 90 minutes*

From the financial statements of Henrietta Carrot Ltd, for the year ended 31 December 2000, prepare a cash flow statement in the format used by most major UK plcs.

Henrietta Carrot Ltd acquired a long-term investment in an associate company during the year 2000, and revalued its fixed assets upwards by £200,000 in the year.

Henrietta Carrot Ltd issued 10,000 additional £1 ordinary shares during the year.

Fixed assets additions during the year 2000 were £200,000.

Depreciation charge for the year to 31 December 2000 was £100,000.

Henrietta Carrot Ltd
Balance sheet as at 31 December 2000

	2000 £000	1999 £000
Fixed assets		
Tangible	1,300	1,000
Investments	100	–
	1,400	1,000
Current assets		
Stocks	220	200
Debtors	230	200
Investments	75	50
Cash and bank	135	100
	660	550

Current liabilities (less than 1 year)

Overdraft	60	50
Creditors	250	100
Dividends	50	40
Taxation	50	40
	410	230
Net current assets	250	320
Total assets less current liabilities	1,650	1,320
less		
Long-term liabilities (over 1 year)		
Debenture	200	250
Net assets	1,450	1,070
Capital and reserves		
Share capital	310	300
Share premium	390	320
Revaluation reserve	200	–
Profit and loss account	550	450
	1,450	1,070

Henrietta Carrot Ltd
Profit and loss account for the year ended 31 December 2000

	£000
Turnover	720
Cost of sales	(400)
Gross profit	320
Distribution and administrative costs	(100)
Profit before interest and tax	220
Net interest	(20)
Profit before tax	200
Tax on profit on ordinary activities	(50)
Profit on ordinary activities after tax	150
Dividends	(50)
Retained profit for the financial year	100

5 Business performance analysis

LEARNING OBJECTIVES

Completion of this chapter will enable you to:

- carry out a performance review of a business, including the use of SWOT analysis

- critically evaluate the limitations of the performance review process

- analyse business performance through the use of ratio analysis of profitability; efficiency; liquidity; investment

- use both profit and cash flow in the measurement of business performance

- critically compare the use of cash flow versus profit as the best measure in the evaluation of financial performance

- use earnings before interest, tax, depreciation and amortisation (EBITDA) as a close approximation of a cash flow performance measure

- appreciate the importance of both financial and non-financial indicators in the evaluation of business performance

- consider the use of both financial and non-financial measures incorporated into performance measurement systems such as the balanced scorecard

Introduction

Chapters 2, 3, and 4 introduced us to the financial statements of limited companies. This chapter is concerned with how the performance of a business may be reviewed through analysis and evaluation of the balance sheet, the profit and loss account, and the cash flow statement. Business performance may be considered from outside or within the business for a variety of reasons. The performance review process provides an understanding of the business which, together with an analysis of all the relevant information, enables interpretation and evaluation of its financial performance during successive accounting periods and its financial position at the ends of those accounting periods.

The chapter begins with an outline of the steps involved in the performance review process and also considers the limitations of such a process. Financial ratio analysis looks at the detailed use of profitability, efficiency, liquidity and investment ratios in the evaluation of financial performance. The use of earnings per share and cash flow in performance measurement are discussed along with the measurement of earnings before interest, tax, depreciation and amortisation (EBITDA) as an approximation of cash flow. The debate continues as to whether cash flow or profit represents the best basis for financial performance measurement.

The chapter closes with an examination of the important area of non-financial indicators in the evaluation of business performance. The contribution of financial and non-financial measures is examined in their incorporation into performance measurement systems such as the balanced scorecard, developed by David Norton and Robert Kaplan in the early 1990s. In Chapter 6 we shall build on the knowledge gained from the current chapter when we examine the published report and accounts of a major UK plc, Johnson Matthey.

The performance review process

A performance review using financial statements may be undertaken for a number of reasons, for example:

- to assist investment decisions
- to identify possible take-over targets
- to evaluate the financial strength of potential or existing customers or suppliers.

The main aim of a performance review is to provide an understanding of the business, and, together with an analysis of all the relevant information, provide an interpretation of the results. A performance review is generally undertaken using a standard format and methodology. The performance review process begins with a **SWOT analysis** and works through a number of steps to the conclusions, as outlined in Fig. 5.1. A SWOT analysis includes an internal analysis of the company, and an analysis of the company's position with regard to its external environment.

1. SWOT analysis

SWOT is shorthand for strengths, weaknesses, opportunities and threats. The first look at a company's performance usually involves listing the key features of the company by looking internally at its particular strengths and weaknesses, and externally at risks or threats to the company and opportunities that it may be able to exploit. The SWOT analysis may give some indication of, for example, the strength of the company's management team, how well it is doing on product quality, and areas as yet untapped within its market place.

To keep the analysis focused, a cruciform chart may be used for SWOT analysis. An example is outlined in Fig. 5.2, relating to a fictitious company in the 1990s which manufactured components for supply to automotive manufacturers.

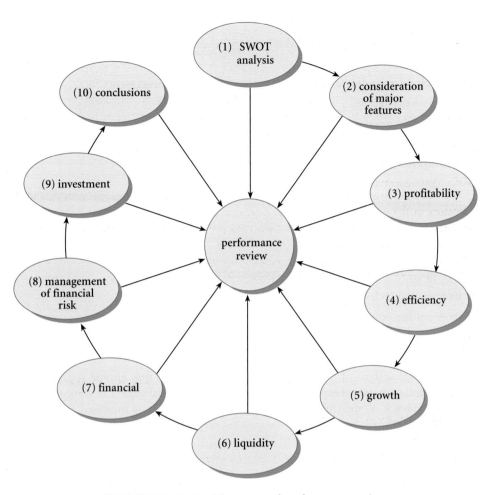

FIGURE 5.1   The stages of performance review

STRENGTHS	WEAKNESSES
Market share	Slow product development
Part of a large diversified group	Products designed not easy to manufacture
OPPORTUNITIES	**THREATS**
European joint ventures	Japanese transplant manufacturers
Market share of Japanese manufacturers	European economic recession

FIGURE 5.2   An example of a SWOT analysis

2. *Consideration of major features*

The increasing amount of information now provided in published financial statements enables the analyst to look in detail at the various industrial and geographical sectors of the business and the trends within these and the business in general. Further background information may be extracted from the accounting policies, the auditors' report, chairman's report and details of any significant events that have been highlighted.

3. Profitability

A number of financial indicators and ratios may be considered to assess the profitability of the company, which include:

- ROCE (return on capital employed), or ROI (return on investment)
- return on sales (ROS)
- gross margin to sales
- asset turnover
- earnings per share (eps)
- dividend cover
- price earnings ratio (P/E).

4. Efficiency

The efficiency of the company may be considered in terms of

- its operating cycle – its debtor days, creditor days, and stock days
- its operating gearing
- vertical analysis of its profit and loss account (which we will look at in Chapter 6)

In a vertical analysis of the profit and loss account (which may also be applied to the balance sheet) each item is expressed as a percentage of the total sales. The vertical analysis provides evidence of structural changes in the accounts such as increased profitability through more efficient production.

5. Growth

Growth of the organisation may relate to sales growth and gross margin growth. Horizontal analysis (which we will look at in Chapter 6), or common size analysis, of the profit and loss account allows a line-by-line analysis of the accounts compared with those of the previous year. It may provide over a number of years a trend of changes showing either growth or decline in these elements of the accounts by calculation of annual percentage growth rates in profits, sales, stock or any other item.

6. Liquidity

Liquidity is concerned with the short-term solvency of the company. It is assessed by looking at a number of key ratios:

- current ratio
- acid test
- defensive interval
- cash ROCE
- cash interest cover

7. Finance

How the company is financed is concerned with the long-term solvency of the company. It is assessed by looking at a number of other key ratios:

- **gearing** – the proportion of capital employed financed by lenders rather than shareholders, expressed in a number of ways, for example the **debt/equity** ratio (long-term loans and preference shares/ordinary shareholders' funds)
- **interest cover** (profit before interest and tax/interest payable)
- various forms of off balance sheet financing.

Off balance sheet financing is defined as the funding or refinancing of a company's operations in such a way that, under legal requirements and existing accounting conventions, some or all of the finance may not be disclosed in its balance sheet. The Accounting Standards Board (ASB) has tried to introduce regulations forcing the inclusion of this type of financing.

8. Management of financial risk

The global market is here. Companies increasingly trade multinationally with greater levels of sophistication in products, operations, and finance. Risk assessment and the management of risk are therefore now assuming increasing importance. The main areas of risk are the areas of investment, foreign currency exchange rates and interest rates, and levels of trade credit.

9. Investment

Investment ratios examine whether or not the company is undertaking sufficient investment to ensure its future profitability. These ratios include, for example:

- capital expenditure/sales
- capital expenditure/depreciation
- capital expenditure/gross fixed assets.

10. Conclusions

The conclusion of the performance review will include consideration of the company's SWOT analysis and the main performance features. It will consider growth and profitability and whether or not this is maintainable, as well as levels of finance and investment, and whether there is sufficient cash flow, and the future plans of the business.

All performance review must use some sort of benchmark. Comparisons may be made against past periods and against budget; they may also be made against other companies and using general data relating to the industry within which the company operates. Later in this chapter we will look in more detail at the use of profitability, efficiency, liquidity, and investment ratios. Growth and financing will be considered in Chapter 14.

Describe each of the stages in a business performance review process.	Progress check 5.1

Limitations of the performance review process

There are many obvious limitations to the above approach. In comparing performance against other companies (and sometimes within the company in comparing past periods), or looking at industrial data, it should be borne in mind that:

Pokemon helps to lift Menzies
By Mark Court

Pikachu, the cuddly Pokémon character, helped to propel John Menzies, the distribution, retail and aviation services group, to pre-tax profits of £15.7 million before exceptionals, compared with just £4.1 million last time.

But David Mackay, John Menzies' chief executive, believes the Pokémon craze is dying out and the company will not extend the exclusive distribution agreement with Nintendo, maker of games consoles and Pokémon games.

Mr Mackay said: 'Pokémon was a unique and wonderful phenomenon but it is on the decline.' He added that the games market was volatile, unpredictable and about to suffer intense competition.

John Menzies is in the throes of being transformed into an aviation services business and, unsurprisingly, a raft of exceptionals clouded its interim account.

A £2.5 million gain on one disposal was more than offset by a £26.4 million loss on another, resulting in a pre-tax loss after exceptionals of £8.2 million.

A fall in operating losses at the Early Learning Centre, the toyshop chain, means that its disposal is likely.

Mr Mackay said: 'We are on track to be in profit this year but there will be no fire sale.'

John Menzies bought Ogden Ground Services, a major airport services group, for £76 million last November and will seek a reclassification from distribution to support services once ELC has been sold.

Robin Althaus, an analyst at Seymour Pierce, said: 'Menzies cannot be faulted so far in its re-invention but it is still an emerging picture.'

The interim dividend rises to 5.5p a share from 5p. The shares rose 5½p to 426½p yesterday.

© *The Times*, London, 24 January 2001

- there may be a lack of uniformity in accounting definitions and techniques
- the balance sheet is only a snapshot in time, and only represents a single estimate of the company's position
- there may actually be no standards for comparison
- changes in the environment and changes in money values, together with short-term fluctuations may have a significant impact
- the past should really not be relied on as a good predictor of the future.

The volatility and unpredictability of the computer games market is well understood by John Menzies who enjoyed considerable success with their sales of Pokemon games. The press cutting above indicates that John Menzies did not assume that they would continue indefinitely to be profitable in that market.

As the press cutting illustrates, John Menzies decided (as a likely result of a strategic review of their business) that it may not continue its distribution agreement with Nintendo, the maker of games consoles and the Pokemon games, and may also dispose of its toyshop chain the Early Learning Centre.

Diversified companies present a different set of problems. Such companies, by their very nature are comprised of companies engaged in various industrial sectors, each having different market conditions, financial structures and expectations of performance. The notes to the accounts which appear in each company's annual report and accounts invariably present a less than comprehensive picture of the company's position.

Progress check 5.2

What are the main limitations encountered in carrying out the performance review of a business?

As time goes by, and accounting standards and legislation get tighter and tighter, the number of loopholes which allow any sort of window dressing of a company's results are reduced. Inevitably, however, there will always remain the possibility of the company's position being presented in ways that may not always represent the 'truth'. We will now look at the type of information that may be used and the important financial ratios and their meaning and relevance.

Ratio analysis

The reasons for a performance review may be wide and varied. Generally, it is required to shed light on the extent to which the objectives of the company are being achieved. These objectives may be

- to earn a satisfactory return on capital employed (ROCE)
- to maintain and enhance the financial position of the business with reference to the management of working capital, fixed assets and bank borrowings
- to achieve cost targets and other business targets such as improvements in labour productivity.

Ratio analysis is an important area of performance review. It is far more useful than merely considering absolute numbers, which on their own may have little meaning. Ratios may be used

- for a subjective assessment of the company or its constituent parts
- for a more objective way to aid decision-making
- to provide **cross-sectional analysis** and **inter-firm comparison**
- to establish models for loan and credit ratings
- to provide equity valuation models to value businesses
- to analyse and identify underpriced shares and take-over targets
- to predict company failure.

There are various models that may be used to predict company failure such as those developed by John Argenti (*Corporate Collapse – the Causes and Symptoms*, 1976), and Edward Altman (*Corporate Financial Distress – A Complete Guide to Predicting, Avoiding and Dealing with Bankruptcy*, 1983). Altman's model is sometimes used for prediction of corporate failure by calculating what is called a *z score* for each company. If the *z score* is greater than 2.99 then it is unlikely to fail, and if the score is less than 1.81 then it is likely to fail. Statistical analyses of financial ratios may further assist in this area of prediction of corporate failure, using for example time series and line of business analyses.

As we saw in our examination of the performance review process, the key ratios include the following categories:

- profitability
- efficiency
- liquidity
- investment.

The further performance evaluation areas of growth and financial structure (gearing) will be considered in Chapter 14 when we look at sources of finance and the cost of capital. We will use the financial statements of Flatco plc, an engineering company, shown in Figs 5.3 to 5.9, to illustrate the calculation of the key financial ratios. The profit and loss account and cash flow statement are for the year ended 31 December 2000 and the balance sheet as at 31 December 2000. Comparative figures are shown for 1999.

Flatco plc
Balance sheet as at 31 December 2000

Figures in £000

	2000	1999
Fixed assets		
Intangible	416	425
Tangible	1,884	1,921
Financial	248	248
	2,548	2,594
Current assets		
Stocks	311	268
Debtors	573	517
Prepayments	589	617
Cash	327	17
	1,800	1,419
Current liabilities (less than 1 year)		
Financial debt	50	679
Creditors	553	461
Taxation	50	44
Dividends	70	67
Accruals	82	49
	805	1,300
Net current assets	995	119
Total assets less current liabilities	3,543	2,713
less Long-term liabilities		
Financial debt	173	–
Creditors	154	167
	327	167
less Provisions	222	222
Net assets	2,994	2,324
Capital and reserves		
Capital	1,200	1,000
Premiums	200	200
Profit and loss account	1,594	1,124
	2,994	2,324

FIGURE 5.3 Flatco plc balance sheet as at 31 December 2000

Flatco plc
Profit and loss account for the year ended 31 December 2000

Figures in £000		2000		1999
Turnover				
Continuing operations		3,500		3,250
Discontinued operations		–		–
		3,500		3,250
Cost of sales		(2,500)		(2,400)
Gross profit		1,000		850
Distribution costs	(300)		(330)	
Administrative expenses	(155)		(160)	
Other operating costs				
Exceptional items: redundancy costs	(95)		–	
		(550)		(490)
Other operating income		100		90
Operating profit				
Continuing operations	550		450	
Discontinued operations	–		–	
		550		450
Income from other fixed asset investments		100		80
Profit before interest and tax		650		530
Net interest		(60)		(100)
Profit before tax		590		430
Tax on profit on ordinary activities		(50)		(44)
Profit on ordinary activities after tax		540		386
Dividends		(70)		(67)
Retained profit for the financial year		470		319

Additional information
Authorised and issued share capital 31 December 2000, 1,200,000 £1 ordinary shares (1,000,000 in 1999).
Total assets less current liabilities 31 December 1998, £2,406,000.
Trade debtors 31 December 1998, £440,000.
Market value of ordinary shares in Flatco plc 31 December 2000, £2.75 (£3,00, 1999).
Tangible fixed assets depreciation provision 31 December 2000, £1,102,000 (£779,000, 1999).

FIGURE 5.4 Flatco profit and loss account for the year ended 31 December 2000

Flatco plc
Cash flow statement for the year ended 31 December 2000
Reconciliation of operating profit to net cash flow from operating activities

Figures in £000

	2000	1999
Operating profit	550	450
Depreciation charges	345	293
Increase in stocks	(43)	(32)
Increase in debtors and prepayments [− 573 + 517 − 589 + 617]	(28)	(25)
Increase in creditors and accruals [553 − 461 + 82 − 49 + 154 − 167]	112	97
Net cash inflow from operating activities	936	783

FIGURE 5.5 Reconciliation of operating profit to net cash flow from operating activities

Cash flow statement

Figures in £000	2000	1999
Net cash inflow from operating activities	936	783
Returns on investments and servicing of finance (note 1)	40	(20)
Taxation	(44)	(40)
Capital expenditure (note 1)	(299)	(170)
	633	553
Equity dividends paid	(67)	(56)
	566	497
Management of liquid resources (note 1)	–	–
Financing (note 1)	373	290
Increase in cash	939	787

FIGURE 5.6 Cash flow statement

Reconciliation of net cash flow to movement in net debt (note 2)

Figures in £000	2000	1999
Increase in cash for the period	939	787
Cash inflow from increase in long-term debt	(173)	–
Change in net debt	766	787
Net debt at 1 January [17 − 679 − 0]	(662)	(1,449)
Net funds/net debt at 31 December [327 − 50 − 173]	104	(662)

FIGURE 5.7 Reconciliation of net cash flow to movement in net debt

Note 1 to the cash flow statement – gross cash flows

Figures in £000		
Returns on investments and servicing of finance	**2000**	**1999**
Income from investments	100	80
Interest received	11	–
Interest paid	(71)	(100)
	40	(20)
Capital expenditure		
Payments to acquire tangible fixed assets	(286)	(170)
Payments to acquire intangible fixed assets	(34)	–
Receipts from sales of tangible fixed assets	21	–
	(299)	(170)
Management of liquid resources		
Purchase of treasury bills	(200)	–
Sale of treasury bills	200	–
	–	–
Financing		
Issue of ordinary share capital	200	300
Debenture loan	173	–
Expenses paid in connection with share issues	–	(10)
	373	290

FIGURE 5.8   Note 1 – gross cash flows

Note 2 to the cash flow statement – analysis of change in net debt/funds

Figures in £000	At 1 January 2000	Cash flows	At 31 December 2000
Cash in hand and at bank	17	310	327
Overdraft	(679)	629	(50)
Debenture	–	(173)	(173)
Total (debt)/funds	(662)	766	104
	At 1 January 1999	**Cash flows**	**At 31 December 1999**
Cash in hand and at bank	–	17	17
Overdraft	(1,449)	770	(679)
Total (debt)/funds	(1,449)	787	(662)

FIGURE 5.9   Note 2 – analysis of change in net debt/funds

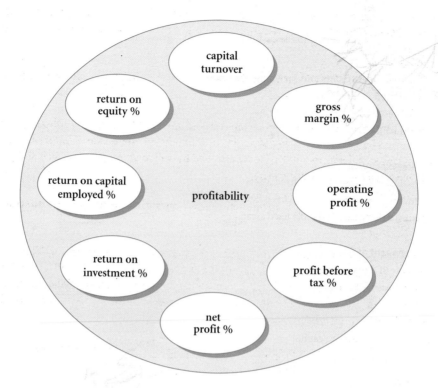

FIGURE 5.10   Profitability ratios

Profitability ratios

It is generally accepted that the primary objective for the managers of a business is to maximise the wealth of the owners of the business. To this end there are a number of other objectives, subsidiary to the main objective. These include:

- survival
- stability
- growth
- maximisation of market share
- maximisation of sales
- maximisation of profit
- maximisation of return on capital.

Each group of financial ratios is concerned to some extent with survival, stability, growth and maximisation of shareholder wealth. We will first consider ratios in the broad area of profitability (see Fig. 5.10), which give an indication of how successful the business has been in its achievement of the wealth maximisation objective.

$$\text{gross margin \%} = \frac{\text{gross margin}}{\text{sales}} = \frac{\text{sales} - \text{cost of sales (COS)}}{\text{sales}}$$

This is used to gain an insight into the relationship between production/purchasing costs and sales revenues. The gross margin needs to be high enough to cover all other costs incurred by the company, and leave an amount for profit. If the gross margin percentage is too low then sales prices may be too low, or the purchase costs of materials or production costs may be too high.

$$\textbf{operating profit \%} = \frac{\textbf{operating profit}}{\textbf{sales}} = \frac{\textbf{sales} - \textbf{COS} - \textbf{other operating expenses}}{\textbf{sales}}$$

The operating profit (or profit before interest and tax (PBIT) excluding other operating income) ratio is a key ratio that shows the profitability of the business before incurring financing costs. If the numerator is not multiplied by 100 to give a percentage, it shows the profit generated by each £1 of turnover.

$$\textbf{profit before tax (PBT) \%} = \frac{\textbf{profit before tax}}{\textbf{sales}} = \frac{\textbf{operating profit} +/- \textbf{net interest}}{\textbf{sales}}$$

This is the profit ratio that uses profit after financing costs, that is having allowed for interest payable and interest receivable. It should be remembered that PBT is a profit measure that goes further than dealing with the trading performance of the business, in allowing for financing costs. It provides an indication of pre-tax profit-earning capability from the sales for the period.

$$\textbf{net profit \%} = \frac{\textbf{net profit}}{\textbf{sales}} = \frac{\textbf{profit before tax (PAT)} - \textbf{corporation tax}}{\textbf{sales}}$$

This is the final profit ratio after allowing for financing costs and corporation tax. Net profit or return on sales (ROS) is the profit available for distribution to shareholders in the form of dividends and/or future investment in the business.

$$\begin{array}{c} \textbf{return on investment (ROI)} \\ \textbf{or return on capital employed (ROCE) \%} \end{array} = \frac{\textbf{operating profit}}{\textbf{total assets} - \textbf{current liabilities}} \\ \textbf{(usually averaged)}$$

This is a form of return on capital employed (using pre-tax profit) which compares income with the operational assets used to generate that income. Profit is calculated before financing costs and tax. This is because the introduction of interest charges introduces the effect of financing decisions into an appraisal of operating performance, and tax levels are decided by external agencies (governments).

The average cost of the company's finance (equity, debentures, loans), weighted according to the proportion each element bears to the total pool of capital, is called WACC, the weighted average cost of capital. The difference between a company's ROI and its WACC is an important measure of the extent to which the organisation is endeavouring to optimise its use of financial resources. In their 1999 annual report, Tomkins plc reported on the improvement in their ROI versus WACC gap and stated that 'to be successful a company must consistently deliver a return on investment (ROI) above its weighted cost of capital (WACC) and must actively manage both variables'. A company manages its ROI through monitoring its operating profit as a percentage of its capital employed. A company manages its WACC by planning the proportions of its financing through either equity (ordinary shares) or debt (loans), with regard to the relative costs of each, dividends and interest.

In looking at acquisitions the importance of WACC is emphasised in the Tomkins plc 1999 annual report: 'Tomkins' strategy is to focus on strategic business activities and within this only to make acquisitions which add to shareholder value by enhancing earnings in the first year and deliver an ROI above the WACC hurdle rate (internal cost of capital) within three years'. This refers to the importance of WACC as a factor used in the evaluation of investment in projects undertaken (or not) by a business (see Chapters 13 and 14).

$$\text{return on equity (ROE)} = \frac{\text{profit after tax}}{\text{equity}}$$

Another form of return on capital employed, ROE measures the return to the owners on the book value of their investment in a company. The return is measured as the residual profit after all expenses and charges have been made, and the equity is comprised of share capital and reserves.

$$\text{capital turnover} = \frac{\text{sales}}{\text{average capital employed in year}}$$

The capital turnover expresses the number of times that capital is turned over in the year, or alternatively the sales generated by each £1 of capital employed. This ratio will be affected by capital additions that may have taken place throughout a period but have not impacted materially on the performance for that period. Further analysis may be required to determine the underlying performance.

The profitability performance measures discussed above consider the general performance of organisations as a whole. It is important for managers also to be aware of particular areas of revenue or expenditure that may have a significant importance with regard to their own company and that have a critical impact on the net profit of the business. Companies may, for example:

● suffer large warranty claim costs
● have to pay high royalty fees
● receive high volumes of customer debit notes (invoices) for a variety of product or service problems deemed to be the fault of the supplier.

All managers should fully appreciate such key items of cost specific to their own company and be innovative and proactive in identifying ways that these costs may be reduced and minimised.

Managers should also be aware of the general range of costs for which they may have no direct responsibility, but nevertheless may be able to reduce significantly by

● improved communication
● involvement
● generation of ideas for waste reduction, increased effectiveness and cost reduction.

Such costs may include:

● the cost of the operating cycle
● costs of warehouse space
● project costs
● costs of holding stock
● depreciation (as a result of capital expenditure)
● warranty costs
● repairs and maintenance
● stationery costs
● telephone and fax costs
● photocopy costs.

The relative importance of these costs through their impact on profitability will of course vary from company to company.

Example 5.1

Calculate the profitability ratios for Flatco plc for 2000 and the comparative ratios for 1999, and comment on the profitability of Flatco plc.

Answer

Gross margin, GM

$$\text{gross margin \% 2000} = \frac{\text{gross margin}}{\text{sales}} = \frac{£1,000 \times 100\%}{£3,500} = 28.6\%$$

$$\text{gross margin \% 1999} = \frac{£850 \times 100\%}{£3,250} = 26.2\%$$

Profit before interest and tax, PBIT

$$\text{PBIT \% 2000} = \frac{\text{PBIT}}{\text{sales}} = \frac{£650 \times 100\%}{£3,500} = 18.6\%$$

$$\text{PBIT \% 1999} = \frac{£530 \times 100\%}{£3,250} = 16.3\%$$

Net profit, PAT (return on sales, ROS)

$$\text{PAT \% 2000} = \frac{\text{net profit}}{\text{sales}} = \frac{£540 \times 100\%}{£3,500} = 15.4\%$$

$$\text{PAT \% 1999} = \frac{£386 \times 100\%}{£3,250} = 11.9\%$$

Return on capital employed, ROCE (return on investment, ROI)

$$\text{ROCE \% 2000} = \frac{\text{operating profit}}{\substack{\text{total assets} - \text{current liabilities} \\ \text{(average capital employed)}}} = \frac{£550 \times 100\%}{(£3,543 + £2,713)/2}$$

$$= \frac{£550 \times 100\%}{£3,128} = 17.6\%$$

$$\text{ROCE \% 1999} = \frac{£450 \times 100\%}{(£2,713 + £2,406)/2} = \frac{£450 \times 100\%}{£2,559.5} = 17.6\%$$

Return on equity, ROE

$$\text{ROE \% 2000} = \frac{\text{PAT}}{\text{equity}} = \frac{£540 \times 100\%}{£2,994} = 18.0\%$$

$$\text{ROE \% 1999} = \frac{£386 \times 100\%}{£2,324} = 16.6\%$$

▶

◀ **Capital turnover**

$$\text{capital turnover 2000} = \frac{\text{sales}}{\text{average capital employed in year}} = \frac{£3,500}{£3,128} = 1.1 \text{ times}$$

$$\text{capital turnover 1999} = \frac{£3,250}{£2,559.5} = 1.3 \text{ times}$$

Report on the profitability of Flatco plc

Sales for the year 2000 increased by 7.7% over the previous year, partly through increased volumes and partly through higher selling prices.

Gross margin improved from 26.2% to 28.6% of sales, as a result of increased selling prices but also lower costs of production.

PBIT improved from 16.3% to 18.6% of sales (and operating profit improved from 13.8% to 15.7%). If the one-off costs of redundancy of £95,000 had not been incurred in the year 2000 operating profit would have been £645,000 (£550,000 + £95,000) and the operating profit ratio would have been 18.4% of sales, an increase of 4.6% over 1999. The underlying improvement in operating profit performance (excluding the one-off redundancy costs) was achieved from the improvement in gross margin and from the benefits of lower distribution costs and administrative expenses.

ROCE was static at 17.6% because the increase in capital employed as a result of additional share capital of £200,000 and long-term loans of £173,000 was matched by a similar increase in operating profit.

Return on equity increased from 16.6% to 18%, despite the increase in ordinary share capital. This was because of improved profit after tax (up 3.5% to 15.4%) arising from increased income from fixed asset investments and lower costs of finance. Corporation tax was only marginally higher than the previous year despite higher pre-tax profits.

Capital turnover for 2000 dropped to 1.1 times from 1.3 times in 1999. The new capital introduced into the company in the year 2000 to finance major new projects is expected to result in significant increases in sales levels over the next few years, which will see improvements in capital turnover over and above 1999 levels.

Progress check 5.3

How may financial ratio analysis be used as part of the process of review of business performance?

Efficiency ratios

The range of efficiency ratios is illustrated in Fig. 5.11.

Efficiency generally relates to the maximisation of output from resources devoted to an activity or the output required from a minimum input of resources. Efficiency ratios measure the efficiency with which such resources have been used.

$$\textbf{debtor days} = \frac{\textbf{trade debtors} \times \textbf{365}}{\textbf{sales}}$$

Debtor days indicate the average time taken, in calendar days, to receive payment from credit customers. Adjustment is needed if the ratio is materially distorted by VAT (or other

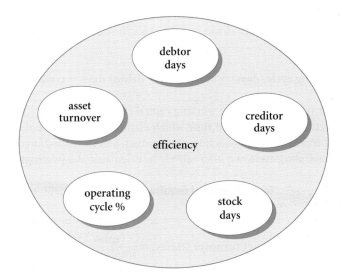

FIGURE 5.11   Efficiency ratios

taxes). This is because sales invoices to customers, and therefore trade debtors (accounts receivable) include the net sales value plus VAT. However, sales are reported net of VAT. To provide a more accurate ratio, VAT may be eliminated from the trade debtors' figures as appropriate. (Note: for example, export and zero-rated sales invoices, which may be included in debtors, do not include VAT and so an adjustment to total trade debtors by the standard percentage rate for VAT may not be accurate.)

$$\text{creditor days} = \frac{\text{trade creditors} \times 365}{\text{cost of sales}} \quad \text{(or purchases)}$$

Creditor days indicate the average time taken, in calendar days, to pay for supplies received on credit. For the same reason, as in the calculation of debtor days, adjustment is needed if the ratio is materially distorted by VAT or other taxes.

$$\text{stock days} = \frac{\text{stock value}}{\text{average daily cost of sales in period}}$$

Stock days (or stock turnover) are the number of days that stocks could last at the forecast or most recent usage rate. This may be applied to total stocks, finished goods, raw materials, or work in progress. The weekly internal efficiency of stock utilisation is indicated by the following ratios:

$$\frac{\text{finished goods}}{\text{average weekly despatches}} \qquad \frac{\text{raw materials}}{\text{average weekly raw material usage}} \qquad \frac{\text{work in progress}}{\text{average weekly production}}$$

These ratios are usually calculated using values but may also be calculated using quantities where appropriate.

$$\text{stock weeks} = \frac{\text{total stock value}}{\text{average weekly cost of sales}} \quad \text{(total COS for the year divided by 52)}$$

Financial analysts usually only have access to published accounts and so they often use the stock weeks ratio using the total closing stocks value in relation to the cost of sales for the year.

$$\textbf{operating cycle (days)} = \textbf{stock days} + \textbf{debtor days} - \textbf{creditor days}$$

We discussed the operating cycle, or working capital cycle, in Chapter 2 when we looked at the balance sheet. It is the period of time which elapses between the point at which cash begins to be expended on the production of a product, and the collection of cash from the customer. The operating cycle may alternatively be calculated as a percentage using:

$$\textbf{operating cycle \%} = \frac{\textbf{working capital requirement}}{\textbf{sales}} \text{ (stocks + debtors - creditors)}$$

$$\textbf{asset turnover (times)} = \frac{\textbf{sales}}{\textbf{total assets}}$$

Asset turnover measures the performance of the company in generating sales from the assets under its control. The denominator may alternatively be average net total assets.

Example 5.2

Calculate the efficiency ratios for Flatco plc for 2000 and the comparative ratios for 1999, and comment on the working capital performance of Flatco plc.

Answer

Debtor days

$$\text{debtor days 2000} = \frac{\text{trade debtors} \times 365}{\text{sales}} = \frac{£573 \times 365}{£3,500} = 60 \text{ days}$$

$$\text{debtor days 1999} = \frac{£517 \times 365}{£3,250} = 58 \text{ days}$$

Creditor days

$$\text{creditor days 2000} = \frac{\text{trade creditors} \times 365}{\text{cost of sales}} = \frac{£553 \times 365}{£2,500} = 81 \text{ days}$$

$$\text{creditor days 1999} = \frac{£461 \times 365}{£2,400} = 70 \text{ days}$$

Stock days (stock turnover)

$$\text{stock days 2000} = \frac{\text{stock value}}{\text{average daily cost of sales in period}} = \frac{£311}{£2,500/365}$$
$$= 45 \text{ days (6.5 weeks)}$$

$$\text{stock days 1999} = \frac{£268}{£2,400/365} = 41 \text{ days (5.9 weeks)}$$

Operating cycle days

operating cycle 2000 = stock days + debtor days − creditor days = 45 + 60 − 81 = 24 days

operating cycle 1999 = 41 + 58 − 70 = 29 days

Operating cycle %

$$\text{operating cycle \% 2000} = \frac{\text{working capital requirement}}{\text{sales}}$$

$$= \frac{(£311 + £573 - £553) \times 100\%}{£3,500} = 9.5\%$$

$$\text{operating cycle \% 1999} = \frac{(£268 + £517 - £461) \times 100\%}{£3,250} = 10.0\%$$

Asset turnover

$$\text{asset turnover 2000} = \frac{\text{sales}}{\text{total assets}} = \frac{£3,500}{£4,348} = 0.80 \text{ times}_{[2,548 + 1,800]}$$

$$\text{asset turnover 1999} = \frac{£3,250}{£4,013} = 0.81 \text{ times}_{[2,594 + 1,419]}$$

Report on the working capital performance of Flatco plc

The major cash improvement programme introduced late in the year 2000 began with the implementation of new cash collection procedures and a reinforced credit control department. This was not introduced early enough to see an improvement in the figures for the year 2000. Average customer settlement days actually worsened from 58 to 60 days.

The purchasing department negotiated terms of 90 days with a number of key large suppliers. This had the effect of improving the average creditors settlement period from 70 to 81 days.

A change in product mix during the latter part of the year 2000 resulted in a worsening of the average stock turnover period from 41 to 45 days. This is expected to be a temporary situation. An improved just in time (JIT) system and the use of vendor managed inventory (VMI) with two main suppliers in the year 2001 are expected to generate significant improvements in stock turnover.

Despite the poor stock turnover, the operating cycle improved from 29 days to 24 days (operating cycle % from 10.0% to 9.5%). Operating cycle days are expected to be zero or better by the end of year 2001.

Asset turnover dropped from 0.81 in 1999 to 0.80 times in the year 2000. The new capital introduced into the company in 2000 to finance major new projects is expected to result in significant increases in sales levels over the next few years which will see improvements in asset turnover over and above 1999 levels.

Progress check 5.4

What do profitability and efficiency ratios tell us about the performance of a business?

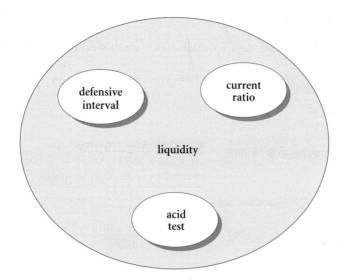

FIGURE 5.12 Liquidity ratios

Liquidity ratios

The degree to which assets are held in a cash or near cash form is determined by the level of obligations that need to be met by the business. Liquidity ratios (see Fig. 5.12) reflect the health or otherwise of the cash position of the business and its ability to meet its short-term obligations.

$$\textbf{current ratio (times)} = \frac{\textbf{current assets}}{\textbf{current liabilities}}$$

The current ratio is an overall measure of the liquidity of the business. It should be appreciated that this ratio will be different for different types of business. For example, an automotive manufacturer may have a higher ratio because of its relatively high level of stock (mainly work in progress), compared with a supermarket retailer which holds a very high percentage of fast-moving stocks.

$$\textbf{acid test (times)} = \frac{\textbf{current assets} - \textbf{stocks}}{\textbf{current liabilities}}$$

The acid test (or quick ratio) indicates the ability of the company to pay its creditors in the short term. This ratio may be particularly meaningful for supermarket retailers because of the speed with which their stocks are converted into cash.

$$\textbf{defensive interval (days)} = \frac{\textbf{quick assets}}{\textbf{average daily cash from operations}} \quad \text{(current assets} - \text{stocks)}$$

The defensive interval shows how many days a company could survive at its present level of operating activity if no inflow of cash were received from sales or other sources.

Example 5.3

Calculate the liquidity ratios for Flatco plc for 2000 and the comparative ratios for 1999, and comment on the liquidity of Flatco plc.

Answer
Current ratio

$$\text{current ratio 2000} = \frac{\text{current assets}}{\text{current liabilities}} = \frac{£1,800}{£805} = 2.2 \text{ times}$$

$$\text{current ratio 1999} = \frac{£1,419}{£1,300} = 1.1 \text{ times}$$

Acid test (quick ratio)

$$\text{quick ratio 2000} = \frac{\text{current assets} - \text{stocks}}{\text{current liabilities}} = \frac{£1,800 - £311}{£805} = 1.8 \text{ times}$$

$$\text{quick ratio 1999} = \frac{£1,419 - £268}{£1,300} = 0.9 \text{ times}$$

Defensive interval

$$\text{defensive interval 2000} = \frac{\text{quick assets}}{\text{average daily cash from operations}}$$

$$= \frac{£1,800 - £311}{(£517 + £3,500 - £573)/365} = 158 \text{ days}$$

$$\text{defensive interval 1999} = \frac{£1,419 - £268}{(£440 + £3,250 - £517)/365} = 132 \text{ days}$$

Report on the liquidity of Flatco plc

Net cash flow from operations improved from £783,000 in 1999 to £936,000 in 2000. Investments in fixed assets were more than covered by increases in long-term finance in both years. Therefore, the operational cash flow improvement was reflected in the net cash flow of £939,000 (£787,000 1999).

The improved cash flow is reflected in increases in the current ratio (1.1 to 2.2 times) and the quick ratio (0.9 to 1.8 times). The increase in the defensive interval from 132 to 158 days has strengthened the position of the company against the threat of a possible downturn in activity.

Although there has been a significant improvement in cash flow, the increase in investment in working capital is a cause for concern. Actions have already been taken since the year end to try and maximise the returns on investment: reduction in stock levels (noted above); further reductions in trade debtors and prepayments; investment of surplus cash in longer term investments.

Progress check 5.5

What are liquidity ratios and why are they so important?

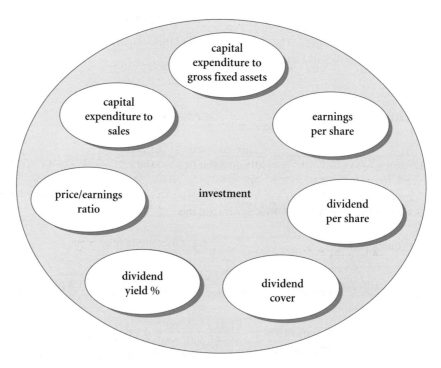

FIGURE 5.13 Investment ratios

Investment ratios

Investment ratios (see Fig. 5.13) generally indicate the extent to which the business is undertaking capital expenditure to ensure its survival, and stability and its ability to sustain current revenues and generate future increased revenues.

$$\text{earnings per share} = \frac{\text{profit after tax} - \text{preference share dividends}}{\text{number of ordinary shares in issue}}$$

Earnings per share or eps measures the return per share of earnings available to shareholders. The eps of companies may be found in the financial pages sections of the daily press.

$$\text{dividend per share} = \frac{\text{total dividends paid to ordinary shareholders}}{\text{number of ordinary shares in issue}}$$

Dividend per share is the total amount declared as dividends per each ordinary share in issue. It is the dividend per share actually paid in respect of the financial year. The amount must be adjusted if additional equity shares are issued during the financial year.

$$\text{dividend cover} = \frac{\text{earnings per share}}{\text{dividend per share}}$$

This shows the number of times the profits attributable to equity shareholders cover the dividends payable for the period.

$$\text{dividend yield \%} = \frac{\text{dividend per share}}{\text{share price}}$$

The dividend yield shows the dividend return on the market value of the shares, expressed as a percentage.

$$\text{price/earnings ratio} = \frac{\text{current share price}}{\text{eps}}$$

The price/earnings or P/E ratio shows the number of years it would take to recoup an equity investment from its share of the attributable equity profit. The P/E ratio values the shares of the company as a multiple of current or of prospective earnings, and therefore gives a market view of the quality of the underlying earnings.

$$\text{capital expenditure to sales \%} = \frac{\text{capital expenditure for year}}{\text{sales}}$$

This ratio gives an indication of the level of capital expenditure incurred to sustain a particular level of sales.

$$\text{capital expenditure to gross fixed assets \%} = \frac{\text{capital expenditure for year}}{\text{gross value of tangible fixed assets}}$$

This is a very good ratio for giving an indication of the replacement rate of new for old fixed assets.

Example 5.4

Calculate the investment ratios for Flatco plc for 2000 and the comparative ratios for 1999, and comment on the investment performance of Flatco plc.

Answer

Earnings per share, eps

$$\text{eps 2000} = \frac{\text{profit after tax} - \text{preference share dividends}}{\text{number of ordinary in issue}} = \frac{£540,000 \times 100}{1,200,000} = 45p$$

$$\text{eps 1999} = \frac{£386,000 \times 100}{1,000,000} = 38.6p$$

Dividend per share

$$\text{dividend per share 2000} = \frac{\text{total dividends paid to ordinary shareholders}}{\text{number of ordinary shares in issue}}$$

$$= \frac{£70,000}{1,200,000} = 5.8p \text{ per share}$$

$$\text{dividend per share 1999} = \frac{£67,000}{1,000,000} = 6.7p \text{ per share}$$

◀ **Dividend cover**

$$\text{dividend cover 2000} = \frac{\text{earnings per share}}{\text{dividend per share}}$$

$$= \frac{45p}{5.8p} = 7.8 \text{ times}$$

$$\text{dividend cover 1999} = \frac{38.6p}{6.7p} = 5.8 \text{ times}$$

Dividend yield %

$$\text{dividend yield 2000} = \frac{\text{dividend per share}}{\text{share price}}$$

$$= \frac{5.8p \times 100\%}{£2.75} = 2.11\%$$

$$\text{dividend yield 1999} = \frac{6.7p \times 100\%}{£3.00} = 2.23\%$$

Price/earnings ratio, P/E

$$\text{P/E ratio 2000} = \frac{\text{current share price}}{\text{eps}} = \frac{£2.75}{45p} = 6.1 \text{ times}$$

$$\text{P/E ratio 1999} = \frac{£3.00}{38.6p} = 7.8 \text{ times}$$

Capital expenditure to sales %

$$\text{capital expenditure to sales 2000} = \frac{\text{capital expenditure for year}}{\text{sales}} = \frac{£286 \times 100\%}{£3,500} = 8.2\%$$

$$\text{capital expenditure to sales 1999} = \frac{£170 \times 100\%}{£3,250} = 5.2\%$$

Capital expenditure to gross fixed assets %

$$\frac{\text{capital expenditure to}}{\text{gross fixed assets 2000}} = \frac{\text{capital expenditure for year}}{\text{gross value of tangible fixed assets}} = \frac{£286 \times 100\%}{(£1,884 + £1,102)} = 9.6\%$$

$$\begin{array}{c} \text{net book} + \text{cumulative} \\ \text{value} \quad \text{depreciation} \\ \text{provision} \end{array}$$

$$\frac{\text{capital expenditure to}}{\text{gross fixed assets 1999}} = \frac{£170 \times 100\%}{(£1,921 + £779)} = 6.3\%$$

Report on the investment performance of Flatco plc

The improved profit performance was reflected in improved earnings per share from 38.6p to 45p. However, the price/earnings ratio dropped from 7.8 to 6.1 times.

The board of directors reduced the dividend for the year to 5.8p per share from 6.7p per share in 1999, establishing a dividend cover of 7.8 times. The dividend yield reduced from 2.23% at 31 December 1999 to 2.11% at 31 December 2000.

The increase in the capital expenditure to sales ratio from 5.2% to 8.2% indicates the company's ability to both sustain and improve upon current sales levels.

The increase in the capital expenditure to gross fixed assets ratio from 6.3% to 9.6% demonstrates the policy of Flatco for ongoing replacement of old assets for new in order to keep ahead of the technology in which the business is engaged.

In this chapter we have looked at most of the key ratios for review of company performance and their meaning and relevance. However, the limitations we have already identified generally relating to performance review must always be borne in mind. Extreme care should be taken with the conclusions used in any performance review to avoid reaching conclusions that may perhaps be erroneous.

If all the financial literature were thoroughly researched the number of different ratios that would be discovered would run into hundreds. It is most helpful to use a limited set of ratios and to fully understand their meaning. The ratios will certainly help with an understanding of the company but do not in themselves represent the complete picture.

Calculation of the ratios for one company for one year is also very limited. It is more relevant to compare companies operating in the same market and to analyse how a company has changed over the years. However, difficulties inevitably arise because it is sometimes impossible to find another company that is strictly comparable with the company being analysed. In addition, the company itself may have changed so much over recent years as to render meaningless any conclusions drawn from changes in ratios.

Progress check 5.6

What are investment ratios and what is their purpose?

The best performance measure – cash or profit?

The importance of cash flow versus profit (or earnings per share) as a measure of company performance has increased over the past few years. The advantages and disadvantages in the use of each are shown in Figs 5.14 and 5.15.

Cash flow has assumed increasing importance and has gained popularity as a measure of performance because the profit and loss account has become somewhat discredited due to the unacceptable degree of subjectivity involved in its preparation. Some of the financial ratios that we have already looked at may be considered in cash terms, for example:

$$\text{cash ROCE \%} = \frac{\text{net cash flow from operations}}{\text{average capital employed}}$$

advantages	disadvantages
	there are a number of different methods of analysing cash flow
it cannot be hidden – like air in a balloon, one can see if it is going in or out	
	cash flow analysis is not straightforward, it can sometimes be extremely complex
generation of long-term cash flow is the real value of a company	
	it is sometimes difficult to obtain cash flow information
use of the discounted cash flow (DCF) method shows the added value to a company	
	it is difficult to compare the cash flows of different companies

FIGURE 5.14 The advantages and disadvantages of using cash flow as a measure of company performance

---

Example 5.5

Calculate the cash ROCE % for Flatco plc for 2000 and the comparative ratio for 1999, and compare with the equivalent profit ratio for Flatco plc.

Cash ROCE %

$$\text{cash ROCE \% 2000} = \frac{\text{net cash flow from operations}}{\text{average capital employed}} = \frac{£936 \times 100\%}{(£3,543 + £2,713)/2}$$

$$= \frac{£936 \times 100\%}{£3,128} = 29.9\%$$

$$\text{cash ROCE \% 1999} = \frac{£783 \times 100\%}{(£2,713 + £2,406)/2} = \frac{£783 \times 100\%}{£2,559.5} = 30.6\%$$

Report on the cash and profit ROCE of Flatco plc

Whilst the profit ROCE % was static at 17.6% for 1999 and 2000, the cash ROCE % reduced from 30.6% to 29.9%. Operating cash flow for 2000 increased by only 19.5% over 1999, despite the fact that operating profit for 2000 increased by 22.2% over 1999.

Operating profit before depreciation (EBITDA) was £895,000 [£550,000 + £345,000] for 2000, which was an increase of 20.5% over 1999 [£450,000 + £293,000 = £743,000]. If pre-depreciation operating profit had been used to calculate ROCE, it would have been 28.6% for 2000 compared with 29.0% for 1999, a reduction of 0.4% and more in line with the picture shown by the cash ROCE.

advantages	disadvantages
	the 1980s boom led to some creative accounting, e.g. Coloroll, Polly Peck, Maxwell, all based on accounting conventions
simple method to use	different bases are used from one company to another
easy to compare companies	use of the historical cost convention means that there is no account taken of expected growth or inflation
possible to see the company relative to the market	there is no account taken of market risk
	the numbers are too easy to manipulate
profit is easily identifiable	the imprecise area of the treatment of extraordinary items and provisions has now been resolved but there still remain dubious areas such as acquisition accounting, depreciation rates, and provisioning

FIGURE 5.15 The advantages and disadvantages of using earnings per share (eps) as a measure of company performance

The chairman of Flatco plc expects that ROCE will be improved in 2001 as a result of

- increased profitability resulting from higher sales levels generated from the investments in new projects
- reduction in levels of working capital, with more efficient use of company resources.

The increasing importance of cash flow as a measure of performance has led to new methods of measurement:

- the Rappaport method uses DCF looking ten years ahead as a method of valuing a company
- the economic value added (EVA™) method, which we will discuss in Chapter 14 (p. 513)
- enterprise value, which is a very similar method to EVA, which excludes the peripheral activities of the company.

* EBITDA is profit before interest, exceptional items, tax,
depreciation and goodwill amortisation

FIGURE 5.16   Tomkins plc EBITDA for 1996 to 2000

Progress check 5.7

What are the benefits of using cash flow instead of profit to measure financial performance? What are the disadvantages of using cash flow?

A profit-based measure of financial performance EBITDA, or earnings before interest, tax, depreciation, and amortisation is now becoming widely used as an approximation to operational cash flow. Amortisation, in the same way as depreciation applies to tangible fixed assets, is the systematic write-off of the cost of an intangible asset. The way in which EBITDA may be used has been illustrated in the Flatco plc Example 5.5.

Tomkins plc, in their 1999 annual report, comment on their use of EBITDA as a performance measure. 'Sophisticated investors increasingly employ a range of measures when assessing the financial health and value of a company, diversifying into cash-based yardsticks from a simplistic earnings per share test. EBITDA is becoming widely accepted as a reliable guide to operational cash flow.'

A graph showing Tomkins plc's EBITDA for the years 1996 to 2000, which was included in the group's annual report for the year 2000, is shown in Fig. 5.16.

We have seen that the method of performance measurement is not a clear cut cash or profit choice. It is generally useful to use both. However, many analysts and the financial press in general continue to depend heavily on profit performance measures with a strong emphasis on earnings per share (eps) and the price/earnings ratio (P/E).

Non-financial performance indicators

The externally published financial reports and internal financial information do not give a full picture of what is actually happening in an organisation. Such financial information is necessarily historical, and is open to manipulation and interpretation within the scope of the various accounting standards, practices and current legislation. The numbers presented are invariably the numbers the organisation wishes to be seen, and usually to present a favourable impression, while ignoring problems and areas for improvement.

Financial reporting does not tell us how well the company is, for example, meeting its delivery schedules or how satisfied its customers really are with its products and after sales service. Although in themselves these and other such performance indicators are not given a value, which is shown on the balance sheet, they certainly have significant value in terms of the underlying strength of the company and its ability to create sustained increases in shareholder wealth in the future.

The use of non-financial performance indicators is assuming increasing importance. These are measures of performance based on non-financial information, which may originate in and be used by operating departments to monitor and control their activities without any accounting input. Non-financial performance measures may give a more timely indication of the levels of performance achieved than do financial ratios, and may be less susceptible to distortion by factors such as uncontrollable variations in the effect of market forces on operations.

Some examples of non-financial performance indicators are:

Customer service quality
- number of customer complaints
- % of repeat orders
- customer waiting time
- number of on-time deliveries
- % customer satisfaction index
- number of cut orders

Manufacturing performance
- % waste
- number of rejects
- set-up times
- output per employee
- material yield %
- adherence to production schedules
- % of rework
- manufacturing lead times

Purchasing/logistics
- number of suppliers
- number of days stock held
- purchase price index

Customer development
- number of new accounts
- number of new orders
- % annual sales increase
- % level of promotional activity
- % level of product awareness within company

Marketing
- market share trends
- growth in sales volume
- number of customer visits per salesman
- client contact hours per salesman
- sales volume actual versus forecast
- number of customers
- customer survey response information

New product development
- number of new products developed
- number of on-time new product launches
- % new product order fulfilment

Human resources/ Communications/ Employee involvement	● staff turnover ● absenteeism days and % ● accident/sickness days lost ● training days per employee ● training spend % to sales ● % of employees having multi-competence ● % of employees attending daily team briefings
Information technology	● number of PC breakdowns ● number of IT training days per employee ● % system availability ● number of hours lead time for queries/problem solving.

Progress check 5.8

Explain, giving some examples, what are meant by non-financial performance measures and what they may add to our understanding of business performance.

The balanced scorecard

In 1990 David Norton and Robert Kaplan were involved in a study of a dozen companies that covered manufacturing and service, heavy industry and high technology to develop a new performance measurement model. The findings of this study were published in the *Harvard Business Review* in January 1992 and gave birth to an improved measurement system, the **balanced scorecard**.

The balanced scorecard concept had evolved by 1996 from a measurement system to a core management system. *The Balanced Scorecard* published by Kaplan and Norton in 1996 illustrates the importance of both financial and non-financial measures incorporated into performance measurement systems; these are included not on an *ad hoc* basis but are derived from a **top-down process** driven by the company's **mission** and strategy.

An example of a balanced scorecard is shown in Fig. 5.17. It provides a framework for translating a strategy into operational terms.

The balanced scorecard includes headings covering the following four key elements:

● financial

● internal business processes

● learning and growth

● customer.

From Fig. 5.17 it can be seen that although

● objectives

● measures

● targets

● initiatives.

are implied within each of the elements, the financial element represents only one quarter of the total.

How the company appears to its shareholders is an important underlying factor of the balanced scorecard approach. But it is interesting to see that the measures that are considered by the company in satisfying shareholders go much further than just financial ones:

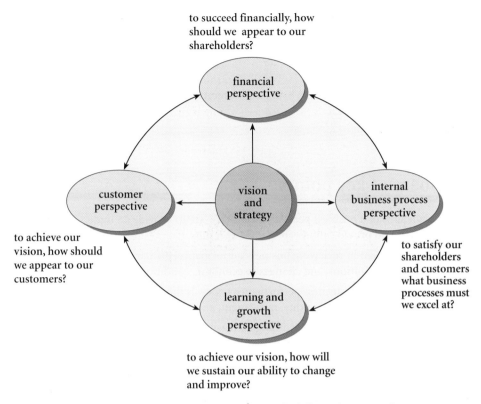

to succeed financially, how should we appear to our shareholders?

to achieve our vision, how should we appear to our customers?

to satisfy our shareholders and customers what business processes must we excel at?

to achieve our vision, how will we sustain our ability to change and improve?

FIGURE 5.17   *An example of a balanced scorecard*

● to satisfy our shareholders and customers, what business processes must we excel at?

● to achieve our vision, how will we sustain our ability to change and improve?

● to achieve our vision, how should we appear to our customers?

Norton and Kaplan comment on the dissatisfaction of investors who may see only financial reports of past performance. Investors increasingly want information that will help them forecast future performance of companies in which they have invested their capital. In 1994 the American Certified Public Accountants (CPA) Special Committee on Financial Reporting in New York reinforced this concern with reliance on financial reporting for measuring business performance. 'Users focus on the future while today's business reporting focuses on the past. Although information about the past is a useful indicator of future performance, users also need forward-looking information.'

The CPA committee was concerned on how well companies are creating value for the future and how non-financial measurement must play a key role. 'Many users want to see a company through the eyes of management to help them understand management's perspective and predict where management will lead the company. Management should disclose the financial and non-financial measurements it uses in managing the business that quantify the effects of key activities and events.'

The subject of non-financial performance measures and concepts like the balanced scorecard have been introduced in this book as an illustration and to provide some balance against the dominance of financial-based measures that are used to measure and evaluate performance in most businesses. It also serves to highlight the recognition that the accountancy profession itself has given to these wider business issues and the way in which professional accounting bodies, in particular the Chartered Institute of Management Accountants, have led the thinking away from their narrowly focused beginnings.

> **Progress check 5.9**
>
> Describe the framework of the balanced scorecard approach and explain what you think it tries to achieve.

Summary of key points

- The main aims of a business performance review are to provide an understanding of the business and provide an interpretation of results.

- Care must be taken in reviewing business performance, primarily because of lack of consistency in definitions, and changes in economic conditions.

- An important area of business performance review is the use of ratio analysis looking at profitability, efficiency, liquidity, investment, and also growth and financial structure.

- Cash flow and cash ratios are becoming increasingly as important as profit and profitability ratios in the measurement of business performance.

- There is no best way of evaluating financial performance and there are advantages and disadvantages in using earnings per share or cash flow as the basis of measurement.

- Earnings before interest, tax, depreciation and amortisation – EBITDA is now commonly used as a close approximation of a cash flow performance measure.

- The use of non-financial indicators is important in the evaluation of business performance.

- Both financial and non-financial measures are now incorporated into performance measurement systems such as the balanced scorecard.

Glossary of key terms

acid test Quick assets (current assets excluding stocks) divided by current liabilities measures the ability of the business to pay creditors in the short-term.

balanced scorecard An approach to the provision of information to management to assist strategic policy formulation and achievement. It emphasises the need to provide the user with a set of information which addresses all relevant areas of performance in an objective and unbiased fashion. The information provided may include both financial and non-financial elements, and cover areas such as profitability, customer satisfaction, internal efficiency and innovation.

cash interest cover Net cash inflow from operations plus interest received, divided by interest paid, calculates the number of times the interest payable is covered by cash flow available for such payments.

creditor days Average trade creditors divided by average daily purchases on credit terms indicates the average time taken, in calendar days, to pay for supplies received on credit.

cross-sectional analysis Cross-sectional analysis provides a means of providing a standard against which performance can be measured and uses ratios to compare difference businesses at the same points in time (see inter-firm comparison).

current ratio Current assets divided by current liabilities is an overall measure of liquidity.

debt/equity ratio A gearing ratio that relates to financial gearing, which is the relationship between a company's borrowings, which includes both prior charge capital and long-term debt, and its ordinary shareholders' funds (share capital plus reserves).

debtor days Average trade debtors divided by average daily sales on credit terms indicates the average time taken, in calendar days, to receive payment from credit customers.

defensive interval Quick assets (current assets excluding stocks) divided by average daily cash from operations shows how many days a business could survive at its present level of operating activity if no inflow of cash was received from sales or other sources.

dividend cover Earnings per share divided by dividend per share indicates the number of times the profits attributable to the equity shareholders cover the actual dividends payable for the period.

EBITDA Earnings before interest, tax, depreciation, and amortisation.

gearing Financial gearing calculations can be made in a number of ways. Gearing is generally seen as the relationship between a company's borrowings, which include both prior charge capital (capital having a right of interest or preference shares having fixed dividends) and long-term debt, and its ordinary shareholders' funds (share capital plus reserves).

horizontal analysis (or common size analysis) An analysis of the profit and loss account (or balance sheet) that allows a line-by-line analysis of the accounts with those of the previous year. It may provide over a number of years a trend of changes showing either growth or decline in these elements of the accounts through calculation of annual percentage growth rates in profits, sales, stock or any other item.

interest cover Profit before interest and tax divided by interest payable, calculates the number of times the interest payable is covered by profits available for such payments. It is particularly important for lenders to determine the vulnerability of interest payments to a drop in profit.

inter-firm comparison Systematic and detailed comparison of the performance of different companies generally operating in a common industry. Normally the information distributed by the scheme administrator (to participating companies only) is in the form of ratios, or in a format, which prevents the identity of individual scheme members from being identified.

mission The mission of an organisation, not necessarily written, is its general sense of purpose and underlying inherent beliefs, that creates and reflects a 'common thread', common values and culture throughout the organisation. An organisation's written mission statement usually includes a summary of goals and policies together with its purpose and what business it is in, what it provides and for whom its exists, its values and commitment to its employees and suppliers, its policies and behaviour standards and principles of business, quality and professionalism, and its strategy and long-term vision.

non-financial performance indicators Measures of performance based on non-financial information which may originate in and be used by operating departments to monitor and control their activities without any accounting input. Non-financial performance measures may give a more timely indication of the levels of performance achieved than do financial ratios, and may be less susceptible to distortion by factors such as uncontrollable variations in the effect of market forces on operations.

operating gearing The relationship of fixed costs to total costs. The greater the proportion of fixed costs, the higher the operating gearing, and the greater the advantage to the business of increasing sales volume. If sales drop, a business with high operating gearing may face a problem from its high level of fixed costs.

price/earnings ratio (P/E) The market price per ordinary share divided by earnings per share shows the number of years it would take to recoup an equity investment from its share of the attributable equity profit.

return on capital employed (ROCE) ROCE, or return on investment (ROI), is the profit before interest and tax divided by average capital employed. It indicates the profit-generating capacity of capital employed.

return on investment (ROI) See return on capital employed (ROCE).

stock days Stocks value divided by average daily cost of sales calculates the number of days stocks at the current usage rate.

SWOT analysis Performing a SWOT analysis is a means of gaining a clear picture of the Strengths, Weaknesses, Opportunities, and Threats, which made the organisation what it is. SWOT analysis can apply across diverse management functions and activities, but is particularly appropriate to the early stages of formulating strategy.

top-down process A top-down approach usually relates to a particular type of budgeting process where a budget allowance is set or imposed without permitting the ultimate budget holder to have the opportunity to participate in the budgeting process.

vertical analysis An analysis of the profit and loss account (or balance sheet) in which each item is expressed as a percentage of the total. The vertical analysis provides evidence of structural changes in the business such as increased profitability through more efficient production.

weighted average cost of capital (WACC) The average cost of the company's finance (equity, debentures, bank loans) weighted according to the proportion each element bears to the total pool of capital. Weighting is usually based on market valuations, current yields and costs after tax.

Assessment material

Questions

Q5.1 (i) Who is likely to carry out a business performance review?

(ii) Describe what may be required from such reviews giving some examples from different industries and differing perspectives.

Q5.2 (i) Outline how the business performance review process may be used to evaluate the position of a dot.com company like Amazon UK.

(ii) What are the limitations to the approach that you have outlined?

Q5.3 How is ratio analysis, in terms of profitability ratios, efficiency ratios, liquidity ratios, and investment ratios, used to support the business review process?

Q5.4 Why should we be so careful when we try to compare the profit and loss account of a limited company with a similar business in the same industry?
(Hint: Research Tesco and Sainsbury on the Times CD-ROM for 1999 and 2000 for USA earnings and Far East earnings.)

Q5.5 (i) Why does profit continue to be the preferred basis for evaluation of the financial performance of a business?

(ii) In what ways can cash flow provide a better basis for performance evaluation, and how may cash flow be approximated?

Q5.6 (i) What does financial performance not tell us about the health of a business?

(ii) Give examples, from each of the key areas of business activity, of non-financial measures that may fill these gaps.

Q5.7 (i) Why has the balanced scorecard become such an essential part of so many business management toolkits in recent years?

(ii) How can the balanced scorecard be used to achieve improved business performance?

Discussion points

D5.1 In what ways may the performance review process be used to anticipate and react to change?

D5.2 'Lies, damned lies, and statistics.' In which of these categories do you think ratio analysis sits, if at all?

D5.3 The balanced scorecard is a recently developed concept, but it also appears to be the grouping together of a number of well-established principles and techniques. In what ways does it represent a new technique?

Exercises

Solutions are provided in Appendix 4 to all exercise numbers highlighted in colour.

Level I

E5.1   *Time allowed – 60 minutes*

From the financial statements of Freshco plc, a Lancashire-based grocery and general supplies chain supplying hotels and caterers, for the year ended 30 June 2000, prepare a report on performance using appropriate profitability ratios for comparison with the previous year.

Freshco plc
Balance sheet as at 30 June 2000

	2000 £m	1999 £m
Fixed assets	146	149
Current assets		
Stocks	124	100
Debtors	70	80
Cash and bank	14	11
	208	191
Current liabilities (less than 1 year)		
Creditors	76	74
Dividends	20	13
Taxation	25	20
	121	107
Net current assets	87	84
Total assets less current liabilities	233	233
less		
Long-term liabilities (over 1 year)		
Debenture	20	67
Net assets	213	166
Capital and reserves		
Capital	111	100
General reserve	14	9
Profit and loss account	88	57
	213	166

Freshco plc
Profit and loss account for the year ended 30 June 2000

	2000 £m	1999 £m
Turnover	894	747
Cost of sales	(690)	(581)
Gross profit	204	166
Distribution and administrative costs	(101)	(79)
Operating profit	103	87
Other costs	(20)	(5)
Profit before interest and tax	83	82
Net interest	(2)	(8)
Profit before tax	81	74
Tax on profit on ordinary activities	(25)	(20)
Profit on ordinary activities after tax	56	54
Retained profit brought forward	57	16
	113	70
Dividends	(20)	(13)
	93	57
Transfer to general reserve	(5)	–
Retained profit for the financial year	88	57

Additional information

(i) Authorised and issued share capital 30 June 2000, £222m £0.50 ordinary shares (£200m, 1999).

(ii) Total assets less current liabilities 30 June 1998, £219m. Trade debtors 30 June 1998, £60m.

(iii) Market value of ordinary shares in Freshco plc 30 June 2000, £3.93 (£2.85, 1999).

(iv) Fixed assets depreciation provision 30 June 2000, £57m (£44m, 1999).

(v) Depreciation charge for the year to 30 June 2000, £13m (£10m, 1999).

Freshco plc
Cash flow statement for the year ended 30 June 2000

Reconciliation of operating profit to net cash flow from operating activities

	2000 £m	1999 £m
Operating profit	103	87
Depreciation charges	13	10
Increase in stocks	(24)	(4)
Increase in debtors	(10)	(20)
Increase in creditors	2	4
Net cash inflow from operating activities	84	77

Cash flow statement

	2000 £m	1999 £m
Net cash inflow from operating activities	84	77
Returns on investments and servicing of finance	(2)	(8)
Taxation	(20)	(15)
Capital expenditure	(10)	(40)
	52	14
Equity dividends paid	(13)	(11)
	39	3
Management of liquid resources	–	–
Financing	(36)	7
Increase in cash	3	10

E5.2 *Time allowed – 60 minutes*

Using the financial statements of Freshco plc from Exercise E5.1, for the year ended 30 June 2000, prepare a report on performance using appropriate efficiency ratios for comparison with the previous year.

E5.3 *Time allowed – 60 minutes*

Using the financial statements of Freshco plc from Exercise E5.1, for the year ended 30 June 2000, prepare a report on performance using appropriate liquidity ratios for comparison with the previous year.

E5.4 *Time allowed – 60 minutes*

Using the financial statements of Freshco plc from Exercise E5.1, for the year ended 30 June 2000, prepare a report on performance using appropriate investment ratios for comparison with the previous year.

Level II

E5.5 *Time allowed – 90 minutes*

The chief executive of Laurel plc, Al Chub, wants to know the strength of the financial position of Laurel's main competitor, Hardy plc. From Hardy's financial statements for the past three years he has asked you to write a report that evaluates the financial performance of Hardy plc and to include

(i)   as full a ratio analysis as possible with the information available

(ii) an identification of the top five areas which should be investigated further

(iii) details of information that has not been provided, but if it were available would improve your analysis of Hardy's performance

Hardy plc
Balance sheet as at 31 March 2000

Figures in £m	1998	1999	2000
Fixed assets	106	123	132
Current assets			
Stocks	118	152	147
Debtors	53	70	80
Cash and bank	26	29	26
	197	251	253
Current liabilities (less than 1 year)			
Trade creditors	26	38	38
Other creditors	40	52	55
	66	90	93
Net current assets	131	161	160
Total assets less current liabilities	237	284	292
less			
Long-term liabilities (over 1 year)			
Debenture	37	69	69
Net assets	200	215	223
Capital and reserves			
Capital	50	50	50
Profit and loss account	150	165	173
	200	215	223

Hardy plc
Profit and loss account for the year ended 31 March 2000

Figures in £m	1998	1999	2000
Turnover	420	491	456
Cost of sales	(277)	(323)	(295)
Gross profit	143	168	161
Distribution and administrative costs	(93)	(107)	(109)
Operating profit	50	61	52
Other costs	–	–	–
Profit before interest and tax	50	61	52
Net interest	(3)	(7)	(9)
Profit before tax	47	54	43
Tax on profit on ordinary activities	(22)	(26)	(23)
Profit on ordinary activities after tax	25	28	20
Dividends	(12)	(12)	(12)
Retained profit for the financial year	13	16	8

Published report
and accounts

LEARNING OBJECTIVES

Completion of this chapter will enable you to:

● explain why annual reports and accounts of limited companies are
filed and published

● recognise the key elements of the contents of the annual report
and accounts of a typical public limited company

● evaluate the information disclosed within the annual report and
accounts

● carry out an horizontal analysis of the profit and loss account and
the balance sheet

● carry out a vertical analysis of the profit and loss account and the
balance sheet

● interpret the information provided by segmental reporting

● critically evaluate the quality of environmental reporting within
annual reports

● appreciate the impact of inflation on the financial performance of
companies

● prepare and describe an alternative perception of the profit and
loss account illustrated by the value added statement

Introduction

This chapter builds on the business performance analysis techniques we
introduced in Chapter 5. It is concerned with the type of information, both
financial and non-financial, that is included in company annual reports and
accounts. We will use the annual report and accounts of Johnson Matthey plc
for the year 2000 to illustrate the financial statements of a large UK plc. We will
not consider the whole of the Johnson Matthey plc annual report, a copy of

which may be obtained from their head office in Trafalgar Square, London, UK. Further information and copies of the report and accounts 2000 (and for the year 2001) may be obtained from the Johnson Matthey website which is linked to the website accompanying this book at www.mcgraw-hill.co.uk/textbooks/davies.

We will look at extracts from Johnson Matthey plc's report and accounts 2000, including the

- chairman's statement
- chief executive's statement
- financial review
- accounting policies
- financial highlights
- financial statements
- segmental reporting
- **environmental reporting**
- directors' report.

The information disclosed in Johnson Matthey plc's report and accounts 2000 provides us with a broad picture of what sort of company Johnson Matthey is. The report and accounts include not only Johnson Matthey's historical financial performance, but also an indication of Johnson Mathey's prospects for the future. Included within the financial review is an example of how such a group manages financial risk.

In Chapter 5 we considered ratio analysis in our review of business performance. In this chapter we will look at some further tools of analysis. The first is horizontal analysis, or common size analysis, which provides a line-by-line comparison of the accounts of a company (profit and loss account and balance sheet) with those of the previous year. The second approach is the vertical analysis, where each item in the profit and loss account and balance sheet is expressed as a percentage of the total. The chapter closes with a look at the nature and purpose of the value added statement and its preparation. The value added statement is a variation on the profit and loss account and is concerned with measuring the value added by a business rather than the profit earned by the business.

An area of increasing importance now reported on in the annual reports and accounts of UK plcs is **corporate governance**. Corporate governance, including the role of auditors, will be covered in detail in Chapter 7.

Why are annual accounts filed and published?

After each year end, companies prepare their annual report and accounts, which include the financial statements and the auditors' report, for their shareholders. Copies of the annual report and accounts must be filed with the Registrar of Companies, and presented for approval by the shareholders at the company's annual general meeting (AGM). Further copies are usually made available to other interested parties such as financial institutions, major suppliers and other investors. The annual report and accounts of a plc usually takes the form of a glossy booklet which includes photographs of the directors, products and activities and other promotional material, and many non-financial performance measures, as well as the statutory legal and financial information. Large companies also issue half yearly, or interim reports which include the standard financial information, but the whole report is on a much smaller scale than the annual report.

The following press cutting includes comments on the interim financial report published by Johnson Matthey plc for the first half of their financial year to 30 September 2000.

Johnson Matthey has the mettle

Chris Clark, chief executive of chemicals and metals group Johnson Matthey, claimed his company was 'on the side of the angels' yesterday. High metals prices, excitement over fuel cell technology and the market's confidence in Mr Clark, has driven the company's share price up 70pc this year, to a high of £11.21.

Johnson Matthey delivered a 40pc jump in profits before tax and exceptionals to £86m yesterday, prompting most analysts to upgrade their full-year profit forecasts for at least the second time this year to around £176m. The company's shares rose 24 to £10.73 in sympathy.

Things are certainly looking stellar for Johnson Matthey, but analysts are unsure whether the company's affair with the heavens makes its shares worth buying any more. With fears over climate change, car companies and power generators are busying themselves developing pollution-free fuel cells which make electricity out of hydrogen and oxygen. Johnson Matthey has over 100 scientists working on this technology and claims to be at the forefront.

Some analysts believe this business could be worth £300m to £400m within 10 years. This, combined with a seemingly endless increase in the price of platinum and the strength of the dollar – Johnson Matthey's main earning currency – makes the company's future look bright.

The only cloud on Johnson Matthey's horizon is a slackening global car market, plagued by overcapacity, which is bound to hit Johnson Matthey's catalyst business sooner or later. Priced at 18 times forecast earnings the shares are not expensive. But they have risen fivefold in the last two years.

© *The Daily Telegraph*, 30 November 2000

On the strength of Johnson Matthey plc's interim results, financial analysts were prompted to upgrade their profit forecast for the group for the year to 31 March 2001. The publication of the annual report and accounts is of course always the time when such forecasts may be seen to have been justified. Johnson Matthey plc's report and accounts 2001 did indeed justify such optimism with a profit of £180.3m.

Financial statements, whether to internal or external parties, are defined as summaries of accounts to provide information for interested parties. The key reports and statements within the published annual report and accounts are illustrated in Fig. 6.1.

In 1993 the Accounting Standards Board (ASB) issued a statement of good practice that supported the earlier suggestion made in the report of the **Cadbury Committee** (1992) that companies should include in their annual reports an operating and financial review (OFR) of the business. The reason for this suggestion was that businesses had become increasingly diversified and complex, and it had become increasingly difficult to understand information contained in financial reporting. Complex financial and organisational structures made it difficult to analyse and interpret financial information. It was felt that the OFR was needed to provide a greater insight into the affairs of the company, in addition to the information traditionally already provided by the chairman's statement and the directors' report.

The OFR was intended to cover the business as a whole for the year under review, and to include issues relevant to the assessment of future prospects. The OFR should include:

- brief reports that are easy to understand
- reports on each of the individual aspects of the business
- explanations of non-recurring aspects of the business
- discussion of matters that underpin the financial results for the period
- consideration of factors that might impact on the future performance of the business.

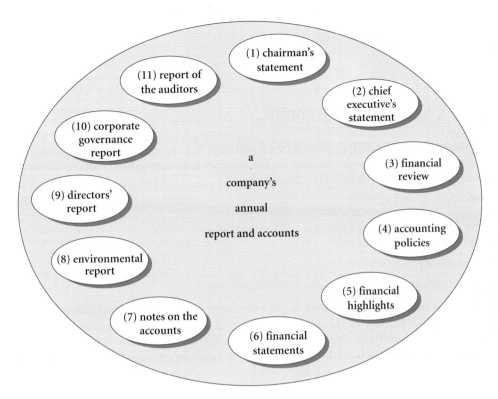

FIGURE 6.1 The key reports and statements within a company's annual report and accounts

The OFR includes two separate reports:

● an operating review, which includes
  – new product development information
  – details of shareholders' returns
  – sensitivities of the financial results to specific accounting policies
  – risks and uncertainties
  – future investment
● a financial review, which includes
  – current cash position
  – sources of funding
  – treasury policy
  – capital structure
  – confirmation that the business is a going concern
  – factors outside the balance sheet impacting on the value of the business
  – taxation.

We will look at each of the reports and statements included in Fig. 6.1 in this chapter, using the annual report and accounts 2000 of Johnson Matthey plc as an illustration, except for the last two reports, 10) the corporate governance report and, 11) the report of the auditors, which will be discussed in Chapter 7. It should be noted that Johnson Matthey's operating review is included within the chief executive's statement. With regard to the notes on the accounts, in this chapter we will consider only note 1 that relates to **segmental reporting**.

Why are annual accounts filed and published?

(1) Chairman's statement

In addition to the profit and loss account and cash flow statement for the year and the balance sheet as at the year-end date, the annual report and accounts includes much more financial and non-financial information such as:

● company policies
● financial indicators
● directors' remuneration
● employee numbers
● business analysis.

The annual report and accounts includes the chairman's statement. This offers an opportunity for the chairman of the company to report in unquantified and unaudited terms on the performance of the company during the past financial period and on likely future developments. Let's take a look at the Johnson Matthey chairman's statement from its chairman, Michael Miles, OBE (see pp. 192–3).

The Johnson Matthey chairman's statement can be seen to include his general comments about the performance of the company over the past year, its current position, and its outlook for the future. A couple of paragraphs describe the strategy of the group. As with most chairmen's statements, Johnson Matthey's statement includes comments about the board of directors, and the achievements of the management team and other employees over the preceding year. The Johnson Matthey statement devotes a large section to the importance of the company's employees, their training and development. It also includes reference to the importance of social and environmental issues (which we will deal with later in this chapter). Michael Miles' report concludes with a return to corporate strategy and a reinforcement of his confidence in the continuing growth of the business.

What is the purpose of a chairman's statement?

(2) Chief executive's statement

Chief executives' statements generally include detail on the performance of the business particularly relating to products, markets, technology and the various geographical areas of activity. These statements include brief comments on the financial highlights of the preceding year and the recommended dividend payable to shareholders. The chief executive's statement includes a review of operations which outlines the main factors underlying the business and identifies any changes or expected future changes which may impact on the business. It normally concludes with an outlook on the future prospects of the business.

The Johnson Matthey chief executive's statement for 2000, presented by Chris Clark (see pp. 194–7), emphasises the group's change in focus, and disposal of its electronic materials division. This report provides a great deal of information of particular interest to current and potential new shareholders relating to future growth opportunities, planned major investments, the development of new and existing technologies, and new product development. This report includes some detail of the headline financial results, but its main focus is the operating review containing the sort of information referred to earlier.

(3) Financial review

The financial review goes into further financial detail than the chief executive's statement and is normally prepared by the finance director. In the case of Johnson Matthey, the financial review has been prepared by its group finance director, John Sheldrick. The purpose of the financial review is to review the results for the past year and to provide an overview of financial policy. Let's look at the Johnson Matthey financial review, included in its annual report and accounts for the year 2000 (see pp. 198–200).

The Johnson Matthey financial review begins with a review of the results for the year to 31 March 2000, with an initial focus on sales, profit before tax, earnings per share and dividends. The review goes on to look in a little more detail at sales and margins, return on investment, exceptional items, interest and exchange rates, taxation, and cash flow. We can see that the review includes many of the financial performance measures we have discussed in Chapter 5. Examples are return on sales and return on investment, which are analysed by each area of business activity.

Johnson Matthey is one of the growing band of companies using economic value added (EVA) to measure performance. A comment was made with regard to the adverse impact of the strength of £ sterling against the **euro** and other foreign currencies. The group benefited from the stronger US$ with nearly one half of the group's operating income being derived from North America. The group's net cash flow improved primarily as a result of the sale of the group's electronic materials division. This was despite a deterioration in the group's free cash flow (net operating cash flow after interest, tax, dividends and capital expenditure), due to an increase in platinum prices.

The first part of the financial review concludes with a comment on the movement in shareholders' funds over the year. Two thirds of the review is devoted to the group's policy on financial **risk management**. Risk management is a key strategic area for the type of business in which Johnson Matthey is involved. Policy is explained relating to interest rate, liquidity, and foreign currency **risk** and the **financial instruments** that are used by Johnson Matthey to manage financial risks.

The final area of risk, that of precious metals prices, is also outlined in terms of policy and way in which this area of risk is managed. The group finance director emphasised the extent to which the group is risk averse; the group's treasury department, which is responsible for managing risk, is run as a service centre rather than a profit centre.

Johnson Matthey have not reported on their share price performance in their report and accounts for the year 2000. This information, available from Johnson Matthey plc, is illustrated in Fig. 6.2 for each 31 March from 1991 to 2000.

Chairman's Statement

Michael Miles
Chairman

I am pleased to report that 1999/2000 was a very good year for Johnson Matthey with all three of its operating divisions contributing to strong growth in profits. Excellent progress has continued to be made towards our goal of enhancing shareholder value. Johnson Matthey's strong technology and market leadership positions are widely recognised as providing a firm platform for continued growth as well as presenting exciting opportunities for the development of new global businesses such as fuel cells.

The strategy that we announced 18 months ago of refocusing the group on its core activities where we have genuine leadership and a strong market position has made good progress during the year. The sale of our Electronic Materials business to AlliedSignal Inc. was completed during the first half. The year has seen continued progress in the reshaping of the group with rationalisation of our Colours & Coatings Division's Tableware activities and the exit from its non-core organic pigments businesses. At the same time we have continued to invest in research and development, in new technology and in new production facilities to ensure that we maintain our leadership positions. It is gratifying to see that Johnson Matthey is increasingly recognised as a leading global speciality chemicals company with a strong franchise in catalysts, chemicals and precious metals.

Fuel cells have been the centre of a great deal of interest over the last year. Through its commitment to research and development and strong relationships with the world's leading developers of fuel cell technology, Johnson Matthey is in a uniquely strong position to benefit from the growth of new fuel cell industries. As the world leader in catalysts and catalysed components for fuel cells the advent of fuel cell engines for cars and fuel cell based micro combined heat and power units for homes offer Johnson Matthey a major opportunity for growth. The board is fully committed to supporting management in growing this exciting new business. On pages 14 and 15 we have a special feature on fuel cell technology and the role that Johnson Matthey is playing in bringing fuel cell systems to market.

Board

The board of Johnson Matthey continues to pay particularly close attention to the group's future strategic direction and opportunities for growth. We are fortunate to have the support of a strong team of non-executive directors who bring a wealth of experience to the board. I am grateful for their efforts and wise counsel over the last year.

2 Johnson Matthey

In July 1999 Mike Cleare retired from the board following the agreement to sell our Electronic Materials business to AlliedSignal Inc. Mike joined the board of Johnson Matthey in September 1995 following a succession of senior management positions with the group in both the United Kingdom and the United States. He headed Electronic Materials Division from January 1997. On behalf of the board I wish Mike well in his retirement.

In June this year we announced that George Wells would retire from the board at the end of July 2000. George has been a valuable member of our board since joining us in March 1998 and I should personally like to thank him for his contribution.

People and the Community

People are Johnson Matthey's major asset and the company is fortunate to have an extremely dedicated and highly professional workforce. On behalf of the board I would like to thank all our employees for their hard work during the year.

At the end of April 2000 Dr George McGuire retired as Director of Johnson Matthey's Technology Centre after a distinguished 30 year career with Johnson Matthey. I would like to take this opportunity to thank George for his hard work and dedication and to wish him all the best for his retirement.

The company's future is embodied in its employees and I can not stress highly enough the importance of developing the management talent of tomorrow. This receives a great deal of attention throughout the company and is acknowledged as a primary responsibility of today's management. Our Training and Development of People policy is set out on page 24 of this annual report.

While Johnson Matthey is at the forefront of a number of important environmentally beneficial technologies, such as emission control catalysts and fuel cells, we also strive to ensure that all our operations around the world meet and exceed our responsibilities to the environment. We also seek to achieve the highest standards of health and safety performance in all our operations. Our corporate Environment, Health and Safety policies and information on our performance in these areas are detailed on pages 20 and 21.

Our current Charity of the Year programme is in support of the National Asthma Campaign. During the year we have also made donations to the Royal London Society for the Blind, with whom we have a relationship dating back over 160 years, and to the NSPCC in support of their FULL STOP campaign.

Conclusion

The board is pleased with the progress that has been made with implementing the strategy that we announced in November 1998. We believe that Johnson Matthey's strong technology and market positions in catalysts, fine chemicals and precious metals mean that we are uniquely placed to achieve strong growth as the world seeks to meet the environmental challenges of this new century.

Michael Miles OBE
Chairman

Chief Executive's Statement

Chris Clark
Chief Executive

Johnson Matthey's strategy announced in November 1998 to change the focus of the group has been successfully implemented. Electronic Materials Division (EMD) was established as a stand alone entity and sold for a good price. Our core businesses achieved 17% growth in profits following 20% growth in 1998/99.

The prospects for future growth are very encouraging. We are undertaking a significant investment programme to take advantage of opportunities in the strongly growing autocatalyst market. We have recently announced an investment of £10 million to build a new autocatalyst facility at Royston in the UK to meet the increasing demand in Europe for more technologically advanced catalysts. The new factory will initially have capacity to manufacture 3.5 million catalysts a year. In February 2000 we announced the establishment of a new autocatalyst facility in China which will initially have capacity to produce 0.6 million car catalysts and 1 million motorcycle catalysts.

We are doubling the capacity of our very successful Indian business at a new site in Harayana state which will have capacity for 2 million car catalysts and 4 million motorcycle catalysts.

We are also investing in our global manufacturing technology with expenditure of £20 million over the next 3 years. This investment will give Johnson Matthey a significant competitive edge enabling the production of catalysts to the much tighter specifications required for the next generation of clean cars.

4 Johnson Matthey

In March 2000 Johnson Matthey unveiled its SCRT™ system which represents a major step forward in diesel emission control. This will make heavy duty diesel truck and bus engines as clean as those of the very latest passenger cars. In the next few years much more stringent emission control limits will be introduced for heavy duty diesel engines both in the US and Europe. This new technology will enable manufacturers to meet these new limits within industry cost targets.

New catalyst development is increasing in other areas. In January 2000 we acquired an equity stake in Oy Smoptech Ab as part of a phased acquisition of the company. Smoptech, which is based in Turku, Finland, has developed a range of advanced polymer fibres for use as innovative supports for catalysts and in other chemical process applications in the pharmaceutical and chemical industries. In Pharmaceutical Materials the major capacity expansion at West Deptford in the US is well underway and should be operational during calendar year 2001 to meet anticipated demand arising from new product introductions.

Fuel cells represent a major opportunity for growth with their application in vehicles and in our homes soon to become a reality. It is expected that there will be several thousand fuel cell vehicles on the road by 2005 and industry estimates are that between 600,000 and 1 million fuel cell cars will be produced per year by 2010. Johnson Matthey is the world leader in catalysts and catalysed components for fuel cells. We are investing £12 million in the expansion of our fuel cell development, testing and pilot production facilities both at our Technology Centre at Sonning Common and in the US.

Our technology lead in fuel cells has enabled us to secure an unrivaled list of fuel cell customer partnerships. These include XCELLSIS, VW, General Motors, Siemens, Ballard, IFC, Plug Power and Energy Partners. We recently announced a new collaboration and supply agreement with James Cropper PLC. This represents an important step in the development of high volume manufacturing processes for Johnson Matthey's Membrane Electrode Assembly (MEA), the key component at the heart of Polymer Electrolyte Membrane (PEM) fuel cells.

Johnson Matthey continues to be the largest fabricator of platinum group metal (pgm) products in the world and has a distribution capability second to none. Our platinum marketing activities support demand for platinum products worldwide which is expected to show continued growth in the coming years. The group is sole marketing agent for Anglo American Platinum Corporation Limited, the world's leading primary producer of pgms, a relationship which goes back over 70 years. Many of the new uses for pgms have been developed in Johnson Matthey's own laboratories. We are increasing our investment in this area, which will underpin the continued long term growth of our core Precious Metals Division.

Colours & Coatings Division continues to make excellent progress since we acquired full ownership in February 1998. Return on sales has risen to 11.6%. We expect the return to continue to improve as the benefits of the restructuring programme for Tableware come through. We will be investing £10 million on new production facilities at Castellon in Spain to meet rapid growth in demand from tile manufacturers in southern Europe and around the world. We are also planning to put further investment in our factory in Maastricht, Holland which makes specialised automotive glass enamels and other decorative products for the glass industry.

Chief Executive's Statement

The programme to manage the millennium IT risk was completed well in advance of the deadline and the group achieved a smooth and successful transition into 2000. New investment in Information Technology infrastructure to support the rapid growth of the business continues to be made. The Internet and related technology provide significant opportunities to further enhance the capabilities of our businesses in improving efficiency and better serving our customers. These opportunities and other ways of realising value via the Internet form the basis of our e-Commerce strategy and are being pursued energetically. Johnson Matthey's established US catalogue sales business Alfa Aesar has been trading on the Internet since 1997 and is currently in the process of being upgraded to offer improved facilities for customers with a growing interest in e-Commerce.

The group is also looking at the opportunity to grow its core businesses by strategic acquisitions, and is actively pursuing a number of opportunities. Following the sale of EMD the group is well positioned to fund these opportunities out of existing resources.

Financial Highlights

In the year to 31st March 2000 operating profit from continuing operations rose by 17% to £146.5 million on sales that were 27% up at £3,769 million. On 17th August 1999, EMD was sold to AlliedSignal Inc. for US$655 million. EMD made a £0.1 million contribution to profits compared with £22.1 million for the full year 1998/99. Despite the shortfall in EMD, Johnson Matthey earned profits before tax and exceptionals of £143.8 million, 10% up on prior year.

Earnings per share excluding exceptionals were 7% up at 47.5 pence. Including exceptionals earnings per share were 4% up at 51.4 pence.

As a result of the sale of EMD net cash flow for the group was strongly positive at £393.3 million. Johnson Matthey ended the year with net cash of £165.8 million compared with net borrowings of £221.6 million last year. Shareholders' funds rose by £202.6 million to £755.4 million.

The board is recommending to shareholders a final dividend of 14.2 pence making a total dividend for the year of 20.3 pence, an increase of 7%. The dividend would be covered 2.3 times by earnings.

Operations

Catalysts & Chemicals Division increased its sales by 26% over last year to £856 million. The growth reflected increased sales volume and the effect of higher palladium prices on autocatalysts. The division's operating profit rose by 14% to £84.8 million.

The Autocatalyst business achieved good growth in operating profit with unit sales 11% higher than last year driven by strong car sales and tightening emission standards in all the world's major car markets. These tighter standards are resulting in more catalysts per vehicle and growing demand for more technologically sophisticated catalysts.

In August 1999 we announced that Johnson Matthey had agreed with General Motors Corporation to settle a long-standing commercial dispute. As part of the settlement agreement Johnson Matthey has entered into collaboration with General Motors on a significant research and development project on fuel cells for transportation applications.

Testing the latest catalysts for motorcycle applications at Johnson Matthey's European Autocatalyst Technology Centre in Royston, UK

The Chemicals business also achieved good growth in operating profit benefiting from strong demand for pgm refining and good sales of platinum group metal compounds. As anticipated, profits in our Pharmaceutical Materials business were flat as a result of the increased competition in methylphenidate as two new generic suppliers entered the market and prices declined. This was offset by strong sales of carboplatin, fentanyl and hydromorphone and initial income from a new product in late stage clinical trials.

Precious Metals Division's (PMD's) sales were 31% ahead of last year at £2,672 million. Sales of platinum group metals rose as a result of increasing demand and higher prices. Gold sales also increased with higher levels of refining activity in the Far East. Operating profit for the division rose by 22% to £45.4 million.

Another year of unpredictable Russian supplies supported pgm prices and ensured continued market volatility. PMD's marketing operations benefited from the trading opportunities and record demand for metal from the autocatalyst and jewellery sectors. Buoyant demand for industrial products underpinned a good performance from PMD's platinum fabrication facilities.

Gold and Silver operations had a satisfactory year. Good levels of business for refining and bullion products were offset by weaker margins in a competitive marketplace.

Johnson Matthey's new facility to manufacture heterogeneous catalysts for the bulk chemicals industry

Colours & Coatings Division's sales were 1% down on last year at £241.2 million. Much of the division's operations are based in Europe and sales growth was adversely affected by exchange translation because of the weakness of the euro. On a constant currency basis sales grew by 3%. Operating profits grew by 11% to £27.9 million despite adverse exchange translation. Margins improved to 11.6% as a result of both a shift to higher margin products and continued emphasis on reducing costs.

The Structural Ceramics segment was well up on last year with strong demand for decorative products from tile producers in southern Europe. The Glass business also performed well led by continued growth in sales of automotive glass enamels. The division's inorganic pigments businesses produced encouraging results with good sales of products for woodstains, paints and plastics. The division's organic pigments businesses made a loss of £0.4 million and were sold at the end of the year.

The Tableware business saw a further decline in its market and a rationalisation programme was introduced in the second half of the year to streamline operations by closing one site, reducing administration costs and cutting headcount by more than 200. The cost of this programme is £9.8 million of which £5.2 million had been spent by 31st March 2000. It will give rise to savings of around £4 million in the financial year 2000/01 and £7 million per annum in following years.

Outlook

Prospects for all the group's businesses are very encouraging. We are investing in new technology to maintain continued growth and pursuing a number of opportunities to add further to our core businesses.

Chris Clark
Chief Executive

Financial Review

Review of Results

In the year to 31st March 2000 operating profit from continuing operations rose by 17% to £146.5 million on sales that were 27% up at £3,769 million. On 17th August 1999, Electronic Materials Division (EMD) was sold to AlliedSignal Inc. for US$655 million. EMD made a £0.1 million contribution to profits compared with £22.1 million for the full year 1998/99. Despite the shortfall in EMD, Johnson Matthey earned profits before tax and exceptionals of £143.8 million, 10% up on prior year.

Earnings per share excluding exceptionals were 7% up at 47.5 pence. Including exceptionals earnings per share were 4% up at 51.4 pence. The board is recommending to shareholders a final dividend of 14.2 pence making a total dividend for the year of 20.3 pence, an increase of 7%. The dividend would be covered 2.3 times by earnings.

Sales and Margins

Johnson Matthey's turnover is heavily impacted by the high value of precious metals sold by the group particularly in the Precious Metals Division. The total value of sales each year varies according to the mix of metals sold and level of trading activity. The value of the precious metals included in sales is generally separately invoiced and payment made within a few days. Consequently, although return on sales (operating profit / total external sales) for the precious metals businesses is low, profit growth has been relatively stable and return on investment is high.

To provide a more useful measure of return on sales, the adjacent table shows sales by division excluding the value of precious metals. Total sales for the continuing businesses excluding precious metals were £841.4 million which was 13% up on last year and return on sales averaged 17.4% compared with 16.8% in 1998/99. The group's target for each of its divisions is to achieve a return on sales excluding precious metals in excess of 10%. In 1999/2000 Catalysts & Chemicals and Precious Metals were well above that target, Colours & Coatings showed a good improvement and also came in above the target.

Return on Investment

We set a target of 20% for the pre-tax return on assets (ROA) for all our businesses. This target is based on operating profit divided by average net operating assets (including goodwill). Catalysts & Chemicals and Precious Metals were both well ahead of the group target. Colours & Coatings improved its return but was still a little below the group target.

Return on Sales (ROS)

| | Total External Sales | | ROS | |
	1999	2000	1999	2000
	£ million	£ million	%	%
Catalysts & Chemicals	677	856	11.0	9.9
Precious Metals	2,041	2,672	1.8	1.7
Colours & Coatings	244	241	10.3	11.6
Continuing Businesses	2,963	3,769	4.2	3.9

| | Sales Excluding Precious Metals | | ROS | |
	1999	2000	1999	2000
	£ million	£ million	%	%
Catalysts & Chemicals	408	494	18.2	17.2
Precious Metals	96	114	38.8	40.0
Colours & Coatings	240	234	10.5	11.9
Continuing Businesses	744	841	16.8	17.4

For the continuing businesses return on assets reached 24.2% in 2000. For the group as a whole (including EMD for part of the year), return on assets was 18.4% (see pages 68 and 69). On a post-tax basis this equates to a return of 13.2% which is comfortably above the group's current average long run cost of capital of 10%. Economic value added, which measures earnings after charging the cost of capital, was £32 million including exceptionals compared with £16 million last year.

Exceptional Items

Overall, exceptional items gave rise to a net profit of £13.6 million on a pre-tax basis. Most of the gain arose from the sale of EMD for US$655 million in cash which was completed in August 1999. Some peripheral assets, mainly property, amounting to £13.7 million were retained. The sale generated a net gain of £152.2 million compared with book value. After writing back £123.7 million of goodwill it gave rise to an exceptional profit of £28.5 million.

At the end of the year the group sold its organic pigments businesses in Venezuela and the United States to Dominion Colour Corporation and Continuous Link Color Inc. respectively. The businesses were sold at a loss of £4.5 million compared with book value. After writing back £1.7 million of goodwill the disposals gave rise to an exceptional loss of £6.2 million.

An exceptional charge of £9.8 million has been included in operating profit to cover the cost of the rationalisation programme for the group's Tableware business. An exceptional gain of £1.1 million arose in the year on disposal of surplus properties.

Interest and Exchange Rates

The interest charge fell by £13.5 million to £2.4 million as a result of the interest earned on the sale proceeds of EMD. In the second half of the year the group had net interest income of £2.8 million. Interest for the year includes £2.2 million of leasing costs for gold and silver which increased from £1.3 million last year.

Operating profit from continuing operations rose significantly in North America, Asia and in the rest of the world but fell slightly in Europe. The increase in the rest of the world included additional autocatalyst manufacturing in South Africa and Argentina for the European market.

Exchange rates had a mixed impact on the group's results. The strength of sterling against the euro and other foreign currencies had an adverse impact on the group's businesses that export from the UK, particularly in Colours & Coatings. However the US dollar was also stronger which benefited the translation of our US subsidiaries' earnings. Overall, exchange translation improved profits by £0.2 million compared with last year.

Taxation

The group's average tax rate, excluding exceptional items, was slightly higher than last year at 28.1%. Tax payable in the UK rose compared with last year as a result of the change in the rules for Advance Corporation Tax. Tax payable fell in the US following the disposal of EMD but increased in the rest of the world reflecting the higher level of profit earned in those countries.

Cash Flow

The group's net cash flow for the year was very strong at £393.3 million as a result of the sale of EMD. Free cash flow (net cash flow from operating activities after interest, tax, dividends and capital expenditure) for the continuing businesses was slightly negative at £7.6 million after two years in which the group had generated £54.8 million at this level. The outflow was mainly the result of the sharp increase in platinum group metal prices which occurred towards the end of the year and which resulted in additional funding requirements for debtors and stocks in Catalysts & Chemicals Division.

The group ended the year with net cash of £165.8 million compared with net borrowings of £221.6 million last year. Shareholders' funds rose by £202.6 million to £755.4 million.

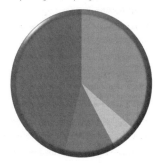

Operating Profit by Region

North America 47% (£69.3 million)
Europe 36% (£52.2 million)
Asia 6% (£8.8 million)
Rest of the World 11% (£16.2 million)

Financial Review

Financial Risk Management

The group uses financial instruments, in particular forward currency contracts and currency swaps, to manage the financial risks associated with the group's underlying business activities and the financing of those activities. The group does not undertake any trading activity in financial instruments. Our Treasury department is run as a service centre rather than a profit centre.

Interest Rate Risk

Following the sale of EMD the group used the proceeds to repay borrowings and deposited the remainder with a range of high quality international banks. The deposits are mainly held in sterling with relatively short maturities. The group occasionally uses interest rate swaps to generate the desired interest profile. The group has £62.7 million (US$100 million) of long term fixed rate borrowings in the form of an issue of US dollar bonds which carry an interest coupon of 6.36%. At 31st March 2000 the group had £53.5 million of floating rate borrowings, largely in the form of foreign currency loans to fund overseas operations (see page 57). A 1% change in all interest rates would have a 1.4% impact on group profit before tax. This is well within the range the group regards as acceptable.

Liquidity Risk

The group's policy on funding capacity is to ensure that we always have sufficient long term funding and committed bank facilities in place to meet foreseeable peak borrowing requirements. Following the sale of EMD the group reduced its committed bank facilities to £40 million. None of these facilities was drawn down at 31st March 2000. The group also has a number of uncommitted facilities and overdraft lines.

Foreign Currency Risk

Johnson Matthey's operations are global in nature with the majority of the group's operating profits earned outside the UK. The group has operations in 34 countries with the largest single investment being in the USA. In order to protect the group's sterling balance sheet and reduce cash flow risk, the group finances most of its US investment by US dollar borrowings. Although most of this funding is obtained by directly borrowing US dollars, some is achieved by using currency swaps to reduce costs and credit exposure. The group also uses local currency borrowings to fund its operations in other countries (see page 57).

The group uses forward exchange contracts to hedge foreign exchange exposures arising on forecast receipts and payments in foreign currencies. Currency options are occasionally used to hedge foreign exchange exposures, usually when the forecast receipt or payment amounts are uncertain. Details of the contracts outstanding on 31st March 2000 are shown on page 59.

Precious Metals Prices

Fluctuations in precious metal prices can have a significant impact on Johnson Matthey's financial results. Our policy for all our manufacturing businesses is to limit this exposure by hedging against future price changes where such hedging can be done at acceptable cost. The group does not take material exposures on metal trading.

All the group's stocks of gold and silver are fully hedged by leasing or forward sales. Currently the majority of the group's platinum group metal stocks are unhedged because of the lack of liquidity in the platinum metal markets.

John Sheldrick
Group Finance Director

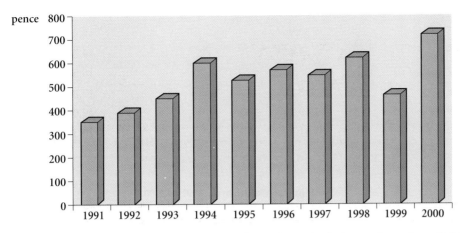

FIGURE 6.2 Johnson Matthey plc year-end 31 March share price 1991 to 2000

(4) Accounting policies

The statement of accounting policies informs readers of the policies the company has pursued in preparation of the report and accounts, and of any deviation from the generally accepted fundamental accounting concepts and conventions. Johnson Matthey devote a large part of their statement of accounting policies to the management of risk, (see pp. 203–4).

Progress check 6.3

What information do the chief executive's statement and the financial review provide and how do these reports differ?

(5) Financial highlights

The section headed financial highlights serves to focus on the headline numbers of sales, profit before tax, earnings per share, dividends, and return on investment. Johnson Matthey's financial highlights are illustrated in both summary and graphical form on p. 205.

Example 6.1

Refer to the Johnson Matthey plc ten-year record, which you will find on pp. 234–5 in the **Exercises** section at the end of this chapter, and present earnings per share and dividends per share for 1991 to 2000

(i)   in tabular form, and

(ii) in one bar chart for comparison.

	Earnings per share (pence)	Dividends per share (pence)
1991	23.6	9.25
1992	25.5	9.65
1993	26.5	10.30

1994	23.1	11.40
1995	32.9	13.50
1996	34.4	14.50
1997	36.0	15.50
1998	48.2	17.80
1999	49.3	19.00
2000	51.4	20.30

(6) Profit and loss account, balance sheet, and cash flow statement

The three financial statements that are shown on pp. 206–8, illustrate Johnson Matthey plc's consolidated profit and loss account, and consolidated cash flow statement for the year to 31 March 2000, and its consolidated and parent company balance sheets as at 31 March 2000.

The profit and loss account is consolidated to include the results of all the companies within the group, which together with the parent company, Johnson Matthey plc, total around 30. Profit is stated both before exceptional items and after exceptional items, and the consolidated profit and loss account also shows previous year comparative figures.

The balance sheet is presented in consolidated form, also showing previous year comparative figures, and includes a separate balance sheet for the parent company only.

The cash flow statement is consolidated to include the cash flows of all the companies within the group, and includes the parent company, Johnson Matthey plc.

We will look at the financial performance of Johnson Matthey in Examples 6.2 and 6.3 using the two approaches to ratio analysis that were mentioned in the introduction to this chapter:

- horizontal analysis, or common size analysis, which provides a line-by-line comparison of the profit and loss account (and balance sheet) with those of the previous year
- vertical analysis, where each item in the profit and loss account (and balance sheet) is expressed as a percentage of the total sales (total assets).

Accounting Policies

for the year ended 31st March 2000

Accounting convention: The accounts are prepared in accordance with applicable accounting standards under the historical cost convention.

Basis of consolidation: The consolidated accounts comprise the accounts of the parent company and all its subsidiary undertakings and include the group's interest in associates and joint ventures.

The results of companies acquired or disposed of in the year are dealt with from or up to the effective date of acquisition or disposal respectively. The net assets of companies acquired are incorporated in the consolidated accounts at their fair values to the group at the date of acquisition.

The parent company has not presented its own profit and loss account as permitted by section 230 of the Companies Act 1985.

Turnover: Comprises all invoiced sales of goods and services exclusive of sales taxes.

Financial instruments: The group uses financial instruments, in particular forward currency contracts and currency swaps, to manage the financial risks associated with the group's underlying business activities and the financing of those activities. The group does not undertake any trading activity in financial instruments.

A discussion of how the group manages its financial risks is included in the Financial Review on page 10. Financial instruments are accounted for as follows:

- Forward exchange contracts are used to hedge foreign exchange exposures arising on forecast receipts and payments in foreign currencies. These forward contracts are revalued to the rates of exchange at the balance sheet date and any aggregate unrealised gains and losses arising on revaluation are included in other debtors / other creditors. At maturity, or when the contract ceases to be a hedge, gains and losses are taken to the profit and loss account.

- Currency options are occasionally used to hedge foreign exchange exposures, usually when the forecast receipt or payment amounts are uncertain. Option premia are recognised at their historic cost in the group balance sheet as prepayments. At maturity, or upon exercise, the option premia net of any realised gains on exercise are taken to the profit and loss account.

- Interest rate swaps are occasionally used to hedge the group's exposure to movements on interest rates. The interest payable or receivable on such swaps is accrued in the same way as interest arising on deposits or borrowings. Interest rate swaps are not revalued to fair value prior to maturity.

- Currency swaps are used as balance sheet hedging instruments to hedge foreign currency assets and borrowings. Currency swaps are used to reduce costs and credit exposure where the group would otherwise have cash deposits and borrowings in different currencies. The difference between spot and forward rate for these contracts is recognised as part of the net interest payable over the period of the contract. These swaps are revalued to the rates of exchange at the balance sheet date and any aggregate unrealised gains or losses arising on revaluation are included in other debtors / other creditors. Realised gains and losses on these currency swaps are taken to reserves in the same way as for the foreign investments and borrowings to which the swaps relate.

The aggregate fair values at the balance sheet date of the hedging instruments described above are disclosed as a note on the accounts.

The group has taken advantage of the exemption available for short term debtors and creditors.

Foreign currencies: Profit and loss accounts in foreign currencies and cash flows included in the cash flow statement are translated into sterling at average exchange rates for the year. Foreign currency assets and liabilities are translated into sterling at the rates of exchange at the balance sheet date. Gains or losses arising on the translation of the net assets of overseas subsidiaries and associated undertakings are taken to reserves, less exchange differences arising on related foreign currency borrowings. Other exchange differences are taken to the profit and loss account.

Research and development expenditure: Charged against profits in the year incurred.

Johnson Matthey **43**

Accounting Policies

for the year ended 31st March 2000

Goodwill: Goodwill arising on acquisitions made after 1st April 1998 is capitalised and amortised over the estimated useful economic life of 20 years. Goodwill previously eliminated against reserves has not been reinstated, but will be charged to the profit and loss account on subsequent disposal of the businesses to which it relates.

Depreciation: Freehold land and certain office buildings are not depreciated. The depreciation charge and accumulated depreciation of these properties would be immaterial and they are reviewed for impairment annually. Other fixed assets are depreciated on a straight line basis at annual rates which vary according to the class of asset, but are typically; leasehold property 2% (or at higher rates based on the life of the lease), freehold buildings 3.33%, plant and equipment 10% - 33%.

Leases: The cost of assets held under finance leases is included under tangible fixed assets and the capital element of future lease payments is included in borrowings. Depreciation is provided in accordance with the group's accounting policy for the class of asset concerned. Lease payments are treated as consisting of capital and interest elements and the interest is charged to the profit and loss account using the annuity method. Rentals under operating leases are expensed as incurred.

Grants in respect of capital expenditure: Grants received in respect of capital expenditure are included in creditors and released to the profit and loss account in equal instalments over the expected useful lives of the related assets.

Precious metal stocks: Stocks of gold, silver and platinum group metals are valued according to the source from which the metal is obtained. Metal which has been purchased and committed to future sales to customers or hedged in metal markets is valued at the price at which it is contractually committed or hedged, adjusted for unexpired contango. Leased metal is valued at market prices at the balance sheet date. Other precious metal stocks owned by the group, which are unhedged, are valued at the lower of cost and net realisable value.

Other stocks: These are valued at the lower of cost, including attributable overheads, and net realisable value.

Deferred taxation: Provided using the liability method on all timing differences to the extent that they are expected to reverse in the foreseeable future.

Pensions and other retirement benefits: The group operates a number of contributory and non-contributory schemes, mainly of the defined benefit type, which require contributions to be made to separately administered funds. The cost of these schemes is charged to the profit and loss account over the service lives of employees in accordance with the advice of the schemes' independent actuaries. Variations from the regular cost are spread over the average expected remaining service lives of current employees.

The cost of post-retirement health care benefits is charged to the profit and loss account on a systematic basis over the expected service lives of employees. The actuarial liability for the cost of these benefits is fully provided for in the balance sheet.

Change of accounting policies: Under the provisions of FRS 15 - 'Tangible Fixed Assets', which the group adopted on 1st April 1999, the group has restated the carrying amount of tangible fixed assets to depreciated historic cost. Consequently the group has restated its comparatives for the year to 31st March 1999. The effect on operating profit is immaterial, but the profit on disposal of surplus properties has been increased by the difference between book value and historical cost at the date of disposal (£6.9 million). Most of this gain (£6.4 million) related to the disposal of the group's former head office site in Hatton Garden. The revaluation reserve, which was £9.0 million at 31st March 1999, has been eliminated. The current year profit on disposal of surplus properties has been increased by £0.7 million following the change in accounting policy.

Financial Highlights

Group Results Summary						
	1999	2000	%		1999	2000
	£ million	£ million	Inc.		£ million	£ million
Total turnover	3,385.4	**3,866.0**	14%	Net cash flow	20.1	393.3
Divisional operating profit						
Catalysts & Chemicals	74.2	84.8	14%	Net (borrowings) / cash	(221.6)	165.8
Precious Metals	37.3	45.4	22%	Shareholders' funds	552.8	755.4
Colours & Coatings	25.1	27.9	11%			
Corporate	(11.6)	(11.6)		Economic value added[2]	16	32
Operating profit-continuing[1]	125.0	146.5	17%	Return on assets (ROA)[2]	16.1%	18.4%
Discontinued operations	22.1	(0.3)				
Operating profit[1]	147.1	146.2	-1%			
Interest	(15.9)	(2.4)				
Profit before tax and exceptionals[1]	131.2	143.8	10%			
	pence	pence				
Earnings per share	49.3	51.4	4%	[1] Excluding exceptional items and goodwill amortisation		
Earnings per share excluding exceptionals[1]	44.3	47.5	7%	[2] See page 8		
Dividend per share	19.0	20.3	7%			

Profit before tax and exceptionals[1]

£ million

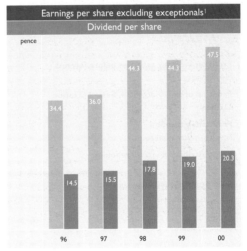

Earnings per share excluding exceptionals[1]
Dividend per share

pence

Consolidated Profit and Loss Account

for the year ended 31st March 2000

	NOTE	2000 Before exceptional items and goodwill amortisation £ million	2000 Exceptional items and goodwill amortisation £ million	2000 Total £ million	1999 Total restated £ million
Turnover	1				
Continuing operations		3,769.0	–	3,769.0	2,962.7
Discontinued operations	3	97.0	–	97.0	422.7
Group turnover		3,866.0	–	3,866.0	3,385.4
Operating profit	1				
Continuing operations before goodwill amortisation		146.5	–	146.5	124.7
Goodwill amortisation		–	(0.2)	(0.2)	–
Continuing operations before exceptional items		146.5	(0.2)	146.3	124.7
Exceptional items	2	–	(9.8)	(9.8)	(1.9)
Total continuing operations		146.5	(10.0)	136.5	122.8
Discontinued operations	3	(0.3)	–	(0.3)	22.1
Group operating profit	4	146.2	(10.0)	136.2	144.9
Share of profit in associates		–	–	–	0.3
Total operating profit		146.2	(10.0)	136.2	145.2
Profit on sale - continuing operations					
Profit on disposal of surplus properties		–	1.1	1.1	7.2
Profit on sale - discontinued operations					
Sale of Electronic Materials	2	–	28.5	28.5	–
Sale of Organic Pigments	2	–	(6.2)	(6.2)	–
Sale of UK Minerals		–	–	–	1.6
Profit on ordinary activities before interest		146.2	13.4	159.6	154.0
Net interest	5	(2.4)	–	(2.4)	(15.9)
Profit on ordinary activities before taxation	6	143.8	13.4	157.2	138.1
Taxation	7	(40.4)	(4.9)	(45.3)	(31.9)
Profit after taxation		103.4	8.5	111.9	106.2
Equity minority interests		(0.2)	–	(0.2)	0.7
Profit attributable to shareholders		103.2	8.5	111.7	106.9
Dividends	9	(44.3)	–	(44.3)	(41.3)
Retained profit for the year	25	58.9	8.5	67.4	65.6

	NOTE			pence	pence
Earnings per ordinary share	8			51.4	49.3
Diluted earnings per ordinary share	8			51.0	49.3
Earnings per ordinary share excluding exceptional items and goodwill amortisation	8			47.5	44.3
Dividend per ordinary share	9			20.3	19.0

The notes on pages 45 to 67 form an integral part of the accounts.

38 Johnson Matthey

Consolidated and Parent Company Balance Sheets

as at 31st March 2000

| | | Group | | Parent company | |
	NOTE	2000 £ million	1999 restated £ million	2000 £ million	1999 restated £ million
Fixed assets					
Goodwill	11	5.1	4.2	–	–
Tangible fixed assets	12	311.3	480.2	112.7	70.6
Investments	13	1.0	1.8	209.9	210.0
		317.4	486.2	322.6	280.6
Current assets					
Stocks	15	253.2	243.7	149.6	87.7
Debtors: due within one year	16	333.5	336.4	546.0	537.5
Debtors: due after one year	16	97.9	94.0	238.0	351.2
Short term investments	17	16.3	9.2	12.2	4.9
Cash at bank and in hand	18	282.0	58.6	208.4	3.9
		982.9	741.9	1,154.2	985.2
Creditors: Amounts falling due within one year					
Borrowings and finance leases	18	(46.2)	(165.6)	(24.5)	(102.7)
Precious metal leases	20	(60.6)	(24.7)	(76.8)	(29.1)
Other creditors	21	(315.6)	(289.2)	(602.4)	(298.6)
Net current assets		560.5	262.4	450.5	554.8
Total assets less current liabilities		877.9	748.6	773.1	835.4
Creditors: Amounts falling due after more than one year					
Borrowings and finance leases	18	(70.0)	(114.6)	(62.7)	(106.8)
Other creditors	21	(0.2)	(1.1)	(1.2)	(0.3)
Provisions for liabilities and charges	22	(47.8)	(74.3)	(17.9)	(18.5)
Net assets		759.9	558.6	691.3	709.8
Capital and reserves					
Called up share capital	24	221.1	218.5	221.1	218.5
Share premium account	25	116.7	103.9	116.7	103.9
Associates' reserves	25	(0.1)	0.1	–	–
Profit and loss account	25	417.7	230.3	353.5	387.4
Shareholders' funds		755.4	552.8	691.3	709.8
Equity minority interests		4.5	5.8	–	–
		759.9	558.6	691.3	709.8

The accounts were approved by the Board of Directors on 6th June 2000 and signed on its behalf by:

C R N Clark

Directors

J N Sheldrick

The notes on pages 45 to 67 form an integral part of the accounts.

Consolidated Cash Flow Statement

for the year ended 31st March 2000

	NOTE	2000 £ million	1999 £ million
Reconciliation of operating profit to net cash inflow from operating activities			
Operating profit		136.2	144.9
Depreciation and amortisation charges		46.6	64.3
Profit on sale of tangible fixed assets and investments		(0.9)	(0.4)
(Increase) / decrease in owned stocks		(26.7)	4.8
Increase in debtors		(77.2)	(23.9)
Increase / (decrease) in creditors and provisions		52.3	(13.7)
Net cash inflow from operating activities		130.3	176.0
Cash Flow Statement			
Net cash inflow from operating activities		130.3	176.0
Dividends received from associates		0.1	0.1
Returns on investments and servicing of finance	27	(2.5)	(16.5)
Taxation		(33.5)	(32.4)
Capital expenditure and financial investment	27	(65.7)	(61.4)
Acquisitions and disposals			
Acquisitions	27	(2.9)	(8.7)
Disposals	27	393.7	4.4
Net cash inflow / (outflow) for acquisitions and disposals		390.8	(4.3)
Equity dividends paid		(42.2)	(39.8)
Net cash inflow before use of liquid resources and financing		377.3	21.7
Management of liquid resources	27	(169.8)	4.9
Financing			
Issue and purchase of share capital	27	8.0	(1.6)
Decrease in borrowings and finance leases	27	(163.7)	(22.4)
Net cash outflow from financing		(155.7)	(24.0)
Increase in cash in the period		51.8	2.6
Reconciliation of net cash flow to movement in net debt			
Increase in cash in the period		51.8	2.6
Cash outflow from movement in borrowings and finance leases	28	163.7	22.4
Cash outflow / (inflow) from term deposits included in liquid resources		169.8	(4.9)
Change in net debt resulting from cash flows		385.3	20.1
Borrowings disposed of with subsidiaries		8.0	–
Translation difference	28	(5.9)	(16.6)
Movement in net debt in year		387.4	3.5
Net debt at beginning of year	28	(221.6)	(225.1)
Net funds / (debt) at end of year	28	165.8	(221.6)

The notes on pages 45 to 67 form an integral part of the accounts.

Horizontal analysis

We introduced the technique of horizontal analysis in Chapter 5. The following example illustrates the technique applied to a summary of the Johnson Matthey plc profit and loss account for the years to 31 March 2000 and 31 March 1999.

Example 6.2

We are required to prepare an horizontal analysis using a summary of the profit and loss account results for Johnson Matthey plc for 1999 and 2000, using 1999 as the base year.

Johnson Matthey plc
Summary consolidated profit and loss account for the year ended 31 March 2000

Figures in £m		2000		1999
Turnover				
Continuing operations		3,769.0		2,962.7
Discontinued operations		97.0		422.7
		3,866.0		3,385.4
Operating profit before exceptional items	146.0		147.1	
Exceptional items	(9.8)		(1.9)	
Operating profit				
Continuing operations	136.5		123.1	
Discontinued operations	(0.3)		22.1	
		136.2		145.2
Profit on disposals				
Continuing operations	1.1		7.2	
Discontinued operations	22.3		1.6	
		23.4		8.8
Profit on ordinary activities before interest		159.6		154.0
Net interest		(2.4)		(15.9)
Profit on ordinary activities before taxation		157.2		138.1
Taxation		(45.3)		(31.9)
Profit after tax		111.9		106.2
Equity minority interests		(0.2)		0.7
Profit attributable to shareholders		111.7		106.9
Dividends		(44.3)		(41.3)
Retained profit for the year		67.4		65.6

◀ Answer

Johnson Matthey plc
Consolidated profit and loss account for the year ended 31 March 2000

Horizontal analysis	1999	2000
Turnover		
Continuing operations	100.0	127.2
Discontinued operations	100.0	23.0
Total turnover	100.0	114.2
Operating profit before exceptional items	100.0	99.3
Exceptional items	100.0	515.8
Operating profit		
Continuing operations	100.0	110.9
Discontinued operations	100.0	(1.4)
Total operating profit	100.0	93.8
Profit on disposals		
Continuing operations	100.0	15.3
Discontinued operations	100.0	1,393.8
Total profit on disposals	100.0	265.9
Profit on ordinary activities before interest	100.0	103.6
Net interest	100.0	15.1
Profit on ordinary activities before taxation	100.0	113.8
Taxation	100.0	142.0
Profit after tax	100.0	105.4
Equity minority interests	100.0	(28.6)
Profit attributable to shareholders	100.0	104.5
Dividends	100.0	107.3
Retained profit for the year	100.0	102.7

Example 6.2 has considered only two years, and has used 1999 as the base year 100. This means, for example:

If turnover for 1999 of £3,385.4m = 100

Then turnover for 2000 of £3,866.0m = $\dfrac{£3,866.0m \times 100}{£3,385.4m} = 114.2$

Subsequent years may be compared with 1999 as base 100, using the same sort of calculation.

This technique is particularly useful to make a line-by-line comparison of a company's accounts for each accounting period over say five or ten years, using the first year as the base year. When we look at a set of accounts we may by observation automatically carry out this process of assessing percentage changes in performance over time. However, presentation of the information in tabular form, for a number of years, gives a very clear picture of trends in performance in each area of activity and may provide the basis for further analysis.

We can see from the above horizontal analysis how the net profit for the year has been derived compared with that for 1999. Despite an increase of 14.2% in sales, operating profit was reduced by 6.2%. Before allowing for exceptional costs, operating profit had reduced by 0.7%. Johnson Matthey were able to increase the level of profit before tax through gains from disposals of £23.4m (165.9% above the previous year), and reductions in net interest from £15.9m down to £2.4m.

Profit before tax for 2000 was 13.8% above 1999. Higher average corporation tax levels incurred by the company reduced the amount of profit attributable to shareholders for 2000 to 4.5% above that earned in 1999.

Progress check 6.4

What can an horizontal analysis of the information contained in the financial statements of a company add to that provided from ratio analysis?

Vertical analysis

Example 6.3 uses total turnover (**continuing operations** plus **discontinued operations**) as the basis for calculation. The following analysis confirms the conclusions drawn from the horizontal analysis.

Example 6.3

We are required to prepare a vertical analysis using a summary of the consolidated profit and loss account results for Johnson Matthey plc for 1999 and 2000.

Answer

Johnson Matthey plc
Consolidated profit and loss account for the year ended 31 March 2000

Vertical analysis	2000	1999
Total turnover	100.0	100.0
Operating profit before exceptional items	3.8	4.3
Exceptional items	(0.3)	(0.0)
Operating profit		
Continuing operations	3.5	3.6
Discontinued operations	(0.0)	0.7
Total operating profit	3.5	4.3
Profit on disposals		
Continuing operations	0.0	0.2
Discontinued operations	0.6	0.1
Total profit on disposals	0.6	0.3
Profit on ordinary activities before interest	4.1	4.6
Net interest	(0.0)	(0.5)
Profit on ordinary activities before taxation	4.1	4.1

Taxation	(1.2)	(0.9)
Profit after tax	2.9	3.2
Equity minority interests	(0.0)	0.0
Profit attributable to shareholders	2.9	3.2
Dividends	(1.2)	(1.2)
Retained profit for the year	1.7	2.0

Operating profit before exceptional items was reduced from 4.3% in 1999 to 3.8% in 2000, and after exceptional items from 4.3% to 3.5% of sales. There was an improvement in profit on disposals from 0.3% in 1999 to 0.6% in 2000, which gave a profit before interest of 4.1% (1999 4.6%).

Interest charges were reduced from the previous year, in both value and percentage of sales, at 0.0% (1999 0.5%), with profit after tax reduced to 2.9% (1999 3.2%).

An increased burden of taxation appears to be one of the main reasons for the reduction in profit attributable to shareholders from 3.2% in 1999 to 2.9% in 2000. Dividends were 1.2% of sales (1999 1.2%), giving a retained profit for the year of 1.7% (1999 2.0%).

Progress check 6.5

What can a vertical analysis of the information contained in the financial statements of a company add to the information provided from an horizontal analysis and ratio analysis?

(7) Notes on the accounts

The section headed Notes on the Accounts in the annual report and accounts contains information that must be reported additional to, and in support of, the financial statements. This may be used to comment on financial performance. Generally, the information disclosed in notes to the accounts includes:

- segmental information – analysis by business and geographical area relating to turnover, operating profit and net assets
- exceptional items
- discontinued operations
- operating profit
- net interest
- profit before taxation
- taxation
- earnings per share
- dividends
- employees/directors information – employee numbers, costs, and retirement benefits
- fixed assets
- stocks

- debtors
- investments
- borrowings
- derivatives and financial instruments
- creditors
- finance leases
- provisions
- share capital
- reserves
- commitments and **contingent liabilities**
- cash flows
- net debt
- acquisitions and disposals
- **post balance sheet events**

Segmental reporting

The first note in the notes on the accounts in Johnson Matthey's report and accounts for 2000 is headed segmental information. Accounting standard SSAP 25, Segmental Reporting, requires large companies to disclose segmental information by each class of business, and by geographical region, unless the directors feel that by doing so they may seriously damage the competitive position of the company. This analysis is required in order that users of financial information may carry out more meaningful financial analysis.

Most large companies are usually comprised of diverse businesses supplying different products and services, rather than being engaged in a single type of business. Each type of business activity may have

- a different structure
- different levels of profitability
- different levels of growth potential
- different levels of risk exposure

The financial statements of such diversified companies are consolidated to include all business activities, which is a potential problem for the users of financial information. For analysis and interpretation of financial performance, aggregate figures are not particularly useful for the following reasons:

- difficulties in evaluation of performance of a business which has interests that are diverse from the aggregated financial information
- difficulties of comparison of trends over time and comparison between companies because the various activities undertaken by the company are likely to differ in size and range in comparison with other businesses
- differences in conditions between different geographical markets, in terms of levels of risk, profitability and growth
- differences in conditions between different geographical markets, in terms of political and social factors, environmental factors, currencies and **inflation** rates

Segmental reporting analysis enables

● the further analysis of segmental performance to determine more accurately the likely growth prospects for the business as a whole

● evaluation of the impact on the company of changes in conditions relating to particular activities

● improvements in internal management performance, because it may be monitored through disclosure of segmental information to shareholders

● evaluation of the acquisition and disposal performance of the company.

Example 6.4

The information in the table below relates to global sales by Guinness plc for the years 2000 and 1999.

Figures in £m	2000	1999
Global Sales	4,730	4,681
Asia/Pacific – B	349	324
Asia/Pacific – S	454	426
North America – B	166	151
North America – S	491	551
Rest of Europe – B	1,025	954
Rest of Europe – S	723	741
Rest of the World – S	402	384
Rest of the World – B	203	198
UK – B	519	495
UK – S	398	457

S = spirits B = beer

(i) Using the information provided you are required to prepare a simple table that compares the sales for 1999 with the sales for the year 2000.

(ii) Discuss how a simple sales analysis can provide an investor with information that is more useful than just global sales for the year.

Answer

(i)

Global sales	2000 £m Spirits	2000 v 1999 %	2000 £m Beers	2000 v 1999 %	2000 £m Total	2000 v 1999 %	1999 £m Spirits	1999 £m Beers	1999 £m Total
UK	398	−12.9	519	+4.8	917	−3.7	457	495	952
Rest of Europe	723	−2.4	1,025	+7.4	1,748	+3.1	741	954	1,695
North America	491	−10.9	166	+9.9	657	−6.4	551	151	702
Asia/Pacific	454	+6.6	349	+7.7	803	+7.1	426	324	750
Rest of the World	402	+4.7	203	+2.5	605	+3.9	384	198	582
Total global sales					4,730	+1.0			4,681

(ii) Numbers that are blandly presented in a global format do not usually reveal trends. Analysis of information by area, for example, may reveal trends and may illustrate the impact of new policies or the changes in specific economic environments. The analysis of the Guinness sales for two years shows

- in which geographical area sales have increased or decreased
- in which products sales have increased or decreased.

Analysis of the results over several years is usually needed to provide meaningful trend information as a basis for investigation into the reasons for increases and decreases.

Class of business is a part of the overall business, which can be identified as providing a separate product or service, or group of related products or services. A geographical segment may comprise an individual country or a group of countries in which the business operates.

If a company operates in two or more classes of business activity or two or more geographical segments, there should normally be separate disclosure of information for each segment, which should include:

- sales to external customers and sales to other segments within the business, according to origin, and also by destinations of the goods and services if they are substantially different from the geographical region from which they were supplied
- operating profit before accounting for finance charges, taxation, minority interests and extraordinary items
- net assets.

Let's take a look at Johnson Matthey's segmental reporting, (see pp. 216–7). This may be used to provide even more useful information through horizontal and vertical analysis of the numbers. Such an analysis over a five or ten-year period would be particularly useful to identify trends in performance, and changes that may have taken place in the activities of the business and the areas of the world in which the company has operated.

There are many problems relating to the principle of disclosure of segmental information, some of which we have already identified:

- directors may be reluctant to disclose information that may damage the competitive position of the company – foreign competitors may not have to disclose similar data
- segmental information may not be useful since the total company results are what should be relevant to shareholders
- some users of information may not be sufficiently financially expert to avoid being confused by the segmental information
- conglomerates may choose not to disclose segmental information, whereas a single activity company by definition is unable to hide anything.

There are, in addition, some accounting problems concerned with the preparation of segmental reports:

- identification of business class and geographical segments is not defined in SSAP 25, but is left to the judgement of the directors of the company
- lack of definition of segments results in difficulty in comparison of companies
- difficulties in analysis and apportionment of costs that are common between activities and geographical regions
- difficulties in the treatment of costs of transfers of goods and services between segments.

Notes on the Accounts

for the year ended 31st March 2000

1 Segmental information

	Turnover		Operating profit		Net operating assets	
	2000	1999 restated	2000	1999 restated	2000	1999 restated
Activity analysis	£ million	£ million	£ million	£ million	£ million	£ million
Catalysts & Chemicals	856.2	677.2	84.8	74.2	350.0	298.6
Precious Metals	2,671.6	2,041.3	45.4	37.3	76.5	75.5
Colours & Coatings	241.2	244.2	27.9	25.1	170.4	169.7
Corporate	–	–	(11.6)	(11.6)	(2.8)	(18.3)
	3,769.0	2,962.7	146.5	125.0	594.1	525.5
Discontinued operations	97.0	422.7	(0.3)	22.1	–	254.7
Total turnover	3,866.0	3,385.4				
Goodwill amortisation			(0.2)	–		
Exceptional items included in total operating profit (note 2)			(9.8)	(1.9)		
			136.2	145.2	594.1	780.2
Other exceptional items			23.4	8.8		
Net interest			(2.4)	(15.9)		
Profit on ordinary activities before taxation			157.2	138.1		
Net cash / (borrowings and finance leases)					165.8	(221.6)
Net assets					759.9	558.6

	Turnover		Operating profit		Net operating assets	
	2000	1999 restated	2000	1999 restated	2000	1999 restated
Geographical analysis by origin	£ million	£ million	£ million	£ million	£ million	£ million
Europe	2,450.5	2,087.7	52.2	58.1	365.3	350.6
North America	1,052.0	807.8	69.3	54.1	126.0	90.4
Asia	887.2	505.1	8.8	3.6	57.0	38.3
Rest of the World	195.8	159.5	16.2	9.2	45.8	46.2
	4,585.5	3,560.1	146.5	125.0	594.1	525.5
Discontinued operations	110.2	451.0	(0.3)	22.1	–	254.7
	4,695.7	4,011.1				
Less inter-segment sales	(829.7)	(625.7)				
Total turnover	3,866.0	3,385.4				
Goodwill amortisation			(0.2)	–		
Exceptional items included in total operating profit (note 2)			(9.8)	(1.9)		
			136.2	145.2	594.1	780.2
Other exceptional items			23.4	8.8		
Net interest			(2.4)	(15.9)		
Profit on ordinary activities before taxation			157.2	138.1		
Net cash / (borrowings and finance leases)					165.8	(221.6)
Net assets					759.9	558.6

Notes on the Accounts

for the year ended 31st March 2000

1 Segmental information continued

	2000	1999 restated
External turnover by geographical destination	£ million	£ million
Europe	1,306.4	1,711.1
North America	1,261.0	1,147.4
Asia	1,083.9	349.3
Rest of the World	214.7	177.6
Total turnover	3,866.0	3,385.4

Turnover by destination relating to the United Kingdom amounted to £831.5 million (1999 £825.4 million).

The group sold its Electronic Materials Division and Organic Pigments businesses during the year and their results are reported as discontinued operations (note 3).

2 Exceptional items

An exceptional charge of £9.8 million (1999 £1.9 million) has been included in total operating profit. This comprises:

	2000	1999
	£ million	£ million
Cost of rationalising Tableware	(9.8)	–
Profit on sale of shares in Ballard Power Systems, Inc.	–	3.0
Loss on closure of Australian autocatalyst manufacturing business	–	(2.4)
Closure costs on withdrawal from plating and bushings manufacture	–	(2.5)
	(9.8)	(1.9)

These charges arise in Europe (£9.2 million, 1999 £0.4 million credit), North America (£ nil, 1999 £0.3 million), Asia (£0.6 million, 1999 £0.1 million) and the Rest of the World (£ nil, 1999 £1.9 million).

The sale of the group's Electronic Materials Division produced a net profit of £28.5 million, and the sale of the group's Organic Pigments businesses produced a net loss of £6.2 million (note 30).

3 Discontinued operations

	Turnover		Operating profit	
	2000	1999	2000	1999
	£ million	£ million	£ million	£ million
Electronic Materials (note 30)	91.6	414.7	0.1	22.1
Organic Pigments (note 30)	5.4	6.3	(0.4)	(0.3)
UK Minerals (note 30)	–	1.7	–	0.3
	97.0	422.7	(0.3)	22.1

Progress check 6.6

Describe what is meant by segmental reporting and to whom is it useful?

Example 6.5

Refer to note 1 in the Johnson Matthey plc Notes on the Accounts in their annual report and accounts 2000 and identify activity – turnover for 1999 and 2000.

You are required to present the data in both pie chart and bar chart format.

What do the charts you have prepared tell you about JM's sales for 1999 and 2000?

Answer

Johnson Matthey plc turnover 2000

Johnson Matthey plc turnover 1999

Johnson Matthey plc turnover 1999 and 2000

The pie charts give a broad indication of turnover by type of business, and show that for both years precious metals provide just below three quarters of the turnover, catalysts and chemicals provide around one quarter of the turnover and colours and coatings is a small sector that provides the balance. The bar chart is probably more useful in showing more clearly that turnover from the two largest sectors has increased in 2000 over 1999 but the smallest sector has remained at the same volume.

(8) Environmental reporting

An inspection of Johnson Matthey's report and accounts 2000 will reveal that environmental issues and the health and safety of its employees, customers, and the community, ranks highly amongst the company's priorities. This is demonstrated in the coverage given to such issues in the chairman's statement and in the two separate pages devoted to these issues (see pp. 220–1).

Throughout the past ten years or so companies have started to show greater interest about their position with regard to environmental issues. General corporate awareness has increased as to how the adoption of particular policies may have adverse social and environmental effects. Environmental issues naturally focus on our inability to sustain our use of non-renewable resources, the disappearance of the ozone layer and forestation, pollution and waste treatment. Social issues may include problems associated with race, gender, disability, sexual orientation, and age, and the way that companies manage bullying, the incidence of accidents, employee welfare, training and development.

The increase in awareness of environmental and social issues has followed the concern that the focus of traditional reporting has been weighted too heavily towards the requirements of shareholders, with too little regard for the other stakeholders. This has led to an over-emphasis on the financial performance, particularly the profitability, of the business. The accountancy profession and other interested parties have given thought to the widening of the annual report and accounts to meet the requirements of all stakeholders, and not just the shareholders of the business.

There is currently no consensus of 'best practice' in the area of social and environmental reporting. Neither is there a compulsory requirement for companies to include such statements in their annual reports and accounts. However, most large companies have reacted positively to the need for such reporting, although the quality, style and content, and the motives for inclusion, vary greatly. Motives may range from simple reassurance to attempts to mould and change opinion, and political lobbying.

Most companies that include environmental reporting in their annual reports and accounts have yet to get beyond the outline of environmental and social policies. Some companies include reports expanding on these policies in qualitative terms which explain the performance of the business in its compliance with national and international standards. Few companies have yet taken the next step to provide detailed quantitative reports of targets, and performance and the financial impact of environmental issues.

Environmental reporting is still in its infancy. It seems likely that as the focus on standardisation of targets, indicators and audit of environmental performance increases, then the pressure for wider reporting will increase, and be supported by an environmental financial reporting standard.

Environment, Health and Safety

Johnson Matthey places high priority on its responsibility for the environment and the health and safety of its employees, customers and the community.

The Group Managing Director retains overall board responsibility for Environment, Health and Safety (EHS) issues. EHS risks are reviewed by the EHS Committee, which meets every two months and reports to the board. The EHS Committee is chaired by the Group Managing Director and consists of divisional directors and the EHS Director. The EHS Committee has approved the group EHS policies. The policies, and accompanying guidance notes, reflect relevant legislation and best practice, and are issued to all site managers and EHS personnel. A full review of the policies is made triennially, with interim amendments made when needed. The overall aim is to ensure consistent standards at all JM sites around the world and to promote continuous improvement, based on careful risk assessment and comprehensive EHS management systems. The high level summary policies are set out adjacent.

Each of our locations around the world is required to formulate its own particular arrangements, including performance targets, to meet the objectives set out in the corporate policies and to ensure that all employees have received adequate training on the policies and their individual responsibilities. A number of current environmental projects are discussed on page 21.

The group EHS department audits all operating sites against the policies on a regular basis, with the frequency dependant on the nature of operations at the individual sites. During 1999/2000, 24 EHS audits were carried out with exit interviews held with site management on key points. Audit reports are distributed to site and divisional management, and important issues arising from audits are discussed by the EHS Committee. A further 20 occupational health visits were made by the Group Occupational Physician. A monthly

report on site, divisional and group health and safety performance is prepared for discussion at the EHS Committee, and circulated to all site management. Environmental data is collected and analysed internally on an annual basis.

Environment Policy

- Ensure that site operations meet legal and company requirements.
- Design and manufacture products to optimise their environmental performance.
- Eliminate all polluting releases from operations. Where elimination is not presently achievable, the intermediate goal is reduction.
- Promote high standards of energy management.
- Undertake comprehensive waste management programmes based on the following hierarchy of options – prevent, minimise, re-use, recycle and safely dispose.
- Minimise the impacts of past, present and future operations through effective planning and adequate provision of resources.
- Ensure that operations cause minimal visual impact or nuisance to the public.

Health and Safety Policy

- Ensure that all locations meet all legal and company health and safety requirements.
- Manufacture current products in a manner which ensures a safe working environment through each phase of the production process.
- Strive toward an end goal of eliminating unsafe practices at all locations.
- Promote high standards of safety awareness through employee involvement and management commitment at each location.
- Operate processes at all times to minimise danger to the surrounding community.
- Provide immediate and effective response in event of accidents and emergencies.

Once again, a pair of swans has returned to Mossops Creek alongside Johnson Matthey's Brimsdown refinery to rear their young

During 1999, the Chemicals business unit at Royston, UK, initiated a four year £2 million project with the dual aims of reducing gaseous emissions, and minimising waste. The project to reduce gaseous emissions has involved, in the first instance, installation of additional abatement and monitoring plant. Ten-fold reductions in emissions of acid gases have already been achieved, with further planned improvements over the next phases. The waste minimisation aspect will focus on the recovery and recycling of waste streams throughout the processes. To date, a significant reduction in reagent consumption has been achieved in the platinum group metals refinery, together with a decrease in the numbers of effluent tankers transporting waste away from the site. Additional waste minimisation opportunities are actively being planned for the next phases of this project.

Johnson Matthey's Environmental Products business provides unique catalytic solutions to air quality problems caused by emissions from industrial processes and power generation plants. The opportunity to utilise this internal expertise was taken in a recent project to fit a selective catalytic reduction system at Johnson Matthey's autocatalyst plant at Devon, USA. The system has delivered not only a 92% reduction in NOx emissions, but also resulted in significant operational benefits.

This year, Noble Metals UK, part of the Precious Metals Division, became the second Johnson Matthey business unit to achieve ISO14001, joining the Chemicals business unit (Royston and Brimsdown sites, UK). As part of ISO14001, all employees receive training to ensure they are aware of environmental issues affecting the business, and progress is being made towards a number of targets for environmental improvements at the facility. Some projects, such as a review of the degreasing process, will result in a number of benefits including reductions in emissions, cost savings and a better workplace environment for employees.

Colours & Coatings have completed a project this year to reduce gaseous emissions during production of base colours. This multidisciplinary project brought together production management, sales, environmental management and research in a comprehensive review of the existing product range, looking at raw material selection, process optimisation and abatement systems. Where possible, products have been reformulated to avoid use of problematic ingredients, or improvements to process management have been made to reduce emissions. For the products where this has not been possible, abatement systems have been upgraded, and in a few cases products removed entirely from the product range.

Progress check 6.7

What is environmental reporting and why is it becoming increasingly important to companies?

(9) Directors' report

The directors' report includes financial and non-financial information, and it is a statutory requirement for a copy of this report, along with the accounts of the business, to be sent to shareholders. The directors' report includes a great deal of detail, for example:

- details of the principal activities of the business
- information about directors and their share ownership
- details about auditors
- company employment policy
- proposed dividends payable to shareholders
- major fixed assets acquisitions and disposals, and changes in valuation
- changes to share capital
- charitable and political donations made by the company.

The Johnson Matthey plc directors' report (see pp. 224–5), includes a section on each of the headings we have outlined above. In addition, it includes a section on directors' (lack of) material interests in contracts, and the group policy on payment of commercial debts. The inclusion of the company's 'creditor days' performance is important. There has been general pressure for companies to rely less on funding from extended credit from suppliers, over and above agreed terms.

Following the publication of the Cadbury Committee report in 1992, the directors' report now includes a section on corporate governance (see Chapter 7), and includes details about the company's system of internal control, and its various committees, for example the remuneration committee. Johnson Matthey have reported on the many committees they have in place, and their functions:

- chief executive's committee: strategy, planning and executive management
- audit committee: financial reporting, corporate control, internal and external audit
- nomination committee: appointment of executive and non-executive directors
- management development and remuneration committee: senior management remuneration.

Inflation and reporting

Inflation is a general increase in the price level over time. We will consider the impact of inflation on the financial statements prepared under the traditional, historical cost convention. In this book we will not cover in detail the alternative approaches to reporting the effect of inflation, other than to highlight the level of awareness of the problem. The accountancy profession has, over the years, considered many proposals of methods to try and deal with inflation-related problems requiring financial reports to reflect the effects of inflation. The proposals relating to the treatment of inflation in financial reporting have revolved around two schools of thought:

- the purchasing power approach, using a price index like the Retail Price Index, to adjust the historical costs of transactions
- the current cost accounting approach, which requires fixed assets and stocks to be included in the accounts at their current value rather than their historical cost.

Progress check 6.8

What purpose does the directors' report serve and what information does it usually include?

We have previously discussed the reasons for using money as the unit of measurement, which include its properties as a medium of exchange and a store of value. Its use implies some stability in its value, which in the real world is patently not the case. One £ held today does not have the same value as one £ held in a year's time; it will purchase less in a year's time despite the relatively low levels of inflation prevailing in the UK over recent years – but note how in the mid-1970s the inflation level reached nearly 25% per annum!

The basic problem of inflation in financial reporting is that it tends to overstate profit calculated using traditional historical costs. In periods of inflation the impact on profit is seen in four key areas:

- borrowing and extended credit received are worth less in real terms when settled compared to when the borrowing took place or the credit was received, which is a gain for the business
- financial investments made and extended credit allowed are worth less in real terms when settled compared to when the investments took place or the credit was granted, which is a loss for the business
- depreciation of fixed assets is understated, being based on fixed assets' historical costs and so when assets eventually have to be replaced the replacement cost will be higher, for which the company may have provided insufficient cash resources
- closing stocks will be more likely to have higher values, on a like-for-like basis, compared with opening stocks and so profit may be overstated, but the pressure on cash resources will be felt when stocks have been sold and then need to be replaced at higher prices.

It is important for the non-accounting specialist to be aware that the published financial statements of UK limited companies have not been adjusted to allow for the effects of inflation. Over extended periods there is therefore significant distortion in the accounting information that has been presented based on historical costs. However, the non-specialist may be assured that the accountancy profession continues to grapple with the problem of inflation in financial reporting.

Progress check 6.9

Why should users of financial information be aware of the effects of inflation on financial reporting?

Directors' Report

The directors submit to shareholders their one hundred and ninth annual report, together with the audited accounts of the group for the year ended 31st March 2000. Pages 1 to 37 are an integral part of the report.

Principal Activities

The group's principal activities are summarised on page 11.

Dividends

The interim dividend of 6.1 pence per share, up 0.4 pence, was paid in February 2000. A final dividend of 14.2 pence per share, up 0.9 pence, is being proposed to shareholders as Resolution 2 at the Annual General Meeting (AGM), making a total for the year of 20.3 pence, an increase of 7% over last year. Dividends for the year total £44.3 million.

Share Capital

Allotments of ordinary shares of £1 each of the company were made during the year as set out in note 24 on page 61.

In accordance with the resolution approved by shareholders at the 1999 Annual General Meeting, the company's share capital was reduced on 17th September 1999, by the cancellation of the 450,000 5% (prior to 6th April 1999, 3.5%) cumulative preference shares (300,000 of which had been issued) and the nominal value (£0.3 million) repaid to the shareholders.

The board has decided to seek shareholders' approval to renew the authority for the company to make purchases of its own ordinary shares through the market. Johnson Matthey has no present intention to exercise this authority and would only do so in circumstances where the directors believe that it would result in an increase in earnings per share and is in the best interests of the shareholders generally.

The resolutions relating to the company's share capital to be proposed at the AGM are set out in the circular enclosed with this annual report.

Employment Policies

It is the policy of the group to train and develop employees at all levels so that group objectives can be met. We recruit, train and manage our employees regardless of sex, ethnic origin or religion. Employees who become disabled and disabled people are offered employment consistent with their capabilities. Close attention under the direction of the Management Development and Remuneration Committee is given to the group's recruitment and training procedures as well as career development to meet current and future group requirements. The group's Training and Development of People policy is set out on page 24.

Johnson Matthey recognises the importance of effective employee communications. Information and comment is exchanged with employees through the company's in-house magazine, regular news bulletins, presentations to staff and team briefings.

45% of employees worldwide are shareholders in Johnson Matthey through the group's employee share schemes, which held 2,639,638 shares (1.19% of ordinary share capital) at 31st May 2000. A total of 677 current and former directors and employees hold options over 5,274,164 shares through the company's executive share option schemes. A total of 882,466 shares have been allocated to directors and key executives under the long term incentive plan.

Directors' Report

Directors

Details of the directors of the company are shown on pages 22 and 23. Mr N A P Carson and Mr D W Morgan, appointed to the board on 1st August 1999, offer themselves for election at the forthcoming AGM. In accordance with the company's Articles of Association, Mr D G Titcombe (who is employed on a service contract subject to two years' notice), Mr H M P Miles (Chairman) and Mr P F Retief retire by rotation and, being eligible, offer themselves for re-election at the AGM. Mr G D Wells, who was a director throughout the financial year, will retire from the board on 31st July 2000. Directors interests in the company's shares are detailed in the Remuneration Report on pages 30 to 37.

Directors' Material Interests in Contracts

Other than service contracts, no director had any material interest in any contract of significance with any group company at any time during the year.

Substantial Shareholdings

The company has been advised of the following notifiable interests in its ordinary share capital as at 31st May 2000:

Schroder Investment Management Ltd	17.33%
Fidelity Investments	7.22%

The directors are not aware of any other notifiable holdings of 3% or more of the ordinary share capital of the company.

Auditor

In accordance with section 384 of the Companies Act 1985, a resolution is to be proposed at the forthcoming AGM for the reappointment of KPMG Audit Plc as auditor of the company.

Policy on Payment of Commercial Debts

The group's policy in relation to the payment of all suppliers (set out in its Group Control Manual, which is distributed to all group operations) is that payment should be made within the credit terms agreed with the supplier. At 31st March 2000, the company's aggregate level of "creditor days" amounted to 6 days. Creditor days are calculated by dividing the aggregate of the amount which were owed to trade creditors at the end of the year by the aggregate of the amounts the company was invoiced by suppliers during the year and multiplying by 365 to express the ratio as a number of days.

Donations

During the year the group donated £208,000 (1999 £267,000) to charitable organisations, of which £168,000 (1999 £198,000) was in the UK. There were no political donations made in the year (1999 £ nil).

This report was approved by the directors on 6th June 2000 and is signed on their behalf by:

Simon Farrant
Company Secretary

Value added statements

Value added is a measure of the wealth created by a company through its activities. It is the difference between the value of its sales and the cost of the materials and services that it has bought in.

The **value added statement** is effectively a rearrangement of the profit and loss account. It shows how value added is distributed among the relevant parties:

- employees
- lenders
- shareholders
- Government

and the amount to provide maintenance and expansion of the business.

The value added statement has often been compared with a cake or a pie (see Fig. 6.3 and Fig. 6.4), with interested parties asking 'are we getting our fair share of the cake?' This question is often the basis of trade union employee wage negotiations with companies.

The Accounting Standards Committee in 1975 published *The Corporate Report*, which described the value added statement as 'the simplest and most immediate way of putting profit into a proper perspective *vis à vis* the whole enterprise as a collective effort of capital, management and employees'. The value added statement has certain advantages as a business performance measure:

- simple to calculate
- enables comparison between companies with different activities
- improves relationships between shareholders, managers and employees
- cannot be manipulated to the same extent as accounting profit
- enables further analysis for example vertical analysis against turnover
- lends itself to integration with employee incentive schemes.

Example 6.6

We are required to prepare a value added statement for Johnson Matthey plc using the consolidated profit and loss accounts, and consolidated cash flow statements for 2000 and 1999. Employee costs for 2000 were £187.6m (1999, £263.4m).

Answer

Johnson Matthey plc
Consolidated value added statement for the year ended 31 March 2000

Figures in £m	2000	1999
Turnover (from the consolidated profit and loss account)	3,866.0	3,385.4
Bought in materials and services (balancing number)	3,472.4	2,903.0
Value added	393.6	482.4
Applied as follows:		
To pay employees	187.6	263.4
To pay providers of capital (from the consolidated profit and loss account)		
Net interest on loans	2.4	15.9
Dividends to shareholders	44.3	41.3

To pay Government

Corporation tax	45.3	31.9

To provide maintenance and expansion

Depreciation (from the consolidated cash flow statement)	46.6	64.3
Retained profits (from the consolidated profit and loss account)	67.4	65.6
	393.6	482.4

The value added statement for Johnson Matthey plc shown in Example 6.6 illustrates how value added has been derived and how it has been applied in absolute terms for the years 1999 and 2000. A vertical analysis of the numbers would perhaps provide a better basis for comparison, which is illustrated in Example 6.7.

Example 6.7

Using the value added statement from Example 6.6 we are required to

(i) prepare a vertical analysis of the data

(ii) present the results in a pie chart format

Answer

Johnson Matthey plc
Consolidated vertical analysis value added statement for the year ended 31 March 2000

Figures in £m	2000	1999
Value added	100.0	100.0
Applied as follows:		
To pay employees	47.7	54.6
To pay providers of capital		
Net interest on loans	0.6	3.3
Dividends to shareholders	11.3	8.6
To pay Government		
Corporation tax	11.5	6.6
To provide maintenance and expansion		
Depreciation	11.8	13.3
Retained profits	17.1	13.6

The vertical analysis of the value added statement for Johnson Matthey plc shows us that around one half of the value generated by the business is distributed to employees in the form of salaries, wages and benefits (54.6% for 1999 down to 47.7% for 2000). This is far greater than the proportion distributed to the providers of capital (lenders and share-holders), which is at 11.9% for both years, although the proportion paid to lenders was higher in 1999 than 2000.

This presentation illustrates the significant increase in the burden of taxation, which has nearly doubled from 1999 to 2000. The company may face a question at its annual general meeting (AGM), where the directors may be asked to explain the increase in taxation, which will almost certainly have had an impact on the flow of dividends to the shareholders.

The remainder of value added is retained for maintenance and expansion of assets. This has increased from 26.9% in 1999 to 28.9% in 2000, indicating an increase in the financing of growth of the business through internally generated sources.

Of course, the value added statement also has disadvantages:

● some difficulty encountered in measurement and reporting

● classification of items – for example taxation, which normally excludes employee tax and National Insurance, and business rates

● unstandardised format with varying treatment of the items in the value added statement

● current lack of popularity among companies, despite the inclusion of a value added statement by a large percentage of large companies up to the early 1980s in their annual reports and accounts.

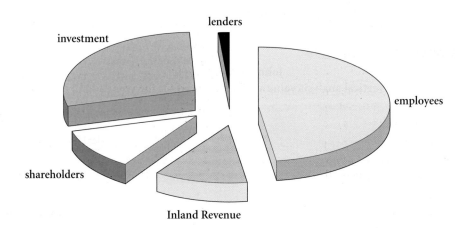

FIGURE 6.3 Johnson Matthey plc % distribution of value added for the year 2000

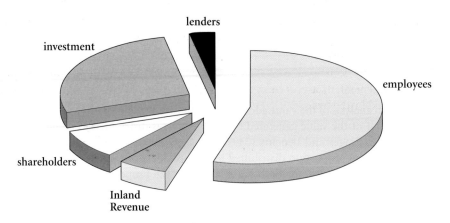

FIGURE 6.4 Johnson Matthey plc % distribution of value added for the year 1999

The value added statement seems unlikely to replace the conventional profit and loss account, or cash flow statement as a decision-making tool or as a measure of business performance. However, it may continue to be useful for internal communication of company financial performance to employees, and in support of employee incentive schemes.

Progress check 6.10

What is a value added statement and what does it tell us?

Summary of key points

● Limited companies prepare their annual reports and accounts to keep shareholders informed about financial performance and the financial position of the business.

● The annual report and accounts of a public limited company now requires disclosure of a great deal of both financial and non-financial information in addition to the financial statements.

● The annual report and accounts allows evaluation of a public limited company in a wider context than was possible from the sort of financial information traditionally required by the shareholders.

● Horizontal analysis of the profit and loss account (which may also be applied to the balance sheet) for two or more years starts with a base year 100 and shows each item, line-by-line, indexed against the base year, and is particularly useful in looking at performance trends over a number of years.

● Vertical analysis of the profit and loss account (which may also be applied to the balance sheet) shows every item as a percentage of turnover (balance sheet–total assets), and is also particularly useful in looking at performance trends over a number of years.

● Segmental reporting provides a further dimension to the financial statements through analysis of turnover, operating profit and net assets, by business class and geographical segments.

● The quality and depth of environmental and social reporting, in both qualitative and quantitative terms, is becoming increasingly important as annual reports and accounts are required to meet the needs of all stakeholders, not just the shareholders.

● Although the financial statements of limited companies are not adjusted for the effects of inflation the impact of inflation is a factor that must be considered in evaluation of business performance.

● The value added statement, which is an alternative presentation of the traditional profit and loss statement, measures wealth as the value added by the business rather than the profit earned by the business.

Glossary of key terms

Cadbury Committee Report of the Cadbury Committee (December 1992) on the Financial Aspects of Corporate Governance, set up to consider issues in relation to financial reporting and accountability, and to make recommendations on good practice, relating to:

- responsibilities of executive and non-executive directors
- establishment of company audit committees
- responsibility of auditors
- links between shareholders, directors, and auditors
- any other relevant matters.

The report established a Code of Best Practice, now succeeded by the Combined Code of Practice.

contingent liability A possible obligation that arises from past events and whose existence will be confirmed only by the occurrence of one or more uncertain future events not wholly within the entity's control; or

A present obligation that arises from past events but is not recognised because: it is not probable that a transfer of benefits will be required to settle the obligation; or, the amount of the obligation cannot be measured with sufficient reliability (FRS12).

continuing operations Operations not satisfying all the conditions relating to discontinued operations (see below).

corporate governance The system by which companies are directed and controlled. Boards of directors are responsible for the governance of their companies. The shareholders' role in governance is to appoint the directors and the auditors and to satisfy themselves that an appropriate governance structure is in place.

discontinued operations Operations of the reporting entity that are sold or terminated and that satisfy certain criteria (FRS 3):

- the sale or termination is completed either in the period or before the earlier of three months after the commencement of the subsequent period and the date on which the financial statements are approved

- if a termination, the former activities have ceased permanently
- the sale or termination has a material effect on the nature and focus of the reporting entity's operations, and represents a material reduction in its operating facilities resulting from its withdrawal from a particular market (whether class of business or geographical) or from a material reduction in turnover in the reporting entity's continuing markets
- the assets, liabilities, results of operations and activities are clearly distinguishable physically, operationally and for financial reporting purposes.

environmental reporting A statement included within the annual report and accounts that sets out the environmental policies of the company and an explanation of its environmental management systems and responsibilities. The environmental report may include reporting on the performance of the business on environmental matters in qualitative terms regarding the extent to which it meets national and international standards. It may also include a quantitative report on the performance of the business on environmental matters against targets, together with an assessment of the financial impact.

euro The common currency of the European Union, which came into being on 1 January 1999. Financial transactions and/or financial reporting of member states may now be undertaken in either the functional domestic currencies, or in euros.

financial instrument Any contract that gives rise to both a financial asset of one entity and a financial liability or equity instrument of another entity. Financial instruments include both primary financial instruments – such as bonds, debtors, creditors and shares – and derivative financial instruments whose value derives from the underlying assets.

inflation A general increase in the price level over time. In a period of hyper inflation the rate at which the price level rises has become extremely high, and possibly out of control.

post balance sheet events Favourable and unfavourable events, which occur between the balance sheet date and the date on which the financial statements are approved by the board of directors.

risk A condition in which there exists a quantifiable dispersion in the possible outcomes from any activity. For example: credit risk – the risk that a borrower may default on his obligations; currency risk – the possibility of loss or gain due to future changes in exchange rates.

risk management The process of understanding and managing the risks that the organisation is inevitably subject to in attempting to achieve its corporate objectives. For management purposes, risks are usually divided into categories such as operational; financial; legal compliance; information; personnel.

segmental reporting The inclusion in a company's report and accounts of analysis of turnover, profits and net assets by class of business and by geographical segments (Companies Acts 1985/89 and SSAP 25).

value added statement An alternative presentation of the traditional profit and loss account that measures the wealth created by a company through its activities, through value added by the business rather the profit earned by the business. It shows how value added is distributed among the relevant parties: employees; lenders; shareholders; Government, and the amount to provide maintenance and expansion of the business.

Assessment material

Questions

Q6.1   (i)   Why, and for whom, do the annual reports and accounts of limited companies have to be prepared?

      (ii)   Where do they have to be filed?

      (iii) Who are the main users of the information contained in the annual report and accounts?

      (iv) How do they use the information?

Q6.2   (i)   Why do you think that the chairman, chief executive, and finance director of a plc each need to provide a statement or report for inclusion in the annual report and accounts?

      (ii)   What purpose do these reports serve and in what ways do they differ?

Q6.3   (i)   Describe the key elements of Johnson Matthey's financial review that is included in their report and accounts for 2000, and what they say about the performance of the business.

      (ii)   Why do you think that a third of this report is devoted to financial risk management?

      (iii) What does risk management mean?

      (iv) What are the financial risks faced by Johnson Matthey?

Q6.4   Describe the technique of horizontal analysis and how it may be used to evaluate, explain and compare company performance.

Q6.5   Describe the technique of vertical analysis and how it may be used to evaluate, explain and compare company performance.

Q6.6   (i)   What were the inadequacies in financial statement reporting that SSAP 25, Segmental Reporting, sought to address and how did it do this?

      (ii)   What are the practical problems that companies face associated with their compliance with SSAP 25?

Q6.7   (i)   Why do you think that environmental reporting has become increasingly important in terms of corporate awareness, and with regard to the awareness of the non-business community?

      (ii) Examine the annual reports and accounts of a number of large UK plcs to compare and critically evaluate the approach taken by Johnson Matthey to their environmental reporting in their 2000 report and accounts.

Q6.8 (i) How does inflation distort accounting information that has been prepared under the historical cost convention?

(ii) In what ways have the accountancy profession considered some alternative approaches to try and deal with the problem of inflation?

Q6.9 (i) Explain what is meant by a value added statement.

(ii) In what ways may a value added statement be used to measure financial performance?

(iii) What are the disadvantages in using value added statements?

(iv) Why do you think the levels of popularity they enjoyed in the 1980s have not been maintained?

Discussion points

D6.1 'The annual reports and accounts prepared by the majority of UK plcs serve to ensure that shareholders, and other stakeholders, are kept very well informed about the affairs of their businesses.' Discuss.

D6.2 'In the global competitive world in which we live, company directors should be able to exercise their full discretion as to the amount of information they disclose in their annual reports and accounts. If they are not allowed this discretion in disclosure, their companies may be driven out of business by their competitors, particularly foreign competitors who may not have the restriction of such extensive reporting requirements.' Discuss.

D6.3 'The main reason that companies increasingly include environmental reports in their annual reports and accounts is to change the views of users and regulators about the activities in which their businesses are engaged, in order to pre-empt and avoid any negative or harmful reactions.' Discuss this statement by drawing on examples of the type of businesses to which this might apply.
(Hint: You may wish to research Railtrack, and British Gas, as well as Johnson Matthey plc, to provide material for this discussion.)

Ten Year Record

	1991 £ million	1992 £ million	1993 £ million	1994 £ million	1995 £ million
Turnover					
Parent and subsidiaries	1,728.1	1,744.5	1,853.7	1,955.0	2,177.8
Share of joint ventures	–	–	–	–	97.1
Total	1,728.1	1,744.5	1,853.7	1,955.0	2,274.9
Operating profit	62.3	62.9	71.6	81.6	100.4
Goodwill amortisation	–	–	–	–	–
Exceptional items	0.5	(2.1)	–	–	–
Total operating profit	62.8	60.8	71.6	81.6	100.4
Other exceptional items	–	4.4	3.7	(11.7)	(0.7)
Profit before interest	62.8	65.2	75.3	69.9	99.7
Net interest	3.2	1.9	(1.5)	(4.6)	(4.3)
Profit before taxation	66.0	67.1	73.8	65.3	95.4
Taxation	(22.0)	(19.2)	(23.7)	(20.7)	(30.5)
Profit after taxation	44.0	47.9	50.1	44.6	64.9
Equity minority interests	(0.2)	(0.2)	(0.3)	(0.2)	(1.0)
Profit attributable to shareholders	43.8	47.7	49.8	44.4	63.9
Dividends	(16.7)	(17.9)	(19.1)	(21.8)	(25.9)
Profit retained	27.1	29.8	30.7	22.6	38.0
Earnings per ordinary share (graph 1)	23.6p	25.5p	26.5p	23.1p	32.9p
Earnings per ordinary share excluding exceptional items and goodwill amortisation (graph 2)	23.4p	24.2p	25.2p	27.0p	33.2p
Dividend per ordinary share (graph 3)	9.25p	9.65p	10.3p	11.4p	13.5p
Summary Balance Sheet					
Assets employed:					
Goodwill	–	–	–	–	–
Tangible fixed assets	189.2	219.7	263.1	281.1	256.1
Fixed assets investments / joint ventures / associates	8.7	5.1	1.1	1.1	70.9
Stocks	217.8	148.6	155.0	153.6	153.2
Debtors and short term investments	165.3	163.4	185.7	207.2	190.9
Other creditors and provisions	(339.8)	(273.2)	(232.8)	(242.1)	(207.5)
	241.2	263.6	372.1	400.9	463.6
Financed by:					
Net borrowings and finance leases / (cash)	22.1	9.9	90.6	76.1	102.4
Retained earnings	30.6	64.7	90.3	129.0	167.5
Share capital and share premium	188.1	188.5	190.3	194.4	195.7
Equity minority interests	0.4	0.5	0.9	1.4	(2.0)
Capital employed	241.2	263.6	372.1	400.9	463.6
Cumulative goodwill taken directly to reserves	39.6	41.2	49.6	50.5	57.5
Return on assets	21.6%	21.5%	19.7%	18.7%	20.6%

(Total operating profit before exceptional items and goodwill amortisation / average capital employed and cumulative goodwill taken directly to reserves)

1999 and prior years have been restated to reflect changes in accounting policies. The earnings per ordinary share for 1995 and prior years have been adjusted for the bonus element in the 1 for 8 rights issue made on 19th September 1995.

Ten Year Record

1996 £ million	1997 £ million	1998 £ million	1999 £ million	2000 £ million
2,528.9	2,423.2	3,138.8	3,385.4	3,866.0
156.7	156.9	128.8	–	–
2,685.6	2,580.1	3,267.6	3,385.4	3,866.0
111.0	116.3	139.2	147.1	146.2
–	–	–	–	(0.2)
–	–	(4.5)	(1.9)	(9.8)
111.0	116.3	134.7	145.2	136.2
–	–	4.4	8.8	23.4
111.0	116.3	139.1	154.0	159.6
(8.8)	(8.0)	(9.0)	(15.9)	(2.4)
102.2	108.3	130.1	138.1	157.2
(30.5)	(29.2)	(25.2)	(31.9)	(45.3)
71.7	79.1	104.9	106.2	111.9
(1.7)	(1.2)	(0.3)	0.7	(0.2)
70.0	77.9	104.6	106.9	111.7
(31.4)	(33.6)	(38.7)	(41.3)	(44.3)
38.6	44.3	65.9	65.6	67.4
34.4p	36.0p	48.2p	49.3p	51.4p
34.4p	36.0p	44.3p	44.3p	47.5p
14.5p	15.5p	17.8p	19.0p	20.3p
–	–	–	4.2	5.1
321.7	337.7	461.5	480.2	311.3
100.4	84.2	4.2	1.8	1.0
196.6	184.7	244.8	243.7	253.2
232.2	252.6	381.1	439.6	447.7
(284.2)	(267.5)	(382.8)	(389.3)	(424.2)
566.7	591.7	708.8	780.2	594.1
134.2	143.7	225.1	221.6	(165.8)
119.6	131.0	158.0	230.4	417.6
313.6	316.8	319.6	322.4	337.8
(0.7)	0.2	6.1	5.8	4.5
566.7	591.7	708.8	780.2	594.1
150.3	156.3	171.4	171.4	46.0
17.9%	15.9%	17.1%	16.1%	18.4%

1 Earnings per share

pence

91 23.6 | 92 25.5 | 93 26.5 | 94 23.1 | 95 32.9 | 96 34.4 | 97 36.0 | 98 48.2 | 99 49.3 | 00 51.4

2 Earnings per share excluding exceptionals

pence

91 23.4 | 92 24.2 | 93 25.2 | 94 27.0 | 95 33.2 | 96 34.4 | 97 36.0 | 98 44.3 | 99 44.3 | 00 47.5

3 Dividends per share

pence

91 9.25 | 92 9.65 | 93 10.3 | 94 11.4 | 95 13.5 | 96 14.5 | 97 15.5 | 98 17.8 | 99 19.0 | 00 20.3

Johnson Matthey **69**

Exercises

Solutions are provided in Appendix 4 to all exercise numbers highlighted in colour.

Level I

E6.1   *Time allowed – 30 minutes*

The fixed assets in the balance sheet of Ace plc have been summarised as follows:

		£m
Land at valuation		3.0
Buildings at cost		1.0
Plant and equipment – cost	2.0	
– depreciation	1.5	0.5
		4.5

Explain the meaning of this £4.5m figure to one of the company's shareholders, who has asked for an explanation of the numbers in the year-end balance sheet, included in the company's annual report and accounts.

E6.2   *Time allowed – 60 minutes*

(i) **Use the ten-year record of Johnson Matthey (see pp. 234–5) to prepare an horizontal analysis of the profit and loss account for the five years years 1996 to 2000, using 1996 as the base year.**

(ii) **What does this analysis tell us about Johnson Matthey's financial performance over that period?**

E6.3   *Time allowed – 60 minutes*

(i) **Use the ten-year record of Johnson Matthey (see pp. 234–5) to prepare an horizontal analysis of the balance sheet for the five years years 1996 to 2000, using 1996 as the base year.**

(ii) **What does this analysis tell us about Johnson Matthey's financial position over that period?**

Level II

E6.4   *Time allowed – 60 minutes*

(i) **Use the ten-year record of Johnson Matthey (see pp. 234–5) to prepare a vertical analysis of the profit and loss account for the five years years 1996 to 2000.**

(ii) **What does this analysis tell us about Johnson Matthey's financial performance over that period?**

E6.5 *Time allowed – 90 minutes*

Note 1 to the report and accounts of Johnson Matthey provides segmental analysis for the years 2000 and 1999.

Prepare an horizontal analysis from this information, with 1999 as the base year, and use it to explain the appropriate elements of financial performance and the changes in the financial position of the business.

E6.6 *Time allowed – 90 minutes*

Refer to the financial statements included in Johnson Matthey's report and accounts 2000 to calculate the appropriate ratios for comparison with the previous year, and include them in a report on the profitability of the group (see Chapter 5).

E6.7 *Time allowed – 90 minutes*

Refer to the financial statements included in Johnson Matthey's report and accounts 2000 to calculate the appropriate ratios for comparison with the previous year, and to give your assessment of the company's sources and uses of cash, and include them in a report on the group's cash position (see Chapter 5).

E6.8 *Time allowed – 90 minutes*

Refer to the financial statements included in Johnson Matthey's report and accounts 2000 to calculate the appropriate ratios for comparison with the previous year, and include them in a report on the working capital of the group (see Chapter 5).

E6.9 *Time allowed – 90 minutes*

Refer to the financial statements included in Johnson Matthey's report and accounts 2000 to calculate the appropriate ratios for comparison with the previous year, and include them in a report on the investment performance of the group (see Chapter 5).

E6.10 *Time allowed – 90 minutes*

The notes and five-year profit and loss account extracts from the financial statements of Guinness plc are shown below.

You are required to use these to carry out an appropriate analysis and provide a report on the likely explanations of differences in performance over the five years.

Notes

- The group sells alcohol-based products to consumers and operates in nearly every major country throughout the world
- Local and global competition is intense in many markets
- Brands have been sold during the five years
- New products are invariably variants on the group's basic products of beers, wines and spirits

- The group share price had been relatively static due to the maturity of the market and the pattern of profits
- Other investment income shown in the five-year analysis related to an investment in a French luxury goods group
- Soon after year six the group merged with another international food and drinks business, which also had an extensive portfolio of own and purchased brands
- After the merger several brands were sold to competitors
- After the merger many of the directors left the group's management team
- Exchange rates over the five-year period in several of the group's markets were quite volatile
- The group had £1.4 billion of brands in its balance sheet.

Guinness plc five-year profit and loss account

Figures in £m	Year 5	Year 4	Year 3	Year 2	Year 1
Turnover	4,730	4,681	4,690	4,663	4,363
Gross profit	961	943	956	938	1,023
Other investment income	113	47	89	(48)	(24)
Profit before interest and tax (operating profit)	1,074	990	1,045	890	999
Net interest	(99)	(114)	(130)	(188)	(204)
Profit before tax	975	876	915	702	795
Tax on profit on ordinary activities	(259)	(251)	(243)	(247)	(242)
Profit on ordinary activities after tax	716	625	672	455	553
Minority interests	(31)	(30)	(31)	(22)	(29)
Profit for financial year	685	595	641	433	524
Dividends	(295)	(302)	(279)	(258)	(237)
Retained profit	390	293	362	175	287
Earnings per share	35.1p	29.4p	31.8p	22.9p	28.1p
Interest cover	10.8	8.7	8.0	4.7	4.9
Dividend cover	2.2	2.0	2.3	1.8	2.3

7

Corporate governance

LEARNING OBJECTIVES

Completion of this chapter will enable you to:

● describe how the framework for establishing good corporate governance and accountability has been established in a Combined Code of Practice, developed from the work of the Cadbury, Greenbury, and Hampel Committees

● explain the statutory requirement for the audit of limited companies, the election by shareholders of suitably qualified, independent auditors, and the role of the auditors

● outline directors' specific responsibility to shareholders, and responsibilities to society in general, for the management and conduct of companies

● recognise the fiduciary duties that directors have to the company, and their duty of care to all stakeholders and to the community at large, particularly with regard to the Companies Acts 1985/1989, Health and Safety at Work Act 1974, and Financial Services Act 1986

● appreciate the importance of directors' duties regarding insolvency and the Insolvency Act 1986

● consider the implications for directors of wrongful trading, and recognise the difference between this and the offence of fraudulent trading, and the possibility of criminal penalties

● outline the implication for directors of the Company Directors Disqualification Act 1986

● explain the actions that directors of companies should take to ensure compliance with their obligations and responsibilities, and to protect themselves against possible non-compliance

CONTENTS

Introduction

In Chapter 6 we saw that a large part of Johnson Matthey plc's report and accounts 2000 was devoted to the subject of corporate governance, the systems by which companies are directed and controlled. This chapter turns to the statutory and non-statutory rules that surround the accounting for limited companies.

In earlier chapters we discussed the way in which the limited company exists in perpetuity as a legal entity, separate from the lives of those individuals who both own and manage it. The limited company has many rights, responsibilities, and liabilities in the same way as individual people. As a separate legal entity the company is responsible for its own liabilities. These are not the obligations of the shareholders who have paid for their shares, being the limit of their obligations to the company.

The directors of a limited company are appointed by, and are responsible to, the shareholders for the management of the company, maintained through their regular reporting on the activities of the business. The responsibilities of directors, however, are wider than to just the shareholders. They are also responsible for acting correctly towards their employees, suppliers, customers, and to the public at large.

The annual audit of the accounts is a statutory requirement for all limited companies, excluding smaller limited companies. As with directors, the auditors of a limited company are also appointed by, and are responsible to, the shareholders. Their primary responsibility is to make an objective report to shareholders and others as to whether, in their opinion, the financial statements show a true and fair view, and compliance with statutory, regulatory and accounting standard requirements. Therefore, the management and regulation of a company as a separate legal entity lies with the directors and the auditors. The directors are within, and part of, the company, and the auditors are external to, and not part of, the company.

This chapter will look at roles and responsibilities of directors and auditors. It will also consider the obligations of directors, particularly with regard to the corporate governance Combined Code of Practice, and the many Acts that are now in place to regulate the behaviour of directors of limited companies. The chapter closes with a look at some of the steps that directors may take to protect themselves against possible non-compliance.

Corporate governance code of practice

Concerns about financial reporting and accountability, and the impact on the business community (see Fig. 7.1), grew during the 1980s following increasing numbers of company failures and financial scandals.

During the 1980s and 1990s there was huge concern within the business community following the financial scandals surrounding BCCI, Polly Peck and Robert Maxwell's companies. These concerns were seen in a lack of confidence in financial reporting, and in shareholders and others being unable to rely on auditors to provide the necessary safeguards for their reliance on company annual reports.

The main factors underlying the lack of confidence in financial reporting were:

- loose accounting standards, which allowed considerable latitude (an example has been the treatment of extraordinary items and exceptional items in financial reporting)
- lack of a clear framework to ensure **directors** were able to continuously review business controls
- competitive pressure within companies and on auditors, making it difficult for auditors to maintain independence from demanding boards

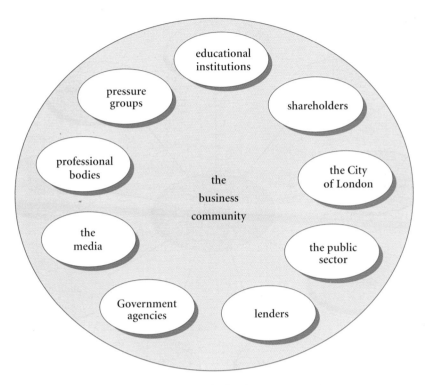

FIGURE 7.1   The business community

● lack of apparent accountability regarding directors' remuneration and compensation for loss of office.

The Cadbury Committee, chaired by Sir Adrian Cadbury, was set up in May 1991 by the Financial.Reporting Council, the London Stock Exchange, and the accountancy profession, to address these concerns and make recommendations on good practice.

The Cadbury Committee defined corporate governance as 'the system by which companies are directed and controlled (see Fig. 7.2). Boards of directors are responsible for the governance of their companies. The shareholders' role in governance is to appoint the directors and the auditors and to satisfy themselves that an appropriate governance structure is in place. The responsibilities of the board include setting the company's strategic aims, providing the leadership to put them into effect, supervising the management of the business and reporting to shareholders on their stewardship. The board's actions are subject to laws, regulations and the shareholders in general meeting.'

The financial aspects within the framework described by Cadbury are the ways in which the company's board sets financial policy and oversees its implementation, the use of financial controls, and how the board reports on activities and progress of the company to shareholders.

The framework for establishing good corporate governance and accountability set up by the Cadbury Committee was formulated as the Committee's Code of Best Practice. This provided a benchmark against which to assess compliance. These provisions have since been updated following the reports of the Greenbury Committee (and the **Hampel Committee** in January 1998), resulting in a **Combined Code of Practice**.

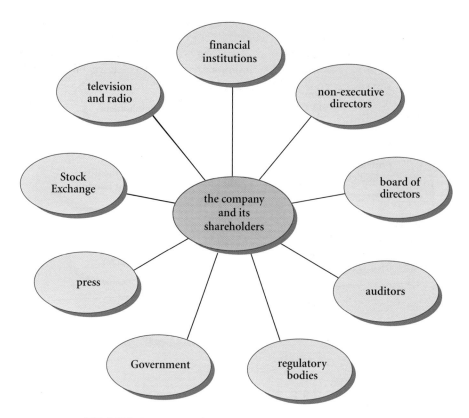

FIGURE 7.2 The context of corporate governance

The underlying principles of the Code are:

- openness
- integrity
- accountability.

Openness

Openness from companies is constrained within the limits of their competitive position but is the basis for the confidence that needs to exist between business and all those who have a stake in its success. Openness in disclosure of information adds to the effectiveness of the market economy. It forces boards to take action and allows shareholders and others to be able to look more closely and thoroughly into companies.

Integrity

Integrity means straightforward dealing and completeness. Financial reporting should be honest and present a balanced view of the state of the company's affairs. The integrity of the company's reports will depend on the integrity of the people responsible for preparing and presenting them.

The annual reports and financial statements of the majority of UK plcs now include a section headed *Corporate Governance*. These sections of the annual reports are required to aim to comply with provisions set out in a Combined Code of Practice (principles of good governance and code of best practice), embracing the principles of the Cadbury, Greenbury and Hampel Committees, appended to the Listing Rules of the London Stock Exchange.

The corporate governance section of a company's annual report and accounts should contain details under the following headings:

- directors' biographies
- board responsibilities
- board composition and functions
- board committees
    - audit committee
    - nomination committee
    - remuneration committee
    - IT committee
    - capital expenditure committee
    - **non-executive directors'** committee
- directors' remuneration
- relations with shareholders
- internal financial control
- incentive compensation
- directors' pensions
- corporate strategy.

This may not be a complete list but it gives a broad indication of the areas of compliance under the Combined Code of Practice. This compliance can be seen in the annual reports and accounts of UK plcs.

Accountability

Accountability of boards of directors to their shareholders requires the commitment from both to make the accountability effective. Boards of directors must play their part by ensuring the quality of information that is provided to shareholders. Shareholders must exercise their responsibilities as owners of the business. The major investing institutions (for example, pension funds and insurance companies) are in regular contact with the directors of UK plcs to discuss past, current, and future performance.

Companies listed on the Stock Exchange are requested to comply with the Code, but other companies may benefit from compliance. It is not compulsory for any company, but rather a target of best practice to aim for. Companies listed on the Stock Exchange, however, are required to include in their annual report and accounts a statement as to whether or not they have complied with the Code throughout the accounting period.

Progress check 7.1

What is corporate governance and how is it implemented?

Example 7.1

Outline some of the basic problems that shareholders with small shareholdings encounter as they enter a new relationship with the company they effectively part own.

Answer

Most major plcs are owned by shareholders with both large and small shareholdings, the analysis of which can be found in their annual reports and accounts.

Usually within a very short time of acquiring their shares, most new small shareholders realise they have neither influence nor power.

As plcs have become multi-activity and multinational, so the directors have become more distanced from the shareholders. (Compare this with, for example, locally based building societies.)

During the move towards growth and expanded activities by companies, considerable disquiet regarding accountability developed in the business community and the Committee on the Financial Aspects of Corporate Governance (Cadbury Committee) was appointed, which produced its report in December 1992.

There has been unease regarding remuneration, bonus schemes, option schemes and contracts. The various committees on corporate governance, subsequent to Cadbury, have reviewed each of these areas.

Let's take a look at the Johnson Matthey section on corporate governance, included in their report and accounts 2000, and reproduced on pages 245–7. The company states that 'throughout the year [2000], the company has been in compliance with the provisions of the Code with the exception of the matter noted on page 29'. The company states this non-compliance as 'three of the executive directors are employed on contracts subject to two years' notice . . . in the event of early termination of contracts the MRDC [Management Development and Remuneration Committee] strongly endorses the principle of requiring the directors to mitigate their loss.'

A number of the headings required as part of corporate governance reporting are not included within Johnson Matthey plc's main corporate governance report, but are shown elsewhere in the report and accounts. Directors' biographies, board responsibilities, composition and functions are shown on pages 22 and 23 of the report, and remuneration policies and remuneration of the directors are shown on pages 30 to 37 of the report, none of which are reproduced here.

Non-executive directors are represented on all the main committees, except the chief executive's committee. The company does not appear to have an information technology (IT) committee or a capital expenditure committee, and so IT and capital expenditure are presumably the responsibility of the chief executive's committee.

The audit and the role of auditors

As we have noted earlier, an annual audit of the accounts is a statutory requirement for all limited companies, except for those currently having an annual turnover of less than £350,000 and a balance sheet total of less than £1.4 million (refer to the Department of Trade and Industry website www.dti.com for changes to these limits). The shareholders of a limited company are responsible for appointing suitably qualified, independent persons, either individually or as a firm to act as auditors. The external auditors are not part of

Corporate Governance

The company has applied all of the principles set out in section 1 of the Combined Code on Corporate Governance (the Code) relating to the structure and composition of the board, the remuneration of the directors, relations with shareholders and procedures for financial reporting, audit and internal control of the group. This statement describes how the principles of the Code have been applied.

Throughout the year, the company has been in compliance with the provisions of the Code with the exception of the matter noted on page 29.

Directors and the Board

The board is responsible to the company's shareholders for the group's system of corporate governance, its strategic objectives and the stewardship of the company's resources. The board meets at least seven times per year and delegates specific responsibilities to board committees, as described below. The board reviews the key activities of the business, and receives papers and presentations to enable it to do so effectively. The Company Secretary is responsible to the board, and is available to individual directors, in respect of board procedures.

The board comprises the Chairman, the Chief Executive, four other executive directors and six other independent non-executive directors. The role of non-executive directors is to enhance independence and objectivity of the board's deliberations and decisions. The executive directors have specific responsibilities, which are detailed on pages 22 and 23, and have direct responsibility for all operations and activities.

All directors submit themselves for re-election every three years.

Committees of the Board

The Chief Executive's Committee is responsible for the recommendation to the board of strategic and operating plans and on decisions reserved to the board where appropriate. It is also responsible for the executive management of the group's business. The Committee is chaired by the Chief Executive and meets monthly. It comprises the executive directors and three senior executives of the company.

The Audit Committee is a sub-committee of the board whose purpose is to assist the board in the effective discharge of its responsibilities for financial reporting and corporate control. The Committee is chaired by Mr H R Jenkins and meets twice a year. It comprises all the non-executive directors with the Chief Executive, the Finance Director and the external and internal auditors in attendance.

The Nomination Committee is a sub-committee of the board responsible for advising the board and making recommendations on the appointment of new directors. The Committee is chaired by Mr H M P Miles and comprises all the non-executive directors.

The Management Development and Remuneration Committee (MDRC) is a sub-committee of the board which determines on behalf of the board the remuneration of the Chief Executive, executive directors and senior management. The Committee is chaired by Mr H M P Miles and comprises all the non-executive directors. The Chief Executive and Director of Human Resources attend by invitation except when their own performance and remuneration are discussed.

Directors' Remuneration

The Remuneration Report on pages 30 to 37, includes details of remuneration policies and of the remuneration of the directors.

Corporate Governance

Relations with Shareholders

The company reports formally to shareholders twice a year, when its half year and full year results are announced and an interim report and a full report are issued to shareholders. At the same time, executive directors give presentations on the results to institutional investors, analysts and the media in London and other international centres.

The Annual General Meeting (AGM) of the company takes place in London and formal notification is sent to shareholders with the annual report at least 20 working days in advance of the meeting. The directors are available, formally during the AGM, and informally afterwards, for questions. Details of the 2000 AGM are set out in the notice of the meeting enclosed with this annual report.

During the year, the Chief Executive, Finance Director and executive directors maintain a dialogue with institutional shareholders on the company's progress through a programme of meetings. All executive directors speak regularly at external conferences and presentations.

Accountability, Audit and Internal Control

The statement of directors' responsibilities in relation to the accounts is set out on page 37.

In its reporting to shareholders, the board aims to present a balanced and understandable assessment of the group's financial position and prospects.

The group has adopted the transitional approach to Internal Control under the Combined Code as outlined in the letter from the London Stock Exchange to listed companies in September 1999. As a result the directors confirm that they have reviewed the effectiveness of the group's system of internal financial controls.

The existing risk management and internal control processes necessary to implement the guidance 'Internal Control: Guidance for Directors on the Combined Code' have been modified and a report on the application of the Internal Control principle D.2 will be included in the annual report and accounts for the year ending 31st March 2001.

The board has overall responsibility for the group's system of internal controls, which are designed to meet the group's needs and address the risks to which it is exposed. Such a system can provide reasonable but not absolute assurance against material misstatement or loss.

The group's organisational structure is focused on its three wholly owned divisions. These entities are all separately managed, but report to the board through a board director. The executive management team receive monthly summaries of financial results from each division through a standardised reporting process.

The board meets annually to consider the strategy for individual divisions and again annually to review three year financial plans. The group has in place a comprehensive annual budgeting process including forecasts for the next two years. Variances from budget are closely monitored. The group's treasury policies are discussed in the financial review on page 10. The principal aspects of these policies are approved by the board. Specific criteria exist for the approval of significant contracts and other legal agreements. A committee of the board reviews significant items of this nature.

The Group Control Manual, which is distributed to all group operations, clearly sets out the composition, responsibilities and authority limits of the various board and executive committees and also specifies what may be decided without central approval. It is supplemented by other specialist policy and procedures manuals issued by the group, divisions and individual business units or departments. The high intrinsic value of many of the metals with which the group is associated necessitates stringent physical controls over precious metals held at the group's sites.

The internal audit function is responsible for monitoring the group's systems of internal financial controls and the control and the integrity of the financial information reported to the board. The Audit Committee receives the reports produced by the internal audit function on a regular basis. Actions are agreed with management in response to the internal audit reports produced.

In addition, significant business units through a programme of self-assessment provide assurance on the maintenance of financial controls and compliance with group policies. These assessments are summarised by the internal audit function and a report is made annually to the Audit Committee.

Non-Compliance with the Combined Code

The item in the Code with which the company did not comply in full throughout the period together with the appropriate Code reference is stated below:

Three of the executive directors are employed on contracts subject to two years' notice at any time, which the MDRC considers appropriate in the overall context of the executive directors' terms of employment. It is not currently proposed that this should be reduced further for existing service contracts. In the event of early termination of service contracts the MDRC strongly endorses the principle of requiring the directors to mitigate their loss (B.1.7).

Going Concern

The directors have a reasonable expectation that the group has sufficient resources to continue in operational existence for the foreseeable future and have, therefore, adopted the going concern basis in preparing the accounts.

the company but are responsible to the shareholders, with the main duty of objectively reporting to shareholders and others as to whether, in their opinion, the financial statements show a true and fair view, and comply with statutory, regulatory and accounting standard requirements. Such an opinion is referred to as an unqualified opinion.

The report of the auditors is usually very short and additionally includes:

- reference to the directors' responsibility for preparation of the annual report and accounts
- reference to the responsibility as auditors being established by
  - UK statute
  - the **Auditing Practices Board (APB)**
  - the Listing Rules of the Financial Services Authority
  - the accountancy profession's ethical guidance.

The auditors are required to explain the basis of the audit, and report if in their opinion:

- the directors' report is not consistent with the accounts
- the company has not kept proper accounting records
- they have not received all the information and explanations required for the audit
- information specified by law, or the Listing Rules regarding directors' remuneration and transactions with the company, is not disclosed
- company policies are appropriate and consistently applied and adequately disclosed
- all information and explanations considered necessary provide sufficient evidence to give reasonable assurance that the accounts are free from material misstatement
- the overall presentation of information in the accounts is adequate.

There may very occasionally be circumstances when the financial statements may be affected by an inherent, and fundamental uncertainty. In such cases the auditors are obliged to draw attention to the fundamental uncertainty. If the fundamental uncertainty is adequately accounted for and disclosed in the financial statements then the opinion of the auditors may remain unqualified. If there is inadequate disclosure about the fundamental uncertainty then the auditors must give what is termed a qualified opinion. A qualified **audit report** is something that may destroy company credibility and create uncertainty, and is obviously something to be avoided.

In addition to their reporting on the financial statements of the company, the auditors' reports now include a statement of the company's corporate governance compliance with the seven provisions of the Combined Code of Practice. This review is in accordance with guidelines issued by the Auditing Practices Board. The auditors are not required to:

- consider whether the statements by the directors on internal control cover all risks and controls
- form an opinion on the effectiveness of the company's corporate governance procedures or its risk management and internal control procedures
- form an opinion on the ability of the company to continue in operational existence.

The audit and the perceived role of auditors has been the subject of much criticism over the years. The responsibility of the auditors does not include guarantees that:

- the financial statements are correct
- the company will not fail
- there has been no fraud.

This gap, 'the expectations gap', between public expectation and what the audit actually provides is understandable in the light of the numerous examples of company failures and financial scandals in the 1980s and 1990s. These have led to a lack of confidence of the business community in financial reporting, and in shareholders being unable to rely on safeguards they assumed would be provided by their auditors.

The problem is that 'correctness' of financial statements is an unachievable result. We have seen from our consideration of both the balance sheet and profit and loss account the inconsistency in asset valuation and the level of subjective judgement required in their preparation. Directors are required to prepare, and auditors give an opinion on, accounts that give a true and fair view rather than accounts that are deemed 'correct'.

Companies increasingly face a greater diversity and level of risk:

- financial risk
- commercial risk
- operational risk

and the increasing possibility of corporate failure is very real. Although the financial statements of companies are based on the going concern concept, the directors and auditors cannot realistically give any assurance that those businesses will not fail.

An area of risk that is of increasing concern to companies is fraud. This is perhaps due to:

- increasing pace of change
- widespread use of computer systems
- ease and speed of communications and transfer of funds
- use of the Internet
- increase in staff mobility
- increasing dependence on specific knowledge (for example, Nick Leeson and Barings, and dot.com companies' IT experts).

Fraud is perhaps something on which auditors may arguably be expected to give an opinion. This is not something that is currently required from an external audit. It is something for which an **internal audit** department may be responsible. In the same way, external auditors could be requested to report on the adequacy or otherwise of systems of internal control.

Most major corporate fraud is now associated with communications and information technology systems. The use of internal (or external) audit for the:

- detection of fraud
- minimisation of fraud
- elimination of fraud

therefore tends to be specialised and is something for which the costs and benefits must be carefully evaluated.

Progress check 7.2

What is the audit and to whom are the auditors responsible, and for what?

The report of the auditors to the shareholders of Johnson Matthey plc, included in the report and accounts 2000, is illustrated on page 250. It can be seen to have complied with the standard audit reporting requirements outlined above. It may be interesting to compare

Report of the Auditors

to the members of Johnson Matthey Public Limited Company

We have audited the accounts on pages 38 to 41 and 43 to 67.

Respective Responsibilities of Directors and Auditor

The directors are responsible for preparing the annual report. As described on page 37 this includes responsibility for preparing the accounts in accordance with applicable United Kingdom law and accounting standards. Our responsibilities, as independent auditors, are established in the United Kingdom by statute, the Auditing Practices Board, the Listing Rules of the Financial Services Authority, and by our profession's ethical guidance.

We report to you our opinion as to whether the accounts give a true and fair view and are properly prepared in accordance with the Companies Act. We also report to you if, in our opinion, the directors' report is not consistent with the accounts, if the company has not kept proper accounting records, if we have not received all the information and explanations we require for our audit, or if information specified by law or the Listing Rules regarding directors' remuneration and transactions with the group is not disclosed.

We review whether the statement on pages 27 to 29 reflects the company's compliance with the seven provisions of the Combined Code specified for our review by the Financial Services Authority, and we report if it does not. We are not required to consider whether the board's statements on internal control cover all risks and controls, or form an opinion on the effectiveness of the group's corporate governance procedures or its risk and control procedures.

We read the other information contained in the annual report, including the corporate governance statement, and consider whether it is consistent with the audited accounts. We consider the implications for our report if we become aware of any apparent misstatements or material inconsistencies with the accounts.

Basis of Audit Opinion

We conducted our audit in accordance with Auditing Standards issued by the Auditing Practices Board. An audit includes examination, on a test basis, of evidence relevant to the amounts and disclosures in the accounts. It also includes an assessment of the significant estimates and judgements made by the directors in the preparation of the accounts, and of whether the accounting policies are appropriate to the group's circumstances, consistently applied and adequately disclosed.

We planned and performed our audit so as to obtain all the information and explanations which we considered necessary in order to provide us with sufficient evidence to give reasonable assurance that the accounts are free from material misstatement, whether caused by fraud or other irregularity or error. In forming our opinion we also evaluated the overall adequacy of the presentation of information in the accounts.

Opinion

In our opinion the accounts give a true and fair view of the state of affairs of the company and the group as at 31st March 2000 and of the profit of the group for the year then ended and have been properly prepared in accordance with the Companies Act 1985.

KPMG Audit Plc
Chartered Accountants
Registered Auditor
London
7th June 2000

the auditors report for, say, 1990 with the same report for the year 2000, in which so many more areas are covered, to confirm the importance of corporate governance.

Example 7.2

The audit is the objective review (or sometimes the detailed examination) of business systems and transactions. A business may employ internal and external auditors. The latter are considered the more independent, although both are paid by the business. External auditors are appointed by, and report to, the shareholders, whereas the internal auditors report to the company's audit committee.

(i) Why should the external auditors of a plc report direct to the shareholders and not to the chairman of the company?

(ii) Why should the internal auditors of a plc report to the audit committee and not to the finance director?

Answer

(i) The external auditors are appointed by and are responsible to the shareholders. The annual general meeting (AGM) is the formal meeting of directors, shareholders and auditors. Conceivably, the chairman could shelve the report, with shareholders unaware of the contents. The law is quite strict on auditors' access to the shareholders.

(ii) The finance director is responsible for the system of recording transactions. The finance director could prevent vital information from the internal auditors being distributed to others in the organisation.

(iii) The audit committee may request the non-executive directors to review specific areas, for example, the output from the internal auditors. The audit committee meets many times during the year and it offers a degree of objectivity. The careers of its members do not depend on the continuance of their directorship.

We will now consider the role of directors and their responsibilities in more detail, and with regard to the corporate governance Combined Code of Practice. We will also look at some of the circumstances in which directors of limited companies are particularly vulnerable, and how these may lead to disqualification of directors.

The fact that a corporate governance Code of Practice exists or even that the appropriate corporate governance committees have been established is not necessarily a guarantee of effective corporate governance. Tomkins plc, a large diversified multinational corporation had corporate governance committees in place relating to directors and their remuneration, relations with shareholders, accountability and audit. However, as the press cutting on page 252 illustrates, this was not sufficient to allay concern by shareholders over corporate governance practices following a fall in the group's share price by more than 50% over a two-year period.

The chief executive of Tomkins plc, Greg Hutchings resigned in October 2000 following allegations that he had awarded himself excessive perks (his wife and his cleaner on the company payroll, personal use of company jets and London apartments) and had authorised corporate donations for the campaign to make Lord Archer Mayor of London. Following his claim that an unpublished report from Ernst and Young exonerated him from any malpractice, Greg Hutchings went to court to recover shares in Tomkins plc he claimed were owed to him, and also claimed salary, bonus and pension benefits that were due to him at the time he left the company – a total of around £7m.

Tomkins probes four-jets chief
By George Tregarne
Financial Correspondent

Tomkins, the conglomerate which owns Smith & Wesson handguns, has responded to criticism of chief executive Greg Hutchings by launching an investigation into his executive perks.

The review will be conducted by the company's auditors, Arthur Andersen. It follows complaints by fund manager J O Hambro Capital that, among other things, Mr Hutchings's wife and cleaner had both been on the Tomkins payroll. Tomkins also has four corporate jets.

Investors' concern over corporate governance practices at the group has been triggered by a fall in the share price, from more than 370p two years ago. Yesterday the shares dropped to 166p, down 3.

David Mayhew, the senior partner of house broker Cazenove, told Mr Hutchings earlier this year that Tomkins would have to smarten up its act. Sir Brian Pitman, former chairman of Lloyds, soon joined the board and David Newlands, former GEC finance director, was made non-executive chairman. Mr Newlands is personally overseeing the perks inquiry.

© *Daily Telegraph*, 10 October 2000

Directors' responsibilities

The responsibilities of directors, in terms of the Combined Code of Practice, can be seen to be important and far-reaching. It has been said that being a director is easy, but being a responsible director is not. It is important for all directors to develop an understanding and awareness of their ever-increasing legal obligations and responsibilities to avoid the potential personal liabilities, and even disqualification, which are imposed if those obligations are ignored.

It can be seen that the aims of most of the codes of practice and legislation have been to promote better standards of management in companies. This has also meant penalising irresponsible directors, the effect of which has been to create an increasingly heavy burden on directors regardless of the size or nature of the business they manage. The Government is actively banning offending directors.

Directors' duties are mainly embodied in the:

- Companies Act 1985/1989
- Insolvency Act 1986
- Company Directors Disqualification Act 1986
- Health and Safety at Work Act 1974
- Financial Services Act 1986

and there is

- potential for legal action on corporate manslaughter.

In addition, it should be noted that further statutory provisions giving rise to vicarious liability of directors for corporate offences are included in Acts of Parliament, which currently number well over 200! Directors can be:

- forced to pay a company's losses
- fined
- prevented from running businesses
- imprisoned.

Many smaller companies without continuous legal advice are unaware about how much the rules have tightened. It is usually not until there is wide publicity surrounding high-profile business problems that boards of directors are alerted to the demands and penalties to which they may be subjected if things go wrong.

It was not only the 1980s and early 1990s that saw corporate scandals and irregularities (for example, Polly Peck, and the Maxwell companies). Corporate misdemeanours continued, perhaps on an even larger scale, through the late 1990s and on into the twenty-first century (note the Barings debacle).

At the end of 1999, accounting irregularities caused trading in engineering company TransTec shares to be suspended, with Arthur Andersen called in as administrative receiver. The case was fuelled by the revelation by former TransTec chief accountant Max Ayris that nearly £500,000 of a total of £1.3m in grants from the Department of Trade and Industry was obtained fraudulently. TransTec, founded by former Government minister Geoffrey Robinson, collapsed in December 1999, after the accounting irregularities were discovered, with debts of more than £70m. Following the collapse of the company the role of the auditors to the company, PricewaterhouseCoopers, was also to be examined by the Joint Disciplinary Scheme, the accountancy professions' senior watchdog.

Also during 1999, the trade finance group Versailles discovered that there had been some double counting of transactions, which prompted the Department of Trade and Industry to take a close interest in its affairs.

Non-executive directors are legally expected to know as much as executive directors about what is going on in the company. Ignorance is not a defence. Directors must be aware of what is going on and have knowledge of the law relating to their duties and responsibilities. Fundamentally, directors must

● use their common sense
● be careful in what they do
● look after shareholders
● look after creditors
● look after employees.

Progress check 7.3

What are the main responsibilities of directors with regard to the accounting and financial reporting of their companies?

Duty of care

It is the duty of a director to exercise his/her powers in the best interests of the company, which includes not acting for his/her personal benefit, nor for an improper use. As we have seen, in the year 2000 the chairman of a major plc was criticised for alleged excessive perks, unauthorised donations, and inclusion of members of his family and household staff on the company payroll, without proper disclosure. Investors' concern over corporate governance practices at the group had been triggered by a fall in the share price of over 50% in two years. The resignation of the chairman followed an initial investigation. The new chairman very quickly launched a full inquiry into executive perks within the group, overseen by him personally.

Duty of care means doing the job with the skill and care that somebody with the necessary knowledge and experience would exercise if they were acting on their own behalf. Delegation of directors' power must be 'properly and sensibly done'. If a director of a company does not choose the right people or supervise them properly, all the directors may be liable for the misdeeds and mistakes of the people they have appointed.

When a company fails and is found to be insolvent, the **receiver** appointed will leave no stone unturned to identify whether any money may be recovered in order to pay off creditors. This will include checking for any oversights by directors for items they should have spotted 'if they had exercised their proper level of skill'.

Fiduciary duty

Directors must act in the best interests of the company. Courts will support directors who act honestly and in good faith. Acting in the best interests of the company includes not making personal profit at the company's expense, letting personal interest interfere with the proper running of the business, or doing business which favours directors or their close associates. In the year 2000 there were several business failures within the dot.com sector, where directors did act in the best interests of the company although their business plans may not have been commercially successful (for example, breathe.com).

Corporate manslaughter

Before 1999 there were only five prosecutions in the UK for corporate manslaughter, resulting in two convictions. The risk for directors is therefore remote, but nonetheless it should not be ignored.

In earlier years companies were outside the criminal law. As one judge put it 'a company had a soul to damn and no body to kick', meaning that because a company did not have an actual existence it could not be guilty of a crime because it could not have a guilty will. In 1965 a case established the validity of the indictment of a company for manslaughter. Since then over 19,000 people have been killed as a result of corporate activity, but no company stood trial for manslaughter, apart from P&O European Ferries (Dover) Ltd after the capsize and sinking of the *Herald of Free Enterprise* off Zeebrugge in 1987. The directors of P&O Ferries did stand trial, but were acquitted because the trial collapsed halfway through. Obstacles in the law included the need to prove gross negligence and to prove that at least one sufficiently senior official was guilty of that same gross negligence.

Although each year hundreds of people are killed at work or in commercially related activity, if companies have been prosecuted at all they have been charged under the Health and Safety at Work Act (1974) and other regulatory legislation. Many of the companies implicated in work fatalities and public transport disasters operate with diffuse management systems and much delegated power. Such systems that appear to have no 'controlling mind' make it difficult to meet the requirement of the law because of the difficulty in identifying the individual(s) who may possess the mental element for the crime.

A case that was successfully prosecuted involved a small company, OLL Ltd, which organised a canoe expedition at Lyme Bay in 1993, in which four teenage schoolchildren died. In 1994 the jury in the case found OLL Ltd guilty of manslaughter – an historic decision. Peter Kite, the managing director of the activity centre responsible for the canoeing disaster, was jailed for three years for manslaughter, and OLL Ltd was fined £60,000. OLL Ltd was the first company in the UK ever to be found guilty of manslaughter, in a decision that swept away 400 years of legal history.

The Lyme Bay case was atypical of corporate homicide incidents. The company was small, so it was relatively easy to discover the 'controlling mind'; the risks to which pupils were exposed were serious and obvious and, critically, they were not technical or esoteric in any way. Moreover, very unusually, the directors could not claim ignorance of the risks because of a damning letter they had received from former instructors telling them to improve safety at the centre.

The directors of Great Western Trains were acquitted over the Southall (1997) rail crash, but the Paddington (1999) rail crash case had not reached a satisfactory conclusion, when another case – the Hatfield (2000) rail crash – began in 2001.

A few years ago the legal profession considered that the promised review of the Law Commission's recommendation for an Involuntary Homicide Act 'could result in company directors being made personally responsible for safety and therefore potentially liable in cases of avoidable accidents'. The Government confirmed that an Act was likely to be on the statute books by the end of 2001.

Other responsibilities

Directors do not owe a direct duty to shareholders, but to the company itself. Directors have no contractual or fiduciary duty to outsiders and are generally not liable unless they have acted in breach of their authority. Directors must have regard to the interests of employees but this is enforceable against directors only by the company and not by the employees.

Progress check 7.4

What is meant by a duty of care and fiduciary duty with regard to company directors?

Insolvency

Insolvency, or when a company becomes insolvent, is when the company is unable to pay creditors' debts in full after realisation of all the assets of the business. The penalties imposed on directors of companies continuing to trade, while insolvent, may be disqualification and personal liability. Many directors have lost their houses (as well as their businesses) as a result of being successfully pursued by the receivers appointed to their insolvent companies.

The Insolvency Act 1986 provides guidance on matters to be considered by liquidators and receivers in the reports, which they are required to prepare on the conduct of directors. These matters include:

- breaches of fiduciary and other duties to the company
- misapplication or retention of monies or other property of the company
- causing the company to enter into transactions which defrauded the creditors
- failure to keep proper accounting and statutory records
- failure to make annual returns to the Registrar of Companies and prepare and file annual accounts.

If a company is insolvent, the courts assess the directors' responsibility for:

- the cause of the company becoming insolvent
- the company's failure to supply goods or services which had been paid for
- the company entering into fraudulent transactions or giving preference to particular creditors
- failure of the company to adhere to the rules regarding creditors' meetings in a creditors' **voluntary winding-up**
- failure to provide a **statement of affairs** or to deliver up any proper books or information regarding the company.

Progress check 7.5

How does insolvency impact on directors and what are their responsibilities in this regard?

Wrongful trading

A major innovation of the Insolvency Act 1986 was to create the statutory tort (civil wrong) of **wrongful trading**. It occurs where a director knows or ought to have known before the commencement of winding up that there was no reasonable prospect of the company avoiding insolvency and he/she does not take every step to minimise loss to creditors. If the court is satisfied of this it may:

(i)   order the director to contribute to the assets of the business, and

(ii) disqualify him/her from further involvement in corporate management for a specified period.

A director will not be liable for wrongful trading if he/she can show that from the relevant time he/she 'took every step with a view to minimising the potential loss to the company's creditors as (assuming him/her to have known that there was no reasonable prospect that the company would avoid going into insolvent liquidation) he/she ought to have taken'. A company goes into insolvent liquidation, for this purpose, if it does so at a time when its assets are insufficient for the payments of its debts and other liabilities and the expenses of winding up.

Both subjective tests and objective tests are made with regard to directors. A director who is responsible, for example, for manufacturing, quality, purchasing, or human resources, is likely to have less skill and knowledge regarding the financial affairs of the company than the **finance director**, unless otherwise fully briefed. Directors with financial or legal experience will certainly be expected to bear a greater responsibility than other directors because of their specialist knowledge.

Fraudulent trading

Fraudulent trading is an offence committed by persons who are knowingly party to the continuance of a company trading in circumstances where creditors are defrauded, or for other fraudulent purposes. Generally, this means that the company incurs more debts at a time when it is known that those debts will not be met. Persons responsible for acting in this way are personally liable without limitation for the debts of the company. The offence also carries criminal penalties.

The offence of fraudulent trading may apply at any time, not just in or after a winding-up. If a company is wound up and fraudulent trading has taken place, an additional civil liability arises in respect of any person who was knowingly a party to it.

Progress check 7.6

Are there any differences between wrongful trading and fraudulent trading? If so, what are they?

Disqualification of directors

Example 7.3

A director of a Hampshire building and double-glazing contractor was disqualified for six years after his company collapsed owing creditors £364,000. Ronald Norris, director of the Aldershot-based Berg Group, which was wound up on 6 January 1999, was found guilty of trading while insolvent since 3 December 1997. Norris from West Sussex, stood before Reading County Court on 8 January 1999. The other grounds for his disqualification were the transfer of a pension fund, of which Norris was a beneficiary on a property owned by Berg, failing to ensure that VAT was collected as due, and failing to ensure that monies due to Berg from connected companies were collected.

Outline some of the basic reasons why it is necessary for society to ban persons from becoming directors of limited companies.

Answer

The limited liability company is a very efficient means of conducting business, but if used by unscrupulous persons then innocent people can lose money, through no fault of their own.

The limited liability company can offer a financial shield to protect employees and investors if things go wrong and the company ceases trading, unable to pays its creditors.

UK law is now quite strict and will attack an obvious unscrupulous person taking advantage of the limited liability company and leaving various creditors out of pocket.

In recent times the UK Government has been banning an increasing number of persons from becoming directors, as well as publishing their names in the public domain (for example, the Internet). Almost certainly the recently introduced regime is showing its teeth and punishing guilty directors in a most practical manner.

Disqualification means that a person cannot be, for a specified period of time, a director or manager of any company without the permission of the courts. Disqualification is governed under the Company Directors (Disqualification) Act 1986, and may result from breaches under:

- the Companies Act 1985/1989
  - from cases of fraud or other breaches of duty by a director
- the Insolvency Act 1986
  - if the courts consider that the conduct of a director makes him/her unfit to be concerned in the future management of a company.

Whilst there are serious implications for directors of companies under the Company Directors (Disqualification) Act 1986, it should be noted that the Act is not restricted to company directors. Over one half of the liabilities fall on 'any persons' as well as company directors. 'Any persons' in this context potentially includes any employee within the organisation.

The following offences, and their penalties, under the Act relate to any persons:

- being convicted of an indictable offence – disqualification from company directorships for up to five years, and possibly for up to 15 years
- fraud in a winding up – disqualification from company directorships for up to 15 years
- participation in fraudulent or wrongful trading – disqualification from company directorships for up to 15 years

- acting as a director while an undischarged bankrupt, and failure to make payments under a County Court administration order – imprisonment for up to two years, or a fine, or both

- personal liability for a company's debts where the person acts while disqualified – civil personal liability

The following offences, and their penalties, under the Act relate to directors (but in some instances include other managers or officers of the company):

- persistent breaches of company legislation – disqualification from company directorships for up to five years

- convictions for not less than three default orders in respect of a failure to comply with any provisions of companies' legislation requiring a return, account or other document to be filed, delivered, sent, etc., to the Registrar of Companies (whether or not it is a failure of the company or the director) – disqualification from company directorships for up to five years

- finding of unfitness to run a company in the event of the company's insolvency – disqualification from company directorships for a period of between two years and 15 years

- if after investigation of a company the conduct of a director makes him unfit to manage a company – disqualification from company directorships for up to 15 years

- attribution of offences by the company to others if such persons consent, connive or are negligent – imprisonment for up to two years, or a fine, or both, or possibly imprisonment for not more than six months, or a fine.

In some circumstances directors may be disqualified automatically. Automatic disqualification occurs in the case of an individual who revokes a County Court administration order, or the case of an undischarged bankrupt unless **leave of the court** is obtained. In all the other situations the right to act as a director may be withdrawn only by an order of the court, unless a company through its Articles of Association provides for specific circumstances in which a director's appointment may be terminated. The City of London has seen a major toughening of the regime where persons have found themselves unemployable (for example, the fallout from the Baring Bank debacle in the mid-1990s).

Progress check 7.7	**In what circumstances may a director be disqualified?**

Summary of directors' obligations and responsibilities

In summary, the following may serve as a useful checklist of directors' obligations and responsibilities:

- both executive and non-executive directors must act with care, look after the finances and act within their powers, and look after employees

- directors are responsible for keeping proper books and presenting shareholders with accounts, and failure to do so can result in disqualification

- directors should understand the accounts and be able to interpret them

- the board of directors is responsible for filing accounts with the Registrar of Companies and must also notify changes to the board of directors and changes to the registered address

- shareholders must appoint auditors
- the directors are responsible for calling and holding annual general meetings, and ensuring minutes of all meetings are appropriately recorded
- directors are responsible for ensuring that the company complies with its memorandum and articles of association
- if a company continues to trade while technically insolvent and goes into receivership a director may be forced to contribute personally to repaying creditors
- a director trading fraudulently is liable to be called on for money
- any director who knew or ought to have known that insolvency was unavoidable without minimising loss to the creditors becomes liable
- directors can be disqualified for paying themselves too much
- inadequate attention paid to the financial affairs of the company can result in disqualification.

We have seen the onerous burden of responsibility placed on directors of limited companies in terms of compliance with guidelines and legislation. The obligations of directors continue to grow with the increase in Government regulation and legislation. Sixteen new directives were introduced during the two years to 2001, relating to such issues as employee working conditions, health and safety and, for example, administration of a minimum wage policy.

How can directors make sure that they comply and cover themselves in the event of things going wrong?

Actions to ensure compliance

Directors of companies need to be aware of the dividing line between the commission of a criminal offence and the commission of technical offences of the Companies Act. Directors should take the necessary actions to ensure compliance with their obligations and responsibilities, and to protect themselves against possible non-compliance:

- directors may delegate their responsibilities within or outside the company and in such circumstances they must ensure that the work is being done by competent, able and honest people
- directors of small companies in particular should get professional help to ensure compliance with statutory responsibilities
- directors must ensure that they are kept fully informed about the affairs of the company by having regular meetings and recording minutes and material decisions
- directors should ensure they have service contracts that cover the company's duties, rights, obligations, and directors' benefits
- directors must ensure that detailed, timely management accounts are prepared, and, if necessary, professional help sought to provide for example monthly reporting systems and assistance with interpretation of information produced and actions required.

It is essential that directors carefully watch for warning signs of any decline in the company's position, for example:

- falling sales/market share
- overdependence on one product/customer/supplier
- overtrading (see Chapter 15)

- pressure on bank borrowings
- increases in trade creditors
- requirements for cash paid in advance
- increasing stock levels
- poor financial controls.

The protection that directors may obtain is extremely limited. All directors should certainly take out individual professional liability insurance. But above all it is probably more important that all directors clearly understand their obligations and responsibilities, closely watch company performance, and take immediate, appropriate action as necessary, to ensure compliance and minimise their exposure to the type of personal risks we have discussed above.

Progress check 7.8

What actions should directors take to ensure they meet their obligations, and to protect themselves should things go wrong?

Summary of key points

- The framework for establishing good corporate governance and accountability has been established in a Combined Code of Practice, developed from the work of the Cadbury, Greenbury, and Hampel Committees.
- There is a statutory requirement for the audit of the accounts of limited companies, except for smaller limited companies.
- The election of suitably qualified, independent auditors is the responsibility of the shareholders, to whom they are responsible.
- Directors of limited companies have a specific responsibility to shareholders, and general responsibilities to all stakeholders and the community, for the management and conduct of companies. (Note the continued activities of pressure groups such as Greenpeace and the Friends of the Earth.)
- Directors of limited companies have a fiduciary duty to act in the best interests of the company, and a duty of care to all stakeholders and to the community at large, particularly with regard to the Companies Acts 1985/1989, Health and Safety at Work Act 1974, Financial Services Act 1986, and Insolvency Act 1986.
- The implications for directors for wrongful trading may be to contribute to the assets of the business, and disqualification from further involvement in corporate management for a specified period.
- The implications for directors for fraudulent trading may be to contribute to the assets of the business without limit, disqualification, and possible criminal and civil penalties.
- The implications of the Company Directors (Disqualification) Act 1986 apply not only to company directors, and over 50% of the provisions relate to any persons.
- Directors of limited companies, in addition to taking out individual professional liability insurance, must ensure that they clearly understand their obligations and responsibilities.

Glossary of key terms

Auditing Practices Board (APB) A body formed in 1991 by an agreement between the six members of the Consultative Committee of Accountancy Bodies, to be responsible for developing and issuing professional standards for auditors in the United Kingdom and the Republic of Ireland.

audit report An objective verification to shareholders and other users that the financial statements have been prepared properly and in accordance with legislative and regulatory requirements; that they present the information truthfully and fairly and that they conform to the best accounting practice in their treatment of the various measurements and valuations.

Combined Code of Practice The successor to the Cadbury Code, established by the Hampel Committee. The code consists of a set of principles of corporate governance and detailed code provisions embracing the work of the Cadbury, Greenbury and Hampel Committees. Section 1 of the code contains the principles and provisions applicable to UK listed companies, while section 2 contains the principles and provisions applicable to institutional shareholders in their relationships with companies.

director A person elected under the company's articles of association to be responsible for the overall direction of the company's affairs. Directors usually act collectively as a board and carry out such functions as are specified in the articles of association or the Companies Acts, but they may also act individually in an executive capacity.

finance director The finance director of an organisation is actively involved in broad strategic and policy-making activities involving financial considerations. The finance director provides the board of directors with advice on financing, capital expenditure, acquisitions, dividends, the implications of changes in the economic environment, and the financial aspects of legislation. The finance director is responsible for the planning and control functions, the financial systems, financial reporting, and the management of funds.

fraudulent trading An offence committed by persons who are knowingly party to the continuance of a company trading in circumstances where creditors are defrauded or for other

fraudulent purposes. Generally, this means that the company incurs more debts at a time when it is known that those debts will not be met. Persons responsible for so acting are personally liable without limitation for the debts of the company. The offence also carries criminal penalties.

Hampel Committee The 1998 report of the Hampel Committee on Corporate Governance was set up to conduct a review of the Cadbury Code and its implications:

- review of the role of directors
- matters arising from the Greenbury Study Group on directors' remuneration
- role of shareholders and auditors
- other relevant matters.

The Hampel Committee was responsible for the corporate governance Combined Code of Practice.

insolvency The inability of a company, partnership or individual to pay creditors' debts in full after realisation of all the assets of the business.

internal audit An independent appraisal function established within an organisation to examine and evaluate its activities as a service to the organisation. The objective of internal auditing is to assist members of the organisation in the effective discharge of their responsibilities. To this end, internal auditing furnishes them with analyses, appraisals, recommendations, counsel and information concerning the activities reviewed (Institute of Internal Auditors – UK).

leave of the court This is where the court will make a decision after hearing all the relevant information.

non-executive director A director who does not have a particular function to perform within the company's management. The usual involvement is to attend board meetings only.

receiver A person appointed by secured creditors or by the court to take control of company property, usually following the failure of the company to pay principal sums or interest due to debenture holders whose debt is secured by fixed or floating charges over the assets of the company. The receiver takes control of the charged assets and may operate the company's business with a view to selling it as a going concern. In practice receivership is closely followed by liquidation.

statement of affairs Details submitted to the Official Receiver during the winding-up of a company identifying the assets and liabilities of the company. The details are prepared by the company directors, or other persons specified by the Official Receiver, and must be submitted within 14 days of the winding-up order or the appointment of a provisional liquidator.

voluntary winding-up A voluntary winding-up of a company occurs where the company passes a resolution that it shall liquidate and the court is not involved in the process. A voluntary winding-up may be made by the members (the shareholders) of the company or by its creditors, if the company has failed to declare its solvency.

wrongful trading Wrongful trading occurs where a director knows or ought to have known before the commencement of winding-up that there was no reasonable prospect of the company avoiding insolvency and he/she does not take every step to minimise loss to creditors. If the court is satisfied of this it may (i) order the director to contribute to the assets of the business, and (ii) disqualify him/her from further involvement in corporate management for a specified period (Insolvency Act 1986).

Assessment material

Questions

Q7.1 (i) How was the corporate governance Combined Code of Practice developed?

(ii) Why was it considered necessary?

Q7.2 Refer to the Johnson Matthey section on corporate governance in their annual report and accounts 2000, pp. 245–7 to illustrate the areas of compliance under the Combined Code of Practice.

Q7.3 (i) Which areas of the business do auditors' opinions cover?

(ii) What happens if there is any fundamental uncertainty as to compliance?

Q7.4 Explain the implications of the 'expectation gap' with regard to external auditors.

Q7.5 Explain the obligations of directors of limited companies in terms of their duty of care, their fiduciary duty, and the forthcoming introduction of an Involuntary Homicide Act.

Q7.6 If the severity of the penalty is determined by the seriousness of the offence, describe the half dozen or so most serious offences under the Company Directors (Disqualification) Act 1986, which relate to directors of limited companies.

Q7.7 Outline the general responsibilities of a director of a limited company with regard to the company, its shareholders, and other stakeholders.

Q7.8 What are the key actions that a director of a limited company may take to ensure compliance with his/her obligations and responsibilities?

Discussion points

D7.1 Discuss, and illustrate with some examples, how far you think the corporate governance Combined Code of Practice goes to preventing the kind of corporate excesses we have seen in the recent past.

D7.2 'I pay my auditors a fortune in audit fees. I look upon this almost as another insurance premium to make sure that I'm protected against every kind of financial risk.' Discuss.

D7.3 'Everyone who embarks on a career in industry or commerce aspires to becoming a director of their organisation, because then all their troubles are over! Directors just make a few decisions, swan around in their company cars, and pick up a fat cheque at the end of each month for doing virtually nothing.' Discuss.

D7.4 In an age of increasingly sophisticated computer systems is the traditional role of the auditor coming to an end?

Exercises

Solutions are provided in Appendix 4 to all exercise numbers highlighted in colour.

Level I

E7.1 *Time allowed – 30 minutes*

Discuss why users of financial statements should have information on awards to directors of share options, allowing them to subscribe to shares at fixed prices in the future.

E7.2 *Time allowed – 30 minutes*

Outline the basic reasons why there should be openness regarding directors' benefits and 'perks'.

E7.3 *Time allowed – 30 minutes*

Can you think of any reasons why directors of UK plcs found that their contracts were no longer to be open-ended under the new regime of corporate governance?

E7.4 *Time allowed – 60 minutes*

William Mason is the managing director of Classical Gas plc, a recently formed manufacturing company in the chemical industry, and he has asked you as finance director to prepare a report that covers the topics, together with a brief explanation, to be included in a section on corporate governance in their forthcoming annual report and accounts.

Level II

E7.5 *Time allowed – 60 minutes*

After the birth of her twins Vimla Shah decided to take a couple of years away from her career as a company lawyer. During one of her coffee mornings with Joan Turnbull, Joan confided in her that although she was delighted at her husband Ronnie's promotion to commercial director of his company, which was a large UK plc in the food industry, she had heard many horror stories about problems that company directors had encountered, seemingly through no fault of their own. She was worried about the implications of these obligations and responsibilities (whatever they were) that Ronnie had taken on. Vimla said she would write some notes about what being a director of a plc meant, and provide some guidelines as to the type of things that Ronnie should be aware of, and to include some ways in which Ronnie might protect himself, that may all offer some reassurance to Joan. **Prepare a draft of what you think Vimla's notes for Joan may have included.**

E7.6   *Time allowed – 60 minutes*

Li Nan has recently been appointed managing director of Pingers plc, which is a company that supplies table tennis equipment to clubs and individuals throughout the UK and Europe. Lin Nan is surprised at the high figure that appeared in last year's accounts under audit fees.

Li Nan is not completely familiar with UK business practices and has requested you to prepare a detailed report on what the audit fees cover, and to include the general responsibilities of directors in respect of the external audit.

E7.7   *Time allowed – 60 minutes*

Use the following information, extracted from Tomkins plc report and accounts for 2000, as a basis for discussing the users of financial information's need for information on directors' remuneration.

	Basic salary	Benefits in kind	Bonuses
G Hutchings, executive director	£975,000	£45,000	£443,000
G Gates (USA), non-executive director	nil, but has a 250,000 US$ consultancy agreement		
R Holland, non-executive director	£23,000	nil	nil

Case Study I

BUZZARD LTD

Buzzard Ltd is a first-tier supplier to major passenger car and commercial vehicle manufacturers. As a first-tier supplier Buzzard provides systems that fit directly into motor vehicles, which they have manufactured from materials and components acquired from second, third, fourth-tier, etc., suppliers. During the 1990s, through investment in R&D and technology, Buzzard became regarded as one of the World's leaders in design, manufacture and supply of innovative automotive systems.

In the mid-1990s Buzzard started business in one of the UK's many development areas. It was established through acquisition of the business of Firefly from the Stonehead Group. Firefly was a traditional, mass production automotive component manufacturer, located on a brownfield site in Gentbridge, once a fairly prosperous mining area. Firefly had pursued short-term profit rather than longer-term development strategies, and had a poor image with both its customers and suppliers. This represented a challenge but also an opportunity for Buzzard to establish a World Class manufacturing facility.

A major part of Buzzard's strategic plan was the commitment to investing £30m to relocate from Gentbridge to a new fully-equipped 15,000 square metre purpose-built factory on a 20-acre greenfield site in Bramblecote, which was finally completed during the year 2000. At the same time, it introduced the changes required to transform its culture and implement the operating strategies required to achieve the highest level of industrial performance. By the year 2000 Buzzard Ltd had become an established supplier of high quality and was close to achieving its aim of being a World Class supplier of innovative automotive systems.

In December 2000 a seven-year bank loan was agreed with interest payable half yearly at a fixed rate of 8% per annum. The loan was secured with a floating charge over the assets of Buzzard Ltd.

The financial statements of Buzzard Ltd, its accounting policies and extracts from its notes to the accounts, for the year ended 31 December 2000 are shown below, prior to the payment of any proposed dividend. It should be noted that Note 3 to the accounts – Profit on ordinary activities before taxation – reports on some of the key items included in the profit and loss account for the year and is not a complete analysis of the profit and loss account.

Required

(i) Prepare a SWOT analysis for Buzzard Ltd based on the limited information available.

(ii) What do you consider to be the main risks faced by Buzzard Ltd, both internally and external to the business, based on your SWOT analysis and your own research about the automotive industry in the UK?

(iii) Prepare a report for shareholders that describes Buzzard's performance, supported by the appropriate profitability, efficiency, liquidity, and investment ratios required to present as complete a picture as possible from the information that has been provided.

(iv) The company has demonstrated its achievement of high levels of quality and customer satisfaction but would you, as a shareholder, be satisfied with the financial performance of Buzzard Ltd?

Profit and loss account
for the year ended 31 December 2000

	Notes	2000 £000	1999 £000
Turnover	1	115,554	95,766
Cost of sales		(100,444)	(80,632)
Gross profit		15,110	15,134
Distribution costs		(724)	(324)
Administrative expenses		(12,348)	(10,894)
Operating profit		2,038	3,916
Net interest	2	(868)	(972)
Profit on ordinary activities before taxation	3	1,170	2,944
Taxation		–	–
Profit for the financial year		1,170	2,944

The company has no recognised gains and losses other than those included above, and therefore no separate statement of total recognised gains and losses has been presented.

Balance sheet
as at 31 December 2000

	Notes	2000 £000	1999 £000
Fixed assets			
Tangible assets	8	42,200	29,522
Current assets			
Stocks	9	5,702	4,144
Debtors	10	18,202	16,634
Cash at bank and in hand		4	12
		23,908	20,790
Creditors: amounts falling due within one year	11	(23,274)	(14,380)
Net current assets		634	6,410
Total assets less current liabilities		42,834	35,932
Creditors: amounts falling due after more than one year			
Borrowings and finance leases	12	(6,000)	–
Provisions for liabilities and charges	13	(1,356)	(1,508)
Accruals and deferred income	14	(1,264)	(1,380)
Net assets		34,214	33,044
Capital and reserves			
Share capital	15	22,714	22,714
Profit and loss account		11,500	10,330
Shareholders' funds	16	34,214	33,044

Cash flow statement
for the year ended 31 December 2000

	2000 £000	1999 £000
Net cash inflow from operating activities	12,962	3,622
Returns on investments and servicing of finance		
Interest received	268	76
Interest paid	(1,174)	(1,044)
Net cash outflow from returns on investments and servicing of finance	(906)	(968)
Capital expenditure		
Purchase of tangible fixed assets	(20,490)	(14,006)
Sale of tangible fixed assets	12	30
Government grants received	1,060	1,900
Net cash outflow from investing activities	(19,418)	(12,076)
Net cash inflow/(outflow) before financing	(7,362)	(9,422)
[Hint: 12,962 − 906 − 19,418]		
Financing		
Issue of ordinary share capital	–	8,000
Increase in borrowings	6,000	–
Net cash (outflow)/inflow from financing	6,000	8,000
Decrease in cash in the period	(1,362)	(1,422)

	2000 £000	1999 £000
Note – reconciliation of net cash flows to the movement in net funds		
Decrease in cash in the period	(1,362)	(1,422)
Cash inflow from movement in borrowings	(6,000)	–
Opening net debt	(1,974)	(552)
Closing net debt	(9,336)	(1,974)

	1999 £000	Cash flow £000	2000 £000
Note – analysis of changes in net debt during the year			
Cash at bank and in hand	12	(8)	4
Overdraft	(1,986)	(1,354)	(3,340)
Borrowings due after one year	–	(6,000)	(6,000)
Net debt	(1,974)	(7,362)	(9,336)

Accounting policies

The financial statements have been prepared in accordance with applicable accounting standards. A summary of the more important accounting policies which have been applied consistently is set out below.

Basis of accounting The accounts are prepared under the historical cost convention.

Research and development Expenditure on research and development is written off as it is incurred.

Tangible fixed assets Tangible fixed assets are stated at their purchase price together with any incidental costs of acquisition.

Depreciation is calculated so as to write off the cost of tangible fixed assets on a straight line basis over the expected useful economic lives of the assets concerned. The principal annual rates used for this purpose are:

Freehold buildings	20 years
Plant and machinery (including capitalised tooling)	4–8 years
Office equipment and fixtures and fittings	5–8 years
Motor vehicles	4 years

Freehold land is not depreciated.

Government grants Grants received on qualifying expenditure or projects are credited to deferred income and amortised in the profit and loss account over the estimated useful lives of the qualifying assets or over the project life as appropriate.

Stocks and work in progress Stocks and work in progress are stated at the lower of cost and net realisable value. In general, cost is determined on a first in first out basis; in the case of manufactured products cost includes all direct expenditure and production overheads based on the normal level of activity. Net realisable value is the price at which stocks can be sold in the normal course of business after allowing for the costs of realisation and, where appropriate, the cost of conversion from their existing state to a finished condition. Provision is made where necessary for obsolescent, slow moving and defective stocks.

Foreign currencies Assets, liabilities, revenues and costs denominated in foreign currencies are recorded at the rate of exchange ruling at the date of the transaction; monetary assets and liabilities at the balance sheet date are translated at the year end rate of exchange or where there are related forward foreign exchange contracts, at contract rates. All exchange differences thus arising are reported as part of the results for the period.

Turnover Turnover represents the invoiced value of goods supplied, excluding value added tax.

Warranties for products Provision is made for the estimated liability arising on all known warranty claims. Provision is also made, using past experience, for potential warranty claims on all sales up to the balance sheet date.

Notes to the accounts

1 Segmental analysis

	Turnover		Profit on ordinary activities before taxation	
	2000 £000	1999 £000	2000 £000	1999 £000
Class of business				
Automotive components	115,554	95,766	1,170	2,944
Geographical segment				
United Kingdom	109,566	92,020		
Rest of Europe	5,290	3,746		
Japan	698	–		
	115,554	95,766		

2 Net interest

	2000 £000	1999 £000
Interest payable on bank loans and overdrafts	(1,182)	(1,048)
Interest receivable	314	76
	(868)	(972)

3 Profit on ordinary activities before taxation

	2000 £000	1999 £000
Profit on ordinary activities before taxation is stated after crediting:		
Amortisation of Government grant	1,176	796
(Loss)/profit on disposal of fixed assets	(18)	10
And after charging		
Depreciation charge for the year:		
Tangible owned fixed assets	7,782	4,742
Research and development expenditure	7,694	6,418
Auditors' remuneration for:		
Audit	58	58
Other services	40	52
Hire of plant and machinery – operating leases	376	346
Hire of other assets – operating leases	260	314
Foreign exchange losses	40	20

4 Directors and employees

The average weekly number of persons (including executive directors) employed during the year was:

	2000 number	1999 number
Production	298	303
Engineering, quality control and development	49	52
Sales and administration	56	45
	403	400

	2000 £000	1999 £000
Staff costs (for the above persons):		
Wages and salaries	6,632	5,837
Social security costs	562	483
Other pension costs	286	218
	7,480	6,538

8 Tangible fixed assets

	Freehold land and buildings £000	Motor vehicles £000	Plant, machinery and tooling £000	Office equipment, fixtures and fittings £000	Total £000
Cost					
At 1 January 2000	15,450	114	20,648	4,600	40,812
Additions	20	28	19,808	634	20,490
Disposals	–	–	(80)	(10)	(90)
At 31 December 2000	15,470	142	40,376	5,224	61,212
Depreciation					
At 1 January 2000	834	54	7,932	2,470	11,290
Charge for year	734	22	6,226	800	7,782
Eliminated in respect of disposals	–	–	(58)	(2)	(60)
At 31 December 2000	1,568	76	14,100	3,268	19,012
Net book value at 31 December 2000	13,902	66	26,276	1,956	42,200
Net book value at 31 December 1999	14,616	60	12,716	2,130	29,522

9 Stocks

	2000 £000	1999 £000
Raw materials and consumables	4,572	3,274
Work in progress	528	360
Finished goods and goods for resale	602	510
	5,702	4,144

10 Debtors

	2000 £000	1999 £000
Amounts falling due within one year		
Trade debtors	13,364	8,302
Other debtors	4,276	7,678
Prepayments and accrued income	562	654
	18,202	16,634

11 Creditors: amounts falling due within one year

	2000 £000	1999 £000
Overdraft	3,340	1,986
Trade creditors	13,806	8,646
Other taxation and social security payable	2,334	1,412
Other creditors	122	350
Accruals and deferred income	3,672	1,986
	23,274	14,380

12 Borrowings

	2000 £000	1999 £000
Bank and other loans repayable otherwise than by instalments		
Over five years	6,000	–

13 Provisions for liabilities and charges

	Pensions £000	Warranties for products £000	Total £000
At 1 January 2000	732	776	1,508
Expended in the year	(572)	(494)	(1,066)
Charge to profit and loss account	562	352	914
At 31 December 2000	722	634	1,356

14 Accruals and deferred income

	2000 £000	1999 £000
Government grants		
At 1 January 2000	1,380	2,176
Amount receivable	1,060	–
Amortisation in year	(1,176)	(796)
At 31 December 2000	1,264	1,380

15 Share capital

	2000 £000	1999 £000
Authorised		
28,000,000 (1999: 28,000,000) ordinary shares of £1 each	28,000	28,000
Issued and fully paid		
22,714,000 (1999: 22,714,000) ordinary shares of £1 each	22,714	22,714

16 Reconciliation of movement in shareholders' funds

	2000 £000	1999 £000
Opening shareholders' funds	33,044	22,100
Issue of ordinary share capital	–	8,000
Profit for the financial year	1,170	2,944
Closing shareholders' funds	34,214	33,044

17 Capital commitments

	2000 £000	1999 £000
Capital expenditure that has been contracted for but has not been provided for in the financial statements	1,506	162
Capital expenditure that has been authorised by the directors but has not yet been contracted for	6,768	5,404

18 Financial commitments

At 31 December 2000 the company had annual commitments under non-cancellable operating leases as follows:

	Land and buildings 2000 £000	Other 2000 £000	Land and buildings 1999 £000	Other 1999 £000
Expiring within one year	–	96	112	210
Expiring within two to five years	–	254	–	360
Expiring after five years	–	120	–	90
	–	470	112	660

PART II

Management accounting

Part II is about management accounting. In contrast with financial accounting, which deals with historical information, management accounting is more concerned with looking ahead and providing information to assist managers in decision-making, forecasting, planning and achievement of plans.

Chapter 8 provides an introduction to management accounting and the framework in which it operates. It looks at the nature and behaviour of costs and how they change in response to changes in levels of activity.

Chapter 9 takes a broad approach to the management of costs, and the relationships between costs, activity volumes, and profit. This chapter introduces the topic of break-even analysis, and various approaches to the treatment of costs, and goes on to consider some of the more recently developed techniques of cost management.

Chapter 10 considers how some of the techniques of management accounting may be used in the decision-making process. Decision-making is looked at in the context of both costs and sales pricing.

Chapter 11 deals with the way in which businesses, as part of their strategic management process, translate their long-term objectives and plans into forecasts, short-term plans and budgets.

Chapter 12 deals with budgetary control. This is concerned with the periods after the budgeting process has been completed, in which actual performance may be compared with the budget. This chapter looks at how actual performance comparisons with budget may be made and analysed to explain deviations from budget, and to identify appropriate remedial actions.

Cost behaviour

LEARNING OBJECTIVES

Completion of this chapter will enable you to:

- outline the additional accounting concepts that relate to management accounting

- explain what is meant by the term cost, its nature and limitations

- identify the bases for allocation and apportionment of costs

- determine the costs of products, services or activities using the techniques of absorption costing and marginal costing

- critically compare the techniques of absorption costing and marginal costing

Introduction

The chapters included in Part I of this book were concerned with financial accounting, with particular emphasis on the three key financial statements: balance sheet; profit and loss account; cash flow statement. This has necessarily focused on the historical aspect of accounting. To use a car driving analogy, we have made far more use of the rear view mirror than the view through the windscreen. We have concentrated on the accumulation of data and the reporting of past events, rather than the consideration of current and future activities.

We have previously identified accounting as having the three roles of maintaining the scorecard, problem solving, and attention directing. The scorecard role, although primarily a financial accounting role, remains part of the responsibility of management accounting. However, its more important roles are those of problem solving and attention directing. These roles focus on current and future activities, with regard to the techniques involved in decision-making, planning and control that will be covered in this and subsequent chapters.

This chapter introduces management accounting by looking at some further concepts to those that were covered in Chapter 1. Management accounting is

Rover saved by £10 sale to Phoenix

By Sophie Barker, Maurice Weaver and George Jones

Rover was saved from closure yesterday after one of the most dramatic rescue missions in the history of British industry.

The Phoenix consortium, headed by John Towers, a former chief executive of the car firm, sealed a deal with BMW to buy the ailing company for a nominal £10. He received a hero's welcome from Longbridge workers as he arrived at the Midlands plant. Mr Towers pledged to recreate a 'world class' car maker which would return to profit within two years.

Under BMW's ownership, Rover was said to be losing £2 million a day – a figure which Mr Towers rejected. The deal, signed at 8.30 am, brought to an end a two-month 'rollercoaster' of uncertainty about Rover's future – and put a former flagship of the car industry back in British ownership.

The Phoenix consortium, made up mainly of Midlands businessmen, only opened serious negotiations last Tuesday but worked around the clock over the past two weeks to put together a viable business plan. Until yesterday, there had been widespread doubts that Phoenix could save a company which BMW dubbed its 'English Patient' and had been suffering from the effects of the high pound.

Mr Towers will make about 1,000 of the 8,500 workers redundant – but that is considerably fewer than the 50 per cent expected if the company had been bought by the venture capitalists Alchemy Partners or if BMW had closed the plant. The deal has removed – at least for the time being – the threat of thousands of further job losses among suppliers in the West Midlands and the nationwide network of Rover dealers.

Phoenix will fund the redundancies from a £500 million BMW loan. It has also received a £200 million loan from an American bank – but no Government money has yet been sought or promised. Tony Blair, who was closely involved in behind-the-scenes negotiations between Phoenix and BMW, described the rescue as 'good news' and a 'real start to the process of giving Longbridge a good future'.

He said the Government had resisted calls to re-nationalise Rover – but had not stood by idly. Instead it had worked to bring about a viable commercial solution. Mr Towers was given a champagne reception by delighted workers, who downed tools early to greet their new boss. He admitted it had been an 'emotional day' for the car industry.

He plans to keep Longbridge production at 200,000 cars a year – about the same as BMW made last year. Despite the euphoria among the workers – and the evident relief in Government – motor industry experts warned that Phoenix faced a struggle to become profitable at a time when there was over-capacity in the industry.

Phoenix has formed a new company to take over the development, production and distribution of Rover cars. This includes responsibility for the Rover 25, 45 and 75 models as well as the MGF sports car and the existing Mini – which is soon to be superseded by BMW's new Mini.

A new estate version of the Rover 75 is also in the pipeline. The Rover 75 will shift from BMW's Cowley plant, near Oxford, to Longbridge – a move which is not expected to amount to any substantial job losses. Phoenix will also own all Rover's 'heritage' brands, apart from Triumph and Riley.

Mr Towers said he had pushed for these to be included but BMW refused and the issue could have become 'a deal breaker' if he had insisted. He also said he was in talks with other firms to forge a deal in which a rival to Rover would step into Longbridge and provide car bases for a new model. Honda and Volkswagen have been mentioned as potential candidates.

While Mr Towers stressed that he had 'always maintained a good working relationship' with Honda, which until 1994 owned a 20 per cent stake in Rover, the Japanese car company yesterday said it was not in talks with the consortium. Stephen Byers, the Trade and Industry Secretary, who was cheered by Labour MPs, acknowledged that an alliance with another global car manufacturer was essential to Rover's long-term survival.

He said the deal secured the firm's 'short and medium-term future' – but Mr Towers' 'hard-headed' approach gave Rover a chance of success. Mr Towers will remain at the helm of the new Rover Group, alongside Nick Stephenson, a fellow Phoenix member and West Midlands businessman, until he finds a chief executive. An appointment is understood to be imminent.

Pressed on how he planned to make a success of a company that had defeated one of the world's leading car makers, Mr Towers said: 'We are going to have a completely different approach to BMW. They have spent huge amounts creating excellent products, charging premium prices and creating a 'British BMW'. We will strip a lot of the overheads out and change the style and culture of the business'.

Mr Towers is expected to launch a marketing campaign to 'engage people's imagination' and to develop a 'sportier' image, possibly using the MG badge on upgraded existing models, in a bid to capture younger buyers. John Edmonds, general secretary of the GMB union, said: 'This is the best deal that we could have hoped for and gives the company a breathing space. John Towers can be assured of the strongest support from the workforce'.

Alchemy, which had been waiting in the wings in case the deal collapsed, issued a statement wishing Phoenix and its employees good luck.

© *Daily Telegraph*, 10 May 2000

concerned with costs. We will look at what cost is, how costs behave and how costs are ascertained. This will include some of the approaches used to determine the costs of products and services. Management accountants may be involved in the preparation of financial information that frequently requires senior management attention, resulting in decisions that are not always popular (for example down-sizing of businesses), as seen in the Rover example on the opposite page.

Early in the year 2000 the Phoenix consortium headed by John Towers was successful in its quest to acquire the Rover group following BMW's withdrawal. This was expected to avoid redundancies and put Rover back into British ownership. As the press cutting shows, this case highlighted some important business activities in which management accounting is involved:

- planning – the consortium needed to prepare a viable business plan very quickly to support their offer to take over the group, which involved directing attention to specific areas and providing proposed solutions to actual and anticipated problems

- evaluation of the impact of current and future losses – formulation of cost-cutting proposals including some redundancies

- forecasting – preparation of forecasts to support negotiation with bankers for funding

- business analysis – analysis and interpretation of factors internal and external to the company to support the strategic decision-making of the new company.

By the beginning of 2001 the business world remained sceptical that Rover, the £2m-a-day loss-maker, could be turned into a profitable, independent car maker. The company still faced major problems, including the patchy mess of the Longbridge, Birmingham site, and a shortage of cash for new product development. However, the consortium expected to start making small profits by the year 2002.

Management accounting concepts

Management accounting is an integral part of management, requiring the identification, generation, presentation, interpretation and use of information relevant to the activities outlined in Fig. 8.1:

- formulating business strategy involves setting the long-term objectives of the business

- planning and controlling activities deal with short-term objectives and investigations into the differences that may arise from actual outcomes against the plan and the recommendation and implementation of remedial actions

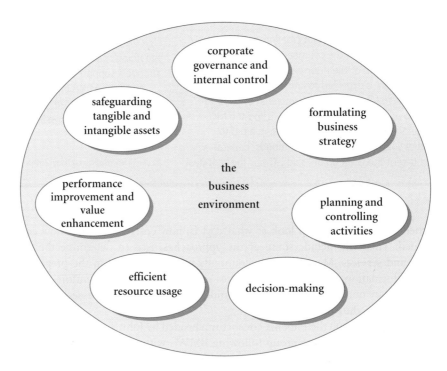

FIGURE 8.1 The areas of business activity supported by management accounting

- decision-making includes identification of those items of information relevant to a particular decision and those items that may be ignored
- efficient resource usage may be determined from the process of setting short-term budget plans and in their implementation
- performance improvement and value enhancement includes cost reduction and profit improvement exercises and the implementation of improvement initiatives such as quality costing, continuous improvement, and benchmarking
- safeguarding tangible and intangible assets – the management of fixed assets and working capital (which we shall look at in more detail in Chapter 15) are key accounting responsibilities in ensuring that there is no undue diminution in the value of assets such as buildings, machinery, stocks and debtors, as a result, for example, of poor management, and weak physical controls, and to ensure that every endeavour is made to maximise returns from the use of those assets
- corporate governance and internal control were considered in Chapter 7 and are concerned with the ways in which companies are controlled, the behaviour and accountability of directors and their levels of remuneration, and disclosure of information.

Therefore, it can be seen that management accounting, although providing information for external reporting, is primarily concerned with the provision of information to people within the organisation for:

- product costing
- forecasting, planning and control
- decision-making.

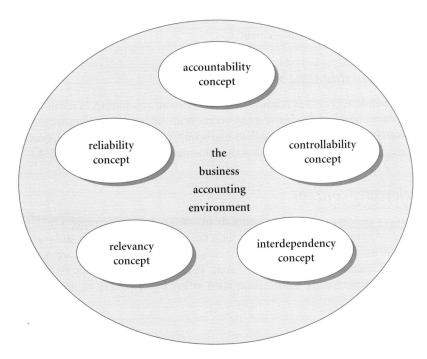

FIGURE 8.2 Management accounting concepts

Outline what is meant by management accounting and give examples of areas of business activity in which it may be involved.

In addition to the fundamental accounting concepts that were discussed in Chapter 1, there are further fundamental management accounting concepts (see Fig. 8.2). These do not represent any form of external regulation but are fundamental principles for the preparation of internal management accounting information. A brief outline of these principles is as follows.

The accountability concept

Management accounting presents information measuring the achievement of the objectives of an organisation and appraising the conduct of its internal affairs in that process. In order that further action can be taken, based on this information, the accountability concept makes it necessary at all times to identify the responsibilities and key results of individuals within the organisation.

The controllability concept

The controllability concept requires that management accounting identifies the elements or activities which management can or cannot influence, and seeks to assess risk and sensitivity factors. This facilitates the proper monitoring, analysis, comparison and interpretation of information which can be used constructively in the control, evaluation and corrective functions of management.

The interdependency concept

The **interdependency concept** requires that management accounting, in recognition of the increasing complexity of business, must access both internal and external information sources from interactive functions such as marketing, production, personnel, procurement and finance. This assists in ensuring that the information is adequately balanced.

The relevancy concept

The **relevancy concept** ensures that flexibility in management accounting is maintained in assembling and interpreting information. This facilitates the exploration and presentation, in a clear, understandable and timely manner, of as many alternatives as are necessary for impartial and confident decisions to be taken. This process is essentially forward-looking and dynamic. Therefore, the information must satisfy the criteria of being applicable and appropriate.

The reliability concept

The **reliability concept** requires that management accounting information must be of such quality that confidence can be placed on it. Its reliability to the user is dependent on its source, integrity and comprehensiveness.

Example 8.1

During 1999 the UK Government promoted the building of the Dome in Greenwich, London, to celebrate the Millennium. It was opened on time for 31 December 1999. The projected number of visitors during the year was 12 million. That target was not reached.

Discuss the above situation and its relationship with the controllability concept.

(Hint: Research the Internet, for example www.telegraph.co.uk)

Answer

The visitor numbers proved to be a major problem from the outset. Various attempts were made to increase the number of visitors, for example free tickets to schools. The visitor numbers were frequently reported in the national press. The management was changed to try and get somewhere near the targets. All measures taken and effort expended throughout the year unfortunately failed.

Progress check 8.2

Explain in what ways the additional concepts have been developed to support the profession of management accounting.

The nature of costs

Costs and revenues are terms that are inextricably linked to accounting. Revenues relate to inflows of assets such as cash and accounts receivable from debtors, or reductions in liabilities, resulting from trading operations. Costs generally relate to what was paid for a product or a service. It may be a past cost:

● a particular use of resources forgone to achieve a specific objective

● a resource used to provide a product or a service

● a resource used to retain a product or a service.

A cost may be a future cost in which case the alternative uses of resources other than to meet a specific objective may be more important, or relevant, to the decision whether or not to pursue that objective.

Cost is not a word that is usually used without a qualification as to its nature and limitations. On the face of it cost may obviously be described as what was paid for something. Cost may, of course, be used as a noun or a verb. As a noun it is an amount of expenditure (actual or notional) incurred on, or attributable to, a specified thing or activity; it relates to a resource sacrificed or forgone, expressed in a monetary value. As a verb, we may say that to cost something is to ascertain the cost of a specified thing or activity.

A number of terms relating to cost are regularly used within management accounting. A comprehensive glossary of key terms appears at the end of this chapter. These terms will be explained as we go on to discuss each of the various topics and techniques.

Progress check 8.3

What does 'cost' mean?

Cost accumulation relates to the collection of cost data. Cost data may be concerned with past costs or future costs. Past costs, or historical costs are the costs that we have dealt with in Chapters 2, 3 and 4, in the preparation of financial statements.

Costs are dependent on, and generally change with, the level of activity. The greater the volume or complexity of the activity, then normally the greater is the cost. We can see from Fig. 8.3 that there are three main elements of cost:

● fixed cost

● variable cost

● semi-variable cost (or semi-fixed, or mixed cost).

Fixed cost is a cost which is incurred for an accounting period, and which, within certain manufacturing output or sales turnover limits, tends to be unaffected by fluctuations in the level of activity (output or turnover). An example of a fixed cost is rent of premises that will allow activities up to a particular volume, but which is fixed regardless of volume, for example a car production plant. In the longer term, when volumes may have increased, the fixed cost of rent may also increase from the need to provide a larger factory. Discussion on fixed overheads invariably focuses on when should the fixed costs be no longer 'fixed'? Since most businesses these days need to be dynamic and constantly changing, changes to fixed costs inevitably follow changes in their levels of activity.

A variable cost varies in direct proportion to the level, or volume, of activity, and again strictly speaking, within certain output or turnover limits. The variable costs incurred in production of a car: materials, labour costs, electricity costs, and so on, are the same for each

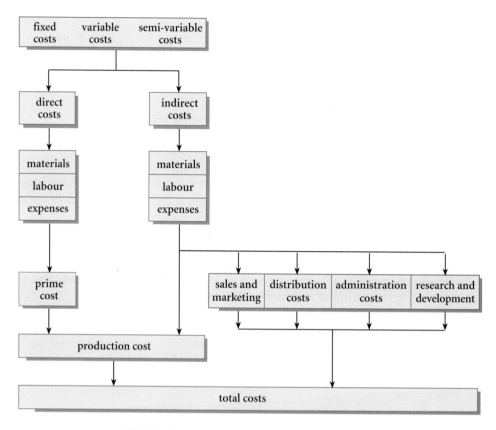

FIGURE 8.3 The elements of total costs

car produced and so the total of these costs varies as volume varies. The relationship holds until, for example, the cost prices of materials or labour change.

Progress check 8.4

Discuss whether or not knowledge of labour costs can assist management in setting prices for products or services.

A semi-variable cost is a cost containing both fixed and variable components and which is thus partly affected by a change in the level of activity, but not in direct proportion. Examples of semi-variable costs are maintenance costs comprising regular weekly maintenance and breakdown costs, and telephone expenses that include line and equipment rental in addition to call charges.

An example of the quarterly telephone charges that may be incurred by a business at various levels of call usage is shown below, and in the chart in Fig. 8.4. If the business makes no calls at all during the quarter it will incur costs of £200, which cover line rentals and rental of equipment.

Calls (units)	1,000	2,000	3,000
Charges	£700	£800	£900

FIGURE 8.4 An example of how a quarterly semi-variable telephone cost comprises both fixed and variable elements

The total costs of an entity comprise three categories:

● staff costs, the costs of employment which include

- gross pay
- paid holidays
- employer's contributions to National Insurance
- pension schemes
- sickness benefit schemes
- other benefits, for example protective clothing and canteen subsidies

● materials include

- raw materials purchased for incorporation into products for sale
- consumable items
- packaging

● expenses, relating to all costs other than materials and labour costs.

Each of the above three categories may be further analysed into:

● **direct costs**

● **indirect costs**

Are managers really interested in whether a cost is fixed or variable when assessing cost behaviour within an organisation?

Direct costs are those costs that can be traced and identified with, and specifically measured with respect to a relevant cost object. A **cost object** is the thing we wish to determine the cost of. Direct costs include **direct labour**, **direct materials**, and direct overheads. The total cost of direct materials, direct labour and direct expenses, or overheads, is called prime cost.

Indirect costs, or overheads, are costs untraceable to particular units (compared with direct costs). Indirect costs include expenditure on labour, materials or services, which cannot be identified with a saleable cost unit. The term 'burden' used by American companies is synonymous with indirect costs or overheads.

Indirect costs may relate to:

● the provision of a product
● the provision of a service
● other 'sales and administration' activities.

Total indirect costs may therefore be generally categorised as:

● production costs
● sales and marketing costs
● distribution costs
● administration costs
● research and development costs.

Indirect costs relating to production activities have to be allocated, that is, assigned as allocated overheads to any of the following:

● a single **cost unit**
a unit of product or service in relation to which costs are ascertained
● a **cost centre**
a production or service location, function, activity or item of equipment for which costs are accumulated
● a **cost account**
a record of the expenditure of a cost centre or cost unit
● a time period.

Example 8.2

Discuss whether managers are really interested in whether a cost is fixed or variable when assessing cost behaviour within their departments.

Answer

A manager must know how a cost will behave when setting a departmental budget. As time goes by and the manager routinely reports actual compared to budget, several differences will be caused by the behaviour of the cost. For example, certain wage costs may be greater per hour for hours worked after 6.00 pm each day.

Progress check 8.6

Explain costs in terms of the hierarchy of costs that comprise the total costs of a business.

Within the various areas of management accounting there is greater interest in future costs. The future costs that result from management decisions are concerned with **relevant costs** and **opportunity costs**, which are described briefly below but which will be illustrated in greater detail when we consider the techniques of decision-making in Chapter 10.

Relevant costs (and revenues) are the costs (and revenues) appropriate to a specific management decision. They are represented by future cash flows whose magnitude will vary depending upon the outcome of the management decision made. If stock is sold to a retailer, the relevant cost, used in the determination of the profitability of the transaction, would be the cost of replacing the stock, not its original purchase price, which is a sunk cost. **Sunk costs**, or irrecoverable costs, are costs that have been irreversibly incurred or committed prior to a decision point and which cannot therefore be considered relevant to subsequent decisions.

An opportunity cost is the value of the benefit sacrificed when one course of action is chosen in preference to an alternative. The opportunity cost is represented by the forgone potential benefit from the best of the alternative courses of action that have been rejected. A student, for example, may have a Saturday job that pays £7 per hour. If the student gave up one hour on a Saturday to clean the car instead of paying someone £5 to clean it for them, the opportunity cost would be

One hour of the student's lost wages	£7
less: **Cost of car cleaning**	£5
Opportunity cost	£2

Cost allocation and cost apportionment

The indirect costs of service departments may be allocated both to other service departments and to production departments. An idea of the range of departments existing in most large businesses can be gained by simply looking at the newspaper job advertisements of major companies, where each department may represent an 'allocation of costs' problem.

Allocation of overheads is the charging to a cost centre those overheads that result solely from the existence of that cost centre. Cost assignment defines the process of tracing and allocating costs to the cost object. Overheads are allocated where possible, but allocation can only be done if the exact amount incurred is known without having to carry out any sort of sharing. For example, a department in a factory may have a specific machine or a type of skilled labour that is only used in that department. The depreciation cost of the specific machine and the cost of the skilled labour would be allocated to that department. If the amount is not known and it is not possible to allocate costs then the total amount must be apportioned.

Example 8.3

A degree of subjectivity is involved in the allocation of expenses to a cost centre, which can frequently cause problems.

Discuss why the allocation of wage costs to the Millennium Dome project should have been fairly straightforward.

Answer

The Dome was very unusual since it was a large capital project with a very short life, starting on 31 December 1999 and finishing 31 December 2000. The ticket office would also have a very short life – it would have had no tickets to sell after 31 December 2000! The costs of staff working in the ticket office would also be easy to identify.

Apportionment is the charging to a cost centre of a fair share of an overhead on the basis of the benefit received by the cost centre in respect of the facilities provided by the overhead. For example, a factory may consist of two or more departments that occupy different amounts of floor space. The total factory rent cost may then be apportioned between the departments on the basis of floor space occupied.

Therefore, if an overhead cannot be allocated then it must be apportioned, involving use of a basis of apportionment, a physical or financial unit, so that the overhead will be equitably shared between the cost centres. Bases of apportionment, for example, that may be used are:

● area – for rent, heating and lighting, building depreciation

● number of employees – for personnel and welfare costs, safety costs

● weights or sizes – for materials handling costs, warehousing costs.

The basis chosen will use the factor most closely related to the benefit received by the cost centres.

Example 8.4

The Millennium Dome had many areas that were financed by outside companies that had signed contracts for the year. The contracts would have included clauses regarding recovery of certain costs from them, by the Millennium Company.

Discuss which of the costs of cleaning and security would be more difficult to apportion.

Answer

The cleaning costs would have been fairly straightforward to apportion, probably on a surface area basis (square metres).

The security costs may have been more problematical, for example using a basis of value of contents, area of concession and so on.

Once overheads have been allocated and apportioned, perhaps via some service cost centres, ultimately to production cost centres, they can be charged to cost units. For example, in a factory with three departments the total rent may have been apportioned to the manufacturing department, the assembly department, and the goods inwards department. The total overhead costs of the goods inwards department may then be apportioned between the manufacturing department and the assembly department. The total costs of the manufacturing department and the assembly department may then be charged to the units being produced in those departments, for example television sets, or cars. The same process may be used in the service sector, for example theatre seats, and hospital beds. A cost unit is a unit of product or service in relation to which costs are ascertained. A **unit cost** is the average cost of a product or service unit based on total costs and the number of units.

The unit cost ascertainment process (illustrated in Fig. 8.5) involves taking each cost centre and sharing its overheads among all the cost units passing through that centre. This process is similar to apportionment but in this case cost units are charged instead of cost centres. This process of charging costs to cost units is absorption and is defined as the charging of overheads to cost units.

The cost of converting material into finished products, that is, direct labour, direct expense and production overhead, is called the conversion cost. An example of this may be seen in the manufacture of a car bumper, which may have started out as granules of plastic and 'cans of paint'. After the completion of carefully controlled processes that may use some labour and incur overhead costs, the granules and paint are converted into a highly useful product.

	Number of units	Manufacturing department					Charge per unit
		Production time	Rate per hour	Total charge on the basis of hours			
Overhead costs	3,000 product A	1,000 hours	£5	£5,000	[£5,000/3,000]		£1.67
for January	2,000 product B	4,000 hours	£5	£20,000	[£20,000/2,000]		£10.00
£50,000	5,000 product C	5,000 hours	£5	£25,000	[£25,000/5,000]		£5.00
	10,000 units	10,000 hours		£50,000			

FIGURE 8.5 An example of unit cost ascertainment

Progress check 8.7

What is cost allocation and cost apportionment? Give some examples of bases of cost apportionment.

Absorption costing

In this section we are looking at profit considered at the level of total revenue less total cost. If a CD retailer, for example, uses absorption costing it includes a proportion of the costs of its premises, such as rent and utilities costs, in the total unit cost of selling each CD. The allocation and apportionment process that has been outlined in the past few paragraphs is termed **absorption costing**, or full costing. This process looks at costing in terms of the total costs of running a facility like a hospital, restaurant, retail shop, or factory, being part of the output from that facility. This is one method of costing that, in addition to direct costs, assigns all, or a proportion of, production overhead costs to cost units by means of one or a number of **overhead absorption rates**. There are two steps involved in this process:

- computation of an overhead absorption rate
- application of the overhead absorption rate to cost units.

The basis of absorption is chosen in a similar way to choosing an apportionment base. The overhead rate is calculated using:

$$\text{overhead absorption rate} = \frac{\text{total cost centre overheads}}{\text{total units of base used}}$$

Example 8.5

Albatross Ltd budgeted to produce 44,000 dining chairs for the month of January, but actually produced 48,800 dining chairs (units). Its sales were 40,800 units at a price of £100 per unit.

Budgeted costs for January:

Direct material	£36 per unit
Direct labour	£8 per unit
Variable production costs	£6 per unit

Fixed costs

Production costs	£792,000
Administrative expenses	£208,000
Selling costs	£112,000

Sales commission is paid at 10% of sales revenue. There was no opening stock and budgeted costs were the same as actual costs.

We are required to prepare the profit and loss account for January using absorption costing techniques, on the basis of the number of budgeted units of production.

Answer

$$\text{Overhead absorption rate} = \frac{\text{budgeted fixed production cost}}{\text{budgeted units of production}} = \frac{£792,000}{44,000} = £18 \text{ per unit}$$

Over-absorption of fixed production overheads

$= (\text{actual production} - \text{budgeted production}) \times \text{fixed production overhead rate per unit}$

$= (48,800 - 44,000) \times £18 \text{ per unit} = £86,400$

Production costs per unit

	£	
Direct material	36	
Direct labour	8	
Variable production overhead	6	
Variable production cost	50	
Fixed production overhead	18	see above
Full production cost per unit	68	

Profit and loss account

	£	£
Sales (40,800 × £100)		4,080,000
Full production costs (48,800 × £68)	3,318,400	
plus Opening stock	—	
less Closing stock (8,000 units × £68)	(544,000)	
Cost of sales		2,774,400
Gross profit		1,305,600
less Other expenses		
Sales commission (£4,080,000 × 10%)	408,000	
Administrative expenses	208,000	
Selling costs	112,000	
		728,000
		577,600
plus Over-absorbed fixed production overheads		86,400 see above
Net profit for January, before tax		664,000

Under/over-absorbed overheads represent the difference between overheads incurred and overheads absorbed. Over-absorbed overheads are credited to the profit and loss account, increasing the profit, as in the above example (refer to Appendix 1 to refresh your knowledge of debits and credits). Under-absorbed overheads are debited to the profit and loss account, reducing the profit. In this example, the over-absorption of overheads was caused by the actual production level deviating from the budgeted level of production. Deviations, or variances, can occur due to differences between actual and budgeted volumes and/or differences between actual and budgeted expenditure.

There are many bases that may be used for calculation of the overhead absorption rate, for example:

- units of output
- direct labour hours
- machine hours.

Desktop IT systems can assist in these calculations and provide many solutions to the problem of the 'overhead absorption rate', allowing consideration of a number of 'what-if' scenarios before making a final decision.

It can be seen that absorption costing is a costing technique whereby each unit of output is charged with both fixed and variable production costs. The fixed production costs are treated as part of the actual production costs. Stocks, in accordance with SSAP 9, are therefore valued on a full production cost basis and 'held' within the balance sheet until the stocks have been sold, rather than charged to the profit and loss account in the period in which the costs of the stocks are incurred. When the stocks are sold in a subsequent accounting period these costs are matched with the sales revenue of that period and charged to the profit and loss account. The objective of absorption costing is to obtain an overall average economic cost of carrying out whatever activity is being costed.

In order for costings to be carried out from the first day of operations, overhead rates are invariably calculated on the basis of expected future, or budgeted overheads and the number of units of manufacturing capacity. Actual overheads and levels of production are unlikely to exactly equal budgeted amounts and so the use of budgeted overhead absorption rates will inevitably lead to an **overhead over or under-absorption** (as we have seen in Example 8.5), which is transferred (usually) monthly to the profit and loss account, for internal management accounting reporting.

Progress check 8.8

What is absorption costing and how is it used? Give some examples of bases that may be used for the calculation of overhead absorption rates applied to cost units.

We shall now consider another costing technique, **marginal costing**, which is also known as variable costing or **period costing**. We will return later to Example 8.5, using the marginal costing technique and contrast it with the absorption costing technique.

Marginal costing

We have considered above a costing method that looks at profit considered at the level of total revenue, or total sales, less total cost. We will now look at another way of considering profitability, called **contribution**, and its corresponding costing system called marginal costing (see Fig. 8.6).

$$\textbf{contribution} = \textbf{total revenue} - \textbf{variable costs}$$

Marginal costing, variable costing, or period costing, is a costing technique whereby each unit of output is charged only with variable production costs. The costs which are generated solely by a given cost unit are the variable costs associated with that unit, including the variable cost elements of any associated semi-variable costs. Marginal cost ascertainment includes all unit direct costs plus the variable overhead cost per unit incurred by the cost unit. The marginal cost of a unit may be defined as the additional cost of producing one such unit. The marginal cost of a number of units is the sum of all the unit marginal costs. Whereas absorption costing deals with total costs and profits, marginal costing deals with variable costs and contribution. Contribution is defined as the sales value less the variable cost of sales. Contribution may be expressed as:

- total contribution
- contribution per unit
- contribution as a percentage of sales.

If a business provides a series of products that all provide some contribution, the business may avoid being severely damaged by the downturn in demand of just one of the products. Fixed production costs are not considered to be the real costs of production, but costs which provide the facilities, for an accounting period, that enable production to take place. They are therefore treated as costs of the period and charged to the period in which they are incurred against the aggregate contribution. Stocks are valued on a variable production cost basis that excludes fixed production costs.

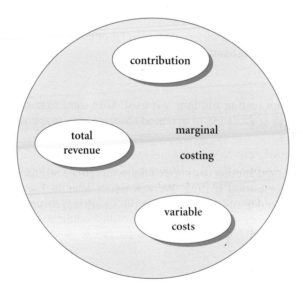

F I G U R E   8 . 6   The elements of marginal costing

Marginal cost ascertainment assumes that the cost of any given activity is only the cost that that activity generates; it is the difference between carrying out and not carrying out that activity. Each cost unit and each cost centre is charged with only those costs that are generated as a consequence of that cost unit and that cost centre being a part of the company's activities.

We will now return to Example 8.5 and consider the results using marginal costing techniques, and contrast them with those achieved using absorption costing in Example 8.6.

Example 8.6

Using the information for Albatross Ltd from Example 8.5, we are required to prepare a profit and loss account for January using marginal costing.

Answer

The variable (marginal) production costs per unit from Example 8.5 are:

	£
Direct material	36
Direct labour	8
Variable production overhead	6
Variable production cost	50

Profit and loss account

	£	£
Sales (40,800 × £100)		4,080,000
Variable production costs (48,800 × £50)	2,440,000	
plus Opening stock	–	
less Closing stock (8,000 units × £50)	(400,000)	
Cost of sales		2,040,000
Gross contribution		2,040,000
less Sales commission (£4,080,000 × 10%)		408,000
Net contribution		1,632,000
less Fixed costs		
Production costs	792,000	
Administrative expenses	208,000	
Selling costs	112,000	1,112,000
Net profit for January, before tax		520,000

It can be seen that profit calculated using the marginal costing technique is £144,000 less than that using the absorption costing technique, because under absorption costing stock is valued at full production costs, the fixed production costs being carried forward in the stock to the next period instead of being charged to the current period as under marginal costing.

Note: The activity is the same regardless of the costing technique that has been used. It is only the method of reporting that has caused a difference in the profit.

Stock valuation difference

Closing stock units × (absorption cost per unit − marginal cost per unit) = profit difference

8,000 units × (£68 − £50) = £144,000

Some specific features of the marginal costing technique are:

● its recognition of cost behaviour, providing better support for sales pricing and decision-making, which we shall explore further in Chapter 10

● it allows better control reports to be prepared because contribution is based on, and varies with, the sales level, which we shall examine when we look at cost and overhead relationships in Chapter 9

● fixed costs may be addressed within the period that gives rise to them.

However, marginal costing is not suitable for stock valuation in line with accounting standard SSAP 9, because there is no fixed cost element included. SSAP 9 requires closing stocks to consist of direct materials, direct labour and appropriate overheads. A great many companies, large and small, adopt marginal costing for monthly management reporting and stocks valuation for each of their accounting periods throughout their financial year. Such companies overcome the problems of non-compliance with SSAP 9 by making an adjustment to their stocks valuation and their profit and loss accounts to include an allowance for fixed overhead costs, in the final accounting period at their year-end.

Absorption costing versus marginal costing

A more comprehensive list of the advantages and disadvantages of both techniques is summarised in Figs 8.7 and 8.8.

Progress check 8.9	**Should managers participate in the accounting exercise of allocation of fixed costs? (Hint: You may wish to consider the cyclical nature of the building industry as an example that illustrates the difficulty of allocating fixed costs.)**

In the long run, over several accounting periods, the total recorded profit of an entity is the same regardless of whether absorption costing or marginal costing techniques are used. The difference is one of timing. The actual amounts of the costs do not differ, only the period in which they are charged against profits. Thus, differences in profit occur from one period to the next depending on which method is adopted.

Figure 8.9 illustrates and contrasts the formats of the trading and profit and loss account using absorption costing and marginal costing.

Marginal costing is a powerful technique since it focuses attention on those costs which are affected by, or associated with, an activity. We will return to marginal costing in Chapter 9, with regard to cost/volume/profit (CVP) relationships and break-even analysis. It is also particularly useful in the areas of decision-making and relevant costs, and sales pricing which we shall be looking at in Chapter 10.

Progress check 8.10	**What is marginal costing and in what ways is it different from absorption costing?**

advantages	disadvantages
it is simple to use, and based on a formula that uses an estimated or planned fixed overhead rate included in the calculation of unit costs of products and services	fixed costs are not necessarily avoidable and they have to be paid regardless of whether sales and production volumes are high, low or zero
it is easy to apply using cost or a percentage mark-up to achieve a reasonable profit	fixed costs are not variable in the short run
apportionment and allocation of fixed costs to cost centres makes managers aware of costs and services provided and ensures that they remember that all costs need to be covered for the company to be profitable	there are different alternative bases of overhead allocation which therefore result in different interpretations
cost price or full cost pricing ensures that all costs are covered	the capacity levels chosen for overhead absorption rates are based on historical information and are therefore open to debate
it conforms with the accrual concept of SSAP 2 by matching costs with revenue for a particular accounting period, as in the full costing of stocks	activity must be equal to or greater than the budgeted level of activity or else fixed costs will be under-absorbed
stock valuation complies with SSAP 9, as an element of fixed production costs is absorbed into stocks	if sales are depressed then profits can be artificially increased by increasing production thus increasing stocks
it avoids the separation of costs into fixed and variable elements, which are not easily and accurately identified	
analysis of over and under-absorbed overheads highlights any inefficient utilisation of production resources	

FIGURE 8.7   Advantages and disadvantages of absorption costing

advantages	disadvantages
it is market based not cost based; exclusion of fixed production costs on a marginal basis enables the company to be more competitive	pricing at the margin may lead to underpricing with too little contribution and non-recovery of fixed costs, particularly in periods of economic downturns
it covers all incremental costs associated with the product, production and sales	stock valuation does not comply with SSAP 9, as no element of fixed production costs is absorbed into stocks
it enables the analysis of different market price/volume levels to allow selection of optimal contributions and it enables the strategic analysis of competitors and customers	
it enables the company to determine break-even points and plan profit, and to use the opportunity cost approach	
it avoids the arbitrary apportionment of fixed costs and avoids the problem of determining a suitable basis for the overhead absorption rate, e.g. units, labour hours, machine hours etc.	
most fixed production overheads are periodic, or time-based, and incurred regardless of levels of production, and so should be charged to the period in which they are incurred, e.g. factory rent, salaries and depreciation	
fixed production costs may not be controllable at departmental level and so should not be included in production costs at the cost centre level – control should be matched with responsibility	
profits cannot be manipulated by increasing stocks in times of low sales because stocks exclude fixed costs and profits therefore vary directly with sales	
it facilitates control through easier pooling of separate fixed costs and variable costs totals, and preparation of flexible budgets to provide comparisons for actual levels of activity	
stock valued on a variable cost basis supports the view that the additional cost of stock is limited to its variable costs	
marginal costing is prudent because fixed costs are charged to the period in which they are incurred, not carried forward in stock which may prove to be unsaleable and result in earlier profits having been overstated	

FIGURE 8.8 Advantages and disadvantages of marginal costing

Absorption costing		Marginal costing	
	Net turnover		Net turnover
less:		**less variable costs:**	
Direct materials		Direct materials	
Direct labour		Direct labour	
Production overhead		Variable production overhead	
		Variable selling and distribution overhead	
	Production cost of sales		Production cost of sales
	Gross profit		**Contribution**
less:		**less fixed costs:** Production overhead	
Selling overhead		Selling overhead	
Distribution overhead		Distribution overhead	
Administrative expenses		Administrative expenses	
Research and development costs		Research and development costs	
	Non-production overhead		Total fixed costs
	Net profit before tax		**Net profit before tax**

FIGURE 8.9   Trading and profit and loss account absorption and marginal costing formats

Example 8.7

Management accounting provides information to various departments within a business. Fast-moving businesses need this information very quickly. Hotel groups have invested in central booking systems and these systems are used to reveal times of the year when reservations are down because of national and local trends.

Discuss how the marketing department and the management accounting function might work together to generate extra bookings.

Answer

The marketing department may assess the periods and times in which each hotel has gaps in its reservations. The management accountant may assess the direct costs associated with each reservation, for example the costs of cleaning and food. The two departments may then suggest a special offer for a fixed period of time (for example, Travelodge special offers in the press during January and February 2001). The special offer may allow for local conditions by varying the price within a range, for example £20 to £30 per night.

Management accounting continues to change and develop as it meets the needs presented by:

- changing economic climates
- globalisation

- information technology
- increasing competition.

Marginal costing developed from absorption costing in recognition of the differences in behaviour between fixed costs and variable costs. In most industries, as labour costs continue to become a smaller and smaller percentage of total costs, traditional costing methods, which usually absorb costs on the basis of direct labour hours, have been seen to be increasingly inappropriate.

In Chapter 9, we will look at some of the more recent management accounting techniques that have been developed in response to some of the criticisms of traditional costing methods:

- **activity based costing (ABC)**
- **throughput accounting (TA)**
- **life cycle costing**
- **target costing**
- benchmarking
- *kaizen*

Summary of key points

- There is a number of additional accounting concepts that relate to management accounting.
- Cost (as a noun) is an amount of expenditure attributable to a specified thing or activity, but also relates to a resource sacrificed or forgone, expressed in a monetary value.
- Cost (as a verb) may be used to say that to cost something is to ascertain the cost of a specified thing or activity, but cost is not a word that is usually used without a qualification as to its nature and limitations.
- Direct costs are directly identified with cost objects.
- Indirect costs have to be allocated or apportioned to cost units, cost centres, or cost accounts using appropriate bases for allocation and apportionment.
- Unit costs of products, services or activities may be determined using the traditional costing techniques of absorption costing and marginal costing.
- There are many arguments for and against the use of the techniques of both absorption costing and marginal costing, revolving mainly around the basis chosen for allocation and apportionment of overheads.

Glossary of key terms

absorption costing A method of costing that, in addition to direct costs, assigns all, or a proportion of, production overhead costs to cost units by means of one or a number of overhead absorption rates.

accountability concept Management accounting presents information measuring the achievement of the objectives of an organisation and appraising the conduct of its internal activities in that process. In order that further action can be taken, based on this information, it is necessary at all times to identify the responsibilities and performance of individuals within the organisation.

activity based costing (ABC) An approach to costing and monitoring of activities which involves tracing resource consumption and costing final outputs. Resources are assigned to activities and activities to cost objects based on consumption estimates. The latter utilise cost drivers to attach activity costs to outputs.

allocation The charging to a cost centre those overheads which result solely from the existence of that cost centre.

apportionment The charging to a cost centre of a fair share of an overhead on the basis of the benefit received by the cost centre in respect of the facilities provided by the overhead.

benchmarking The establishment, through data gathering, of targets and comparators, whereby relative levels of performance (and particularly areas of underperformance) can be identified. By the adoption of identified best practices it is hoped that performance will improve.

contribution Sales value less variable cost of sales, which may be expressed as total contribution, contribution per unit, or as a percentage of sales.

controllability concept Management accounting identifies the elements or activities which management can or cannot influence, and seeks to assess risk and sensitivity factors. This facilitates the proper monitoring, analysis, comparison and interpretation of information which can be used constructively in the control, evaluation and corrective functions of management.

cost The amount of expenditure (actual or notional) incurred on, or attributable to, a specified thing or activity. To cost something is to ascertain the cost of a specified thing or activity. Cost also relates to a resource sacrificed or forgone, expressed in a monetary value.

cost centre A production or service location, function, activity or item of equipment for which costs are accumulated and to which they are charged.

cost object The thing that we wish to determine the cost of.

cost unit A unit of product or service in relation to which costs are ascertained.

direct cost A traceable cost, or expenditure which can be economically identified with and specifically measured in respect of a relevant cost object.

direct labour Labour costs which can be economically identified with and specifically measured in respect of a relevant cost object.

direct materials Materials costs which can be economically identified with and specifically measured in respect of a relevant cost object.

fixed cost A cost which is incurred for an accounting period, and which, within certain output or turnover limits, tends to be unaffected by fluctuations in the levels of activity (output or turnover).

indirect cost An indirect cost is a cost that is untraceable to particular units. It is expenditure on labour, materials or services which cannot be economically identified with a specific saleable cost unit. Such costs have to be allocated, that is assigned to a single cost unit, cost centre, or cost account or time period. The term 'burden' used by American companies is synonymous with indirect costs or overheads.

interdependency concept Management accounting, in recognition of the increasing complexity of business, must access both internal and external information sources from interactive functions such as marketing, production, personnel, procurement and finance. This assists in ensuring that the information is adequately balanced.

kaizen Continuous improvement in all aspects of performance, at every level within the organisation.

life cycle costing The maintenance of physical asset records over the entire asset life, so that decisions concerning the acquisition, use or disposal of the asset can be made in a way that achieves the optimum assets usage at the lowest possible cost to the business. The term may be applied to the profiling of cost over a product's life, including the pre-production stage and to company and industry life cycles.

marginal costing A costing technique whereby each unit of output is charged with variable production costs. Fixed production costs are not considered to be real costs of production, but costs which provide the facilities for an accounting period that enable production to take place.

opportunity cost The value of the benefit sacrificed when one course of action is chosen, in preference to an alternative. The opportunity cost is represented by the forgone potential benefit from the best rejected course of action.

overhead absorption rate A means of attributing overhead to a product or service, based, for example, on direct labour hours, direct labour cost or machine hours.

overhead over and under-absorption (or overhead over and under-recovery) The difference between overhead incurred and overhead absorbed, using an estimated rate, in a given period.

period cost A cost which relates to a time period rather than to the output of products or services.

relevancy concept Management accounting must ensure that flexibility is maintained in assembling and interpreting information. This facilitates the exploration and presentation, in a clear, understandable and timely manner, of as many alternatives as are necessary for impartial and confident decisions to be taken. This process is essentially forward-looking and dynamic. Therefore, the information must satisfy the criteria of being applicable and appropriate.

relevant cost Cost appropriate to a specific management decision.

reliability concept Management accounting information must be of such quality that confidence can be placed in it. Its reliability to the user is dependent on its source, integrity and comprehensiveness.

semi-variable cost A cost containing both fixed and variable components and which is thus partly affected by a change in the level of activity.

sunk cost A cost which has already been incurred and which cannot now be recovered.

target cost A product cost estimate derived by subtracting a desired profit margin from a competitive market price. This may be less than the planned initial product cost, but will be expected to be achieved by the time the product reaches the mature production stage.

throughput accounting (TA) A method of performance measurement which relates production and other costs to throughput. Throughput accounting product costs relate to usage of key resources by various products.

unit cost The average cost of a product or service unit based on total costs and the number of units.

variable cost Cost that varies in direct proportion to the volume of activity.

Assessment material

Questions

Q8.1   (i) What are the main roles of the management accountant?

       (ii) How does management accounting support the effective management of a business?

Q8.2   (i) What are the differences between fixed costs, variable costs and semi-variable costs?

       (ii) Give some examples of each.

Q8.3   (i) Why do production overheads need to be allocated and apportioned, and to what?

       (ii) Describe the processes of allocation and apportionment.

Q8.4   (i) Which costing system complies with the provisions outlined in SSAP 9?

       (ii) Describe the process used in this technique.

Q8.5   What is marginal costing and how does it differ from absorption costing?

Q8.6   What are the main benefits to be gained from using a system of marginal costing?

Discussion points

D8.1   Surely an accountant is an accountant! Why does the function of management accounting need to be separated from financial accounting and why is it seen as such an integral part of the management of the business? Discuss.

D8.2   Do the benefits from using marginal costing outweigh the benefits from using absorption costing sufficiently to replace absorption costing in SSAP 9 as the basis for stock valuation and the preparation of financial statements?

Exercises

Solutions are provided in Appendix 4 to all exercise numbers highlighted in colour.

Level I

E8.1 *Time allowed – 45 minutes*

Bluebell Woods Ltd produces a product for which the following standard cost details have been provided based on production and sales of 4,300 units in a four-week period:

Direct material cost	£0.85 per kg
Direct material usage	2 kg per unit
Direct labour rate	£4.20
Direct labour time per unit	42 minutes
Selling price	£5.84 per unit
Variable production costs	£0.12 per unit
Fixed production costs	£3,526 per four-week period

Prepare a standard profit statement for a four-week period using

(i) absorption costing

(ii) marginal costing

E8.2 *Time allowed – 45 minutes*

The total costs for one specific manufacturing process have been incurred at various levels of output as follows:

Output units	Total cost £
28,750	256,190
30,000	261,815
31,250	267,440
32,500	273,065
33,750	278,690
35,000	284,315

(i)   Discuss why total cost needs to be analysed into its behavioural elements to enable its effective management and control.

(ii) From the table above, draw a graph that analyses the fixed and variable components of the total costs of the process.

(iii) What is the fixed cost of the process shown from the graph?

(iv) What are the variable costs per unit for this process?

Level II

E8.3 *Time allowed – 75 minutes*

Square Gift Ltd is located in Wales, where the national sales manager is also based, and has a sales force of 15 salesmen covering the whole of the UK. The sales force, including the national sales manager all have the same make and model of company car. A new car costs £16,000, and all cars are traded in when they are two years old for a guaranteed £6,000.

- The salesman with the lowest annual mileage of 18,000 miles, operates in the South East of England.
- The salesman with the highest annual mileage of 40,000 miles, operates throughout Scotland.
- The annual average mileage of the complete sales team works out at 30,000 miles per car.

The average salesman's annual vehicle running cost is:

	£
Petrol and oil	3,000
Road tax	155
Insurance	450
Repairs	700
Miscellaneous	300
Total	4,605

- Annual vehicle repair costs include £250 for regular maintenance.
- Tyre life is around 30,000 miles and replacement sets cost £350.
- No additional repair costs are incurred during the first year of vehicle life because a special warranty agreement exists with the supplying garage to cover these, but on average £200 is paid for repairs in the second year – repair costs are averaged over the two years with regular maintenance and repairs being variable with mileage rather than time.
- Miscellaneous vehicle costs include subscriptions to motoring organisations, vehicle cleaning costs, parking, and garaging allowances.

Analyse the total vehicle costs into fixed costs and variable costs separately to give total annual costs for

(i) the lowest mileage per annum salesman

(ii) the highest mileage per annum salesman

You may ignore cost of capital, and possible impacts of tax and inflation.
(Hints: Assume that insurance costs are the same for each area.
Assume that miscellaneous operating costs are fixed.
Repairs are based on amount of mileage.)

E8.4   *Time allowed – 75 minutes*

Rocky Ltd manufactures a single product, the budget for which was as follows for each of the months July and August 2000:

		Total £		Per unit £
Sales (6,000 units)		60,000		10.00
Production cost of sales:				
Variable overhead	45,000		7.50	
Fixed overhead	3,000	48,000	0.50	8.00
		12,000		2.00
Selling and distribution costs (fixed)		4,200		0.70
Administrative expenses (fixed)		3,000		0.50
Profit		4,800		0.80

Actual units produced, sold and in stock in July and August were:

	July	August
Opening stock	–	900
Production	5,300	4,400
Sales	4,400	5,000
Closing stock	900	300

Prepare profit and loss accounts for each of the months July and August, assuming that fixed production overhead is absorbed into the cost of the product at the normal level shown in the monthly budget.
(Hint: This is the absorption costing approach).

E8.5   *Time allowed – 75 minutes*

Using the data for Rocky Ltd from Exercise E8.4, prepare profit and loss accounts for each of the months July and August, assuming that fixed production overhead is not absorbed into the cost of the product, but is treated as a cost of the period and charged against sales.
(Hint: This is the marginal costing approach).

E8.6   *Time allowed – 75 minutes*

Using your answers to Exercises E8.4 and E8.5, explain why the profits for July and August are different using the two costing methods, and support your explanation with an appropriate reconciliation of the results.

9

Cost management

LEARNING OBJECTIVES

Completion of this chapter will enable you to:

● explain cost/volume profit (CVP) relationships and break-even analysis

● identify the limitations of CVP analysis

● outline the more recently developed techniques of activity based costing (ABC), and throughput accounting (TA)

● identify the conditions appropriate to the use of life cycle costing

● apply the principles of target costing

● consider benchmarking as a technique to identify best practice and enable the introduction of appropriate performance improvement targets

● outline *kaizen* as a technique for continuous improvement of all aspects of business performance

● use cost of quality (COQ) to identify areas for improvement and cost reduction within each of the processes throughout the business

Introduction

In Chapter 8 we introduced costs, contribution and profit. This chapter develops the importance of contribution as a measure of profitability and begins with an examination of the relationship between costs, volumes of activity, and profit, or CVP analysis. We will look at a particular application of CVP analysis in break-even analysis, and consider some of the advantages and limitations of its use.

This chapter looks at some of the more recently developed management accounting techniques, some of which have been developed in response to the criticisms of traditional costing methods, for example activity based costing; throughput accounting; life cycle costing; target costing; benchmarking; *kaizen*; quality costing.

Paffard's team finds satisfying the chocaholics a trifle tricky

Thorntons' job should not be so difficult. The company is the biggest specialist manufacturer and retailer of chocolates in a nation of chocaholics; it provides the ideal gift for men who can't think of anything else to buy their wives; and it has a reassuring family firm image.

Unfortunately, the management never seems to get it right. Last October, they blamed poor results on too many products, at Christmas they failed to cope with a late rush and in May they sent the shares plummeting with a profits warning after customers decided their Easter eggs were boring.

Three years into Roger Paffard's five-year plan to modernise the business, this is a trifle worrying. Some of Thorntons' problems were perennials for the British luxury goods sector – ordering and distribution systems were outdated, and advertising was out of touch.

Mr Paffard was the first non-Thorntons' chief executive, but his reforms have produced mixed results. He opened a shiny new factory, but forgot to develop new products during the Easter chocolate binge – like-for-like sales fell 3.7pc as a result.

He invested heavily in infrastructure, some of it vital for survival – such as computerised point-of-sale ordering systems – and some of it innovative. Thorntons is now one of a select bunch of companies that can produce coloured chocolates.

If people decide they want to eat red chocolate, this could be a winner. But that remains to be seen, while Mr Paffard's aggressive store opening plans pose the risk of overstretching. He wants 500 stores and 90 Thorntons' cafés by 2002 – an ambitious programme for a company whose shares have fluctuated between 250p and 171.5p since May.

© *Daily Telegraph*, 6 October 1999

The broadening of the range of activities supported by management accounting has resulted in a gradual disappearance of the boundaries between itself and financial management. Management accounting continues to develop with an emphasis on decision-making and strategic management, and financial management. Financial management is usually defined as the management of the processes that deal with the efficient acquisition and deployment of short and long-term financial resources. It was interesting to note in September 2000 that CIMA renamed its monthly journal from *Management Accounting* to *Financial Management*.

Thorntons' disastrous Easter 1999 (see the press cutting above) highlighted the need for evaluation of the impact, and a company's possible response, to changes to levels of demand for current products and products in development. It also emphasised the focus that is required on service departments (ordering and distribution) so that companies can ensure they meet promises made to their customers.

By the beginning of 2000 Thorntons had invested heavily to improve its stores outlets and to increase its number of production lines to support the chief executive's promise of a good spring. Investors' lack of confidence in Mr Paffard's optimism resulted in his resignation in March 2000. Another misjudged Easter 2000 left Thorntons with a glut of Easter eggs worth £1.4m. A year after the appointment of a new chief executive in April 2000 Thorntons began to show signs of extricating itself from its sticky mess when in March 2001 it produced six-month financial results in line with expectations.

Cost/volume/profit (CVP) relationships and break-even analysis

Cost/volume/profit (CVP) analysis studies the effects on future profit of changes in fixed costs, variable costs, volume, sales mix and selling price. Break-even (B/E) analysis is one application of CVP, which can be useful for profit planning, sales mix decisions, production capacity decisions and pricing decisions.

There are three fundamental cost/revenue relationships which form the basis of CVP analysis:

total costs = variable costs + fixed costs

contribution = total revenue − variable costs

profit (or operating income) = total revenue − total costs

The **break-even point** is the level of activity at which there is neither profit nor loss. It can be ascertained by using a break-even chart or by calculation. The break-even chart indicates approximate profit or loss at different levels of sales volume within a limited range. Break-even charts may be used to represent different cost structures and also to show contribution break-even positions and profit–volume relationships (see Figs 9.1, 9.2, 9.3, and 9.4). Computerised spreadsheets can be used to convert profit–volume relationship 'what-ifs' into either charts or tables that may be used for presentation or decision-making purposes. They provide the means of exploring any area within fixed costs, variable costs, semi-variable costs, and sales, in terms of values and volumes.

The slopes of the total cost lines in Fig. 9.1 and Fig. 9.2 represent the unit variable costs.

The break-even chart shown in Fig. 9.1 shows a relatively low level of fixed costs with variable costs rising quite steeply as the level of activity increases. Where the total sales (or income) line intersects the total cost line is the point at which total sales or total revenue equals total costs. This activity of 40 units is the break-even point.

The break-even chart shown in Fig. 9.2 shows the impact of a higher level of fixed costs with a higher break-even point at around 60 units, even though variable costs are lower than the cost structure shown in Fig. 9.1. If variable costs had stayed the same, the break-even point would be even higher at over 80 units of activity.

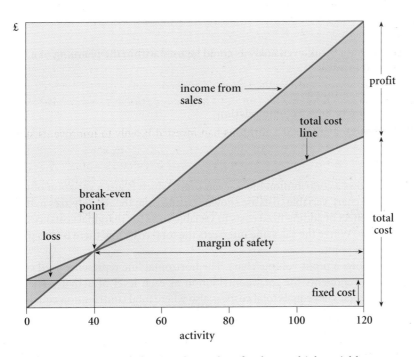

FIGURE 9.1 Break-even chart – low fixed costs, high variable costs

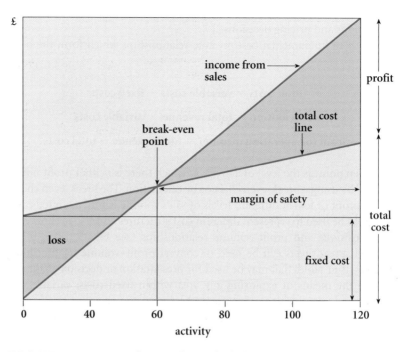

FIGURE 9.2 Break-even chart – high fixed costs, low variable costs

 The margin of safety shown in each of these charts will be explained when we look a little further at some break-even relationships.

Explain how a break-even analysis could be used within the planning of a 'one-off' event that involves

- **the sales of tickets**
- **provision of hotel accommodation**
- **live music**

Fig. 9.3 shows a contribution break-even chart, which is just a variation of the previous charts. In this chart, variable costs are shown starting from the zero x/y axes in the same way as sales. The effect of adding fixed costs to variable costs (or marginal costs) is shown in the total costs line. Where the sales line intersects the total costs line there is zero profit. This is the break-even point.

Fig. 9.4 shows a profit volume chart. The horizontal line represents fixed costs and the diagonal line represents the total contribution at each level of activity. The break-even point, where total sales equals total costs, is also where total contribution equals fixed costs.

We will look at why the break-even point is where total contribution equals fixed costs and also consider some further break-even relationships.

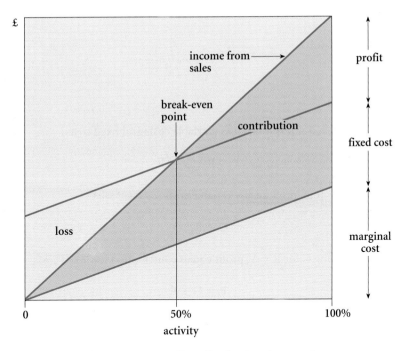

FIGURE 9.3 Contribution break-even chart

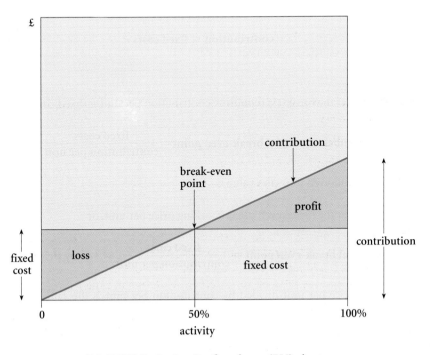

FIGURE 9.4 Profit volume (PV) chart

Consider

Total revenue = R
Variable costs = V
Fixed costs = F
Profit = P
Contribution = C

Profit equals total revenue less total costs (variable costs and fixed costs)

$$\mathbf{P = R - V - F}$$

Contribution equals total revenue less variable costs

$$\mathbf{C = R - V}$$

Therefore, substituting C for R − V, profit equals contribution less fixed costs

$$\mathbf{P = C - F}$$

At the break-even point total revenue equals totals costs, and profit is zero, therefore

$$\mathbf{0 = C - F}$$

Or at the break-even point

$$\mathbf{C = F}$$

$$\textbf{contribution = fixed costs} \qquad \text{(BE1)}$$

It follows that the

Number of units at the break-even point × contribution per unit = fixed costs, or

$$\textbf{number of units at break-even point} = \frac{\textbf{fixed costs}}{\textbf{contribution per unit}} \qquad \text{(BE2)}$$

Therefore the break-even in £ sales value is

Number of units at the break-even point × selling price per unit, or

$$\textbf{£ sales value at break-even point} = \frac{\textbf{fixed costs}}{\textbf{contribution per unit}} \times \textbf{selling price per unit}$$

But the selling price per unit divided by contribution per unit is the same as total sales revenue divided by total contribution, which is

The reciprocal of the contribution to sales ratio percentage

So, an alternative expression is

$$\textbf{£ sales value at break-even point} = \frac{\textbf{fixed costs}}{\textbf{contribution to sales ratio \%}} \qquad \text{(BE3)}$$

The term 'margin of safety' is used to define the difference between the break-even point and an anticipated or existing level of activity above that point.   (BE4)

In other words, the margin of safety measures the extent to which anticipated or existing activity can fall before a profitable operation turns into a loss-making one (see Figs 9.1 and 9.2).

Progress check 9.2

Discuss how departmental stores might use the concept of contribution and break-even analysis when analysing their financial performance.

The following example uses the relationships we have discussed to illustrate the calculation of a break-even point.

Example 9.1

	£
Sales (1,000 units)	10,000
Variable costs (direct materials and direct labour)	6,000
Contribution	4,000
Fixed costs	2,000
Profit	2,000

We are required to find the break-even point in number of units and the sales value at that point.

Answer

Number of units sold   1,000

Therefore, contribution/unit $\dfrac{£4,000}{1,000} = £4$ per unit

And, contribution to sales ratio % $= \dfrac{£4,000}{£10,000} \times 100\% = 40\%$

Using BE2   number of units at break-even point $= \dfrac{\text{fixed costs}}{\text{contribution per unit}}$

$= £2,000/£4$

$= 500$ units

Using BE3   £ sales value at break-even point $= \dfrac{\text{fixed costs}}{\text{contribution to sales ratio \%}}$

$= £2,000/40\%$

$= £5,000$

The CVP technique may also be used to derive a target cost estimate, by subtracting a desired margin or target profit from a competitive market price. This cost may be less than the planned initial product cost, but will be a cost that is expected to be achieved by the time the product reaches the mature production stage. Sales volumes or sales values may be calculated that are required to achieve a range of profit targets.

Example 9.2

Bill Jones, who had worked for many years as an engineer in the automotive industry, had recently been made redundant. Bill, together with a number of colleagues, now had the opportunity to set up a business to make and sell a specialised part for motor vehicle air-conditioning units. Bill had already decided on a name for the company. It would be called Wilcon Ltd. Bill had some good contacts in the industry and two automotive components manufacturers had promised him contracts that he estimated would provide sales of 15,000 units per month, for the foreseeable future.

The business plan was based on the following data

Selling price per unit	£17.50	
Variable costs per unit	£13.00	
Fixed costs for month	£54,000	including salaries for 5 managers @ £1,500 each

We are required to find the break-even volume and sales value for Wilcon Ltd.

Answer
Contribution/unit

	£
Selling price	17.50
Variable cost	13.00
Contribution/unit	4.50

Break-even volume

If the number of units sold is n \qquad Total contribution $= n \times £4.50$

At the break-even point fixed costs equal total contribution (see BE1)

$$£54,000 = £4.50 \times n$$

Therefore, $n = £54,000/£4.50 = 12,000$ units

Sales value at break-even point $=$ number of units at break-even point
$\times$ selling price per unit
$= 12,000 \times £17.50 = £210,000$

Example 9.3

Using the data from Example 9.2 we are required to find the margin of safety (volume and value) for Wilcon Ltd if the predicted sales volume is 12,500 units per month.

Answer

Margin of safety (volume and value) if the predicted sales volume is 12,500 units per month

The predicted or forecast volume is 12,500 units, with a sales value of $12,500 \times £17.50$

$$= £218,750$$

The margin of safety is predicted volume – break-even volume (see BE4)

$$= 12,500 - 12,000 = 500 \text{ units}$$

Margin of safety sales value $= £218,750 - £210,000$

$$= £8,750$$

Example 9.4

Using the data from Example 9.2 we are required to find the reduction in break-even volume if one less manager were employed by Wilcon Ltd.

Answer

Reduction in break-even volume if one less manager were employed

Fixed costs become $£54,000 - £1,500$

$$= £52,500$$

If the number of units sold is n

$$£52,500 = £4.50 \times n$$

Therefore, $n = £52,500/£4.50 = 11,667$ units

Therefore reduction in volume from break-even is $12,000 - 11,667$, or 333 units

Example 9.5

Using the data from Example 9.2 we are required to find the volume of units to be sold by Wilcon Ltd to make £9,000 profit per month.

Answer

Volume of units to be sold to make £9,000 profit

Profit = contribution − fixed costs

If n equals the number of units, for a profit of £9,000

£9,000 = $(n \times £4.50) − £52,500$ [54,000 − 1,500]

Or, $n = £61,500/£4.50 = 13,667$ units

Example 9.6

Using the data from Example 9.2 we are required to find the revised break-even volume if fixed costs are reduced by 10% and variable costs are increased by 10% by Wilcon Ltd.

Answer

Revised break-even volume if fixed costs are reduced by 10% and variable costs are increased by 10%

If fixed costs are 90% × £54,000 = £48,600

And variable costs are 110% × £13 = £14.30

Then unit contribution becomes £17.50 − £14.30 = £3.20

£48,600 = £3.20 × n

Therefore, $n = £48,600/£3.20 = 15,188$ units

Example 9.7

Using the data from Example 9.2 we are required to find the revised selling price that must be charged by Wilcon Ltd to show a profit of £6,000 on 10,000 sales units.

Answer

Revised selling price that must be charged to show a profit of £6,000 on 10,000 sales units

Profit = contribution − fixed costs

If total contribution is TC

$$£6,000 = TC − £54,000$$
$$TC = £60,000$$

Therefore

Contribution/unit = £60,000/10000 = £6 per unit

Variable cost is £13 per unit

Therefore revised selling price is

$$£13 + £6 = £19 \text{ per unit}$$

Examples 9.1 to 9.7 have used the technique of sensitivity analysis. We have considered the sensitivity of the break-even point against expected volumes of activity. We have also considered the impact on the break-even point of changes to fixed costs and variable costs, and how costs and price levels need to change to achieve a planned level of profit. Sales price sensitivity may be considered in terms of volume through analysis of fixed labour and overhead costs, and variable material, labour and overhead costs.

CVP analysis may therefore be used in:

- profit planning
- project planning
- establishing points of indifference between projects
- make or buy decision-making
- shut down or continuation decisions
- product mix decisions
- sales pricing.

We shall consider many of these applications of CVP analysis in Chapter 10 when we look at decision-making.

Progress check 9.3

What is a break-even point? Why is it important for a business to know its break-even point, and what types of sensitivity can it be used to analyse?

Limitations of CVP analysis

We have seen that break-even analysis is just one of the applications of cost/volume/profit (CVP) analysis. It should be noted that CVP analysis relies on a great many assumptions:

- that output is the only factor affecting costs – there may be others including inflation, efficiency, economic and political factors
- the simplistic approach to cost relationships: that total costs are divided into fixed and variable costs – in reality costs cannot be split easily, even into variable and fixed costs
- the likelihood that fixed costs do not remain constant beyond certain ranges
- the behaviour of both costs and revenue is linear – linearity is rare with regard to costs and revenue
- there is no uncertainty – there is much uncertainty involved in the prediction of costs and sales
- there is a single product – businesses usually provide more than one product and sales mix is not constant but continually changes due to changes in demand
- that stock levels do not change
- the time value of money is ignored (see Chapter 13)
- that these assumptions hold over the relevant range (the activity levels within which assumptions about cost behaviour in break-even analysis remain valid: it is used to mitigate the impact of some of the limitations of CVP analysis mentioned above).

In real life situations the above assumptions clearly do not hold because, as has been noted previously cost relationships are not simple and straightforward. Companies usually provide more than just one product or service, and factors affecting their costs and volumes do change frequently. Such factors do not usually change only one at a time but more usually change all at once. Nevertheless, the principles of CVP analysis continue to hold true. A greater degree of sophistication may be achieved from more dynamic and complex models, and using computerised simulation models. Uncertainty will always remain. The impact of the results of the occurrence of uncertain events, within given constraints, may also be evaluated using more sophisticated methods of sensitivity analysis.

Some of the above limitations may not apply since IT spreadsheets can now provide very sensitive 'what-if' solutions to the original problem areas. Users can use the link facilities in modelling systems that can speedily provide a range of alternative values.

Progress check 9.4	Discuss the usefulness of a sensitivity analysis of the factors used in calculation of the break-even point of a national chain fast food outlet that uses television advertising campaigns.

The above limitations to CVP analysis are very real and should be borne in mind when using the technique, for example, to consider alternative pricing options that use both the marginal and full absorption costing approach.

In addition to break-even analysis, cost/volume/profit (CVP) analysis techniques may be used in a number of decision-making scenarios, some of which we will look at in Chapter 10. Very often, for example, in a decision-making scenario there are two or more limiting factors, in which case a linear programming model would need to be used to determine optimum solutions; linear programming is not covered in this book.

Progress check 9.5	What is CVP analysis and on what assumptions is it based?

Activity based costing (ABC)

The activities of businesses across the entire chain of value-adding organisational processes have a considerable impact on costs and therefore profit. A recently developed management accounting approach to evaluating the extent of this impact and to dealing with the root causes of costs is activity based costing (ABC).

Activity based costing (ABC) provides an alternative approach to the costing of products in response to some of the criticisms that have been aimed at the more traditional approaches. Before we examine the concept of ABC let's look at a simple example, which puts these criticisms in context.

Example 9.8	

Traditional Moulding Ltd manufactures two plastic fittings, the RX-L and the RX-R. Both products are produced in the Moulding2 department, which has total overheads of £5,000 for the month of March. Moulding2 uses 4,000 hours of direct labour to produce the RX-L (2,000) and RX-R (2,000). The other activities within the Moulding2 department are ten machine set-ups (eight to produce the RX-L and two to produce the RX-R) which cost £3,200, and the processing of ninety sales orders (fifty for the RX-L and forty for the RX-R) costing £1,800.

We are required to determine the costs charged to each product using absorption costing on a direct labour hours basis, and alternatively determine the costs on the basis of the other activities within the department.

Answer

Absorption costing basis

Cost per labour hour = £5,000/4,000 hours = £1.25 per direct labour hour

	RX-L £	RX-R £	Total £
2,000 hours at £1.25	2,500		2,500
2,000 hours at £1.25		2,500	2,500
	2,500	2,500	5,000

Alternative activities basis

	RX-L	RX-R	Total	
Machine set-ups	8	2	10	(cost £3,200)
Sales orders	50	40	90	(cost £1,800)
				(total cost £5,000)

	RX-L £	RX-R £	Total £
Machine set-ups at £320 each	2,560	640	3,200
Sales orders at £20 each	1,000	800	1,800
	3,560	1,440	5,000

There is obviously a considerable difference between the overhead costs attributed to each of the products, depending on which basis we have used. We may question whether or not the absorption basis is fair and whether or not the activity basis provides a fairer method.

Increasing competition is a fact of life within any industry, public or private, and whatever product or service is being offered to customers in the marketplace. Globalisation has brought increased pressures of competition. Pressures on a company's profit margins inevitably follow from the increasing pace of technological change, which results in shortened life cycles of products that have been manufactured by the company as they are replaced by completely new models. Thus, the obsolescence of capital equipment is accelerated. This all means that the basis of competition has changed.

The effects on businesses are significant, and those that do not respond successfully may fail, or be acquired by other companies. Costs such as development costs and costs of capital equipment must be recovered over a shorter time period. The phases within the product life cycle must be managed more effectively and efficiently. The faster pace of business and the need for quick decisions and action mean that effective computerised information systems are required to provide relevant and timely information.

The above changes in the manufacturing business environment have led to changes in the patterns of cost behaviour. Technological and other changes have meant a lowering

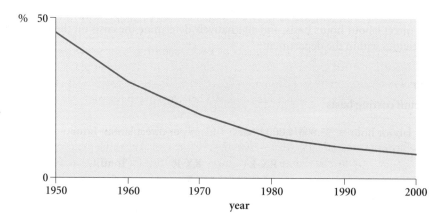

FIGURE 9.5   Estimated UK direct labour costs as
% of manufacturing costs over the past 50 years

of the percentage of direct labour costs as a proportion of total manufacturing costs. An indication of the trend, and the scale of this reduction in percentage of direct labour cost are shown in Fig. 9.5. In many industries materials and components costs have become an increasingly large proportion of total manufacturing costs. Automation and decreasing equipment life spans have led to capital equipment costs forming a higher percentage of total costs. The costs of information technology and other overhead and indirect costs have also increased as a percentage of total cost. There has therefore been increasing dissatisfaction with traditional costing and decision-making techniques and the search for other, perhaps more relevant and meaningful methods.

Traditional decision-making and control have looked at cost/volume relationships and the splitting of fixed and variable costs. The consideration of 'other characteristics' has not been emphasised. Activity based costing (ABC) was developed by Kaplan and Cooper in 1984 and was aimed to get accountants to consider 'other characteristics' in terms of the causes of cost, or what are defined as the **cost drivers**.

Kaplan and Cooper said that one cost system was not enough, and that three were needed:

● for stock valuation
● for operational control
● for product cost measurement.

Together with Cooper, Kaplan proposed ABC as a method for dealing with the latter two requirements. ABC involves the examination of activities across the entire chain of value-adding organisational processes underlying the causes, or drivers, of cost and profit. Kaplan and Cooper have defined ABC as an approach to costing and monitoring of activities which involves tracing resource consumption and costing final outputs. Resources are assigned to activities and activities to cost objects based on consumption estimates. The latter utilise cost drivers to attach activity costs to outputs.

Progress check 9.6

Why does traditional analysis of fixed and variable costs within a fast moving company (for example, a company that supplies computer hardware, software and helpline services) not appear to provide managers with enough information?

An activity driver is defined as a measure of the frequency and intensity of the demands placed on activities by cost objects. An example is the number of customer orders which measures the consumption of order entries by each customer. A cost driver is defined as any factor which causes a change in the cost of an activity. For example, the quality of parts received by an activity is a determining factor in the work required by that activity and therefore affects the resources required. An activity may have multiple cost drivers associated with it.

If a company produces only one product then all overheads may be allocated to that product. The unit cost of the product is then the average cost. The difficulty of allocation of overheads arises when the company produces many products using many different resources consumed in different proportions by products. It is the sharing of overheads and the feasibility of monitoring the costs that causes the difficulty.

Traditional cost allocation approaches allocate overheads, for example, on the basis of direct labour hours, or units produced. They are therefore volume driven, based on a scientific management basis of mass production with standard design, a high labour content percentage of total costs, large volumes, low fixed costs, and with demand greater than supply. This incidentally resulted in competitive advantage gained from cost leadership.

ABC starts by considering four different groups of activities giving rise to overheads: movement, production demands, quality, and design, rather than the volume of production. ABC is based on the premise that activities consume resources, and products consume activities. There is a need to identify how labour and machinery is actually used through

- interview
- questionnaire
- observation
- process activity mapping.

Activities are often cross-functional, for example a company buying function that involves purchasing, finance, administration, and personnel (human resources) departments in the whole procurement process. This speeds up and improves communication and may avoid a great deal of unnecessary and duplicate clerical and administrative tasks.

ABC requires the analysis of total overhead costs into variable costs and fixed costs, with variable costs split into short-term and long-term variable costs. Within an ABC system it is assumed that fixed costs do not vary with any measure of activity volume for a given time period. Short-term variable costs – volume-based costs – are defined in the same way as traditional volume driven variable costs – materials and direct labour. Long-term variable costs – activity based costs – are defined as those costs which vary with the level of activity, which may be non-productive, and the variation may not be instant. Examples of these are machine set-up costs, and goods receiving costs, which are driven by the activities of the number of production runs and number of customer orders, respectively.

The diagram in Fig. 9.6 represents an example of the framework of ABC. The bases of ABC are:

- it is activities that cause costs, not products
- it is activities and not costs that can be managed
- control of costs is best achieved through the management of activities
- each cost driver, or activity, is evaluated by setting up its own individual cost centre, to see if it is worth undertaking or buying in, and to see how it may be managed, reported on and evaluated.

The search for alternative methods such as ABC also highlights many weaknesses in traditional cost accounting methods. Indiscriminate use of a single performance measure

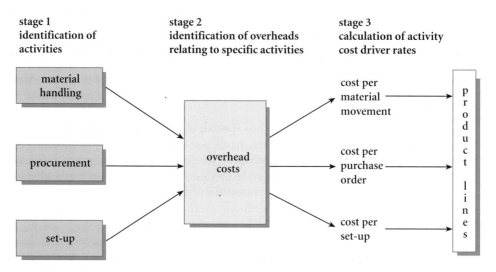

stage 1
identification of
activities

stage 2
identification of overheads
relating to specific activities

stage 3
calculation of activity
cost driver rates

material
handling

procurement

set-up

overhead
costs

cost per
material
movement

cost per
purchase
order

cost per
set-up

product lines

FIGURE 9.6   Framework of activity based costing (ABC)

can lead to misleading conclusions about profit and cost performance. Traditional cost accounting methods lead to a failure to understand the activities that are causing costs, and a compartmentalised approach to costing which does not look at the processes and activities that cross departmental boundaries.

Progress check 9.7

Use an example of a media group to provide the basis for a discussion on how ABC analysis considers departmental activities as the causes of costs rather than the products that are being produced.

These weaknesses result in:

● pricing and profitability errors
● misidentified cause and effect relationships
● improper make or buy decisions
● improper design initiatives
● irrelevant and untimely variance analysis
● misallocations of capital and resources
● non-productive activities.

The ABC methodology requires all cost types to be identified and classified into those that are volume based, those that are activity based, and those that may have some other basis.

Example 9.9

Consider how costs of a wine-bottling process, for example, for supply to one large customer, may be classified into those that are volume based, activity based, or on some other basis.

Answer

The bottle-filling process costs may be totally volume related. The labelling and corking processes may be related to stocking and handling of materials and the set-up of the processes required to align labels and corks. Alternatively, costs may in some way be related to the different grades of product, perhaps the perceived quality of the wine as cheap plonk or fine wine.

Volume-based costs are then computed on a product unit costs basis, for example, materials costs. Activity based costs are computed relative to each activity. For each product the cost of using each activity for the output level is calculated. The total costs for each product are then calculated and divided by the output volume in order to calculate the unit cost for each product.

The ABC accounting system may be used to develop an **activity based management (ABM)** system. This is a system of management which uses activity based information for a variety of purposes including cost reduction, cost modelling and customer profitability analysis. The system involves four key operations: activity analysis; activity costings; activity costs per product; activity performance measurement and management. A good ABM system should promote more effective cross-function management.

Major companies involved with providing consumers with customer service and advice found the resources required on site were quite expensive, both in capital and management time. As a result of various experiments during the latter part of the 1990s, the UK has seen a major move towards the out-sourcing of these services to specialist call centres located in 'low cost' areas, away from 'high cost' city centres. This illustrates the ABM process applied to the customer service activity. Decisions are taken following analyses of activities and their costs, followed by the evaluation of various alternative options that might be available, their implementation and subsequent management. In a similar way, many companies have investigated the out-sourcing of a number of routine accounting functions to specialist contractors.

The activity analysis identifies all activities and analyses all inputs and outputs of each activity. Activity costings identify all relevant and important costs of all activities. The activity volume that is chosen is the one that most directly influences costs, and the total costs are expressed in terms of activity per unit of activity volume.

Next, the activity costs per product are calculated by identifying the activity which each product consumes and measuring the consumption rates of activities per product. Using the unit activity cost consumption rates, costs are then allocated to each product.

The final step is activity performance measurement and management. This involves evaluation of the major elements in the performance of an activity. Changes in activity levels are then evaluated and performance reviewed which may then result in re-engineering of the methods used in that activity. The results are evaluated by

● measuring, and

● monitoring, and

● controlling the re-engineered activity.

Example 9.10

Assume that Traditional Moulding Ltd (from Example 9.8) had achieved improvements in the processes that resulted in a reduction in the costs and number of machine set-ups required, so that the RX-L and the RX-R each required only one set-up and the total cost was only £640. What would be the revised costs?

Answer

	RX-L	RX-R	Total	
Machine set-ups	1	1	2	(cost £640)
Sales orders	50	40	90	(cost £1,800)

	RX-L	RX-R	Total
	£	£	£
Machine set-ups at £320 each	320	320	640
Sales orders at £20 each	1,000	800	1,800
	1,320	1,120	2,440

There is another considerable difference between the overhead costs attributed to each of the products. We have used the same basis as previously, but an improvement in one of the processes has brought the costs attributed to each product virtually in line with each other whereas previously one product bore almost three times the cost of the other product.

A full worked example will clarify the ABC accounting concepts we have discussed and show the results obtained using ABC compared with those using an alternative traditional absorption costing method.

Example 9.11

A clothing manufacturer, Brief Encounter Ltd, manufactures two products, the Rose and the Rouge, using the same equipment and similar processes. Activities have been examined to identify the relevant cost drivers as machine hours, set-ups and customer orders. August budget data has been provided relating to the cost drivers, in addition to material, labour and overhead costs and quantities produced.

August budget ABC data	Rose	Rouge
Budgeted number of units manufactured	20,000	10,000
Direct material cost per unit	£5	£20
Direct labour hours per unit	0.5	0.5
Direct labour cost per hour	£8	£8
Machine hours per unit	2	4
Set-ups during the month	30	70
Customer orders handled in the month	40	160

Overhead costs for the month: relating to machine activity	£300,000
relating to set-ups of production runs	£50,000
relating to order handling	£70,000

To illustrate ABC and to provide a comparison with traditional costing methods we are required to calculate the full production cost of each unit of the Rose and the Rouge using both a traditional absorption costing approach and an ABC costing approach. The results should be illustrated in both tabular and graphical form.

Answer

Absorption costing

Using a traditional absorption costing approach the full production cost of each unit of Rose and Rouge may be calculated:

Budget direct labour hours (20,000 units × 0.5 hours) + (10,000 units × 0.5 hours)

= 15,000 hours

Overhead absorption rate per direct labour hour

$$= \frac{\substack{\text{machine activity} \\ \text{costs}} + \substack{\text{set-up} \\ \text{costs}} + \substack{\text{order handling} \\ \text{costs}}}{\text{direct labour hours}}$$

$$= \frac{(£300{,}000 + £50{,}000 + £70{,}000)}{15{,}000 \text{ hours}} = £28 \text{ per direct labour hour}$$

Full unit production costs of the Rose and the Rouge:

		Rose £		Rouge £
Direct materials		5.00		20.00
Direct labour	(0.5 hours × £8)	4.00	(0.5 hours × £8)	4.00
Factory overhead	(0.5 hours × £28)	14.00	(0.5 hours × £28)	14.00
Unit production costs		23.00		38.00

Total costs (20,000 × £23) + (10,000 × £38) = £840,000

ABC

Using an ABC costing approach the full production cost of each unit of the Rose and the Rouge may be calculated:

Planned for the month of August:

Machine hours (20,000 units × 2 hours) + (10,000 × 4 hours)	= 80,000 hours
Machine costs	= £300,000
Machine rate per hour	= £3.75
Number of set-ups (30 + 70)	= 100 set-ups
Set-up costs	= £50,000
Cost per set-up	= £500
Number of orders handled (40 + 160)	= 200 orders
Order handling costs	= £70,000
Cost per order handled	= £350

◀ Overhead costs per unit of the Rose and the Rouge on an ABC basis:

		Rose £		Rouge £
Machine activity	(2 hours × £3.75)	7.50	(4 hours × £3.75)	15.00
Set-ups	(30 × £500)/20,000	0.75	(70 × £500)/10,000	3.50
Order handling	(40 × £350)/20,000	0.70	(160 × £350)/10,000	5.60
Unit overhead costs		8.95		24.10

ABC unit production costs of the Rose and the Rouge:

		Rose £		Rouge £
Direct materials		5.00		20.00
Direct labour	(0.5 hours × £8)	4.00	(0.5 hours × £8)	4.00
Factory overhead		8.95		24.10
Unit production costs		17.95		48.10

Total costs (20,000 × £17.95) + (10,000 × £48.10) = £840,000

Summary of unit product costs

	Rose £	Rouge £
Full absorption cost per unit	23.00	38.00
ABC cost per unit	17.95	48.10

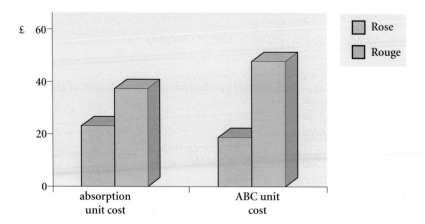

There are large differences between the two alternative calculations of unit costs. In practice, this can have a significant impact on pricing policies adopted by companies, and on other decision-making, for example with regard to discontinuation of apparently unprofitable products.

It can be seen from Example 9.11 that all costs have been accounted for and included in the unit costs for the Rose and the Rouge using both the absorption costing and ABC methods. However, using absorption costing, the Rose has been shown to be far less profitable, and the Rouge shown to be far more profitable than by using the ABC approach. In this brief example, the ABC approach has probably shown the more correct and realistic unit costs applying to the Rose and the Rouge because it has identified the activities, the causes of costs, directly related to the manufacture of each product. The pooling of the costs associated with each activity has enabled costs to be attributed directly to each product, rather than using an estimate based on, say, direct labour costs. Therefore, a more informed approach may be taken to improving machine set-up, and order-handling performance, and their cost reduction and better pricing decisions may be made regarding both the Rose and the Rouge.

There are benefits to be gained from the use of ABC: it facilitates improved understanding of costs; it enables improvements and overhead savings to be made; it focuses on activities and not production volumes; it examines the profitability of products; it identifies loss-making products; it leads to development of activity based management systems.

However, there are also many problems associated with the implementation and use of an ABC system:

- it does not comply with statutory stock valuation requirements
- it is as subjective as absorption costing
- it is historical
- it uses cost pooling (points of focus for the costs relating to particular activities), but also requires the use of apportionment, which involves the same problems of subjectivity identified in the use of absorption costing
- it requires identification of cost drivers, the right ones; it requires the measurement of cost drivers and activity costs
- it requires the relating of activities to products
- it requires the measurement of cross-product drivers, which are factors that cause changes in costs of a number of activities and products
- there are always other consequences that ABC does not address
- there is a novelty, or flavour of the month factor associated with ABC which is questionable
- it is an expensive and time-consuming exercise.

Despite the problems associated with the implementation of ABC, its acceptance is becoming more widespread in UK. Nevertheless, there is as yet little evidence as to improved profitability resulting from the implementation of ABC. Dr Stephen Lyne and Andy Friedman from Bristol University carried out research into 11 companies to study the impact of activity based techniques in real-life situations over a six-year period up to 1999 (*Success and Failure of Activity Based Techniques*).

The Lyne/Friedman research involved defining exactly what was meant by success and failure, and using the researchers' criteria five companies failed, and six were deemed a partial success. Interestingly, the research highlighted some key factors that influenced the success or otherwise of implementing ABC:

- the positive and negative roles of individuals
- the degree to which ABC was an embedded system
- the degree of integration with information technology systems
- the use of consultants
- relations between accountants and operational managers.

ABC should perhaps not be regarded totally as the panacea, the answer to all the problems associated with cost accounting. ABC, no doubt, represents an enlightened approach and adds something more meaningful than traditional costing methods. Its implementation requires very large and complex data-collection exercises in which involvement of all activities throughout the whole organisation is necessary. ABC is very time-consuming and costly. Care needs to be taken in evaluation of the results of ABC. It is very useful for identification and management of the activities that cause costs. It is a useful tool to assist in product pricing decisions. It is not yet a costing method which may replace absorption costing for use in financial reporting.

Progress check 9.8	Describe the activity based costing (ABC) process and in what ways it may be most effectively used.

Throughput accounting (TA)

Another recent development in management accounting has been the introduction of throughput accounting (TA). It has its roots in the development of the production scheduling software, **optimised production technology (OPT)**, from the mid-1970s. Through the 1980s and 1990s Eli Goldratt further developed and refined these ideas to construct the **theory of constraints (TOC)**, which was outlined in 1984 by Goldratt and Cox in their book *The Goal*.

As part of the OPT approach, TA, developed from Goldratt's TOC, provides a new measurement system. This approach takes labour and overhead costs as given and concentrates on the flow of production through the factory. TA recognises that maybe only one or two variables limit the ability of the organisation to achieve its goal to make money. Concentration only on those specific variables, and putting the efforts where the problems are, can result in huge overall gains.

A simple definition of TA has been provided by Yoshikawa in *Contemporary Cost Management* (1993). Throughput accounting (TA) is an approach to accounting which is largely in sympathy with the **just in time (JIT)** philosophy. In essence, TA assumes that a manager has a given set of resources available. These (fixed resources) comprise existing buildings, capital equipment, and a labour force. Using these resources, purchased materials and parts must be processed to generate sales revenue. Given this scenario the most appropriate financial objective to set for doing this is the maximisation of **throughput**.

Just in time (JIT) is a philosophy with an objective to produce or to procure products or components as they are required by a customer or for use, rather than for stock. A JIT system is a 'pull' system, which responds to demand, in contrast to a 'push' system, in which stocks act as buffers between the different elements of the system, such as purchasing, production and sales.

There is a link between TA and JIT in that throughput is not directly generated by producing for stock but only by effecting sales from finished output. TA is probably more usefully regarded as a new general approach within which a number of different measures can be constructed, rather than a new set of accounting techniques. This then needs to be supported by a change from traditional cost thinking to throughput thinking as a means of improving profitability.

TA is similar to the approach of contribution per unit of scarce resource, but whereas

contribution = sales revenue − total variable costs

	£	£
Sales		x
Direct materials		(x)
Throughput		x
Direct labour	(x)	
Production overhead	(x)	
Administrative expenses	(x)	
Selling costs	(x)	
		(x)
Operating profit		x

FIGURE 9.7 Throughput report

Throughput is defined as

throughput = sales revenue − direct materials cost

An advantage of TA over traditional methods is that decisions made on standard costing 'efficiencies' are thus avoided. An example of such decisions are those based on apparent improvements in labour productivity gained from manufacturing increased volumes (and build-ups of unnecessary stocks), not supported by increased customer orders. TA concentrates on identification and management of **bottlenecks** (which is in itself a process of continuous improvement) and so priority may be given to investment in bottlenecks. The concentration on throughput highlights the critical profit improvement areas of sales prices, volume, and material costs.

TA is a method of performance measurement, which relates production and other costs to throughput. The product costs calculated using TA relate to the usage of key resources by various products. As the costs of all factors other than materials are deemed fixed, the objective of maximisation of throughput will motivate management to generate the greatest profit for the business. TA is therefore an extreme form of marginal costing. The similarity can be seen in Fig. 9.7 from the example of a throughput report developed by Yoshikawa.

In *The Goal*, Goldratt defines

- throughput as the rate at which the system generates money through sales
- inventory is all the money that the system invests in purchasing things which it intends to sell (not to be confused with inventory as the American term for stocks)
- operational expense is all the money the system spends in order to turn inventory into throughput

Goldratt's three measures are operationalised through a number of simple calculations:

- throughput = sales revenue − outside purchases of product related materials and services
- inventory (in Goldratt's terminology) includes materials stocks plus machines and buildings
- operational expense covers conversion cost, including direct and indirect employee costs, operating, or idle time

From these three measures Goldratt defines two important relationships:

$$\textbf{net profit} = \textbf{throughput} - \textbf{operational expense}$$

$$\textbf{return on investment (ROI)} = \frac{\textbf{throughput} - \textbf{operational expense}}{\textbf{inventory}}$$
$$\textbf{(in the TA world)}$$

(Note the difference between this definition of ROI and the financial accounting definition that we looked at in Chapter 5.)

The three elements of the throughput accounting ROI ratio belong to three different 'worlds':

● throughput – the throughput world
● operational expense – the cost world, which is obsessed and involved with cost cutting
● inventory – the just in time (JIT) world, concentrating on reducing stocks and the costs of holding stocks and with the aim of reducing waste.

Goldratt sees throughput as the priority, with inventory second, and operational expense last. This is a big change in managers' mind sets in which it is crucial for cost accounting not to interfere with the improvement of manufacturing performance. Traditional cost accounting methods may be criticised for reporting efficiency gains from longer production runs and increased volumes of production. Such efficiencies may be illusory if the result is high levels of unsold stock.

Progress check 9.9

Discuss the relationship between throughput and the traditional ratio of return on capital employed (ROCE) or return on investment (ROI).

Goldratt's approach broadened from a concentration on 'bottlenecks' (in production) to a general concern with constraints. A constraint may be defined as anything which prevents a system from achieving a higher performance relative to its goal. Constraints do not necessarily have to be within the production processes, but may, for example, be concerned with

● demand
● skills
● accounting systems.

Note how in 2000 and 2001, the UK general public saw the Government attempting to solve constraint problems by allocating further funds to the health service and schools.

There are four key influences on throughput, and therefore profitability:

● selling prices
● direct materials purchase costs
● direct material usage
● volume of throughput.

Progress check 9.10

Discuss the connection between TA and the electronic point of sale (EPOS) systems used by all the major supermarket chains.
Hint: Start the discussion by considering just in time (JIT).

To maximise throughput it is first necessary to identify the constraints, the factors that currently limit the expansion of throughput. Constraints may be:

● the existence of uncompetitive selling prices
● the need for on-time deliveries
● the lack of product quality and reliability
● the lack of reliable materials supplies
● shortages of production resources.

Attention may then be given by managers to minimisation or elimination of these constraints.

TA then focuses on some key activities:

● identification of bottlenecks and constraints, through profiling of processes and identification of buffer stocks
● close attention to decision-making on new capital equipment investments
● project teams investigating and implementing reductions in lead times, set-up times and waiting times.

Along with its inventive approach to performance measurement and control, the overriding benefit of TA is that it forces everyone, and management in particular, to get back to understanding what is actually happening where the products and services are being provided, and to appreciate the critical need for adherence to customer schedules.

Example 9.12

An aim of throughput accounting (TA) is maximisation of throughput, defined as sales revenue less direct material cost. Purchased materials and parts must be processed to generate this sales revenue.

Discuss how the modern clothing manufacturing scenario of manufacturing in the Far East and selling in London's West End may generate stress within the UK managers of such a business.

Answer

Competition between the clothing retailers is severe. There is no guarantee that what is on the racks will sell out, ready for the next range. Anything not sold by a certain date must be discounted for a short time or sold at a greatly reduced price to other specialist retailers. Time is of the essence as the selling seasons are fashion, weather and temperature driven. There must be continuous contact with the Far East factory to boost production of fast sellers and reduce excess stocks and production of the slow sellers to the minimum. Note how 'throughput' as defined by Goldratt and Cox is sales (and money) driven.

Progress check 9.11

What is throughput and what do we mean by throughput accounting (TA)? In what ways can TA be used to improve productivity?

Life cycle costing

Life cycle costing has an ultimate aim of minimising total expenditure over the lifetime of a product, or over the lifetime of an item of a fixed asset. Life cycle costing involves the maintenance of physical asset records over the entire asset life, so that decisions concerning the acquisition, use or disposal of the asset can be made in a way that achieves the optimum assets usage at the lowest possible cost to the business.

With a focus on maximising reliability and minimising maintenance and repair costs, acquisition of machinery or equipment involves an examination of the original cost and the support cost of the asset over the number of years of its expected lifetime. Depending on the type of equipment, support costs may range from 10 to 100 times the cost of acquisition. The approach may be applied to smaller items such as computer hardware and software, and vehicles, to very large equipment like buildings and aircraft. The construction industry has become increasingly aware of the need to adopt an holistic approach to the design, building and disposal of structures. It has been estimated that around 60% of a typical total construction budget is spent on repair and maintenance and so there is an obvious need to design for reliability and durability, with more carefully planned maintenance and repair schedules.

As distinct from the service sector, the manufacturing environment has become more advanced in response to customer requirements for higher and higher levels of quality, durability and reliability. Such factors have to be designed into the product at the planning stage in addition to design for ease and speed of manufacture. Prototype and pre-production stages of a product's development have a significant impact on the product, and its cost over the entire life of the product. Life cycle costing may be applied to the profiling of cost over a product's life, including the prototyping and pre-production stages and in terms of the life cycles of both the business and the industry.

Example 9.13

Powerful IT resources are now widely available, and all types of business may benefit from their acquisition and use. Fixed asset registers used to be maintained manually or not at all. Now they can be maintained with ease on a computer.

Discuss how a major plc can benefit from maintaining its fleet of company cars (say 100 vehicles) on a computer system, using a spreadsheet costing around £100.

Answer

Any spreadsheet can easily hold all the records relating to 100 cars.

The records should include acquisition cost, date of acquisition, supplier, specification, insurance, maintenance, mileages, market values (from external sources), and depreciation.

The spreadsheet should be robust enough to last several years and may export to other IT packages for report and update purposes.

Managers should be able to interrogate the data to make decisions on the future management of their fleet, and expansion of the system and retrieval of data may be available at all times.

Progress check 9.12

How can life-cycle costing achieve its aims of improving reliability and minimising costs?

Target costing

Management accounting traditionally supported pricing decisions based on, for example, the calculation of the selling price required to be charged for a product or service that covered total costs plus a margin for profit for the business. Such an approach took no account of the price which the market might accept for the particular product or service. Neither did this approach encourage the objective of total cost minimisation. In fact, one could argue that such an approach encouraged costs to be increased since the higher the cost, the higher was the level of total profit. Increased pressures on businesses to provide higher and higher specifications and levels of quality at more competitive prices has prompted changes to traditional approaches to the costing of products and services.

Target costing policies have been developed from wide usage in Japan based on the principle that a product must have a target price that will succeed in winning a share of the market. A target cost is a product cost estimate (for example, a car at £12,000) derived by subtracting a desired profit margin (for example, £2,000) from a competitive market price (for example £14,000), determined through customer analysis and market research. The target cost may be less than the planned initial product cost (which may have been say £13,500). The cost reduction (in this case £1,500) will be expected to be achieved by the time the product reaches the mature production stage, through continuous improvement and replacement of technologies and processes.

Target costing has also been described as a structured approach to determining the cost at which a proposed product with specified functionality and quality must be produced in order to generate the desired level of profitability at the product's anticipated selling price. Target costing focuses on reducing the cost of a product through design changes.

The traditional Western approach of 'cost plus' involved the setting of a target selling price by adding an expected margin to expected costs. If actual costs were more than expected then the selling price would be higher. Using target costing, in the long run, costs must come down to below the target price for the product to be worth manufacturing. This is saying that market prices determine product costs and not vice versa.

Target costs are determined by setting specific goals. Better performance then emerges from specific, challenging goals rather than a company's general goal of merely doing its best. Over many years, car manufacturers have been replacing metal with composites, and upgrading vehicle specifications without increasing prices. Examples of this could be seen from car advertisements appearing in the UK press during the year 2000.

Example 9.14

UK computer buyers saw major improvements to the specification of PCs, costing around £1,000, during the year 2001.

Discuss why the market place should change so quickly, regarding the functionality of a PC.

Answer

The suppliers of peripherals into the PC market regularly find that economies of scale drive down unit prices. DVD players have followed printers, scanners and CD writers. The majority of PCs that were sold for around £1,000 in the UK in early part of 2001 included, as standard, DVD players and CD writers. Most retailers and dealers also included printers and scanners. Obviously the consumer may prefer to buy this type of package off the shelf from one source, whereas the dealer aims to maintain the unit price as high as possible.

There are three factors that affect the structure of a target-costing system:

- type of product – complex, capital intensive products that have a long development time tend to require more sophisticated target costing systems that are closely linked to the use of value engineering techniques
- the market – where goods are supplied to the general public, the target costing system is based on a heavier bias towards consumer analysis and a focus on functionality; examples were apparent in UK press advertisements during 2001, where PCs were offered with CD writers, whereas earlier advertisements would have offered merely a CD player
- influence over suppliers – the target costing system creates a downward pressure on supplier prices, assuming that the customer company has greater power and is more important than the supplier company; in the UK during 2000, many manufacturers found themselves being pressurised by the major retailers to hold or reduce their prices in the electrical goods sector, for example, which reflected 'target costing' by those retailers.

Example 9.15

In the UK, two companies selling PCs called Time and Tiny have both advertised in the same national daily newspapers, with advertisements promoting packages comprising a computer with printer, camera, scanner, and a range of software, and with very similar prices.

What sort of pressure do you think these two companies are able to exert on suppliers of DVD players and CD rewriters?

Answer

Neither company should let the other company drive down prices unilaterally. One of the key ways of remaining competitive is to examine 'ways and means' of reducing the number of constituent parts of the package and unit prices from various individual sources. Almost certainly both companies may have alternative sources, to enable them to play one off against the other, which is really standard buyer practice.

Example 9.16

Until 1999, there were articles in the business press on how Marks and Spencer plc were working with suppliers as a 'partnership' at the factory floor level. These suppliers were all aware of other suppliers making the same products for Marks and Spencer plc.

Discuss how Marks and Spencer plc might put pressure on its suppliers.

Answer

There may always be several potential manufacturers that can supply a garment or a food product, for example, to a retailer. The national retailers are aware of this and may use these circumstances to negotiate volumes, prices, quality and deliveries. There will always be such 'tension' between the retailer and manufacturer.

Target costs may be used to exert pressure on suppliers to reduce costs. However, target costing creates a great deal of pressure within the organisation and the targets set must be achievable. It is not a method of cost control in the traditional sense, but rather provides a goal and a focus for cost reduction. Target costing is something that must be applied at the design stage of new product development, and cross-functional support and co-operation are absolute requirements for its success. The cross-functional support might involve:

- the designer wanting to change from one material used in manufacture to another
- the buyer sourcing materials or components from a new supplier
- the factory floor agreeing that the new product will cause no problems during assembly.

Example 9.17

Nissan operates in the automotive market where functionality continues to increase at a quite rapid pace. Consider the target costing system that may be used by Nissan.

Answer

Nissan's target costing system would tend to be determined by market factors, using the following process:

- identification of the major characteristics of the car model, its engine, air conditioning system, etc.
- determination of current costs
- calculation of the 'allowable cost' of each function
- assessment of the level of cost reductions required
- use of an iterative process looking at costs and possible reductions in levels of functionality, in consultation with the marketing department
- assessment of first draft target costs achievable using value engineering
- detailed review of target costs to assess feasibility
- acceptance of draft target costs to be implemented in product development
- implementation of target costs using value engineering as appropriate.

After products are in production, costs are constantly monitored against targets. If costs are not in line with target costs then further cost reduction exercises are introduced to achieve targets.

Progress check 9.13

Outline what is meant by target costing and why it has become increasingly popular for large manufacturers of consumer products.

Benchmarking

Benchmarking is the establishment, through data gathering, of targets and comparators, through whose use relative levels of performance (and particularly areas of under-performance) can be identified. Through the adoption of identified best practices it is hoped that performance will improve.

The performance of other companies should be continually benchmarked. This should look at, for example, design, quality, cost, and delivery, and is known as internal benchmarking, which is a method of comparing one operating unit or function with another within the same industry.

Benchmarking need not be restricted to companies with similar products or companies in the same industry. Lessons may be learned and costs reduced by comparing the company's processes with processes in other non-related companies or industries. Functional benchmarking (also known as operational, or generic benchmarking), compares internal functions with those of the best external practitioners of those functions, regardless of the industry they are in. A well known airline achieved such improvements from benchmarking a photocopier manufacturer.

Competitive benchmarking compares performance from information gathered about direct competitors, through techniques such as **reverse engineering**. Reverse engineering relates to the decomposition and analysis of competitors' products in order to determine how they are made, their costs of production and the way in which future development may proceed. This is a technique favoured by Japanese manufacturers who have used it to advantage to copy and improve on quality and reliability of competing products and to manufacture at lower cost. Another type of competitive benchmarking is strategic benchmarking, which is aimed at strategic action and organisational change.

Benchmarking is a very useful tool that companies may use to develop suitable performance measures and also targets for improvement in each part of their business. A number of further techniques and concepts may be adopted to achieve such improvements, for example:

- **value analysis/value engineering**
- **concurrent engineering**
- **cost of quality**
- *kaizen.*

We will look at two of most important of these concepts and techniques, *kaizen*, and cost of quality (COQ), in the next two sections.

Progress check 9.14

What is benchmarking and how can it be used in support of business performance improvement?

Kaizen

Change management is sometimes considered an oxymoron by many people, who say that change is usually, by its very nature, unplanned and independent of human purpose and is therefore unmanageable. However, the management of change was for many years one of the fundamental sources of competitive advantage that Japanese businesses had over their Western counterparts. The management of change is the basis of the concept of *kaizen*, which simply means improvement. It was a concept so natural and obvious to most Japanese managers that they often did not realise they possessed it.

The tools of *kaizen* were introduced to Japan in the 1950s from the USA by Deming and Juran. However, the concept continued to be rejected for a long time in the West until the Japanese postwar 'economic miracle' began to be studied more seriously and the techniques applied to achieve the same improvements in productivity.

Kaizen means continuous improvement involving everyone, including both managers and operators – the people actually doing things. The *kaizen* philosophy assumes that

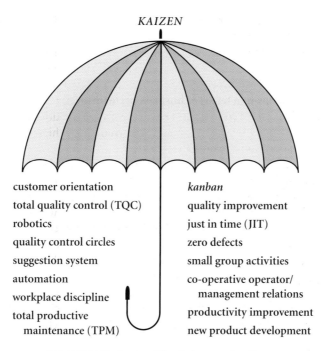

FIGURE 9.8 The *kaizen* umbrella

everyone's way of life, whether it is working life, social life, or home life, deserves to be constantly improved. *Kaizen* signifies small continuous improvements to the *status quo* as a result of constant efforts rather than drastic investment/improvement programmes.

In his book *Kaizen* (1986), Imae described *kaizen* as an umbrella concept (see Fig. 9.8), covering most of those 'uniquely Japanese' practices that have achieved such worldwide fame.

Kaizen teams are small multi-disciplined groups that are brought together to brainstorm and develop improvement ideas. A prerequisite for *kaizen* is a culture within the organisation that is conducive to change – from top to bottom. Two of the fundamentals of **total quality control (TQC)**, **policy deployment** and **cross-function management**, provide an important framework in which *kaizen* may operate. Policy deployment is a process of internalising improvement policies throughout the company from translation of customer requirements, through each process of specification, design, etc. to final manufacturing and delivery. *Kaizen* usually involves first line maintenance becoming the responsibility of operators in what is termed **total productive maintenance (TPM)**.

An organisation that has a cross-functional structure has an horizontal, cross-departmental organisation as opposed to the traditional vertical, functional, chimney organisation of separate departments or functions. This allows for improved communication and team-working, and develops better relationships and quicker decision-making.

It is always beneficial for a business to have at least one continuous improvement team running at any one time to look at:

- products
- materials
- processes
- purchasing
- logistics
- any of the support functions.

The make up of the *kaizen* teams should be changed frequently and the process should ensure that employees are involved in assessing, and auditing, departments and tasks other than their own departments.

Progress check 9.15

What does *kaizen* mean in terms of business performance?

Cost of quality (COQ)

Quality, once a deviation from the 'normal' product by providing extra 'luxury' and more features, is now a given. Quality means doing what the customer wants every time at the lowest internal cost. It involves:

● getting it right
● getting it right first time
● only doing the right things and doing them right
● doing the right things better.

In many businesses that have no quality systems, or neglected quality systems, the cost of quality is usually in excess of 20% of turnover. Within service industries this cost may be 40% or more! Organisations that have implemented well-developed quality systems may be able to reduce the cost of quality down to below 20% and perhaps as low as 2% of turnover.

Cost of quality (COQ) is a technique that is used to measure the difference between the actual costs incurred within each of the processes of manufacture and/or supply of goods, and services, and the equivalent costs if there were no failures within each of those processes. It may be defined as the additional cost incurred in non-added-value activities and events in a business in fully satisfying customers' agreed requirements for products and services delivered. It is the cost of both not doing the right things and not doing things right first time.

Example 9.18

Amazon.com was set up to be able to take orders in the UK for books and CDs through the Internet. If a customer complained regarding poor delivery, the order would be re-sent by courier, even if Amazon were sure that the original had been despatched, if there was a reasonable excuse for the delay.

Discuss a simple internal report that may be used to reveal to the managers of Amazon whether or not they were delivering a quality service.

Answer

The managers of Amazon may obtain, at any time, reports in detail or summary of deliveries by courier, because of the availability of their powerful IT resources. The reports should identify causes of delay and identify whether these are within or outside the control of Amazon. The managers may then accept the reasonable excuses for delay from customers (snow or earthquake?), or take the appropriate corrective action regarding their operations.

In the UK, the Department of Trade and Industry (DTI) quality standard BS6143 (1990) defines quality costs using four categories:

- two types of cost of achieving quality
  - prevention costs
  - appraisal costs
- two costs of not achieving quality
  - internal failure costs
  - external failure costs.

In addition, there are two further important categories, which are the costs of exceeding requirements, and the cost of lost opportunities.

These six costs of quality are fertile areas for cost reduction and performance improvement:

Quality costs

- prevention costs – costs of activities that prevent failure from occurring
  - training employees
  - quality awareness programmes
  - planning and continuous improvement teams
  - costs of supplier assurance
  - costs of calibration, test and control equipment
- appraisal costs – costs incurred to determine conformance with quality standards
  - inspection
  - checking
  - auditing or expediting parts or documentation
  - performance testing
  - costs of stock evaluation and storage records (e.g. traceability).

Non-quality costs

- internal failure costs – costs of correcting products or services which do not meet quality standards prior to delivery to customers
  - scrap
  - rework
  - design changes after process implementation
  - obsolete inventory
  - absenteeism
  - costs of downtime
- external failure costs – costs incurred to correct products and services after delivery to customers
  - customer credits
  - replaced products
  - customer invoice errors and adjustments
  - unplanned field service costs
  - costs of complaints
  - warranty claims
  - concessions (deviations from specification)
  - product liability

● cost of exceeding requirements – costs incurred providing information or services which are unnecessary or unimportant, or for which no known requirement has been established

  – excess inventory
  – redundant copies of documents
  – reports which are not read
  – detailed analytical effort when simple estimates would suffice

● cost of lost opportunities – lost revenues resulting from the loss of existing customers, the loss of potential customers and the loss of business growth arising from the failure to deliver products and services at the required quality standards

  – cancellations due to inadequate service response times
  – ordering of competitors' products because the company's products are not available
  – wrong products offered for the specific customer's application.

Example 9.19

Flatco plc has calculated the following costs of quality for 2000, which have been categorised as:

● PR prevention   ● AP appraisal   ● ER exceeding requirements
● IF internal failure   ● EF external failure.

In the year 2000 Flatco plc's sales turnover was £3.5m, and its profit before tax was £590,000. We are required to comment on Flatco plc's cost of quality for the year 2000.

Flatco plc
Costs of quality

Department	Description	Cost £000	Category
Logistics	Unnecessary storage space	12	IF
Management	Ineffective meetings	10	IF
Production	Scrap	10	IF
Finance	Computer maintenance records	15	PR
Purchasing	Order errors	13	IF
Human resources	Health and Safety and environmental costs	20	PR
Human resources	Unplanned absenteeism	30	IF
Quality	Customer warranty returns	55	EF
Logistics	Excess stocks	14	ER
Quality	Costs of inspection equipment	14	AP
Management	Training in problem solving	7	PR
Production	Unused production floor space	9	ER
Human resources	Training in skill improvement	32	PR
Purchasing	Inefficient scheduling	19	IF
Design and development	Design changes	21	IF
Design and development	Project overruns	31	IF
Total		312	

Answer

The costs of quality were first identified in each of the departments in the company and then a cost and a category allocated to them. Excess stocks of £14,000, for example, were calculated from an average of £35,000 surplus stock through the year, which was unusable inventory with no value, multiplied by 40%, its inventory carrying costs (space, handling, funding, etc.). The purchasing department employed a person, costing £20,000 per annum, who was employed for two thirds of her time on correction of purchase orders, therefore costing £13,000. The total cost of quality at £312,000 can be seen to be 8.9% of sales of £3.5m. Whilst not perhaps at disastrous levels this is nevertheless a big number at 53% of profit before tax. The analysis of costs of quality shows prevention costs £74,000; appraisal costs £14,000, and analysis of costs of non-quality shows internal failure costs £146,000; external failure £55,000; costs of exceeding requirements £23,000. The total quality costs of £88,000 are incurred to maintain a high level of quality. The balance of £224,000 non-quality costs is incurred as a result of low quality. These costs should be prioritised for inclusion in a cost-reduction plan to minimise or eliminate. This may involve spending on additional quality costs but would result in significant profit improvement.

The traditional view was to consider quality as a cost. The perception of this cost was therefore:

- as prevention and appraisal costs increase, the level of defects reduces

Therefore:

- as failure costs reduce, the total costs of prevention, appraisal and failure then reduce

And so:

- diminishing returns take effect, and the optimum is at the point just before total costs start to increase where defects are at a level of say x%

Therefore:

- x% defects are established as the accepted level of the cost of quality.

The total quality view considers cost of quality as a cost to be minimised with an aim of Zero defects:

- prevention and appraisal costs are initially high as the total quality initiative starts
- a large part of the initial costs, for example familiarisation and training, will not be repeated and so prevention and appraisal costs start to reduce

So:

- defects start to reduce and costs of defects reduce, so total costs of quality reduce

So:

- defects continue to reduce as the total quality programme becomes increasingly effective and awareness increases

Therefore:

- total costs of quality continue to reduce as continuous improvement takes place.

To achieve an improvement in performance, and therefore an increase in profit, the business must take the following approach:

- identify the cost of quality categories
- identify the activities and events within these categories that result in cost of quality
- prioritise as high, medium, low to categorise each activity and specify the cost of quality category to determine areas of high opportunity
- use the information to focus on improvement actions
- monitor progress towards reducing the cost of quality.

This represents a **total quality management (TQM)** approach to company performance by raising quality awareness and reducing the costs of quality through implementation of improvement actions.

Progress check 9.16

How does the total quality approach to cost of quality differ from the traditional approach to quality and how may this result in improved profitability?

Summary of key points

- Cost/volume/profit (CVP) analysis may be used to determine the break-even position of a business and provide sensitivity analyses on the impact on the business of changes to any of the variables used to calculate break-even.

- There are a great many limitations to CVP analysis, whether it is used to consider break-even relationships, decision-making or sales pricing.

- The more recently developed techniques of activity based costing (ABC) and throughput accounting (TA) are approaches that attempt to overcome the problem of allocation and apportionment of overheads.

- Life cycle costing uses maintenance of cost records over entire asset lives so that decisions regarding acquisition or disposal may be made in a way that optimises asset usage at the lowest cost to the business.

- A target cost is a product cost estimate (that may be less than the planned initial product cost but which will be expected to be achieved by the time the product reaches the mature production stage through continuous improvement and replacement of technologies and processes), derived by subtracting a desired profit margin from a competitive market price, determined through customer analysis and market research.

- Benchmarking processes of the best performing organisations within the industry, or within any other industry, can identify best practice, the adoption of which may improve performance.

- *Kaizen*, an 'umbrella' concept covering most of the 'uniquely Japanese' practices, is a technique used for continuous improvement of all aspects of business performance.

- Cost of quality (COQ) is used to identify areas for improvement and cost reduction within each of the processes throughout the business.

Glossary of key terms

activity based management (ABM) System of management which uses activity based cost information for a variety of purposes including cost reduction, cost modelling and customer profitability analysis.

bottleneck An activity within an organisation which has a lower capacity than preceding or subsequent activities, thereby limiting throughput. Bottlenecks are often the cause of a build-up of work-in-progress and idle time.

break-even point The level of activity at which there is neither profit nor loss, ascertained by using a break-even chart or by calculation.

concurrent engineering A means of reducing product development time and cost by managing development processes so they can be implemented simultaneously rather than sequentially.

cost driver Any factor which causes a change in the cost of an activity. For example, the quality of parts received by an activity is a determining factor in the work required by that activity and therefore affects the resources required. An activity may have multiple cost drivers associated with it.

cost of quality (COQ) The cost of quality may be defined as the additional cost incurred in non-added value activities and events in a business in fully satisfying customers' agreed requirements for products and services delivered. It is the cost both of not doing the right things and not doing things right first time.

cross-function management Horizontal cross-departmental organisation as opposed to the traditional vertical, functional, chimney organisation.

just in time (JIT) The management philosophy that incorporates a 'pull' system of producing or purchasing components and products in response to customer demand, which contrasts with a 'push' system where stocks act as buffers between each process within and between purchasing, manufacturing, and sales.

limiting factor (or key factor) Anything which limits the activity of an entity. An entity seeks to optimise the benefit it obtains from the limiting factor. Examples are a shortage of supply of a resource or a restriction on sales demand at a particular price.

margin of safety The difference between the break-even point and an anticipated or existing level of activity above that point.

optimised production technology (OPT) OPT is a manufacturing philosophy combined with a computerised system of shop-floor scheduling and capacity planning. It is a philosophy that focuses on factors such as manufacture to order, quality, lead times, batch sizes and set-up times, and differs from a traditional approach of balancing capacity as near 100% as possible and then maintaining flow. The aim of OPT is to balance flow rather than capacity. The goal of OPT is to make money by increasing throughput and reducing stocks and operating expenses, by making better use of limited capacity by tightly controlled finite scheduling of bottleneck operations.

policy deployment The process of internalising improvement policies throughout the company from translation of customer requirements, through each process of specification, design, etc. to final manufacturing and delivery.

reverse engineering The decomposition and analysis of competitors' products in order to determine how they are made, their costs of production and the way in which future development may proceed.

theory of constraints (TOC) An approach to production management which aims to maximise sales revenue less materials (throughput), whilst simultaneously reducing 'inventory' and operational expense. It focuses primarily on factors which act as constraints to this maximisation.

throughput The rate of production of a defined process over a stated period of time. Rates may be expressed in terms of units of products, batches produced, turnover, or other meaningful measurements.

total productive maintenance (TPM) Where first line maintenance, cleaning, checking for irregularities, leaks etc., and simple maintenance, become the responsibility of operators rather than of the maintenance department.

total quality control (TQC) A concept of the quality operation of a business that includes policy deployment, quality control teams, cross-function quality groups, 5S techniques of good housekeeping, the seven tools of quality, and the Deming cycle of plan–do–check–act, to involve everyone in all areas of the business to meet customer needs.

total quality management (TQM) An integrated and comprehensive system of planning and controlling all business functions so that products or services are produced which meet or exceed customer expectations. TQM is a philosophy of business behaviour, embracing principles such as employee involvement, continuous improvement at all levels and customer focus, as well as being a collection of related techniques aimed at improving quality. In addition to the features included in TQC, TQM additionally includes JIT, *heijunka*, and *jidoka*.

value analysis A technique for examination, by multi-disciplined teams, of design attributes and any other factors affecting the cost of the product to identify and implement the means of achieving the specified purpose most economically at the required standard of quality and reliability. Value analysis is the broad term usually used to include both value analysis and value engineering. Value engineering applies to products under development, whilst value analysis applies to products currently in production.

value engineering The method of value analysis that applies to products under development.

Assessment material

Questions

Q9.1 How may cost/volume/profit (CVP) analysis be used to determine the break-even point of a business?

Q9.2 Are the assumptions on which CVP analysis is based so unrealistic that the technique should be abandoned?

Q9.3 (i) What are the principles on which activity based costing (ABC) is based?

(ii) How does ABC differ from traditional costing methods?

Q9.4 (i) Is throughput accounting (TA) an alternative to traditional costing methods?

(ii) What may be some of the real benefits from the use of TA?

Q9.5 Describe the process of life cycle costing, together with some examples that illustrate its aims and benefits.

Q9.6 (i) Describe the various approaches to target costing.

(ii) Critically evaluate the differences between target costing approaches and traditional cost plus pricing.

Q9.7 The *kaizen* philosophy includes a wide range of practices and techniques concerned with achievement of continuous improvement. Describe the role of three of these and how you think they may support the implementation of *kaizen* in a business within a service industry.

Q9.8 How may benchmarking add value to a business?

Q9.9 (i) Describe what is meant by cost of quality, giving examples within each of the categories of cost of quality you have outlined.

(ii) Explain how quality costing may be used to achieve business performance improvement.

Discussion points

D9.1 Is activity based costing (ABC) a serious contender to replace the traditional costing methods? What are some of the drawbacks in implementing this?

D9.2 'Many companies benchmark every element of every process, at great cost, but seem to lose sight of what they are trying to achieve.' Discuss.

D9.3 '*Kaizen* is probably the Japanese business tool that has had the most significant impact on performance improvement in the West.' Why should that be so?

Exercises

Solutions are provided in Appendix 4 to all exercise numbers highlighted in colour.

Level I

E9.1   *Time allowed – 15 minutes*

Break-even sales	£240,000
Marginal cost of sales	£240,000
Sales for January	£320,000

What is the profit?

E9.2   *Time allowed – 15 minutes*

Sales for January	£120,000, on which profit is £10,000
Fixed cost for January	£30,000

What is the break-even point?

E9.3   *Time allowed – 15 minutes*

Selling price	£15
Marginal cost	£9
Fixed cost for January	£30,000
Sales for January	£120,000

What is the break-even point and what is the profit?

E9.4   *Time allowed – 30 minutes*

In the UK, the newsagents' shelves are full of computer magazines with very similar cover prices, for example, £2.99 each.

How may a marketing department of a magazine publishing company become involved in the target costing process as a new magazine is being developed for the market?

E9.5   *Time allowed – 60 minutes*

Atlas plc, a large UK manufacturer and supplier of business equipment had a total turnover for 2000 of £50m. Its profitability has suffered over the past couple of years through competition, lack of innovation, high stock levels, slow introduction of new products, and high levels of rework in production. The managing director has proposed the implementation of a quality costing system to identify the problems in each department and to develop action plans for improvement.

In the sales and marketing department a number of areas have been identified for action. A reduction in the volume of sales orders has revealed that £4m of sales has been lost to competitors' products. The budget had been based on earning a profit before tax of 12% of sales, but the actual profit for the past year was 4% of sales, due to higher costs. The marketing department has discovered that competitors on average have been able to price products at an average premium of 10% over Atlas due to superior quality and the fact that Atlas have been forced to reduce prices to maintain sales levels. 15% of sales orders completed by Atlas salesmen have errors (that does not please the customers at all) resulting in delivery delays, invoicing, pricing and quantity errors. Delays in payments from customers have resulted in debtor levels increasing by £2.5m mainly because of invoicing errors resulting from incorrect sales orders.

We are told that costs of production are 65% of sales, and the number of people in the sales team is 84 and the average gross cost per person is £27k. Rework and error correction costs have been estimated at 25% of original costs, and Atlas's borrowing costs are 9% per annum.

(i)   **Based on the information provided, what is the total cost of quality for the sales and marketing department in value and as a percentage of total sales, and**

(ii) **In which quality cost categories do they fall?**

(iii) **What actions would you recommend to provide a significant reduction to these costs?**

Level II

E9.6   *Time allowed – 45 minutes*

It is a morning in February and Marsha Ighodaro picks up the keys of her brand new Mini from the Rover dealer in a town situated some 29 miles from the village in which she lives. She drives away in the car she has dreamt about since finally choosing and ordering it five weeks earlier (she has very quickly rationalised her acceptance of the red model instead of the British racing green she originally wanted). It's a cold morning and so she moves the heater control lever to the left and switches on the fan. Alas, nothing happens! The heater doesn't work.

Fortunately, these days, such failures rarely occur. But how may a manufacturing company ensure that the complete product offering, such as a Mini, provides the required level of quality and delivery on each of the assemblies making up the product to meet the expectations of the customer, at a cost he/she is willing to pay?

E9.7   *Time allowed – 45 minutes*

The managing director of Flatco plc has agreed with his budget committee that a 20% profit before tax to sales should be achievable for 2001. The sales and marketing department have already agreed to a target of 10% increase in sales for 2001 over 2000. The managing director has suggested that a percentage improvement should be targeted for costs in all areas of the company that will provide a 20% profit before tax. (The Flatco plc profit and loss account for the year 2000 is shown in Fig. 5.4 in Chapter 5.)

(i)   **Calculate the required percentage cost reduction on the assumption that same percentage is applied throughout the company.**

(ii) **How fair do you think this is as a method of target setting?**

(iii) **How may each department assess whether such targets are achievable or not?**

(iv) **What impacts may such targets have on the effectiveness of each of the departments within Flatco?**

E9.8   *Time allowed – 90 minutes*

Crispian Brown Ltd, manufactures two versions of its product the tanbag, the Standard and the Super. The Super was introduced, after many successful years of selling the Standard tanbag, to generate increased sales by taking market share from a competitor. Since that time Super sales increased as planned but profits have declined. The managing director, Crispian, has asked his management accountant Fontella Franklin to look at the accuracy of the costing system and also to consider overhead costs in terms of activities.

Brown's costing system is currently based on full absorption costing using direct labour hours. For 2000 the company forecast production of 5,000 Supers and 40,000 Standards, each taking two hours and one hour of direct labour respectively. Overheads were estimated at £900,000 for the year. Material and labour costs per unit were as follows:

	Super	Standard
Direct material cost per unit	£40	£25
Direct labour per unit (at £7 per hour)	£14	£7

Fontella has determined the following costs in respect of the four key activities traced to production of the Super and the Standard:

Activity	Estimated costs 2000	Number per product Super	Standard
Machine hours	£182,000	20,000	15,000
Shipments made	£135,000	250	650
Scrap/rework jobs	£379,000	1,000	1,000
Purchase orders issued	£204,000	200	400

You are required to:

(i)   calculate the full overhead rate for 2000 and production cost of each unit of the Super and the Standard
(ii) calculate the cost per event or transaction of each of the activities
(iii) use an activity based costing approach to determine the overhead cost assignable to each model
(iv) use an activity based costing approach to determine the overhead cost for per unit of each model for 2000
(v)   use an activity based costing approach to calculate the total production cost per unit of each model for 2000
(vi) identify the factors, using the information you have calculated, to explain the company's declining profits.

Decision-making

LEARNING OBJECTIVES

Completion of this chapter will enable you to:

- explain the scope and importance of decision-making to an organisation

- outline the decision-making process

- explain the significance of the concept of relevant costs

- apply marginal costing techniques to decision-making

- evaluate shut-down or continuation decisions

- critically compare make or buy alternatives

- consider the problem of product mix, scarce resources and limiting factors

- consider the wide range of sales pricing options

- use a decision tree to determine expected values of alternative outcomes

Introduction

In Chapter 9 we looked at the relationship between costs, activity levels, contribution and profit. This chapter will further develop these ideas and introduce some additional ways of looking at costs. One of the most important uses of accounting and financial information is as an aid to decision-making. There are many categories of business decisions. The costs and benefits that result from each type of decision may be very different and so it is useful to identify the different categories of decisions. Broadly, decisions are to do with

- problem solving
- planning
- control
- investment.

This chapter begins by outlining what decision-making means and considering the different types of decision that may be assisted by various accounting techniques. A later chapter has been devoted to the whole area of capital investment decision-making.

We will outline the various types and levels of decision and the process of decision-making. The concept of relevant costs is explored in some detail and we will consider its significance in assessing the information that should be used in calculations to support decision-making.

This chapter will look at the following specific types of decision:

- whether or not to shut down a factory or a department, in a manufacturing or service environment
- whether to buy a component or part used in manufacturing from an outside supplier or to make it internally
- decisions on product or service mix and the constraints of limiting factors
- pricing policy and the alternative sales pricing options available to an entity
- decisions in which risk is a key factor, and the use of decision trees.

The scope of decision-making

The management accountant is involved with providing financial and non-financial information and analysis to enable managers to evaluate alternative proposals and to determine which courses of action they should take. However, decisions are made by managers, not by the management accountant, and the levels of authority within the management hierarchy are determined by company policy. Companies normally establish limits at each management level for each type of decision, and the level of expenditure allowed. The approval of one or more directors is normally required for all capital expenditure. Strategic decision-making is carried out at board level. Operational decisions are normally made at the middle manager level, and tactical decisions made at the junior manager level.

There are obviously different levels of decision-making and different levels and types of decisions. The decision by the chairman of Corus (formerly British Steel) about whether he should wear a blue tie or a red tie is of less significance (although perhaps not to tie-makers) than his decision on whether or not to shut down a steel-producing plant. The scope of decision-making includes the areas of problem solving, planning, control, and investment (see Fig. 10.1).

(1) Problem solving decisions

Decision-making relating to problem solving considers relevant costs (and revenues) which are the costs (and revenues) appropriate to a specific management decision. These include incremental or **differential costs** and benefits, sunk costs and opportunity costs. They are represented by future cash flows whose magnitude will vary depending upon the outcome of the management decision made. If stock is sold to a retailer, the relevant costs used in the determination of the profitability of the transaction would be the cost of replacing the stock, not its original purchase price, which is a sunk cost. Sunk costs, or irrecoverable costs, are costs that have been irreversibly incurred or committed to prior to a decision point and which cannot therefore be considered relevant to subsequent decisions.

An opportunity cost is the value of the benefit sacrificed when one course of action is chosen in preference to an alternative. The opportunity cost is represented by the forgone potential benefit from the best of the alternative courses of action that have been rejected.

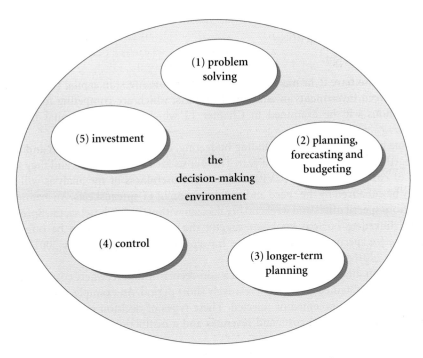

FIGURE 10.1 The scope of decision-making

(2) *Planning, forecasting and budgeting decisions*

Planning, forecasting and budgeting decisions require best estimates of costs and the use of cost/volume/profit (CVP) analysis.

(3) *Long-term planning decisions*

Longer-term planning decisions assume that in the long run all costs are variable and that scarce resources, and over or under-capacity, are problems that can be overcome.

(4) *Control decisions*

Control decisions use historical information and comparisons such as variance analysis and actual/budget comparisons.

(5) *Investment decisions*

Investment decisions tend to be longer term, and cash flow and the time value of money are important appraisal factors.

Decision-making is a crucially important process within any organisation. It is used to select, hopefully, the correct future course of action in, for example

● whether to make or buy equipment
● levels of order quantities and stock holding

- whether or not to replace an asset
- determination of selling prices
- contract negotiation.

Decisions also have to be made as to whether or not to invest in capital projects and on choices between investments in alternative projects, which are competing for resources. Such decisions will be examined in Chapter 12 which deals with capital investment decisions.

Routine planning decisions, including budgeting, commonly analyse fixed and variable costs, together with revenues, over a year. These costs are often estimated and may support the use of cost/volume/profit (CVP) analysis. The usefulness of the analysis will almost certainly be enhanced by the speed and sophistication of IT spreadsheets. An example may be seen from special offers and weekend breaks seen within the UK hotel sector. Spreadsheet 'what-ifs' linked to current bookings suggest the capacity available to be offered at a special rate for specific periods (note the Travelodge 'book by 23 January 2001 – stay by 15 February 2001' offer).

Decisions on short-run problems are of a non-recurring nature, where costs are incurred and benefits are obtained all within a relatively short period. An example is whether or not a contract should be accepted or rejected. These types of decision need identification of incremental or differential costs and revenues and a distinction between sunk costs and opportunity costs.

Investment and disinvestment decisions, such as whether to buy a new machine, or shut down a department, often have long-term consequences, and so ideally the time value of money should be allowed for, using **discounted cash flow** (DCF) techniques. The long-term consequences may span several accounting periods and the economies of more than just one country may be involved, for example international motor manufacturers with plants established throughout the world.

Longer-range decisions are made once and reviewed infrequently. They are intended to provide a continuous solution to a continuing or recurring problem. They include decisions about selling and distribution policies, for example, whether to sell direct to customers or through an agent. In the long run all costs are variable. In the short-term, fixed costs, or resource and capacity problems that may be encountered, can be changed or overcome over time.

Such changes may be determined by the board of directors at the strategic level, where the priorities of the business may be changed, or at the operational and tactical levels where change may be achieved through, for example, bottom-up continuous improvement initiatives. The process may therefore take several months and even years (especially, for example, in trying to sell a site or a building). The timespan may be shorter; for example, UK retailers are able to announce the impact of their Christmas trading results very early in January, which suggests that analyses of variances are undertaken on a daily, or even perhaps an hourly, basis.

Control decisions involve deciding whether or not to investigate disappointing perform-ance, and expected benefits should exceed the costs of investigation and control. Historical information such as comparison of costs, revenues or profits to budget, is used to carry out variance analysis to indicate what control decisions need to be taken. Variance analysis can be used to look at just one factory, or several factories. Manufacturers will often locate new plant and equipment in subsidiaries where there are few 'disappointing performances'.

Example 10.1

The UK motor manufacturer Vauxhall began producing police cars and rally cars based on its 'family saloons'.

Discuss the short-run problems that may have been encountered by Vauxhall during the decision-making process relating to these products.

Answer

The specification of the police car was customer driven and the changes to the standard saloons could be costed in order that a price could be proposed to the customer. The operatives on the production line could easily modify the existing model to the new specification.

The rally car was almost certainly going to create problems because the specification may need to change throughout the season. Production-line disruptions would inevitably ensue. The rally car would probably require specialists amongst the work force to design and produce it.

Why is decision-making so important to any organisation and what types of decision do they face?

The decision-making process

We have seen that it is possible to analyse decisions into five main categories:

- short-run problem decisions
- routine planning decisions
- long-range decisions
- control decisions
- investment and disinvestment decisions.

This is useful because the relevant costs and benefits are likely to differ between each type of decision. The decision-making process comprises the seven steps outlined in Fig. 10.2.

First, the objectives, either long term or short term, need to be identified.

Short-term objectives may be financial, such as:

- profit maximisation
- loss avoidance
- profit growth
- sales growth

or non-financial, such as:

- improved product quality
- customer service
- employee welfare
- environmental friendliness.

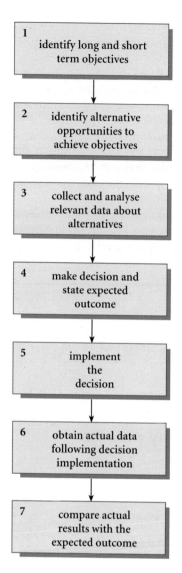

FIGURE 10.2   The seven steps of the decision-making process

Long-term objectives may be more to do with:

- the financial risk of the company
- long-term growth
- debt/equity financing
- dividend growth
- the relationships between these factors.

Second, alternative opportunities must be identified which might contribute to achieving the company's objectives. The ability to identify opportunities, or things to do which might help the company reach its objectives, is a major test of how good management is. Failure to recognise opportunities that exist may result in decisions not taken or opportunities missed.

Third, the relevant data about each of the alternatives must be collected and analysed. For example, this may relate to decisions on whether to manufacture or buy from an external supplier, or to use an existing site or establish a new site.

Fourth, the decision must then be made and the expected outcome stated. If a board of directors, for example, makes a decision, then the minute of that decision should formally refer back to the various documentation, forecasts, etc. that were an integral part of that decision.

Fifth, the decision must be implemented. The minutes of meetings of the board of directors should confirm that a specific decision has been implemented, along with an overview of progress to date.

Sixth, data needs to be obtained about actual results following implementation of the decision.

Finally, the actual results are compared with the expected outcome, and the achievements that have resulted from the decision are evaluated. It must be appreciated that not every decision will generate achievements, as a UK major retailer found out when it launched a new range of clothes in 1999 and again in 2000. The subsequent evaluation of results revealed a series of disappointments.

Of course, in practice things rarely work out as planned, or in an orderly way. In reality the decision-making process usually appears to be overtaken by events, requiring very quick response and without the time for perhaps a more considered response.

Outline the decision-making process.	**Progress check 10.2**

Relevant costs

In the Millennium Dome example in Chapter 4 we saw the importance of appropriate planning and control of cash to be sunk into major projects. The amount that was expected to have been spent on the attraction by December 2000 (some £800m) would be a past cost already committed and spent and would therefore not be considered in any decision about to whom the attraction may be sold or for how much. However, if future cash outlays were proposed, on which a sale was dependent, then these costs would be relevant costs with regard to the sale decision (see the newspaper cutting on the next page).

An Anglo-Irish consortium called Legacy that wanted to develop the site, continued to try and secure financial backers for its attempt to acquire the Dome (despite the Government having said in 2000 that it had reached a sale agreement with them in principle). However, the question of the future of the Dome continued to rumble on unanswered through 2001 during which time taxpayers' money, sunk costs which would not be recovered from any potential sale, continued to be spent on supporting this project.

Let the Dome go!
City Editor's comment

A few well-intentioned but muddle-headed souls have been suggesting that there should be life after death for the Millennium Dome. They want it to remain open and desperately hope that Pierre-Yves Gerbeau will ride in with a thirteenth-hour offer to trump Legacy's bid and keep it open as a visitor attraction.

Let's get this straight. The Dome was a financial fiasco of Ozymandian proportions. Last year it made an operating loss of £130m. That's an operating loss, quite apart from the obscene cost of building the thing and fitting it out.

In other words, the company lost more than £20 for each man, woman and child that set foot in the big tent. It would have been cheaper (and more entertaining) to close the thing a year ago and employ the buffoonish Lord Falconer to stand outside North Greenwich Tube and hand crisp tenners to all comers to persuade them to take their kids to the zoo or the pictures instead.

I have learnt that internal forecasts in the New Millennium Experience Company suggest that the Dome would have lost a further £75m this year had it remained open. And this forecast is based on the heroic assumption that visitor numbers would rise. This, of course, is a nonsense since the only reason the Dome persuaded so many people to visit was that this was a one-year only opportunity. If they were told you could visit any time, they would stay away in their millions.

David James, NMEC's chairman, is absolutely right to close down this financial embarrassment as quickly and painlessly as possible, since realistically no one is prepared to fund further losses. And Legacy is absolutely right to turn this godforsaken corner of South East London into what it should have always been – a mixture of residential and light industrial property and cheap office space.

The only sadness is that Legacy's plans have to incorporate the Dome itself when it should really have been taken down and moved to somewhere in the Home Counties to be used for Scout camps and the occasional rock festival.

© *Daily Telegraph*, 7 January 2001

Example 10.2

During the year 2000 a car manufacturer evaluated two proposals regarding the production of a new car. The car could be built in France or England. In 2001 the company chose England.

Discuss the basic relevant costs and opportunity cost relating to the company's decision.

Answer

The relevant costs are those of setting up the production line of the new car in England and these costs can be linked back to the decision made by the board of directors. The opportunity cost is the projected profit of the alternative French production facility.

Accounting information used in absorption costing, for example, may be different from relevant information used in decision-making. Relevant information may relate to costs or revenues; compared with accounting information, it may be qualitative as well as quantitative.

Relevant costs are costs that arise as a direct consequence of a decision. These may differ between the alternative options. They are sometimes referred to as incremental or differential costs.

Relevant costs are future costs, not past costs. A decision is about the future and it cannot alter what has been done already. A cost incurred, or committed to, in the past is irrelevant to any decision that is made now.

Relevant costs are cash flows, not accounting costs. All decisions are assumed to maximise the benefit to the shareholders. The time value of money impacts on longer-term decisions but all short-term decisions are assumed to improve shareholder wealth if they increase net cash flows.

Only cash flow information is required for a decision and so costs or charges that do not reflect additional cash spend are ignored for the purpose of decision-making. It should be appreciated that depreciation is not a cash-based expense, but an entry in the accounts of the business that reflects an estimate for 'wear and tear' of the particular item of capital expenditure.

Example 10.3

A hotel group with a central booking system is required to make a decision on whether to market empty rooms at a special offer through the press, or other media such as television or the Internet.

Discuss the cash outflow information that might influence the final decision.

Answer

Almost certainly the major cash outflow will be the cost of the advertising itself. There is an element of a 'gamble' for the company, even if it has used this strategy in the past. However, if the company follows this strategy each year then it may gain experience and an understanding of the relationship between advertising and extra bookings. It will also be able to determine the relationship between the discounts and volume of bookings and type of advertising options.

Relevant costs may also be referred to as opportunity costs. An opportunity cost is the benefit forgone by choosing one option instead of the next best alternative. A car manufacturer is constrained to making a maximum number of cars in a particular period. Regardless of whether they are saloons or estates, there is always a maximum. A waiting list may have to be instituted, with the factory deciding which type of vehicle and which of the models to produce. The decision may result in lost sales and/or lost benefits in production.

Example 10.4

An opportunity cost is the benefit forgone by choosing one option instead of the next best alternative.

Discuss why the managers of the Millennium Dome might have embarked on a policy of offering thousands of heavily discounted tickets to schools.

Answer

The managers knew how much cash they would lose on certain days if the tickets were sold at the discounted price. They knew how much they would lose if no discounted tickets were sold. On the basis of their current tickets sold they knew how many they would sell on a particular day in the future. It was obvious to them that the only way to build up ticket sale numbers was to discount tickets in a very formal way, generating cash, even at a lower rate per head.

Unless there is some evidence to the contrary, it is always assumed that variable costs are relevant costs and that fixed costs are not relevant to a decision. However, some variable costs may include some non-relevant costs. For example, direct labour costs are normally accounted for as variable costs, but if the work-force is paid a fixed rate per person per week, in some circumstances this may be a committed cost and therefore not relevant to decision-making.

Depreciation cost per hour may be accounted for as a variable cost. But, depreciation is never a relevant cost because it is a past cost and does not represent cash flow that will be incurred in the future.

There are several costs: sunk costs; committed costs; notional costs, that are termed irrelevant to decision-making because they are either not future cash flows or they are costs which will be incurred anyway, regardless of the decision that is taken.

A sunk cost is a cost which has already been incurred and which cannot now be recovered. It is a past cost which is not relevant to decision-making. Such costs may be, for example, the costs of dedicated fixed assets and development costs already incurred. Most consumer goods currently being sold are the final version of earlier versions, which will have cost considerable sums of money to develop.

A committed cost is a future cash outflow that will be incurred anyway, whatever decision is taken now about alternative opportunities. Committed costs may exist because of contracts already entered into by the company. During the year 2000 Internet providers in the UK found themselves in loss-making contracts with their customers. Several providers closed their operations, incurring considerable bad publicity.

 A **notional cost**, or imputed cost, is a hypothetical accounting cost to reflect the use of a benefit for which no actual cash expense is incurred. Examples are notional rents charged by a company to its subsidiary companies, or to cost centres, for the use of accommodation that the company owns, and notional interest charged on capital employed within a cost centre or profit centre of the company.

There are many examples of the use of relevant costs in decision-making: profit planning – for example, the contribution implications of pricing and advertising decisions, and the sales mix and contribution implications of constraints on resources; profit and product mix planning – for example with regard to the contribution per limiting factor.

The following is a summary which illustrates the general rules for identifying relevant costs:

Materials

The relevant cost of raw materials is generally their current replacement cost, unless the materials are already owned and would not be replaced if used. If the materials are already owned, the relevant cost is the higher of the current resale value and the value obtained if the materials were put to alternative use. The higher of these costs is the opportunity cost. If there is no resale value and there is no other use for the materials then the opportunity cost is zero.

Depreciation

Depreciation on equipment that has already been purchased is not a relevant cost for decision-making.

Capital expenditure

The historical cost of equipment that has already been purchased is not a relevant cost for decision-making. If the capital equipment has not already been purchased, and the decision would involve such a purchase, the situation is different. The relevant cost of equipment, of which the purchase would be a consequence of the decision, can be measured in two alternative ways, using the discounted cash flow (DCF) method:

- the cost of the equipment treated as an initial cash outlay in year zero, with the relevant costs and benefits of the decision assessed over the life of the project
- the cost of the equipment converted into an annual charge to include both the capital cost and a notional interest charge over the expected life of the equipment.

Future cash costs

Future cash costs are relevant if they have a direct consequence on the decision. These are costs not yet incurred or committed to. For example, you may have an old car which you would like to sell. The price you paid for it is irrelevant to your sale decision. However, if you needed to pay out large sums for a garage to work on the car to make it saleable, then those future cash costs would be very relevant to your decision to sell, or not, and at what price.

Differential costs

The relevant differential cash costs are the differences between two or more optional courses of action. If we return to the example of the sale of your old car, we may find that the cost of the work required to make it saleable is prohibitive and that you may be forced to keep the car rather than sell it. However, the difference between the price quoted by the garage may be undercut sufficiently by another garage to prompt you to reverse your decision.

Example 10.5

A machine requires repair and the relevant costs of two different repair options are as follows:

	£
Repair machine on site	
Cost of spares	1,250
Labour cost	750
Reduction to contribution resulting from lost production	4,200
Take machine away to workshop for repair	
Cost of spares	1,250
Labour cost	400
Reduction to contribution resulting from lost production	5,800

We are required to prepare a statement of differential costs.

Answer

Statement of differential costs		£
Additional labour cost of repair on site	[750 − 400]	(350)
Lower reduction to contribution from repair on site	[5,800 − 4,200]	1,600
Differential benefit of repair on site		1,250

Opportunity costs

The benefit forgone in choosing one option over the next best alternative is relevant. Many successful businesses find themselves in an expanding market, where most of their products are selling well, and each new product is becoming profitable. Inevitably, competing products from within the same company may have to be weeded out. Therefore, the company will have to forgo current benefits as a result of culling a profitable product.

The UK motor industry has several examples of product options that were dropped in favour of others. The German motor industry has seen two products dropped, only for them to reappear: the beetle (VW) car and boxer (BMW) motor cycle. In these cases, management decided to forgo the benefit of producing the products in favour of new models. Eventually they had to change their minds as the benefits forgone needed to be reassessed and updated versions were eventually brought back.

Sunk costs, committed costs and notional costs

None of these costs are relevant. They include, for example, costs of dedicated fixed assets and development costs already incurred.

Example 10.6

A company bought a computer system two years ago for £57,000. After allowing for depreciation its book value is now £19,000. Because computer technology moves so quickly resulting in obsolescence and price reductions, this equipment has no resale value. Although the company may continue to use the computer system for another year, with the limited facilities it provides, it would prefer to scrap it now and replace it with a much enhanced system providing many more functions.

Consider the implications of the company's decision to replace its computer system.

Answer

The original computer system initial cost of £57,000, which now has a net book value of £19,000, is a sunk cost, and therefore ignored, in terms of decisions made to replace the computer system. The money has been spent and the asset has no alternative use.

Fixed costs

Fixed costs are not relevant costs, unless they result from the decision. For example, the cost of employing an extra salesman would normally be categorised as a fixed cost. Conceptually, fixed costs stay at the same level irrespective of the changes in level of activity. In practice, management needs to make decisions regarding future fixed costs. Longer-term forecasts and budgets may indicate that changes in activity levels require changes to levels of fixed costs. For example, if higher education in the UK saw the falling-off of student numbers in certain courses then that might result in the universities cutting back on their fixed overheads, such as premises and staff numbers.

Example 10.7

The UK saw two attractions open in London in 2000: the Millennium Dome and the London Eye.

Compare what you may consider to be the fixed costs of the two attractions.

Answer

One basic difference between the two attractions is that the Dome was to remain open for one year and the London Eye would remain open for a number of years. Obviously the majority of the Dome's fixed costs would cease with its closure, but charges like insurance would need to continue to be paid. The London Eye became popular and fully booked very quickly. Unlike the Dome, its capacity is limited to the number of passengers each gondola would hold. In the Eye's case an analysis of the fixed costs should reveal that the costs are indeed genuinely fixed and there will be little 'movement' from year to year, whereas the headlines during 2000 would suggest that most of the Dome's expenses were varying throughout the year!

Variable costs

Variable costs are generally relevant costs but care must be taken with regard to the provisos outlined above. Variable costs may be non-relevant costs in some circumstances.

Example 10.8

A company is planning a small new project that requires 1,000 hours of direct labour, costing £9 per hour. However, the company pays its direct labour work-force a fixed wage of £342 per person for a 38-hour week.

The company has a 'no redundancy' agreement, and has enough spare capacity to meet the additional hours required for the project.

We are required to consider the relevant costs relating to the new project.

Answer

The direct labour cost for accounting purposes is regarded as a variable cost of £9 per hour. But, it is really a committed cost, and therefore a fixed cost of £342 per week. The relevant cost of the new project for direct labour is therefore zero.

It should be noted that the company may similarly treat depreciation of say £2.40 per hour as an accounting variable cost. However, for decision-making, depreciation is never considered as a relevant cost. It is a past cost, and therefore not a cash flow to be incurred in the future.

Attributable costs

We may consider fixed costs as comprising divisible fixed costs, and indivisible fixed costs. A fixed cost is divisible if significant changes in activity volumes require increases or decreases in that cost.

An **attributable cost** is the cost per unit that could be avoided, on the average, if a product or function were discontinued entirely without changing the supporting organisational structure. An attributable cost consists of:

● short-run variable costs
● divisible fixed costs
● only those indivisible fixed costs that are traceable.

Example 10.9

A company employs 55 people, who are paid fixed monthly wages, within four departments in its factory. Each department is headed by a departmental manager who is paid a salary.

How should each of the staff costs be regarded in a decision relating to the possible shut-down of one of the departments?

Answer

The direct labour costs of the 55 operators are divisible fixed costs (if there were only one operator, then the direct labour cost would be an indivisible fixed cost).

Each departmental manager's salary is an indivisible fixed cost that is traceable to their department. This is because if a department were to be shut down, the manager would no longer be required and therefore no cost would be incurred.

Scarce resources

The relevant cost of a scarce resource to be included in a decision-making calculation is the benefit forgone (the opportunity cost) in using the resource in another way, in addition to the direct cost of purchasing the resource. Let's look at an example.

Example 10.10

Mr and Mrs Green are willing to pay £22,000 to Steamy Windows Ltd to build a conservatory. The general manager of Steamy Windows estimates that the job requires the following materials:

Material	Total units required	Units in stock	Book value of units in stock £/unit	Realisable value £/unit	Replacement cost £/unit
A	1,000	0	0.0	0.0	6.0
B	1,000	600	2.0	2.5	5.0
C	1,000	700	3.0	2.5	4.0
D	200	200	4.0	6.0	9.0

B is regularly used by Steamy Windows Ltd and if it is required for this job it needs to be replaced to meet other production demands.

C and D are in stock because of previous overbuying, and have restricted use.

No other use can be found for C, but D could be used as a substitute for 300 units of E, which currently costs £5/unit and Steamy Windows Ltd currently has none in stock.

We are required to determine the relevant costs of the project and decide whether or not the job should be taken on.

Answer

Relevant costs:

		£	
A	1,000 × £6/unit	6,000	replacement cost because these materials have not yet been purchased
B	1,000 × £5/unit	5,000	replacement cost because these materials are used regularly and so the stock items would have to be replaced
C	(300 × £4/unit) + (700 × £2.50/unit)	2,950	300 must be bought at the replacement cost of £4/unit – 700 will not be replaced but could have been sold for £2.50 per unit
D	(300 E × £5/unit)	1,500	200 could be sold for £6/unit, but this is less than the opportunity cost of substitution of E
		15,450	

The relevant costs of the job are £15,450.

If the difference of £6,550 is an acceptable level of profit to Steamy Windows Ltd, before allowing for labour and overhead costs, then the job should be accepted.

Progress check 10.3

Outline three examples of costs that are usually relevant, and three costs that are not usually relevant in decision-making.

We will now look at examples of four specific areas of decision-making, outlined in Fig. 10.3.

(1) Marginal costing and shut-down or continuation decisions

We have already discussed the importance of the marginal costing technique as an aid to costing and break-even decision-making. In the UK, during December 2000 a major car manufacturer decided that production of cars would cease at its Luton (Bedfordshire) plant. The group company explained that over-capacity forced it to cut back on production. The employees on the second shift were sent home on full pay in February 2001 since there was no point in producing cars that would not sell. It was quite obvious from the public announcements that the company had carried out many 'what-ifs' on the corporate spreadsheets. However, it was apparently unable to justify continuation of production at the Luton site, despite its presence in the town for the past 90 years or so. The following example looks at the use of marginal costing in a decision regarding the possible closure of an apparent loss-making activity.

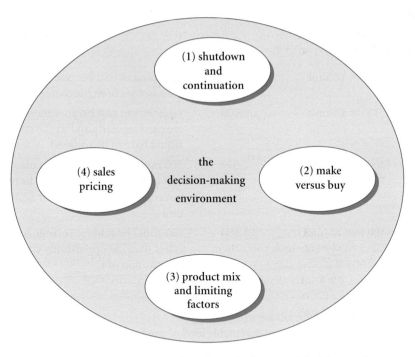

FIGURE 10.3 Examples of practical areas of decision-making

Example 10.11

Ron G Choice Ltd has three departments: C chairs; D desks; T tables, manufacturing three separate ranges of office furniture. Choice Ltd's sales manager, Jim Brown, has just started a course on cost accounting and has reviewed the company's accounts for last year with renewed interest.

	C	D	T
	£	£	£
Sales	60,000	80,000	40,000
Variable costs	40,000	60,000	34,000
Fixed costs allocated	6,000	10,000	8,000

It appeared to Jim that all was not well with the table department T. He was about to recommend to the managing director that department T should be closed down because it appeared to be making a loss. However, Jim felt he should first run his ideas past the company's accountant, Tony White to check his figures and gain some support.

Jim provided the following analysis, using an absorption costing basis

	C	D	T	Total
	£	£	£	£
Sales	60,000	80,000	40,000	180,000
Total costs	46,000	70,000	42,000	158,000
Profit/(loss)	14,000	10,000	(2,000)	22,000

On this basis, Jim said, department T was making a loss and should be closed.

Answer

Tony asked Jim if he had considered the position using a marginal costing basis. Jim said he had not and so Tony provided the following analysis

	C £	D £	T £	Total £
Sales	60,000	80,000	40,000	180,000
Variable costs	40,000	60,000	34,000	134,000
Contribution	20,000	20,000	6,000	46,000
less: Fixed costs				24,000
Profit				22,000

Tony explained to Jim that the profit for the company was the same using both techniques because there is no closing-stock adjustment involved.

However, Tony said that the way in which the fixed costs had been allocated to each department was fairly arbitrary and so perhaps they could consider the position of Choice Ltd following the closure of department T on a marginal costing basis.

The result was as follows:

	C £	D £	T £	Total £
Sales	60,000	80,000	–	140,000
Variable costs	40,000	60,000	–	100,000
Contribution	20,000	20,000	–	40,000
less: Fixed costs				24,000
Profit				16,000

Jim could see that closure of the tables department T would result in a reduction in total company profit of £6,000 to £16,000, compared with the original £22,000. Tony explained that this was caused by the loss of contribution of department T.

Jim thanked Tony for helping him avoid an embarrassing visit to the managing director's office. He would now also be better prepared for the next part of his costing course – on marginal costing!

This simple example shows that despite what the absorption costing approach indicated, department T should be kept open because it yields a contribution towards covering the fixed costs.

The marginal costing approach, as we have previously seen, focuses on the variable costs which are affected by the decision and separates them from the fixed costs which are unaffected by the decision and are therefore irrelevant to it. In Example 10.11, the closure of department T would not save any of the allocated fixed costs – they would then have to be shared amongst departments C and D. If the fixed costs had been directly attributable to each department rather than allocated then there would have been an £8,000 saving by closing department T. Since that is higher than the department's contribution of £6,000, then Jim's advice would have been correct to close department T.

Progress check 10.4

In what way is marginal costing useful in shut-down decisions?

(2) Make versus buy

Make versus buy decisions are made when a component used in one of the manufacturing processes to produce a product may either be bought in from outside suppliers or manufactured within the factory. It would seem that the choice is simply a straightforward comparison between the extra cost to make the component, the marginal cost, and the price charged by suppliers. In fact, the decision involves consideration of a number of other factors, for example:

- cost price sensitivity to changes in volumes
- accuracy of data
- reliability of bought-in and/or self-manufactured components
- supplier switching costs
- reliability of suppliers in terms of delivery and financial stability
- length of time the cost price will be held
- opportunity cost.

If the component were not made in-house what activities would be carried out using the relevant facilities? If other manufacturing activities have to be forgone so as to make the component in-house then there is a loss of the contribution that this work would otherwise have earned. The contribution sacrificed is the opportunity cost of not carrying out the alternative activities. The opportunity cost must be added to the marginal cost of making the component to compare with suppliers' prices in making a make versus buy decision. The technique usually used to determine loss of contribution is contribution per unit of a **key factor** (limiting factor) of production.

Example 10.12

Procrastinate Ltd makes a product A, which takes 30 hours using the Dragon machine. Its marginal cost and selling price are £1,400 and £2,000 respectively. Component X, which is used in the manufacture of product A, could be made on the Dragon machine in 5 hours with a marginal cost of £400. The best outside supplier price for one component X is £450.

Should Procrastinate make or buy component X?

Answer

Contribution of product A = £2,000 − £1,400 = £600

Contribution per hour of use of the Dragon machine = £600/30 = £20

If component X is made in 5 hours then 5 × £20, or £100 contribution is lost

Opportunity cost plus marginal cost = £100 + £400 = £500, which is greater than the best outside supplier price of £450 so component X should be bought rather than made in-house.

In this example, we have assumed that the Dragon machine is working at full capacity in order to calculate the opportunity cost of lost production. If this were not so and the Dragon machine were idle for a significant amount of time then there would be no loss of contribution. The only cost of making component X would then be its marginal cost of £400 which, being less than the best supplier price of £450, would indicate a decision to make in-house rather than buy.

Illustrate the process used to make a make/buy decision.

(3) Product mix decisions and limiting factors

An organisation may not have access to an unlimited supply of resources to allow it to exploit every opportunity to continue indefinitely to increase contribution. Such scarce resources, for example may be:

● labour hours
● levels of labour skills
● machine capacity
● time
● market demand
● components
● raw materials
● cash
● credit facilities.

A limiting factor, or key factor, is anything that limits the activity of the organisation. The organisation has to decide what mix of products or services to provide, given the restricted resources available to it, with its volume of output constrained by the limited resources rather than by sales demand. It can do this by seeking to maximise profit by optimising the benefit it obtains from the limiting factor. Machine time would be an example of a limiting factor for a company if all the machines in the company were operating at full capacity without being able to provide the output required to meet all the sales demand available to the company.

The technique used for decisions involving just one scarce resource assumes that the organisation is aiming to maximise profit. This further assumes that fixed costs are unchanged by the decision to produce more or less of each product. The technique therefore is to rank the products in order of their contribution-maximising ability per unit of the scarce resource. The following two examples illustrate this technique. The first example assumes that product demand is unlimited, whilst the second example assumes given levels of product demand.

Example 10.13

Need The Dough, a small village bakery, makes only two types of loaf, small and large. There is unlimited demand for this bread and both products use the same skilled labour of bakers, which is in short supply. The product data are as follows:

	Small	Large
Sales price per loaf	£0.71	£0.85
Variable cost per loaf	£0.51	£0.61
Contribution per loaf	£0.20	£0.24
Minutes of skilled labour per loaf	20	30

We are required to determine the contribution-maximising strategy for Need The Dough. ▶

◀ **Answer**

If we consider the contribution per unit of scarce resource, one hour of skilled labour, we can see that the contribution for each loaf per hour is

Small loaves earn   £0.60 per labour hour   [60/20 × 20p]
Large loaves earn   £0.48 per labour hour   [60/30 × 24p]

So even though large loaves generate a larger unit contribution of 24p compared to 20p earned by small loaves, the contribution-maximising strategy for Need The Dough is to bake and sell as many small loaves as possible which generate a contribution of 60p, compared with 48p for large loaves, per each hour of scarce labour.

Example 10.14

Felinpot Ltd are potters who make only two products, two ornamental pots called the Bill and the Ben. The product data are as follows:

	Bill	Ben
Contribution per pot	£5	£7.20
Volume of special blue clay per pot	1 kg	2 kg
Monthly demand	470	625

In one month the maximum amount of specialist blue clay available is 1,450 kg
We are required to determine the contribution-maximising strategy for Felinpot Ltd.

Answer

For each pot the contribution per unit of blue clay is

Bill   £5/1 kg   = £5   per kg
Ben   £7.20/2 kg = £3.60 per kg

The contribution-maximising strategy for Felinpot Ltd should therefore be to make Bill pots in preference to Ben pots, even though the unit contribution of a Ben is greater than a Bill.

Output of Bill pots should be maximised to meet the monthly demand of

470 pots, using 1 kg × 470 = 470 kg   contribution = 470 × £5   = £2,350
The balance of 980 kg of clay (1,450 kg less 470 kg) should be used to make Ben pots
980 kg/2 kg = 490 pots   contribution = 490 × £7.20 = £3,528
                                                   total contribution   = £5,878

Example 10.14 showed that because special blue clay was in short supply, every endeavour should be made to maximise the contribution to Felinpot Ltd for every kilogram of clay used. Regardless of the high level of demand for the other product, the product with the highest contribution per kilogram of special clay used is the one which should be produced to its maximum demand level. All the clay left over from that should then be used to produce the 'less profitable' product in terms of its return per kilogram of special clay.

More complex actual scenarios may be encountered. For example, there may be limited product demand with one scarce resource. The same technique applies whereby the factors are ranked in order of their contribution per unit of scarce resource. Optimum profit is earned from the decision to produce the top-ranked products up to the limit of demand.

Many situations occur where there are two or more scarce resources. The technique of ranking items in order of contribution per unit of limiting factor cannot be used in these situations. In these cases **linear programming** techniques need to be used – the graphical method or the simplex (algebraic) method – which are beyond the scope of this book.

Progress check 10.6

What are limiting factors and how do they impact on decisions related to product mix?

(4) Sales pricing

Pricing policy is just one of the four categories of decision-making included in the 'marketing mix'. The others are the product, place (where sold and how distributed), and promotion (selling, advertising and promotion). Pricing decisions must have some regard for cost, in order to ensure that the selling price exceeds the average unit cost in order to make a profit. Pricing decisions must also recognise the importance of the range of factors that comprise the general heading of 'demand'.

Examples 10.15 to 10.19 look at various sales pricing methods that are concerned solely with cost, and assuming unlimited demand, that may be used to achieve a break-even position or a targeted profit. These methods illustrate both the marginal and full absorption costing approach.

Example 10.15

Chip Pendale's company Pendale Ltd has a maximum production output of 500 chairs. It has been asked to tender for a contract to supply 300 chairs.

The costing information for Pendale Ltd for 300 chairs (or units) is as follows:

	£
Assembly cost centre costs:	
Wages for 300 units	1,500
Materials – timber and glue	300
Direct costs	1,800
Production overheads absorbed:	
Machine maintenance	150
Machine depreciation	250
Supervision	100
	2,300
General overheads absorbed:	
Factory rent, rates	100
Administrative expenses	100
Heating and lighting	130
Total costs	2,630

◀ Initially, we may assume a selling price of £11 per chair.

We are required to calculate the unit cost of a chair at output levels of 300 and 500 chairs, using:

(i) absorption costing

(ii) marginal costing

(iii) and compare the profits of both methods at output levels of 200, 300 and 500 chairs.

Answer

Calculation of the unit cost of a chair at output levels of 300 and 500 chairs:

		300 chairs unit costs £	Output	500 chairs unit costs £
Wages	(£1,500/300 units)	5.00	(£1,500/300 units)	5.00
Materials	(£300/300 units)	1.00	(£300/300 units)	1.00
Variable cost per chair, unchanged on changes in output		6.00		6.00
Production overhead	(£500/300 units)	1.67	(£500/500 units)	1.00
General overhead	(£330/300 units)	1.10	(£330/500 units)	0.66
Full cost per chair		8.77		7.66

Although total fixed costs remain unchanged, the unit costs of £8.77 and £7.66 are different due to costs being based on output of either 300 or 500 units.

On an absorption costing basis:

Assuming a full cost of £8.77 per chair on output of 300 units, we can consider sales volumes for 200, 300, and 500 chairs:

Chairs	200 £	300 £	500 £
Sales revenue at £11 per unit	2,200	3,300	5,500
Total costs at £8.77 per unit (volume × full cost per unit)	1,754	2,630	4,385
Net profit	446	670	1,115

On a marginal costing basis:

Chairs	200 £	300 £	500 £
Sales revenue at £11 per unit	2,200	3,300	5,500
Variable costs at £6.00 per unit	1,200	1,800	3,000
Contribution	1,000	1,500	2,500

Fixed costs (the same regardless of output):

Production overheads	500	500	500
General overheads	330	330	330
Profit	170	670	1,670

The differences in profit between the two approaches   (276)   –   555
are due to the under or overcharge of the fixed cost element being
£8.77 − £6.00 = £2.77 × (−100 or +200) the volume difference against 300 chairs.

Example 10.16

Using the data from the Pendale Ltd Example 10.15 consider the pricing approach of minimum pricing at specified volumes of 300 and 500 chairs.

Answer
Minimum pricing at specified volumes:

If we assume 300 units

Total revenue = total costs   which = £2,630   [(300 × £6.00) + £500 + £330]

The break-even price = £2,630/300 units = £8.77 per unit

At 500 units the break-even price = {(500 × £6.00) + £500 + £330}/500 units
$$= £3,830/500 \text{ units} = £7.66 \text{ per unit}$$

Example 10.17

Using the data from the Pendale Ltd Example 10.15 consider the pricing approach of break-even volume at specified prices of £11 and £13 per chair.

Answer
Break-even volume at specified prices:

If we assume that the selling price is £11 per unit

Contribution = revenue − direct costs = £11 − £6 = £5 per unit

$$\text{The break-even volume} = \frac{\text{total fixed costs}}{\text{contribution per unit}} = \frac{£830}{£5} = 166 \text{ units}$$

If we assume that the selling price is £13 per unit

Contribution = revenue – direct costs = £13 − £6 = £7 per unit

$$\text{The break-even volume} = \frac{\text{total fixed costs}}{\text{contribution per unit}} = \frac{£830}{£7} = 119 \text{ units}$$

Example 10.18

Using the data from the Pendale Ltd Example 10.15 consider the pricing approach of cost plus pricing at outputs of 300 and 500 chairs.

Answer

Cost plus pricing:

This method uses the full cost per unit plus a mark up:

If we assume 300 units

Full cost per unit plus 25% mark-up	= £8.77
New selling price	= £11.00 (rounded up)

If we assume 500 units

Full cost per unit plus 25% mark-up	= £7.66
New selling price	= £9.60 (rounded up)

Example 10.19

Using the data from the Pendale Ltd Example 10.15 consider the pricing approach of volume required to achieve a target profit of £1,000 at a selling price of £11 per chair, and of £1,200 at a selling price of £13 per chair.

Answer

Volume required to achieve a target profit:

If we assume that the target profit is £1,000

And assume that the selling price is £11 per unit

Contribution = £11 − £6 = £5 per unit

$$\text{Therefore required volume} = \frac{\text{total fixed costs} + \text{required profit}}{\text{contribution per unit}} = \frac{(£830 + £1,000)}{£5}$$

$$= 366 \text{ units}$$

If we assume that the target profit is £1,200

And assume that the selling price is £13 per unit

Contribution = £13 − £6 = £7 per unit

$$\text{Therefore required volume} = \frac{\text{total fixed costs} + \text{required profit}}{\text{contribution per unit}} = \frac{(£830 + £1,200)}{£7}$$

$$= 290 \text{ units}$$

In considering each of the above pricing methods we need to ask ourselves:

● which selling price is most appropriate, and
● which cost base is most appropriate?

The prices we have calculated have no relationship with market demand; the cost-based approach is not market based; there has been no identification of profit potential at different output or market demand levels; there has been no attempt to maximise profit.

Progress check 10.7

Outline four methods of sales pricing that do not make use of market data.

Maximum contribution using market data

The final sales pricing option we shall consider looks at a range of selling prices per unit and uses a graphical representation of profits and losses at various volume levels to determine the maximum contribution, and therefore maximum profit level (see Example 10.20).

There is difficulty in estimating a demand curve but certain practical steps can be taken to reach a pricing decision based on demand analysis as follows:

● establish the variable cost per unit and the fixed costs for the period, and using a number of different prices construct a profit line for each price on a profit/volume (PV) chart
● make a rough estimate of demand at each price and calculate the profit at this level of demand, and plot this profit on the profit lines on the PV chart, a different profit value for each selling price
● join up the profit values for each selling price and so construct a contribution curve to determine the highest point on the contribution curve which is the highest contribution and highest profit and so the approximate price that the company should consider.

Progress check 10.8

How may a business use market data to price its product in order to maximise contribution?

Example 10.20

Turning again to Pendale Ltd, let's assume the following price and market information for its one product, its chair:

Selling price per unit	p1 £11	p2 £12	p3 £13	p4 £14
Sales volume units demand	500	420	300	250
Variable cost per unit	£6	£6	£6	£6
Contribution per unit	£5	£6	£7	£8
Total contribution	£2,500	£2,520	£2,100	£2,000

Directly attributable fixed costs are assumed to be £1,830

We are required to use a profit/volume (PV) chart contribution curve to determine a selling price at which profit may be maximised.

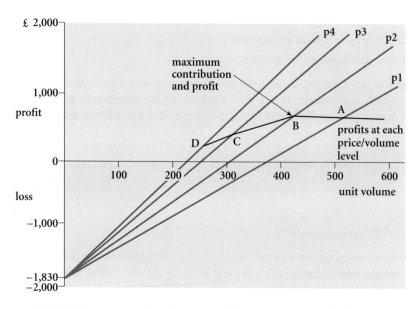

FIGURE 10.4 Profit volume (PV) chart and contribution curve

Answer

The PV chart shown in Fig. 10.4 shows profit lines for each selling price plotted as p1, p2, p3, p4.

The expected profit at each price is plotted at points A, B, C and D.

Selling price			Profit
p1	£11	A	£670
p2	£12	B	£690
p3	£13	C	£270
p4	£14	D	£170

The line drawn through A, B, C and D is the contribution curve which shows how contribution is maximised at or around point B and at a price of £12.

Since demand estimates at any price are likely to be approximate it may be useful to show bands of profit rather than single numbers, illustrated in Example 10.21.

Example 10.21

We may take the concept introduced in Example 10.20 a step further.

We may assume a band of demands around each of the estimated demands in example 10.20, for example:

a range of 480 to 520 around the estimate of 500 units

a range of 400 to 440 around the estimate of 420 units, and so on

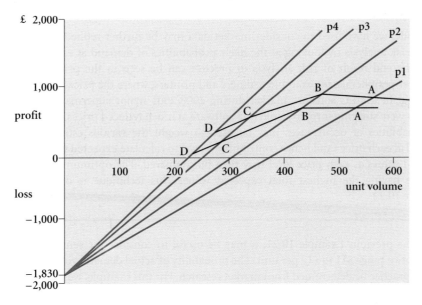

FIGURE 10.5 Profit volume (PV) chart and contribution curve band

Selling price per unit	Contribution per unit	Demand units	Contribution £	Profit £
£11	£5	480–520	2,400–2,600	570–770
£12	£6	400–440	2,400–2,640	570–810
£13	£7	280–320	1,960–2,240	130–410
£14	£8	230–270	1,840–2,160	10–330

We are required to prepare the contribution curve as a band to illustrate the selling price at which profit may be maximised.

Answer

The PV chart will then show the contribution curve as a band, as shown in Fig. 10.5.

Selling price			Profit
p1	£11	A	£570–£770
p2	£12	B	£570–£810
p3	£13	C	£130–£410
p4	£14	D	£10–£330

This indicates an optimal price of around £12.

Risk analysis and sales pricing

The model we have used to consider market data may be further refined by providing a simple risk analysis by looking at the likely probabilities of demand at each selling price level. The end result of risk analysis in practice can be seen in the pricing of various computer peripherals, for example scanners and printers, where the prices are continually changing. In the PC software market during 2000/2001 major supermarkets and other retailers were stocking formerly 'sold out' software at much reduced prices.

Probabilities of occurrences may be used to weight the various estimated levels of demand at each price (and hence contribution) level to calculate expected values. The total expected values at each price level may then be compared. The optimum selling price is the one having the highest total expected value. This technique is demonstrated in Example 10.22.

Example 10.22

Using the previous Example 10.21, it may be useful to consider the sensitivity over the selling price range £11 to £12 per unit. The probability of actual demand volumes for chairs may in practice be determined from market research. For this example, we may assume the following probability distribution to provide an illustration of the principle. Note that the total of each of the probabilities of volumes of demand at each price totals one. This means that demand is assumed to be certainly at one of the volume levels, but we don't know with certainty which one.

Price £11		Price £11.50		Price £12	
Demand estimate Units	Probability	Demand estimate Units	Probability	Demand estimate Units	Probability
480	0.1	410	0.3	400	0.4
490	0.2	420	0.5	420	0.4
500	0.3	430	0.2	440	0.2
510	0.3				
520	0.1				
	1.0		1.0		1.0

The profit maximising price may then be estimated on the basis of this risk analysis, the optimum price being the price that gives the highest total expected value.

Price £11 Cont./unit £5				Price £11.50 Cont./unit £5.50				Price £12 Cont./unit £6			
Est. demand Units	Cont. £	Prob.	Exp. value £	Est. demand Units	Cont. £	Prob.	Exp. value £	Est. demand Units	Cont. £	Prob.	Exp. value £
480	2,400	0.1	240	410	2,255	0.3	677	400	2,400	0.4	960
490	2,450	0.2	490	420	2,310	0.5	1,155	420	2,520	0.4	1,008
500	2,500	0.3	750	430	2,365	0.2	473	440	2,640	0.2	528
510	2,550	0.3	765								
520	2,600	0.1	260								
		1.0	2,505			1.0	2,305			1.0	2,496

This risk analysis would point to an optimum selling price of around £11 per unit, having the highest total expected value at £2,505.

Pricing policy

We have seen that the traditional approach to sales pricing policy is full cost plus pricing. The disadvantages are that it:

- ignores competition and the relationships between demand and price
- does not necessarily maximise profit
- requires the apportionment of shared costs when several products are produced
- may ignore the distinction between variable, fixed and opportunity costs.

We have looked at other cost-based models like minimum pricing and we have seen that the company will maximise profits where marginal cost equals marginal revenue. We have further considered sales pricing using market data and taking account of risk and uncertainty. To complete our discussion on pricing policy three other factors should also be considered:

- **price elasticity**: the percentage change in the quantity demanded arising from a percentage change in price
  - elastic demand is where a fall or rise in price will increase or reduce demand such that total revenue will be higher or lower than at the current price
  - inelastic demand (for example cigarettes) is the converse
- price discrimination occurs when an organisation sells the same products at different prices in two or more different markets (note the extensive use of this practice by the oil companies which sell petrol at a range of prices throughout their garages' distribution outlets in different locations)
- pricing decisions should always take account of **competitive pricing**.

In real life business situations many further factors may impact on the company's pricing policy, for example, scarcity of production resources and limiting factors of production. Profit-maximising budgets may be established through the ranking of products in order of contribution earned per unit of the scarce resource or limiting factor. However, as we have previously discussed, very often there are two or more limiting factors, in which case a linear programming model would need to be used to determine optimum solutions. Such approaches are beyond the scope of this book.

Progress check 10.9

Describe how sensitivity analysis may be used to evaluate alternative sales pricing policies.

Decision trees

A **decision tree** is a pictorial method of showing a sequence of interrelated decisions and their expected outcomes. Decision trees can incorporate both the probabilities of, and values of, expected outcomes.

Example 10.23

The sales department of Billy Ardtable Ltd has the opportunity to promote a new children's toy, which will provide a unit contribution of £20. Market research has indicated that if the promotion is undertaken at a cost of £50,000, there is a 60% chance of selling 50,000 units, and a 40% likelihood of selling 30,000 units. Market research has also shown that if the product is not promoted then there is a 50/50 chance of selling either quantity.

The sales manager is not sure whether it is worthwhile promoting the product. What should he do? We have been asked to advise.

Answer

We first need to draw a decision tree, which shows the start point and the two alternatives of promoting or not promoting the product (see the decision tree diagram in Fig. 10.6).

The branch of the tree indicating that Ardtable should promote is labelled with the cost of that activity, £50,000.

The branch of the tree indicating that Ardtable should not promote is labelled with the cost of that activity, £0.

The next step is to label the probabilities of occurrences (sales volumes in this example) on the branches following the decision to promote, being 0.6 (60%) for sales of 50,000 toys and 0.4 (40%) for sales of 30,000 toys.

The same thing is done on the branches following the decision not to promote, being 0.5 (50%) for sales of 50,000 toys and 0.5 (50%) for sales of 30,000 toys.

The expectations of contributions are then calculated by multiplying sales volumes by unit contribution and probability.

The contribution expectation following no promotion is

£500,000 + £300,000 = £800,000

The contribution expectation following the promotion is

£600,000 + £240,000 = £840,000

but, the promotion option also involves a cost of £50,000 and so the net expectation is £790,000.

The £790,000 net expectation following the promotion may be compared with the net expectation from not promoting of £800,000.

On the above basis we should advise the sales manager of Billy Ardtable Ltd not to promote the sales of toys.

Example 10.23 is a very simple illustration of the use of a decision tree in decision-making. In practice, a more complex situation would require trees bearing many alternative branches and probability branches to solve the problem.

Progress check 10.10

Outline the principles in the use of decision trees in decision-making.

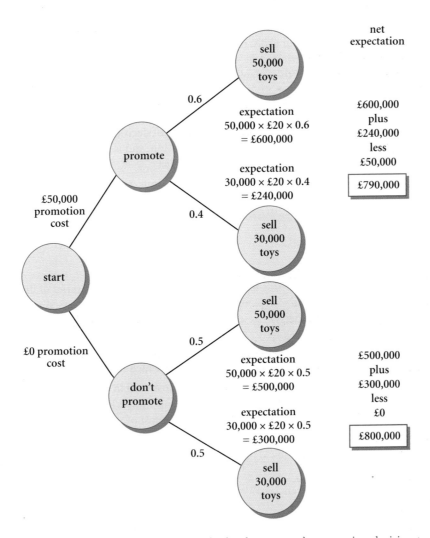

FIGURE 10.6   Billy Ardtable Ltd sales department's promotion decision tree

Summary of key points

- Decision-making is of fundamental importance to organisations, for example in the areas of problem solving, planning, control and investment.
- The decision-making process includes identification of relevant costs, and starts with the identification of objectives. Following the implementation of decisions, the process ends with the comparison of actual results with expected outcomes.
- Relevant costs, or incremental or differential costs, arise as a direct consequence of a decision, and may differ between alternative options.
- Marginal costing may be used to assist in shut-down or continuation decisions.
- Make versus buy decisions involve consideration of a wider range of factors than simply the differences in the basic cost.

- Organisations do not have access to unlimited supplies of resources, for example, labour hours, levels of labour skills, machine capacity, time, market demand, components and raw materials, cash – a limiting factor is the lack of any resource which limits the activity of the organisation.

- Product mix decisions are influenced by the scarcity of resources and the availability of limiting factors.

- Sales pricing policy is just one of the four categories of decision included in the marketing mix of price, product, place, and promotion, and is based on cost and market factors that influence demand for the product.

- Decision trees enable a sequence of interrelated decisions, and their expected outcomes, to be reported pictorially.

Glossary of key terms

attributable cost The cost per unit that could be avoided, on the average, if a product or function were discontinued entirely without changing the supporting organisational structure.

competitive pricing Setting a price by reference to the prices of competing products.

decision tree A pictorial method of showing a sequence of interrelated decisions and their expected outcomes. Decision trees can incorporate both the probabilities of, and values of, expected outcomes, and are used in decision-making.

differential cost The difference in total cost between alternatives, calculated to assist decision-making.

discounted cash flow (DCF) The discounting of the projected net cash flows of a capital project to ascertain its present value, using a yield or internal rate of return (IRR), net present value (NPV) or discounted payback.

expected value The financial forecast of the outcome of a course of action multiplied by the probability of achieving that outcome. The probability is expressed as a value ranging from zero to 1.

key factor (or limiting factor) Anything which limits the activity of an entity. An entity seeks to optimise the benefit it obtains from the limiting factor. Examples are a shortage of supply of a resource or a restriction on sales demand at a particular price.

linear programming The use of a series of linear equations to construct a mathematical model. The objective is to obtain an optimal solution to a complex operational problem, which may involve the production of a number of products in an environment in which there are many constraints.

notional cost A cost used in product evaluation, decision-making and performance measurement to represent the cost of using resources which have no conventional 'actual cost'. Notional interest, for example, may be charged for the use of internally generated funds.

price elasticity A measure of the responsiveness of the demand for a product or service to a change in the price of that product or service. Products with an inelastic demand show relatively little changes in demand to relatively large changes in price (for example, the necessities of life) – demand is therefore not significantly price sensitive. Products with an elastic demand show relatively large changes in demand to relatively small changes in price.

risk analysis The evaluation and quantification of all currently known uncertainty, in order to predict likely outcomes and identify strategies for reducing risk to an acceptable level and controlling residual risk.

Assessment material

Questions

Q10.1 Why is decision-making so important to organisations?

Q10.2 What are short and long-range decisions, and control decisions?

Q10.3 What are the seven steps used in the decision-making process?

Q10.4 Use some examples to illustrate, and explain what are meant by relevant costs, sunk costs, and opportunity costs.

Q10.5 In what ways may marginal costing provide a better approach to decision-making than absorption costing?

Q10.6 What are the key factors that should be considered in make versus buy decisions?

Q10.7 How should limiting factors be considered if a business is seeking to maximise its profits?

Q10.8 (i) What are scarce resources?
  (ii) What factors does an entity need to consider to make optimising decisions related to product mix?

Q10.9 Outline the five main approaches to sales pricing decisions.

Q10.10 How may risk analysis be applied to sales pricing decisions?

Q10.11 What is a decision tree and what is its relevance as an aid to decision-making?

Discussion points

D10.1 'What is all the fuss about decision-making? Surely it's simply a question of adding up a few numbers and the decision makes itself.' Discuss.

D10.2 The selling price of a product is the amount that the average customer will pay. Discuss.

Exercises

Solutions are provided in Appendix 4 to all exercise numbers highlighted in colour.

Level I

E10.1 *Time allowed – 30 minutes*

McPrentill Publishing Ltd has estimated that the costs of printing one of their new books called *A Feng Shui Approach To Accounting* will be as follows:

Identifiable fixed costs (setting the type, preparing the press, etc.)	£20,000
Marginal cost	£12 per book

McPrentill normally mark up their break-even prices by 40% to cover fixed costs of marketing administration and their profit margin.

(i) **What price should McPrentill charge to customers for each book if demand is estimated at 5,000 books?**

(ii) **What discount could McPrentill allow to a large customer for 5,000 books (that would take total sales to 10,000 books) while still maintaining their 40% margin? What discount could McPrentill allow to all customers while still maintaining their 40% margin?**

(iii) **What discount could McPrentill allow to a large customer for 15,000 books (that would take total sales to 20,000 books) while still maintaining their 40% margin? What discount could McPrentill allow to all customers while still maintaining their 40% margin?**

E10.2 *Time allowed – 60 minutes*

Calvin Williams had been running his own desktop publishing company for a couple of years after which time demand for his services had started to increase. He needs to buy a photocopying machine that will help to meet the increased workload. The model that seems to best fit his needs is available from the manufacturer at a retail price of £12,600. To save some money, Calvin has made enquiries regarding the availability of a second-hand model. One is available at a price of £8,100. After taking a look at this machine Calvin believes that it is basically fine but is concerned that a main component, the central copying unit, may not be acceptable. From experience, he feels there is around a 40% chance that the main component will not be acceptable. A new central copying unit will cost £7,200. Calvin thinks that after buying the second-hand photocopying machine, he may find that the main component will prove unacceptable, and a new one would have to be bought for £7,200.

(i) **(a)** **You are required to present this information in a decision tree, and recommend the course of action that Calvin should follow.**

    (b) **What other factors should Calvin consider when making his decision?**

Prior to making a decision, the second-hand photocopying machine could be sent for a thorough checking and testing by a local photocopier service and repair centre. This would cost £600, but Calvin would then know for certain whether the main component was acceptable or not.

(ii) **Using this additional information revise your decision tree and advise Calvin accordingly.**

Level II

E10.3 *Time allowed – 60 minutes*

Hurdle Ltd makes and sells wooden fencing in a standard length. The material cost is £10 per length which requires one half hour of skilled labour at £10 per hour (which is in quite short supply).

Hurdle Ltd has no variable overheads but has fixed overheads of £60,000 per month. Each length of fencing sells for £28, and there is a heavy demand for the product throughout the year.

A one-off contract has been offered to Hurdle Ltd to supply a variation to their standard product.

(a) The labour time for the contract would be 100 hours.

(b) The material cost would be £600 plus the cost of additional special components.

(c) The special components could be purchased from an outside supplier for £220 or could be made by Hurdle Ltd for a material cost of £100 and additional labour time of 4 hours.

You are required to advise the company:

(i)   **whether the special component should be manufactured by Hurdle Ltd or purchased from the outside supplier**

(ii)   **whether the contract should be accepted, and**

(iii) **how much should be charged to the customer to enable Hurdle Ltd to make a profit of 20% mark-up on the total cost of the contract.**

(Hint: Do not forget to include opportunity costs in the total costs of the contract.)

E10.4 *Time allowed – 60 minutes*

Muckraker Ltd prepares four types of peat mix for supply to garden centres. Thanks to the popularity of Charlie Dymock and the success of the Ground Force television programme, Muckraker's output has increased in successive months and demand continues to increase. For example, total peat production increased from 2,580 kg April to June to 3,460 kg in the third quarter. Muckraker has now reached a crisis because output cannot be increased by more than another 5% from the current work-force, who are working flat out, and which cannot be increased. In the third quarter of its year Muckraker's financial data are as follows:

	Peat A	Peat B	Peat C	Peat D
Peat production kg	912	1,392	696	460
Selling price per kg	£8.10	£5.82	£4.96	£6.84
Cost data per kg				
Direct labour (£10 per hour)	£0.98	£0.65	£0.50	£0.85
Direct materials	£3.26	£2.45	£2.05	£2.71
Direct packaging	£0.40	£0.35	£0.30	£0.35
Fixed overheads	£1.96	£1.30	£0.99	£1.70
Total costs	£6.60	£4.75	£3.84	£5.61

Fixed overheads are absorbed on a direct labour cost basis.

Another company, Bogside Products, has offered to supply 2,000 kg of peat B at a delivered price of 80% of Muckraker's selling price. Muckraker will then be able to produce extra peat A in its place up to the plant's capacity.

Should Muckraker Ltd accept Bogside Products' offer?

E10.5 *Time allowed – 60 minutes*

Ceiling Zero plc has manufactured six CZ311 aircraft for a customer who has now cancelled the order. An alternative buyer, Coconut Airways, would be prepared to accept the aircraft if certain agreed modifications were completed within one month. The CZ contracts manager has prepared a costs schedule as a basis for establishing the minimum price that should be charged to Coconut Airways:

	£000	£000
Original cost of manufacture of 6 CZ311 aircraft		
Based on direct costs + 100% overheads charge		6,400
less: Deposit retained when order cancelled		1,000
		5,400
Costs of modification		
Direct materials	520	
Direct labour	200	
		720
Fixed overheads at 75% of direct costs of modification [0.75 × 720]		540
Administration costs at 25% of direct costs [0.25 × 720]		180
Total costs		6,840
The contracts manager has suggested an additional mark up of 25%		1,710
Suggested minimum price to Coconut airways		8,550

Two types of material were used in the original aircraft manufacture:

Melunium could be sold as scrap for reuse for £400,000, but it would take 60 hours of labour at £100 per hour to prepare the melunium for sale. The department required to carry out this work is particularly slack at the moment.

Polylindeme could be sold for £300,000 and would also require 60 hours' preparation by the same department at the same rate per hour. Alternatively, polylindeme could be kept for a year and used on another contract instead of metalindeme which would cost £400,000. To do this, a further 120 hours of labour at £150 per hour would be required in addition to the 60 hours above.

The materials used in the modifications for Coconut Airways were ordered last year at a cost of £840,000. The delivery was late and the realisable value fell to £200,000. Because of this the suppliers of the materials have given CZ a discount of £320,000. CZ can not use this material on any other contracts.

The direct labour for the modifications is a temporary transfer from another department for 4 weeks. That department usually contributes £1,000,000 per week to overhead and profits. 75% of that level could be maintained if a special piece of equipment were hired at a one-off cost of £300,000 to compensate for the reduction in labour force.

If the aircraft were not sold, the specifications, plans and patents could be sold for £350,000.

Additional interim managers would need to be hired at £180,000 for the modifications, included in overhead costs. The fixed overhead rate included straight line depreciation (included in overheads at £140,000), staff expenses and lighting. Hand tools will be used for the modifications. No other overheads are affected by the modifications.

CZ's normal profit mark-up is 50%. The contracts manager has reduced this to 25% because it is felt that this is probably what Coconut Airways would be willing to pay.

You are required to redraft the contract manager's schedule to give a more meaningful price and to explain all assumptions and alterations.

E10.6 *Time allowed – 60 minutes*

Use the data for Muckraker Ltd from Exercise E10.4 to calculate the most profitable combination of output of peats A, B, C and D from subcontracting 2,000 kg of one of the products at a price of 80% of its selling price and producing extra quantities of another product up to Muckraker's total capacity.

You should assume that demand for Muckraker's products will be sufficient to meet the extra output, and that Muckraker's levels of quality and delivery performance will be maintained.

E10.7 *Time allowed – 90 minutes*

Mr Threefingers Ltd manufactures three DIY tools, the Rimbo, the Cutzer, and the Brazer. The numbers for the financial year just ended are as follows:

	Rimbo £	Cutzer £	Brazer £	Total £
Sales	100,000	80,000	120,000	300,000
(units)	(10,000)	(4,000)	(10,000)	
Variable costs	60,000	50,000	70,000	180,000
Contribution	40,000	30,000	50,000	120,000
Fixed costs	34,000	36,000	40,000	110,000
Profit/(loss)	6,000	(6,000)	10,000	10,000

£10,000 of the fixed costs of producing Cutzers are costs which would be saved if their production ceased.

Mr Threefingers Ltd is considering a number of options:

(a) Cease production of Cutzers.

(b) Increase the selling price of Cutzers by 15%.

(c) Reduce the selling price of Cutzers by 10%.

(d) Resurrect a tool which was popular 10 years ago, the Thrad, on the following basis:

- use the resources released by ceasing production of Cutzers
- incur variable costs of £48,000 and extra fixed costs of £12,000, for sales of 20,000 units
- sales of 20,000 Thrads, according to market research, could be made at a price of £5 each

(i)   **Evaluate the options (a) to (d), stating any assumptions that are made to support your calculations.**

(ii) **What other factors should be considered by Mr Threefingers Ltd in their decision on which option(s) to adopt?**

(iii) **Which option(s) would you recommend and why?**

11

Planning and budgeting

LEARNING OBJECTIVES

Completion of this chapter will enable you to:

- identify budgeting as one part of the strategic management process

- define a budget, its purpose and uses

- recognise the importance of forecasting within the budget process

- outline how a business may apply the budgeting process in practice

- explain the preparation of budgets for planning purposes

- prepare the elements of an operating budget and a financial budget to derive the master budget

- describe the system of responsibility accounting and identify the four different types of responsibility centre

- appreciate the motivational and behavioural aspects of budgeting

- explain the preparation of budgets for control purposes and how performance against budget may be evaluated

- identify the potential problems that may be encountered during budget preparation

Introduction

Chapter 10 looked at decision-making as one application of the management accounting roles of problem solving and attention directing. This chapter looks at a further application of those roles and is concerned with how businesses attempt to plan their activities for the year ahead, or for a shorter period, to enable them to plan and maintain control of the business. Budgeting is the part of the strategic management of the business to do with planning and control. In this chapter we will consider the budget for planning and control purposes.

This chapter considers the role of forecasting in the budget process, and looks at the budget setting process in detail. The budgeting process will be used to construct a simple budget for a company based on its organisational objectives, and its best estimates of future activities.

We return to the use of budgets for control purposes in discussing the motivational aspects of budgeting and how performance against budget may be evaluated. The chapter closes by identifying some of the important conflicts and problems encountered in the budgeting process.

Budgeting, planning and control

The situation surrounding Malcolm Walker's departure in February 2001 as Iceland's executive chairman poses interesting questions with regard to the way in which a company's actual performance is reported compared with its planned performance (see the press cutting on the opposite page). Mr Walker claimed that he was unaware that the company's Christmas trading had deteriorated so badly. However, this case highlights just how important it is that the planning and budgeting process ensures that it enables accurate feedback of actual performance at the right time to the appropriate people within the organisation.

The investigation into the sale of Mr Walker's shares by the FSA would have included consideration of how the budgetary control systems operated within Iceland to ensure that information was regularly communicated and evaluated by the organisation's key decision makers.

The long-term (strategic) and short-term (budget) planning processes are core management tasks that are critically important to the future survival and success of the business. The budget prepared for planning purposes, as part of the strategic planning process, is the quantitative plan of management's belief of what the business's costs and revenues will be over a specific future period. The budget prepared for control purposes, even though it may have been based on standards that may not be reached, is used for motivational purposes to influence improved departmental performance. Monitoring of actual performance against the budget is used to provide feedback in order take the appropriate action necessary to reach planned performance, and to revise plans in the light of changes.

The following case study of a catering equipment hirer illustrates the importance of the preparation of business plans and what can result if there is a lack of preparation for unexpected future events. The business was involved in hiring out catering equipment for corporate and private entertainment functions. A gradual economic downturn saw corporate demand decrease as businesses cut back their entertaining and hospitality budgets. The catering equipment hire business had been doing very well and the proprietor felt confident of being able to continue to meet overhead payments even with a reduced sales level, because a reasonable bank balance had been built up. The proprietor did not quantify the change in position in a revised financial plan. After a few months the business needed overdraft facilities and began to delay its payments to creditors. The bank manager was not sympathetic since he had received no prior warning of the potential problem. Goodwill with creditors began to diminish. The business failed, but may not have if the proprietor had:

- attempted to quantify the effect of the economic downturn on profit and cash flow
- warned the bank of the problem
- tried to negotiate the overdraft facility
- negotiated favourable terms with creditors.

Walker quits after Iceland sales dive
By Kate Rankine, Deputy City Editor

Malcolm Walker abruptly quit yesterday as Iceland's executive chairman, resigning ahead of a crisis board meeting to discuss his future at the troubled frozen food company.

Mr Walker's sudden departure from the company he founded 30 years ago follows his £13.5m share sale last month, which took place only five weeks before the company issued a severe profits warning. His share sale is currently being examined by the Financial Services Authority as company directors are not allowed to deal within two months of a price sensitive announcement.

On January 22, Iceland shares plunged on the profits warning, and have continued to fall sharply. Yesterday they closed down another 5 at 187.5p. On December 20, Mr Walker sold his 4m Iceland shares at 339p each, just short of the company's five-year high of 346p. He retains 1.65m shares.

Last night, it was unclear whether Mr Walker, 54, will receive compensation for loss of office. He had a two-year employment contract and was paid about £550,000 a year. After yesterday's board meeting in the City, Iceland will today confirm Mr Walker's resignation and will appoint non-executive director David Price non-executive chairman. Mr Price is currently chairman of Foreign & Colonial Management.

Last night, it was also uncertain whether executive director Andrew Pritchard will remain at the company. When Bill Grimsey became chief executive at the beginning of the month, he axed Russell Ford as Iceland's managing director and promoted Mr Pritchard from finance director to managing director. However, it is understood that Mr Grimsey, the highly regarded former chief executive of DIY retailer Wickes, has since been horrified by what he regards as Iceland's poor financial controls and systems.

Sources close to Mr Walker last night claimed that he did not know that Christmas trading had deteriorated so sharply when he sold his shares. One source said: 'Malcolm simply didn't know how bad it was. Now he's had enough and decided it is time to go. What is the point of carrying on? Bill [Grimsey] is extremely capable. It was Malcolm's decision to go. Bill didn't force him into it'.

However, other sources insisted that Mr Walker would have received daily sales figures throughout December. Another source said: 'Malcolm saw those sales figures every day. It would have been inconceivable that he didn't look at them. He lived and breathed Iceland'.

On January 22, Iceland revealed that like-for-like sales crashed by 5.5pc for the four weeks to December 29. On December 13 and 14, Iceland flew City analysts to its Deeside head office where it told them it was 'positive on the group's future prospects' and 'confident that all the expected benefits of the merger with Booker are real and achievable'.

Mr Walker was executive chairman and chief executive from Stuart Rose's abrupt departure on November 13 for Arcadia Group until Mr Grimsey took over as chief executive on January 2. Mr Grimsey is today expected to report on his 'thorough evaluation' of Iceland's integration with Booker, the cash and carry group which it bought last year.

© *Daily Telegraph*, 4 February 2001

This is a not uncommon example that illustrates how preparation, and regular revision, of financial plans is vital to be prepared against the risk of unexpected events and changes in circumstances.

Another case study gives a good example of the importance of business plans. The managing director of a company that manufactured wrought iron garden furniture wanted to increase the turnover of the business by 25% in the coming year. He had identified the requirements necessary to fulfil this increase:

- spare capacity in existing retail outlets
- additional new equipment
- one extra employee.

However, the managing director had failed to recognise the cost of financing the increased turnover:

- cash outflow for additional raw materials before cash flowed in from increased sales
- financing costs of additional equipment
- additional wages.

The managing director had focused only on the positive aspects of the expansion

- increased sales (although sales prices remained constant)
- increased cash flowing into the business.

The business ran into cash flow problems because it didn't inform its bankers of its expansion plans and therefore didn't submit a business plan (projected profit and loss account and cash flow) or negotiate a new overdraft facility. For any business it is crucial that any major change, whether expansion or diversification, must be quantified financially in revised business plans. Smaller businesses are particularly vulnerable and should prepare projections more frequently than on an annual basis incorporating realistic expectations for existing activities and plans for any changes in the business in order to

- alert the business owner to risks and difficulties which may arise
- allow time for remedial action to be taken.

The broad picture of **planning** and **control** includes budgeting, **strategic planning**, **management control**, and operations control. The process involves:

- identification of objectives, involving factors such as profit, market share, value, etc.
- identification of potential strategies using facts as well as opinion
- evaluation of options, including a selection of courses of action and preparation of forecasts

- implementation of long-term plans, and finalising the planning before going on to provide control
- monitoring of actual outcomes, which will highlight whether the **budget** was too easy or unachievable
- provision of responses regarding actual outcomes against plans through feedback.

Strategic planning

Strategic planning is the process of deciding:

- on the objectives of the organisation
- on changes in these objectives
- on the resources used to attain these objectives
- on the policies that are to govern the acquisition, use and disposition of these resources.

It is not correct to assume that strategic planning is just an extension of budgeting, but there is a close relationship between these processes. A budget is a quantified statement, for a defined period of time, which may include planned revenues, expenses, assets, liabilities and cash flows. A budget provides a focus for the organisation, aids the co-ordination of activities, and facilitates control.

The way in which a typical strategic planning process may be carried out in an organisation is best illustrated in the flow charts in Fig. 11.1 and 11.2. The chart in Fig. 11.1 shows how analysis is used to develop strategies and actions. The chart in Fig. 11.2 shows the sequences of each step in the process and the relationship between strategic planning and budgeting.

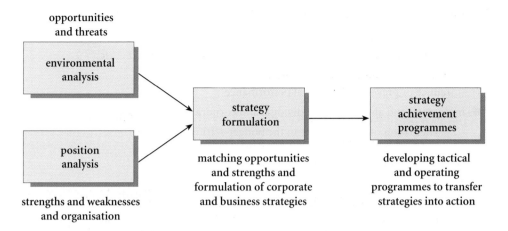

FIGURE 11.1 The strategic planning process

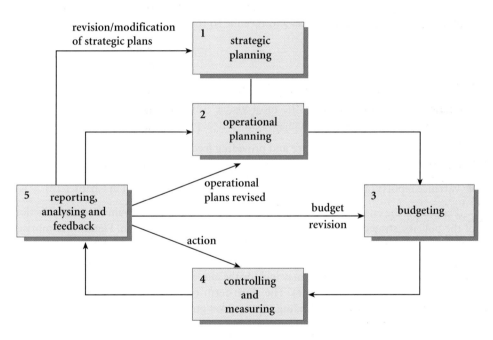

FIGURE 11.2 The strategic planning relationship with budgeting

Budgeting

The broad purposes of budgeting include:

● planning and control, through

  – exception reporting of financial and non-financial indicators, which
  – economises on managerial time, and
  – maximises efficiency

- co-ordination, which
  - assists goal congruence
- communication, through
  - the feedback process, which should
  - reduce or prevent sub-optimal performance
- motivation and alignment of individual and corporate goals, through
  - participation of many people in the budget-setting process
- evaluation of performance, to
  - facilitate control.

Budgetary control establishes a basis for internal audit by regularly evaluating departmental results. The budget process should ensure that scarce resources are allocated in an optimal way, and so enable expenditure to be controlled. Management is forced to plan ahead so that long-term goals are achieved.

The budget provides a yardstick for performance rather than rely on comparisons with past periods, since when conditions and expectations will have changed. Areas of efficiency and inefficiency are identified through reporting of **variances**, and **variance analysis** will prompt remedial action where necessary. Part of the budget process should identify the people responsible for items of cost and revenue so that areas of responsibility are clearly defined.

Planning

Planning and control are two of the most visible ways that financial and non-financial information may be used in the management control process. This is done by:

- setting standards of performance and providing feedback, and therefore
- identifying areas for improvement, by means of
- variance reports (a subject to which we shall return in more detail in Chapter 12).

Planning is the establishment of objectives and the formulation, evaluation and selection of the policies, strategies, tactics and action required to achieve them. Planning comprises long-term/strategic planning, and short-term operational planning. The latter usually refers to a period of one year. With regard to a new retail product, the strategic (long-term) plan of the business, for example, may include the aim to become profitable, and to become a market leader within three years. The short-term operational plan may be to get the product stocked by at least one leading supermarket group within 12 months.

Control

Control and monitoring are the continuous comparison of actual results with those planned, both in total, and for the separate divisions within the organisation, and taking appropriate management action to correct adverse variances and to exploit favourable variances. The UK has seen the growth of 'call centres', and the press have exposed the constant monitoring by management as unpleasantly intrusive. There appears to be a high turnover of staff in these new hi-tech businesses, where they are regarded as cheap labour but do not necessarily meet management targets.

Management control is the process by which managers assure that resources are obtained and used effectively and efficiently in the accomplishment of the organisation's objectives. The UK company Railtrack plc found itself forced into diverting extra resources into rail maintenance during the autumn months of 2000, as it was felt that it was not achieving the basic objective of safety of passengers and employees.

Operational control is concerned with day-to-day activities of organisations, and is the process of assuring that specific tasks are carried out effectively and efficiently. For example, the UK Government decided in the year 2000 to allocate further funds to hospitals for the recruitment of more nurses, to enable the hospitals to carry out specific tasks 'effectively and efficiently'.

Whereas planning is achieved by means of a fixed master budget, control is generally exercised through the comparison of actual costs with a flexible budget. A flexible budget is a budget which, by recognising different cost behaviour patterns, is designed to show changes in variable costs as the volume of activity of the organisation changes. Over the short time-spans that budgets normally cover (one year or six months), fixed costs are assumed to remain unchanged. The mobile telephone market in 2000/2001 is probably one of the best illustrations of a 'high profile' market having the need for flexible budgeting, as the number of units sold in successive periods continued to make the headlines in the media.

<table>
<tr><td>**What is budgeting, and how does it fit into the overall strategic planning process?**</td><td>Progress check 11.1</td></tr>
</table>

Forecasting and planning

The budget is a plan. The planning activity of the budget process should reflect real beliefs of each company's management, reflecting what they think will happen, flexible to changes in circumstances, and providing feedback.

A forecast is not a budget but a prediction of future environments, events, and outcomes. Forecasting is required in order to prepare budgets. This should start with projected sales volumes/market share of current and new products. Examples of forecasts by product, or sector, can be found regularly in the press, for example car sales and mobile telephone sales.

Large companies need to be very sensitive to trends and developments within their forecasting process as mistakes can prove very expensive. For example, a major UK chocolate manufacturer made too many eggs for Easter 2000, which did not sell; its forecasts and therefore its budgets were proved to be very wide of the mark, and the impact on the business was extremely costly.

In order to highlight more clearly some of the issues around forecasting it may be useful to consider it in the context of budgeting in terms of large group plcs, comprising many companies that may be either diversified or within the same industrial sector.

Sales volume projections are required to evaluate turnover and product margins. Marketing policy may or may not be centralised. Centralised marketing information may not always be congruent with individual company expectations and may allow little scope for negotiation.

Sales prices are usually negotiated by individual companies with their customers, to ensure that group margin targets are met. However, in the case of large group companies, relationships with major customers may mean that this is not always an autonomous process, resulting in inevitable acceptance of group agreements in many cases. Whilst this may achieve corporate goals, it may conflict with individual company objectives in trying to meet targeted gross margins. Conversely, commercial managers may try to set sales budgets that may be too easily achievable through understatement of price increase expectations.

Increased market share through new innovation is commonly a primary objective of individual companies. However, new product development, financed out of internally generated funds, involves very large investments and long lead times. This creates competition for resources, and difficulties whilst also trying to achieve group targets for return on investment (ROI). Resources may come off second best, but without any relaxation in product development objectives.

The production manager forecasts production resource requirements, materials and labour, based on sales forecasts, stock-holding policies, and performance improvement targets. The production manager may have an easier job in an expanding rather than a declining market. Each type of market receives wide coverage in the financial press, for example the mobile telephones and coal, respectively, in the UK.

Many companies within large groups may be suppliers and customers within the group. The prices to be charged between companies within large groups, transfer prices, are usually set by the parent company and based on pre-determined formulae. Some companies within the group may lose and some companies may gain, the objective being that the group is the overall winner. As a consequence, transfer pricing may provide prices that are disagreed and cause disputes, which rarely result in acceptable outcomes for individual companies. Optimal pricing for the group must take precedence over individual company requirements to meet group profitability objectives (despite the impact on individual company profit performance bonuses)!

There are groups of companies where materials or components may be supplied from group-nominated suppliers, or certainly from suppliers where unit price is the dominant procurement criterion. Purchase indices are an important performance measure of the purchasing function, but may not relate to total procurement cost. Group purchasing performance objectives may therefore subvert those of the individual companies, which seek to minimise total costs, on which delivery costs, for example, and the impact of foreign currency exchange rate fluctuations may have a significant impact.

The above examples illustrate some important conflicts at the forecasting stage, arising from policy decisions where group goals inevitably dominate individual company goals, which in turn may also lack congruence with individual goals. Quite frequently a subsidiary company must comply with a group instruction, which may result in an apparently successful local product being dropped, in favour of a group-wide product. An example of this was seen in the year 2001 where the group goals of General Motors (USA) were not appreciated by a wide cross-section of the UK community, because so many lost their jobs (and businesses) as a result of Vauxhall cutbacks initiated by the group board of directors.

Forecasting usually relies on the analysis of past data to identify patterns used to describe it. Patterns may then be extrapolated into the future to prepare a forecast. There are many forecasting methods, qualitative and quantitative, with no one best model. It is usually a question of fitting the pattern of historical data to the model that best fits. It could be argued that it is easier to forecast the sales of ice-cream than the sales of CDs by a new band. Apparently, the major music-based groups have also found this a mystery over the years.

Progress check 11.2	What is the role of forecasting in budgeting?

Qualitative forecasting

Qualitative forecasting uses expert opinion to predict future events and includes:

- the Delphi method – use of a panel of recognised experts
- technological comparisons – independent forecasters predicting changes in one area by monitoring changes in another area
- subjective curve fitting – for example, similar product life cycles for similar products like CD players and mini disc players.

Quantitative forecasting

Quantitative forecasting uses historical data to try to predict the future, and includes univariate models and causal models. Univariate models predict future values of time series when conditions are expected to remain the same, for example exponential smoothing and the use of moving averages.

Causal models involve the use of the identification of other variables related to the variable being predicted. For example, linear regression may be used to forecast sales, using the independent variables of:

- sales price
- advertising expenditure
- competitors' prices.

The major UK retailers have been seen to be highly pro-active in revising their sales prices and their advertising activities (and expenditure) as a result of changes in the market place.

Whichever method is used it is important that the basis and the methodology of the forecasting is understood. All assumptions made and the parameters of time, availability of past data, costs, accuracy required, and ease of use must be clearly stated to maintain any sort of confidence in the forecasts.

Progress check 11.3

Give examples of some of the techniques used to forecast the demand for a product?

The budget process

The budgeting process normally aims to:

- identify areas of efficiency/inefficiency
- allow people participation
- allocate responsibility to enable performance evaluation through exception reporting of actual versus budget.

Whilst participation may be encouraged, insufficient attention may be given to managers' differing motivational tendencies either to achieve success or to avoid failure. The budget process therefore may not always achieve desired results, nor provide the appropriate rewards for success.

We will use Supportex Ltd in Examples 11.1 to 11.7 to illustrate a step-by-step approach to the budget preparation process.

Sales and gross margin budget

The complete budget preparation process is outlined in Fig. 11.3. Once the sales forecast has been prepared the budgeted gross margin may be calculated. The budgeted gross margin is derived from estimated:

- sales volumes, and prices
- materials usage, and prices
- direct labour hours, and rates
- overhead costs.

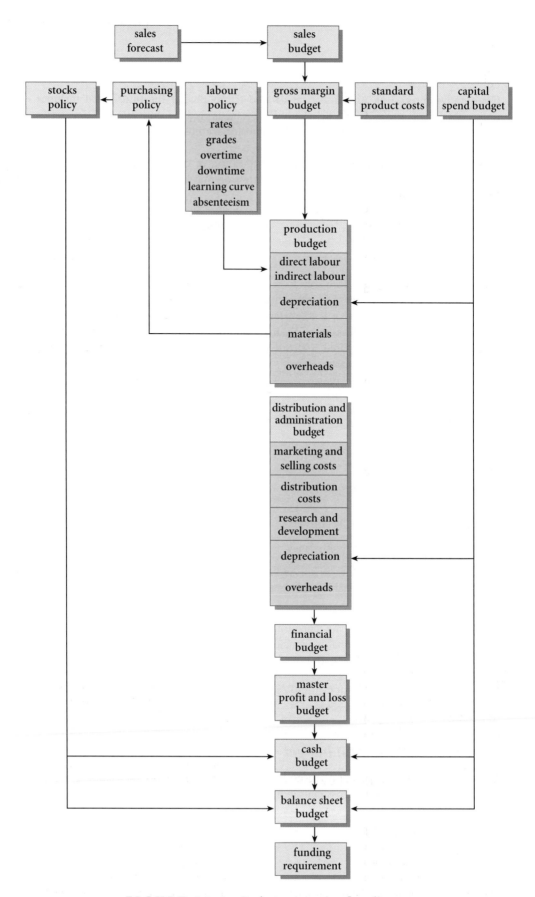

FIGURE 11.3   Budget preparation flow diagram

Progress check 11.4

> What are the decisions to be made and the policies established by a business before embarking on the budget preparation process?

Example 11.1

Supportex Ltd manufactures three only specialist types of lintels: Small; Medium; Large. Supportex has received sales forecasts prepared by its sales manager, Ms Ball. Taking account of trends in the building industry and an analysis of competitive performance, Crystal has used a linear regression computer model to forecast demand for Supportex's products and sales prices for the year from 1 April 2000. Crystal Ball's sales forecast data are as follows:

Lintel	Demand	Price
Small	5,000	£20
Medium	8,000	£30
Large	6,000	£40

We are required to prepare an unphased sales budget for the year ended 31 March 2001.

Answer
Sales budget

Lintel	Demand	Price	£ sales
Small	5,000	£20	100,000
Medium	8,000	£30	240,000
Large	6,000	£40	240,000
			580,000

Production budget

The production budget may be prepared by allowing for expected stock movements in the period, based on company policy and targets for improvement. Budgeted materials requirements are based on a **bill of materials (BOM)**, which is the 'list of ingredients and recipe' for each product. The purchasing function ensures that the right materials, components and packaging are procured in the right quantities, at the right time to the right location, in line with production and stockholding requirements.

Budgeted labour requirements are based on standard labour hours required for each product. Conflicts arise between manufacturing and engineering in respect of estimates of standard hours. Engineering changes may be made continuously, but may not always be reflected in up-to-date bills of materials.

In practice, the calculation of the standard hours required to manufacture each product is not a straightforward process. There is always much debate between managers with regard to how standard labour hours are adjusted in respect of, for example, absenteeism, downtime, training, efficiency, and the extent to which they should be reflected in the standard labour rate. These factors have an obvious impact on the manufacturing director's requirements for direct labour resources for given levels of production, inevitably conflicting with the human resources director's headcount objectives.

Many companies have structures comprised of business units, each with responsibility for production areas relating to specific products/customers. Responsibility for estimating budget production overheads and indirect labour requirements is devolved to business unit managers, the remaining above-the-line overheads and indirect labour requirements being provided by quality, purchasing, logistics and maintenance managers. Each manager may also submit his/her capital expenditure requirements, which are then used for subsequent calculation of depreciation, and the assessment of cash flow implications.

Depreciation charged to production overhead is calculated based on existing plant and equipment and the plans for new plant and equipment that have been submitted by managers responsible for production and production support activities. It must be emphasised that the method of determining the depreciation charge is highly subjective, and the marketplace has seen many products last much longer than the most extreme original estimates made by managers. An example has been the Rover Mini car, which was not expected to be in production for over 35 years!

Example 11.2

The purchasing manager of Supportex Ltd, Mr Daley, has obtained what he believes are the most competitive prices for materials used to make and package Supportex's products. Supportex's cost prices and the standard quantities used in each product for the budget year are as follows:

Materials

	Labels	Packaging	Rubbers	Steels
Cost prices	£1	£2	£3	£6
Standard quantities				
Small	2	1	1	0.5
Medium	1	1	2	1
Large	2	2	1	1

Material handlers and operators are employed to make the Supportex products. The company's production manager, Ben Drools has provided the following hourly rates and the standard times used in production:

	Material handlers	Operators
Hourly rates	£6	£7.50
Standard minutes		
Small	5	12
Medium	5	20
Large	10	40

Production overheads are forecast at £38,000, which are absorbed into product costs on the basis of direct labour hours.

At 31 March 2000 stock levels have been estimated by Arthur Daley at:

Finished product	Quantity	Materials	Quantity
Small	1,000	Labels	15,000
Medium	1,500	Packaging	10,000
Large	1,000	Rubbers	15,000
		Steels	10,000

The Managing Director has set Ben a target of a 20% reduction in component stocks by 31 March 2001 and the company expects finished goods stock to be up by 10% by the same time.

We are required to prepare the following unphased budgets for the year ended 31 March 2001:

(i) Production

(ii) Direct labour

(iii) Unit gross margin

(iv) Materials usage and purchases.

Answer

(i) Production budget

	Sales units	Stock increases	Production units
Small	5,000	100	5,100
Medium	8,000	150	8,150
Large	6,000	100	6,100

(ii) Direct labour budget

	Production units	Material handlers hours	Operators hours		
Small	5,100	425	1,020		
Medium	8,150	679	2,717		
Large	6,100	1,017	4,067		
Direct labour hours		2,121	7,804	Total	9,925 hours
Direct labour rates		£6/hour	£7.50/hour		
Direct labour cost		£12,726	£58,530	Total	£71,256

(iii) Unit gross margin budget

Unit product costs

	Small	Medium	Large
	£	£	£
Materials:			
Labels	2	1	2
Packaging	2	2	4
Rubbers	3	6	3
Steels	3	6	6
(a)	10	15	15
Direct labour:			
Material handlers	0.5 [5 × £6/60]	0.5 [5 × £6/60]	1 [10 × £6/60]
Operators	1.5 [12 × £7.50/60]	2.5 [20 × £7.50/60]	5 [40 × £7.50/60]
(b)	2	3	6

▶

		Small £	Medium £	Large £
Total production overheads £38,000 ÷ 9,925 = £3.8287 per hr	(c)	£1.0848	£1.5953	£3.1906
Total unit production costs (a + b + c)	(d)	£13.0848	£19.5953	£24.1906
Sales prices	(e)	£20	£30	£40
Unit gross margins (e − d)		£6.9152	£10.4047	£15.8094
rounded to		£6.92	£10.40	£15.81

(iv) Materials usage budget

Units	Labels	Packaging	Rubbers	Steels
Small	10,200	5,100	5,100	2,550
Medium	8,150	8,150	16,300	8,150
Large	12,200	12,200	6,100	6,100
Total usage	30,550	25,450	27,500	16,800
Stocks 31 March 2000	15,000	10,000	15,000	10,000
Stocks reduction by 31 March 2001 targeted at 20% of 31 March 2000 levels	3,000	2,000	3,000	2,000

Materials purchases budget

Units	Labels	Packaging	Rubbers	Steels	Total
Total usage	30,550	25,450	27,500	16,800	
Stock decrease	3,000	2,000	3,000	2,000	
Purchase requirements	27,550	23,450	24,500	14,800	
Unit costs	£1	£2	£3	£6	
Purchase requirements	£27,550	£46,900	£73,500	£88,800	£236,750

Distribution and administration budget

The below-the-line overhead costs of:

● marketing and selling
● distribution
● administration
● research and development

and also planned capital expenditure, are provided by managers responsible for departments such as:

● commercial and marketing
● finance

- information technology
- administration
- human resources
- engineering
- product development.

Financial budget

Costs of financing and/or interest receivable from the investment of surplus funds may be estimated for the first draft budget. As the phased profit and loss accounts, capital expenditure, and cash budget become finalised the financial budget can be refined with a little more accuracy.

Master profit and loss budget

The master budget is prepared by pulling together each of the elements outlined above to provide a budgeted:

- trading account
- manufacturing account
- profit and loss account

for the year.

These may then be phased to show expected month-by-month results. The ways in which the various items within the budget are phased are determined by the type of revenue or cost. Some items may be related to the volume of sales, or production levels, whilst others may be spread evenly on a monthly, weekly or daily basis.

The budget preparation procedure described above is usually a negotiation process between budget holders and the budget committee. Conflicts may arise as budgets are very often seen as 'finance' budgets, perceived as a pressure device, with a corresponding demotivating effect on personnel.

Problems ensue due to lack of information, ignorance, and misunderstanding of the budget process (probably through a lack of training), which may result in generally inflated budgets. Judgement is required to identify whether apparently inflated budgets reflect real needs, or some degree of 'padding' due to a fear of cutbacks. Padding relates to the overestimation of budgeted costs (or underestimation of budgeted revenues) by managers with the expectation that their budgets may be cut, so that their final agreed budgets may be at levels that they feel are achievable.

Further conflicts arise between departments within a company, through competition for resources, and also poor communication, resulting in duplication in cost budgets or padding. Examples of costs omitted, or duplicated, are health and safety costs (human resources or manufacturing?), training costs (human resources or decentralised into the operational departments?), and the question of centralised/decentralised costs generally. This often results in each department blaming the other if services are not provided, or if cost targets are not achieved.

Padding may occur where budget holders are allowed to be excessively prudent regarding costs and expenses or achievement of sales. If the company or a sector of its business is expanding, the padding may be tolerated. When competition is fierce or the industry is in decline, then the padding could prove quite harmful and lead to decisions being based on an incorrect cost base. It is inevitable that managers may be prudent when constructing their budgets, and this can take the form of putting a little extra into expense categories that may be difficult to verify, or a little less into certain categories of sales.

The budget preparation process is a continuous process of:

- setting objectives
- forecasting
- draft budget preparation
- evaluation
- feedback
- forecast and budget revisions.

Within most organisations this process continues, limited by budget preparation timetable constraints, until an acceptable final budget has been achieved.

During the budget process, cost reductions are inevitably requested from all areas within the organisation. This poses obvious dilemmas for all managers. Whilst wanting to co-operate in meeting profitability objectives, they must still maintain the same levels of service for both internal and external customers.

Example 11.3

Supportex Ltd have budgeted selling and administrative costs of £80,000 for the following year. The overheads and selling and administrative costs include total depreciation budgeted for the year of £23,569. There are not expected to be any financing costs over the coming year.

We are required to prepare an unphased profit and loss account budget, using absorption costing, for the year ended 31 March 2001.

Answer

Profit and loss account master budget

	Small		Medium		Large		Total
	Total	**Unit**	**Total**	**Unit**	**Total**	**Unit**	
Sales units	5,000		8,000		6,000		
	£		£		£		£
Sales	100,000	£20	240,000	£30	240,000	£40	580,000
Cost of sales (derived from sales less gross margin)	65,400		156,800		145,140		367,340
Gross margin	34,600	£6.92	83,200	£10.40	94,860	£15.81	212,660
Using unit gross margins from example 11.2 (iii)							
Selling and administrative costs							80,000
Profit							132,660

Cash budget

Cash flow is an extremely important element in the budget preparation process. The master profit and loss budget, together with the planned capital expenditure, the outflow of cash on fixed asset acquisitions and investments, may then be used to prepare an initial cash budget. This will also include the impact of the operating cycle:

● materials purchases become stock items held for a period before use, and creditors to be paid out of cash at a later date

● production uses up stock to generate sales which become debtors to be received into cash at a later date

● the more immediate payment of staff costs and other operational expense.

The final cash budget, phased to show monthly cash surpluses or cash requirements, will also include the effect of non-operational events such as cash raised through the issue of shares and loans, and cash paid in respect of taxation and dividends to shareholders.

Example 11.4

Supportex Ltd have prepared an estimated balance sheet for 31 March 2000 as follows:

	£	£
Fixed assets	362,792	
Stocks	206,669	
Trade debtors	46,750	
Cash and bank	2,432	618,643
Trade creditors	35,275	
Share capital	200,000	
Retained earnings	383,368	618,643

Trade debtors all pay in the month following the month of sale and Arthur Daley has negotiated trade creditors' payments in the second month following the month of purchase. Direct labour, production overheads, and selling and administrative costs are all paid in the month they are incurred. There is no planned capital expenditure for the budget year and trading is expected to be evenly spread over the 12 months, except for month 12 when the changes is stock levels are expected to occur.

We are required to prepare an unphased cash budget for the year ended 31 March 2001.

Answer
Cash budget

Cash inflows from customers:	£	Cash outflows to creditors:	£
Trade debtors at 31/3/00	46,750	Trade creditors at 31/3/00	35,275
Sales 2000/01	580,000	Purchases 2000/01	236,750
less: Trade debtors at 31/3/01	(48,333)	less:Trade creditors at 31/3/01	(39,458)
(1 month sales)	578,417	(2 months purchases)	232,567
Cash outflows for overheads:		Cash outflow for capital:	zero
Production overheads	38,000	Cash outflow for tax:	zero
Sales and administration	80,000	Cash outflow for dividends:	zero
less: Depreciation	(23,569)	Cash outflow for direct labour:	71,256
	94,431	Cash inflow for shares/loans:	zero

	£
Inflows from customers	578,417
Outflows to creditors	(232,567)
Outflows for overheads	(94,431)
Outflow for direct labour	(71,256)
Budgeted cash flow 2000/01	180,163 [see Example 11.5]
Forecast cash and bank 31/3/00	2,432
Budgeted cash and bank 31/3/01	182,595

The calculation of the budgeted cash flow statement, shown in Example 11.4, was carried out by preparing a direct cash flow statement (see Chapter 4). This may be checked by the preparation of a more conventional indirect cash flow statement, as shown in Example 11.5.

Example 11.5

We are required to prepare an unphased budgeted indirect cash flow statement for Supportex Ltd for the year ended 31 March 2001.

Answer
Cash flow statement

	£	
Budgeted operating profit 2000/01	132,660	
plus: Depreciation	23,569	
plus: Decrease in stocks	21,334	[206,669 − 185,335]
less: Increase in debtors	(1,583)	[48,333 − 46,750]
plus: Increase in creditors	4,183	[39,458 − 35,275]
Budgeted cash flow 2000/01	180,163	[see Example 11.4]
Forecast cash and bank 31/3/00	2,432	
Budgeted cash and bank 31/3/01	182,595	

The budgeted cash flow figure of £180,163 calculated in Example 11.5 can be seen to agree with the budgeted cash flow figure calculated in Example 11.4.

Balance sheet budget

The budget balance sheet may be prepared with reference to:

- information relating to sales, costs, etc., from the master profit and loss budget
- the capital expenditure budget
- operating cycle assumptions on stock days, debtor days, creditor days
- the cash budget.

As with the profit and loss budget and cash budget, the balance sheet budget may be phased to show the expected month-by-month financial position of the organisation.

Example 11.6

Using the information from the last four Examples 11.1 to 11.5 we are now required to prepare an unphased balance sheet budget for Supportex Ltd as at 31 March 2001.

Answer

Stock valuations at 31 March 2001

	Quantity	£ unit price (see Example 11.2)	£
Finished product			
Small	1,100	13.0848	14,393
Medium	1,650	19.5953	32,332
Large	1,100	24.1906	26,610
Total			73,335
Materials			
Labels	12,000	1.00	12,000
Packaging	8,000	2.00	16,000
Rubbers	12,000	3.00	36,000
Steels	8,000	6.00	48,000
Total			112,000
Budgeted stocks at 31 March 2001			185,335

Fixed assets

	£
Fixed assets at 31 March 2000	362,792
Budgeted depreciation 2000/01	(23,569)
Budgeted fixed assets at 31 March 2001	339,223

Retained earnings

	£
Retained earnings at 31 March 2000	383,368
Budgeted profit 2000/01 (see Example 11.3)	132,660
Budgeted retained earnings at 31 March 2001	516,028

Using the budgeted stocks, fixed assets, and retained earnings calculations above, and the budgeted cash and bank balance, trade debtors and trade creditors calculated in Example 11.4, we now have the complete information to construct the budgeted balance sheet as at 31 March 2001:

Balance sheet:

	£	£
Fixed assets	339,223	
Stocks	185,335	
Trade debtors	48,333	
Cash and bank	182,595	755,486
Trade creditors	39,458	
Share capital	200,000	
Retained earnings	516,028	755,486

The budget balance sheet as at 31 March 2001 shown in Example 11.6 has been prepared by calculating:

- the effect on fixed assets of depreciation for the year 2000/01
- the closing valuation of stocks at 31 March 2001
- the closing valuation of trade debtors at 31 March 2001
- the cash and bank balance at 31 March 2001
- the closing valuation of trade creditors at 31 March 2001
- the addition to retained earnings, the budgeted profit for the year 2000/01.

There is an alternative way of deriving the balance sheet that may be used in practice, which also clarifies the links between stock movements and the profit and loss account and its links with the balance sheet. This method requires a calculation of the materials cost of products actually sold (compared with the materials used in production in Example 11.2). It also requires a calculation of the direct labour and production overheads cost of products actually sold (compared with the cash paid out in Example 11.4). The cash paid out for direct labour and overheads in the budget year will be absorbed into the valuation of stock of finished product. Not all that finished product will be sold in the period. Some will have been left in stock at 31 March 2001. The same situation applied at 31 March 2000.

Therefore finished product stocks at 31 March 2001 will need to be adjusted by the amount of direct labour and overheads in their valuation that relates to the difference in the finished goods stock level between 31 March 2000 and 31 March 2001. The balance of what is paid out for direct labour and overheads in the budget year is charged to the profit and loss account.

Example 11.7

We are required to derive the budget balance sheet for Supportex Ltd at 31 March 2001 by plotting the expected movements for the budget year 2000/1 relating to each type of activity, and totalling across each line from the starting balance sheet 31 March 2000. This is an alternative approach to Example 11.6, which also shows the relationship between sales, costs, cash and the balance sheet.

Materials cost of goods sold

Units	Labels		Packaging		Rubbers		Steels	
Small	[5,000 × 2]	10,000	[5,000 × 1]	5,000	[5,000 × 1]	5,000	[5,000 × 0.5]	2,500
Med.	[8,000 × 1]	8,000	[8,000 × 1]	8,000	[8,000 × 2]	16,000	[8,000 × 1]	8,000
Large	[6,000 × 2]	12,000	[6,000 × 2]	12,000	[6,000 × 1]	6,000	[6,000 × 1]	6,000
Total		30,000		25,000		27,000		16,500
Unit costs		£1		£2		£3		£6
Materials cost of sales		£30,000		£50,000		£81,000		£99,000

Total = £260,000

Direct labour in finished stock increase 31 March 2001

	Stock increases	£ direct labour/unit	£ stock adjustment
Small	100	2	200
Medium	150	3	450
Large	100	6	600
			1,250

Production overhead in finished stock increase 31 March 2001

	Stock increases	£ production overhead/unit (see Example 11.2)	£ stock adjustment
Small	100	1.0848	108
Medium	150	1.5953	239
Large	100	3.1906	319
			666

Sales, materials purchases, depreciation, cash receipts, and cash payments have previously been calculated (see Examples 11.1 to 11.5).

Balance sheet

Figures in £	31/03/00	Sales	Cash recs.	Purchases	Cash pays.	Depn.	Materials cost of sales	Direct labour	Production overheads	31/03/01
Fixed assets	362,792					(23,569)				339,223
Stocks	206,669			236,750			(260,000)	1,250	666	185,335
Trade debtors	46,750	580,000	(578,417)							48,333
Cash and bank	2,432		578,417		(232,567)			(71,256)	(94,431)	182,595
	618,643									755,486
Trade creditors	35,275			236,750	(232,567)					39,458
Share capital	200,000									200,000
Retained earnings	383,368	580,000				(23,569)	(260,000)	(70,006)	(93,765)	516,028
	618,643									755,486

Progress check 11.5

Describe a typical budget preparation process.

Funding requirements

The final budget should not be accepted until the projected financial position of the business has been reviewed in terms of the adequacy, or otherwise, of funding. The budget for the forthcoming period may have been based on higher or lower activity than the previous period, or it may include new product development, or other major new projects. Risk analysis and risk assessment is essential to be carried out on each of the uncertain areas of the budget, to determine any requirement for additional funding and to safeguard the future of the business.

Additional funding may be by way of extended overdraft facilities, loans or additional share capital. The appropriate funding decision may be made and matched with the type of activity for which funding is required. For example, major capital expenditure projects would not normally be funded by an overdraft; the type of longer-term funding generally depends on the nature of the project.

Example 11.8

Magic Moments have planned to sell fluffy puppies between October and December to meet the Christmas demand. They have forecast the following sales at £20 each to be received in cash in the month of sale.

	Oct	Nov	Dec	Total
Units	500	750	1,500	2,750

Magic Moments have contracted to buy fluffy puppies at £12 each. They will have to buy 300 in September. Month end stocks are planned to be:

October 30% of November sales

November 20% of December sales

December zero

Magic Moments must pay for fluffy puppies in the month following purchase.

We are required to prepare:
– a schedule of opening stocks, purchases, and closing stocks in units for September to December
– a direct cash flow forecast phased for October to January
How have Magic Moments funded their activities?

Answer

Stocks and purchases:

Units	Sep	Oct	Nov	Dec
Opening stock	–	300	225	300
Purchases (derived)	300	425	825	1,200
Sales	–	500	750	1,500
Closing stock	300	225	300	–

Cash flow:

Figures in £		Oct		Nov		Dec		Jan
Opening balance		–		6,400		16,300		36,400
Cash inflow	(500 × £20)	10,000	(750 × £20)	15,000	(1,500 × £20)	30,000		–
Cash outflow	(300 × £12)	3,600	(425 × £12)	5,100	(825 × £12)	9,900	(1,200 × £12)	14,400
Closing balance		6,400		16,300		36,400		22,000

Magic Moments have funded their business through managing their operating cycle. Effectively, their creditors have financed the business.

Regardless of whether higher or lower activity is expected and budgeted for future periods, it is absolutely essential that the company's bankers are kept fully informed of expectations. Bankers do not like surprises. The corporate graveyard is littered with small businesses in particular who have ignored this basic requirement.

Performance evaluation and control

The many uses of budgeting may be summarised as follows:

- a system for optimal allocation of scarce resources, for example a factory capable of a specific process like plate glass manufacture
- a yardstick for performance, better than past performance, since conditions may have changed
- people participation to provide motivation for improved performance and alignment of individual and corporate goals
- improved communication to enable co-ordination of various parts of the business and so avoid sub-optimisation
- thinking ahead to achieve long-term goals and identify short-term problems
- a system of authorisation and for clear identification of responsibility
- internal audit by evaluating efficiency and effectiveness of departmental performance for prompt remedial action as necessary
- a system of control and management by exception reporting.

Prior to budget preparation, targets may be issued, for example, for:

- sales
- gross margin
- return on investment
- stock days
- debtor collection days
- creditor payment days.

Whilst the responsibility for the budget usually rests with a budget committee, for the budget to achieve its aims, it is important for relevant managers to have full participation in the process and receive communication of the guidelines. Uncertainties, limiting factors and constraints, along with all assumptions, must be made available to all managers with budget responsibility.

It is by ensuring that full communication and participation take place that the most effective use may be made of budgeting as a tool of control. Actual departmental results may then be regularly reported against control budgets that have had full acceptance by the relevant managers and based on up-to-date and realistic standards of performance. The budget is used as a tool for control of the business by monitoring actual performance and comparing how closely it is in line with the plan. For this purpose the overall budget plan is broken down into the individual elements, representing the areas of responsibility of each of the budget holders, which are called **responsibility centres**.

Responsibility centres

As part of the budgetary process, in order to co-ordinate an organisation's activities, responsibility is assigned to managers who are accountable for their actions. Each manager, therefore is in charge of a responsibility centre. A responsibility centre is a department or organisational function whose performance is the direct responsibility of a specific manager. **Responsibility accounting** is the system used to measure and compare actual results against budget for each centre. Costs are traced to the activities causing them, or to the individuals knowledgeable about why they arose, and who authorised them.

There are four main types of responsibility centre, and within each type, the responsibilities of the manager of each centre are defined in a different way:

- cost centre is a production or service location, function, activity or item of equipment for which costs are accumulated – the manager is accountable for costs only

- **revenue centre** is a centre devoted to raising revenue with no responsibility for costs, for example, a sales centre – the manager is responsible for revenues only (revenue centres are often used in not-for-profit organisations)

- **profit centre** is a part of the business that is accountable for both costs and revenues – the manager is responsible for revenues and costs

- **investment centre** is a profit centre with additional responsibilities for capital investment and possibly for financing, and whose performance is measured by its return on investment – the manager is responsible for investments, revenues and costs.

Responsibility must be matched with control, otherwise a manager is more likely to be demotivated. The manager must be able to influence the costs in question over specific time spans. Problems may also arise when costs may be influenced by more than one manager. Many very large businesses have pursued the policy of devolving spending responsibility down through the organisation. Employees are frequently motivated by being given spending responsibility and fully accepting control, which may be supported by sophisticated IT techniques as hardware and software has become more economic, by, for example, file sharing or remote interrogation of files.

Budget holders can only be responsible for controllable costs or revenues within their areas of responsibility. For example, a production manager may be responsible for ensuring that he/she does not exceed the number of direct labour hours allowed within their area of responsibility for a given level of output. Uncontrollable costs, for example the level of depreciation on the machines and equipment used within the production manager's department, may appear within budget holders' areas of activity but cannot realistically be used to measure performance. Further examples of such costs may be business taxes, or rents on property that may have been the subject of long-term agreements.

In a similar way, a budget holder may be responsible for controlling costs of a department that relate to sales volumes or other variable activities. The costs of that department, the variable costs and possibly the fixed costs, will vary according to the level of activity that takes place. For this reason, the budget for control purposes is flexed in line with actual levels of activity to provide more realistic levels of expected costs against which to measure performance.

Outline the system of responsibility accounting in its various forms and describe what it aims to achieve.

For control purposes, therefore, the master budget needs to be:

● phased by reporting period – usually by week, calendar month, or four-week periods
● broken down to provide a separate budget for each responsibility centre
● flexed to show the costs (or revenues) expected as a result of changes in activity levels from those planned within the master budget.

We will look at the mechanics of **flexed budgets** in Chapter 12, together with the method of comparison with actual performance. We shall look at the way in which standards are used for this purpose in budget preparation to enable meaningful exception reporting to be provided for analysis of differences, or variances, to the budget plan.

Motivation and the behavioural aspects of budgeting

We have discussed the importance of participation and communication in the budget process and so it can be seen that key aspects of budgeting are behavioural. One of the main objectives is to influence the behaviour of the people in the organisation so that efficiency is maximised and corporate goals are attained. It is important therefore that the evaluation of performance does not degenerate into a blame culture. It follows then that motivation is an important underlying factor in ensuring that achievable budgets are set and that the managers with the responsibility for each of the elements of the budget have a very good chance of achieving their objectives.

The question of motivation is a very large subject in its own right. It is sufficient for our purposes to outline some of the many motivational factors without going into much further detail. Key motivational factors include:

● pay
● bonuses
● feedback of information
● communication and discussion of control reports
● success, and reward for target achievement
● training in the budget process
● the identification of controllable and uncontrollable costs
● the setting of fair, achievable standards
● the avoidance of short-run wins at the expense of long-run considerations, leading to dysfunctional decision-making

- flexibility in meeting the requirements of the budgeting system
- performance appraisal using budgets flexed to actual activity levels
- inclusion of non-financial performance indicators.

Many writers, including Hopwood, Argyris, Hofstede, McGregor, Becker and Green have identified the various motivational problems which may be encountered in budgeting. The ways they have suggested these problems can be alleviated, and how motivation can be enhanced is beyond the scope of this book, and may be followed up with further reading.

Progress check 11.7

As Supportex Ltd's purchasing manager, Arthur Daley is responsible for negotiating the best deals with suppliers. For planning purposes the budget that has been prepared for 2000/01 has used current materials' prices and suppliers' credit that have been negotiated by Arthur. Within a control budget, give examples of the type of performance targets that may be set for Arthur and how these targets may be set and monitored.

Problems in budgeting

Within most companies budgeting is a high-profile, formal process, prepared on either a yearly or half-yearly basis. The budget is prepared within the context of a company's strategic management process, and includes current year performance projections. It should ideally emphasise the strategies and priorities of the company and focus on both financial and non-financial performance.

Information provided from the budget process generally falls into the following main categories:

- sales, relating to
  - customers
  - demand volumes
  - market share
  - price index expectations
- product margins
- purchase price index expectations
- overheads
- headcount
- new product development
- capital investment
- working capital
- cash
- non-financial performance indicators, in areas such as
  - product quality
  - staff development
  - delivery performance
  - customer satisfaction.

Many companies have developed dynamic budgeting models, using packaged IT solutions that may link financial and non-financial performance measures.

The major purposes of budgeting may be identified as:

- compelling planning and forcing management to look ahead by
  - setting targets
  - anticipating problems
  - giving the organisation purpose and direction
- formalising the communication of ideas and plans to all appropriate individuals
- co-ordinating activities of different business units and departments
- establishing a system of control, by
  - allocating responsibility
  - providing a plan against which actual performance may be measured and evaluated
- motivating improved performance of personnel.

It may be seen from many job advertisements how motivation is recognised as being extremely important in providing a vital link with individual performance, which in turn links with achievement of corporate budget targets.

The emphasis given to each budget purpose varies, and is very much dependent upon:

- company policy
- the way in which information is provided/received and by whom
- the negotiating skills of each manager with the company's budget team.

Problems of conflict arise out of actual and perceived fulfilment of each of the purposes of the budget. Each area is a minefield of potential problems of conflict. For example, it was revealed in 2000, that the chief executive of a major UK retailer only wanted to hear good news about the company's position in the marketplace. The managers were afraid to give him bad news.

There are basic problems within the process of setting targets. Organisations can be very unforgiving when targets are not achieved. The budget preparation process has become easier to manage with the introduction of powerful IT resources; but it has also resulted in more accuracy required within the estimates and also within a shorter time-frame.

During the budget-setting process, it is essential that individual budget holders 'buy-in' to their budgets to enable subsequent meaningful monitoring and evaluation of actual performance. Their budgets, while representing difficult-to-meet targets, must also be achievable to provide the necessary motivation to reach their goals.

Responsibility must be matched with control. Costs that should be considered uncontrollable, may not necessarily be treated as such in evaluating individual performance, resulting in discontent and demotivation. Similar conflicts arise if there is insufficient clarification, or if costs are controlled by more than one person; for example, special transport costs incurred to meet production needs through supplier non-performance – a manufacturing or purchasing responsibility?

Performance against budgeted costs at the operating level should be flexed to reflect current activity. This may not always happen, resulting in unfair appraisal of individual performance and misrepresentation of company performance. It is quite obvious that managers have no influence on the basic 'health' of their company's industrial sector; we have previously noted the examples seen in the latter part of the twentieth century of mobile telephones (expanding in the UK) and coal (declining in the UK).

Business unit/manager performance may be considered measuring return on investment (ROI) rather than in absolute terms using **residual income (RI)**. Business unit managers may decide to replace old equipment (resulting in lower ROI and worsened cash flow)

thereby increasing residual income, or to make do with old equipment (resulting in higher ROI and improved cash flow) giving reduced RI. The ROI measure may therefore result in a sub-optimisation decision for the company as a whole. There have been many case studies based on UK manufacturers which showed that the age of their plant was much older than that used by overseas competitors.

Budgeted levels of training, particularly operator quality training, must be evaluated considering short-term profitability performance objectives and longer-term goals of zero defects. The aim must be of course to achieve both! A famous UK car manufacturer used the pressure of telephone calls from customers direct to the factory floor, to reduce defects in the finished motor cars, especially those going into the export markets. Another UK manufacturer of motor cars required the engines to be signed for by the appropriate engineer, so that the customer could identify who was responsible for that particular engine.

Many materials may be procured in foreign currency. Should the performance of the purchasing department (responsible for supplier selection) reflect the impact of any resultant currency rate variances? Or should performance be measured using standard exchange rates prevailing at the outset, with, say, the finance department (usually responsible for hedging activities) bearing the cost of currency movements?

Major conflicts arise out of management of the operating cycle, the objective being its minimisation, through reduced debtor and stock days and extended creditor days. The company treasurer must respect this objective, while maintaining good relationships with customers and suppliers, and ensuring no threat to operations. The purchasing and manufacturing directors must ensure low stock days, while maintaining buffer stocks to cover disasters and ensuring that schedules are met, through perhaps the use of JIT processes.

When extremely tight time constraints are imposed for the budget-setting process (which is invariably the case in practice) this may conflict with the degree of accuracy possible in reporting. It also means that top management commitment is critical in providing timely:

- direction
- communication
- feedback

required for the budget process.

The final budget is inevitably a quantitative representation of future plans and targets, and the ways in which each company will reach its short-term goals. Whilst increasing attention is now paid to non-financial measures, the focus remains on performance in financial terms. That being so, traditional cost allocation methods continue to distort the way in which product profitability is reported. This, together with the short-term emphasis of the budgeting activity, therefore provides potentially misleading results. It may also have a demotivating effect on managers involved in both commercial and manufacturing activities, which may result in poor performance.

The problems encountered in the budgeting process may be summarised to include:

- the need for good planning
- difficulties with attitudes including lack of motivation, trust and honesty
- the problems in gathering information
- timeliness of the information
- the amount of detail required
- responsibility for the budget and the key performance areas within the budget.

This outline of the some of the problems that may be encountered in the budgeting process may appear to give a negative perspective to its use as an instrument of planning and control. However, the conflicts, by their very nature, ideally serve to highlight the important issues and ensure that budgeting is not just a mechanical exercise carried out once or twice a year but a dynamic part of the strategic planning process contributing to successful management of the business.

Progress check 11.8

What are the key aims of budgeting and what sort of problems are encountered that may prevent those aims being met?

Summary of key points

- A budget is a plan and budgeting is one part of the strategic planning process, which is concerned with planning and control.
- Planning budgets are management's belief of what the business's costs and revenues will be over a specified future time period, the budget period.
- Control budgets are used for management motivational purposes and are used in this way to influence improved departmental performance.
- Forecasts are not plans but predictions of the future, which are required as an important prerequisite to the budget process.
- Prior to budget preparation, in addition to forecasting, decisions must be made and policies formulated regarding stock days and purchasing, debtor and creditor days, staff costs, capital expenditure, and standard costs.
- The master profit and loss budget is prepared from each of the elements of the operating budget: sales; production; distribution and administration; and the financial budget.
- The master budget is comprised of the profit and loss budget, cash budget, and balance sheet budget.
- Risk assessment and risk analysis should be applied to the master budget, and it must be closely reviewed in terms of additional funding requirements.
- As part of the control function of the budget, the system of responsibility accounting is used to measure actual results against budget for each of the various types of responsibility centre.
- Control budgets are usually flexed to reflect actual activity levels, and performance against budget provided from exception reporting is evaluated so that corrective actions may be implemented as appropriate.
- The preparation of budgets for planning and control purposes needs the involvement of people to provide realistic plans and the motivation for performance targets to be achieved.
- There are usually many conflicts and problems associated with the budget preparation process in most organisations, the majority of which are concerned with the 'softer' human resources issues of managers' behaviour.

Glossary of key terms

bill of materials (BOM) A detailed specification, for each product produced, of the sub-assemblies, components and materials required, distinguishing between those items which are purchased externally and those which are manufactured in-house.

budget A quantified statement, for a defined period of time, which may include planned revenues, expenses, assets, liabilities and cash flows.

control The ability to direct the financial and operating policies of an entity with a view to gaining economic benefits from its activities (FRS 8).

flexed budget The budgeted cost ascribed to the level of activity achieved in a budget centre in a control period. It comprises variable costs in direct proportion to volume achieved and fixed costs as a proportion of the annual budget.

forecast A prediction of future events and their quantification for planning purposes.

investment centre A profit centre with additional responsibilities for capital investment and possibly for financing, and whose performance is measured by its return on investment – the manager is responsible for investments, revenues and costs.

management control The process by which managers assure that resources are obtained and used effectively and efficiently in the accomplishment of the organisation's objectives.

planning The establishment of objectives, and the formulation, evaluation and selection of the policies, strategies, tactics and action required to achieve them. Planning comprises long-term/strategic planning, and short-term operational planning, the latter being usually for a period of up to one year.

profit centre A part of the business that is accountable for both costs and revenues – the manager is responsible for revenues and costs.

residual income (RI) Profit before tax less an imputed interest charge for invested capital, which may be used to assess the performance of a division or a branch of a business.

responsibility accounting A system in which a budget holder is given responsibility for all revenues and costs that can be traced to clearly defined areas of their responsibility.

responsibility centre A department or organisational function whose performance is the direct responsibility of a specific manager.

revenue centre A centre devoted to raising revenue with no responsibility for costs, for example, a sales centre – the manager is responsible for revenues only (revenue centres are often used in not-for-profit organisations).

strategic plan A statement of long-term goals along with a definition of the strategies and policies which will ensure achievement of those goals.

variance The difference between a planned, budgeted or standard cost and the actual cost incurred. The same comparisons may be made for revenues.

variance analysis The evaluation of performance by means of variances, whose timely reporting should maximise the opportunity for managerial action. These variances will be either favourable variances (F) or adverse variances (A).

Assessment material

Questions

Q11.1 (i) Why do businesses need to prepare budgets?

(ii) What are they used for?

Q11.2 If there are differences between budgets prepared for planning purposes and budgets prepared for control purposes, what are these differences?

Q11.3 Describe and illustrate the differences between qualitative and quantitative forecasting techniques.

Q11.4 (i) Give some examples of the forecasts that are required to be able to prepare the complete master budget.

(ii) What are the most suitable techniques for each of these forecasts?

Q11.5 Draw a flow diagram to illustrate the budget preparation process.

Q11.6 Explain and illustrate the way in which a business may approach the strategic management process.

Q11.7 (i) What are the internal and external sources of funding for a business?

(ii) How may a business use the budget process to assess its future funding requirements?

Q11.8 How does the assignment of individual budget responsibility contribute to improved organisational performance?

Q11.9 Discuss the ways in which a budget may be used to evaluate performance.

Q11.10 Outline some of the major problems that may be encountered in budgeting.

Discussion points

D11.1 'Once I know what the forecast sales are for next year I can tell you how much profit we will make within five minutes, so there's no need for this annual time-wasting and costly budgeting ritual.' Discuss.

D11.2 'The area of budgeting is a minefield of potential problems of conflict.' How can these problems be usefully used as a learning experience to ultimately improve the performance of the business?

D11.3 You are the general manager of a newly formed subsidiary company. The group managing director has declared that he has targeted your company to make a profit of £250,000 in its first year. What assumptions, decisions and policies are concerned with preparing a budget by working backwards from a starting point of budgeted profit?

Exercises

Solutions are provided in Appendix 4 to all exercise numbers highlighted in colour.

Level I

E11.1 *Time allowed – 15 minutes*

Earextensions plc set up a new business to assemble mobile phones from kits. They planned to make and sell one model only and expected to sell 441,200 units between January and June in their first year of trading. February, March, and April volumes were each expected to be 20% above the preceding month and May, June, and July volumes were expected to be the same as April. The selling price was £50 each.

Cost prices for the parts used in making a phone were as follows:

Electronic assembly	Keypad	Case
£23.30	£1	£2

Operators and assemblers were employed to make the phones with the following hourly rates and standard times used in production:

	Assemblers	Operators
Hourly rate	£10	£8
Standard minutes	3	1.5

Production overheads were forecast at £4.1m, which was incurred on an equal monthly basis and absorbed into product costs on the basis of direct labour hours.

At 31 December the numbers of units in stock were estimated at:

Finished product	Quantity	Materials	Quantity	
	zero	Electronic		
		Assembly	10,000	
		Keypad	30,000	} purchased in December
		Case	20,000	

Materials stock levels at the end of each month were planned to be 50% of the following month's usage. Finished product stock levels at the end of each month were planned to be 20% of the following month's sales.

Earextensions plc have budgeted selling and administration costs of £4.5m for the six months. The first three months were evenly spread at 60% of the total and the second three months evenly spread at 40% of the total. Production overheads included total depreciation of £50,000 budgeted for six months. Financing costs over the six months were expected in line with sales at 0.2% of sales value.

Earextensions plc prepared an estimated balance sheet for its new subsidiary at 31 December as follows:

	£	£
Fixed assets	495,000	
Stocks	303,000	
Trade debtors	–	
Cash and bank	355,000	1,153,000
Trade creditors	303,000	
Loans	450,000	
Share capital	400,000	
Retained earnings	–	1,153,000

Trade debtors were expected to pay in the second month following the month of sale and trade creditors were planned to be paid in the third month following the month of purchase. Direct labour, production overheads, and selling and administrative costs are all paid in the month in which they are incurred. There was no further planned capital expenditure during the first six months.

You are required to prepare a phased sales budget in units and values for the six months January to June.

E11.2   *Time allowed – 30 minutes*

Using the information from Exercise E11.1 prepare a phased finished product stocks and a phased production budget in units for the six months January to June.

Level II

E11.3   *Time allowed – 30 minutes*

Using the information from Exercise E11.1 prepare a unit gross margin budget and a phased direct labour budget for the six months January to June.

E11.4   *Time allowed – 30 minutes*

Using the information from Exercise E11.1 prepare a phased materials stocks, materials usage and purchases budget in units and values for the six months January to June.

E11.5   *Time allowed – 30 minutes*

Using the information from Exercise E11.1 prepare a phased selling and administrative costs budget, and financial budget for the six months January to June, and a phased profit and loss account budget, using absorption costing, for the six months January to June.

E11.6   *Time allowed – 30 minutes*

Using the information from Exercise E11.1 prepare a finished product valuation budget for the six months January to June.

E11.7 *Time allowed – 60 minutes*

Using the information from Exercise E11.1 prepare a creditors' budget and a debtors' budget, and a phased cash budget for the six months January to June.

E11.8 *Time allowed – 60 minutes*

Using the information from Exercise E11.1 prepare a phased balance sheet budget for the six months January to June.

12 Budgetary control

LEARNING OBJECTIVES

Completion of this chapter will enable you to:

● use standard costing in the budget process

● use standard costing in performance evaluation and control

● identify the use of flexible budgeting in performance evaluation and control

● prepare flexed budgets in line with changes in activity levels

● explain what is meant by a variance between actual and standard performance

● appreciate the importance of variance analysis in exception reporting

● calculate the individual variances used to explain differences between actual and standard performance

● summarise variances in the form of standard cost operating statements

● explain the reasons for variances between actual and standard performance

● appreciate the differences between planning and operational variances

Introduction

In Chapter 11 we illustrated the budget preparation process with the construction of budgets using:

● forecast volumes
● forecast prices
● policy decisions relating to capital expenditure and working capital
● unit product costs.

This chapter will explore in greater detail how the costs of units of a product or a process are determined. We will look at how standards may be used in the budgeting process to cost each unit or process. The budgeted unit or process cost is called its standard cost.

This chapter will explain the technique of standard costing and the ways in which actual performance may be measured and compared with the budget through the use of variance analysis. We will look at how, using standard costs, the budget may be flexed to reflect actual levels of activity, and then used to calculate individual variances. Individual variances may then be investigated to explain the reasons for the differences between actual and expected performance.

The process of explaining significant variances from standard continues to be considered as a powerful management tool. This chapter closes by introducing a further refinement to variance analysis through the use of planning and operational variances.

We referred to the Marks and Spencer case in Chapter 2 with regard to valuation of assets. From the press cutting on the opposite page we can see that M&S's fortunes continued to decline through 2001, despite the chairman and chief executive's forecast in November 2000 that the following Christmas would be 'one of the best for M&S'.

The Marks and Spencer case emphasises the need for forecasting and budgeting systems that reflect realistic expectations, and the need to include control systems that enable:

- fast reporting of performance
- quick response in the implementation of remedial actions
- timely revision of forecasts.

Standard costing

As part of the budgeting process, or at any other time when actual costs need to be compared with planned costs, a basis for comparison must be established. Standard costing provides such a basis through the setting of predetermined cost estimates.

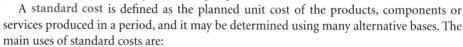

A **standard cost** is defined as the planned unit cost of the products, components or services produced in a period, and it may be determined using many alternative bases. The main uses of standard costs are:

- measurement of business performance
- control of processes
- valuation of stocks
- establishment of selling prices.

Standards may be defined as benchmark measurements of resource usage, set in defined conditions, and can be set on a number of bases:

- on an *ex ante* (before the event) estimate of expected performance
- on an *ex post* (after the event) estimate of attainable performance
- on a prior level of performance by the same organisation
- on the level of performance achieved by comparable organisations
- on the level of performance required to meet organisational objectives.

Standards may also be set at attainable levels which assume efficient levels of operation, but which include allowances for normal loss, waste and machine downtime, or at ideal levels, which make no allowance for the above losses, and are only attainable under the most favourable conditions.

Out-of-fashion M&S hits new lows
By Kate Rankine, Deputy City Editor

Luc Vandevelde, Marks & Spencer's chairman and chief executive, came under increasing pressure yesterday as the troubled retailing giant disclosed a sharp decline in Christmas sales for the third successive year.

Mr Vandevelde, who joined M&S as executive chairman almost a year ago, blamed too many unfashionable and unattractive clothes for a 5.1pc fall in like-for-like sales for the 16 weeks to January 20. 'We should have had more trendy, casual ranges. We weren't fashionable enough', he said. Analysts, who yesterday cut their profit forecasts by £30m to £450m pre-tax for the year ending March 2001, estimated that underlying clothing sales plunged by 11pc over Christmas and New Year.

Sheilagh Brown is taking early retirement as M&S's head of women's wear design, and a new design team, including external recruits, will be appointed shortly.

Despite the disappointing sales figures, and his prediction only last November of 'one of the best Christmases' for M&S, Mr Vandevelde yesterday said he believes that he can turn round the company by next year. 'When I joined M&S, the company was about a year into a restructuring', he said. 'As executive chairman I said that we should see some signs of a recovery in two years. I like a challenging target. I believe it is still possible. Hopefully we shall see signs of a recovery in the spring. I'm as confident as I can be,' he added.

However, analysts doubt that Mr Vandevelde will succeed within his two-year target. Tony Shiret, an analyst at investment bank CSFB, said: 'Perhaps Luc Vandevelde should make less upbeat statements in future. This is a very poor set of figures. It shows how far M&S has come down, that people look at the numbers and think that they are okay relative to expectations.' M&S shares yesterday rose 5.5 to 205.5p, partly owing to relief that the sales figures were not even worse.

Another analyst, who declined to be named, said: 'I am mystified why the shares are up. The prospects for the spring and summer still aren't good. Margins have improved, but the quality of the clothes is going down and that will put off customers. M&S is a bit like the *Titanic*, gracefully sinking. Luc doesn't seem to have a clue what to do to solve it. He certainly won't turn it round in two years.'

In a leaked internal memo to M&S employees yesterday, Mr Vandevelde said: 'The management team has been working hard to develop our longer term plan and it will shortly be in a position to share it with you.' Yesterday he described the plan as 'part of the normal planning process'.

Asked whether Mr Vandevelde was embarrassed by his prediction of 'one of the best Christmases', he replied: 'Embarrassed? No. Disappointed? Yes. I should have expected better results than I got. I was convinced there were signs of a Christmas upturn.'

He partly blamed the unfashionable ranges on last year's upheaval at the company's Baker Street head office. Almost half of its 4,000 employees were forced to re-apply for their jobs in a shake-up of its buying and marketing operations.

'The organisation didn't have much confidence last year', said Mr Vandevelde. 'People were disturbed by the change. They took their eye off the ball.'

© *Daily Telegraph*, 24 January 2001

Budgeted costs and standard costs are sometimes used to mean the same thing but this is not always so. All amounts in a budget are budgeted amounts, but not all budgeted amounts are standard amounts. Budgeted costs are usually used to describe the total planned costs for a number of products. Standard amounts relate to a series of specific processes. For example, one of the processes included in producing of a bottle of beer, the sticking of the label on to the bottle, is a process that includes the time and the cost of the label.

A standard product specification is a statement containing a full breakdown of the cost elements, which are included in the standard cost of a product or service. For each cost element (direct labour, direct material, overhead) a standard input quantity and standard unit input cost are shown as well as standard cost per unit of output produced.

A bill of materials is a detailed specification, for each product produced, of the sub-assemblies, components and materials required, distinguishing between those items that are purchased externally and those which are manufactured in-house. Having established the quality and other specifications of materials required, the purchasing department estimates costs based on suppliers prices, inflation and the availability of bulk discounts, in order to establish direct material unit costs.

The standard direct labour cost is the planned average cost of direct labour, based on the standard time for the job and standard performance. A standard hour is the amount of work achievable, at standard efficiency levels, in an hour. Work study and analysis of the learning curve are techniques that may be used to assist in determining standard hours. The standard time for a job is the time in which a task should be completed at standard performance.

Standard performance is the level of efficiency, which appropriately trained, motivated and resourced employees can achieve in the long run. Initially, the time taken to produce a specific level of output is longer than the time taken after 'normal' employees have been adequately trained and have gained experience of the process. Time taken to achieve specific levels of output will reduce over time, but the amount of the reductions in time will also reduce over time until almost negligible. This is called the learning curve effect, and when time reductions have virtually ceased the curve becomes horizontal. It is that level, where the long-term time for the particular activity has been established, that may be considered standard performance for the activity. The standard direct labour cost is then calculated by multiplying a standard direct labour hour by a standard hourly rate. Direct labour rates per hour are determined with reference to the type of skills to be used, union agreements, inflation and market rates.

Progress check 12.1

What is meant by the standard cost of a product and what type of specifications and analyses are required prior to being able to calculate a standard cost?

A typical standard cost for a unit of a product may be illustrated in the following example.

Example 12.1

Applejack Ltd manufactures drums of high grade apple pie filling that uses two types of material, apples and sugar, and requires one grade of direct labour. The company additionally incurs some variable and fixed production overheads, which are absorbed into the unit costs of the product. The standard cost for a drum (one unit) of the product may be represented as follows, where overheads have been absorbed on the basis of direct labour hours.

		£
Direct materials		
Sugar	1 kilo at £2 per kilo =	2
Apples	2 kilos at £3 per kilo =	6
		8

Direct labour	
1 hour at £8 per hour	8
Variable production overhead	
1 hour at £2 per hour	2
Fixed production overhead	
1 hour at £3 per hour	3
Standard full production cost per drum	21

Advantages of standard costs

There are several advantages in using a standard costing system:

- it is a basis for budget preparation
- it may be used in planning and control
- it can be used to highlight areas of strength and weakness
- it can be used in evaluation of performance by comparing actual costs with standard costs and so assisting in implementation of responsibility accounting
- it should result in the use of the best resources and best methods and so increase efficiency
- it may be used as a basis for stock valuation
- it can be used as a basis for pay incentive schemes
- it can be used for decision-making in its estimation of future costs
- it fits in with management by exception, whereby only significant variances (differences between actual and expected results) are investigated, and so making effective use of management time
  - control action is immediate because, for example, as soon as materials are issued from stores into production they can be compared with the standard materials which should be required for actual production
  - transfer prices (the prices at which goods or services are transferred from one process or department to another or from one company in the group to another) may be based on standard rather than actual costs to avoid inefficiencies in the form of excess costs.

Disadvantages of standard costs

There are also a number of disadvantages in using a standard costing system, not least of which is the difficulty in the establishment of the standard fixed overhead rate if standard absorption costing is used as opposed to standard marginal costing.

Standard costing requires a great deal of input data, which can prove time-consuming and expensive, as can the maintenance of the cost database. The amount of detail required, together with a lack of historical detail, and lack of experience and further training requirements all add to this administrative burden.

Standard costing is usually used in organisations where the processes or jobs are repetitive. It is important to set accurate standards or else evaluation of performance will be meaningless. If the standard is weak then the comparison is of little value. However, it is difficult to strike a balance in setting accurate standards so that they both motivate the workforce and achieve the organisation's goals. There may be difficulties in determining which variances against standard are significant, and too narrow a focus on certain variances may exclude other useful information.

If performance evaluation is linked to **management by exception**, which assumes actual equals standard unless variances contradict that, there may be attempts by managers to cover up negative results. Morale may suffer if reprimands follow poor results and managers are not praised for positive results.

Further adverse impacts on behaviour may occur if managers and supervisors feel that they do not have an overall view and are involved only in limited areas, seeing only a small part of the big picture. Responsibility accounting must also ensure that controllable and non-controllable variances are separately identified.

Operating difficulties and frustration may be encountered through, for example, technological and environmental factors, assessment of standards of performance, departmental interdependence, variances reported at the wrong levels, the timing of revisions to standards, over-reaction to results, and the constant need to estimate. It is important to remember that there is a great deal of uncertainty in setting standards costs. This can arise due to inflation, economic and political factors. Standards therefore need to be continually updated and revised – once a year is usually not often enough.

Progress check 12.2	To what extent do the advantages of the use of standard costing outweigh its disadvantages?

Types of standard

In addition to current costs there are three types of standard that may be used as the basis for a standard costing system. The use of current standards by definition relates to current circumstances with regard to performance levels, wastage and inefficiencies. It may be observed from the following explanations that 'standard costing' can be seen to be flexible and dynamic. It should not be seen as a straitjacket.

Basic standards are those that remain unchanged since the previous period and probably many previous periods. They may be used for comparison but are likely to be out of date and irrelevant. As business circumstances may change dramatically in the market-place, so the original basic standard will not reflect the current situation.

Ideal standards are the results expected from perfect performance under perfect conditions. They assume no wastage, nor inefficiencies. However, although they may be aimed for they will be impossible to achieve and therefore provide a poor motivational tool.

Attainable standards are the results expected under normal operating conditions, having some allowances for wastage and a degree of inefficiency. Attainable standards should be set to be difficult but not impossible to achieve; they may therefore provide the most challenging targets and give the greatest motivation for achievement.

Progress check 12.3	What are the different types of standard that may be used as the basis for standard costing and which one may be the most appropriate?

Flexed budgets

We discussed flexible budgeting in Chapter 11. Control budgets need to be revised in line with actual levels of activity to provide more realistic levels of expected costs against which to measure performance. Such a revised budget is called a flexed budget which shows the costs (and revenues) expected as a result of changes in activity levels from those planned within the master budget.

The standards chosen for use in the budget preparation are also used in the revised flexed budget to provide a method of comparison with actual performance. This method allows comparison of costs on a like-for-like basis and so enables meaningful exception reporting of the analysis of variances.

This system of management control uses a **closed-loop system**. This is a system which allows corrective action using a feedforward or a feedback basis. A feedback control system is shown in Fig. 12.1 and provides the measurement of differences between planned outputs and actual outputs and the modification of subsequent actions or plans to achieve future required results. Fig. 12.2 illustrates a feedforward control system which forecasts

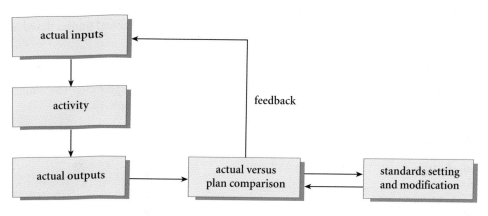

FIGURE 12.1   Feedback control system

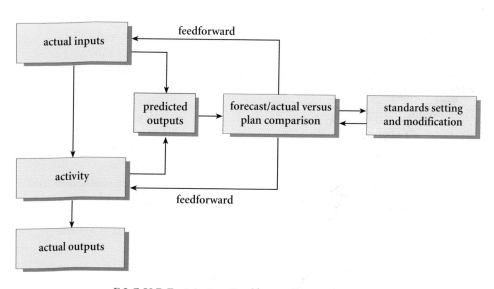

FIGURE 12.2   Feedforward control system

differences between actual and planned outcomes and implements action before the event to avoid such differences.

Normally, fixed overheads by definition are fixed over the short-term regardless of changes in the level of activity, for example, units sold, units produced, number of invoices. Equally, direct labour and direct materials costs may be assumed to vary directly with sales. In practice, there is usually a wide band of activity over which direct labour costs may not vary.

Care should be taken in using the above assumptions but we may consider that they hold true for the purpose of illustration of flexed budgets and variance analysis. The variance analysis can be routine but decisions resulting from the interpretation can be far-reaching. Consider how, following the public's reaction to buying products originating from genetically modified foodstuffs (soya or maize), many UK supermarkets publicly announced they would cease stocking them.

Progress check 12.4

Describe the way in which flexed budgets are used in a management control system.

We will consider an example which shows how a straight comparison of actual with budgeted performance may be refined through the preparation of a revised budget flexed in line with the actual activity level.

Example 12.2

Applejack Ltd planned to produce 600 drums of pie filling during September. The budget for September was prepared using the standard costs shown in Example 12.1.

Budget costs for September

Production	600 units
	£
Direct materials	
Sugar 600 kilos at £2 per kilo =	1,200
Apples 1,200 kilos at £3 per kilo =	3,600
	4,800
Direct labour	
600 hours at £8 per hour	4,800
Variable production overhead	
600 hours at £2 per hour	1,200
Fixed production overhead	
600 hours at £3 per hour	1,800
Total production cost	12,600

600 drums of filling were planned to be produced in the month at a manufacturing cost of £12,600.

At the end of September the actual output turned out to be 650 drums as follows:

Actual costs for September

Production		650 units
		£

Direct materials

Sugar	610 kilos at £2.10 per kilo =	1,281
Apples	1,210 kilos at £3.20 per kilo =	3,872
		5,153

Direct labour

500 hours at £9 per hour	4,500

Variable production overhead

500 hours at £1.50 per hour	750

Fixed production overhead

500 hours at £3.60 per hour	1,800
Total production cost	12,203

650 drums of filling were actually produced in the month at a manufacturing cost of £12,203.

We are required to prepare a flexed budget for September as the basis for subsequent variance analysis.

Answer

A flexed budget for Applejack Ltd must be prepared for 650 drums output. The flexed budget will use the standard costs shown in Example 12.1 to show what the costs would have been if the budget had been based on 650 drums instead of 600 drums.

Flexed budget costs for September

Production		650 units
		£

Direct materials

Sugar	650 kilos at £2 per kilo =	1,300
Apples	1,300 kilos at £3 per kilo =	3,900
		5,200

Direct labour

650 hours at £8 per hour	5,200

Variable production overhead

650 hours at £2 per hour	1,300

Fixed production overhead

650 hours at £3 per hour	1,950
Total production cost	13,650

If 650 drums of filling had been planned to be produced in the month the standard manufacturing cost would be £13,650.

Using Example 12.2, if we compare the total manufacturing cost of the flexed budget with the total actual cost for the month, the performance looks even better than the comparison with the total budgeted cost; the total cost is £1,447 less than expected at that level of output. However, whilst the comparison of total cost is favourable, this does not tell us anything about individual performance within each element of the budget; the impacts of the differences between the actual and the flexed budget with regard to:

- amounts of materials used
- materials prices
- direct labour hours
- direct labour rates
- overheads.

The analysis of the detailed variances in respect of each cost can identify each element making up the cost, the unit costs and the unit quantities, and tell us something about whether the individual cost performances were good or bad. In the year 2000 the UK saw an amazing upward demand for mobile telephones and a decline in the demand for university places (as a percentage of available places). Both sectors would have carried out an 'analysis of the detailed variances' during that year to assist in the determination of conclusions regarding cost performance.

Progress check 12.5

In what ways does a flexed budget provide a more realistic measure of actual performance than comparison with the original budget?

Variance analysis

A variance is the difference between a planned, budgeted or standard cost and the actual cost incurred. The same comparisons may be made for revenues. Variance analysis is the evaluation of performance by means of variances, whose timely reporting should maximise the opportunity for managerial action. These variances will be either favourable variances (F) or adverse variances (A). Neither should occur if the standard is correct and actual performance is as expected. A favourable variance is not necessarily good – it may be due to a weak standard. Management by exception assumes that actual performance will be the same as the standard unless variances contradict this.

Detailed variances can identify each difference within the elements making up cost or revenue by looking at unit prices and unit quantities. Variances may be due to:

- measurement errors
- use of standards that are out of date
- operations that are out of control
- random factors.

When variances occur it must then be considered as to whether these variances should be investigated or not. The variances may not be material, or it may not be cost effective to carry out such an investigation.

Calculation of variances

Let's look at the individual variances that occurred for the month of September in Apple-jack's manufacture of apple pie filling. We will analyse each of the variances and provide a detailed, line-by-line comparison of actual versus budget performance of each of the items that comprise the total actual to budget favourable variance of £397. The simplest way to start to examine the differences is to present the original budget, flexed budget and actual results in three columns for further analysis.

Example 12.3

We saw from Example 12.2 that on the face of it Applejack's performance for September was very good – higher than budget output (650 versus 600 units) at lower than budget costs (£12,203 versus £12,600).

Is it a good performance? If it is, how much of a good performance is it?

To determine how good Applejack's performance was for September we are required to provide an analysis of variances to explain the favourable total cost variance of £397 against budget (£12,600 − £12,203).

Answer

Applejack Ltd's budget, actual and flexed budget (from Example 12.2) for the production of apple pie filling for the month of September may be summarised as follows:

	Budget		**Flexed**			**Actual**	**Difference Actual– Flexed**
Units	600		650			650	–
	£		£			£	£
Direct materials							
Sugar	(600 × £2)	1,200	(650 × £2)	1,300	(610 × £2.10)	1,281	19
Apples	(1,200 × £3)	3,600	(1,300 × £3)	3,900	(1,210 × £3.20)	3,872	28
		4,800		5,200		5,153	47
Direct labour							
	(600 × £8)	4,800	(650 × £8)	5,200	(500 × £9)	4,500	700
Variable production overhead							
	(600 × £2)	1,200	(650 × £2)	1,300	(500 × £1.50)	750	550
Fixed production overhead							
	(600 × £3)	1,800	(650 × £3)	1,950	(500 × £3.60)	1,800	150
Total cost		12,600		13,650		12,203	1,447

A graphical representation, as shown at the top of page 430, of each of the cost elements and the total of actual costs compared with the flexed budget for output of 650 units gives a broad picture of Applejack Ltd's good performance.

Let's look at the detailed variances.

We have prepared a flexed budget, which in effect gives us a new starting point against which to compare actual performance more realistically. We have therefore already built in a variance, arising out of the change in volume from 600 drums to 650 drums. At a unit cost of £21 the total of this difference, or variance, is an adverse volume variance of £1,050 (50 × £21).

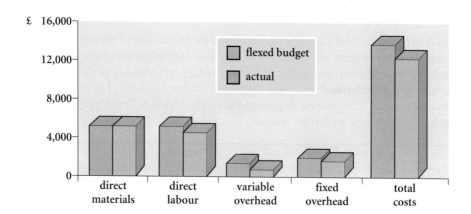

Volume:

Variance 650 drums less 600 drums at a total unit cost of £21 per drum £1,050A

We also need to consider the individual cost element variances, between actual costs and the flexed budget costs.

Materials:

Sugar usage was 40 kilos less than it should have been at a standard cost of £2 per kilo £80F

The sugar price was 10p more per kilo than standard for the 610 kilos used £61A

Apples usage was 90 kilos less than it should have been at a standard cost of £3 per kilo £270F

The apple price was 20p more per kilo than standard for the 1,210 kilos used £242A

Total materials variance actual versus flexed budget £47F

Direct labour:

Hours worked were 150 hours less than they should have been at a standard rate of £8 per hour £1,200F

The labour rate was £1 more per hour than standard for the 500 hours worked £500A

Total direct labour variance actual versus flexed budget £700F

Variable production overhead:

Hours worked were 150 hours less than they should have been at a standard rate of £2 per hour £300F

The overhead rate was 50p less per hour than standard for the 500 hours worked £250F

Total variable production overhead variance actual versus flexed budget £550F

Fixed production overhead:

Hours worked were 150 hours less than they should have been at a standard rate of £3 per hour £450F

Hours worked were 100 less (at £3 per hour) than required to absorb total fixed costs £300A

Total fixed production overhead variance actual versus flexed budget £150F

Total variances [£1,050A + £47F + £700F + £550F + £150F] =	£397F
Budget total costs	£12,600
Actual total costs	£12,203
Total variance (favourable)	£397

Several variances are calculated to quantify the difference in activity or volume. Most of the other variances show the impact of:

● differences in prices

– price variances
– rate variances
– expenditure variances

and

● differences in quantities

– usage variances
– efficiency variances

between those prices and quantities actually incurred and those which should have been expected at the actual level, or volume of output. The exception to this is the fixed production overhead variance, which is comprised of a fixed production overhead expenditure variance (budget minus actual cost) and a fixed production overhead volume variance.

The total fixed production variance is the difference between:

● the actual cost

and

● the cost shown in the flexed budget.

The two components of the total fixed production volume variance are:

● the fixed production overhead efficiency variance

– a 'normal' one that calculates the difference between actual and flexed hours at the standard overhead absorption rate

● the fixed production overhead capacity variance

– calculates the difference between actual and budgeted hours at the standard overhead absorption rate
– measures the amount by which overheads have been under or over-absorbed (under-absorbed in the Applejack example), caused by the actual hours worked differing from the hours originally budgeted to be worked.

In the Applejack example we have used the absorption costing approach to calculate unit standard costs for the product and therefore in the calculation of variances. Marginal costing may also be used to calculate unit standard costs for the product and calculation of variances. Some of the differences between the variances that are calculated are as one would expect, using contribution instead of profit. Another difference is in respect of production fixed costs, which of course are not absorbed into unit marginal product costs. The fixed production overhead variance using marginal costing is simply the difference between the actual and the budgeted cost.

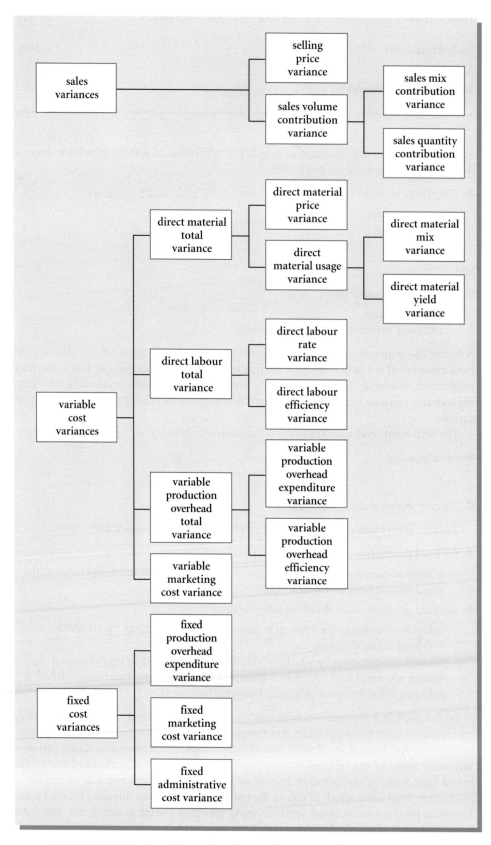

FIGURE 12.3 Chart of variances using marginal costing principles

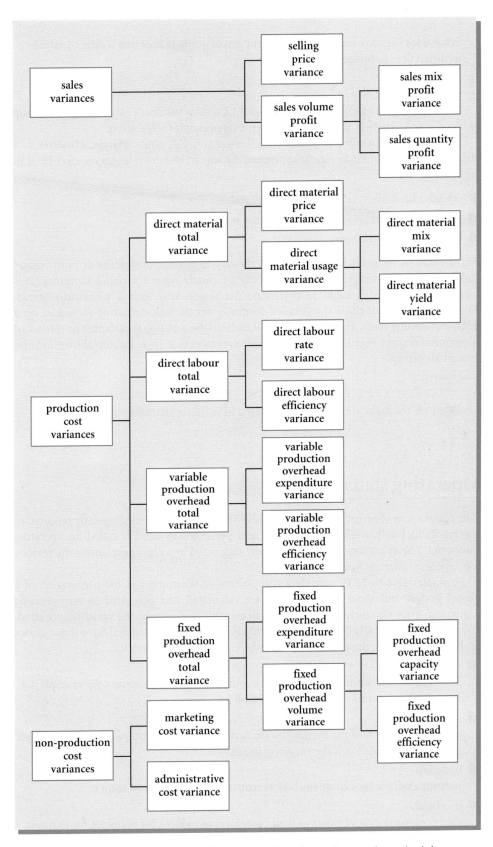

FIGURE 12.4 Chart of variances using absorption costing principles

Progress check 12.6

What does variance analysis tell us about actual performance that a direct analysis of differences to budget cannot tell us?

The hierarchy of variances in Figs 12.3 and 12.4 show variances using marginal costing principles and variances using absorption costing principles respectively.

A non-accountant will not usually be called upon to calculate variances. However, as a manager, it is important to clearly appreciate the way in which variances are calculated to be better able to:

- consider their materiality
- investigate the reasons for their occurrence if necessary
- take the appropriate corrective actions.

Explanation of variances is usually part of the day-to-day responsibilities of most budget holding managers. Unless there is knowledge of exactly what a variance represents it is virtually impossible to begin to determine the reason why such a variance occurred. Figs 12.5 and 12.8 include the detailed formulae for the calculation of variances, on a marginal costing basis. Figs 12.9 and 12.10 include the additional variances in respect of absorption costing. Figs 12.6 and 12.7 include variances that apply to both absorption and marginal costing.

Progress check 12.7

What are the main areas of cost considered in variance analysis?

Operating statements

The comparison of actual costs and revenues with budget is normally regularly reported to management (daily, weekly or monthly) and presented in what is called an operating statement. The operating statement is usually supported by a report explaining the reasons why specific variances have occurred.

Examples 12.4 to 12.10 provide a comprehensive illustration of the preparation of a flexed budget and show how variances are calculated and presented in an operating statement. They also include explanations of possible reasons why the variances occurred. While not including all possible variances that may be considered according to those shown in Figs 12.3 to 12.10, these examples show the key variances relating to:

- sales
  note how the marketing department of a company can use the results, for example, UK supermarkets' consumer products special offers
- labour
  note for example how the human resources department of a company may be involved in further investigation if the variances are material
- materials
  note for example how company buyers may need to look for new sources
- overheads
  many companies move closer to their customers or to low-cost premises, for example, in order to reduce overheads.

Sales contribution variances

Sales volume contribution

(budgeted sales quantity × standard contribution per unit) − (actual sales quantity × standard contribution per unit)

Which can be split into:

Sales quantity contribution

(budgeted sales quantity × budgeted weighted average standard contribution per unit) − (total actual sales quantity × budgeted weighted average standard contribution per unit)

Sales mix contribution

(actual sales quantity × budgeted weighted average standard contribution per unit) − (actual sales quantity × individual standard contribution per unit)

Sales price

(actual sales quantity × standard selling price per unit) − actual sales revenue

FIGURE 12.5   Sales variances on a marginal costing basis

Materials variances

Direct material price

(actual quantity of material purchased × standard price) − actual cost of material purchased

Direct material usage

(standard quantity for actual production × standard material cost per unit) − (actual material quantity used × standard cost per unit)

Which can be split into:

Direct material mix

(actual input quantity − standard material input quantity for the output produced) × (standard weighted average cost per input unit − standard cost per input unit)

Direct material yield

(actual material input quantity − standard material input quantity for the output produced) × standard weighted average cost per unit of material input

Or

(actual material input quantity × standard cost per unit) − (total actual material input in standard proportions × standard cost per unit)

FIGURE 12.6   Direct materials variances

Labour variances

Direct labour rate

(actual hours paid × standard direct labour rate per hour) − (actual hours paid × actual direct labour rate per hour)

Direct labour efficiency

(actual production in standard hours × standard direct labour rate per hour) − (actual direct labour hours worked × standard direct labour rate per hour)

FIGURE 12.7   Direct labour variances

Overhead variances

Variable production overhead expenditure

actual cost incurred − (actual hours worked × standard variable production overhead absorption rate per hour)

Variable production overhead efficiency

(actual hours worked × standard variable production overhead absorption rate per hour) − (actual production in standard hours × standard variable production overhead absorption rate per hour)

Fixed production overhead expenditure

budgeted fixed production overhead − actual fixed production overhead

FIGURE 12.8   Overheads variances on a marginal costing basis

Sales profit variances

Sales volume profit

(budgeted sales quantity × standard profit per unit) − (actual sales quantity × standard profit per unit)

Which can be split into:

Sales quantity profit

(budgeted sales quantity × budgeted weighted average standard profit per unit) − (total actual sales quantity × budgeted weighted average standard profit per unit)

Sales mix profit

(actual sales quantity × budgeted weighted average standard profit per unit) − (actual sales quantity × individual standard profit per unit)

FIGURE 12.9   Sales variances on an absorption costing basis

Overheads variances

Fixed production overhead volume

(actual production in standard hours × standard fixed production overhead absorption rate per hour) − budgeted fixed production overhead

Which can be split into:

Fixed production overhead efficiency

(actual hours worked × standard fixed production overhead absorption rate per hour) − (actual production in standard hours × standard fixed production overhead absorption rate per hour)

Fixed production overhead capacity

(actual hours worked × standard fixed production overhead absorption rate per hour) − (budgeted hours to be worked × standard fixed production overhead absorption rate per hour)

FIGURE 12.10   Overheads variances on an absorption costing basis

Example 12.4

Dymocks Ltd manufactures large ornamental garden pots, called the El Greco, the standards for which are as follows:

Direct labour	1 hour at £4 per hour
Direct materials	2 kgs at £7.50 per kg
Variable overheads	£3 per direct labour hour
Selling price	£50 per unit

Fixed overheads are budgeted at £4,000 and absorbed on a direct labour hours basis. Dymocks have budgeted to produce and sell 800 Grecos in the month of July.

Using standard costs, the budget for El Grecos for July was:

		£
Sales	800 × £50 per unit	40,000
Direct labour	800 × 1 hour × £4 per hour per unit	(3,200)
Direct materials	800 × 2 kg × £7.50 per kg per unit	(12,000)
Variable overheads	800 × 1 hour × £3 per direct labour hour	(2,400)
Fixed overheads	800 × 1 hour × £5 per direct labour hour	(4,000)
Budgeted profit for July		18,400

The standard profit per unit used in the budget $= \dfrac{£18,400}{800 \text{ units}} = £23$ per unit

Actual results for July were:		£
Sales	900 × £48	43,200
Direct labour	850 hours × £3.50 per hour	(2,975)
Direct materials	1,400 kgs × £8 per kg	(11,200)
Variable overheads	actual	(2,750)
Fixed overheads	actual	(5,000)
Actual profit for July		21,275

We are required to prepare:

(i) a flexed budget for July

(ii) a summary comparing the actual results for July with the budget and the flexed budget.

◀ **Answer**

The flexed budget for July for sales of 900 units is:

		£
Sales	900 × £50 per unit	45,000
Direct labour	900 × 1 hour × £4 per hour per unit	(3,600)
Direct materials	900 × 2 kg × £7.50 per kg per unit	(13,500)
Variable overheads	900 × 1 hour × £3 per direct labour hour	(2,700)
Fixed overheads		(4,000)
Flexed budgeted profit for July		21,200

The July results for Dymocks Ltd may be summarised as follows:

	£ Budget	£ Actual	£ Flexed	£ Difference Actual − Flexed
Sales	40,000	43,200	45,000	(1,800)
Direct labour	(3,200)	(2,975)	(3,600)	625
Direct materials	(12,000)	(11,200)	(13,500)	2,300
Variable overheads	(2,400)	(2,750)	(2,700)	(50)
Fixed overheads	(4,000)	(5,000)	(4,000)	(1,000)
Profit	18,400	21,275	21,200	75

The variance or the difference between the budget and the flexed budget of £2,800 (£21,200 − £18,400) is only due to volume. The profit variances for sales volume and fixed overheads volume are the only ones that will need to be considered between the flexed budget and the budget. All other variances are between actual results and the flexed budget.

Example 12.5

Using the summary of results for Dymocks Ltd for July from Example 12.4 we are required to prepare an analysis of sales variances, and give an explanation of why these variances might have occurred.

Answer

Sales variances

Sales volume profit

(budgeted sales quantity × standard profit per unit) − (actual sales quantity × standard profit per unit)

measuring the effect of changing sales volumes on profit

(800 × £23) − (900 × £23)   = £2,300 (F)   (one part of the profit variance of £2,800 noted in Example 12.4)

Sales price

(actual sales quantity $\times$ standard selling price per unit) $-$ actual sales revenue

measuring the effect of selling prices different to those budgeted

$(900 \times £50) - £43,200 \qquad = £1,800$ (A) \qquad (see Example 12.4 summary)

Possible reasons for the above variances:

– selling prices are likely to affect sales volumes

– external factors such as economic recession, changes in demand, or increased competition

– prices not achievable perhaps due to lack of market research or bad planning.

Example 12.6

Using the summary of results for Dymocks Ltd for July from Example 12.4 we are required to prepare an analysis of materials variances, and give an explanation of why these variances might have occurred.

Answer

Materials variances

Direct material price

(actual quantity of material purchased $\times$ standard price) $-$ actual cost of material purchased

$(1,400 \times £7.50) - £11,200 \qquad = £700$ (A)

Direct material usage

(standard quantity for actual production $\times$ standard material cost per unit) $-$ (actual material quantity used $\times$ standard cost per unit)

$(1,800 \times £7.50) - (1,400 \times £7.50) \quad = £3,000$ (F)

Total materials variances $\qquad\qquad £2,300$ (F) \qquad (see Example 12.4 summary)

Possible reasons for the above variances

– market conditions have changed

– foreign currency exchange rates may have changed (if applicable)

– supplier discounts have been reduced

– changes in the quality levels of materials used

– there may be a supplier invoicing error

– stock control has improved

– the skills of the labour force has changed

– production methods have changed.

Note that materials price variances occur at two points: standard price compared to receipt of goods price; receipt of goods price compared to invoiced price.

Example 12.7

Using the summary of results for Dymocks Ltd for July from Example 12.4 we are required to prepare an analysis of direct labour variances, and give an explanation of why these variances might have occurred.

Answer

Direct labour variances

Direct labour rate

(actual hours paid × standard direct labour rate per hour) − (actual hours paid × actual direct labour rate per hour)

(850 × £4) − (850 × £3.50) = £425 (F)

Direct labour efficiency

(actual production in standard hours × standard direct labour rate per hour) − (actual direct labour hours worked × standard direct labour rate per hour)

(900 × £4) − (850 × £4)   = £200 (F)

Total direct labour variances   £625 (F)   (see Example 12.4 summary)

Possible reasons for the above variances:

– wage rate negotiations
– changes in the skills of the labour force
– better than expected impact of the effect of the learning curve
– impact of machinery efficiency, levels of maintenance, or use of different materials, with changed levels of quality.

Example 12.8

Using the summary of results for Dymocks Ltd for July from Example 12.4 we are required to prepare an analysis of variable overhead variances, and give an explanation of why these variances might have occurred.

Answer

Variable overhead variances

Variable production overhead expenditure

actual cost incurred − (actual hours worked × standard variable production overhead absorption rate per hour)

£2,750 − (850 × £3.50)   = £225 (A)

Variable production overhead efficiency

(actual hours worked × standard variable production overhead absorption rate per hour) − (actual production in standard hours × standard variable production overhead absorption rate per hour)

(850 × £3.50) − (900 × £3.50) = £175 (F)

Total variable overhead variances   £50 (A)   (see Example 12.4 summary)

Possible reasons for the above variances may be:

- related to the direct labour variances
- due to a number of individual variances within total variable overheads
- changes in the overhead rate with different levels of activity.

Example 12.9

Using the summary of results for Dymocks Ltd for July from Example 12.4 we are required to prepare an analysis of fixed overhead variances, and give an explanation of why these variances might have occurred.

Answer

Fixed overhead variances

Fixed production overhead expenditure

budgeted fixed production overhead − actual fixed production overhead

£4,000 − £5,000   = £1,000 (A)   (see Example 12.4 summary)

Fixed production overhead volume

(actual production in standard hours × standard fixed production overhead absorption rate per hour) − budgeted fixed production overhead

(900 × £5) − £4,000   = £500 (F)   (one part of the profit variance of £2,800 noted in Example 12.4)

Possible reasons for the above variances:

- due to a number of individual variances within total fixed overheads

---

Example 12.10

Using the variances calculated for Dymocks Ltd for July we are required to prepare an operating statement that reconciles the actual profit for July to the budgeted profit for July.

Answer

The actual profit for July may be reconciled with the budgeted profit by summarising the variances:

Operating statement

	£	£	£
Budget profit (Example 12.4)			18,400
Sales variances			
Sales volume (Example 12.5)	2,300 (F)		
Sales price (Example 12.5)	1,800 (A)	500 (F)	
Direct materials variances			
Materials price (Example 12.6)	700 (A)		
Materials usage (Example 12.6)	3,000 (F)	2,300 (F)	

◀ **Direct labour variances**

Labour rate (Example 12.7)	425 (F)	
Labour efficiency (Example 12.7)	200 (F)	625 (F)
Variable overheads variances		
Expenditure (Example 12.8)	225 (A)	
Efficiency (Example 12.8)	175 (F)	50 (A)
Fixed overheads variances		
Expenditure (Example 12.9)	1,000 (A)	
Volume (Example 12.9)	500 (F)	500 (A)
		2,875 (F)
Actual profit (Example 12.4)		21,275

Progress check 12.8

What are the main differences between variance analysis using marginal costing and variance analysis using absorption costing?

The reasons for variances

Although not an exhaustive list of possible causes, the following provides the reasons for most of the common variances encountered in most manufacturing and service businesses:

- direct material price: skills of purchasing department, quality of materials, price inflation, supplier discounts, foreign currency exchange rate fluctuations, invoicing errors
- direct material usage: quality of materials, labour efficiency, pilfering, stock control, quality control
- direct labour rate: use of higher or lower skilled labour than planned, wage inflation, or union agreement
- direct labour efficiency: use of higher or lower skilled labour than planned, quality of materials, efficiency of plant and machinery, better or worse than expected learning curve performance, inaccurate time allocation – employees have to learn a new process and then repeat that process for real many times, within times established during the learning curve evaluation
- overhead expenditure: inflation, wastage, resource usage savings, changes in services – many companies are outsourcing basic in-house services, for example accounting
- overhead efficiency: labour efficiency, efficiency of plant and machinery, technological changes
- overhead capacity: under or over-utilisation of plant capacity, idle time.

Progress check 12.9

Most of the reasons for materials variances may be identified so that the appropriate corrective actions can be taken. What are the types of action that may be taken?

Without exploring the detail, we have also already mentioned materials mix and yield variances that show the effects on costs of changing the mix of materials input, and of materials input yielding either more or less output than expected.

Planning and operational variances

The above discussion has necessarily focused on the description, calculation and understanding of the most common variances that one may come across on a day-to-day basis in a manufacturing or service environment. Regarding each resource, such variances are normally based on the questions:

● what did it cost?

and

● what should it have cost?

or

● how long did it take?

and

● how long should it have taken?

Further light may be shown on the reasons for differences between actual and planned performance through taking variance analysis to a greater level of sophistication than those outlined in the charts and examples above.

There are inevitably problems with traditional variance analyses, which are invariably due to:

● failure to distinguish variances due to an incorrect standard from those that are real operational variances

● failure to indicate which variances are controllable and which are uncontrollable

● failure to identify responsibility for variances

● lack of updating standards to current efficiency levels.

It is sufficient for our purposes to be aware of *ex post* variance analysis, which distinguishes between planning and operational variances. **Planning variances** are due to inaccuracies in the original (*ex ante*) budget. The variances between the new budget that is drawn up to reflect actual conditions during the budget (the *ex post* budget) can then be compared with actual performance to show **operational variances**.

There are a number of variance investigation decision models:

● the percentage rule, which prompts investigation if variances are greater than a certain percentage of the standard

● statistical significance rule, which investigates variances that are 'unusual' occurrences using a normal distribution

● statistical control charts, which provide warning limits and action limits.

It is useful for non-financial managers to be aware of some of these further uses of variances, even though the detail of these is outside the scope of this book.

Summary of key points

- Standard costing can be used to calculate costs of units or processes that may be used in budgeted costs.
- Not all budgeted amounts are standard amounts, as the latter will be precise by nature, unlike budgeted amounts.
- Standard costing provides the basis for performance evaluation and control from comparison of actual performance against budget through the setting of predetermined cost estimates.
- A flexed budget reflects the costs or revenues expected as a result of changes in activity levels from those planned in the master budget.
- A flexed budget provides a more realistic basis for comparison of actual performance.
- Flexed budgets enable comparison of actual costs and revenues on a like-for-like basis through the calculation of differences, or variances.
- Variances are the difference between planned, budgeted or standard costs (or revenues) and actual costs incurred and may be summarised in an operating statement to reconcile budget with actual performance.
- Variances between actual and standard performance may be investigated to explain the reasons for the differences through preparation of a complete analysis of all variances, or alternatively through the use of exception reporting that highlights only significant variances.
- Inaccuracies in original budgets may be identified through planning variances, and actual performance may then be compared with a subsequently revised budget to show operational variances.

Glossary of key terms

attainable standard A standard that assumes efficient levels of operation, but which includes allowances for normal loss, waste and machine downtime.

basic standard A standard that remains unchanged since the previous period and probably many previous periods, that may be used for comparison but is likely to be out of date and irrelevant.

closed-loop system A control system that includes a provision for corrective action, taken on either a feedback or a feedforward basis.

ex ante Means before the event. An *ex ante* budget, or standard, is set before a period of activity commences, and is based on the best information available at that time on expected levels of cost, performance, etc.

ex post Means after the event. An *ex post* budget, or standard, is set after the end of a period of activity, when it can represent the optimum

achievable level of performance in the conditions which were experienced. Thus the budget can be flexed, and the standards can reflect factors such as unanticipated changes in technology and in price levels.

ideal standard A standard that is only attainable under the most favourable conditions and makes no allowance for normal loss, waste and machine downtime.

management by exception The practice of focusing on activities which require attention and ignoring those which appear to be conforming to expectations.

materiality Information is material if its omission or misstatement could influence the economic decisions of users taken on the basis of financial information. Materiality depends on the size of the item or error judged in the particular circumstances of its omission or misstatement.

operational variance A classification of variances in which non-standard performance is defined as being that which differs from an *ex post* standard. Operational variances can relate to any element of the standard product specification.

planning variance A planning or revision variance is a classification of variances caused by *ex ante* budget allowances being changed to an *ex post* basis.

standard A benchmark measurement of resource usage, set in defined conditions.

standard cost The planned unit cost of the products, components or services produced in a period. The standard cost may be determined on a number of bases. The main uses of standard costs are in performance measurement, control, stock valuation and in the establishment of selling prices.

Assessment material

Questions

Q12.1 How is standard costing used in the preparation of budgets?

Q12.2 (i)   What are the benefits of using standard costing?

(ii)   What type of standard may best ensure that those benefits are achieved?

(iii) How are standards used to achieve those benefits?

Q12.3 Describe and illustrate the technique of flexible budgeting.

Q12.4 (i)   What is management by exception?

(ii)   How is variance analysis used to support this technique?

Q12.5 (i)   Outline the main variances that may be reported using the bases of absorption costing and marginal costing.

(ii)   What do these variances tell us about direct labour, direct materials, and overhead costs?

Q12.6 Describe the main reasons why usage and efficiency variances may occur and illustrate these with some examples.

Q12.7 What are mix and yield variances?

Q12.8 (i)   Explain some of the problems associated with traditional variance reporting.

(ii)   What are the roles of planning and operational variances?

Discussion points

D12.1 'We set the budget once a year and then compare the actual profit after the end of the financial year. If actual profit is below budget, then everyone needs to make more effort to ensure this doesn't happen the following year.' Discuss.

D12.2 'The standard-setting process is sometimes seen as management's way of establishing targets that demand better and better manufacturing performance.' To what extent do you think that is true, and if it is true how effectively do you think the standard-setting process achieves that objective?

D12.3 To what extent do you think that the techniques of flexed budgets and variance analysis complicate the otherwise simple process of comparing the various areas of actual performance against budget?

Exercises

Solutions are provided in Appendix 4 to all exercise numbers highlighted in colour.

Level I

E12.1 *Time allowed – 60 minutes*

Nilbog Ltd makes garden gnomes. It uses standard costs and has budgeted to produce and sell 130,000 Fishermen (their top of the range gnome) in 2001. Nilbog's budget for the year is phased over 13 four-week periods, and production and sales are spread evenly in the budget.

Budgeted standards costs and selling prices for the Fisherman are:

		£
Direct materials	3 cu. yds at £3.60	10.80
Direct labour	2 hours at £6.60 per hour	13.20
Variable overheads	2 hours at £2.40 per hour	4.80
Fixed overheads	2 hours at £4.80 per hour	9.60
Standard cost of one Fisherman		38.40
Standard profit		9.60
Standard selling price		48.00

The actual results for period five, a four-week period, were:

Sales	9,000 Fishermen at £48 each
Production	9,600 Fishermen
Purchase of direct materials	30,000 cu. yards at a cost of £115,200
Direct materials usage	28,000 cu. yards
Direct labour cost	£142,560 over 22,000 hours
Variable overhead	£44,000
Fixed overhead	£100,000

There was no work-in-progress at the start or at the end of period 5. Finished goods and materials stocks are valued at standard cost.

You are required to prepare a flexed budget and an operating statement for Nilbog Ltd for period 5, showing the profit for the period and all standard variances with their detailed calculations, together with an explanation of their likely causes.

E12.2 *Time allowed – 90 minutes*

Cyclops plc is an electronics business that manufactures television sets, and uses a standard costing system. The TV cabinets division of Cyclops manufactures, for sale within the company, the plastic cases for one of their most popular models, the F24. The results for the F24 for October 2000 were as follows:

	Actual	**Budget**
Sales units	61,200	40,800
	£	£
Sales	348,840	244,800
Direct labour	133,280	81,600
Direct materials	114,240	81,600
Variable overheads	27,200	16,320
Contribution	74,120	65,280
Fixed overheads	25,000	20,400
Profit	49,120	44,880

The budget had been finalised for 2000 using standard costs for that year.

Sales volumes were increasing and just prior to October the TV cabinets division expected around 50% increase in sales volumes for the month. The division had unused capacity to take up this expected increase in volume. Vimla Patel had recently been appointed as commercial manager and she proposed a 30p selling price reduction per unit, which was effective from 1 October.

Melanie Bellamy, Cyclops purchasing manager had negotiated a 4% discount on the standard price of raw materials purchased and used from October. The production manager Graham Brown had been having problems with quality due to the learning curve and some operators who were still receiving training. Training had been completed by the end of September. This meant some increase in operator pay rates but the planned productivity rate was maintained and there was less materials wastage in October. The variable costs of utilities increased in October, primarily due to electricity and gas price increases.

Graham Brown was able to keep stock levels of materials and finished product at the same level at the start and end of October.

You are required to:

(i)   **prepare an operating statement that provides an analysis of the variances between actual and budget for October on a marginal costing basis, highlighting the performance of each of the managers**

(ii) **give full explanations of why the variances may have occurred**

(iii) **and (iv) prepare the same analysis and explanations as (i) and (ii) above using absorption costing**

(v)   **explain whether absorption costing provides the best basis for assessment of manager performance.**

Level II

E12.3 *Time allowed – 90 minutes*

White Heaven Ltd manufactures a bathroom basin, the Shell and uses standard costing based on a monthly output of 50,000 units. White Heaven uses two types of direct labour and two items of raw material.

Variable costs include

Indirect labour costs of materials handlers and stores persons

Maintenance labour costs

General production overheads

Fixed costs include

Supervisory salaries

Other overheads such as

Factory rent

Electricity standing charges

Gas standing charges

The **ideal** standard cost of a Shell is as follows:

Direct labour	1 hour at £7.20 per hour	grade A
	0.75 hours at £6.00 per hour	grade B
Direct materials	5 kgs at £2 per kg	clay
	3 kgs at £4 per kg	glaze
Indirect labour	0.25 hours at £5.00 per hour	
Maintenance	0.05 hours at £10.00 per hour	
Variable overheads	15% of direct materials cost, plus 10% of direct labour cost	
Supervisory salaries	£95,000 per month	
Other fixed overheads	£109,000 per month	

In June 2000 adjustments were agreed as the basis for the following month's **attainable** standard costs:

Grade A labour rates increased by 40p, grade B by 30p and indirect and maintenance labour by 20p

Grade B labour hours increased by 0.05 hours because of process delays due to a tool change problem

Turnover of operators has meant recruiting some inexperienced, untrained operators

10% of grade A operators with 50% efficiency

25% of grade B operators with 60% efficiency

The clay is to be upgraded in quality with the supplier imposing a 10% surcharge

The glaze will be purchased in larger batches with a 12.5% discount but resulting in an increase in variable overheads to 20% of materials cost for this type of material.

For the July output of 49,000 Shells you are required to calculate:

(i)   the ideal standard cost for a Shell

(ii)   the attainable standard cost for a Shell for July 2000

(iii) the total variance between the ideal and attainable standards.

E12.4 *Time allowed – 90 minutes*

White Heaven Ltd (see Exercise E12.3) actually produced 49,000 Shells during July 2000 and the actual costs for the month were as follows:

Direct labour	52,000 hours at £7.60 per hour	grade A
	43,500 hours at £6.30 per hour	grade B
Direct materials	247,000 kgs at £2.16 per kg	clay
	149,000 kgs at £3.60 per kg	glaze
Indirect labour	12,000 hours at £5.20 per hour	
Maintenance	2,250 hours at £10.20 per hour	
Variable overheads	£251,000	
Supervisory salaries	£97,000	
Other fixed overheads	£110,000	

You are required to:

(i)   calculate the variances between actual costs for July 2000 and the attainable standard

(ii)   prepare an operating statement that summarises the variances

(iii) reconcile the actual cost for July with the expected total attainable cost

(iv)   comment on the likely reasons for each of the variances.

E12.5 *Time allowed – 90 minutes*

Millennium Models Ltd manufactured an ornamental gift for the tourist trade. The standard variable cost per unit was:

Materials price	£0.85 per kg
Unit material usage	2 kgs
Direct labour rate	£4.20 per hour
Standard labour per unit	42 minutes
Selling price per unit	£5.84

Fixed overhead is recovered on the basis of units produced at the rate of £0.82 per unit and Millennium planned to sell 4,300 units in November 1999.
     In November 1999 Millennium's actual performance was:

Units manufactured and sold	4,100
Sales	£24,805
Materials used	6,600 kgs at £0.83
	1,900 kgs at £0.89
Direct labour paid	2,975 at £4.50 per hour
Overheads incurred	£3,800

You are required to:

(i) prepare a budget to actual profit reconciliation for November 1999 including an analysis of sales, materials, and labour variances

(ii) calculate the fixed overhead expenditure variance and fixed overhead volume variances for November 1999.

E12.6 *Time allowed – 90 minutes*

Using the information about Millennium Models Ltd from Exercise E12.5:

(i) explain what you think are the advantages and disadvantages of the implementation of a standard costing system by Millennium Ltd

(ii) explain how the analyses of variances may have helped Millennium Models Ltd control the business

(iii) prepare a report that explains the variance analysis you have carried out in Exercise E12.5 above and provides explanations of Millennium's performance.

Case Study II

ARTHURSTONE

During the 1990s, Sir William Kiloshake began work on a project that had been a dream he had wished to realise for many years.

Bill was a keen botanist and environmentalist and had been brought up close to a large country house called Arthurstone, which stood in a 500-acre estate in which there had once been extensive gardens. The house had long since gone into disrepair and the gardens had been untended for around 50 years.

Bill had brought together a consortium of experts to investigate how Arthurstone could be developed into a national educational and tourist facility.

After many years of feasibility studies, market research, soil analyses, and Government grant applications, the project became a reality by 1997. The project would cost £35m to restore the building and re-establish the gardens. This was supported by a National Lottery grant of £17m. It was expected that around 350,000 people would visit Arthurstone every year, mostly during the summer months.

The net project cost investment of £18m (£35m total cost less £17m grant) had been obtained from sponsorship from the private sector. However, the project needed to be self-financing from its first day of opening to the public, which was 1 May 2000. The costs associated with running the house and gardens are broadly:

Variable operational costs

Fixed operational costs

Variable marketing and administrative costs

Fixed marketing and administrative costs.

The initial price for admission to Arthurstone was £6 per person.

Although market research had been carried out, there was still some uncertainty about the reliability of visitor estimates. Equally, the management of Arthurstone did not have much information about the elasticity of demand for garden attractions and were not convinced that the admission price of £6 was the optimum price. For its first year of operation there were to be no discounts for children, senior citizens, or job seekers/ unemployed persons; neither were there to be volume discounts for large parties of visitors.

The following budget information relates to the first four months that Arthurstone would be open to the public:

	Month 1		Month 2		Month 3		Month 4	
	Visitors	£	Visitors	£	Visitors	£	Visitors	£
Sales	85,000	510,000	90,000	540,000	95,000	570,000	85,000	510,000
Variable operational costs		153,000		162,000		171,000		153,000
Fixed operational costs		45,000		45,000		45,000		45,000
Variable marketing and administrative costs		51,000		54,000		57,000		51,000
Fixed marketing and administrative costs		52,500		52,500		52,500		52,500

The budget for 2000/2001 was prepared on the assumption that during its first year of operation there would be no visitors during the months September to April. During that period of course no variable costs would be incurred.

Required

(i) Prepare the budgeted profit and loss account for each of the first six months, and the total for the year to 30 April 2001, on a marginal costing basis.

(ii) Explain the reasons for the differences in profit levels between the first four months of operation (with supporting calculations).

(iii) Draw a break-even chart that shows the admission price to be charged at the break-even point for Arthurstone.

(iv) What admission price to Arthurstone should be charged to achieve a profit of 10% mark-up on full absorption costs?

(v) What admission price to Arthurstone should be charged to achieve a target profit of £500,000 for the year May 2000 to April 2001?

(vi) What may be the possible impact of charging the prices calculated in (iv) and (v) above, and to what factors may that impact be sensitive?

(vii) At the prices calculated in (iv) and (v), by what percentage levels may the visitor numbers drop from that budgeted before Arthurstone started to make a loss?

(viii) Prepare a short report, which includes any calculations that you consider relevant, outlinings the factors that may be discussed with regard to a proposal that has been made to introduce a revised pricing structure for 2001/2002 which includes discounting for children, senior citizens, job seekers/unemployed persons, and large parties of visitors.

PART III

Business finance

Part III is about business finance, and provides an introduction to financial management. Financial management is broadly defined as the management of all the processes associated with the efficient acquisition and deployment of both short and long-term financial resources. Businesses raise money from shareholders and lenders to invest in assets, which are used to increase the wealth of the business and its owners. The underlying fundamental economic objective of a company is to maximise shareholder wealth.

Chapter 13 considers how businesses make decisions about potential investments that may be made, in order to ensure that the wealth of the business will be increased. This is an important area of decision-making that usually involves a great deal of money and relatively long-term commitments that therefore requires techniques to ensure that the financial objectives of the company are in line with the interests of the shareholders.

Chapter 14 deals with sources of business finance for investment in businesses. This relates to the various types of funding available to business, including the raising of funds from the owners of the business (the shareholders) and from lenders external to the business. Chapter 14 also shows how the costs of the alternative sources of capital are used in the calculation of the overall cost of capital that may be used by companies as the discount rate to evaluate proposed investments in capital projects, and in the calculation of economic value added (EVA) to evaluate company performance.

Finally, in Chapter 15, we look at one of the areas of funds management internal to the business, the management of working capital. Working capital comprises the short-term assets of the business, stock, trade debtors, and cash and claims on the business, trade creditors. This chapter deals with how these important items may be effectively managed.

Capital investment decisions

LEARNING OBJECTIVES

Completion of this chapter will enable you to:

- explain what is meant by an investment

- outline the key principles underlying investment selection criteria

- outline the strengths and weaknesses of the five investment appraisal criteria

- explain what is meant by discounted cash flow (DCF)

- consider investment selection using the appraisal criteria of net present value (NPV) and internal rate of return (IRR)

- explain the effects of inflation, working capital requirements, length and timing of projects, taxation, and risk and uncertainty on investment criteria calculations

- evaluate the impact of risk and the use of sensitivity analysis in decision-making

- consider the ways in which capital projects may be controlled and reviewed

- appreciate the importance of the project post-completion audit

Introduction

We have seen in Part II how the management accountant is involved with providing financial and non-financial information and analysis to enable managers to evaluate alternative proposals and to make decisions.

In Chapter 10 we had an introduction into the ways in which accounting and financial information may be used as an aid to decision-making. This chapter looks at the specific area of decision-making that relates to investment. Such decisions may relate to whether or not to invest in a project, or choices between investment in alternative projects which are competing for resources.

We will begin by looking at exactly what an investment is, and outlining the techniques used to decide on whether or not to invest, and how to choose between alternative investments.

We shall evaluate the advantages and disadvantages of the five main investment appraisal criteria used by companies and consider examples that demonstrate their use. The most important of these are the discounted cash flow methods of net present value (NPV), and internal rate of return (IRR). The technique of discounted cash flow (DCF) will be fully explained.

In addition to the initial costs of an investment and the returns expected from it, a number of other factors usually need to be taken into account in investment decision-making. These include, for example, inflation, the need for working capital, the length and timing of the project, and taxation. We will consider the possible impact of these factors and how the effects of risk and uncertainty on the appraisal of investments may be quantified using sensitivity analysis.

Appraisal of an investment is more than an accounting exercise. An investment decision is a crucially significant and important decision for a business. It is usually a highly politically charged area in the management of an organisation, which if mismanaged is capable of destroying shareholder value. Once an investment decision has been made the project may then be planned and implemented. This chapter closes with an introduction to the ways in which capital investment projects may be controlled and reviewed.

What is an investment?

For the accountant an investment appears on the assets side of the balance sheet under fixed assets. For the finance director an investment is any decision that implies expenditure today with the expectation that it will generate cash inflows tomorrow.

Investment decisions are extremely important because they are invariably concerned with the future survival, prosperity and growth of the organisation. The organisation's primary objective of maximisation of shareholder wealth is a basic assumption that continues to hold true. Investments must be made both to maintain shareholder wealth and to increase it. To meet the shareholder wealth maximisation objective it is crucial that those managing the organisation make optimal decisions that are based on the best information available and use of the most appropriate appraisal techniques.

At the corporate level, investment (in shares) relates to the amount that shareholders are willing to invest in the equity of a company in the expectation of future cash flows in the form of dividends and enhancement of share price. The level of future dividends and share price enhancement are in turn dependent on to what extent the company is able to optimise returns on 'real' investment (investment in companies, plant, machinery, working capital) in new products, projects, new business, and so on. There is a great deal of pressure on chief executives to ensure that profitable 'real' investments are made to provide sustained dividend growth and increasing share prices.

Investment decisions faced by companies are therefore financially driven, and so if performance is deemed inadequate or unlikely to meet shareholder expectations, then the pressure becomes even greater to identify alternative, more profitable projects. Decisions are made by managers and not by the management accountant. Levels of authority within the management hierarchy are determined by company policy. Companies normally establish limits at each management level for each type of decision, and the level of expenditure allowed. The approval of one or more directors is normally required for all capital expenditure and for major projects.

Investment may appear in the balance sheet within fixed assets in line with the accountants' definition, for example, land, buildings, plant, machinery, etc. It may also appear in the profit and loss account in terms of public relations, staff training, or research and development. In some cases the amount of money gained as a result of making an investment is relatively easy to measure, such as cost savings, capacity increases, etc. In other cases, it may be impossible to measure the gains – company image, education, and so on. The amount of spend may be easily forecast, for example the costs of computerisation of a process to reduce the production of non-quality products. In other projects, such as research and development, costs may be more uncertain.

Regardless, an investment decision is required before spending shareholders' and lenders' funds. The decision made needs to be one that shareholders and lenders would be happy with; it is one that is expected to provide anticipated gains in real terms that greatly exceed the funds spent today, in other words a good return on the money invested. Otherwise the investment should not be made.

Progress check 13.1

Describe what is meant by investment.

Investment appraisal criteria

The five main methods used in investment appraisal are shown in Fig. 13.1:

- the **accounting rate of return (ARR)** for appraising capital investment projects is based on profits and the costs of investment; it takes no account of cash flows or the time value of money
- the **payback** method for appraising capital investment projects is based on cash flows, but also ignores the time value of money

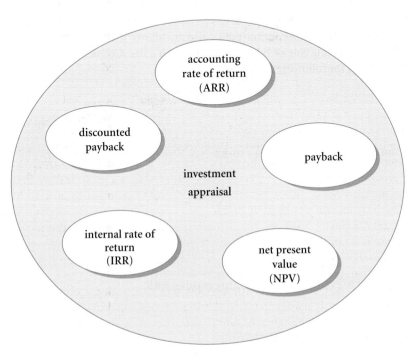

FIGURE 13.1   The five main investment appraisal criteria methods

- net present value (NPV) is one of the two most widely used investment decision criteria, which are based on cash flow and the time value of money
- internal rate of return (IRR) is the second of the two most widely used investment decision criteria, which are based on cash flow and the time value of money
- the discounted payback appraisal method is also based on cash flow and the time value of money.

We will look at examples of each of the five appraisal criteria and the advantages and disadvantages of using each of them.

Accounting rate of return (ARR)

ARR is a simple measure which is sometimes used in investment appraisal. It is a form of return on capital employed. It is based on profits rather than cash flows and ignores the time value of money.

ARR may be calculated using

$$\frac{\text{average accounting profit over the project}}{\text{initial investment}} \times 100\%$$

There are alternative ways of calculating ARR. For example, total profit may be used instead of average profit, or average investment may be used instead of initial investment. It should be noted that in such a case if, for example, a machine originally cost £800,000 and its final scrap value was £50,000 then the average investment is £850,000/2, or £425,000. This is because the investment at the start is valued at £800,000, and the investment at the end of the project is £50,000. The average value over the period of the project is then the addition of these two values divided by two.

Example 13.1

Alpha Engineering Ltd is a company that has recently implemented an investment appraisal system. Its investment authorisation policy usually allows it to go ahead with a capital project if the accounting rate of return is greater than 25%. A project has been submitted for appraisal with the following data:

	£000	
Initial investment	100	(residual scrap value zero)

Per annum profit over the life of the project:

Year	
1	25
2	35
3	35
4	25

We are required to evaluate the capital project using ARR.

Answer

Average profit over the life of the project $= \dfrac{\pounds25,000 + \pounds35,000 + \pounds35,000 + \pounds25,000}{4}$

$$= \pounds30,000$$

Accounting rate of return $= \dfrac{\pounds30,000}{\pounds100,000} \times 100\% = 30\%$

which is greater than 25% and so acceptance of the project may be recommended.

It should be noted that the method of calculation of ARR that is selected must be used consistently. However, ARR although simple to use is not recommended as a primary appraisal method. The method can provide an 'overview' of a new project but it lacks the sophistication of other methods (see the following explanations and methods). The impact of cash flows and time on the value of money really should be considered in investment appraisal, which we will discuss in a later section about key principles underlying investment selection criteria.

Progress check 13.2

What is the accounting rate of return (ARR) and how is it calculated?

Payback

Payback is defined as the number of years it takes the cash inflows from a capital investment project to equal the cash outflows. An organisation may have a target payback period, above which projects are rejected. It is useful and sometimes used as an initial screening process in evaluating two mutually exclusive projects. The project that pays back in the shortest time may on the face of it be the one to accept.

Example 13.2

Beta Engineering Ltd's investment authorisation policy requires all capital projects to pay back within 3 years, and views projects with shorter payback periods even more desirable. Two mutually exclusive projects are currently being considered with the following data:

	Project 1 £000	Project 2 £000	
Initial investment	200	200	(residual scrap value zero)

Per annum cash inflows over the life of each project:

Year	Project 1 Yearly cash flow £000	Project 1 Cumulative cash flow £000	Project 2 Yearly cash flow £000	Project 2 Cumulative cash flow £000
1	60	60	100	100
2	80	140	150	250
3	80	220	30	280
4	90	310	10	290

▶

We are required to evaluate the projects by considering their payback periods.

Answer

> Project 1 derives total cash inflows of £310,000 over the life of the project and pays back the initial £200,000 investment three quarters of the way into year three, when the cumulative cash inflows reach £200,000 [£60,000 + £80,000 + £60,000 (75% of £80,000)].
>
> Project 2 derives total cash inflows of £290,000 over the life of the project and pays back the initial £200,000 investment two thirds of the way into year two, when the cumulative cash inflows reach £200,000 [£100,000 + £100,000 (67% of £150,000)].
>
> Both projects meet Beta Engineering Ltd's three-year payback criteria.
>
> Project 2 pays back within 2 years and so is the preferred project, using Beta's investment guidelines.

Example 13.2 shows how payback may be used to compare projects. The total returns from a project should also be considered, in addition to the timing of the cash flows and their value in real terms. As with ARR, although its use is widespread amongst companies, payback is not recommended as a primary appraisal method. This method can also provide an 'overview' but may not be the primary appraisal method used in the larger companies or with regard to large projects because it ignores the time value of money.

Progress check 13.3

What is payback and how is it calculated?

Key principles underlying investment selection criteria: cash flows, and the time value of money

The first two appraisal criteria we have considered are simple methods that have limitations in their usefulness in making optimal capital investment decisions. The three further appraisal criteria are NPV, IRR and discounted payback. Whichever of these three methods is used, two basic principles apply: *Cash is king* and *Time value of money* (see page 463).

In Part I of this book (Chapters 3, 4 and 5) we discussed the differences between cash flow and profit and the advantages in using cash as a measure of financial performance.

We may assume that a specific sum money may be held in reserve for some unforeseen future need, or used:

- to earn interest in a bank or building society account over the following year
- to buy some bottles of champagne (for example) at today's price
- to buy some bottles of champagne at the price in one year's time, which we may assume will be at a higher price because of inflation.

We may assume that the bank or building society interest earned for one year, or the amount by which the price of champagne goes up due to inflation over one year is say 5%. Then we can see that £100 would be worth £105 if left in the building society for one year, and £100 spent on champagne today would actually buy just over £95 worth of champagne in one year's time because of its price increase.

Cash is king

Real funds can be seen in cash but not in accounting profit.

Interest charges become payable as soon as money is made available, for example, from a lender to a borrower, not when an agreement is made or when a contract is signed.

Time value of money

Receipt of £100 today has greater value than receipt of £100 in one year's time.

There are two reasons for this:

The money could have been invested alternatively in, say, risk-free Government gilt-edged securities – in fact the actual rate of interest that will have to be paid will be higher than the Government rate, to include a risk premium, because neither companies nor individuals are risk-free borrowers. Generally, the higher the risk of the investment, the higher the return the investor will expect from it.

Purchasing power will have been lost over a year due to inflation.

The percentage rate by which the value of money may be eroded over one year is called the discount rate. The amount by which the value of, say, £100 is eroded over one year is calculated by dividing it by what is called the discount factor

$$\frac{£100}{(1 + \text{discount rate \%})}$$

So, for example, we could buy champagne in one year's time worth

$$£100/(1 + 5\%) \text{ or } £100/1.05 = £95.24$$

If the £95.24 were left for another year, and assuming that prices continued to increase at 5% per annum, we could buy champagne after a further year worth

$$£95.24/(1 + 5\%) \text{ or } £95.24/1.05 = £90.70$$

The yearly reduction in buying power continues to be reduced by application of the discount factor (or using the appropriate discount factor if the discount rate has changed). If the money is not used either to earn interest or to buy something, its value therefore normally becomes less and less. The discount factor for each year obviously depends on the discount rate. The successive year-by-year impact on £100 using an unchanging discount rate of 5% per annum may be illustrated using a simple graph showing its cumulative value from the start until the end of ten years. The graph shown in Fig. 13.2 illustrates the concept of the time value of money.

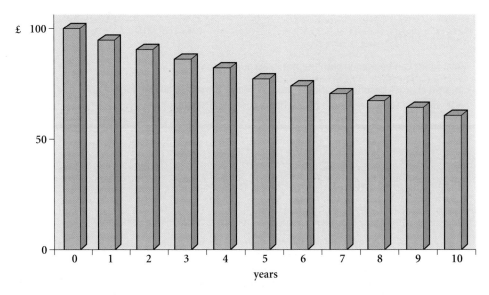

£ 100

50

0

0 1 2 3 4 5 6 7 8 9 10

years

FIGURE 13.2   Future values of £100 using a discount rate of 5% per annum

Discounted cash flow (DCF)

Whichever of the three methods of appraisal is used: NPV; IRR; or discounted payback, a technique of discounting the projected cash flows of the project is used to ascertain its **present value**. Such methods are called discounted cash flow or DCF techniques. They require the use of a discount rate or interest rate to carry out the appropriate calculation.

If we consider a simple company balance sheet:

net assets = equity + financial debt

An investment is an additional asset that may be financed by both equity and debt.

Shareholders and lenders each require a return on their investment that is high enough to pay for the risk they are taking in funding the company and its assets. The expected return on equity will be higher than the cost of debt because the shareholders take a higher risk than the lenders. The average cost of these financial resources provided to the company is called the weighted average cost of capital (WACC). An important rule is that the return generated by a new investment undertaken by a company must be higher than the WACC, which reflects the discount rate – the rate of financing the investment. If, say, a company's WACC is 10%, an investment may be accepted if the expected rate of return is 15% or 16%. The importance of WACC and the significance of the debt/equity financial structure of a business will be examined in more detail in Chapter 14 when we look at sources of finance and the cost of capital.

Other discount rates may be used, such as a borrowing interest rate or even the accounting rate of return. However, the cost of capital – the WACC – is usually the hurdle rate, the opportunity cost of funds, that it used to evaluate new investments.

If i represents the cost of capital (the discount rate), and n the number of periods, e.g. years, these are used to derive a

present value discount factor, which is $1/(1 + i)^n$

where n may have a value from 0 to infinity.

(Note the similarity between this and the way we calculated the future values of £100 illustrated in Fig. 13.2.)

If we consider a project where the initial investment in year 0, is I, and each subsequent year's net cash flows are CF_1, CF_2, CF_3, CF_4 and so on for n years up to CF_n, and the cost of capital is i, then the

present value of the cash flows $= -I + CF_1/(1 + i) + CF_2/(1 + i)^2 + \ldots + CF_n/(1 + i)^n$

The present value of the cash flows using an appropriate cost of capital, or discount rate, is called the net present value or NPV.

What do we mean by discounted cash flow (DCF) and what are the principles on which it is based?

Progress check 13.4

Net present value (NPV)

NPV is today's value of the difference between cash inflows and outflows projected at future dates, attributable to capital investments or long-term projects. The value now of these net cash flows is obtained by using the discounted cash flow method with a specified discount rate.

Example 13.3

An investment of £5,000 is made in year 0, and it generates subsequent yearly cash flows of £1,000, £3,000, £3,000, and £2,000. The cost of capital is 10%.

We are required to evaluate the investment using an NPV approach.

Answer

$NPV = - £5,000 + £1,000/1.1 + £3,000/1.1^2 + £3,000/1.1^3 + £2,000/1.1^4$

$NPV = - £5,000 + (£1,000 \times 0.91) + (£3,000 \times 0.83) + (£3,000 \times 0.75) + (£2,000 \times 0.68)$

$NPV = - £5,000 + £910 + £2,490 + £2,250 + £1,360$

$NPV = + £2,010$ which is greater than 0 and, being positive the investment should probably be made

Such an analysis is more usefully presented in tabular form. The discount rates for each year: $1/1.1$, $1/1.1^2$, $1/1.1^3$, $1/1.1^4$, may be shown in the table as discount factor values which are calculated, or alternatively obtained from present value tables (see the extract below from the Discounted Cash Flow Tables in Appendix 2 at the end of this book).

Rate r %	1	2	3	4	5	6	7	8	9	10	11	12
After n years												
1	0.99	0.98	0.97	0.96	0.95	0.94	0.93	0.93	0.92	**0.91**	0.90	0.89
2	0.98	0.96	0.94	0.92	0.91	0.89	0.87	0.86	0.84	**0.83**	0.81	0.80
3	0.97	0.94	0.92	0.89	0.86	0.84	0.82	0.79	0.77	**0.75**	0.73	0.71
4	0.96	0.92	0.89	0.85	0.82	0.79	0.76	0.74	0.71	**0.68**	0.66	0.64
5	0.95	0.91	0.86	0.82	0.78	0.75	0.71	0.68	0.65	0.62	0.59	0.57

▶

◀ Tabular format of NPV analysis

Year	Cash outflows £	Cash inflows £	Net cash flow £	Discount factor	Present values £
0	−5,000		−5,000	1.00	−5,000
1		1,000	1,000	0.91	910
2		3,000	3,000	0.83	2,490
3		3,000	3,000	0.75	2,250
4		2,000	2,000	0.68	1,360
				NPV	2,010

Progress check 13.5

What is net present value (NPV) and how is it calculated?

Internal rate of return (IRR)

The NPV of a capital investment project is calculated by:

● discounting, using a rate of return, discount rate, or cost of capital, to obtain
● the difference in present values between cash inflows and cash outflows.

The internal rate of return (IRR) method calculates:

● the rate of return, where
● the difference between the present values of cash inflows and outflows, the NPV, is zero.

Through this calculation, the IRR provides the exact rate of return that the project is expected to achieve. An organisation would then undertake the project if the expected rate of return, the IRR, exceeds its target rate of return.

IRR may most easily be determined through interpolation, which assumes a linear relationship between the NPVs of a capital investment project derived using different discount rates. If a project generates a positive NPV of £50,000 using a discount rate of 10% and a negative NPV of £5,000 using a discount rate of 20%, then the IRR (at which point NPV is zero) must be somewhere between 10 and 20%. The exact rate may be determined graphically and calculated algebraically, as illustrated in Fig.13.3. The IRR may also be determined using the appropriate spreadsheet function, in Excel for example.

A similar approach may be adopted if both NPVs are positive. For example, if a project generates a positive NPV of £50,000 using a discount rate of 10% and a positive NPV of £20,000 using a discount rate of 15%, then the IRR (at which point NPV is zero) may be extrapolated as shown in Fig.13.4.

Progress check 13.6

What is the internal rate of return (IRR) and how is it calculated?

Example 13.4 illustrates the use of both NPV and IRR.

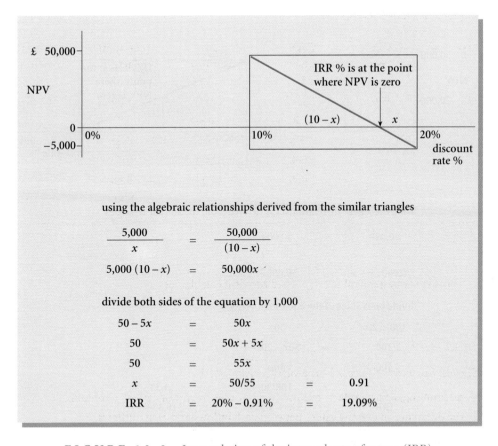

using the algebraic relationships derived from the similar triangles

$$\frac{5,000}{x} = \frac{50,000}{(10-x)}$$

$$5,000\,(10-x) = 50,000x$$

divide both sides of the equation by 1,000

$$50-5x = 50x$$
$$50 = 50x + 5x$$
$$50 = 55x$$
$$x = 50/55 = 0.91$$
$$\text{IRR} = 20\% - 0.91\% = 19.09\%$$

FIGURE 13.3   Interpolation of the internal rate of return (IRR)

Example 13.4

Gamma plc is a diversified multinational group that wishes to acquire a computer system costing £600,000 which is expected to generate cash gains of £170,000 per year over five years. The computer system will have a residual value of zero after five years. The suggested cost of capital is 12%. For this example we may ignore taxation. Gamma has a target IRR of 15%. We are required to evaluate the computer system investment by considering its IRR.

Answer

	£
Yearly cash gains	170,000

Year	Cash outflows £000	Cash inflows £000	Net cash flow £000	Discount factor at 12%	Present values £000
0	−600		−600	1.00	−600.0
1		170	170	0.89	151.3
2		170	170	0.80	136.0
3		170	170	0.71	120.7
4		170	170	0.64	108.8
5		170	170	0.57	96.9
				NPV	13.7

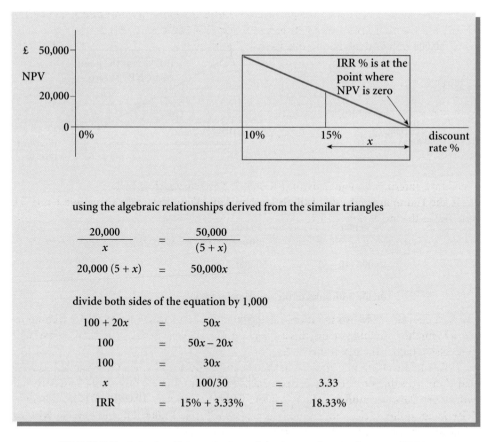

using the algebraic relationships derived from the similar triangles

$$\frac{20,000}{x} = \frac{50,000}{(5+x)}$$

$$20,000\,(5+x) = 50,000x$$

divide both sides of the equation by 1,000

$100 + 20x$	$=$	$50x$	
100	$=$	$50x - 20x$	
100	$=$	$30x$	
x	$=$	$100/30$	$= \quad 3.33$
IRR	$=$	$15\% + 3.33\%$	$= \quad 18.33\%$

FIGURE 13.4   Extrapolation of the internal rate of return (IRR)

Alternatively, using the cumulative present values in the Discounted Cash Flow Tables the present value of £1 at 12% over 5 years is £3.61, therefore

$$\text{NPV} = -£600,000 + (£170,000 \times 3.61) = +£13,700$$

The project gives a positive NPV of £13,700 over 5 years. If Gamma plc used NPV to appraise capital projects then acceptance of this project may be recommended because NPV is positive.

The IRR is the rate of return that would give an NPV of zero.

The interpolation technique shown in Fig. 13.3 may be used to derive the internal rate of return of the project.

If we assume a rate of return of 20%, the 5-year cumulative discount rate is 2.99 (from the cumulative present value of £1 in the DCF tables in Appendix 2).

The new NPV would be:

$$-£600,000 + (£170,000 \times 2.99) = -£91,700$$

(Note that if Gamma plc used NPV to appraise capital projects then acceptance of this project would not be recommended at a cost of capital of 20% because it is negative).

We have already calculated the positive NPV of £13,700 using a cost of capital of 12%. The IRR must be at some point between 20% and 12% (difference 8%).

Using a similar calculation to that used in Fig. 13.3:

$$\frac{£91,700}{x} = \frac{£13,700}{(8 - x)}$$

$$(£91,700 \times 8) - £91,700x = £13,700x$$

$$£733,600 = £105,400x$$

$$x = 7.0$$

Therefore, interpolation gives us an IRR of 20% less 7%, which is 13%.

If the Gamma group uses IRR to appraise capital projects then this project may be rejected as the target rate is 15%.

NPV or IRR?

We have looked at the two main capital appraisal methods which use the DCF technique. Which method should an organisation adopt for the appraisal of capital investment projects? Which is the better method?

IRR is relatively easy to understand particularly for non-financial managers. It can be stated in terms that do not include financial jargon, for example 'a project will cost £1m and will return 20% per annum, which is better than the company's target of 15%.' Whereas, NPV is not quite so clear, for example 'a project will cost £1,000,000 and have an NPV of £250,000 using the company's weighted cost of capital of 12%.'

There are three major disadvantages with the use of IRR

● IRR ignores the size of investment projects
  – two projects may have the same IRR, but
  – one project may return many times the cash flow returned by the other project, and so
  – the projects if judged solely on IRR may seem to rank equally
● if project cash flows do not follow the usual 'outflow at the start of the project followed by inflows over the life of the project' the result may be two or more IRRs, which can lead to uncertainties and difficulties in interpretation
● IRR should not be used to decide between mutually exclusive projects because of its inability to allow for the relative size of investments.

If mutually exclusive projects need to be compared then the following rules for acceptance apply:

● is the IRR greater than the hurdle rate (usually the WACC)?

if so

● the project with the highest NPV should be chosen assuming the NPV is greater than zero.

A company may be considering a number of projects in which it may invest. If there is a limited amount of funds available then **capital rationing** is required. This method requires ranking the competing projects in terms of NPV per each £ of investment in each project. Investment funds may then be allocated according to NPV rankings, given the assumption that the investments are infinitely divisible.

Progress check 13.7

What are the disadvantages in the use of internal rate of return (IRR) in the support of capital investment appraisal decisions?

Discounted payback

The discounted payback appraisal method requires a discount rate to be chosen to calculate the present values of cash inflows and then the payback is the number of years required to repay the original investment.

Example 13.5

A new leisure facility project is being considered by Denton City Council. It will cost £600,000 and is expected to generate the following cash inflows over six years:

Year	£
1	40,000
2	100,000
3	200,000
4	350,000
5	400,000
6	50,000

The cost of capital is 10% per annum.
Evaluate the project using discounted payback.

Answer

Year	Net cash flow £000	Cumulative net cash flow £000	Discount factor at 10%	Present values £000	Cumulative present values £000
0	−600	−600	1.00	−600.0	−600.0
1	40	−560	0.91	36.4	−563.6
2	100	−460	0.83	83.0	−480.6
3	200	−260	0.75	150.0	−330.6
4	350	90	0.68	238.0	−92.6
5	400	490	0.62	248.0	155.4
6	50	540	0.56	28.0	183.4
	540		NPV	183.4	

Taking a simple payback approach we can see that the project starts to pay back at nearly three quarters of the way through year 4. The discounted payback approach shows that with a cost of capital of 10% the project does not really start to pay back until just over a third of the way into year 5. This method also highlights the large difference between the real total value of the project of £183,400 in discounted cash flow terms, and the arithmetic total of cash flows of £540,000.

Progress check 13.8

What is discounted payback and how is it calculated?

Advantages and disadvantages of the five investment appraisal criteria

We have discussed the five capital investment criteria and seen examples of their application. The table in Fig.13.5 summarises each of the methods and the advantages and disadvantages of their practical use in investment appraisal.

It is interesting to note that payback still seemed to be the most popular appraisal method within UK companies, closely followed by IRR! NPV, discounted payback and ARR appeared to be equal third sharing around the same level of popularity (*A Survey of Management Accounting Practices in UK Companies 1993*).

Progress check 13.9

Which technique do you think is the most appropriate to use in capital investment appraisal, and why?

Other factors affecting investment decisions

A number of further factors may have an additional impact on investment criteria calculations:

- the effect of inflation on the cost of capital
- whether additional working capital is required for the project
- the length of the project
- taxation
- risk and uncertainty.

Inflation

If i is the real cost of capital and the inflation rate is I, then the actual (or money) cost of capital a may be calculated as follows:

$$(1 + a) = (1 + i) \times (1 + I)$$

Therefore

actual cost of capital $a = (1 + i) \times (1 + I) - 1$

	definition	advantages	disadvantages
accounting rate of return (ARR)	average accounting profit over the life of the project divided by the initial or average investment	quick and easy to calculate and simple to use	based on accounting profit rather than cash flows
		the concept of a % return is a familiar one	a relative measure and so no account is taken of the size of the project
		very similar to ROCE	ignores timing of cash flows and the cost of capital
payback	the point where the cumulative value of a project's cash flows becomes positive	easily understood	ignores the timing of cash flows
		considers liquidity	ignores cash flows that occur after the payback point
		looks only at relevant cash flows	ignores the cost of capital, i.e. the time value of money
net present value (NPV)	the total present values of each of a project's cash flows, using a present value discount factor	uses relevant cash flows	its use requires an estimate of the cost of capital
		allows for the time value of money	
		absolute measure and therefore useful, for example, for comparison of the change in shareholder wealth	
		it is additive which means that if the cash flow is doubled then the NPV is doubled	
internal rate of return (IRR)	the discount factor at which the NPV of a project becomes zero	does not need an estimate of the cost of capital	it is a relative rate of return and so no account is taken of the size of the project
		because the result is stated as a % it is easily understood	its use may rank projects incorrectly
			as cash flows change signs −ve to +ve or *vice versa* throughout the project there may be more than one IRR
			it is difficult to use if changes in the cost of capital are forecast
discounted payback	the point where the cumulative value of a project's discounted cash flows becomes positive	easily understood	its use requires an estimate of the cost of capital
		considers liquidity	ignores cash flows that occur after the payback point
		looks only at relevant cash flows	
		allows for the time value of money	

FIGURE 13.5   Advantages and disadvantages of the five investment appraisal methods

Example 13.6

We are required to calculate a company's real cost of capital if its actual (money) cost of capital is 11% and inflation is running at 2%.

Answer

Real cost of capital

$$i = \frac{(1 + a)}{(1 + I)} - 1$$

$$i = \frac{1.11}{1.02} - 1 = 0.088 \text{ or } 8.8\%$$

This would normally then be rounded to say 9% and forecast cash flows that have been adjusted for inflation may then be discounted using this real cost of capital. Alternatively, if forecast cash flows have not been adjusted for inflation, then these money cash flows would be discounted using the company's actual cost of capital. The result is the same using either method.

Working capital

Any increases in working capital required for a project in addition to the normal investments need to be shown as cash outflows as necessary in one or more years, offset by cash inflows to bring the total to zero by the end of the project.

Example 13.7

Delta Precision plc, a manufacturing company, has the opportunity to invest in a machine costing £110,000 that will generate net cash inflows from the investment of £30,000 for 5 years after which time the machine will be worth nothing. Cost of capital is 10%. We may ignore inflation and taxation.

We are required to evaluate the project using NPV.

Answer

Year	Cash outflows £000	Cash inflows £000	Net cash flow £000	Discount factor at 10%	Present values £000
0	−110		−110	1.00	−110.0
1		30	30	0.91	27.3
2		30	30	0.83	24.9
3		30	30	0.75	22.5
4		30	30	0.68	20.4
5		30	30	0.62	18.6
				NPV	3.7

The positive NPV of £3,700 would indicate acceptance of this investment.

Suppose that in addition to the above factors, for this project Delta required:

- £20,000 working capital in year 1
- £40,000 working capital in year 2, but then
- zero working capital in years 3, 4 and 5.

◀ The revised cash flows would be:

Year	0	1	2	3	4	5	Total
	£000	£000	£000	£000	£000	£000	£000
Investment	−110						−110
Cash inflows		30	30	30	30	30	150
Working		−20		20			0
capital			−40	40			0
Total	−110	10	−10	90	30	30	40

The total cash flow of the project is still the same at £40,000, but the timings of the cash flows are different.

Year	Net cash flows £000	Discount factor	Present values £000
0	−110	1.00	−110.0
1	10	0.91	9.1
2	−10	0.83	−8.3
3	90	0.75	67.5
4	30	0.68	20.4
5	30	0.62	18.6
		NPV	−2.7

The need for, and the timing of, working capital gives a negative NPV of £2,700 which would now indicate rejection of this investment.

Length of project and taxation

In practice, tax must always be allowed for in any capital investment appraisal calculations. Without getting into too much detail regarding tax, the following examples illustrate the principle.

Example 13.8

Epsilon Ltd, is a company that manufactures and distributes consumer products. It is currently considering the acquisition of a machine costing £2,700,000 to market a new product.

The machine will be worth nothing after 10 years but is expected to produce 10,000 units of a product per year during that period, with variable costs of £35 per unit.

The product can be sold for £120 per unit.

Fixed costs directly attributed to this product will be £300,000 per year.

The company's cost of capital is 10%.

We may assume that all costs and revenues are paid and received during each year. We may further assume that corporation tax is paid in the year that profit is made and calculated at 40% of profit, and that for tax purposes each year's depreciation is equal to capital allowances.

We are required to evaluate the acquisition of the machine using NPV.

Answer

	£000	
Sales revenue	1,200	[10,000 × £120]
Variable costs	(350)	[10,000 × £35]
Depreciation	(270)	[2,700,000 over ten-year life]
Fixed costs	(300)	
Taxable profit	280	
Corporation tax at 40%	(112)	[based on taxable profit plus depreciation less capital allowances]
Profit after tax	168	
Add back depreciation	270	[non-cash flow]
Yearly cash flow	438	

Using the cumulative present value Discounted Cash Flow Tables (see Appendix 2) the present value of £1 at 10% over 10 years is £6.15, therefore:

$$NPV = -£2,700,000 + (£438,000 \times 6.15) = -£6,300$$

The NPV is less than 0 and the project is therefore not profitable.

Corporation tax is normally payable by a company in the year following that in which profit is earned. If a project lasts for say four years then cash in respect of tax must be shown in the fifth year. The length of the project is then effectively five years. Tax payable in respect of operating profit must be shown separately from cash flows in respect of capital allowances. The first investment year is normally shown as year 0 and the first tax allowance year is therefore year one.

Example 13.9

Zeta plc has the opportunity to invest in a machine costing £100,000 that will generate cash profits of £30,000 per year for the next four years after which the machine would be sold for £10,000. The company's after tax cost of capital is 8% per annum.
  We may assume:

– corporation tax at 30%
– annual writing down allowances in each year are on the investment reducing balance at 25%
– there will be a balancing charge or allowance on disposal of the machine.

We are required to consider whether the investment should be made, using an NPV approach.

Answer

Capital allowances:

Year	Opening balance £	Capital allowance at 25% £	Balancing allowance/ (charge) £	Opening balance £
0	100,000	25,000		75,000
1	75,000	18,750		56,250
2	56,250	14,063		42,187
3	42,187	10,547		31,640
4	31,640	7,910		23,730
	23,730			
Proceeds	10,000		13,730	
Total		76,270	13,730	

Note that the totals of the capital allowances and balancing allowance equal £90,000, the net cost of the machine £100,000 less £10,000.

Next, we can calculate the taxable profit, and the tax payable.

Year	0 £	1 £	2 £	3 £	4 £
Profits		30,000	30,000	30,000	30,000
Capital allowances	25,000	18,750	14,063	10,547	21,640
Taxable 'profit'	−25,000	11,250	15,937	19,453	8,360
Tax receivable/ (payable) at 30%	7,500	−3,375	−4,781	−5,836	−2,508

We can now calculate the net cash flows and the present values of the project:

Year	Machine £	Profits £	Tax £	Net cash flow £	Discount factor at 8% pa	Present values £
0	−100,000			−100,000	1.00	−100,000
1		30,000	7,500	37,500	0.93	34,875
2		30,000	−3,375	26,625	0.86	22,897
3		30,000	−4,781	25,219	0.79	19,923
4	10,000	30,000	−5,836	34,164	0.74	25,281
5			−2,508	−2,508	0.68	−1,705
						1,271

The positive NPV of £1,271 would indicate acceptance of this investment.

Capital investment decisions take on a wider dimension for international corporations with the consideration of a further factor, the uncertainty associated with foreign currency exchange rate fluctuations. For UK-based companies this has had a particular significance over the past few years with the uncertainty surrounding the UK's adoption of the euro. Foreign currency exchange rate risk is not discussed in this chapter but is an important topic that was introduced in Chapter 2.

Progress check 13.10

Why and how should inflation and working capital be allowed for in making capital investment decisions?

Nissan's decision to build its new Micra car in Sunderland in the UK illustrated the importance of some of the additional factors that influence investment appraisal decisions, as illustrated in the press cutting on page 478.

The level of Government support, the volatility of the £ sterling against the euro, and the flexibility of the work-force were factors that impacted on the Nissan decision, in addition to the initial financial appraisal of the investment.

Risk and uncertainty and decision-making – sensitivity analysis

In our earlier discussion on the decision-making process we have talked about comparing actual results following implementation of the decision with the expected outcome. Our own experience tells us that actual outcomes usually differ considerably from expected outcomes. In terms of capital investment, the greater the timescale of the project the more time there is for more things to go wrong; the larger the investment, the greater may be the impact.

As a final step in evaluation of the investment in a project it is prudent to carry out some sort of **sensitivity analysis**. Sensitivity analysis may be used to assess the risk associated with a capital investment project. A project having a positive NPV may on the face of it seem viable. It is useful to calculate how much the NPV may change should there be changes to the factors used in the appraisal exercise. These factors are shown in Fig. 13.6.

Sensitivity may be evaluated through numerical analysis, which is illustrated in Examples 13.10 to 13.14. Sensitivity may also be shown graphically:

● NPV may be plotted on the y vertical axis

● the percentage change in the variable factors, used in the appraisal, may be plotted on the x horizontal axis.

This process may be carried out for each variable, for example:

● sales

● cost savings

● investment

● scrap value.

The most sensitive variable is the one with the steepest gradient.

Sunderland beats Paris to £230m Nissan deal

By Sophie Barker, City Staff

Sunderland overcame competition from France yesterday as Nissan promised a £230 million investment to build the new Micra car at its Wearside plant.

The contract spanning 10 years secures the plant's future as Britain's largest car works and ends months of uncertainty for the staff. Production on the new model Micra is to start next year. Nissan's decision also lifts the longer-term threat of closure from the factory, which faced losing production of two other models had the Micra crossed the Channel.

The move confounded most expectations that the new car would be built at a rival factory in Flins, west of Paris, owned by Renault, Nissan's major shareholder. Only four months ago, Carlos Ghosn, Nissan's president, warned that the strength of the pound against the euro was damaging Sunderland's chances of winning the contract.

Speaking in London yesterday, Mr Ghosn said: 'We chose Sunderland because the plant proved it can build cars profitably.' Pressed on his apparent about-turn, the Nissan boss suggested that he had sought assurances from the Government during 'many' meetings over its stance on joining the single currency.

'What has changed is that, during our discussions, we were able to make clear how important the volatility [of the pound against the euro] was for our future investment. We don't want to make profits just because we are lucky.'

Stephen Byers, Trade Secretary, was quick to deny that the Government had given any assurances on the euro. But the Tory MP, Sir Teddy Taylor said: 'Mr Byers should come clean on what he specifically said to Nissan about the single currency.'

Sir Teddy, who is secretary of the European Reform Group, added: 'The buzz going round Westminster is that assurances have been given to Nissan on this issue. It would help a great deal if the Government said openly and clearly what assurances were given about a referendum.'

Other observers attributed Mr Ghosn's change of heart to the euro's changing fortunes. Nissan had complained about the strength of the pound until last October, when the euro began to recover.

Nissan's comments were also seen as part of a campaign to secure swift European approval for the Government's £40 million grant for Sunderland, agreed last week. In the past few weeks, French trade unions have raised the prospect of the Flins factory not being able to modernise its facilities in time for the launch of the new Micra in 2003.

Mr Ghosn said yesterday that he believed that the UK would 'again provide a place where we can build cars competitively'. But the Sunderland operation would protect itself against future currency fluctuations by buying 65 per cent of its car parts in euros.

Nissan currently buys 20 to 25 per cent of its components in euros and sells 65 per cent of Sunderland made Micras into the euro zone. The new purchasing policy threatens Nissan's 132 British suppliers and could lead to job losses for smaller firms unable to invoice in euros.

This fresh cost-cutting move is part of an ongoing programme to slash 30 per cent from the Sunderland factory's cost base. Workers have already been asked to work around the clock on three shifts, turning Sunderland into Britain's first 24-hour car plant.

Both sides of the euro lobby claimed victory following Nissan's decision. Business for Sterling said it was 'a vote of confidence in Britain'. For its part, Britain in Europe said Nissan's move 'showed the danger of ruling out the euro'.

Workers at BMW's Cowley factory in Oxford, where the new Mini will be built, voted yesterday to accept a two-year pay deal, the Transport and General Workers' Union said.

© *Daily Telegraph*, 26 January 2001

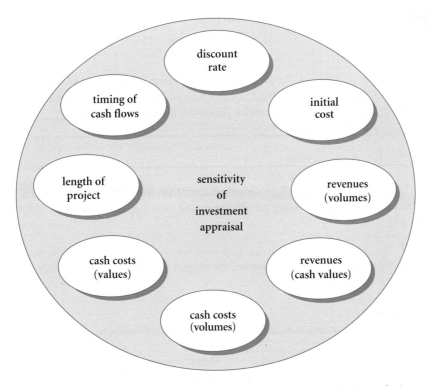

FIGURE 13.6 Project appraisal factors used in sensitivity analysis

Example 13.10

Theta Ltd has the opportunity to invest in a project with an initial cost of £100,000 that will generate estimated net cash flows of £35,000 at the end of each year for five years. The company's cost of capital is 12% per annum. For simplicity we can ignore the effects of tax and inflation.

We are required to evaluate the sensitivity of the initial investment in the project using an NPV approach.

Answer

The cumulative present value tables show us the annuity factor over 5 years at 12% per annum at 3.61 (see Appendix 2).

Therefore the NPV of the project is

$$-£100,000 + (£35,000 \times 3.61)$$
$$= -£100,000 + £126,350$$
$$NPV = £26,350$$

The positive NPV of £26,350 would indicate going ahead with the investment in this project.

◀ We can carry out a sensitivity analysis on the project by considering the effect of a change to the initial investment.

Initial investment

The NPV of the project is £26,350. If the initial investment rose by £26,350 to £126,350 (£100,000 + £26,350) the NPV would become zero and it would not be worth taking on the project. This represents an increase of 26.4% on the initial investment.

Example 13.11

Using the data from Example 13.10 we are required to evaluate the sensitivity of the annual cash flows from the project, using an NPV approach.

Answer

We can carry out a sensitivity analysis on the project by considering the effects of changes to the annual cash flows.

Annual cash flow

If we again consider what needs to happen to bring the NPV to zero

Then
$$\text{NPV} = 0 = -£100,000 + (a \times 3.61)$$

Where a is the annual cash flow

$$a = £100,000/3.61$$
$$a = £27,700$$

Which is a reduction of 20.9% from the original per annum cash flow of £35,000.

Example 13.12

Using the data from Example 13.10 we are required to evaluate the sensitivity of cost of capital on the project for Theta Ltd, using an NPV approach.

Answer

We can carry out a sensitivity analysis on the project by considering the effects of changes to the cost of capital.

Cost of capital

When the NPV is zero the internal rate of return (IRR) is equal to the cost of capital. If the cost of capital is greater than the IRR then the project should be rejected.

In this example we therefore first need to calculate the cumulative discount factor at which the NPV is zero.

$$\text{NPV} = 0 = -£100,000 + (£35,000 \times d)$$

Where *d* is the cumulative discount factor for 5 years

$$d = £100,000/£35,000$$
$$d = 2.857$$

The cumulative present value tables show us that the annuity factor over 5 years of 2.86 represents an interest rate of 22%.

The IRR is therefore approximately 22%, which is an 83.3% increase over the cost of capital of 12%.

Example 13.13

Using the data from Example 13.10 we are required to evaluate the sensitivity of the length of the project for Theta Ltd, using an NPV approach.

Answer

We can carry out a sensitivity analysis on the project by considering the effects of changes to the length of project.

Length of project

The original project was 5 years for which we calculated the NPV at £26,350. We may consider what would be the effect if the project ended after say 4 years or 3 years.

If the project was 4 years, the cumulative discount factor (from the tables) is 3.04 so the NPV of the project is:

$$-£100,000 + (£35,000 \times 3.04)$$
$$= -£100,000 + £106,400$$
$$NPV = £6,400$$

The positive NPV of £6,400 still indicates going ahead with the investment in this project.

If the project was 3 years the cumulative discount factor (from the tables) is 2.40 so the NPV of the project is:

$$-£100,000 + (£35,000 \times 2.40)$$
$$= -£100,000 + £84,000$$
$$NPV = -£16,000$$

The negative NPV of £16,000 indicates not going ahead with the investment in this project if the length of the project drops below four years, which is the year in which NPV becomes negative. This is a change of 20% (that is a drop from 5 years to 4 years).

Example 13.14

Using the data from Examples 13.10 to 13.13 we are required to summarise each of the sensitivities that have been calculated and present some conclusions about the sensitivity of the project that are apparent from the summary.

Answer

The sensitivity analysis we have carried out is more usefully summarised to show each of the factors we have considered, to show

- the values used in the original appraisal
- the critical values of those factors
- the percentage change over the original values that they represent

Factor	Original value	Critical value	% change
Initial investment	£100,000	£126,350	26.4
Annual cash flow	£35,000	£27,700	−20.9
Cost of capital	12%	22%	83.3
Length of project	5 years	4 years	−20

We may draw the following conclusions from our sensitivity analysis:

- none of the factors used in the appraisal was critical, their critical values all being +/− 20%
- cost of capital is the least critical factor at 83.3%, which is useful to know since the accuracy of the calculation of cost of capital may not always be totally reliable

---

The same technique of sensitivity analysis may be used as an early warning system before a project begins to show a loss. It can be seen from the factors outlined in this section, that a board of directors should request a sensitivity analysis on major projects. In the UK, the five years up to 2000 saw several projects concerned with the manufacture of chips for computers become very unprofitable, with timing of cash flows critical to their viability.

However, there are limitations to the use of sensitivity analysis. The example we have considered looked at the effect of changes to individual factors in isolation. In reality two or more factors may change simultaneously. The impact of such changes may be assessed using the more sophisticated technique of linear programming. A further limitation may be the absence of clear rules governing acceptance or rejection of the project and the need for the subjective judgement of management.

When we looked at risk and sales pricing in Chapter 10 we saw that we may apply probabilities to estimated demand estimates at different pricing levels to derive expected values. In the same way, cash flows from investments may be weighted by their probabilities of occurrence to calculate an expected NPV.

Example 13.15

Kappa plc has the opportunity of engaging in a two-year project for a specific client. It would require an initial investment in a machine costing £200,000. The machine is capable of running three separate processes. The process used will depend on the level of demand from the client's final customers. Each process will therefore generate different yearly net cash flows, each with a different likelihood of occurrence. The company's cost of capital is 15% per annum.

The forecast probabilities and net cash flows for each year are:

Process	Probability of occurrence	Per annum cash flow
Process 1	0.5	£150,000
Process 2	0.1	£15,000
Process 3	0.4	£90,000
	1.0	

The total of the probabilities is 1, which indicates that one of the options is certain to occur. Even though one process will definitely be used should Kappa take on the project?

Answer

We first need to use the probabilities to calculate the weighted average of the expected outcomes for each year.

Process	Cash flow £	Probability	Expected cash flow £
1	150,000	0.5	75,000
2	15,000	0.1	1,500
3	90,000	0.4	36,000
Expected per annum cash flows			112,500

To calculate the expected NPV of the project we need to discount the expected annual cash flows using the discount rate of 15% per annum.

Year	Expected cash flow £	Discount rate	Expected present value £
1	112,500	0.87	97,875
2	112,500	0.76	85,500
Total	225,000		183,375
Initial investment			200,000
Expected NPV			−16,625

The negative expected NPV of £16,625 indicates that Kappa plc should reject investment in this project.

◀ Although the technique of expected net present value is a clear decision rule with a single numerical outcome there are caveats:

● this technique uses an average number which in the above example is not actually capable of occurrence

● use of an average number may cloud the issue if the underlying risk of outcomes worse than the average are ignored

● if the per annum cash flow from process 1 had been £300,000 and the expected NPV had been positive consider the impact on Kappa if, for example, if the client had actually required the use of process 2.

<table><tr><td>Progress check 13.11</td><td>Risk and uncertainty increasingly impact on investment decisions. What are these risk factors, and how may we evaluate their impact?</td></tr></table>

Control of capital investment projects

Once a project has been appraised and a sensitivity analysis carried out and the approval has been given at the relevant level in the organisation, project controls must be established and then post-project completion audits carried out. The controls cover the three main areas of:

● capital spend – note the number of subjective areas where things can go wrong

● project-timing – delays appear to be 'routine' in many major projects as evidenced almost daily in the financial press

● benefits – evidenced almost as frequently in the financial press, this is another area where things may not turn out as planned.

Capital spending limits are usually put in place by most organisations with levels of spend requiring authorisation at the appropriate managerial level. Capital expenditure proposals should be documented to show:

● project details, including costs, benefits and the life of the project

● appraisal calculations and comparisons with the organisation's targets

● assumptions

● names of the project manager and the project team

● name(s) and signature(s) of the manager(s) authorising the project

● the period(s) in which expenditure should take place.

Material delays in capital spend or in the progress of the project should prompt a resubmitted proposal together with the reasons for delay. A good project manager with the appropriate level of responsibility and authority should ensure that projects run to plan.

Benefits from projects are not easy to control because they are usually derived over many years. The importance of having a good project manager in place cannot be over-emphasised. He/she should ensure that expected benefits actually materialise and are as large in value as anticipated. The project manager should also ensure that costs are kept in line with expectation.

Post-implementation audits should be carried out for all projects if possible. Although after the event corrective action cannot usually be taken, variances may be analysed to use the project as an information and learning tool:

- to appraise manager performance
- to identify strengths and weaknesses in the forecasting and estimating techniques
- to identify areas of improvement in the capital investment process
- to advertise the fact that both project and manager performance are being monitored.

Progress check 13.12

In what ways can we ensure that capital investment projects are adequately controlled?

Summary of key points

- An investment requires expenditure on something today that is expected to provide a benefit in the future.
- The decision to make an investment is extremely important because it implies the expectation that expenditure today will generate future cash gains in real terms that greatly exceed the funds spent today.
- '£1 received today is worth more than £1 received in a year's time' is an expression of what is meant by the 'time value of money'.
- The principles underlying the investment appraisal techniques that use the DCF method are cash flow (as opposed to profit), and the time value of money.
- Five main criteria are used to appraise investments: accounting rate of return (ARR); payback; net present value (NPV); internal rate of return (IRR); and discounted payback – the last three being discounted cash flow (DCF) techniques.
- The technique of discounted cash flow discounts the projected net cash flows of a capital project to ascertain its present value, using an appropriate discount rate, or cost of capital.
- Additional factors impacting on investment criteria calculations are: the effect of inflation on the cost of capital; working capital requirements; length of project; taxation; risk and uncertainty.
- There may be a number of risks associated with each of the variables included in a capital investment appraisal decision: estimates of initial costs; uncertainty about the timing and values of future cash revenues and costs; the length of project; variations in the discount rate.
- Sensitivity analysis may be used to assess the risk associated with a capital investment project.
- To establish the appropriate levels of control, the appointment of a good project manager with the appropriate level of responsibility and authority, together with regular project reviews, are absolute essentials to ensure that projects run to plan.

Glossary of key terms

accounting rate of return (ARR) Annual profit divided by investment. It is a form of return on capital employed. Unlike NPV and IRR, it is based on profits, not cash flows.

capital rationing This is a restriction on an organisation's ability to invest capital funds, caused by an internal budget ceiling being imposed on such expenditure by management (soft capital rationing), or by external limitations being applied to the organisation, for example when additional borrowed funds cannot be obtained (hard capital rationing).

discounted payback The number of years required to repay an original investment using a specified discount rate.

internal rate of return (IRR) The annual percentage return achieved by a project, at which the sum of the discounted cash inflows over the life of the project is equal to the sum of the discounted cash outflows.

investment Any application of funds which is intended to provide a return by way of interest, dividend or capital appreciation.

net present value (NPV) The difference between the sums of the projected discounted cash inflows and outflows attributable to a capital investment or other long-term project.

payback The number of years it takes the cash inflows from a capital investment project to equal the cash outflows. An organisation may have a target payback period, above which projects are rejected.

present value The cash equivalent now of a sum receivable or payable at a future date.

sensitivity analysis A modelling and risk assessment technique in which changes are made to significant variables in order to determine the effect of these changes on the planned outcome. Particular attention is thereafter paid to variables identified as being of special significance.

Assessment material

Questions

Q13.1 (i) What is capital investment?

(ii) Why are capital investment decisions so important to companies?

Q13.2 Outline the five main investment appraisal criteria.

Q13.3 Describe the two key principles underlying DCF investment selection criteria.

Q13.4 What are the advantages in the use of NPV over IRR in investment appraisal?

Q13.5 What are the factors that impact on capital investment decisions?

Q13.6 (i) What is meant by risk with regard to investment?

(ii) How does sensitivity analysis help?

Q13.7 Describe how capital investment projects may be controlled and reviewed.

Discussion points

D13.1 'I know that cash and profit are not always the same thing but surely eventually they end up being equal. Therefore, surely we should look at the likely ultimate profit from a capital investment before deciding whether or not to invest?' Discuss.

D13.2 'This discounted cash flow business seems like just a bit more work for the accountants to me. Cash is cash whenever it's received or paid. I say let's keep capital investment appraisal simple.' Discuss.

D13.3 'If you don't take a risk you will not make any money.' Discuss.

Exercises

Solutions are provided in Appendix 4 to all exercise numbers highlighted in colour.

Level I

E13.1 *Time allowed – 30 minutes*

Global Sights & Sounds Ltd (GSS) sells multi-media equipment and software through its retail outlets. GSS is considering investing in some major refurbishment of one of its outlets, to enable it to provide improved customer service, until the lease expires at the end of four years. GSS is currently talking to two contractors, Smith Ltd and Jones Ltd. Whichever contractor is used, the improved customer service has been estimated to generate increased net cash inflows as follows:

Year	£
1	75,000
2	190,000
3	190,000
4	225,000

Smith:
The capital costs will be £125,000 at the start of the project, and £175,000 at the end of each of years 1 and 2.

Jones:
The capital costs will be the same in total, but payment to the contractor can be delayed. Capital payments will be £50,000 at the start of the project, £75,000 at the end of each of years 1, 2 and 3, and the balance of capital cost at the end of year 4. In return for the delayed payments the contractor will receive a 20% share of the cash inflows generated from the improved services, payable at the end of each year. In the interim period, the unutilised capital will be invested in a short-term project in another department store, generating a cash inflow of £60,000 at the end of each of years 1, 2 and 3.

It may be assumed that all cash flows occur at the end of each year.
The effects of taxation and inflation may be ignored.

You are required to advise GSS Ltd on whether to select Smith or Jones, ignoring the time value of money, using the appraisal basis of:

(i) accounting rate of return (ARR), and

(ii) comment on the appraisal method you have used.

E13.2 *Time allowed – 30 minutes*

Using the information on Global Sights & Sounds Ltd from Exercise E13.1, you are required to advise GSS Ltd on whether to select Smith or Jones, ignoring the time value of money, using the appraisal basis of:

(i) payback, and

(ii) comment on the appraisal method you have used.

E13.3 *Time allowed – 60 minutes*

An automotive components manufacturing group, Lubosh plc, supplies parts to all the main UK motor vehicle manufacturers. The group is considering a £40m investment in tooling and plant for a new vehicle (codename Mondino) for one of its customers. The project is expected to have a three-year life. In each of the years 1, 2, and 3 the incremental cash inflows are expected to be £50m and the cash outflows £30m in each year. The initial investment is stated in money terms, but all other cash flows include the effects of inflation. The inflation rate is 8% per annum with regard to cash outflows and 7% per annum with regard to cash inflows. Lubosh's cost of capital is 17%.

What is the NPV of the investment?
What is the IRR of the project?
Lubosh normally expects projects to payback within 18 months, with a discounted payback of less than two years? Will the Mondino project do that?
Should Lubosh undertake the Mondino project? What other considerations are there in addition to just looking at the numbers?

Level II

E13.4 *Time allowed – 30 minutes*

Using the information on Global Sights & Sounds Ltd from Exercise E13.1, you are required to advise GSS Ltd on whether to select Smith or Jones, using the appraisal basis of

(i) net present value (NPV), using a cost of capital of 12% per annum to discount the cash flows to their present value, and

(ii) comment on the appraisal method you have used.

E13.5 *Time allowed – 30 minutes*

Using the information on Global Sights & Sounds Ltd from Exercise E13.1, you are required to advise GSS Ltd on whether to select Smith or Jones, using the appraisal basis of

(i) discounted payback, using a cost of capital of 12% per annum to discount the cash flows to their present value, and

(ii) comment on the appraisal method you have used.

E13.6 *Time allowed – 45 minutes*

Using the information on Global Sights & Sounds Ltd from Exercise E13.1, you are required to advise GSS Ltd on whether to select Smith or Jones, using the appraisal basis of:

(i) internal rate of return (IRR), and

(ii) comment on the appraisal method you have used.

E13.7 *Time allowed – 45 minutes*

In Exercise E13.1 we are told that a 20% share of the improved cash inflow has been agreed with Jones Ltd.

You are required to:

(i) calculate the percentage share at which GSS Ltd would be indifferent, on a financial basis, as to which of the contractors Smith or Jones should carry out the work

(ii) outline the other factors, in addition to your financial analyses in (i), that should be considered in making the choice between Smith and Jones.

E13.8 *Time allowed – 60 minutes*

Alive & Kicking Ltd (AAK) owns a disused warehouse in which a promoter runs regular small gigs. There are currently no facilities to provide drinks. The owners of AAK intend to provide such facilities and can obtain funding to cover capital costs. This would have to be repaid over five years at an annual interest rate of 10%.

The capital costs are estimated at £120,000 for equipment that will have a life of five years and no residual value. To provide drinks, the running costs of staff, etc., will be £40,000 in the first year, increasing by £4,000 in each subsequent year. AAK proposes to charge £10,000 per annum for lighting, heating and other property expenses, and wants a nominal £5,000 per annum to cover any unforeseen contingencies. Apart from this, AAK is not looking for any profit as such from the provision of these facilities, because it believes that there may be additional future benefits from increased use of the facility. It is proposed that costs will be recovered by setting drinks prices at double the direct costs.

It is not expected that the full sales level will be reached until year 3. The proportions of that level estimated to be reached in years 1 and 2 are 40% and 70% respectively.

You are required to:

(i) calculate the sales that need to be achieved in each of the five years to meet the proposed targets

(ii) comment briefly on four aspects of the proposals that you consider merit further investigation.

You may ignore the possible effects of taxation and inflation.

E13.9 *Time allowed – 90 minutes*

Lew Rolls plc is an international group that manufactures and distributes bathroom fittings to major building supply retailers and DIY chains. The board of Rolls is currently considering four projects to work with four different customers to develop new bathroom ranges (toilet, bidet, bath, basin, and shower).

Rolls has a limit on funds for investment for the current year of £24m. The four projects represent levels of 'luxury' bathrooms. The product ranges are aimed at different markets. The lengths of time to bring to market, lives of product and timings of cash flows are different for each product range.

The Super bathroom project will cost £3m and generate £5m net cash flows spread equally over five years.

The Superluxury bathroom project will cost £7m and generate £10m net cash flows spread equally over five years.

The Executive bathroom project will take a long time to start paying back. It will cost £12m and generate £21m net cash flows, zero for the first two years and then £7m for each of the next three years.

The Excelsior bathroom project will cost £15m and generate £10m net cash flows for two years.

For ease of calculation it may be assumed that all cash flows occur on the last day of each year.

Projects may be undertaken in part or in total in the current year, and next year there will be no restriction on investment. Lew Rolls plc's cost of capital is 10%.

You are required to:

(i)   calculate the NPV for each project

(ii) calculate the approximate IRR for each project

(iii) advise on the acceptance of these projects on the basis of NPV or IRR or any other method of ranking the projects.

(iv) What are the advantages of the appraisal method you have adopted for Lew Rolls plc?

(v)   What other factors should be used in the final evaluations before the recommendations are implemented?

E13.10 *Time allowed – 90 minutes*

A UK subsidiary of a large multinational is considering investment in four mutually exclusive projects. The managing director, Indira Patel, is anxious to choose a combination of projects that will maximise shareholder wealth.

At the current time the company can embark on projects up to a maximum total of £230m. The four projects require the following initial investments:

£20m in project Doh

£195m in project Ray

£35m in project Mee

£80m in project Fah

The projects are expected to generate the following net cash flows over the three years following each investment. No project will last longer than three years.

Project Year	Doh £m	Ray £m	Mee £m	Fah £m
1	15	45	15	20
2	30	75	25	25
3		180	60	100

The company's WACC is 12% per annum, which is used to evaluate investments in new projects. The impact of tax and inflation may be ignored.

Advise Indira with regard to the projects in which the company should invest on the basis of maximisation of shareholder wealth, given the limiting factor of the total funds currently available for investment.

14 Sources of finance and the cost of capital

LEARNING OBJECTIVES

Completion of this chapter will enable you to:

- identify the different sources of finance available to an organisation

- explain the concept of gearing, or the debt/equity ratio

- explain what is meant by the weighted average cost of capital (WACC)

- calculate the cost of equity and the cost of debt

- appreciate the concept of risk with regard to capital investment

- outline the capital asset pricing model (CAPM), and the β factor

- analyse return on equity as a function of financial structure

- explain the use of economic value added (EVA™) and market value added (MVA) as performance measures and value creation incentives

CONTENTS

Introduction

In Chapter 13 we dealt with decisions related to capital investment. In this chapter we will consider the main sources of external finance available to an entity to finance such investments: loans (or debt) and ordinary shares (or equity). We shall also discuss gearing, which is concerned with the relationship between the debt and equity of the entity.

The appraisal of investment projects by a company inevitably involves calculations which use some sort of discount rate. The discount rate that is normally used is the company's cost of capital. A company's cost of capital is dependent on the financial structure of the entity, its relative proportions and cost of debt (loans) and equity capital (shares). In Chapter 5 and in Chapter 13 we introduced WACC and in this chapter we will consider its calculation and application.

Coral plans rescue financing
By Damian Reece

Coral Group, the country's third largest bookmaker, has crashed to a £52.2m pre-tax loss and has been forced to seek urgent refinancing to stave off financial disaster, including a breach of its banking covenants.

New information contained in the company's filings with the Securities and Exchange Commission in the US reveals a £10m bail-out by its parent, Deutsche Bank. Deutsche owns Coral through its Morgan Grenfell Private Equity arm, which paid £395m for it in 1998. The documents also reveal that the company is working on a refinancing plan to ensure that it meets its debt repayments.

Although it is known that Coral made an operating loss of £4.2m in 2000, the SEC documents show that interest expenses on the company's debt have forced it into a further £48.3m loss, pushing it into a £52.5m pre-tax loss for the full year. The company has to make detailed SEC filings because it has bonds listed on the New York Stock Exchange.

Coral says in the documents: 'On October 11, 2000, after the end of fiscal 2000, the company issued an additional 10m shares of £1 each to the parent for a cash consideration of £10m. The company's directors do not believe that the current capital structure of the group is optimal and are currently assessing alternative refinancing structures. The directors believe the group is likely to be successfully refinanced in the foreseeable future.

However, there can be no certainty that a successful refinancing will be achieved and if a refinancing did not occur, the group may need to change its capital and revenue expansion plans to ensure that it remains able to meet the requirements of its existing facility agreements.'

One adviser to Coral said yesterday: 'What happened was that Deutsche put more money in, otherwise they [Coral] would have breached their banking covenants.' A spokesman for Coral did not return calls yesterday.

Coral now has total debts of £498.9m. It had turnover in 2000 of £1.3bn and a gross profit of £162m. But operating expenses soared in 2000 to £166m compared to £77.3m last year. Much of the additional expense has been incurred in setting up and expanding Eurobet, Coral's internet betting arm which it bought for £4.4m. This business made a loss of £11m last year and was hit by large Far Eastern syndicates betting on the Euro 2000 football championships.

Coral was heading for a £1bn flotation last year which was pulled in October. The company is now understood to be for sale if a buyer can be found. Recent speculation has centred on a possible US buyer. Possible UK buyers include Rank and Stanley Leisure. Rank wants to build a gaming business having sold off non-core operations, while Stanley is thought to be interested in acquiring Coral's 860-strong chain of betting shops but not Eurobet.

The problems at Coral come as speculation increases that Scott Lanphere, one of the senior directors at Morgan Grenfell Private Equity, will leave this week after months of vicious in-fighting.

Lanphere, who was paid a £1m signing-on fee when he joined MGPE three years ago, has clashed with Graham Hutton, the head of the private equity firm. The clashes have centred on MGPE's disastrous sale of its 12.5 per cent stake in Slec, the Formula One motor sport company controlled by Bernie Ecclestone, to EMTV, the German media group.

© *Sunday Telegraph*, 4 February 2001

We will look at how the costs of equity and debt may be determined. One of the fundamental differences between equity and debt is the risk associated with each type of financing and its impact on their cost. The capital asset pricing model (CAPM) is introduced to show how risk impacts on the cost of equity.

This chapter looks briefly at the relationship between the return on equity and the financial structure of the company. The chapter closes with an introduction to economic value added (EVA) and market value added (MVA). These measures are increasingly replacing traditional performance measures in many large corporations. An outline of these recently developed techniques is considered in terms of their use as both performance measures and motivational tools.

In early 2000 the bookmaking group Coral was considering a refinancing plan to ensure it could meet its debt repayments and support its capital and revenue expansion plans.

The press cutting opposite illustrates Coral's weak financial position, which subsequently made it the target for takeover. By April 2001 Stanley Leisure appeared to be established as the front runner most likely to complete a deal to acquire Coral's 850 betting shops.

Sources of finance

There are broadly two main sources of finance available to a company:

- **ordinary shares** (or equity)
- **loan capital** (or debt).

Each type of financing has a unique set of characteristics and rights. The main ones are shown in the table in Fig. 14.1.

Other sources of finance available to a company are:

- retained earnings
- preference shares
- leasing
- trade credit.

equity (ordinary shares)	debt (loans)
the term is unlimited i.e. for life	the term is fixed and has a maturity date
ordinary shares have a nominal or par value	loans require security, e.g. debentures
ordinary shares have voting rights	loans have no voting rights
dividends are payable on ordinary shares, the values of which are dependent on company performance	interest is payable on loans: it may be fixed; variable; rolled over
dividends are an appropriation or a use of profits, and are therefore payable after corporation tax	interest on loans is an allowable expense for corporation tax
if a company is wound up the ordinary shareholders are the last to be considered – it is capital having the highest risk	if a company is wound up, lenders appear near the top of the list for consideration

FIGURE 14.1 Some of the main characteristics and rights of equity capital compared with debt capital

Trade credit will be discussed in Chapter 15 when we look at the management of working capital.

Share capital

The capital of a company is called share capital and may comprise ordinary shares and preference shares (although there are other classes of shares, which are not covered in this book). The company determines the maximum share capital that it is ever likely to need to raise and this level is called its authorised share capital. The amount of shares actually in issue at any point in time is normally at a level for the company to meet its foreseeable requirements. These shares are called the company's issued share capital which, when all the shareholders have paid for them, are referred to as fully paid up issued share capital.

Ordinary shareholders receive a dividend at a level determined usually by company performance and not as a specific entitlement. Preference shareholders receive a dividend at a level that is fixed, subject to the conditions of issue of the shares, and have priority over the ordinary shareholders if the company is wound up.

Additional equity capital may be raised through increasing the number of shares issued by the company through **scrip issues** and **rights issues**. A scrip issue (or bonus issue) increases the number of shares with the additional shares going to existing shareholders, in proportion to their holdings, through capitalisation of the reserves of the company. No cash is called for from the shareholders.

Sportingbet floats with scaled-back fundraising
By Clive Mathieson

Sportingbet.com, the ambitious online bookmaker, yesterday defied investor disillusionment with dot-coms to become the UK's first successful Internet float of 2001.

However, the 'very difficult stock market conditions' forced Sportingbet to scale back its fundraising expectations in an effort to get the company to market. Sportingbet said it had raised £18 million after expenses, below earlier targets of £20 million to £30 million.

The company will list on London's Alternative Investment Market on January 30 after issuing 15 million new shares, representing about 12 per cent of issued capital, at 120p each.

At the issue price, Sportingbet is worth £156 million, with Mark Blandford, the founder and chief executive, retaining a 19.7 per cent stake worth almost £31 million.

Nigel Payne, finance director, said Sportingbet had raised less than analysts' expectations but was 'over the moon' with the final valuation of the company.

He said investors in the float had recognised that Sportingbet was an offline business using the Internet to reach a global market.

'We are a bookmaker and we're using the Internet as a means to market,' he said. 'It's a different model to what has become accepted parlance for a dot.com – an e-tailer.'

Sportingbet operates a global online and telephone sports betting business with about 50,000 customers in 103 countries. Just 7 per cent of gambling turnover comes from the UK. Dresdner Kleinwort Wasserstein (DKW), the float sponsor, expects the global 'e-gambling' market to grow at 32 per cent a year between 2001 and 2004.

DKW forecasts that Sportingbet, which is already cash-flow positive, will increase revenues tenfold to about £270.4 million this year. The company is expected to report its first pre-tax profit in 2003, as sales hit £669 million.

Mr Payne said funds raised in the float would be used to increase marketing spending, enter joint ventures and make acquisitions. He said the company was well advanced in identifying acquisitions: 'I don't expect the money to be sitting on the balance sheet for a year earning interest.'

Source: *The Times*, London, 24 January 2001

In a rights issue, the right to subscribe for new shares (or debentures) issued by the company is given to existing shareholders. The 'rights' to buy the new shares are usually fixed at a price discounted to below the current market price. A shareholder not wishing to take up a rights issue may sell the rights.

The online bookmaker Sportingbet.com is really an offline business that uses the Internet to reach a global market (see the press cutting opposite). This case illustrates how a business may obtain required funding to expand its sales through increased marketing spending, and investments in acquisitions and joint ventures.

Sportinbet.com raised £18m by issuing 15 million shares and became listed on the London Alternative Investment market in January 2001. The bank that sponsored the company's flotation reported massive increases in forecast sales expected in the years 2001 to 2003.

Example 14.1

A company that achieves a profit after tax of 20% on capital employed has the following capital structure:

400,000 ordinary shares of £1	£400,000
Retained earnings	£200,000

In order to invest in some new profitable projects the company wishes to raise £252,000 from a rights issue. The company's current ordinary share price is £1.80.

The company would like to know the number of shares that must be issued if the rights price is £1.60; £1.50; £1.40; £1.20.

Answer

Capital employed is £600,000 [£400,000 + £200,000]

Current earnings are 20% of £600,000 = £120,000

Therefore, earnings per share (eps) $= \dfrac{£120,000}{400,000} = 30p$

After the rights issue earnings will be 20% of £852,000, which equals £170,400.

Rights price £	Number of new shares £252,000/ rights price £	Total shares after rights issue £	Eps £170,400/ total shares pence
1.60	157,500	557,500	30.6
1.50	168,000	568,000	30.0
1.40	180,000	580,000	29.4
1.20	210,000	610,000	27.9

We can see that at a high rights issue share price the earnings per share are increased. At lower issue prices eps are diluted. The 'break-even point', with no dilution, is where the rights price equals the capital employed per share £600,000/400,000 = £1.50.

Example 14.2

A company has 1,000,000 £1 ordinary shares in issue with a market price of £2.10 on 1 June. The company wished to raise new equity capital by a 1 for 4 share rights issue at a price of £1.50. Immediately the company announced the rights issue the price fell to £1.95 on 2 June. Just before the issue was due to be made the share price had recovered to £2 per share, the cum rights price.

We need to calculate the theoretical ex rights price, the new market price as a consequence of an adjustment to allow for the discount price of the new issue.

Answer

The market price will theoretically fall after the issue

1,000,000 shares × the cum rights price of £2	£2,000,000
250,000 shares × the issue price of £1.50	£375,000
Theoretical value of 1,250,000 shares	£2,375,000
Therefore, the theoretical ex-rights price is	$\dfrac{£2,375,000}{1,250,000} = £1.90$ per share

Or to put it another way

Four shares at the cum rights value of £2	£8.00
One new share issued at £1.50	£1.50
	£9.50
Therefore, the theoretical ex-rights price is	$\dfrac{£9.50}{5} = £1.90$ per share

Long-term debt

Generally, companies try and match debt with the type of assets requiring to be financed:

● fixed assets
● working capital.

Long-term debt is usually more expensive and less flexible, but has less risk, than short-term debt. Long-term debt is therefore normally matched to finance the acquisition of fixed assets, which are long-term assets from which the company expects to derive benefits over several periods.

Long-term financial debts are the elements of loans and leases that are payable after one year of the balance sheet date. Debt capital may take many forms: loans, debentures, Eurobonds, mortgages, etc. We will not delve into the particular attributes of each type of debt capital. Suffice to say, each involves interest payment, and capital repayment and security for the loan is usually required.

Progress check 14.1

What are the major differences that may be found in comparing the capital structure of companies?

Security for a loan may be by way of a floating charge, without attachment to specific assets, on the whole of the business's assets. If the company is not able to meet its obligations the floating charge will crystallise on specific assets like debtors or stocks. Security may alternatively, at the outset, take the form of a fixed charge on specific assets like land and buildings.

Loan interest is a fixed commitment, which is usually payable once or twice a year. Although debt capital is burdened with a fixed commitment of interest payable it is a tax efficient method of financing. A 10% debenture, if corporation tax were at 30% would actually cost the company 7%.

Loans, or debentures, may be redeemable in which case the principal, the original sum borrowed will need to be repaid on a specific date.

Example 14.3

Explain the main features of debentures (loans) compared with ordinary shares as sources of finance.

Answer

Ordinary shares represent long-term capital provided by the owners of a company, both new and existing. The owners receive varying levels of dividends that are usually based on the underlying profitability of the company (Tesco plc actually advised their shareholders of this relationship in the late 1990s).

Debentures and loans may be either unsecured, or secured on some or all of the assets of the company. Lenders to a company receive interest, payable yearly or half-yearly, the rate of which may vary with market conditions.

If a company is liquidated the ordinary shareholders are always last to be repaid.

Short-term debt

Short-term financial debts are the elements of overdrafts, loans and leases that are repayable within one year of the balance sheet date. Short-term finance tends to be less expensive and more flexible than long-term debt. Short-term debt is therefore normally matched to finance the fluctuations in levels of the company's net current assets, its working capital.

Such short-term finance represents a higher risk for the borrower. Interest rates are volatile, and an overdraft, for example, is technically repayable on demand. The company may finance its operations by taking on further short-term debt, as levels of working capital increase. Because of the higher risk associated with short-term debt, many companies adopting a conservative funding policy may accept a reduction in profitability and use long-term debt to finance not only fixed assets, but also a proportion of the company's working capital. Less risk-averse companies may use short-term debt to finance both working capital and fixed assets; such debt provides increased profitability because of its lower cost.

Retained earnings

Both debt and equity are sources of finance external to the company. Internal sources of finance may be provided from cash generated by the company in excess of the requirements to finance its operations, and to pay interest, taxation, and dividends. The surplus in cash terms is called retained earnings. Another source of internal finance may be provided from additional cash resources generated from more effective management of the company's working capital.

There is statistical evidence which shows that through the 1990s the majority of capital funding of UK companies continued to be derived from internal sources of finance. However, this is not free. The profit or net earnings generated from the operations of the company belongs to the shareholders of the company. There is a cost, an opportunity cost, which is the best alternative return that shareholders could obtain on these funds elsewhere in the financial markets.

It is the shareholders who decide at the annual general meeting (AGM) how much of those earnings are distributed to shareholders as dividends, the balance being held and reinvested in the business. The retained earnings of the company are increased by net profit less any dividends payable; they are part of the shareholders' funds and therefore appear within the equity of the company. Similarly any losses will reduce the retained earnings of the company. The cost of shareholders' equity is reflected in the level of dividends paid to shareholders, which is usually dependent on how well the company has performed during the year.

Progress check 14.2	Describe what is meant by debt and equity and give some examples. Are these the only sources of finance available to a company?

Gearing

The relationship between debt and equity capital represents the financial structure of an organisation. This relationship is called gearing. We will first take a look at gearing and its application and then consider an example showing the issue of debt capital compared with the issue of shares.

The relationship between the two sources of finance, loans and ordinary shares, or debt and equity gives a measure of the gearing of the company. A company with a high proportion of debt capital to share capital is highly geared, and low geared if the reverse situation applies. Gearing (leverage, or debt/equity) has important implications for the long-term stability of a company because of, as we have seen, its impact on financial risk.

The extent to which the debt/equity is high or low geared has an effect on the earnings per share (eps) of the company:

● if profits are increasing, then higher gearing is preferable

● if profits are decreasing, then lower gearing or no gearing is preferred.

Similarly, the argument applies to the riskiness attached to capital repayments. If a company goes into liquidation, lenders have priority over shareholders with regard to capital repayment. So, the more highly geared the company the less chance there is of ordinary shareholders being repaid in full.

The many types of short and long-term capital available to companies leads to complexity, but also the expectation that overall financial risks may be reduced through improved matching of funding with operational needs. The gearing position of the company may be considered in many ways depending on whether the long-term capital structure or the overall financial structure is being analysed. It may also be analysed by concentrating on the income position rather than purely the capital structure.

Financial gearing relates to the relationship between a company's borrowings, which includes debt, and its share capital and reserves. Concerning capital structure, gearing calculations may be based on a number of different capital values. All UK plcs disclose their net debt to equity ratio in their annual reports and accounts.

The ratios that follow are the two most commonly used. Both ratios relate to financial gearing, which is the relationship between a company's borrowings, which includes both prior charge capital and long-term debt, and its shareholders' funds (share capital plus reserves).

$$\text{gearing} = \frac{\text{long-term debt}}{\text{equity} + \text{long-term debt}}$$

$$\text{debt equity ratio or leverage (D/E)} = \frac{\text{long-term debt}}{\text{equity}}$$

Example 14.4 illustrates the calculation of both ratios.

Example 14.4

Two companies have different gearing. Company A is financed totally by 20,000 £1 ordinary shares, whilst company B is financed partly by 10,000 £1 ordinary shares and a £10,000 10% loan. In all other respects the companies are the same. They both have assets of £20,000 and both make the same profit before interest and tax (PBIT).

	A £	B £
Assets	20,000	20,000
less 10% loan	–	(10,000)
	20,000	10,000
Ordinary shares	20,000	10,000

$$\text{Gearing} = \frac{\text{long-term debt}}{\text{equity} + \text{long-term debt}} \quad \frac{0}{20,000 + 0} = 0\% \quad \frac{10,000}{10,000 + 10,000} = 50\%$$

$$\text{Debt equity ratio} = \frac{\text{long-term debt}}{\text{equity}} \quad \frac{0}{20,000} = 0\% \quad \frac{10,000}{10,000} = 100\%$$

Company B must make a profit before interest of at least £1,000 to cover the cost of the 10% loan. Company A does not have any PBIT requirement because it has no debt.

Company A is lower geared and considered less risky in terms of profitability than company B which is a higher geared company. This is because PBIT of a lower geared company is more likely to be sufficiently high to cover interest charges and make a profit for equity shareholders.

As we have seen, gearing calculations can be made in a number of ways, and may also be based on earnings/interest relationships in addition to capital values. For example:

$$\text{dividend cover (times)} = \frac{\text{earnings per share (eps)}}{\text{dividend per share}}$$

This ratio indicates the number of times the profits attributable to the equity shareholders covers the actual dividends paid and payable for the period. Financial analysts usually adjust their calculations for any exceptional or extraordinary items of which they may be aware.

What is gearing? Outline some of the ways in which it may be calculated.

$$\text{interest cover (times)} = \frac{\text{profit before interest and tax}}{\text{interest payable}}$$

This ratio calculates the number of times the interest payable is covered by profits available for such payments. It is particularly important for lenders to determine the vulnerability of interest payments to a drop in profit. The following ratio determines the same vulnerability in cash terms.

$$\text{cash interest cover} = \frac{\text{net cash inflow from operations} + \text{interest received}}{\text{interest paid}}$$

Example 14.5

Swell Guys plc is a growing company that manufactures equipment for fitting out small cruiser boats. Its planned expansion involves investing in a new factory project costing £4m. The 12-year project will add £0.5m to profit before interest and tax each year. Next year's operating profit is forecast at £5m, and dividends per share are forecast at the same level as last year. Tax is not expected to be payable over the next few years due to tax losses that have been carried forward.

Swell Guys last two years' results are as follows:

	Last year £m	Previous year £m
Profit and loss account for the year ended 31 December		
Sales	18	15
Operating costs	16	11
Operating profit	2	4
Interest payable	1	1
Profit before tax	1	3
Tax on ordinary activities	0	0
Profit after tax	1	3
Dividends	1	1
Retained profit	0	2
Balance sheet as at 31 December		
Fixed assets	8	9
Current assets		
Stocks	7	4
Debtors	4	3
Cash	1	2
	12	9

Creditors due within one year

Bank overdraft	4	2
Trade creditors	5	5
	9	7
Net current assets	3	2
Total assets less current liabilities	11	11
less		
Long-term loans	6	6
Net assets	5	5
Capital and reserves		
Share capital (25p ordinary shares)	2	2
Profit and loss account	3	3
	5	5

Swell Guys is considering two options:

1. Issue of £4m 15% loan stock repayable in five years time
2. Rights issue of 4m 25p ordinary shares at £1 per share after expenses

   For each of the options the directors would like to see:

(i)   how the retained profit (derived from operating profit) will look for next year

(ii)   how earnings per share will look for next year

(iii) how the capital and reserves will look at the end of next year

(iv)   how long-term loans will look at the end of next year

(v)   how gearing will look at the end of next year.

Answer

(i)   **Swell Guys plc forecast profit and loss account for next year ended 31 December**

Operating profit   £5m + £0.5m from the new project

		New debt £m	New equity £m
Operating profit		5.5	5.5
Interest payable	[1.0 + 0.6]	1.6	1.0
Profit before tax		3.9	4.5
Tax on ordinary activities		0.0	0.0
Profit after tax		3.9	4.5
Dividends		1.0	1.5
Retained profit		2.9	3.0

(ii)   **Earnings per share**

Profit available for ordinary shareholders	£3.9m	48.75p	£4.5m	37.5p
Number of ordinary shares	8m		12m	

▶

◄

| | | As at 31 December | | |
		New debt £m		New equity £m
(iii) **Capital and reserves**					
Share capital (25p ordinary shares)		2.0	(8m)	3.0	(12m)
Share premium account		0.0		3.0	
Profit and loss account		5.9		6.0	
		7.9		11.0	
(iv) **Long-term loans**	[6 + 4]	10.0		6.0	
(v) **Gearing**					
$\dfrac{\text{long-term debt}}{\text{equity} + \text{long-term debt}}$	$\dfrac{6 + 4}{7.9 + 6 + 4}$	55.9%	$\dfrac{6}{11 + 6}$	35.3%	

Progress check 14.4

Explain how a high interest cover ratio can reassure a prospective lender.

The weighted average cost of capital (WACC)

The weighted average cost of capital (WACC) may be defined as the average cost of the total financial resources of a company, i.e. the shareholders' equity and the net financial debt.

If we represent shareholders equity as E and net financial debt as D then the relative proportions of equity and debt in the total financing are:

$$\frac{E}{E + D} \text{ and } \frac{D}{E + D}$$

The cost of equity is the expected return on equity, the return the shareholders expect from their investment. If we represent the return on shareholders equity as e and the return on financial debt as d, and t is the rate of corporation tax, then we can provide a formula to calculate WACC. As we saw in Chapter 10, the return on shareholder equity comprises both cash flows from dividends and increases in the share price. We will return to how the cost of equity may be derived in a later section in this chapter.

Interest on debt capital is an allowable deduction for purposes of corporate taxation and so the cost of share capital and the cost of debt capital are not properly comparable costs. Therefore this tax relief on debt interest ought to be recognised in any discounted cash flow calculations. One way would be to include the tax savings due to interest payments in the cash flows of every project. A simpler method, and the one normally used, is to allow for the tax relief in computing the cost of debt capital, to arrive at an after-tax cost of debt. Therefore the weighted average cost of capital is calculated from:

$$\text{WACC} = \left\{ \frac{E}{(E + D)} \times e \right\} + \left\{ \frac{D}{(E + D)} \times d\,(1 - t) \right\}$$

Example 14.6

Fleet Ltd has the following financial structure:

$e = 15\%$ return on equity (this may be taken as given for the purpose of this example)

$d = 10\%$ lower risk, so lower than the return on equity

$t = 30\%$ rate of corporation tax

$\dfrac{E}{E + D} = 60\%$ equity to debt plus equity ratio

$\dfrac{D}{E + D} = 40\%$ debt to debt plus equity ratio

We are required to calculate the WACC for Fleet Ltd, and evaluate the impact on WACC of a change in capital structure to equity 40% and debt 60%.

Answer

Calculation of WACC for Fleet Ltd with the current financial structure:

$$WACC = \left\{ \frac{E}{(E + D)} \times e \right\} + \left\{ \frac{D}{(E + D)} \times d\,(1 - t) \right\}$$

$$WACC = (60\% \times 15\%) + \{40\% \times 10\%\,(1 - 30\%)\} = 11.8\%$$

If the company decides to change its financial structure so that equity is 40% and debt is 60% of total financing, then WACC becomes:

$$(40\% \times 15\%) + \{60\% \times 10\%\,(1 - 30\%)\} = 10.2\%$$

So it appears that the company has reduced its WACC by increasing the relative weight from 40% to 60% of the cheapest financial resource, debt, in its total financing. However, this is not true because as the debt/equity ratio of the company increased from 0.67 (40/60) to 1.50 (60/40) the company's risk has also increased.

Therefore the lenders of the financial resources will require a higher return on their investment. There is a well-established correlation between risk and return. So, it is not correct to calculate the WACC using the same returns on equity and debt, as both will have increased.

The market value of a company may be determined by its WACC. The lower the WACC then the higher the net present values of its future cash flows and therefore the higher its market value. The determination of the optimum D/E ratio is one of the most difficult tasks facing the finance director. One of the consequences of this is the problem of calculating an accurate WACC for a company, which is based on its relative proportions and costs of debt and equity capital.

The risks and costs associated with debt capital and equity capital are different and subject to continual change, and may vary from industry to industry and between different types of business. Measurement of the D/E ratio may therefore not be a straightforward task, particularly for diversified groups of companies. Companies in different markets and indeed diversified companies that have trading divisions operating within different markets and producing different products face different levels of risk. If division A operates with a higher risk than division B then the required rate of return of A's investments should be higher than the hurdle rate of return of B's investments. The difference is 'paying' for the difference in risk. This is an important principle but very difficult to implement in practice.

In a later section, we will look at ways in which both the cost of equity and the cost of debt to the company may be determined.

There are many arguments for and against the use of WACC for investment appraisal. Its use is argued on the basis that:

- new investments must be financed by new sources of funds – retained earnings, new share issues, new loans, and so on
- the cost of capital to be applied to new project evaluation must reflect the cost of new capital
- the WACC reflects the company's long-term future capital structure, and capital costs; if this were not so, the current WACC would become irrelevant because eventually it would not relate to any actual cost of capital.

It is argued that the current WACC should be used to evaluate projects, because a company's capital structure changes only very slowly over time; therefore, the marginal cost of new capital should be roughly equal to the WACC. If this view is correct, then by undertaking investments which offer a return in excess of the WACC, a company will increase the market value of its ordinary shares in the long run. This is because the excess returns would provide surplus profits and dividends for the shareholders.

The arguments against the use of WACC are based on the criticisms of the assumptions made that justify the use of WACC:

- new investments have different risk characteristics from the company's existing operations therefore the return required by investors may go up or down if the investments are made, because their business risk is perceived to be higher or lower
- finance raised to fund a new investment
  - may substantially change the capital structure and perceived risk of investing in the company
  - may determine whether debt or equity used to finance the project will change the perceived risk of the entire company, which
  - must be taken into account in the investment appraisal
- many companies raise floating rate debt capital as well as fixed rate debt capital, having a variable rate that changes every few months in line with current market rates; this is difficult to include in a WACC calculation, the best compromise being to substitute an 'equivalent' fixed debt rate in place of the floating rate.

Progress check 14.5

What is WACC and why is it so important?

Cost of debt and equity capital

We have introduced the concept of risk and its correlation with returns on investments. The relationship between risk and return is also one of the key concepts relating to determination of the cost of debt and equity capital. It is an important concept and so we will briefly explore risk a little further, with regard to investments in companies. We shall discuss the cost of debt based on future income flows, that is, interest. We shall similarly discuss the cost of equity based on future income flows, that is, dividends. This will also provide an introduction to the **beta factor** and the **capital asset pricing model (CAPM)**.

The cost of servicing debt capital, as we have discussed, is the yearly or half yearly interest payment, which is an allowable expense for tax. The cost of repayment of a loan, or debt, depends on the type of loan. Loan capital, a debenture for example, may be irredeemable and traded, with a market value. The cost of capital for a redeemable loan may be calculated using a quite complicated formula.

For our purposes, to demonstrate the principle, we can look at the cost of irredeemable loan capital to a company that may be calculated as follows:

$$d = \frac{i \times (1 - t)}{L}$$

where

d = cost of debt capital
i = annual loan interest rate
L = the current market value of the loan
t = the rate of corporation tax

By rearranging the formula it can be seen that market value of the debt is dependent on the level of future returns, the interest rate paid, which is determined by the level of risk associated with the investment.

Example 14.7

Owen Cash plc pays 12% (i) interest per annum on an irredeemable debt of £1m, with a nominal value of £100. The corporation tax rate (t) is currently 50%. The market value of the debt (L) is currently £90.

What is Owen Cash plc's cost of debt?

Answer

d = cost of debt capital

$$d = \frac{i \times (1 - t)}{L} = \frac{12\% \times (1 - 50\%)}{90}$$

$$d = \frac{0.12 \times 0.50}{90} = 6.7\%$$

In a similar way, the cost of equity to a company may be determined by looking at future income flows. In the case of equity or ordinary shares this future income is dividends. A difference between this method and the method applied to debt is that there is no tax relief for dividend payments.

The value of an ordinary share may be simply expressed as the present value of its expected future dividend flows.

$$S = v_1/(1 + e) + v_2/(1 + e)^2 + v_3/(1 + e)^3 \ldots v_n/(1 + e)^n$$

where

e = cost of equity capital
v = expected future dividends for n years
S = the current market value of the share

If dividends are expected to remain level over a period of time the formula may be simplified to

$$S = \frac{v}{e}$$

Therefore, the cost of equity to the company would be

$$e = \frac{v}{S}$$

Dividends payable on a particular share rarely stay constant from year to year. However, they may grow at a regular rate. This so-called dividend based approach to the cost of equity may then be used with the above formula revised as

$$S = v/(e - G)$$

where G = the expected future dividend growth rate.
The cost of equity may then be stated as

$$e = \frac{v}{S} + G$$

Example 14.8

Cher Alike plc has 3m ordinary shares in issue that currently have a market price (S) of £2.71. The board have already recommended next year's dividend (v) at 17p per share. The chairman, Sonny Daze, is forecasting that dividends will continue to grow (G) at 4.2% per annum for the foreseeable future.
What is Cher Alike plc's cost of equity?

Answer

e = cost of equity capital

$$e = \frac{v}{S} + G = \frac{0.17}{2.71} + 4.2\%$$

$e = 0.063 + 0.042 = 10.5\%$

The interest rate paid on a loan is known almost with certainty. Even if the debt carries a variable interest rate it is far easier to estimate than expected dividend flows on ordinary shares.

The cost of equity to a company may alternatively be derived using the capital asset pricing model (CAPM). We will look at this approach to risk, and how some risk may be diversified away by using a spread (or portfolio) of investments.

Progress check 14.6

In broad terms how are the costs of debt and equity determined?

Cost of equity and risk, CAPM and the β factor

Whenever any investment is made there will be some risk involved. The actual return on investment in ordinary shares (equity capital) may be better or worse than hoped for. Unless the investor settles for risk-free securities a certain element of risk is unavoidable.

However, investors in companies or in projects can diversify their investments in a suitably wide portfolio. Some investments may do better and some worse than expected. In this way, average returns should turn out much as expected. Risk that can be diversified away is referred to as **unsystematic risk**.

Some investments are by their very nature more risky than others. This is nothing to do with chance variations in actual compared with expected returns, it is inherent risk that cannot be diversified away. This type of risk is referred to as **systematic risk** or **market risk**. The investor must therefore accept this risk, unless he/she invests entirely in risk-free investments. In return for accepting systematic risk an investor will expect to earn a return which is higher than the return on risk-free investment.

The amount of systematic risk depends, for example, on the industry or the type of project. If an investor has a balanced portfolio of shares he/she will incur exactly the same systematic risk as the average systematic risk of the stock market as a whole. The capital asset pricing model (CAPM) is mainly concerned with how systematic risk is measured and how systematic risk affects required returns and share prices. It was first formulated for investments in shares on the stock exchange, but is now also used for company investments in capital projects.

Systematic risk is measured using what are known as beta factors. A beta factor β is the measure of the volatility of a share in terms of market risk. The CAPM is a statement of the principles outlined above. An investor can use the beta factor β in such a way that a high factor will automatically suggest a share is to be avoided because of considerable high risk in the past. Consider the impact in January 2001 on the beta factor of Iceland plc, caused by the resignation from the board of the major shareholder together with the issue of a profits warning by the company.

The CAPM model can be stated as follows:

the expected return from a security = the risk-free rate of return, plus a premium for market risk adjusted by a measure of the volatility of the security

If

Rs	is the expected return from an individual security
β	is the beta factor for the individual security
Rf	is the risk-free rate of return
Rm	is the return from the market as a whole
(Rm − Rf)	is the market risk premium

$$\mathbf{Rs = Rf + \{\beta \times (Rm - Rf)\}}$$

There are many analysts that specialise in the charting of the volatility of shares and markets, and their findings may regularly be found in the UK financial press.

A variation of the above β relationship may be used to establish an equity cost of capital to use in project appraisal. The cost of equity *e* equates to the expected return from an individual security Rs, and the beta value for the company's equity capital β *e* equates to beta factor for the individual security β.

So

| the return expected by ordinary shareholders, or the cost of equity to the company | = | the risk-free rate of return plus a premium for market risk adjusted by a measure of the volatility of the ordinary shares of the company |

$$e = Rf + \{\beta\, e \times (Rm - Rf)\}$$

Example 14.9

Bittaboth plc has ordinary shares in issue with a market value four times the value of its debt capital. The debt is considered to be risk free and pays 11% (Rf) before tax. The beta value of Bittaboth's equity capital has been estimated at 0.9 ($\beta\, e$) and the average market return on equity capital is 17% (Rm). Corporation tax is at 50% (t).

Calculate Bittaboth plc's WACC.

Answer

e = cost of equity capital

$e = Rf + \{\beta\, e \times (Rm - Rf)\} = 11\% + \{0.9 \times (17\% - 11\%)\}$

$e = 0.11 + (0.9 \times 0.06) = 0.164 = 16.4\%$

d = cost of debt capital

which after tax is $i \times (1 - t)$ or $11\% \times 50\% = 5.5\%$

Any capital projects that Bittaboth may wish to consider may be evaluated using its WACC, which may be calculated as:

{equity/(debt + equity) ratio × return on equity} + {debt/(debt + equity) ratio × after tax cost of debt}

(4/5 × 16.4%) + (1/5 × 5.5%) = 14.2%

14.2% is Bittaboth's weighted average cost of capital (WACC).

It should be remembered that the CAPM considers systematic risk only, and is based on an assumption of market equilibrium.

β factors may be calculated using market and individual companies' information. β values are also obtainable from a variety of sources and are published quarterly by the London Business School.

Progress check 14.7

Describe what is meant by systematic risk and unsystematic risk.

Return on equity and financial structure

The important formula that follows shows the return on equity (ROE) as a function of return on investment (ROI) and the financial structure, leverage or gearing of the company, where:

D = debt capital
E = equity capital
t = corporation tax rate
i = interest rate on debt
ROI = return on investment

ROS = return on sales = $\dfrac{\text{profit after tax}}{\text{total investment}}$

ROE = {ROI × (1 − t)} + {(ROI − i) × (1 − t) × D/E}

Example 14.10 illustrates the use of this relationship and a general rule derived from it.

Example 14.10

A hospital equipment manufacturing company, Nilby Mouth plc, makes an operating profit (PBIT) of £10m on sales of £100m and with a total investment of £60m. The investment is financed by equity (E) of £40m and debt (D) of £20m with an interest rate (i) of 10%. Assume the corporation tax rate (t) is 50%.

We are required to:

(i)   calculate the current return on equity (ROE)

(ii) calculate the ROE if financing were changed so that debt was £40m and equity was £20m

(iii) calculate the current ROE if operating profit were reduced to £4m

(iv) calculate the ROE if operating profit were reduced to £4m and if financing were changed so that debt was £40m and equity was £20m.

Answer

Figures in £m

(i) **Calculation of return on equity (ROE)**

Profit before interest and tax, or operating profit PBIT = 10

Profit before tax PBT = 10 − (20 × 10%) = 8

Profit after tax PAT = 8 × (1 − 50%) = 4

Return on sales ROS = 4/100 = 4%

Return on investment ROI (pre interest and tax) = 10/60 = 16.7%

Debt/equity ratio D/E = 20/40 = 50%

ROE = ROI × (1 − t) + {(ROI − i) × (1 − t) × D/E}

Return on equity ROE = {16.7% × (1 − 50%)} + {(16.7% − 10%) × (1 − 50%) × 50%}
= 0.10025 or 10%

(ii) **Calculation of ROE if financing is changed so that debt is £40m and equity is £20m**

PBIT = 10   PBT = 10 − (40 × 10%) = 6   PAT = 6 × (1 − 50%) = 3

ROS = 3/100 = 3%

ROI (pre interest and tax) = 10/60 = 16.7%

D/E = 40/20 = 200%

ROE = {16.7% × (1 − 50%)} + {(16.7% − 10%) × (1 − 50%) × 200%}
= 0.15050 or 15.1%

Return on sales has reduced, whereas return on equity has increased.

▶

◀ (iii) **Calculation of ROE if the operating profit were reduced to £4m**

PBIT $= 4$ PBT $= 4 - (20 \times 10\%) = 2$ PAT $= 2 \times (1 - 50\%) = 1$

ROS $= 1/100 = 1\%$

ROI (pre interest and tax) $= 4/60 = 6.7\%$

D/E $= 20/40 = 50\%$

ROE $= \{6.7\% \times (1 - 50\%)\} + \{(6.7\% - 10\%) \times (1 - 50\%) \times 50\%\} = 0.02525$ or 2.53%

(iv) **Calculation of ROE if financing is changed so that debt is £40m and equity is £20m**

PBIT $= 4$ PBT $= 4 - (40 \times 10\%) = 0$ PAT $= 0 \times (1 - 50\%) = 0$

ROS $= 0/100 = 0\%$

ROI (pre interest and tax) $= 4/60 = 6.7\%$

D/E $= 40/20 = 200\%$

ROE $= \{6.7\% \times (1 - 50\%)\} + \{(6.7\% - 10\%) \times (1 - 50\%) \times 200\%\} = 0.00050$ or 0.05%

Return on sales has reduced and return on equity has also reduced.

The general rule apparent from the relationships outlined in Example 14.10 is:

- when ROI is greater than i the higher the D/E, the higher the ROE
- when ROI is less than i the higher the D/E, the lower the ROE.

However, even if the ROI is greater than the debt interest the company's bankers may not automatically allow the D/E to increase indefinitely. The company's risk increases as the D/E or leverage increases, in terms of its commitment to high levels of interest payments, and bankers will not tolerate too high a level of risk; they will also be inclined to increase the debt interest rate as D/E increases. Shareholders will have the same reaction – they are happy with an increase in ROE but realise that they also have to face a higher risk.

For a high growth company, to limit the shareholders' investment, the company will have a tendency to increase D/E and therefore ROE, but also the financial risk. The press (for example Questor in the *Daily Telegraph*) usually comments where a plc is seen to embark on a policy of increased borrowings and increasing its gearing ratio, which alerts the reader to 'increased financial risk'. Plcs are usually prepared and ready for such comments in order to respond with their 'defence' of such a policy.

Progress check 14.8

Discuss why bankers may refuse additional lending to a company as its debt/equity ratio increases?

Growth of a company may be looked at using profit and loss account horizontal analyses. Use of this technique, which was covered in Chapter 6, presents all numbers in the profit and loss account as a percentage using a base year, which is 100, for year-on-year comparison. Financial commentators usually begin articles on the performance of plcs by comparing the current year performance with the previous year, and then attempt a forecast of future performance. This is an example of a basic horizontal analysis that focuses on turnover and profits. Only a few companies actually succeed in growing year on year, over an extended period (for example ten years).

Economic value added (EVA™) and market value added (MVA)

Maximisation of shareholder wealth continues to be the prime objective with which managers of corporations are charged. We have considered various ways in which managers may measure financial performance. The extent to which success in particular performance measures align with shareholder wealth is particularly relevant. Equally important are the ways in which managers are motivated to maximise shareholder wealth. In most organisations managerial remuneration provides the link between the measures of financial performance and shareholder value.

Financial performance measures such as a company's shares price are commonly used to indicate how well the company is doing. However, it may be questioned as to how directly the share price reflects decisions that have been taken by management. In the context of managers' performance against budget targets, and the company's overall financial performance, we have previously discussed the merits and otherwise of other performance measures such as profit after tax, earnings per share, dividends, return on capital employed, and cash flow, etc. Each has its limitations, but cash flow based measures are now becoming accepted as perhaps better indicators than profit related measures.

During the mid-1980s, Rappaport developed shareholder value analysis, from which the American firm Stern Stewart Management Services evolved concepts known as **economic value added (EVA™)** and **market value added (MVA)**. Through EVA, Stern Stewart attempted to reconcile between the need for a performance measure correlated highly with shareholder wealth, and a performance measure which was also responsive to actions taken by managers. By the mid-1990s over 200 global companies had been in discussion with Stern Stewart with regard to adoption of EVA; Lucas Varity in the UK and Coca Cola in the USA were already successful users of EVA.

If we assume that the organisation's objective is to maximise shareholder wealth then this will be achieved if new projects are taken on and existing projects are allowed to continue only if they create value. Investment in capital projects may be made only on the basis of choosing those with a positive net present value (NPV). However, NPV cannot be applied to remuneration schemes because it is a summary measure based on projected cash flows and not realised performance.

Companies usually turn to company earnings and cash flow (which are termed flow measures) for management remuneration schemes. EVA supports the same sort of recommendations that NPV provides at the project level, but also provides a better measure of management performance because it rewards for earnings generated, whilst also including charges for the amount of capital employed to create those earnings.

If profit after tax = PAT
Weighted average cost of capital = WACC
Net assets = adjusted book value of net capital = NA
Then we may define EVA as

$$\textbf{EVA} = \textbf{PAT} - (\textbf{WACC} \times \textbf{NA})$$

Example 14.11 will illustrate the calculation of EVA and its relationship with NPV.

Example 14.11

A manager has to choose between three mutually exclusive projects. The company may invest

    £50,000 in project A,   or

    £110,000 in project B,   or

    £240,000 in project C

Project A is expected to generate incremental profits after tax (PAT) of £50,000 in year 1, £40,000 in year 2 (total £90,000), after which the project is terminated.

Project B is expected to generate incremental PATs of £45,000 in year 1, £70,000 in year 2, £70,000 in year 3 (total £185,000), after which the project is terminated.

Project C is expected to generate incremental PATs of £55,000 in year 1, £75,000 in year 2, £80,000 in year 3 (total £210,000), after which the project is terminated.

The company's WACC is 10% per annum.

Capital levels may be assumed to be maintained throughout the life of each project, that is, each year's new capital investment equals depreciation in that year.

Capital items are sold at their book value in the final year of each project, so free cash flow (operating cash flow less capital expenditure) will be equal to PAT each year except the final years when the capital costs are recovered.

We are required to assess which project the manager will choose if:

(i)   his/her remuneration is tied to the NPV of the project

(ii) his/her remuneration is based on IRR

(iii) his/her remuneration is based on project earnings

(iv) his/her remuneration is based on EVA.

Answer

Using a discount rate of WACC at 10% per annum, we first calculate the NPVs of each project.

Year	Cash outflows £000	Cash inflows £000		Net cash flow £000	Discount factor at 10%	Present values £000
Project A						
0	−50			−50	1.000	−50.0
1		50		50	0.909	45.5
2		90	[40 + 50]	90	0.826	74.3
3		0		0	0.751	0.0
Total	−50	140		90		69.8
Project B						
0	−110			−110	1.000	−110.0
1		45		45	0.909	40.9
2		70		70	0.826	57.8
3		180	[70 + 110]	180	0.751	135.2
Total	−110	295		185		123.9

Project C

0	−240			−240	1.000	−240.0
1		55		55	0.909	50.0
2		75		75	0.826	62.0
3		320	[80 + 240]	320	0.751	240.3
Total	−240	450		210		112.3

The IRR is the rate of return that would give an NPV of zero.

The interpolation/extrapolation technique covered in Chapter 13 may be used to derive the internal rate of return of each project.

For project C, if we assume a discount rate of 30%, we may calculate a revised NPV as follows:

Year	Cash outflows £000	Cash inflows £000	Net cash flow £000	Discount factor at 30%	Present values £000
0	−240		−240	1.000	−240.0
1		55	55	0.769	42.3
2		75	75	0.592	44.4
3		320	320	0.455	145.6
Total	−240	450	210		−7.7

We have already calculated the positive NPV for project C of £112,300 using a cost of capital of 10%. The IRR of project C must be at some point between 30% and 10% (difference 20%).

Using a similar calculation to that used in Fig. 13.3 (Chapter 13):

$$\frac{£7,700}{x} = \frac{£112,300}{(20 - x)}$$

$$(£7,700 \times 20) - £7,700x = £112,300x$$

$$£154,000 = £120,000x$$

$$x = \frac{£154,000}{£120,000} = 1.28$$

Therefore, interpolation gives us an IRR of 30% less 1.28%, which may be rounded to 29%.

The IRRs of projects A and B may be calculated in the same way.

The cash flows, NPVs and IRRs of the three projects may be summarised as

Project	PAT			Cash out	Cash in			Total cash flow	IRR	NPV
	Year 1 £000	Year 2 £000	Year 3 £000	£000	Year 1 £000	Year 2 £000	Year 3 £000	£000	%	£000
A	50	40		−50	50	90 [40+50]		90	93	69.8
B	45	70	70	−110	45	70	180 [70+110]	185	53	123.9
C	55	75	80	−240	55	75	320 [80+240]	210	29	112.3

(i) Based on the highest NPV, project B at £123,900 is best for the company shareholders.

(ii) But if the manager's remuneration is based on IRR then he will choose project A at 93%.

(iii) If the manager is remunerated on total project earnings then he will choose project C at £210,000.

(iv) We can calculate the EVA for each project, which equals profit after tax for each period, less capital employed at the start of each period multiplied by the weighted average cost of capital.

Year	Project A		Project B		Project C	
	£000	EVA £000	£000	EVA £000	£000	EVA £000
1	$50 - (50 \times 10\%)$	45	$45 - (110 \times 10\%)$	34	$55 - (240 \times 10\%)$	31
2	$40 - (50 \times 10\%)$	35	$70 - (110 \times 10\%)$	59	$75 - (240 \times 10\%)$	51
3			$70 - (110 \times 10\%)$	59	$80 - (240 \times 10\%)$	56
Total		80		152		138

We may also calculate the NPV of the EVAs of each project, the present values of the EVAs:

Year	Discount factor at 10%	Project A		Project B		Project C	
		Cash flow £000	NPV £000	Cash flow £000	NPV £000	Cash flow £000	NPV £000
1	0.909	45	40.9	34	30.9	31	28.2
2	0.826	35	28.9	59	48.7	51	42.1
3	0.751			59	44.3	56	42.0
Total		80	69.8	152	123.9	138	112.3

This illustrates that EVAs actually equate to cash flows because their present values are the same as the NPV of each project.

We can see from Example 14.12 that earnings-based remuneration schemes may result in over-investment of capital whereas return on net assets will result in underinvestment of capital. Use of EVA as a basis for management remuneration takes account of the fact that the use of capital is charged for by using WACC; additionally, at the project level, the present value of the EVAs gives the same result as NPVs derived from free cash flows. Compare the results in the project NPV tables with the NPVs of the EVAs of each project in Example 14.12.

Although the free cash flow NPVs give the same result as the present values of the EVAs, EVA is more appropriate for remuneration schemes because, as well as being fundamentally related to shareholder value, it is a flow measure of performance. The reason is that flow measures of performance are needed for periodic remuneration because remuneration is designed to provide a flow of rewards. The other flow measure is cash flow. EVA is a better measure than that because it takes into account the cost of capital invested in the project.

Example 14.12

We are required to compute the EVA for 1999, 2000 and 2001 for a major plc from the following information.

Group cost of capital		5%
		£m
Adjusted net assets	2001	750
	2000	715
	1999	631
Profit after tax	2001	550
	2000	526
	1999	498
Equity	2001	100
	2000	48
	1999	115
Net debt	2001	800
	2000	802
	1999	546

Answer

Year	Profit after tax £m	Adjusted net assets £m	5% cost of capital × net assets £m	EVA £m	EVA % of net profit
2001	550	750	37.50	512.50	93%
2000	526	715	35.75	490.25	93%
1999	498	631	31.55	466.45	94%

Note how the profits are being earned using borrowed funds to finance the group. The plc can earn a very high EVA by using borrowed funds.

We have talked about EVA in respect of projects, and that the present value of future EVAs equals the NPV derived from future free cash flows. At a company level, the present value of EVAs equal the market value added (MVA) of a business. This is defined as the difference between the market value of the company and the adjusted book values of its assets.

Example 14.13

We are required to compute the MVA for 1999 and 2000 from the following extracts from the annual report and accounts of a major plc, using the unadjusted value of net assets.

	2000	**1999**
Number of shares (5p)	950.2m	948.9m
Share price	278p	268p
Net assets	£1,097m	£1,437m

Answer

	2000	**1999**
Net assets	£1,097m	£1,437m
Market value	£2,641m	£2,543m
MVA	£1,544m	£1,106m

EVA is a good financial performance measure because it answers the question of how well has the company performed in generating profits over a period, given the amount of capital tied up to generate those profits. However, the capital base is a difficult element to estimate in calculating EVA. The total net assets value on a balance sheet is not an accurate representation of either the liquidation value or the replacement cost value of the business. Stern Stewart consider more than 250 possible accounting adjustments to a balance sheet to arrive at a valuation of the company's assets. In practice most organisations find that no more than a dozen or so adjustments are truly significant, for example stocks, depreciation, goodwill, deferred tax, and closure costs.

Progress check 14.9

What is economic value added (EVA) and what is it used for?

EVA probably does not change or add anything to the conclusions reached on the basis of conventional cash flow based valuation analysis. EVA is primarily a behavioural tool that corrects possible distortions. However, along with most other financial measures, it fails to measure on an *ex post* basis. EVA is undoubtedly a very useful concept for measuring and evaluating management and company performance. It is not a cure for poor management and poor investment decisions but it raises the profile and the awareness of the costs of capital involved in undertaking projects and in running the business.

Summary of key points

- Two main sources of external finance are available to a company, equity (ordinary shares) and debt (loans).
- Sources of internal finance to a company are its retained earnings, extended credit from suppliers, and the benefits gained from more effective management of its working capital.

- Gearing, or the debt/equity ratio, is the relationship between the two sources of finance, loans and ordinary shares – a company having more debt capital than share capital is highly geared, and a company having more share capital than debt capital is low geared.

- The weighted average cost of capital (WACC) is the average cost of the total financial resources of a company, i.e. the shareholders equity and the net financial debt, that may be used as the discount rate to evaluate investment projects, and as a measure of company performance.

- Both the cost of debt and the cost of equity are based on future income flows, and the risk associated with such returns.

- A certain element of risk is unavoidable whenever any investment is made, and unless a market investor settles for risk-free securities, the actual return on investment in equity (or debt) capital may be better or worse than hoped for.

- Systematic risk may be measured using the capital asset pricing model (CAPM), and the β factor, in terms of its effect on required returns and share prices.

- The return on equity may be considered as a function of the gearing, or financial structure of the company.

- The recently developed techniques of economic value added (EVA) and market value added (MVA) are widely becoming used in business performance measurement and as value creation incentives.

Glossary of key terms

beta factor (β) The measure of the volatility of the return on a share relative to the market. If a share price were to rise or fall at double the market rate, it would have a beta factor of 2. Conversely, if the share price moved at half the market rate, the beta factor would be 0.5.

capital asset pricing model (CAPM) A theory which predicts that the expected risk premium for an individual stock will be proportional to its beta, such that the expected risk premium on a stock = beta × the expected risk premium in the market. Risk premium is defined as the expected incremental return for making a risky investment rather than a safe one.

economic value added (EVA™) Profit after tax adjusted for distortions in operating performance (such as goodwill, extraordinary losses, and operating leases) less a charge for the amount of capital employed to create that profit (calculated from the adjusted book value of net assets times the company's weighted average cost of capital). (Stern Stewart)

loan capital Also called debt, relates to debentures and other long-term loans to a business.

market value added (MVA) The difference between the market value of the company and the adjusted book values of its assets.

ordinary shares Shares which entitle the holders to the remaining divisible profits (and, in a liquidation, the assets) after prior interests, for example creditors and prior charge capital, have been satisfied.

preference shares Shares carrying a fixed rate of dividend, the holders of which, subject to the conditions of issue, have a prior claim to any company profits available for distribution. Preference shares may also have a prior claim to the repayment of capital in the event of a winding up.

rights issue The raising of new capital by giving existing shareholders the right to subscribe to new shares or debentures in proportion to their current holdings. These shares are usually issued at a discount to the market price. A shareholder not wishing to take up a rights issue may sell the rights.

scrip issue (or bonus issue) The capitalisation of the reserves of a company by the issue of additional shares to existing shareholders, in proportion to their holdings. Such shares are normally fully paid-up with no cash called for from the shareholders.

systematic risk Risk that can be diversified away.

unsystematic risk (or market risk) Some investments are by their very nature more risky than others. This is nothing to do with chance variations in actual compared with expected returns; it is inherent risk that cannot be diversified away.

Assessment material

Questions

Q14.1 (i) What are the main sources of finance available to an organisation?

(ii) What are their advantages and disadvantages?

Q14.2 What are the implications for a company of different levels of gearing?

Q14.3 What are the advantages and disadvantages for a company in using WACC as a discount factor to evaluate capital projects?

Q14.4 Describe the ways in which the costs of debt and equity capital may be ascertained.

Q14.5 How does risk impact on the cost of debt and equity?

Q14.6 What is the beta β factor, and how may it be related to WACC?

Q14.7 How may a company's return on equity (ROE) be related to its financial structure?

Q14.8 In what way is company growth of such interest to shareholders?

Q14.9 Business performance may be evaluated to determine ways in which it can be improved upon. If managers are capable of delivering improved performance how can EVA be used to support this?

Discussion points

D14.1 The ex owner/manager of a private limited company recently acquired by a large plc, of which he is now a board member said 'This company has grown very quickly over the past few years so that our turnover is now over £20m per annum. Even though we expect our turnover to grow further and double in the next two years I cannot see why we need to change our existing financing arrangements. I know we need to make some large investments in new machinery over the next two years but in the past we've always operated successfully using our existing overdraft facility, which has been increased as required, particularly when we've needed new equipment. I don't really see the need for all this talk about additional share capital and long-term loans.' Discuss.

D14.2 The marketing manager of a large UK subsidiary of a multinational plc: 'Surely the interest rate that we should use to discount cash flows in our appraisal of new capital investment projects should be our bank overdraft interest rate. I don't really see the relevance of the weighted average cost of capital (WACC) to this type of exercise.' Discuss.

D14.3 In the long run does it really matter whether a company is financed predominantly by ordinary shares or predominantly by loans. What's the difference? Discuss.

D14.4 'Economic value added (EVA) is nothing more than just flavour of the month.' Discuss.

Exercises

Solutions are provided in Appendix 4 to all exercise numbers highlighted in colour.

Level I

E14.1 *Time allowed – 30 minutes*

A critically important factor required by a company to make financial decisions, for example the evaluation of investment proposals and the financing of new projects, is its cost of capital. One of the elements included in the calculation of a company's cost of capital is the cost of equity.

(i) **Explain in simple terms what is meant by the 'cost of equity capital' for a company.**

The relevant data for Normal plc and the market in general is given below

Normal plc

Current price per share on the London Stock Exchange	£1.20
Current annual dividend per share	£0.10
Expected average annual growth rate of dividends	7%
β beta coefficient for Normal plc's shares	0.5

The market

Expected rate of return on risk-free securities	8%
Expected return on the market portfolio	12%

(ii) **Calculate the cost of equity capital for Normal plc, using two alternative methods:**

(a) **the Capital Asset Pricing Model (CAPM)**
(b) **a dividend growth model of your choice.**

E14.2 *Time allowed – 30 minutes*

Normal plc pays £20,000 a year interest on an irredeemable debenture, which has a nominal value of £200,000 and a market value of £160,000. The rate of corporation tax is 30%.

You are required to:

(i) **calculate the cost of the debt for Normal plc**

(ii) **calculate the weighted average cost of capital for Normal plc using the cost of equity calculated in Exercise E14.1 (ii) if Normal plc has only ordinary capital of £300,000.**

(iii) **comment on the impact on a company's cost of capital of changes in the rate of corporation tax**

(iv) **calculate Normal plc's WACC if the rate of corporation tax were increased to 50%.**

E14.3 *Time allowed – 30 minutes*

The information below relates to Priory Products plc's actual results for 1999 and 2000 and their budget for the year 2001.

Figures in £000	1999	2000	2001
Cash at bank	100	0	0
Overdraft	0	50	200
Loans	200	200	600
Ordinary shares	100	200	400
Profit and loss account	200	300	400

You are required to calculate the following investment ratios for Priory Products for 1999, 2000, and 2001:

(i) debt/equity ratio – (net debt to equity)

(ii) gearing – (long-term loans to equity and long-term loans).

Level II

E14.4 *Time allowed – 30 minutes*

Lucky Jim plc has the opportunity to manufacture a particular type of self-tapping screw, for a client company, that would become indispensable in a particular niche market in the engineering field.

Development of the product requires an initial investment of £200,000 in the project. It has been estimated that the project will yield cash returns before interest of £35,000 per annum in perpetuity.

Lucky Jim plc is financed by equity and loans, which are always maintained as two thirds and one third of the total capital respectively. The cost of equity is 18% and the pre-tax cost of debt is 9%. The corporation tax rate is 40%.

If Lucky Jim plc's WACC is used as the cost of capital to appraise the project, should the project be undertaken?

E14.5 *Time allowed – 30 minutes*

You are required to compute the MVA for 1999, 2000 and 2001 from the estimated information for a large supermarket group.

	2001	2000	1999
Number of shares	6.823m	6.823m	6.770m
Share price	261p	169p	177p
Adjusted net assets	£5,000m	£4,769m	£4,377m

E14.6 *Time allowed – 90 minutes*

Sparks plc is a large electronics company that produces components for CD and minidisk players. It is close to the current year end and Sparks is forecasting profits after tax at £60m. The following two years' post-tax profits are each expected to increase by another £15m, and years 4 and 5 by another £10m each.

The forecast balance sheet for Sparks plc as at 31 December is as follows:

	£m
Fixed assets	500
Current assets	
Stocks	120
Debtors	160
	280
Creditors due within one year	
Trade creditors	75
Overdraft	75
	150
Net current assets	130
Long-term loans	150
	480
Capital and reserves	
Share capital (£1 ordinary shares)	220
Share premium	10
Profit and loss account	250
	480

Sparks plc has a large overdraft of £75m on which it pays a high rate of interest at 15%. The board would like to pay off the overdraft and obtain cheaper financing. Sparks also has loan capital of £150m on which it pays interest at 9% per annum. Despite its high level of debt Sparks is a profitable organisation. However, the board is currently planning a number of new projects for the next year, which will cost £75m. These projects are expected to produce profits after tax of £8m in the first year and £15m a year ongoing for future years.

The board has discussed a number of financing options and settled on two for further consideration:

1. A 1 for 4 rights issue at £3.00 a share to raise £150m from the issue of 50m £1 shares.

2. A convertible £150m debenture issue at 12% (pre tax) that may be converted into 45m ordinary shares in two years' time.

The equity share index has risen over the past year from 4,600 to the current 5,500, having reached 6,250. Sparks plc's ordinary shares are currently at a market price of £3.37. Gearing of companies in the same industry as Sparks plc ranges between 25% and 45%. In two years' time it is expected that all Sparks debenture holders will convert to shares or none will convert.

The rate of corporation tax is 50%. Repayment of the overdraft will save interest of £5.625m a year after tax.

The board requires some analysis of the numbers to compare against the current position:

(i)   if they make the rights issue

(ii) if they issue debentures

(iii) if the debentures are converted.

The analysis should show:

(a) the impact on the balance sheet

(b) the impact on the profit after tax

(c) earnings per share

(d) gearing

(e) which option should be recommended to the board and why?

15

Management of working capital

CONTENTS

LEARNING OBJECTIVES

Completion of this chapter will enable you to:

● explain what is meant by working capital and the operating cycle

● describe the management and control of the working capital requirement

● outline some of the working capital policies that may be adopted by companies

● implement the systems and techniques that may be used for the management and control of stocks, and optimisation of stock levels

● outline a system of credit management and the control of debtors

● consider the management of creditors as an additional source of finance

● use the operating cycle to evaluate a company's working capital requirement performance

● consider the actions and techniques to achieve short-term and long-term cash flow improvement

Introduction

Chapters 13 and 14 have been concerned with the longer-term elements of the balance sheet, investments and the alternative sources of funds to finance them. This chapter turns to the shorter-term elements of the balance sheet, the net current assets (current assets less current liabilities) or working capital, which is normally supported with short-term financing, for example bank overdrafts. The chapter begins with an overview of the nature and purpose of working capital.

An emphasis is placed on the importance of good management of the working capital requirement (WCR) for the sustained success of companies.

The techniques that may be used to improve the management of stocks, debtors (accounts receivable), and creditors (accounts payable) are explored in detail.

Regular evaluation of the operating cycle may be used to monitor a company's effectiveness in the management of its working capital requirement. Minimisation of working capital is an objective that reduces the extent to which external financing of working capital is required. However, there is a fine balance between minimising the costs of finance and ensuring that sufficient working capital is available to adequately support the company's operations.

This chapter will close by linking working capital to the effective management of cash and by considering some of the ways that both long-term and short-term cash flow may be improved.

Working capital and working capital requirement

The balance sheet is sometimes presented showing assets on the one side and liabilities on the other. This may be said to be a little unsatisfactory since the various categories of assets and liabilities are very different in nature. Cash, for example, is a financial asset and has very different characteristics to fixed assets and stocks.

If we consider the following relationship

$$\text{assets} = \text{equity} + \text{liabilities}$$

it may be rewritten as

$$\text{fixed assets} + \text{stocks} + \text{debtors} + \text{prepayments} + \text{cash}$$
$$=$$
$$\text{equity} + \text{financial debt} + \text{creditors} + \text{accruals}$$

This may be further rewritten to show homogeneous items on each side of the = sign as follows:

$$\text{equity} + \text{financial debt} - \text{cash}$$
$$=$$
$$\text{fixed assets} + \text{stocks} + \text{debtors} - \text{creditors} - \text{accruals/(prepayments)}$$

Total financial resources of the company are equity plus financial debt minus cash, which represent the total money invested in the company, the total investment.

total investment
=
fixed assets + stocks + debtors − creditors − accruals/(prepayments)

Progress check 15.1

Explain briefly the main components of working capital, using an example of a UK plc.

The total investment in the company can be divided into two types:

● investment in operations
● investment in fixed assets

where investment in operations is

stocks + debtors − creditors − accruals/(prepayments)

Stocks, of course, comprise raw materials, finished product and work in progress (including their share of allocated and apportioned production overheads).

The need for working capital – the operating cycle

The interrelationship of the investment in operations may be represented in the operating cycle (Fig. 15.1), which was introduced in Chapter 2 when we looked at the balance sheet.
  The operating cycle includes:

● acquisition of raw materials and packaging, which are at first stored in warehouses prior to use, are invoiced by suppliers and recorded by the company in trade creditors (or accounts payable), and then normally paid for at a later date
● use of materials and packaging in the manufacturing process to create partly completed finished goods, work in progress, stored as stock in the company's warehouses

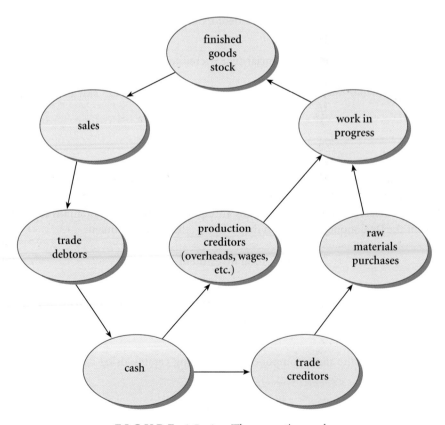

FIGURE 15.1   The operating cycle

- use of materials, packaging, and work in progress to complete finished goods, which are also stored as stock in the company's warehouses
- despatch of finished goods from the warehouses and delivery to customers, who accept the products for which they will pay
- recording as sales by the company its deliveries to customers, which are included in its trade debtors (or accounts receivable) and normally paid by customers at a later date
- use of cash resources to pay overheads, wages and salaries
- use of cash resources to pay trade creditors for production overheads and other expenses
- use of cash resources to pay trade creditors for raw materials.

Example 15.1

Identify which of the following categories you think may be included within a company's operating cycle:

- plant and machinery   - trade creditors   - investments in subsidiaries   - cash
- work in progress   - patents   - accounts receivable   - fixtures and fittings

Answer

Fixed assets are not renewed within the operating cycle. The following items extracted from the above list relate to fixed assets:

| plant and machinery | patents |
| investments in subsidiaries | fixtures and fittings |

The remaining categories therefore relate to the operating cycle, as follows:

| trade creditors | cash |
| work in progress | accounts receivable (trade debtors) |

The company therefore uses some of its funds to finance its stocks, through the manufacturing process, from raw materials to finished goods, and also the time lag between delivery of the finished goods or services and the payments by the customers, the accounts receivable. Short-term funds, for example bank overdrafts, are needed to finance the working capital the company requires as represented in the operating cycle. Many companies use the flexibility of the bank overdraft to finance fluctuating levels of working capital.

Progress check 15.2

How is a company's need for investment in operations explained by the operating cycle?

Working capital requirement (WCR)

Stated in words, the investment in operations (stocks + debtors − creditors +/− accruals/prepayments) is telling us something very important: the company has to raise and use some of its financial resources, for which it has to pay, to invest in its operating cycle. These financial resources are specifically for the company to purchase and create stocks, while it waits for payments from its customers. The impact of this is decreased by the fact that suppliers also have to wait to be paid. Added to this is the net effect of accruals/prepayments. Prepayments may be greater than accruals (requiring the use of funds) or accruals may be greater than prepayments (which is a source of funds). This investment in operations, or the operating cycle, is called the working capital requirement (WCR).

$$\textbf{WCR = stocks + debtors − creditors − accruals/(prepayments)}$$

Example 15.2

From the balance sheet of Flatco plc for 2000 and the comparatives for 1999, we may calculate the working capital requirement for 2000 and the working capital requirement for 1999.

Figures in £000

Working capital requirement:

WCR = stocks + debtors − creditors − accruals/(prepayments)

WCR for 2000 = 311 + 573 − 553 − 82 + 589 = 838

WCR for 1999 = 268 + 517 − 461 − 49 + 617 = 892

In most manufacturing companies the WCR is positive. The smaller the WCR, the smaller are the total financial resources needed, and the stronger is the company. Some businesses, for example supermarkets, may have limited stocks and zero accounts receivable, but high accounts payable. In such cases WCR may be negative and these companies are effectively able to finance acquisition of fixed assets with funds payable to their suppliers.

We will use the financial statements of Flatco plc, an engineering company, shown in Figs 15.2 and 15.3, throughout this chapter to illustrate the calculation of the key working capital ratios. The profit and loss account and cash flow statement are for the year ended 31 December 2000 and the balance sheet is as at 31 December 2000. Comparative figures are shown for 1999.

Progress check 15.3

What is meant by working capital requirement (WCR)?

Working capital (WC)

Working capital (WC) is normally defined as:

$$\text{current assets − current liabilities}$$

or

$$\text{WC = stocks + debtors − creditors − accruals/(prepayments)}$$
$$\text{− short-term debt + cash}$$

Flatco plc
Balance sheet as at 31 December 2000

Figures in £000	2000	1999
Fixed assets		
Tangible	1,884	1,921
Intangible	416	425
Financial	248	248
	2,548	2,594
Current assets		
Stocks	311	268
Debtors	573	517
Prepayments	589	617
Cash	327	17
	1,800	1,419
Current liabilities (less than 1 year)		
Financial debt	50	679
Creditors	553	461
Taxation	50	44
Dividends	70	67
Accruals	82	49
	805	1,300
Net current assets	995	119
Total assets		
less		
Current liabilities	3,543	2,713
less		
Long-term liabilities		
Creditors	154	167
Financial debt	173	–
Provisions	222	222
	549	389
Net assets	2,994	2,324
Capital and reserves		
Capital	1,200	1,000
Premiums	200	200
Profit and loss account	1,594	1,124
	2,994	2,324

FIGURE 15.2   Flatco plc balance sheet as at 31 December 2000

Therefore   **WC = WCR − short-term debt + cash**

The difference between WC and WCR can be seen to be cash less short-term financial debt.

The financial analyst considers the definitions of long and short-term in a different way to the accountant, thinking of long-term as 'permanent' or 'stable' and so will consider WC in an alternative way by calculating the difference between the stable financial resources of the company and its long-term use of funds, its fixed assets.

Flatco plc
Profit and loss account for the year ended at 31 December 2000

Figures in £000		2000		1999
Turnover				
Continuing operations		3,500		3,250
Discontinued operations		–		–
		3,500		3,250
Cost of sales		(2,500)		(2,400)
Gross profit		1,000		850
Distribution costs	(300)		(330)	
Administrative expenses	(155)		(160)	
Other operating costs				
Exceptional items: redundancy costs	(95)		–	
		(550)		(490)
Other operating income		100		90
Operating profit				
Continuing operations	550		450	
Discontinued operations	–		–	
		550		450
Income from other fixed asset investments		100		80
Profit before interest and tax		650		530
Net interest		(60)		(100)
Profit before tax		590		430
Tax on profit on ordinary activities		(50)		(44)
Profit on ordinary activities after tax		540		386
Dividends		(70)		(67)
Retained profit for the financial year		470		319

FIGURE 15.3 Flatco plc profit and loss account
for the year ended 31 December 2000

Since

$$\text{fixed assets} + \text{stocks} + \text{debtors} - \text{creditors} - \text{accruals}/(\text{prepayments})$$
$$=$$
$$\text{equity} + \text{financial debt} - \text{cash}$$

and financial debt comprises two parts:

● long-term debt (payable after one year, in accounting terms)
● short-term debt (payable within one year, in accounting terms)

then an alternative representation of working capital is

$$\textbf{WC} = \textbf{equity} + \textbf{long-term debt} - \textbf{fixed assets}$$

What is meant by working capital (WC)? How may it differ in a manufacturing company compared with a supermarket retailer?

As a general rule, except in certain commercial circumstances WC should always be positive in the long run because if it were negative then the company would be financing its (long-term) fixed assets with short-term debt. Renewal of such debt represents a major liquidity risk. It's the same thing as, say, financing one's house purchase with an overdraft. Since WC has to be positive and the aim should be for WCR to be as small as possible, or even negative, there is a dilemma as to the acceptability of either positive or negative cash. The answer really depends on the quality of the WCR.

If net cash is negative then short-term debt is higher than the cash balance and so WCR is financed partly with short-term debt. So the question may be asked 'will the company suffer the same liquidity risk as with a negative WC?' If stocks are of high quality champagne, the value of which will probably rise year by year, or if receivables are, say, blue chip companies with no credit risk, then a bank is likely to finance such WCR with no restrictions. If the quality of the WCR is poor the bank is unlikely to finance the WCR with short-term debt. The management and control of each of the elements of WCR: stocks; debtors; creditors, which we will look at in the following sections, must be considered in terms of both their quality and their level.

Working capital policy

The financing of its investment in operations, its working capital requirement (WCR), offers a number of options to a company. Choices may be made between internal and external finance. The external financing of WCR is usually provided by bank overdraft. This is because of its flexibility in accommodating the fluctuating nature of net current assets.

Nevertheless, the servicing costs of bank overdrafts, and other short-term funding, are not insignificant and so it is of obvious benefit for companies to maintain their overdraft facility requirements at minimum levels. Such requirements may be reduced by the adoption of appropriate policies with regard to the level of investment in working capital that a company chooses to operate.

The working capital policy adopted will be dependent on individual company objectives that may often be influenced by the type of business and the commercial or industrial sector in which it operates. The choice of objective inevitably presents a conflict between the goals of profitability and liquidity. Working capital policies range between aggressive policies and conservative policies. The former increase profitability through holding low levels of cash and stocks, but run the risk of potential cash shortages and stock-outs. The latter provide greater flexibility, with higher levels of cash and stocks, which provide lower risk at the expense of reduced profitability.

Regardless of the policies adopted, improved management of working capital may have a significant impact on the level of requirement for external financing. Reductions in levels of WCR reduce the requirement for external financing and its associated costs. Maintenance of optimal, and therefore more manageable levels of WCR increase levels of **efficiency** and **effectiveness** and so additionally contribute to increased profitability and a reduction in the requirement for external financing.

Working capital is the 'lubricant' of the investment in operations, enabling the investment in fixed assets to be most effectively exploited. Under-utilised fixed assets can produce extra stocks which then add to the working capital requirement. Good management of their working capital requirement by companies can therefore be seen to be crucially important to both their short and long-term success.

Progress check 15.5

> Why is the good management of the working capital requirement (WCR) crucial to company success?

Stocks management

The Japanese quality experts Shingo and Ohno have identified seven main areas of waste, which relate mainly to stocks in terms of their handling, their movement, and their storage, in addition to the levels held and the proportion of defective and obsolete stocks. These areas of waste emphasise the importance for companies to identify and take the appropriate action for improvements in this aspect of the management of working capital:

Overproduction

- the most serious, which discourages the smooth flow of goods/services and inhibits quality, productivity, communication and causes increases in stocks
- leads to excessive lead and storage times
- lack of early detection of defects
- product deterioration
- artificial work rate pressures
- excessive work in progress
- dislocation of operations and poorer communications
- encourages push of unwanted goods through the system, for example, through the use of bonus systems

- pull systems and *kanban* provide opportunities to overcome overproduction.

Waiting

- occurs when there is no moving or work taking place
- affects materials, products, and people
- waiting time should be used for training, maintenance or *kaizen* but not overproduction.

Transportation

- unnecessary movement and double-handling
- may result in damage and deterioration – for example, in 1999 and 2000 the UK car manufacturers Rover and Vauxhall found themselves with unsold or excess stocks being stored for too long in the open air, and were then forced to cut back production because of storage and damage problems
- increased distance means slower communication or feedback of poor quality, therefore slower corrective action.

Inappropriate processing

- complex solutions to simple procedures
- large inflexible machines instead of small flexible ones – this encourages overproduction to recoup investment, and poor layout leading to excessive transportation and poor communications – the ideal is the smallest machine for the required quality located next to the preceding and succeeding operations
- results from insufficient safeguards, for example, *poka yoke* and *jidoka* – the lack of these lead to poor quality.

Unnecessary stocks

- leading to increased lead time, space, and costs
- prevents rapid identification of problems
- discourages communication
- all leads to hidden problems, found only by reducing stocks
- results in high storage costs.

Unnecessary motion

- refers to the importance of **ergonomics** for quality and productivity
- quality and productivity ultimately affected by operators stretching unnecessarily, bending, and picking up, leading to undue exertion and tiredness.

Product defects

- a direct money cost
- and an opportunity to improve therefore an immediate *kaizen* activity target.

An example of the problems of overproduction resulting in excessive stocks can be seen from the press cutting on the next page. Its immediate effect is to increase the length of the operating cycle and increase the need for further funding, the cost of which has a negative impact on profitability. The other further effects of high stock levels have an additional downward impact on profit from the cost of increased waste in the ways we have examined above.

Despite the light-hearted comments made by some of M&S's rivals, the excess stocks that were known about, in addition to suspected overproduction that had not been reported, represented a serious problem to both M&S (as the UK's largest seller of ladies' underwear) and some of its major suppliers.

Stock levels should be optimised so that neither too little is held to meet orders nor too much is held so that waste occurs. The forecasting of stock requirements must be a part of the management process. In addition, stock level optimisation requires the following:

- establishment of robust stock purchase procedures
- appropriate location and storage of stocks
- accurate and timely systems for the recording, control and physical checks of stocks
- monitoring of stock turnover performance
- implementation of effective stock management and reorder systems.

Knicker manufacturers get their numbers in a twist

By Kate Rankine, Deputy City Editor

Forget butter mountains and wine lakes, the knicker hillock has arrived.

The country's knicker industry has got itself in a twist over widespread rumours that packs of five pairs of knickers have been over-produced in their millions. One chief executive of a major retailer yesterday admitted that he has been contacted by a Marks & Spencer supplier who is sitting on millions of pairs of unwanted knickers.

'It sounded like a disaster for him. He was desperate to get rid of the knickers,' said the chief executive. 'I'm not sure how he or M&S got themselves into this muddle. But it is very much a current problem.'

Two other chief executives at M&S's rivals confirmed that they have also heard tales of too many knickers. 'I wonder whether the bottom will now fall out of the market,' one joked.

But M&S, which is the country's biggest seller of ladies' underwear, yesterday insisted that it had 'no knicker problem'. Rory Scott, who runs M&S's lingerie

business, admitted that the company did have problems almost a year ago.

'In May last year, there was something of a knicker hillock,' he said. 'Our suppliers were over-producing. At the worst point, they had produced 20 weeks of stock and we had committed to buy 50 weeks of knickers.

'But we have worked hard to solve the problem. We now have eight weeks of stock – I'd like to get it down to six,' he added.

This week M&S reduced the price of its five-pair packs of 100pc cotton knickers in black or white from £10 to £7. Describing it as an 'unbeatable deal' and an 'entry price product', Mr Scott denied that the price cut was linked to the stories of excess stock.

However, he admitted: 'I think it is highly unlikely our suppliers have product that they haven't told us about. But it is always possible that there are things we don't know about. If that was the case, it would be nothing to do with us.'

Suppliers of M&S knicker packs include Sara Lee Courtaulds, Delta Textiles and the manufacturing business that was formerly owned by Coats Viyella.

© *Daily Telegraph*, 24 March 2001

Progress check 15.6

Briefly explain how electronic point of sales (EPOS) provides a system of monitoring stock turnover performance.

Stock purchase

For cash flow (and operational efficiency) purposes it is crucial that efficient and effective sales order, materials procurement and stock control systems are in place and operated by highly trained staff. Authority levels for the appropriate purchasing and logistics managers must be established for both price and quantities, for initial orders and reorders.

Stock location

A variety of options exist for the location of stocks and the ways in which they may be stored. Related items of stocks may be grouped together, or they may be located by part number, or by frequency of pick, or located based on their size or weight.

Stock recording and physical checks

Ideally, all stock transactions should be recorded simultaneously with their physical movement. Stock turnover must be regularly reviewed so that damaged, obsolete and slow

E8.5 Rocky

Profit and loss accounts for July and August on a marginal costing basis

	Per unit £	July Units	July £	July £	August Units	August £	August £
Sales	10.00	4,400		44,000	5,000		50,000
Production costs:							
Variable	7.50	5,300	39,750		4,400	33,000	
Opening stock	7.50	0	0		900	6,750	
		5,300	39,750		4,400	33,000	
Closing stock	7.50	900	6,750		300	2,250	
Marginal cost of sales	7.50	4,400		33,000	5,000		37,500
Contribution	2.50	4,400		11,000	5,000		12,500
Fixed costs							
Production costs			3,000			3,000	
Selling/administrative costs			7,200	10,200		7,200	10,200
Net profit				800			2,300

Chapter 9

E9.1 Profit

Contribution for January $=$ sales $-$ variable costs

$$= £320,000 - £240,000$$
$$= £80,000$$

$$\text{Contribution to sales ratio \%} = \frac{£80,000 \times 100\%}{£320,000} = 25\%$$

$$\text{£ sales value at break-even point} = \frac{\text{fixed costs}}{\text{contribution to sales ratio \%}}$$

$$£240,000 = \text{fixed costs}/25\%$$
$$\text{Fixed costs} = £60,000$$

Profit for January $=$ contribution $-$ fixed costs
$$= £80,000 - £60,000$$
$$= £20,000$$

E9.2 Break-even

Contribution for January $=$ profit $+$ fixed costs
$$= £10,000 + £30,000$$
$$= £40,000$$

$$\text{Contribution to sales ratio \%} = \frac{£40,000 \times 100\%}{£120,000} = 33.3\%$$

$$\textbf{£ sales value at break-even point} = \frac{\text{fixed costs}}{\text{contribution to sales ratio \%}}$$

$$= £30,000/33.3\%$$
$$= £90,000$$

(ii) **Marginal costing**

		£
Selling price per unit		5.84

Variable production costs per unit

		£
Direct material	[£0.85 × 2kg]	1.70
Direct labour	[42 × £4.20/60]	2.94
Variable production overhead		0.12
Variable production cost		4.76

Four-week standard profit statement

		£
Sales	[4,300 × £5.84]	25,112
Variable cost of sales		
	[£4,300 × £4.76]	20,468
Contribution		4,644
Fixed production overhead		3,526
Profit for the period		1,118

E8.4 Rocky

Profit and loss accounts for July and August on an absorption costing basis

	Per unit £	July Units	£	£	August Units	£	£
Sales	10.00	4,400		44,000	5,000		50,000
Production costs:							
Variable	7.50	5,300	39,750		4,400	33,000	
Fixed	0.50	5,300	2,650		4,400	2,200	
		5,300	42,400		4,400	35,200	
Opening stock	8.00	0	0		900	7,200	
		5,300	42,400		4,400	35,200	
Closing stock	8.00	900	7,200		300	2,400	
Cost of sales	8.00	4,400		35,200	5,000		40,000
Gross profit	2.00	4,400		8,800	5,000		10,000
Selling/administrative costs			7,200			7,200	
(Under)/over absorption of fixed production costs	0.50		350			800	
				7,550			8,000
Net profit				1,250			2,000

moving stock may be disposed of, possibly at discounted sales prices or for some scrap value.

In cash terms, holding on to unsaleable stocks is a 'waste' of the highest order. It uses up valuable space and time and needs people to manage it. It clogs up the system and reduces efficient order fulfilment and represents money tied up in assets of little value. Businesses need to move on and throw out old, obsolete and slow-moving stocks.

Progress check 15.7

What are the ways in which improvements in a company's management of stocks may contribute to achievement of optimisation of its level of working capital requirement (WCR)?

It is inevitable that stocks will be required to be physically counted from time to time, to provide a check against stock records. This may be by way of a complete physical count two or three times a year, with one count taking place at the company's financial year end. Alternatively, physical **cycle counts** may take place continuously throughout the year. This system selects groups of stocks to be counted and checked with stock records in such a way that all stocks are checked two, three, four or more times up to maybe 12 times a year, dependent on such criteria as value or frequency of usage.

Stock ratios

You may recall from the sections in Chapter 5 about financial ratios that one of the efficiency ratios related to stock turnover is a measure used to monitor stock levels.

$$\text{stock days} = \frac{\text{stock value}}{\text{average daily cost of sales in period}}$$

Stock turnover (or stock days) is the number of days that stocks could last at the forecast or most recent usage rate. This may be applied to total stocks, finished goods, raw materials, or work in progress. The weekly internal efficiency of stock utilisation is shown in the following ratios:

$$\frac{\text{finished goods}}{\text{average weekly despatches}} \qquad \frac{\text{raw materials}}{\text{average weekly raw material usage}} \qquad \frac{\text{work in progress}}{\text{average weekly production}}$$

Stock ratios are usually calculated using values but may also be calculated for individual stock lines using quantities where appropriate.

$$\text{stock weeks} = \frac{\text{total stock units}}{\text{average weekly units cost of sales}}$$

Financial analysts usually only have access to published accounts and so they often calculate the stock weeks ratio using the total closing stocks value in relation to the cost of sales for the year.

| Example 15.3 | From the balance sheet and profit and loss account of Flatco plc for 2000 and the comparatives for 1999, we may calculate the stock turnover for 2000 and the stock days (stock turnover) for 1999. |

$$\text{Stock days } 2000 = \frac{\text{stock value}}{\text{average daily cost of sales in period}} = \frac{£311}{£2,500/365}$$

$$= 45 \text{ days } (6.4 \text{ weeks})$$

$$\text{Stock days } 1999 = \frac{£268}{£2,400/365} = 41 \text{ days } (5.9 \text{ weeks})$$

The performance for 1999, 2000 and future years may be more clearly presented in a trend analysis. If 1999 was the first year in the series, then 41 days may be expressed as the base of 100. The 45 days for the year 2000 is then expressed as 110 [45 × 100/41], and so on for subsequent years. Comparison of 110 with 100 more clearly shows its significance than the presentation of the absolute numbers 45 and 41.

ABC and VIN analysis

The appropriate level of control of stocks may be determined through assessment of the costs of control against the accuracy required and the potential benefits. Use of a **Pareto analysis** (80/20 analysis) allows selective levels of control of stocks through their categorisation into A items, B items, and C items. The ABC method uses Pareto to multiply the usage of each stock item by its value, ranking from the highest to the lowest and then calculating the cumulative result at each level in the ranking.

A items, for example, may be chosen so that the top five stock items make up 60% of the total value. Such items would then be continuously monitored for unit-by-unit replenishment. B items, for example, may be chosen from say 60% to 80% of the total value. Such items would be subject to automated systematic control using cycle counts, with levels of stocks replenished using economic order quantities (see below). C items, for example, may be identified as the 20% of stocks remaining – 'the trivial many' in financial terms. These stocks may be checked by sample counting; because of their low value, more than adequate levels may be held.

Other important factors impact on the choice of stock levels. Total acquisition costs must be considered rather than simply the unit purchase price. There may be requirements to provide items of stock using a just-in-time approach (see the section dealing with JIT later in this chapter). The cost of not having a particular item in stock, even though it may itself have a low cost, may be significant if it is an integral part within a process. Consequently, in addition to ABC categories, stocks are usually allocated vital/important/nice to have (VIN) categories, indicating whether they are

- vital (V) – out of stock would be a disaster
- important (I) – out of stock would give significant operational problems or costs
- nice to have (N) – out of stock would present only an insignificant problem.

Describe how stock turnover may be regularly monitored.

Economic order quantity (EOQ)

A simplistic model called EOQ, or the 'economic order quantity' model, aims to reconcile the problem of the possible loss to a business through interruption of production, or failure to meet orders, with the cost of holding stocks large enough to give security against such loss. EOQ may be defined as the most economic stock replenishment order size, which minimises the sum of stock ordering costs and stockholding costs. EOQ is used in an 'optimising' stock control system.

If

P = the £ cost per purchase order
Q = order quantity of each order in units
N = annual units usage
S = annual £ cost of holding one unit

Then the annual cost of purchasing

= cost per purchase order $\times$ the number of orders to be placed in a year
(annual usage divided by quantity ordered per purchase)

Or $P \times N/Q$

Or PN/Q

The annual cost of holding stock

= annual cost of holding one unit in stock $\times$ average number of units held in stock

$0.5Q \times S$ or $QS/2$

The minimum total cost occurs when the annual purchasing cost equals the annual holding cost,

Or $PN/Q = QS/2$

Cross multiplication gives

$2PN = Q^2S$

Or $Q^2 = 2PN/S$

Therefore when the quantity ordered is the economic order quantity

$$EOQ = \sqrt{2PN/S}$$

Let's look at a simple example.

Example 15.4

E.C.O. Nomic & Sons the greengrocers buy cases of potatoes at £20 per case

£ cost of one purchase order	P = £5 per order
Number of cases turned over in a year	N = 1,000 cases (units)
Annual £ cost of holding one case	S = 20% of purchase price
Then, S = 20% × £20 = £4	

$$EOQ = \sqrt{2PN/S} = \sqrt{2 \times 5 \times 1,000/4}$$
$$EOQ = \sqrt{2,500}$$

The economic order quantity $\quad$ EOQ = 50 cases of potatoes per order

EOQ illustrates the principle of stock ordering and stock holding optimisation but it is extremely limited. In practice, significant divergences from the EOQ may result in only minor cost increases:

● the optimum order quantity decision may more usually be dependent on other factors like storage space, storage facilities, purchasing department resources, logistical efficiency, etc.

● costs of purchasing and holding stock may be difficult to quantify accurately so the resultant EOQ calculation may be inaccurate

● in periods of changing prices, interest rates, foreign currency exchange rates, etc., continual recalculation is required that necessitates constant updates of all purchasing department and warehouse records of purchases and stocks – computerised systems can assist in providing the answers to some of the financial 'what-ifs' presented by changes in the business environment.

The emphasis over the past couple of decades on stock minimisation or stock elimination systems through the implementation of, for example, JIT, *kanban*, and **vendor managed inventory** (**VMI**) has reinforced the disadvantages of holding large stocks. High stock levels reduce the risk of disappointing customers, but it is a costly process not only in the inherent cost of the stock itself, but in the cost resulting from the 'wastes' identified by Shingo and Ohno.

Progress check 15.9

Outline the basic conflict that might arise between the marketing department and the finance department when discussing the practical application of an economic order quantity (EOQ) system.

Just in time (JIT), materials requirement planning (MRP), and optimised production technology (OPT)

Just in time (JIT)

Just in time (JIT) is sometimes incorrectly referred to as a stock reduction or a zero stock system. JIT is a philosophy that is a response to two key factors: the reduction in product life cycles; the increase in levels of quality required from demanding customers.

JIT is a management philosophy that incorporates a 'pull' system of producing or purchasing components and products in response to customer demand. In a JIT system products are pulled through the system from customer demand back down through the supply chain to the level of materials and components. The consumer buys, and the processes manufacture the products to meet this demand. The consumer therefore determines the schedule.

The JIT system contrasts with a 'push' system where stocks act as buffers between each process within and between purchasing, manufacturing, and sales. In a push system, products are produced to schedule, and the schedule may be based on

- a 'best guess' of demand
- last year's sales
- intuition.

Some of the key principles and techniques of waste elimination, which in turn support improved stock management, are embraced within the implementation of the JIT process:

- total quality control (TQC), which embraces a culture of waste elimination and 'right first time'
- *kanban* which is a system of signals used to control stock levels and smooth the rate of production, for example, using cards to prompt top up of materials or components driven by demand from the next process
- set-up time reduction for reduced manufacturing batch sizes
- *heijunka* which is the smoothing of production through levelling of day-to-day variations in schedules in line with longer-term demand
- *jidoka*, or autonomation, is where operators are empowered to stop the line if a quality problem arises, avoiding poor quality production and demanding immediate resolution of the problem
- improved production layout
- *poka yoke* (mistake proofing) fail-safe devices, supporting *jidoka* by preventing parts being fitted in the wrong way, so that poor quality is not passed to the next stage in the production process
- employee involvement including self-quality and operator first-line maintenance
- multi-skilling of employees for increased flexibility
- supplier development for higher quality and greater reliability of supply – in the UK, M&S, for example, have publicised their adoption of this practice.

Two other approaches to stock management

- materials requirement planning (MRP), its development into **manufacturing resource planning (MRPII)**, and
- optimised production technology (OPT)

are sometimes seen as alternatives to JIT, but in fact may be used to complement JIT systems.

Progress check 15.10

Explain briefly what benefits might be gained by both supplier (manufacturer) and customer (national retailer) if they work jointly on optimisation of stock levels and higher quality levels.
(Hint: Research *Daily Telegraph* website www.telegraph.com, Marks and Spencer plc and Bairds plc 1999 and 2000.)

Materials requirement planning (MRP)

MRP is a set of techniques, which uses the bill of materials (BOM), stock data and the **master production schedule** to calculate future requirements for materials. It essentially makes recommendations to release material to the production system. MRP is a 'push' approach that starts with forecasts of customer demand and then calculates and reconciles materials requirements using basic mathematics. MRP relies on accurate BOMs and scheduling **algorithms**, EOQ analyses and allowances for wastage and shrinkage.

Optimised production technology (OPT)

OPT is a philosophy, combined with a computerised system of shop-floor scheduling and capacity planning, that differs from a traditional approach of balancing capacity as near to 100% as possible and then maintaining flow. It aims to balance flow rather than capacity. Like JIT, it aims at improvement of the production process and is a philosophy that focuses on factors such as

- manufacture to order
- quality
- lead times
- batch sizes
- set-up times

and has important implications for purchasing efficiency, stock control and resource allocation.

OPT is based on the concept of throughput accounting (TA), which was outlined in Chapter 8, developed by Eli Goldratt and vividly portrayed in his book *The Goal*. The aim of OPT is to make money, defined in terms of three criteria: throughput (which it aims to increase), and inventory and operating expense, which should at the same time both be reduced. It does this by making better use of limited capacity through tightly controlled finite scheduling of bottleneck operations, and use of increased process batch sizes, which means producing more of a high priority part once it has been set up on a bottleneck machine.

Progress check 15.11

> In the UK there are several low volume car manufacturers. Make an attempt to relate the optimised production technology (OPT) philosophy to their operations. (Hint: Research Morgan Cars of Malvern and TVR of Blackpool.)

Factory scheduling is at the root of OPT and the critical factor in OPT scheduling is identification and elimination or management of bottlenecks. OPT highlights the slowest function. This is crucially important in OPT: if one machine is slowing down the whole line then the value of that machine at that time is equivalent to the value of the whole production line. Conversely, attention paid to improving the productivity of a non-bottleneck machine will merely increase stocks.

Progress check 15.12

> What are some of the systems and techniques that may be used to optimise the levels of stocks held by a manufacturing company?

Debtors and credit management

All companies that sell on credit to their customers should maintain some sort of system of credit control. Improved debt collection is invariably an area that produces significant, immediate cash flow benefits from the reduction of debtor balances. It is therefore an area to which time and resources may be profitably devoted.

Cash flow is greatly affected by the policies established by a company with regard to

- the choice of customers
- the way in which sales are made
- the sales invoicing system
- the speedy correction of errors and resolution of disputes
- the means of settlement
- the monitoring of customer settlement performance
- the overdue accounts collection system.

These are all areas that can delay the important objective of turning a sale into a debtor and a debtor into cash in the shortest possible time. Each area of policy involves a cost. Such costs must be weighed against the levels of risk being taken.

Customers and trading terms

Sales persons are enthusiastic to make sales. It is important that they are also aware of the need to assess customer risk of the likelihood of slow payment or non-payment. If risks are to be taken then this must be with prior approval of the company and with an estimate of the cost of the risk included within the selling price. Similar limits and authorisations must be in place to cover credit periods, sales discounts, and the issue of credit notes.

Credit checks should always be made prior to allowing any level of credit to a potential new customer. Selling on credit with little hope of collection is a way of running out of cash very quickly and invariably resulting in business failure. The procedure for opening a new account must be a formal process that shows the potential customer that it is something that the organisation takes seriously. Many risky customers may thus be avoided.

Before a new account is agreed to be opened, three references should be obtained: one from the customer bank and two from high profile suppliers with whom the customer regularly does business. It is important that these references are followed up in writing with requests as to whether there are any reasons why credit should not be granted. A credit limit should be agreed that represents minimum risk, but at a level that the customer can service. It should also be at a level within which the customer's business may operate effectively.

A copy of the latest annual and interim accounts of a potential customer should be requested from the Registrar of Companies. These will indicate the legal status of the company, who the owners are, and its financial strength. These accounts are by their nature historical. If large volumes of business are envisaged then details of future operations and funding may need to be discussed in more detail with the potential customer. If such large contracts involve special purchases then advance payments should be requested to reduce any element of risk.

Having established relationships with creditworthy customers a number of steps may be taken to further minimise risk associated with ongoing trading:

- sale of goods with reservation of title (**Romalpa clause**) – the goods remain in the ownership of the selling company until they are paid for, and may be recovered should the customer go into liquidation

- credit insurance cover in respect of customers going into liquidation and export risk
- passing of invoices to a factoring company for settlement; the factoring company settles the invoices, less a fee for the service, which therefore provides a type of insurance cover against non-payment – a factoring company can be used as a source of finance enabling short-term funds to be raised raised on the value of invoices issued to customers.

The measures adopted should be even more rigorous in their application to the supply of goods or services to businesses abroad. This is because of the inevitable distance, different trading conditions, regulations, currencies and legislation.

Progress check 15.13	What are the ways in which improvements in the management of debtors and credit management may contribute to achievement of optimal levels of working capital requirement (WCR)?

Settlement methods

Payment collection methods should be agreed with all customers at the outset. The use of cheques, though still popular, is becoming a costly and ineffective collection method. Cash and credit card receipts are the main methods used by retailers and regular speedy banking is the cornerstone of efficient use of funds. Bankers drafts are the next best thing to cash but should be avoided because of the risk involved through their potential for accidental or fraudulent loss. Electronic mail transfers are frequently used for settlement by overseas companies. These tend to be costly and have been known to 'get lost' in the banking systems. **Letters of credit** together with sight drafts are frequently used for payments against large contracts.

Extreme care needs to be taken with letters of credit. They are a minefield of potential problems for non-settlement. Letters of credit must be completed providing full details and with the requisite numbers of copies of all supporting documentation. The conditions stipulated must be fully complied with and particularly regarding delivery of goods at the right time at the right location and in the quantity, quality and condition specified.

Electronic collection methods continue to increase in popularity. Direct debit payments are an option where settlement is made on presentation of agreed sales invoices at the bank. Personal banking is now a feature of the Internet. As its use and level of sophistication continues to be developed, corporate banking transactions conducted through the Internet will inevitably become a major feature. Absolute control is required over both sales and purchase ledger transactions, and all businesses benefit from the strict adherence to routines by the staff involved. Successful control of cash and cheques requires well-thought-out routines. Examples may be seen in the formal recording that takes place in the systems adopted in high volume businesses.

 One of the most acceptable methods is payment through **BACS**, the bankers' automated clearing services. The BACS method requires customers to register as BACS users and to specify the type of payment pattern they wish to adopt for settlement of their creditor accounts (or payroll). Every week, or two weeks or every month, companies supply details of payments to be made – names of payees and amounts. These are then settled by BACS exactly on the day specified and with only one payment transaction appearing on the bank statement. This means that the problems of cost of individual cheques and the uncertainty of not knowing when each payment will be cleared are avoided.

Cash takings must be strictly controlled in terms of a log and the issue of receipts. Regular physical counts must be carried out and cash banked twice daily or at least once daily. Cheques may be lost in the post, or bear wrong dates, or wrong amounts, or the customer may have forgotten to sign. One person should be nominated to receive and bank cash and cheques. A separate person should maintain the sales ledger in order to maintain internal control.

Sales invoices

The sales invoicing system must ensure that prompt, accurate invoices are submitted to customers for all goods and services that are provided. A control system needs to be implemented to prevent supply, without a subsequent sales invoice being issued. An invoicing delay of just one day may result in one month's delay in payment. Incorrect pricing, VAT calculations, invoice totalling, and customer names and addresses may all result in delay. A customer is unlikely to point out an undercharged invoice.

Sales invoices may be routinely followed up with statements of outstanding balances. The credit period offered to customers should obviously be as short as possible. Care should be taken in offering cash discounts for immediate or early payment. This is invariably a disadvantage. Many customers will take the discount but continue to take the extended credit. This is something that may not even be spotted by staff responsible for checking and processing receipts from customers.

Debtor ratios

Another of the efficiency ratios from the sections in Chapter 5 about financial ratios relates to debtor days, which is a measure used to monitor customer settlement performance.

$$\text{debtor days} = \frac{\text{accounts receivable} \times 365}{\text{sales}}$$

Debtor days indicate the average time taken, in calendar days, to receive payment from credit customers. Adjustment is needed if the ratio is materially distorted by VAT or other taxes. Currently, UK sales for exports to countries abroad are not applicable for VAT. Other forms of sales tax may be applicable to sales in those countries.

Example 15.5

From the balance sheet and profit and loss account of Flatco plc for 2000, and the comparatives for 1999, we may calculate the debtor days for 2000 and the debtor days for 1999.

$$\text{Debtor days 2000} = \frac{\text{accounts receivable} \times 365}{\text{sales}} = \frac{£573 \times 365}{£3,500} = 60 \text{ days}$$

$$\text{Debtor days 1999} = \frac{£517 \times 365}{£3,250} = 58 \text{ days}$$

A similar trend analysis to that described in Example 15.3 may be used for greater clarification of performance.

If in 1999, 58 days = 100, then the year 2000 debtor days would = 103.

Progress check 15.14

Describe how customer settlement performance may be regularly monitored.

Collection policy

As a great many experienced businessmen may confirm, perhaps the key factor underlying sustained, successful collection of accounts receivable is identification of 'the person' within the customer organisation who actually makes things happen and who can usually speed up the processing of a payment through the company's systems. Payments are usually authorised and cheques usually signed by the finance director and/or managing director or the accountant. However, 'the person' is the one who prepares payments and pushes them under the noses of the appropriate managers for signature. Cultivation of a good relationship with 'the person' within each customer organisation is an investment that usually pays massive dividends.

The benefit of issue of regular monthly statements of account to customers may be questioned. Most companies pay on invoice and so a brief telephone call to confirm that all invoices have been received, to check on the balance being processed for payment, and the payment date, usually pays greater dividends. Issue of a statement is usually of greater benefit as an *ad hoc* exercise to resolve queries or when large numbers of transactions are involved.

A routine should be established for when settlement of invoices becomes overdue. This process should include having a member of staff who has the specific responsibility for chasing overdue accounts – a credit controller. Chasing overdue accounts by telephone is usually the most effective method. It allows development of good working relationships with customers to enable problems to be quickly resolved and settled.

It is absolutely essential that accurate debtor information is available, up-to-date in terms of inclusion of all invoices that have been issued and allowing for all settlements received, before calling a customer to chase payment. It is also imperative that immediately errors are identified, for example errors in invoicing, they are corrected without delay. These are two of the commonest areas used by customers to stall payment and yet the remedy is within the hands of the company!

An indispensable information tool to be used by the credit controller should be an up-to-date **aged debtors report** giving full details of all outstanding invoices (see Fig. 15.4). This shows the totals of accounts receivable from all customers at a given date and also an analysis of the outstanding invoices in terms of the time between the date of the report and the dates on which the invoices were issued.

In addition, it is useful to have available the full details of each customers' payment record showing exactly what has been paid and when, going back perhaps one year. To provide an historical analysis and assist in resolving possible customer disputes, computerised systems may be used to hold customer data going back many years, for future retrieval. The friendly agreement of the facts on a customer account on the telephone usually goes a very long way towards obtaining settlement in accordance with agreed terms.

Perhaps one of the most effective methods of extracting payment from an overdue account is a threat to stop supply of goods or services. If a debt continues to be unpaid then the next step may be a chasing letter that shows that the organisation means business and will be prepared to follow up with legal action. Prior to sending any such letter the facts should be checked and double-checked – people and computers make mistakes! This letter should clearly explain what is expected and what the implications may be for non-compliance with agreed terms. A solicitor's letter should probably be considered, as a rule of thumb, not before an invoice is, say, 60 days overdue from its expected settlement date.

The last resort is to instruct a solicitor to take action against a customer for non-payment. Small debts may be recovered through the small claims court. The costs are low and the services of a solicitor are not necessarily required. Large debts may be recovered by suing the customer for non-payment. This is an expensive and very time-consuming

Hannagan plc

Aged debtors   As at 30 September 2000

************** ageing ******************************

Customer name	total balance	up to 30 days	over 30, up to 60 days	over 60, up to 90 days	over 90 days
	£	£	£	£	£
Alpha Chemicals Ltd	16,827	7,443	8,352	635	397
Brown Manufacturing plc	75,821	23,875	42,398	6,327	3,221
Caramel Ltd	350,797	324,776	23,464	2,145	412
*	*	*	*	*	*
*	*	*	*	*	*
*	*	*	*	*	*
*	*	*	*	*	*
Zeta Ltd	104,112	56,436	43,565	3,654	457
Total	4,133,714	2,354,377	1,575,477	184,387	19,473
% ageing		56.96%	38.11%	4.46%	0.47%

FIGURE 15.4   Example of an aged debtors report

business. The use of the last resort measures that have been outlined should be kept to a minimum. Their use may be avoided through a great deal of preliminary attention being paid to the recruitment of excellent staff, and the establishment of excellent systems, robust internals controls, and a formal credit control system.

> **Progress check 15.15**
>
> What are some of the ways in which the settlement of accounts receivable from customers may be speeded up?

Creditors management

The balance sheet category of creditors payable within one year comprises taxes, National Insurance, VAT, etc. and accounts payable to suppliers of materials, goods and services provided to the company (trade creditors). Payments to the Government are normally required to be made promptly, but trade creditors are sometimes considered a 'free' source of finance. This really is not the case, and accounts payable are not free debt as the following example illustrates.

Example 15.6

A supplier may offer to Justin Time Ltd payment terms of 90 days from delivery date. If Justin Time Ltd alternatively proposes to the supplier payment terms of 60 days from delivery date the supplier may, for example, offer 1% (or 2%) discount for settlement 30 days earlier.

Annual cost of discount:

At 1% discount $\dfrac{365 \times 1\%}{30} = 12.2\%$ per annum

At 2% discount $\dfrac{365 \times 2\%}{30} = 24.3\%$ per annum

A discount of 1% for settlement 1 month early is equivalent to over 12% per annum (and a discount of 2% is over 24% per annum). Consequently, it becomes apparent that the supplier's selling price must have included some allowance for financial charges; accounts payable are therefore not a free debt.

Many companies habitually delay payments to creditors, in order to enhance cash flow, either to the point just before relationships break down or until suppliers refuse further supply. Creditors may be paid slower than the agreed terms to gain a short-term cash advantage but even as a short-term measure this should only be regarded as temporary. It is very short-term thinking and obviously not a strategy that creates an atmosphere conducive to the development of good supplier relationships. A more systematic approach to the whole purchasing/payables system is the more ethical and professional means of providing greater and sustainable benefits. This is an approach followed by the majority of UK plcs, which is now supported by changes in legislation that were introduced during 1999/2000.

With regard to suppliers, overall business effectiveness and improved control over cash flow may be better served by establishment of policies, in much the same way as was suggested should apply to customers, with regard to:

- the choice of suppliers
- the way in which purchases are made
- the purchase invoicing system
- the speedy correction of errors and resolution of disputes
- the means of settlement
- the monitoring of supplier payment performance.

Progress check 15.16

Explain whether or not trade creditors are a 'free' or even a cheap source of finance for a company, and why.

Suppliers and trading terms

New suppliers should be evaluated perhaps even more rigorously than customers with particular regard to quality of product, quality and reliability of distribution, sustainability of supply, and financial stability. Appropriate controls must be established to give the necessary purchasing authority to the minimum of managers. This requires highly skilled buyers who are able to source the right quality product for the job at the best total acquisition price (base price, delivery, currency risk, etc.), in the delivery quantities and frequencies required and at the best possible terms. Their authority must be accompanied by rules governing:

- which suppliers may be dealt with
- acceptable ranges of product
- purchase volumes
- price negotiation
- discounts
- credit terms
- transaction currencies
- invoicing
- payment methods
- payment terms.

Terms of trading must be in writing. Most companies print their agreed terms on their purchase orders.

Payment methods

Payments to suppliers should be made in line with terms of trading, but advantages may be gained from cheaper payment methods and better control than the issue of cheques. For example, the payables system may automatically prepare weekly payment schedules and trigger automated electronic payments (for example, BACS) directly through the bank. Alternatively, submission of correct supplier invoices directly to the company's bank may also be used to support automatic payment in line with agreed terms. Provided that adequate controls are put in place to check and monitor such transactions these methods provide a cost-effective method of controlling cash outflows and may be an invaluable aid to cash planning.

Purchase invoices

Integrated purchase order, stock control and payables systems, preferably computerised, should be used to control approval of new suppliers, trading terms, prices, etc. When supplier invoices are received by the organisation they must match completely with goods or services received and be matched with an official order. An efficient recording system should allow incorrect deliveries or incorrect invoices to be quickly identified, queried and rectified. The recording system should verify the credit terms for each invoice.

Progress check 15.17

What are some of the ways in which payments to suppliers may be improved to the mutual benefit of the company and its suppliers?

Creditor ratios

Another of the efficiency ratios, from the sections in Chapter 5 about financial ratios, relates to creditor days, which is a measure used to monitor supplier payment performance.

$$\textbf{creditor days} = \frac{\textbf{accounts payable} \times \textbf{365}}{\textbf{cost of sales}} \quad \text{(or purchases)}$$

Creditor days indicate the average time taken, in calendar days, to pay for supplies received on credit. Adjustment is needed if the ratio is materially distorted by VAT or unusual trading terms.

Example 15.7

From the balance sheet and profit and loss account of Flatco plc for 2000, and the comparatives for 1999, we may calculate the creditor days for 2000 and the creditor days for 1999.

$$\text{Creditor days 2000} = \frac{\text{accounts payable} \times 365}{\text{cost of sales}} = \frac{£553 \times 365}{£2,500} = 81 \text{ days}$$

$$\text{Creditor days 1999} = \frac{£461 \times 365}{£2,400} = 70 \text{ days}$$

A trend analysis may also be calculated in the same way as we saw in Examples 15.3 and 15.5.

Payment policy

The priority for the accounts payable manager must be to maintain the level of payables and cash outflows in line with company policy, but at all times ensuring absolutely no interruption to any manufacturing processes or any other operations of the business. Fundamental to this is the development of good working relationships with suppliers so that problems may be quickly resolved and settled, thus avoiding any threats to supply.

The accounts payable manager must have accurate accounts payable information that is up-to-date in terms of all invoices received, invoices awaited and payments made. In the same way as the credit controller deals with customer queries it is also imperative that the accounts payable manager requests corrections of invoice errors, immediately errors are identified. The accounts payable manager should have access to an up-to-date **aged creditors report** (see Fig. 15.5). This shows the totals of accounts payable to all suppliers at a given date and also an analysis of the balances in terms of the time between the date of the report and the dates of the invoices from suppliers.

The accounts payable manager should also have available detailed reports of all unpaid invoices on each account, and full details of each suppliers' payment record showing exactly what has been paid and when, going back perhaps one year. The availability for use of correct, up-to-date information goes a long way to ensuring the avoidance of the build up of any potential disputes.

Progress check 15.18

Describe how supplier payment performance may be regularly monitored.

Hannagan plc

Aged creditors   As at 31 December 2000

************** ageing ****************************

Customer name	total balance	up to 30 days	over 30, up to 60 days	over 60, up to 90 days	over 90 days
	£	£	£	£	£
Ark Packaging plc	9,800	4,355	2,555	455	2,435
Beta Plastics plc	45,337	32,535	12,445	144	213
Crown Cases Ltd	233,536	231,213	2,323	*	*
*	*	*	*	*	*
*	*	*	*	*	*
*	*	*	*	*	*
*	*	*	*	*	*
Zonkers Ltd	89,319	23,213	21,332	12,321	32,453
Total	3,520,811	2,132,133	1,142,144	123,213	123,321
% ageing		60.56%	32.44%	3.50%	3.50%

FIGURE 15.5   Example of an aged creditors report

Operating cycle performance

The operating cycle, or working capital cycle, which was illustrated in Fig. 15.1, is the period of time which elapses between the point at which cash begins to be expended on the production of a product and the collection of cash from the customer. It determines the short-term financing requirements of the business. For a business that purchases and sells on credit the cash operating cycle may be calculated by deducting the average payment period for suppliers from the average stock turnover period and the average customers settlement period.

operating cycle (days) = stock days + debtor days − creditor days

The operating cycle may alternatively be calculated as a percentage using:

$$\textbf{operating cycle \%} = \frac{\textbf{working capital requirement}}{\textbf{sales}} \ \text{(stocks + debtors − creditors)}$$

Example 15.8

From the working capital requirement calculated in Example 15.2 and the stock days, debtor days, and creditor days calculated in Examples 15.3, 15.5, and 15.7, we are required to calculate the operating cycle in days and % for Flatco plc for 2000 and 1999.

Answer

Operating cycle days:

Operating cycle 2000 = stock days + debtor days − creditor days = 45 + 60 − 81 = 24 days

Operating cycle 1999 = 41 + 58 − 70 = 29 days

Operating cycle %:

$$\text{Operating cycle \% 2000} = \frac{\text{working capital requirement}}{\text{sales}} = \frac{(£311 + £573 - £553) \times 100\%}{£3,500}$$

$$= 9.5\%$$

$$\text{Operating cycle \% 1999} = \frac{(£268 + £517 - £461) \times 100\%}{£3,250} = 10.0\%$$

From this example we can see that Flatco plc's operating cycle has improved by 5 days from 1999 to 2000, an improvement of 0.5%. The deterioration in debtor days and stock turnover in this example has been more than offset by the increase in creditor days. Despite the overall improvement, this must be a cause for concern for the company who should therefore set targets for improvement and action plans to reduce its average customer collection period and reduce its number of stock days.

Overtrading

We have seen how important to a company is its good management of WCR. Personal judgement is required regarding choice of optimal levels of working capital appropriate to the individual company and its circumstances. This generally leads to the quest for ever-reducing levels of working capital. However, there is a situation called overtrading which occurs if the company tries to support too great a volume of trade from too small a working capital base.

Overtrading is a condition of a business which enters into commitments in excess of its available short-term resources. This can arise even if the company is trading profitably, and is typically caused by financing strains imposed by a lengthy operating cycle or production cycle. Overtrading is not inevitable. If it does occur then there are several strategies that may be adopted to deal with it:

- reduction in business activity to consolidate and give some breathing space
- introduction of new equity capital rather than debt, to ease the strain on short-term resources
- drastically improve the management of working capital in the ways in which we have outlined.

This chapter has dealt with working capital, and the working capital requirement (WCR). We have looked specifically at management of the WCR. The appreciation by managers of how working capital operates, and its effective management, are fundamental to the survival and success of the company. Cash and short-term debt are important parts of working capital, the management of which we shall consider in the section that follows.

Progress check 15.19

How may a company's investment in operations, its operating cycle, be minimised? What are the potential risks to the company in pursuing an objective of minimisation?

Cash improvement techniques

We have already discussed how profit and cash flow do not mean the same thing. Cash flow does not necessarily equal profit. However, all elements of profit may have been or will be at some time reflected in cash flow. It is a question of timing and also the quality of each of the components of profit:

- day-to-day expenses are usually immediately reflected in an outflow of cash
- fixed assets may have been acquired with an immediate outflow of cash, but the cost of these assets is reflected in the profit and loss account through depreciation which is spread over the life of the assets
- sales of products or services are reflected as revenue in the profit and loss account even though cash receipts by way of settlement of sales invoices may not take place for another month or two or more
- some sales invoices may not be paid at all even though the sales revenue has been recognised and so will subsequently be written off as a cost to bad debts in the profit and loss account
- purchases of materials are taken into stock and may not be reflected in the profit and loss account as a cost for some time after cash has been paid to creditors even though credit terms may also have been agreed with suppliers.

Cash flow is therefore importantly linked to business performance, or profit, which may fluctuate from period to period. There is also a significant impact from non-profit items, which may have a more permanent effect on cash resources.

The non-profit and loss account items that affect short-term and long-term cash flow may be identified within each of the areas of the balance sheet (see Fig. 15.6).

The short-term cash position of a business can be improved by:

- reducing current assets
- increasing current liabilities.

The long-term cash position of a business can be improved by:

- increasing equity
- increasing long-term liabilities
- reducing the net outflow on fixed assets.

We shall consider each of these actions for improvement in the cash position of the business.

Progress check 15.20

Profit and cash do not always mean the same thing. In what way therefore does profit impact on cash flow?

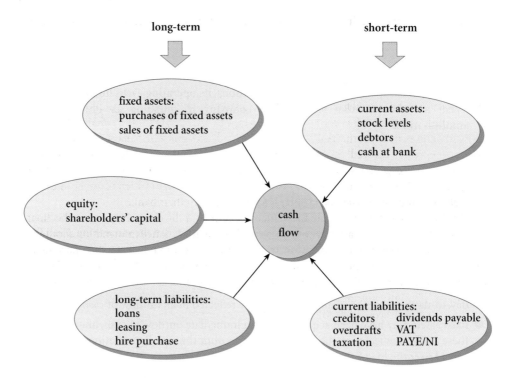

long-term

short-term

fixed assets:
purchases of fixed assets
sales of fixed assets

current assets:
stock levels
debtors
cash at bank

equity:
shareholders' capital

cash
flow

long-term liabilities:
loans
leasing
hire purchase

current liabilities:
creditors   dividends payable
overdrafts   VAT
taxation   PAYE/NI

FIGURE 15.6   Non-profit and loss account balance sheet items
that impact on short-term and long-term cash flow

Short-term cash flow improvement

Stock levels

Stock levels should be optimised so that neither too little is held to meet orders or too much held so that waste occurs. It is a fine balance that requires planning, control and honesty. Many companies either hide or are prepared to turn a blind eye to stock errors, over-ordering or overstocking because managers do not like to admit their mistakes, and in any case the higher the stock then the higher the reported profit!

For cash flow (and operational efficiency) purposes it is crucial to put in place:

● efficient sales order systems

● materials procurement systems

● stock control systems

operated by highly trained staff.

Stock turnover must be regularly reviewed so that damaged, obsolete and slow-moving stock may be disposed of at discounted sales prices or for some scrap value if possible. In cash terms, hanging on to unsaleable stocks is a 'waste' of the highest order. It uses up valuable space and time and needs people to manage it. It clogs up the system, hinders efficient order fulfilment and represents money tied up in assets of little value.

Debtors

Debtors arise from sales of products or services. The methods employed in making sales, the sales invoicing system, the payment terms, and the cash collection system are all possible areas that can delay the important objective of turning a sale into cash in the shortest possible time.

Cash at bank

Whichever method is used for collection from customers, debts will ultimately be converted into a balance in the bank account. It is important to recognise that the balance shown on the bank statement is not the 'real' balance in the bank account. The bank statement balance does not represent 'cleared' funds. **Cleared funds** are funds that have actually been cleared through the banking system and are available for use. It is this balance, if overdrawn, which is used to calculate overdraft interest. There are software packages which routinely monitor bank charges and many users have obtained a refund from their bank.

The difference between the bank statement balance and the cleared balance is the 'float' and this can very often be a significant amount. The cleared balance information should be received from the bank and recorded so that it can be monitored daily. Cash requirements should be forecast in some detail say six months forward and regularly updated. Cleared funds surplus to immediate requirements should be invested. This may be short-term, even overnight, into, say, an interest-bearing account, or longer term into interest-bearing investments or the acquisition of capital equipment or even other businesses.

Creditors

Creditors may be paid more slowly than the agreed terms to gain a short-term cash advantage, but even as a short-term measure this should only be regarded as temporary. A more systematic approach to the whole purchasing/payables system is a more ethical and professional approach that may provide greater and sustainable benefits.

Ordering anything from a third party by any individual within the organisation is a commitment to cash leaking out at some time in the future. Tight controls must be in place to give such authority to only the absolute minimum of employees. This authority must be accompanied by rules governing:

- which suppliers may be dealt with
- acceptable ranges of product
- purchase volumes
- price negotiation
- discounts
- credit terms
- transaction currencies
- invoicing
- payment methods
- payment terms.

A tightly-controlled and computerised system of:

- integrated purchase order
- stock control
- payables

must also feature countersigned approval of, for example:

- new suppliers
- terms
- price ranges.

When supplier invoices are received by the organisation they must match absolutely with goods or services received and be matched with an official order. The recording system should verify the credit terms for each invoice. If payment is made by cheque, these should always bear two signatures as part of the control systems.

Cash improvements may be gained from the purchasing and creditors' system in a number of ways. The starting point must be a highly skilled buyer or buyers who are able to source the right quality product for the job at the best total acquisition price (base price plus delivery costs plus allowance for currency risk, for example), in the delivery quantities and frequencies required and at the best possible terms.

Further gains may be achieved from efficient recording systems that allow incorrect deliveries or incorrect invoices to be quickly identified, queried and rectified. Payments should be made in line with terms but advantages may be gained from less costly payment methods and better control than the issue of cheques. For example, the payables system may automatically prepare weekly payment schedules and trigger automated electronic payments directly through the bank.

Alternatively, submission of correct supplier invoices directly to the company's bank may also be used to support automatic payment in line with agreed terms. Provided that adequate controls are put in place to check and monitor such transactions they provide a cost-effective method of controlling cash outflows and cash planning.

Overdrafts

If an overdraft facility is a requirement then the lowest possible interest rate should be negotiated. As with the purchase of any service, it pays to shop around to obtain the best deal. Bank interest charges should be checked in detail and challenged if they look incorrect – all banks make mistakes. Software packages are available to routinely monitor bank charges.

A bank statement should be received routinely by the company weekly, or daily, and should always be thoroughly checked. A detailed monthly schedule of bank charges should be requested from the bank and checked very carefully. These charges should be strictly in line with the tariff of charges agreed at the outset with the bank. In the same way as interest charges, bank charges should be challenged if they look incorrect.

At all times minimisation of both bank interest and bank charges must be a priority. This can be achieved by cash-flow planning and optimisation of the methods of receipts into and payments out of the bank account. If several bank accounts are held they should be seriously reviewed and closed unless they are really essential and add value to the business.

Taxation

Taxation on corporate profit is a complicated and constantly changing area. Tax experts may be engaged to identify the most tax efficient ways of running a business. At the end of the day, if a business is making profits then tax will become payable. Obvious cash gains may be made from knowing when the tax payment dates are and ensuring they are adhered to. Penalties and interest charges for late and non-payment are something to avoid.

VAT

Value added tax (VAT) is probably an area that is even more complicated than corporate taxation. VAT does not impact on the profit of the business. Businesses are unpaid collectors of VAT. If a business is registered for VAT (currently mandatory for businesses with a turnover of £52,000 or more) it is required to charge VAT at the appropriate rate on all goods and services that are vatable. Accurate records must be maintained to account for all such VAT. Such VAT output tax, as it is called, must be paid over to Her Majesty's Customs and Excise every three months or every month, whichever has been agreed.

VAT charged by suppliers, or input tax, may be offset against output tax so that the net is paid over monthly or quarterly. If input tax exceeds output tax, the VAT is refunded by HM Customs and Excise. It is important to note that VAT offices look very carefully at trends on VAT returns. A return that is materially different to the trend will usually result in a visit from a VAT inspector who will carry out an extremely rigorous audit of all accounting records.

It may benefit an organisation to choose to account either monthly or quarterly for VAT. In the same way as corporate taxation, great care must be taken to submit correct VAT returns, and pay VAT on the correct date to avoid any penalties or interest charges.

PAYE/NI

Pay As You Earn (PAYE) taxation and National Insurance (NI) contributions must be deducted at source from payments to employees. Salaries net of PAYE and NI are paid to employees, and the PAYE and NI and a further contribution for employers' NI is then paid to the Inland Revenue. Employees may be paid weekly or monthly and then PAYE and NI is paid over to the Inland Revenue by the 19th of the following month. In exceptional circumstances the IR may allow an odd day's delay. However, as with all other taxes, payment on the due date without fail is the best advice to avoid unnecessary outflows of cash in penalties and interest for non-compliance.

Dividends payable

Dividends are payable to shareholders by companies as a share of the profits. They are not a cost or a charge against profits but are a distribution of profits. There are some factors for consideration regarding cash flow. The timing of dividend payments is within the control of the company. Dividends may therefore be paid on dates that are most convenient in terms of cash flow and it is important to remember to include them in cash planning.

Progress check 15.21

Which areas within the profit and loss account, and the balance sheet may be considered to identify improvements to the short-term cash position of a company?

Example 15.9

An extract from Flatco plc's balance sheet as at 31 December 2000 and 1999 is shown below. From it we can see that trade debtors at 31 December 1999 were £517,000. Sales were £3,250,000 and so debtor days for 1999 were 58 days. Trade debtors at 31 December 2000 were £573,000, sales were £3,500,000 and debtor days for 2000 had worsened to 60 days. Although new cash collection procedures and a reinforced credit control department were introduced in the latter part of 2000, it was too early to see an improvement by December 2000. A report published on the industry for 1999 indicated that the average time customers took to pay was 35 days, with the highest performing companies achieving 25 days.

We are required to calculate the range of savings that Flatco would expect if it were to implement the appropriate measures to achieve average performance, or if it improved enough to match the best performers. We may assume that sales are more or less evenly spread throughout the year. Flatco's profit before tax for 1999 was £430,000. The average bank interest paid/earned by Flatco plc was 9% per annum.

Flatco plc
Extract of the balance sheet as at 31 December 2000

	2000 £000	1999 £000
Current assets		
Stocks	311	268
Debtors	573	517
Prepayments	589	617
Cash	327	17
	1,800	1,419

Answer

	Flatco	Average (derived)		Best (derived)	
Debtors	£517,000	£312,000		£223,000	
Sales	£3,250,000	£3,250,000		£3,250,000	
Debtor days	58	35		25	
Gain per annum		[517 − 312]	£205,000	[517 − 223]	£294,000
Interest saved/ earned at 9% per annum		£18,450		£26,460	
Improvement to profit before tax		[£18,450 × 100/£430,000] + 4.3%		[£26,460 × 100/£430,000] + 6.2%	

Assuming that Flatco plc's new credit control procedures become effective, at current trading levels it should result in a profit improvement for 2001 of between £25,000 and £37,000 per annum.

Long-term cash flow improvement

Shareholders' capital

Shareholders' capital has many advantages in providing a means of improving long-term cash flow. Provision of additional equity by the shareholders immediately strengthens the balance sheet. It also indirectly strengthens the profit position because equity (ordinary shares) does not bear a commitment to pay interest. Additional equity is an investment in future business, which will ultimately result in dividends payable from successful trading.

When owners of the organisation provide additional equity, a personal cost is imposed on them in that the funding is from their own capital. It also may dilute their own stake or percentage of the business. New shareholders or professional risk capitalists may be another source of equity. This carries the same advantages but also the expectation of rewards is much higher than those from interest-bearing loans.

Loans

Long-term loans have certain advantages, particularly for the acquisition of fixed assets, even though they carry a commitment to regular interest payments which may bear a fixed or variable rate. The period of the loan may be matched with the life of the asset and the agreed repayment schedule may be included in the cash flow plan with reasonable certainty.

Borrowing is always a big decision regardless of the amount. It has a cost and always has to be repaid. The ability to service any borrowing and the ability to repay must be assessed before making the decision to borrow. The real payback on borrowing for investment in fixed assets and working capital should be calculated and cheaper alternatives such as:

- re-use of equipment
- renovation of equipment
- renegotiated terms of trading

fully explored before borrowing.

A disadvantage of long-term loans is that they will invariably need to be secured by lenders on fixed assets to be acquired, or existing, or on other long-term or short-term assets. This reduces some flexibility for the organisation and may limit future short-term or long-term borrowing requirements.

If a company needs to acquire land and buildings in order to trade it has a choice of purchasing leasehold or freehold, or renting. Purchase of premises additionally takes an organisation immediately into the property business. While property prices are rising, this speculation may appear attractive. However, it does represent some risk to the organisation – property speculation has proved disastrous to many companies in the past – and it may result in a lack of flexibility. If a company needs to expand or relocate it may not be able to achieve this quickly and may be hampered by the fixed cost of owning a property.

Renting or short leases may present lower risk and greater opportunities in terms of location and flexibility and with regular payments that may be included in the cash flow plan. It also gives the organisation further financing opportunities, by not having a fixed liability of a loan secured on property.

Leasing and hire purchase

Leasing or hire purchase may be used for financing acquisitions of fixed assets. These two sources of finance require a slightly different accounting treatment. Hire purchase requires a large initial deposit and has VAT included in repayments. Hire purchase and leasing incur interest charges and depreciation, which are charged against profits. The term of either hire purchase or leasing can be matched with the expected life of the assets acquired. Cash flow may be planned in advance whichever method is chosen.

Purchases of fixed assets

The acquisition of fixed assets may represent an immediate outflow of cash. Cash-rich organisations may see advantages in outright purchases. However, the majority of organisations generally need to seek alternative funding. The sources of such funding may be from shares, loans or leasing, either within the UK or from overseas.

The use of an overdraft facility is not usually appropriate for acquisition of fixed assets. Fixed assets by definition have a long life and may be permanent in nature. An overdraft is repayable on demand, which is suitable for working capital requirements but is a risk if used to finance, for example, some machinery which may have an expected life of say 15 years.

Sales of fixed assets

Sales of fixed assets are an obvious means of raising funds. However, the opportunity cost of disposal of an asset must be considered prior to disposal and this should be considered in real terms using discounted cash flows with some allowance for inflation and taxation. An alternative may be to consider the sale of the asset to a leasing company, which then leases it back to the company.

Cash management

Any cash improvement exercise should include the factors we have discussed, which should also be regularly reviewed. However, in order to maintain control over cash flow it is crucial that a cash flow plan or statement is prepared on a month-by-month or week-by-week basis for, say, six months ahead.

The phased cash flow plan should be updated weekly or monthly. It may be continually reviewed and revised in the light of actual performance, and for advantage to be taken of opportunities for improvement through savings and rephasing as a result of consideration of the factors we have discussed above.

The recruitment of honest and reliable staff to deal with the control of cash and working capital is extremely important. Insufficient attention to this point together with a lack of frequent, appropriate training in credit control and cash management is a common occurrence, much to the cost of many companies. Many customers may detect a weak system of credit control and take advantage, resulting in considerable delays in payment of invoices.

Effective, integrated, computerised purchasing, stock control, order processing and sales invoicing systems are the tools necessary for trained and motivated staff to optimise the use of cash resources and safeguard the company's assets. It should be appreciated that until a customer has paid an invoice it remains an asset, which is effectively under the direct control of another business.

Progress check 15.22	Which areas within the profit and loss account and the balance sheet may be considered to identify improvements to the long-term cash position of a company?

Cash shortage is a common reason for business failure. However, businesses that are cash rich may also fail to take full advantage of opportunities to maximise the return on capital employed in the business. Such opportunities may include:

● acquisition of new businesses

● investment in research and development

● investment in new products

● lending to gain the most tax efficient returns.

All investments should, as a matter of company policy, be appraised using one of the recognised discounted cash flow techniques. A realistic company cost of capital should be used to determine whether each project is likely to pay back an acceptable return.

If surplus funds are to be invested for short-term returns, the most tax efficient investments should be sought. An understanding of the relationship between risk and reward is a prerequisite. High-risk investment strategies should only be undertaken if the downside risk is fully understood, and the consequences are what the business could bear and survive should the worst happen. In both the UK and USA there have been some high profile failures of deposit takers, resulting in massive losses by the depositors (note the collapse of BCCI in the UK).

Good banking relationships should be maintained at all times, with regular meetings and the provision of up-to-date information on company performance and new initiatives. The bank should ensure that information is provided to the company as frequently as is required on loans, interest and bank charges detail, bank statements, and daily cleared balance positions, so that they may be thoroughly checked as part of the daily routine. All slow-moving or inactive accounts, particularly, for example, old currency accounts opened for one-off contracts, should be closed to avoid incurring continuing account maintenance charges.

Summary of key points

- The operating cycle of working capital (WC), the net of current assets less current liabilities, is the period of time which elapses between the point at which cash begins to be expended on the production of a product or service, and the collection of cash from the customer.
- The difference between working capital (WC) and working capital requirement (WCR) is cash less short-term financial debt (bank overdraft).
- The working capital requirement is normally financed by bank overdraft because of its flexibility in accommodating the fluctuating nature of net current assets, and the general lower cost of short-term financing.
- Effective management and control of stock requires its appropriate location and storage, establishment of robust stock purchase procedures and reorder systems, and accurate and timely systems for recording, control and physical check of stocks.
- Effective management and control of debtors requires establishment of appropriate policies covering choice of customers, the way in which sales are made, the sales invoicing system, the means of settlement, and the implementation of a credit management and overdue accounts collection system.
- Although not free, trade creditors provide the company with an additional source of finance.
- Effective management and control of creditors requires the establishment of appropriate policies covering choice of suppliers, the way in which purchases are made, the purchase invoicing system, and the means of settlement.
- Regular measurement of the operating cycle, which determines the short-term financing requirements of the business, enables the company to monitor its working capital performance against targets and identify areas for improvement.
- The short-term cash position of an organisation may be improved by reducing current assets, and/or increasing current liabilities.
- The long-term cash position of an organisation may be improved by increasing equity, increasing long-term liabilities, and reducing the net outflow on fixed assets.

Glossary of key terms

aged creditors report The amount owed by creditors, or accounts payable, classified by age of debt.

aged debtors report The amount owed by debtors, or accounts receivable, classified by age of debt.

algorithm A process or set of rules used for a mathematical calculation.

BACS (bankers automated clearing services) An electronic bulk clearing system generally used by banks and building societies for low-value and/or repetitive items such as standing orders, direct debits and automated credits such as salary payments.

cleared funds Cleared funds are funds that have actually been cleared through the banking system and are available for use. It is the cleared funds balance, if overdrawn, which is used to calculate overdraft interest.

cycle count The process of counting and valuing selected stock items at different times, on a rotating basis, so that all stocks are counted two, three, four or more times each year.

effectiveness The utilisation of resources such that the output of the activity achieves the desired result. In other words, efficiency alone is not enough – efficiency in areas from which optimised output is what is required to be effective (to avoid being a 'busy fool').

efficiency The achievement of either maximum useful output from the resources devoted to an activity, or the required output from the minimum resource input.

ergonomics The study of the efficiency of persons in their working environment.

heijunka The smoothing of production through the levelling of schedules. This is done by sequencing orders in a repetitive pattern and smoothing the day-to-day variations in total orders to correspond to longer-term demand.

jidoka Autonomation, which increases productivity through eliminating the non-value adding need for operators to watch machines, thus freeing them for more productive work, for example, quality assurance.

kanban A signal, for example, a card used in JIT production to prompt top up of materials or components driven by demand from the next process.

letter of credit A document issued by a bank on behalf of a customer authorising a third party to draw funds to a specified amount from its branches or correspondents, usually in another country, when the conditions set out in the document have been met.

manufacturing resource planning (MRPII) An expansion of material requirements planning (MRPI) to give a broader approach than MRPI to the planning and scheduling of resources, embracing areas such as finance, logistics, engineering and marketing.

master production schedule A time-phased statement (usually computerised) of how many items are to be produced in a given period (like a giant timetable), based on customer orders and demand forecasts.

materials requirement planning (MRP1 or MRP) A system that converts a production schedule into a listing of the materials and components required to meet that schedule, so that adequate stock levels are maintained and items are available when needed.

Pareto analysis Analysis of a frequency distribution with a small proportion (say 20%) of the items accounting for a large proportion (say 80%) of the total. Examples may be seen in around 80% of sales of a company being derived from about 20% of its customers, and 80% of the value of its stocks being held in 20% of its items.

poka yoke Failsafe devices, support *jidoka* by preventing parts being mounted or fitted in the wrong way and alerting operators by flashing lights, ringing buzzers – it is a method of spotting defects, identifying, repairing and avoiding further defects.

pull system A system whose objective is to produce or procure products or components as they are required for use by internal and external customers, rather than for stock. This contrasts with a 'push' system, in which stocks act as buffers between processes within production, and between production, purchasing and sales.

Romalpa clause A contractual clause, named after a case in which its effect was litigated in 1976, by which the ownership of goods is to remain with the seller until they have been paid for. This can provide a useful protection for the seller in the event of the buyer's insolvency. Its value may be questionable if the goods are mixed with other goods in a manufacturing process or if they are resold to a third party.

vendor managed inventory (VMI) The management of stocks on behalf of a customer by the supplier, the supplier taking responsibility for the management of stocks within a framework that is mutually agreed by both parties. Examples are seen in separate supermarket racks maintained and stocked by merchandising groups for such items as spices, and car parts distributors topping up the shelves of dealers/garages, where the management of the stocks, racking and shelves is carried out by the merchandising group or distributor.

Assessment material

Questions

Q15.1 Describe how a company's financing of its investment in operations may be different from its financing of its investment in fixed assets.

Q15.2 (i) Explain the differences between working capital (WC) and working capital requirement (WCR).

(ii) What are the implications for companies having either negative or positive WCs or WCRs.

Q15.3 Outline the policy options available to a company to finance its working capital requirement (WCR).

Q15.4 Outline the processes and techniques that may be used by a company to optimise its stock levels.

Q15.5 (i) Explain what is meant by economic order quantity (EOQ).

(ii) Describe some of the more sophisticated stock management systems that the EOQ technique may support.

Q15.6 Describe the areas of policy relating to the management of its customers on which a company needs to focus in order to minimise the amount of time for turning sales into cash.

Q15.7 Outline the processes involved in an effective collections and credit management system.

Q15.8 Describe the policies and procedures that a company may implement for effective management of its suppliers.

Q15.9 (i) What is meant by overtrading?

(ii) What steps may be taken by a company to avoid the condition of overtrading?

Q15.10 Describe

(i) a review of the operating cycle, and

(ii) an appropriate action plan that may be implemented to improve the short-term cash position of a business.

Q15.11 (i) For what reasons may some companies require increases in long-term cash resources?

(ii) What sources are available to these companies?

Discussion points

D15.1 If working capital is the 'lubricant' of a company's investment in its operations that enables its investment in fixed assets to be most effectively exploited, how does the company choose the best method of lubrication and how often should this oil be changed?

D15.2 'Management of working capital is simply a question of forcing suppliers to hold as much stock as we require for order and delivery at short notice, and extending payment as far as possible to the point just before they refuse to supply, and putting as much pressure as possible on customers by whatever means to make sure they pay within 30 days.' Discuss.

Exercises

Solutions are provided in Appendix 4 to all exercise numbers highlighted in colour.

Level I

E15.1 *Time allowed – 30 minutes*

Oliver Ltd's sales budget for 2000 is £5,300,000. Oliver Ltd manufactures components for television sets and its production costs as a percentage of sales are:

	%
Raw materials	40
Direct labour	25
Overheads	10

Raw materials, which are added at the start of production, are carried in stock for 4 days and finished goods are held in stock before sale for 7 days. Work in progress is held at levels where products are assumed to be 25% complete in terms of labour and overheads.

The production cycle is 14 days and production takes place evenly through the year. Oliver Ltd receives 30 days' credit from suppliers and grants 60 days' credit to its customers. Overheads are incurred evenly throughout the year.

What is Oliver Ltd's total working capital requirement?

E15.2 *Time allowed – 30 minutes*

Lubosh plc uses plastic granules for its injection moulding machines. It uses 550,000 kgs in a year. It costs £150 to raise and process an order and the supplier delivers one week later. Storage costs for the granules have been calculated at 5p per kg per annum. Lubosh currently orders granules 4 times a year when the stock has fallen to 50,000 kgs.

Is there a more economic method that Lubosh plc may adopt to order plastic granules?

E15.3 *Time allowed – 45 minutes*

Trumper Ltd has recently appointed a new managing director who would like to implement major improvements to the company's management of working capital. Trumper's customers should pay by the end of the second month following delivery. Despite this they take on average 75 days to settle their accounts. Trumper's sales for the current year are estimated at £32m, and the company expects bad debts to be £320,000.

The managing director has suggested an early settlement discount of 2% for customers paying within 60 days. His meetings with all the company's major customers have indicated that 30% would take the discount and pay within 60 days; 70% of the customers would continue to pay within 75 days on average. However, the finance director has calculated that bad debts may reduce by £100,000 for the year, together with savings of £20,000 on administrative costs.

Trumper Ltd has an overdraft facility to finance its working capital on which it pays interest at 12% per annum.

The managing director would like to know how Trumper may gain from introducing early settlement discounts, if it is assumed that sales levels would remain unchanged. The managing director would also like suggestions as to how the company may reduce its reliance on its overdraft, perhaps through better management of its debtors, and whether the overdraft is the best method of financing its working capital.

Level II

E15.4 *Time allowed – 45 minutes*

Josef Ryan Ltd has experienced difficulties in getting its customers to pay on time. It is considering the offer of a discount for payment within 14 days to its customers, who currently pay after 60 days. It is estimated that only 50 per cent of credit customers would take the discount, although administrative cost savings of £10,000 per annum would be gained. The marketing director believes that sales would be unaffected by the discount. Sales for 2001 have been budgeted at £10m. The cost of short-term finance for Ryan is 15% per annum.

What is the maximum discount that Josef Ryan Ltd may realistically offer?

E15.5 *Time allowed – 45 minutes*

Worrall plc's sales for 2000 were £8m. Costs of sales were 80% of sales. Bad debts were 2% of sales. Cost of sales variable costs were 90% and fixed costs were 10%. Worrall's cost of finance is 10% per annum. Worrall plc allows its customers 60 days' credit, but is now considering increasing this to 90 days' credit because it believes that this will increase sales. Worrall plc's sales manager estimated that if customers were granted 90 days' credit, sales may be increased by 20%, but that bad debts would increase from 2% to 3%. The finance director calculated that such a change in policy would not increase fixed costs, and neither would it result in changes to creditors and stock.

Would you recommend that Worrall plc increase customer credit to 90 days?

E15.6 *Time allowed – 45 minutes*

Chapman Engineering plc has annual sales of £39m, which are made evenly throughout the year. At present the company has an overdraft facility on which its bank charges 9% per annum.

Chapman Engineering plc currently allows its customers 45 days' credit. One third of the customers pay on time, in terms of total sales value. The other two thirds pay on average after 60 days. Chapman believes that the offer of a cash discount of 1% to its customers would induce them to pay within 45 days. Chapman also believes that two-thirds of the customers who now take 60 days to pay would pay within 45 days. The other third would still take an average of 60 days. Chapman estimates that this action would also result in bad debts being reduced by £25,000 a year.

(i) **What is the current value of debtors?**

(ii) **What would the level of debtors be if terms were changed and 1% discount was offered to reduce debtor days from 60 days to 45 days?**

(iii) **What is net annual cost to the company of a granting this discount?**

(iv) **Would you recommend that the company should introduce the offer of an early settlement discount?**

(v) **What other factors should Chapman consider before implementing this change?**

(vi) **Are there other controls and procedures that Chapman may introduce to better manage its debtors.**

E15.7 *Time allowed – 60 minutes*

Sarnico Ltd, a UK subsidiary of a food manufacturing multinational group, makes sandwiches for sale by supermarkets. The group managing director, Emanuel Recount, is particularly concerned with Sarnico's cash position. The financial statements for 2000 are as follows:

Profit and loss account for the year ended 30 September 2000

	£m	£m
Sales		49
less: Cost of sales		
Opening stock	7	
add: Purchases	40	
	47	
less: Closing stock	10	37
Gross profit		12
Expenses		(13)
Net loss for the year		(1)

Balance sheet as at 30 September 2000

	£m	£m	£m
Fixed assets			15
Current assets:			
Stock		10	
Debtors		6	
		16	
less			
Creditors due within one year			
Trade creditors	(4)		
Bank overdraft	(11)	(15)	1
			16
less			
Creditors due beyond one year			
Loans			(8)
			8
Capital and reserves			
Ordinary share capital			3
Retained profit			5
			8

We may assume that debtors and creditors were maintained at a constant level throughout the year.

(i) Why should Emanuel Recount be concerned about Sarnico's liquidity?

(ii) What is the 'operating cycle'?

(iii) Why is the operating cycle important with regard to the financial management of Sarnico?

(iv) Calculate the 365-day operating cycle for Sarnico Ltd.

(v) What actions may Sarnico Ltd take to improve its operating cycle performance?

E15.8 *Time allowed – 60 minutes*

Refer to the balance sheet for Flatco plc as at 31 December 2000, and its profit and loss account for the year to 31 December 2000 shown at the beginning of Chapter 15.

A benchmarking exercise that looked at competing companies within the industry revealed that on average debtor days for 2000 were 33 days, average creditor days were 85 days, and average stock days were 32 days. The exercise also indicated that in the best performing companies in the industry the time that customers took to pay was 24 days, with creditor days at 90 days and stock days at 18 days.

You are required to calculate the range of values of savings that Flatco may achieve in 2001 (assuming the same activity levels as 2000) if it were to implement the appropriate measures to achieve average performance or if it improved enough to match the best performers.

You may assume that sales are more or less evenly spread throughout the year. The average bank interest paid/earned by Flatco plc is 9% per annum.

Case Study III

COMPUTACORE LTD

Computacore Ltd produces and sells a range of computer systems. After-sales service work is carried out by local subcontractors, approved by Computacore Ltd. The managing director is considering Computacore carrying out all or some of the work itself and has chosen one area in which to experiment with the new routine.

Some of the computer systems are so large that repair or service work can only be done on site at customers' premises. Others are small enough for subcontractors to take back to their local repair workshops, repair them, and re-deliver them to the customer. If the company does its own after-sales service, it proposes that customers would bring these smaller items for repair to a local company service centre which would be located and organised to deal with visitors.

There is a list price to customers for the labour content of any work done and for parts used. However, the majority of the after-sales service work is done under an annual service contract taken out by customers on purchasing a computer system; this covers the labour content of any service work to be done, but customers pay for parts used.

Any labour or parts needed in the first six months are provided to the customer free of charge under Computacore's product guarantee, and subcontractors are allowed by the company a fixed sum of 2.5% of the selling price of each appliance to cover this work. These sums allowed have proved to be closely in line with the work needed over the past few years.

The price structure is as follows:

Parts
The price to the subcontractor is the Computacore Ltd cost plus 15%
The price to customer is the subcontractor price plus 30%

Labour
The price to the subcontractor is:
80% of list price for work done under a service contract
75% of list price for work not done under a service contract

Records show that 70% by value of the work has to be carried out at customers' premises, whilst the remainder can be done anywhere appropriate.

The annual income Computacore Ltd currently receives from subcontractors for the area in which the experiment is to take place is as follows:

Parts

Under service contract	£360,000
Not under service contract	£120,000

Labour

Under service contract	£600,000
Not under service contract	£240,000
	£1,320,000

The company expects the volume of after-sales work to remain the same as last year for the period of the experiment.

Computacore Ltd is considering the following options:

(a) setting up a local service centre at which it can service small computer systems only – work at customers' premises would continue to be done under subcontract

(b) setting up a local service centre to act only as a base for its own employees who would only service appliances at customers' premises – servicing of small computer systems would continue to be done under subcontract

(c) setting up a local combined service centre plus base for all work – no work would be subcontracted.

If the company were to do service work, it has estimated that annual fixed costs would be budgeted as follows:

	(a) £000	(b) £000	(c) £000
Staff costs			
Managers	180	100	200
Stores	90	70	100
Repair and service	310	1,270	1,530
Rent, rates and lighting	350	100	900
Van and car hire, and transport costs	70	460	470

Required

(i) Prepare an appropriate financial analysis to evaluate each of the alternative options, compared with the current position.

(ii) Recommend which of the three options Computacore Ltd should adopt on the basis of your financial analysis.

(iii) Identify and comment on the non-financial factors, relevant to your recommendation, which might favourably or adversely affect the customer.

(iv) Outline the factors that may be discussed if Computacore Ltd were to propose the establishment of a 'call centre' within or outside the UK, to deal with after-sales service and organisation and scheduling of repair and service work.

APPENDICES

Outline of Appendices

Appendix 1 is about the system used to record accounting transactions and accounting data and provides the fundamental basis for the further analysis and reporting of financial information. It provides an introduction to double-entry bookkeeping. Bookkeeping is a process that records accounting data in such a way that allows subsequent preparation of financial reports in appropriate formats which inform shareholders and others about the financial position and the financial performance of the business. The topics covered may or may not be required by you in order to use the rest of this book. Alternatively, this appendix may be used as a learning aid in support of study of the topics covered in Chapters 1 to 15.

Appendix 2 provides discounted cash flow tables which show the present value of £1 on both a yearly, and a cumulative year basis, up to 15 years for discount rates from 1% up to 50% per annum.

Appendix 3 includes schedules of all Statements of Standard Accounting Practice (SSAPs) and Financial Reporting Standards (FRSs) currently in use. Additions, changes and withdrawals to these standards may be found on the book's accompanying website, which is regularly updated.

Appendix 4 contains solutions to 45% of the chapter-end exercises which include a mix of both Level I and Level II exercises. They refer to the chapter-end exercise numbers which are highlighted in colour. This allows you to attempt the exercises at the end of each chapter and then check on your understanding of the key points and how well you have been able to apply the various learning topics and techniques. Further exercises are included on the book's accompanying website.

Appendix 1

Double-entry – the basics

LEARNING OBJECTIVES	CONTENTS

Completion of this appendix will enable you to:	

<table>
<tr><td>

LEARNING OBJECTIVES

Completion of this appendix will enable you to:

● explain the convention of double-entry bookkeeping

● describe what is meant by 'debit' and 'credit'

● write up business transactions into accounts

● account for closing stocks and other accounting adjustments

● explain the balancing of accounts

● extract a trial balance from a company's accounts

● prepare a profit and loss account, balance sheet and cash flow statement from a trial balance

● appreciate the concepts of accrual accounting and cash accounting

● explain and account for payments in advance (prepayments) and charges not yet received (accruals)

● appreciate the importance of accounting periods

</td><td>

</td></tr>
</table>

Introduction

This appendix begins by explaining what is sometimes referred to as the dual aspect rule. This rule recognises that for all transactions there is a two-sided effect within the entity. A manager in a non-accounting role may not be expected to carry out the recording of transactions in this way, but an appreciation of how accounting data has been recorded will be extremely helpful in the interpretation of financial information. We will go on to describe the processes that deal with the two sides of each transaction, the 'debits' and 'credits' of double-entry bookkeeping.

Don't worry if at first these topics seem a little difficult and confusing. They will become clearer as we follow through some transactions step-by-step into the accounts of a business and show how these accounts are kept in balance.

The appendix continues with an introduction to the way in which each of the accounts are held in what are termed the books of account and ledgers of the business. The balances on all the accounts in an entity are summarised in what is called a trial balance. The trial balance may be adjusted to allow for payments in advance, and charges not yet received, other adjusting entries. From this information we will show how to prepare a simple profit and loss account, balance sheet, and cash flow report.

This appendix refers to some of the accounting concepts introduced in Chapter 1. In that context we will look at the time period chosen by a business, to which the financial reporting relates – the accounting period.

Theory and practice of double-entry bookkeeping

Double-entry bookkeeping has a long history, having been created by the father of modern accounting, the Franciscan monk Lucas Paciolo in Italy in the Middle Ages. His publication, *Summa*, published in 1494 was the first printed work dealing with algebra and also contained the first text on **bookkeeping**, entitled *De Computis et Scripturis*. Book-keeping then spread throughout the world by a series of plagiarisms and imitations of Paciolo.

It is important to remember that the idea of double-entry is a convention. There are two main objectives of bookkeeping: to have a permanent record of transactions; to show the effect of each transaction and the combined effect of all the transactions on the financial position of the entity.

The fundamental idea of double-entry bookkeeping is that all business transactions of a business entity, for example, cash and invoices, shall be recorded twice in the entity's business records. It is based on the principle that every financial transaction involves the simultaneous receiving and giving of value, and is therefore recorded twice. Transactions of course involve both services and goods. We shall find out later in this chapter that there are other accounting entries which do not result directly from invoice or cash transactions but which also result in double-entry records being created. These **accounting adjustment** entries relate, for example, to accounting for **depreciation**, **bad debts**, and **doubtful debts**.

The convention of double-entry assumes that in all business transactions equal and opposite values are exchanged. For example, if a company purchases materials for £1,000 it adds to its stock of materials to the value of £1,000, but reduces its cash balance also to the value of £1,000. The convention uses two terms for convenience to describe the two aspects of each transaction. These terms are debit and credit.

There is sometimes confusion in the use of the terms of debit and credit used in bookkeeping when they are compared with the same terms used on bank statements. Bank statements traditionally refer to receipt of cash as a credit, whereas receipt of cash in bookkeeping terms is referred to as a debit.

Debits and credits

The explanation of debits and credits in terms of value received and value given respectively is not perhaps one that provides the clearest understanding. Neither is the explanation that debits are in the left-hand column and credits are in the right-hand column, or debits are on the side of the room closest to the window!

Debits and credits do represent certain types of account, as we will see later, in both the **balance sheet**: assets and **liabilities**, and the **profit and loss account**: costs and **sales**. However, for the purpose of clarity of explanation we shall propose a couple of basic assumptions with which to work from as we go through some elementary accounting entries.

If we initially consider all business transactions as either goods or services then it is reasonable to assume (unless we are in a barter society) that all these transactions will ultimately end up with cash (or cash equivalents, such as cheques, bank transfers, etc.) changing hands. We can also assume that all these transactions will involve a document being raised, as a record of the transaction and an indication of the amount of cash that will change hands, namely an invoice. A **purchase invoice** records a purchase from a third party and so it represents an account to be payable at some time. A **sales invoice** records a sale to a third party and so it represents an account to be receivable at some time.

Business entities themselves have a separate identity from the owners of the business. When we consider double-entry we will now assume that all the entries we are discussing relate to those of the business entity, in whatever form the entity takes: sole trader; partnership; limited company; public limited company (see Chapter 1).

For the business entity, we shall define the following business transactions:

Transaction		Accounting entries	
CASH RECEIPT	=	DEBIT CASH	and credit something else
CASH PAYMENT	=	CREDIT CASH	and debit something else
PURCHASE INVOICE	=	CREDIT PAYABLES	and debit something else
SALES INVOICE	=	DEBIT RECEIVABLES	and credit something else

These are definitions within the convention of double-entry bookkeeping, which may be usefully remembered as a basis for establishing whether all further subsequent transactions are either debits or credits. It is suggested that the above four statements are kept filed in permanent memory, as a useful aid towards the understanding of further accounting entries.

Progress check A1.1

Outline what is meant by double-entry bookkeeping.

An elementary method of representing and clarifying double-entry is known as the T account. We shall use this method to demonstrate double-entry in action using a simple example. (Note that in the UK there are many computerised accounting packages that automate the double-entry for a business, for example Sage. The purpose of this extensive example is to illustrate how such transactions take place).

Example A1.1

Mr Bean decides to set up a wholesale business, Ayco, on 1 January 2000. He has his own cash resources available for the purpose of setting it up and has estimated that an initial £50,000 would be required for this purpose. During the first month in business, January 2000, **Ayco** (as distinct from Mr Bean) will enter into the following transactions:

	£
Receipt of cheque from Mr Bean	50,000
Purchase for cash the freehold of a shop	30,000
Purchase for cash the shop fittings	5,000
Cash expenses on printing and stationery	200
Purchases of stock, from Beeco, of Aymen toys, payable two months later (12,000 toys at £1 each)	12,000
Sales of Aymen toys to Ceeco for cash (1,000 toys at £2 each)	2,000
Sales of Aymen toys to Deeco, receivable one month later (8,000 toys at £2 each)	16,000

◀ We shall consider each of these transactions in detail and subsequently represent them in T account format for clarity, with debits on the left and credits on the right of the middle line of the T. We will repeatedly refer to the earlier four key double-entry definitions in order to establish the entries required for each transaction.

Receipt of cheque from Mr Bean £50,000 – transaction 1

Ayco will have needed to open a bank account to pay in the money received from Mr Bean. This represents a receipt of cash of £50,000 to Ayco, and so

Debit cash account	£50,000	and credit what?

Answer

This money represents the capital that Mr Bean, as a shareholder, has invested in Ayco and so the account is called the capital account. So:

Debit cash account	£50,000
Credit capital account	£50,000

Example A1.2

Purchase for cash the freehold of a shop £30,000 – transaction 2

This represents a cash payment for the purchase of a shop, something which is called a fixed asset: an asset acquired for retention by the entity for the purpose of providing a service to the business, and not held for resale in the normal course of trading.

Credit cash account	£30,000	and debit what?

Answer

A payment of cash of £30,000 is a credit to the cash account, and so:

Credit cash account	£30,000
Debit fixed assets – shop	£30,000

Example A1.3

Purchase for cash the shop fittings £5,000 – transaction 3

This represents a cash payment for the shop fittings, which are also fixed assets, but a different category of fixed assets from the freehold shop.

Answer

A payment of cash of £5,000 is a credit to the cash account, and so:

Credit cash account	£5,000
Debit fixed assets – fittings	£5,000

Example A1.4

Cash expenses on printing and stationery £200 – transaction 4
This represents a payment of cash of £200 by Ayco in the month, and so:

Credit cash account	**£200**	**and debit what?**

Answer
This money was paid out on day-to-day expenses that have been made to support the business, and is a charge for printing and stationery expenses. So:

Credit cash account	**£200**
Debit printing and stationery expenses	**£200**

Example A1.5

Purchases of stock, from Beeco, of Aymen toys, payable two months later £12,000 – transaction 5
This represents a purchase on credit from Beeco. An invoice is assumed to have been received from Beeco along with the receipt of stock. The invoice from Beeco is a purchase invoice for £12,000 to Ayco, and so:

Credit creditors (accounts payable)	**£12,000**	**and debit what?**

Answer
This represents a purchase of stock which are goods held for resale, and so

Credit creditors	**£12,000**	
Debit stock account	**£12,000**	(a purchase of stock may alternatively be initially debited to a purchases account and then subsequently transferred to a stocks account)

Example A1.6

Sales of Aymen toys to Ceeco for cash £2,000 – transaction 6
This represents a sale for cash to Ceeco. An invoice will be issued by Ayco to Ceeco along with the delivery of stock. The invoice to Ceeco is a sales invoice for £2,000 from Ayco, and so:

Debit debtors (accounts receivable)   £2,000   **and credit what?**

Answer
This represents sales of stock which are called sales, revenue or turnover, and so:

Debit debtors   £2,000
Credit sales account   £2,000

But as a cash sale this sales invoice is being paid immediately with a cash receipt of £2,000, and so:
Debit cash account   £2,000   **and credit what?**

Answer
This £2,000 is immediately paying the receivables, and so

Debit cash account   £2,000
Credit debtors   £2,000

which means that on this transaction the net balance of the receivables account is zero.
   This transaction may be short cut by directly crediting the sales account and debiting cash. However, it is normally recorded in the way described in order to create and record a VAT sales invoice.

Example A1.7

Sales of Aymen toys to Deeco, receivable one month later £16,000 – transaction 7
This represents sales on credit to Deeco. An invoice will be issued by Ayco to Deeco along with the delivery of stock.

Answer
The invoice to Deeco is a sales invoice for £16,000 from Ayco, and so as above

Debit debtors   £16,000
Credit sales account   £16,000

This is different from the transaction in A1.6 because the receivables will not be paid until the following month.

Closing stocks adjustment

In the Ayco example, one further accounting entry needs to be considered, which relates to stocks of toys sold during the period. It is called a **closing stocks** adjustment, which is illustrated in Example A1.8.

Example A1.8

We represented the purchase of 12,000 toys into the stock of Ayco as a debit of £12,000 to the stock account. We have sold 1,000 toys for cash and 8,000 toys on credit. The physical stock of 12,000 toys at 31 January 2000 has therefore been reduced to only 3,000 (12,000 − 1,000 − 8,000). We may value these units that are left in stock at cost, for the purpose of this example, at 3,000 × £1, or £3,000. We have sold a total of 9,000 units during January at a selling price of £2 per unit. These 9,000 units cost £1 each and so these sales have cost Ayco £9,000: cost of sales £9,000. A double-entry accounting transaction is necessary to represent this for two reasons: to show the cost of the 9,000 toys that matches the sale of 9,000 toys; to ensure that the stock account represents only the physical toys that are actually held in stock.

The entries for the original purchase of stock were

Credit creditors	**£12,000**
Debit stock account	**£12,000**

We know that the stock account should now be £9,000 less than the original £12,000, representing the £9,000 cost of sales. Therefore we need to credit the stock account to reduce it and debit something else. The something else is the cost of sales account.

Transaction 8

Credit stock account	**£9,000**
Debit cost of sales account	**£9,000**

Accounting adjustments

The diagram in Fig. A1.1 includes all the main types of accounting transactions that may be recorded in an accounting system. The shaded items represent the prime entries (the first record of transactions) and cash entries. The non-shaded items are the five main accounting adjustment entries.

The closing stocks adjustment, illustrated in Example A1.8, is one of the five main accounting adjustment entries not normally incorporated into the **trial balance** (although they sometimes may be in practice), shown in Fig. A1.2.

Accounting adjustments are made post-trial balance and prior to preparation of the profit and loss account and balance sheet. The other four adjusting entries are **accruals** and **prepayments** (covered later in this appendix), depreciation, and bad and doubtful debts and the **doubtful debt provision** (which are covered together with further detail on closing stocks in Chapter 3).

Each of the T accounts in Fig. A1.3 shows the detailed movement through the month and each account represents the balance on each account at the 31 January 2000, the end of the first month of trading.

Progress check A1.2

Explain broadly what is meant by accounting adjustment entries.

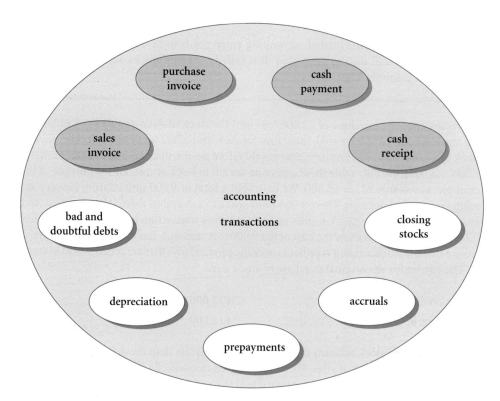

FIGURE A1.1   Accounting transactions

Books of account and the ledgers in action

We saw in the previous section how the principle of double-entry bookkeeping operates to record the detail of transactions. We represented these records in T accounts to provide some clarity in seeing how each entry has been made and the interrelation of the entries. In practice, accounting records are kept along the same lines but in books of account and ledgers rather than T accounts on a piece of paper. The old fashioned manually prepared ledgers maintained by companies have long since been superseded by **computerised accounting systems**. Nevertheless, the same principles apply and the same books of account and ledgers are maintained albeit in an electronic format.

The chart shown in Fig. A1.4 shows the relationship between the main ledger, the general ledger (or nominal ledger) and the other books of account, and subsidiary ledgers:

● **cash book** (receipts and payments)

● **purchase invoice daybook** and **purchase ledger** (or **accounts payable**)

● **sales invoice daybook** and **sales ledger** (or **accounts receivable**).

It also shows the main sources of data input for these ledgers and the basic reporting information produced out of these ledgers and books of account.

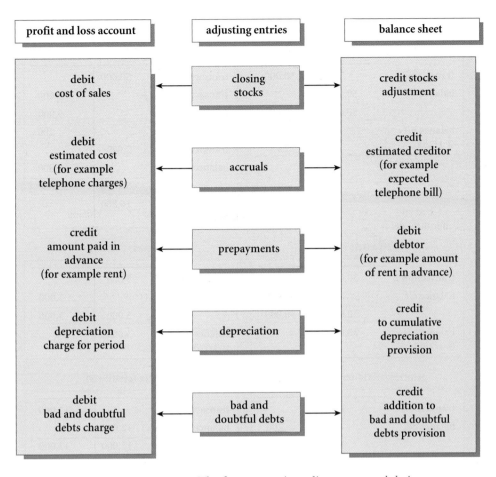

profit and loss account	adjusting entries	balance sheet
debit cost of sales	closing stocks	credit stocks adjustment
debit estimated cost (for example telephone charges)	accruals	credit estimated creditor (for example expected telephone bill)
credit amount paid in advance (for example rent)	prepayments	debit debtor (for example amount of rent in advance)
debit depreciation charge for period	depreciation	credit to cumulative depreciation provision
debit bad and doubtful debts charge	bad and doubtful debts	credit addition to bad and doubtful debts provision

FIGURE A1.2   The five accounting adjustments and their impact on the profit and loss account and the balance sheet

General ledger

In smaller businesses, wages and salaries data are usually recorded in the cash books and subsequently posted to the general ledger. In larger companies, wages and salaries usually have their own ledgers and control accounts in the general ledger.

The main ledger of any company, in which the results of all transactions made by the entity are recorded, is called the **general ledger** or nominal ledger. This ledger is set up to include all accounts whether they are assets, liabilities, sales (or revenues), or costs (or expenses). The detail of every transaction finds its way to this ledger, or is posted to it (to use the technical term), in much the same way as we saw in the T accounts. The general ledger may be said to be the collection of every T account within the entity.

Within the general ledger one account or more will be established to represent cash transactions (including cheques, drafts, bank transfers, etc.). These entries are posted to the general ledger from the analysis of entries made into the cash book. The cash book is a book of original entry maintained to show the detail of all receipts and payments made by the entity; it records the dates, values and unique references of all receipts and payments, and what they are for. These include, for example, payment of salaries, receipts from receivables, purchase of fixed assets, etc.

Figures in £

capital

transaction 1			50,000
balance c/f	50,000		
	50,000		50,000
balance b/f @ 1/2/00			50,000

cash

transaction 1	50,000		
transaction 2			30,000
transaction 3			5,000
transaction 4			200
transaction 6	2,000		
balance c/f			16,800
	52,000		52,000
balance b/f @ 1/2/00	16,800		

fixed assets – shop

transaction 2	30,000		
balance c/f			30,000
	30,000		30,000
balance b/f @ 1/2/00	30,000		

fixed assets – fittings

transaction 3	5,000		
balance c/f			5,000
	5,000		5,000
balance b/f @ 1/2/00	5,000		

printing/stationery expenses

transaction 4	200		
balance c/f			200
	200		200
balance b/f @ 1/2/00	200		

payables (creditors)

transaction 5			12,000
balance c/f	12,000		
	12,000		12,000
balance b/f @ 1/2/00			12,000

stock

transaction 5	12,000		
transaction 8			9,000
balance c/f			3,000
	12,000		12,000
balance b/f @ 1/2/00	3,000		

sales

transaction 6			2,000
transaction 7			16,000
balance c/f	18,000		
	18,000		18,000
balance b/f @ 1/2/00			18,000

receivables (debtors)

transaction 6	2,000		
transaction 6			2,000
transaction 7	16,000		
balance c/f			16,000
	18,000		18,000
balance b/f @ 1/2/00	16,000		

cost of sales

transaction 8	9,000		
balance c/f			9,000
	9,000		9,000
balance b/f @ 1/2/00	9,000		

FIGURE A1.3 T account representation of the January 2000 transactions of Ayco

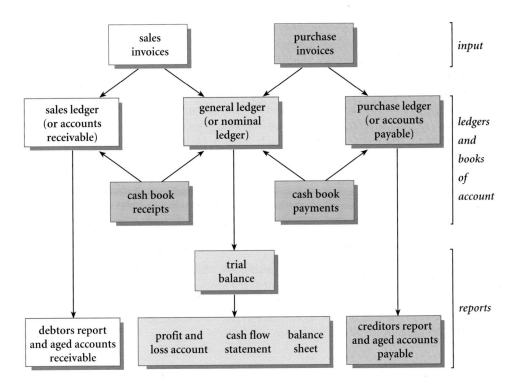

FIGURE A1.4 The general ledger and its relationship with the cash book, purchase ledger and sales ledger

Cash book

The cash book is a book of account that in theory should match exactly with the regular statements issued by the entity's bank. In practice, the cash book is prepared partly from company internally generated **cash payment** information and available information relating to **cash receipts**. Some transactions may appear in the bank account without prior notification, for example bank charges, and so the cash book may also be partly prepared from the bank statement.

There may always be differences in the balances between the cash book and the bank statement because cheques may have been issued but not yet presented to the bank and cash may have been received into the bank account not yet recorded in the cash book. Regular preparation of a **bank reconciliation**, which identifies the differences between the cash book and the bank statement is a necessary function of the finance department.

Each payment and each receipt is posted from the cash book to the cash account in the general ledger as a credit or debit to cash. The opposite entry, either debit or credit, is posted at the same time to its relevant account in the general ledger, for example, payables, printing and stationery expenses, receivables, etc. In the days when such ledgers were maintained manually such postings were made weekly or monthly. With computerised, integrated accounting systems postings may be made simultaneously to the cash book and the general ledger from the same source but avoiding any duplication of effort.

It is most important that the balance on the cash book, the net of all receipts and payments, at all times equals the balance of the cash book represented in the cash account within the general ledger, and that all the opposite entries have also been posted to their relevant accounts. In this way, the equality of total debits and total credits is maintained. The use of computerised accounting systems should guarantee this.

Purchase ledger

Payables are recorded in a ledger, the purchase ledger (or accounts payable) that represents all accounts payable by the entity. Within the general ledger one account or more (control accounts) will be established to represent payables transactions, the purchases by the entity for which invoices have been rendered by suppliers, or vendors. All supplier invoices are recorded in a purchase ledger and analysed into the various items of expense by allocating them to a specific general ledger account. These entries are debited to the appropriate general ledger accounts from the analysis of invoices made in the purchase ledger. The totals of these entries are credited to the account(s) representing accounts payable in the general ledger.

The purchase ledger is maintained to show the detail of all invoices received from suppliers. In addition to the purchase ledger's function of posting the totals of invoices to the accounts payable account in the general ledger, and the analysis of what the invoices represent to the appropriate accounts in the general ledger, it analyses all invoices and groups them by supplier.

Payments made to suppliers from the cash book which have been credited to the cash account and debited to the payables account in the general ledger are also recorded in detail by amount, date and supplier within the purchase ledger. In this way it can be seen that the total balances at any one time of all accounts in the purchase ledger equals the balance on the payables account in the general ledger.

Sales ledger

Receivables are recorded in another ledger – the sales ledger (or accounts receivable) which represents all accounts receivable by the entity. Within the general ledger one account or more will be established (control accounts) to represent receivables transactions – the sales by the entity for which invoices have been issued to customers. All customer invoices are recorded in a sales ledger and analysed into the various items of sale or revenue by allocating them to a specific general ledger account. These entries are credited to the appropriate general ledger accounts from the analysis of invoices made in the sales ledger. The totals of these entries are debited to the account(s) representing accounts receivable in the general ledger.

The sales ledger is maintained to show the detail of all invoices issued to customers. The totals of customer invoices are posted to the accounts receivable account in the general ledger. The analyses of what the invoices represent are posted to the appropriate accounts in the general ledger. The sales ledger may also enable each invoice to be analysed and grouped by customer.

Receipts from customers from the cash book which have been debited to the cash account and credited to the receivables account in the general ledger are also recorded in detail by amount, date and customer within the sales ledger. In this way the total balances at any one time of all accounts in the sales ledger equals the balance on the receivables account in the general ledger.

The cash accounts, payables and receivables accounts in the general ledger are referred to as control accounts because they provide control over the same transactions which are also represented in some further detail, and which must agree in total, in what are termed the books of account and subsidiary ledgers: the cash book, accounts payable (purchase ledger), and accounts receivable (sales ledger).

Progress check A1.3

What are the usual books of account and ledgers you would expect to be used in a company's accounting system?

The trial balance

A trial balance is a list of account balances in a double-entry system. If the records have been correctly maintained, the sum of the debit balance accounts will be equal and opposite to the sum of the credit balance accounts, although certain errors such as omission of a transaction or erroneous entries will not be apparent in the trial balance.

Example A1.9

If we turn again to the Ayco example, we can that see that each of the T accounts we have prepared represent the general (or nominal) ledger balances of the entity. These balances may be listed to form a trial balance for Ayco as at 31 January 2000.

The trial balance for Ayco as at 31 January 2000

	Debit £	Credit £
Capital		50,000
Cash	16,800	
Fixed assets – shop	30,000	
Fixed assets – fittings	5,000	
Printing and stationery expenses	200	
Payables		12,000
Stock	3,000	
Sales		18,000
Receivables	16,000	
Cost of sales	9,000	
	80,000	80,000

From this simple trial balance it is possible to derive three reports that tell us something about the business: the profit and loss account (or income statement); the balance sheet; the cash flow statement.

How do we know which items in the trial balance are balance sheet items and which are profit and loss items? Well, if an item is not a cost (expense) or a sales (revenue) item, then it must be an asset or a liability. The expenses and revenues must appear in the profit and loss account and the assets and liabilities must appear in the balance sheet. Even a computerised accounting system must be told the specific classification of a transaction. Let's examine each of the items in the Ayco trial balance as at 31 January 2000.

Example A1.10

	Debit £	Credit £
Capital		50,000
This represents the original money that the shareholder Mr Bean put into Ayco – not revenue/expense		
Cash	16,800	
This represents the total cash that Ayco has at its disposal at 31 January, an asset – not revenue/expense		
Fixed assets – shop	30,000	
This represents assets purchased out of cash to help run the business – not revenue/expense		
Fixed assets – fittings	5,000	
This represents assets purchased out of cash to help run the business – not revenue/expense		
Printing and stationery expenses	200	
This represents costs incurred on disposable items used in running the business through January – expense		
Payables		12,000
This represents debts which Ayco must pay in the next two months, a liability – not revenue/expense		
Stock	3,000	
This represents items held in stock to sell to customers over future periods, an asset – not revenue/expense		
Sales		18,000
This represents the value of toys delivered to customers in January – revenue		
Receivables	16,000	
This represents debts which Ayco will receive payment for next month, an asset – not revenue/expense		
Cost of sales	9,000	
This represents the cost of toys delivered to customers in January – expense		
	80,000	80,000

Progress check A1.4

What is a trial balance?

Profit and loss account

The profit and loss account shows the profit or loss generated by an entity during an accounting period by deducting all costs from total sales. Within the trial balance we may extract the balances on the costs (expenses) and sales (revenues) accounts in order to construct the profit and loss account. The total sum of these accounts will then result in a balance which is profit or a loss, and which may be inserted back into a restated trial balance in summary form in place of all the individual profit and loss items which comprise that balance.

Example A1.11

The expense and revenue items, or the profit and loss items, may be extracted from the trial balance and summarised as follows:

	Debit £	Credit £
Sales		18,000
Cost of sales	9,000	
Printing and stationery expenses	200	
Balance representing a profit for January	8,800	
	18,000	18,000

Although the £8,800 is shown in the debit column to balance the account, it is in fact a credit balance that is carried forward, that is a balance resulting from £18,000 less debits of £9,200.

Ayco profit and loss account for January 2000

	£
Sales	18,000
less	
Cost of sales	9,000
Gross margin	9,000
Printing and stationery expenses	200
Profit for January 2000	8,800

Progress check A1.5

Outline what a profit and loss account tells us about a company.

Balance sheet

The balance sheet of an entity discloses the assets (debit balances) and liabilities, and shareholders' capital (credit balances), and gains or losses as at a given date. A gain or profit is a credit balance, and a loss is a debit balance. The revised trial balance which includes the net balance of profit or loss, then forms the basis for the balance sheet. The balance sheet may then be constructed by rearranging the balances into an established format.

Example A1.12

The profit is a credit balance of £8,800, and if we substitute this back into the trial balance for the individual revenue and expense items we have:

	Debit £	Credit £
Capital		50,000
Cash	16,800	
Fixed assets – shop	30,000	
Fixed assets – fittings	5,000	
Payables (or creditors)		12,000
Stock	3,000	
Receivables (or debtors)	16,000	
Profit for January		8,800
	70,800	70,800

To construct a balance sheet this needs to be rearranged into a more usual sort of format:

Ayco balance sheet as at 31 January 2000

Assets	£	£	Liabilities	£	£
Fixed assets		35,000	**Equity**		
			Capital	50,000	
			Profit and loss account	8,800	
					58,800
Current assets			**Short-term liabilities**		
Debtors	16,000		Creditors		12,000
Stock	3,000				
Cash	16,800				
		35,800			
		70,800			70,800

Progress check A1.6

Outline what a balance sheet tells us about a company.

Cash flow statement

The final report, the **cash flow statement**, is simply a report on the detail of the movement within the cash account in the trial balance. This starts with the opening balance, shows the receipts and payments during the accounting period and results in the closing balance.

Example A1.13

The final report, the cash flow report, may be constructed by looking at the elements that are included in the cash T account, that is the elements which make up the total movements in the cash account in the general ledger:

	Debit £	Credit £
Cash balance at 1 January 2000	–	
Receipt from Mr Bean – capital for business	50,000	
Payment for freehold shop		30,000
Payment for shop fittings		5,000
Payment for printing and stationery expenses		200
Receipt from customers	2,000	
Cash balance at 31 January 2000		16,800
	52,000	52,000

The £16,800 debit balance carried forward represents a positive cash position of £16,800.

The aim of the last few sections has been to explain the basics of double-entry book-keeping, the sources of accounting data, and to provide an introduction to the accounting ledgers and books of account. This begins to show how the information from double-entry records may be usefully used. The inclusion of the rudimentary financial statements shown above illustrates the importance of the:

- accuracy
- timeliness
- completeness

of the financial data included in the double-entry system.

> **Progress check A1.7**
>
> Outline what a cash flow statement tells us about a company.

Accrual accounting and cash accounting

We have already covered a number of important accounting ideas and concepts, one of which is that profit does not necessarily equal cash. This was apparent from the Ayco example. The net cash movement in that example for the month of January was an inflow, a positive of £16,800. However, the profit and loss account showed a gain, a positive of £8,800. The reason that they were not identical was first (as shown in the cash flow report) due to cash items other than those associated with trading, for example receipt of the original capital, and expenditure on fixed assets. Second, the trading or operational transactions were not all converted into cash within the month of January; they were held as accounts payable, stocks, and accounts receivable.

The approach that we took in the Ayco example demonstrated compliance with the **accruals concept**, or matching concept, the principle that revenue and costs are:

● recognised as they are earned or incurred
● matched with one another
● dealt with in the profit and loss account of the period to which they relate, irrespective of the period of receipt or payment.

Progress check A1.8

In what way does a company's profit and loss account differ from the movements on its cash account during an accounting period

Accruals

It may be that an expense has been incurred within an accounting period, for which an invoice may or may not have been received. For example, electricity used, telephone charges incurred, or stationery supplies received and used. We have talked about the concept of matching costs with sales, or revenues. Costs not necessarily related to sales cannot be matched in that way. Such charges must be matched to the **accounting period** to which they relate, and therefore an estimate of the cost (an accrual) must be made and included as an accounting adjusting entry in the accounts for that period.

Fig. A1.5 shows an invoice dated 15 April 2000 received by a company from its communications provider for charges of £2,000 for the period January to March 2000. At the end of April 2000 the company had not yet received its bill for the next quarter even though it had use of telephone lines and had incurred call charges. We may assume that the company's accounting year runs from January to December. Therefore, before finalising its profit and loss account for January to April the company needed to estimate its telephone costs for April, which are shown as £700.

The estimate of £700 has been charged, or debited, to telephone costs in the profit and loss account, and a temporary creditor, an accrual, credited in the balance sheet for £700. The total telephone costs charged to the profit and loss account for January to April 2000 are therefore £2,700. The accrual carried forward at the end of April would normally be reversed and the position assessed again at the end of May, and the same procedure followed at the end of June. By the end of July the bill would normally be expected to have been received covering the period April to June and so no accrual will be necessary. However, an accrual will be required for the month of July.

Figures in £

Profit and loss account

telephone account

invoice 15 Apr 2000 Jan–Mar	2,000	
Apr accrual	700	
Jan–Apr to profit and loss account		2,700
	2,700	2,700

Balance sheet

accruals

Apr accrual		700
balance c/f	700	
	700	700
balance b/f @ 1 May 2000		700

FIGURE A1.5 T account illustration of accounting for accruals

From the following information we are required to prepare three-column accounts (in an Excel spreadsheet or in a Word table) to reflect the current balances on each account, which are then required to be adjusted for the accruals at 31 December 2000 to show the total transfer to the profit and loss account. We are also required to show a summary of the accruals as at 31 December 2000.

	£
Current balances at 31 December 2000	
Electricity	10,000
Gas	11,000
Telephone	5,000
Interest on overdraft	6,000
Accruals required at 31 December 2000	
Electricity	500
Gas	600
Telephone	500
Interest on overdraft	600

◀ **Answer**

	Debit £	Credit £	Balance £
Electricity			
31 December 2000			10,000
Accrual 31 December 2000	500		10,500
Transfer to profit and loss account		(10,500)	0
Gas			
31 December 2000			11,000
Accrual 31 December 2000	600		11,600
Transfer to profit and loss account		(11,600)	0
Telephone			
31 December 2000			5,000
Accrual 31 December 2000	500		5,500
Transfer to profit and loss account		(5,500)	0
Interest payable on overdraft			
31 December 2000			6,000
Accrual 31 December 2000	600		6,600
Transfer to profit and loss account		(6,600)	0
Accruals 31 December 2000			
Electricity		(500)	(500)
Gas		(600)	(1,100)
Telephone		(500)	(1,600)
Interest payable on overdraft		(600)	(2,200)

The same sort of exercise is carried out within a company for all of the categories of expense for which accruals are likely to be required. Example A1.15 explains how accruals may have been dealt with in Ayco.

Example A1.15

The accruals concept could have been further illustrated in the Ayco scenario by the introduction of a number of additional factors. Assume, for example, that Ayco had used more than £200 of stationery in the month, say £1,000. We know that Ayco had been invoiced for and paid for £200 worth of stationery.

If £500 worth of the additional stationery had been used, and an invoice had been received but not processed through the ledgers, what would be the impact on Ayco? If £300 worth of the additional stationery had been used, and an invoice had not yet been received but was in the mail what would be the impact on Ayco?

The answer is that both would have to be debited to printing and stationery expenses for a total of £800, and credited not to payables but to accruals.

Accruals are treated in a similar way to payables but the invoices for these charges have not yet been processed by the entity. They are charges which are brought into the period because, although goods (or services) have been provided, they have not yet been included in the supplier's accounts.

Expense recognition is an important concept. Expenses should be recognised immediately they are known about. Ayco knew they had used stationery for which there was a cost even though an invoice may not have been processed. On the other hand revenues or profits should not be recognised until they are earned.

The net impact of the above on Ayco would have been a reduction in profit, a debit of £800 and an increase in liabilities, a credit of £800 to accruals. The accruals entries would need to be exactly reversed at the beginning of the following month to avoid a doubling up since the actual transactions will also be processed.

Prepayments

It may be that an expense has been incurred within an accounting period that related to future period(s). For example, business rates, rents, or vehicle licence fees paid in advance. As with accruals, these costs are not necessarily related to sales and cannot be matched with sales. Such charges must also be matched to the period to which they relate and therefore the proportion of the charges that relate to future periods (a prepayment) must be calculated and included as an adjustment in the accounts for that period.

Fig. A1.6 shows a charge of £6,000 that has been incurred by a company from its landlord on 1 January 2000 for rent for the period January to June 2000. At the end of April 2000 the company had paid rent not only for January to April, but rent in advance for May

Figures in £

Profit and loss account

rent account

invoice 1 Jan 2000	Jan–Jun	6,000	
Apr prepayment			2,000
Jan–Apr to profit and loss account			4,000
		6,000	6,000

Balance sheet

prepayments

Apr prepayment	2,000	
balance c/f		2,000
	2,000	2,000
balance b/f @ 1 May 2000	2,000	

FIGURE A1.6 T account illustration of accounting for prepayments and June. Therefore, before finalising its profit and loss account for January to April the company needed to calculate the rent in advance for May and June, which is shown as £2,000.

The rent in advance of £2,000 has been credited to the rent account and a temporary debtor, a prepayment, created in the balance sheet for £2,000. The total rent costs charged to the profit and loss account for January to April 2000 are therefore £4,000. The prepayment carried forward at the end of April would normally be reversed and the position assessed again at the end of May, and the same procedure followed at the end of June. By the end of July a charge would normally be expected to have been received covering the period July to December and so a prepayment will be necessary at the end of July for the period August to December.

Example A1.16

From the following information we are required to prepare three-column accounts (in an Excel spreadsheet or in a Word table) to reflect the current balances on each account, which are then required to be adjusted for the prepayments, deferred income, and accrued income at 31 December 2000, to show the total transfer to the profit and loss account. We are also required to show a summary of the prepayments and accrued income, and accruals and deferred income as at 31 December 2000.

	£
Current balances at 31 December 2000	
Rent payable	12,000
Business rates	13,000
Interest receivable	7,000 (credit)
Rent receivable	8,000 (credit)
Prepayments, accrued income, and deferred income required at 31 December 2000	
Rent payable	700 (normally paid in advance)
Business rates	800 (normally paid in advance)
Interest receivable	700 (normally received in arrears)
Rent received	800 (normally received in advance)

Answer

	Debit £	Credit £	Balance £
Rent payable			
31 December			12,000
Prepayment 31 December 2000		(700)	11,300
Transfer to profit and loss account		(11,300)	0
Business rates			
31 December			13,000
Prepayment 31 December 2000		(800)	12,200
Transfer to profit and loss account		(12,200)	0

Interest receivable

31 December		(7,000)
Accrued income 31 December 2000	(700)	(7,700)
Transfer to profit and loss account	7,700	0

Rent receivable

31 December		(8,000)
Deferred income 31 December 2000	800	(7,200)
Transfer to profit and loss account	7,200	0

Prepayments and accrued income

31 December 2000		0
Rent payable	700	700
Business rates	800	1,500
Interest receivable	700	2,200

Accruals and deferred income

31 December 2000		0
Rent receivable	(800)	(800)

The same sort of exercise is carried out within a company for all of the categories of expense for which prepayments are likely to be required. Example A1.17 explains how prepayments may have been dealt with in Ayco.

Example A1.17

Assume, for example, that Ayco had received an invoice for £2,000 for advertising in January to be paid in March, but the advertising was not taking place until February. An invoice may have been received and processed through the ledgers, but what would be the impact on Ayco?

Answer

Payables would have been credited with £2,000 and advertising expenses debited with £2,000 in the month of January. However, because the advertising had not taken place, the charge of £2,000 would be considered as being in advance, or to use its technical term a prepayment. The payables entry remains as a credit of £2,000, but an additional entry is required to credit advertising expenses with £2,000 and debit prepayments with £2,000.

A prepayment is expenditure on goods (or services) for future benefit, which is to be charged to future operations. Such amounts are similar to debtors and are included in current assets in the balance sheet.

The net impact of the above on Ayco would have been no charge to profit. The prepayment entry would need to be exactly reversed at the beginning of the following month.

Progress check A1.9

What are accruals and prepayments and why are such adjusting entries needed?

Accounting periods

In the Ayco example we were introduced to the idea of an accounting period. An accounting period is that covered by the accounting statements of an entity. Different periods may be chosen within the financial year, for example 13 periods of four weeks, 12 periods using a four, four, five week quarter basis, or 12 calendar periods. The Ayco example assumed 12 periods on a calendar basis. Once an accounting period basis has been chosen, consistency must be maintained. This is an example of both the **periodicity concept** and the **consistency concept** (see Chapter 1).

Progress check A1.10

What is an accounting period?

Summary of key points

- Double-entry bookkeeping is a convention, the two main objectives of which are to have a permanent record of transactions, and to show the effect of each transaction and the combined effect of all the transactions upon the financial position of the entity.

- Double-entry bookkeeping data are recorded as transactions described as 'debits' and 'credits'.

- The meaning of a debit and a credit may most usefully be remembered using the following rule, applying to entries reflected in the accounts of a company:

Cash receipt	=	debit cash account	and credit another account
Cash payment	=	credit cash account	and debit another account
Purchase invoice	=	credit accounts payable	and debit another account
Sales invoice	=	debit accounts receivable	and credit another account

- The main ledger held within the accounting system of a company is called the general ledger, or nominal ledger, in which the results of all transactions made by the company are recorded either in summary or in detail.

- The original books of account, and subsidiary ledgers: cash book (receipts and payments); purchase invoice daybook and purchase ledger (or accounts payable); sales invoice daybook and sales ledger (or accounts receivable), hold the details of transactions that are reflected in the general ledger.

- Wages and salaries data are recorded in the cash books and posted to the general ledger.

- Adjusting accounting entries, such as those relating to closing stock valuations, are made to the accounts prior to preparation of the profit and loss account and balance sheet.

- There are five main accounting adjustments that are made, post trial balance and prior to preparation of the profit and loss account and balance sheet:
  - closing stocks
  - accruals – charges not yet received
  - prepayments – payments in advance (and income accrued)
  - depreciation
  - bad and doubtful debts

- The balances on the individual accounts recorded within the general ledger may be summarised in a trial balance, the total of the debit balances being equal to the total of the credit balances.

- The profit and loss account of an entity shows the profit or loss generated by the entity during an accounting period by deducting all expenses from all revenues.

- The balance sheet of an entity discloses the assets (debit balances) and liabilities, and shareholders' capital (credit balances), and gains (credits) or losses (debits) as at a given date.

- The cash flow statement is a report on the detail of the movement within the cash account in the trial balance, starting with the opening balance and adding the receipts and deducting the payments during the accounting period, resulting in the closing balance.

- The accounting period chosen by a business is the period covered by its accounting statements.

Glossary of key terms

accounting adjustments Accounting entries that do not arise from the basic transactions of cash and invoices. Adjusting entries are made for depreciation, bad and doubtful debts, closing stocks, prepayments, and accruals.

accounting period The period covered by the accounting statements of an entity.

accounts payable Also called trade creditors, is the money owed to suppliers for goods and services.

accounts receivable Also called trade debtors, is the money owed to entities by customers.

accruals Allowances made for costs and expenses payable within one year of the balance sheet date but for which no invoices have yet been recorded.

accruals concept The principle that revenues and costs are recognised as they are earned or incurred, are matched with one another, and are dealt with in the profit and loss account of the period to which they relate, irrespective of the period of receipt or payment. Where a conflict arises, this concept is subservient to the prudence concept.

assets Rights or other access to future economic benefits controlled by an entity as a result of past transactions or events (FRS 5).

bad debt A debt which is considered to be uncollectable and is, therefore, written off either as a charge to the profit and loss account or against an existing doubtful debt provision.

balance sheet A statement of the financial position of an entity at a given date disclosing the assets, liabilities and accumulated funds such as shareholders' contributions and reserves, prepared to give a true and fair view of the financial state of the entity at that date.

bank reconciliation A detailed statement reconciling, at a given date, the cash balance in an entity's cash book with that reported in a bank statement.

bookkeeping Recording of monetary transactions, appropriately classified, in the financial records of an entity, either by manual means, or otherwise.

cash book A book of original entry that includes details of all receipts and payments made by an entity. The details normally include transaction date, method of payment or receipt, amount paid or received, bank statement value (if different), name of payee or payer, general ledger allocation and coding.

cash flow statement A statement which summarises the inflows and outflows of cash for a period, classified under the following standard headings (FRS 1):

- operating activities
- returns on investment and servicing of finance
- taxation
- investing activities
- liquid funds
- equity dividends
- financing.

cash payment A cash payment is the transfer of funds from a business to a recipient (for example, trade creditor or employee).

cash receipt A cash receipt is the transfer of funds to a business from a payer (for example, a customer).

closing stocks All trading companies buy stock with the intention of reselling, at a profit, to a customer. At the end of each accounting period, the company will have unsold stock that will be sold during a subsequent accounting period. That unsold stock is termed 'closing stock' and is deducted from opening stock plus purchases (to derive cost of sales), and will appear in the balance sheet as stocks (within current assets).

computerised accounting system This is a system that maintains business transactions on a computer on a long-term basis.

consistency concept The principle that there is uniformity of accounting treatment of like items within each accounting period and from one period to the next.

cost The amount of expenditure (actual or notional) incurred on, or attributable to, a specified thing or activity. To cost something is to ascertain the cost of a specified thing or activity. Cost also relates to a resource sacrificed or forgone, expressed in a monetary value.

depreciation A measure of the wearing out, consumption or other reduction in the useful economic life of a fixed asset, whether arising from use, effluxion of time or obsolescence through technological or market changes (FRS 11 and FRS 15). Depreciation should be allocated so as to charge a fair proportion of the total cost (or valuation) of the asset to each accounting period expected to benefit from its use.

double-entry bookkeeping The system of bookkeeping based on the principle that every financial transaction involves the simultaneous receiving and giving of value, and is therefore recorded twice.

doubtful debt A debt for which there is some uncertainty as to whether or not it will be settled, and there is a possibility that it may eventually prove to be bad. A doubtful debt provision may be created for such a debt by charging it as an expense to the profit and loss account.

doubtful debt provision An amount charged against profit and deducted from debtors to allow for the estimated non-recovery of a proportion of the debts.

general ledger Also called the nominal ledger, contains all accounts relating to assets, expenses, revenue and liabilities.

liabilities An entity's obligations to transfer economic benefits as a result of past transactions or events (FRS 5).

periodicity concept The requirement to produce financial statements at set time intervals. This requirement is embodied, in the case of UK corporations, in the Companies Act.

prepayments Prepayments includes prepaid expenses for services not yet used, for example rent in advance or electricity charges in advance, and also accrued income. Accrued income relates to sales of goods or services that have occurred and have been included in the profit and loss account for the trading period but have not yet been invoiced to the customer.

profit and loss account (or income statement) The profit and loss account shows the profit or loss generated by an entity during an accounting period by deducting all expenses from all revenues. It measures whether or not the company has made a profit or loss on its operations during the period, through producing and selling its goods or services.

purchase invoice A document received from a supplier by an entity showing the description, quantity, prices and values of goods or services received.

purchase invoice daybook A list of supplier invoices recording their dates, gross values, values net of VAT, the dates of receipt of the invoices, the names of suppliers, and the general ledger allocation and coding.

purchase ledger The purchase ledger contains all the personal accounts of each individual supplier or vendor, and records every transaction with each supplier since the start of their relationship with the company.

sales Also called turnover or revenue, sales are amounts derived from the provision of goods or services falling within the company's ordinary activities, after deduction of sales returns, trade discounts, value added tax, and any other taxes based on the amounts so derived (Companies Act 1985/1989).

sales invoice A document prepared by an entity showing the description, quantity, prices and values of goods delivered or services rendered to a customer.

sales invoice daybook A list of customer invoices recording their dates, gross values, values net of VAT, the names of customers, and the general ledger allocation and coding.

sales ledger The sales ledger contains all the personal accounts of each individual customer, and records every transaction with each customer since the start of their relationship with the company.

trial balance The list of account balances in a double-entry accounting system. If the records have been correctly maintained, the sum of the debit balances will equal the sum of the credit balances, although certain errors such as the omission of a transaction or erroneous entries will not be disclosed by a trial balance.

Assessment material

Questions

QA1.1 What are the four basic business transactions and what are their corresponding debit and credit accounting entries under the convention of double-entry bookkeeping?

QA1.2 (i) Name each of the books of account and ledgers in an accounting system.

(ii) What are they used for?

QA1.3 Describe the use and purpose of the five main accounting adjusting entries.

QA1.4 (i) At a specific point in time, what does a company's trial balance show?

(ii) What may the trial balance not show?

QA1.5 How may the financial performance of a company be ascertained from its trial balance?

QA1.6 How may the financial position of a company be ascertained from its trial balance?

QA1.7 How may the cash position of a company be ascertained from its trial balance?

QA1.8 Why is the profit made during an accounting period not necessarily equal to the cash flow during that period?

QA1.9 What is the relevance of the accounting period?

Discussion points

DA1.1 'Managers who are non-accounting specialists don't need to learn about bookkeeping, debits and credits, etc.' Discuss.

DA1.2 Computerised accounts and information systems have speeded up the recording of accounting data and the presentation of information. What are the other advantages over manual accounting systems and what are the disadvantages?

Exercises

Solutions are provided in Appendix 4 to all exercise numbers highlighted in colour.

Level I

EA1.1 *Time allowed – 30 minutes*

Extracts from the ledgers of Hall Ltd have provided the following information for 1999 and 2000.

	£
Sales 1999	11,000
Sales 2000	12,000
Purchases 1999	7,100
Purchases 2000	8,300
Expenses 1999	2,500
Expenses 2000	2,800
Stock 1 January 1999	600
Stock 1 January 2000	700
Stock 1 January 2001	800
Obsolete stock in purchases 2000	200

You are required to prepare a basic profit and loss account for the years ended 31 December 1999 and 2000.

EA1.2 *Time allowed – 30 minutes*

(a) **Explain why there are always problems at the year-end in the assessment of the costs associated with electricity, gas and telephone.**

(b) **Using the information below, prepare the appropriate year end accounting entries.**

Electricity charges account balance at 15 December 2000: £10,000

Gas charges account balance at 20 December 2000: £5,000

Estimated consumption

Electricity 16 December to 31 December 2000: £300

Gas 21 December to 31 December 2000: £150

EA1.3 *Time allowed – 30 minutes*

Arthur Moment set up a table-making business, Forlegco, on 1 July 2000. He had £10,000 available to invest, which is the amount he estimated was required for setting up costs. In the first month of trading Forlegco entered into the following transactions:

	£
£10,000 from Arthur Moment	10,000
Purchase of hand tools for cash	2,000
Purchase of lathe, power saw and drill on one month's credit	6,000
Purchase of printing and stationery – invoice received for half the order	100

The total order is £200, and it was all delivered in July and used

Purchase of advertising flyers for cash
2,000 at 50p each, of which 1,000 will be used in July, and 500 in August and September

Purchases of timber, glue and varnish, from Woodco, payable within the month £1,500 – half of this stock will be on hand at 31 July 2000

Sales of tables to Gardenfurnco for settlement one month later
(10 tables at £700 each)

You are required to present these transactions in T account format, and then prepare a trial balance for Forlegco for 31 July 2000.

EA1.4 *Time allowed – 30 minutes*

From the trial balance for Forlegco for 31 July 2000 (Exercise EA1.3)

(i) **Prepare a simple profit and loss account for the month of July 2000.**

(ii) **Has Forlegco made a profit in July?**

(iii) **If Forlegco has not made a profit, why not?**

EA1.5 *Time allowed – 30 minutes*

From the trial balance for Forlegco for 31 July 2000 (Exercise EA1.3) prepare a simple balance sheet at that date.

EA1.6 *Time allowed – 30 minutes*

From the trial balance for Forlegco for 31 July 2000 (Exercise EA1.3) prepare a simple cash flow statement for the month of July 2000.

EA1.7 *Time allowed – 30 minutes*

Oblivion Ltd has made a net profit of £41,000 for the month of March 2000, according to its draft accounts. Consider if any of the following additional information should be taken into account, and recalculate the profit accordingly:

(i) discounts allowed to customers in March of £1,248 had not been entered in the accounting records

(ii) a sales invoice of £857 for March had been put into the drawer and not entered in the accounting records

(iii) an invoice for telephone costs for £540 had been entered in the accounting records as £450

(iv) bank charges of £660 on the last bank statement had been missed during the month-end rush

(v) an amount of £1,200 relating to supplier discounts in March had not yet been entered in the accounts.

Level II

EA1.8 *Time allowed – 60 minutes*

David (Dai) Etcoak decided to set up a drinks wholesale business, Etcoakco, on 1 December 2000. He had £100,000 available to invest, which is the amount he felt was required to set up the business. In the first month of trading Etcoakco entered into the following transactions:

	£
£100,000 from Dai Etcoak	100,000
Purchase for cash the freehold of a shop	50,000
Purchase for cash the shop fittings	7,000
Purchase of a labelling machine payable one month later	20,000
Cash expenses on printing and stationery	400
Purchases of stock, from Gasco, of bottles of pop, payable three months later (25,000 bottles at £1.25 each)	31,250
Sales of bottles of Etcoak to Boozah for settlement one month later (10,000 bottles at £2.30 each)	23,000
Sales of bottles of Etcoak to Disco30, receivable in the month (12,000 bottles at £2.30 each)	27,600

You are required to:

(i) **look at these transactions in detail and then present them in T account format, and**

(ii) **state any assumptions you have made particularly relating to how you have valued stock transactions.**

Also:

(iii) **Do you think £100,000 was enough money or too much to invest in the business?**

(iv) **What alternative courses of action are open to Dai?**

Appendix 2

Discounted cash flow tables

Present value of £1

The table shows the value of £1 to be received or paid, using a range of interest rates (r) after a given number of years (n).

The values are based on the formula $V_n r = (1 + r)^{-n}$

Rate r %	1	2	3	4	5	6	7	8	9	10	11	12
After **n years**												
1	0.99	0.98	0.97	0.96	0.95	0.94	0.93	0.93	0.92	0.91	0.90	0.89
2	0.98	0.96	0.94	0.92	0.91	0.89	0.87	0.86	0.84	0.83	0.81	0.80
3	0.97	0.94	0.92	0.89	0.86	0.84	0.82	0.79	0.77	0.75	0.73	0.71
4	0.96	0.92	0.89	0.85	0.82	0.79	0.76	0.74	0.71	0.68	0.66	0.64
5	0.95	0.91	0.86	0.82	0.78	0.75	0.71	0.68	0.65	0.62	0.59	0.57
6	0.94	0.89	0.84	0.79	0.75	0.70	0.67	0.63	0.60	0.56	0.53	0.51
7	0.93	0.87	0.81	0.76	0.71	0.67	0.62	0.58	0.55	0.51	0.48	0.45
8	0.92	0.85	0.79	0.73	0.68	0.63	0.58	0.54	0.50	0.47	0.43	0.40
9	0.91	0.84	0.77	0.70	0.64	0.59	0.54	0.50	0.46	0.42	0.39	0.36
10	0.91	0.82	0.74	0.68	0.61	0.56	0.51	0.46	0.42	0.39	0.35	0.32
11	0.90	0.80	0.72	0.65	0.58	0.53	0.48	0.43	0.39	0.35	0.32	0.29
12	0.89	0.79	0.70	0.62	0.56	0.50	0.44	0.40	0.36	0.32	0.29	0.26
13	0.88	0.77	0.68	0.60	0.53	0.47	0.41	0.37	0.33	0.29	0.26	0.23
14	0.87	0.76	0.66	0.58	0.51	0.44	0.39	0.34	0.30	0.26	0.23	0.20
15	0.86	0.74	0.64	0.56	0.48	0.42	0.36	0.32	0.27	0.24	0.21	0.18

Rate r %	13	14	15	16	17	18	19	20	30	40	50
After **n years**											
1	0.88	0.88	0.87	0.86	0.85	0.85	0.84	0.83	0.77	0.71	0.67
2	0.78	0.77	0.76	0.74	0.73	0.72	0.71	0.69	0.59	0.51	0.44
3	0.69	0.67	0.66	0.64	0.62	0.61	0.59	0.58	0.46	0.36	0.30
4	0.61	0.59	0.57	0.55	0.53	0.52	0.50	0.48	0.35	0.26	0.20
5	0.54	0.52	0.50	0.48	0.46	0.44	0.42	0.40	0.27	0.19	0.13
6	0.48	0.46	0.43	0.41	0.39	0.37	0.35	0.33	0.21	0.13	0.09
7	0.43	0.40	0.38	0.35	0.33	0.31	0.30	0.28	0.16	0.09	0.06
8	0.38	0.35	0.33	0.31	0.28	0.27	0.25	0.23	0.12	0.07	0.04
9	0.33	0.31	0.28	0.26	0.24	0.23	0.21	0.19	0.09	0.05	0.03
10	0.29	0.27	0.25	0.23	0.21	0.19	0.18	0.16	0.07	0.03	0.02
11	0.26	0.24	0.21	0.20	0.18	0.16	0.15	0.13	0.06	0.02	0.01
12	0.23	0.21	0.19	0.17	0.15	0.14	0.12	0.11	0.04	0.02	0.01
13	0.20	0.18	0.16	0.15	0.13	0.12	0.10	0.09	0.03	0.01	0.01
14	0.18	0.16	0.14	0.13	0.11	0.10	0.09	0.08	0.03	0.01	*
15	0.16	0.14	0.12	0.11	0.09	0.08	0.07	0.08	0.02	0.01	*

Cumulative present value of £1

The table shows the present value of £1 per annum, using a range of interest rates (*r*), receivable or payable at the end of each year for *n* years.

Rate *r* % After *n* years	1	2	3	4	5	6	7	8	9	10	11	12
1	0.99	0.98	0.97	0.96	0.95	0.94	0.94	0.93	0.92	0.91	0.90	0.89
2	1.97	1.94	1.91	1.89	1.86	1.83	1.81	1.78	1.76	1.74	1.71	1.69
3	2.94	2.88	2.83	2.78	2.72	2.67	2.62	2.58	2.53	2.49	2.44	2.40
4	3.90	3.81	3.72	3.63	3.55	3.47	3.39	3.31	3.24	3.17	3.10	3.04
5	4.85	4.71	4.58	4.45	4.33	4.21	4.10	3.99	3.89	3.79	3.70	3.61
6	5.80	5.60	5.42	5.24	5.08	4.92	4.77	4.62	4.49	4.36	4.23	4.11
7	6.73	6.47	6.23	6.00	5.79	5.58	5.39	5.21	5.03	4.87	4.71	4.56
8	7.65	7.33	7.02	6.73	6.46	6.21	5.97	5.75	5.54	5.34	5.15	4.97
9	8.57	8.16	7.79	7.44	7.11	6.80	6.52	6.25	6.00	5.76	5.54	5.33
10	9.47	8.98	8.53	8.11	7.72	7.36	7.02	6.71	6.42	6.15	5.89	5.65
11	10.40	9.79	9.25	8.76	8.31	7.89	7.50	7.14	6.81	6.50	6.21	5.94
12	11.26	10.58	9.95	9.39	8.86	8.38	7.94	7.54	7.16	6.81	6.49	6.19
13	12.13	11.35	10.64	9.99	9.39	8.85	8.36	7.90	7.49	7.10	6.80	6.42
14	13.00	12.11	11.30	10.56	9.90	9.30	8.75	8.24	7.79	7.37	6.98	6.63
15	13.87	12.85	11.94	11.12	10.38	9.71	9.11	8.56	8.06	7.61	7.19	6.81

Rate *r* % After *n* years	13	14	15	16	17	18	19	20	30	40	50
1	0.89	0.88	0.87	0.86	0.85	0.85	0.84	0.83	0.77	0.71	0.67
2	1.67	1.65	1.63	1.61	1.59	1.57	1.55	1.53	1.36	1.22	1.11
3	2.36	2.32	2.28	2.25	2.21	2.17	2.14	2.11	1.81	1.59	1.41
4	2.97	2.91	2.86	2.80	2.74	2.69	2.64	2.59	2.17	1.85	1.61
5	3.52	3.43	3.35	3.27	3.20	3.13	3.06	2.99	2.44	2.04	1.74
6	4.00	3.89	3.78	3.69	3.59	3.50	3.41	3.33	2.64	2.17	1.82
7	4.42	4.29	4.16	4.04	3.92	3.81	3.71	3.61	2.80	2.26	1.88
8	4.80	4.64	4.49	4.34	4.21	4.08	3.95	3.84	2.93	2.33	1.92
9	5.13	4.95	4.77	4.61	4.45	4.30	4.16	4.03	3.02	2.38	1.95
10	5.43	5.22	5.02	4.83	4.66	4.49	4.34	4.19	3.09	2.41	1.97
11	5.69	5.45	5.23	5.03	4.83	4.66	4.49	4.33	3.15	2.44	1.98
12	5.92	5.66	5.42	5.20	4.99	4.79	4.61	4.44	3.19	2.46	1.99
13	6.12	5.84	5.58	5.34	5.12	4.91	4.71	4.53	3.22	2.47	1.99
14	6.30	6.00	5.72	5.47	5.23	5.01	4.80	4.61	3.25	2.48	1.99
15	6.46	6.14	5.85	5.58	5.32	5.09	4.88	4.68	3.27	2.48	2.00

Appendix 3

FRSs and SSAPs

Financial Reporting Standards (FRSs) in force in the year 2001

FRS 1	Cash flow statements
FRS 2	Accounting for subsidiary undertakings
FRS 3	Reporting financial performance
FRS 4	Capital instruments
FRS 5	Reporting the substance of transactions
FRS 6	Acquisitions and mergers
FRS 7	Fair values in acquisition accounting
FRS 8	Related party disclosures
FRS 9	Associates and joint ventures
FRS 10	Goodwill and intangible assets
FRS 11	Impairment of fixed assets and goodwill
FRS 12	Provisions, contingent liabilities and contingent assets
FRS 13	Derivatives and other financial instruments: disclosures
FRS 14	Earnings per share
FRS 15	Tangible fixed assets
FRS 16	Current tax
FRS 17	Retirement benefits
FRS 18	Accounting policies
FRS 19	Deferred tax (effective from years ending on or after 23 January 2002)
FRSSE	Financial reporting standard for smaller entities

Statements of Standard Accounting Practice (SSAPs) in force in the year 2001

SSAP 2	Disclosure of accounting policies
SSAP 5	Accounting for value added tax
SSAP 9	Stocks and long-term contracts
SSAP 12	Accounting for depreciation
SSAP 13	Accounting for research and development
SSAP 15	Accounting for deferred taxation (effective up to 2002)
SSAP 17	Accounting for post balance sheet events
SSAP 19	Accounting for investment properties
SSAP 20	Foreign currency translation
SSAP 21	Accounting for leases and hire purchase contracts
SSAP 24	Accounting for pension costs
SSAP 25	Segmental reporting

Appendix 4

Solutions to selected exercises

Solutions are provided for the chapter-end exercise numbers highlighted in colour.

Chapter 2

E2.3 Trainer

Trainer plc
Balance sheet as at 31 December 2000

	£000	£000
Fixed assets		
Land and buildings		320
Plant and machinery		
Cost	200	
Depreciation	80	120
Current assets		
Stocks	100	
Debtors	100	
Bank	73	
	273	
Current liabilities		
Trade creditors	130	
Accruals	5	
Taxation	20	
	155	118
		558
Capital and reserves		
Ordinary shares		320
Profit and loss account		238
		558

Working		£000
Sales		1,000
Cost of sales		600
Gross profit		400
Expenses		(120)
Bad debt		(2)
Depreciation		(20)
Profit before tax		258
Taxation (also a short-term creditor within *Current liabilities*)		(20)
Net profit		238

E2.6 Optical

We first need to adjust Optical plc's trial balance at 31 December 2000 for the additional information we have been given that has not yet been recorded in the trial balance.

Trial balance at 31 December 2000

		Debit £000	Credit £000
Share capital	[400 + 100]		500
Share premium	[100 + 100]		200
Revaluation reserve	[100 − 20]		80
Profit and loss account	[200 − 10]		190
Debentures (15%)	[200 − 50]		150
Land at valuation	[350 − 20]	330	
Buildings – cost		200	
Buildings – depreciation			24
Plant – cost	[450 + 100]	550	
Plant – depreciation			180
Stock		225	
Trade debtors	[200 − 10]	190	
Provision for doubtful debts			20
Trade creditors			220
Expense accruals			11
Expense prepayments		10	
Bank account	[20 + 100 + 100 − 50 − 100]	70	
Total		1,575	1,575

Optical plc
Balance sheet as at 31 December 2000

	£000	£000
Fixed assets		
Land	330	
Buildings	176	
Plant	370	
		876
Current assets		
Stocks	225	
Debtors	170	
Prepayments	10	
Bank	70	
	475	
Liabilities due within 1 year		
Trade creditors	220	
Accruals	11	
	231	
Net current assets		244
Totals assets less current liabilities		1,120
Liabilities due in over 1 year		
Debentures		(150)
Net assets		970
Capital and reserves		
Ordinary shares		500
Share premium		200
Revaluation reserve		80
Profit and loss account		190
		970

E2.7 Pip

Pip Ltd
Balance Sheet as at 31 December 2000

	£000	£000	Working
Fixed assets			
Land and buildings	100,000		
Plant and equipment	100,000		[150,000 − 50,000]
		200,000	
Current assets			
Stocks	45,000		[50,000 − 5000]
Debtors	45,000		[50,000 − 5,000]
Cash in hand and at bank	11,000		[10,000 + 1,000]
	101,000		
Current liabilities			
Bank overdraft	10,000		
Trade creditors	81,000		
	91,000		
Net current assets		10,000	
		210,000	
Capital and reserves			
Ordinary shares (issued)		100,000	
Profit and loss account		110,000	
		210,000	

Note that the intangible assets, brands worth £10,000 in the opinion of the directors, have not been included in the balance sheet on the assumption that they are not purchased brands. Under FRS 10 only brand names that have been purchased may be capitalised and included in the balance sheet.

Chapter 3

E3.3 CDs

Overview
Stocks are regulated by the revised SSAP 9. Stocks should be valued at the lower of cost and net realisable value. Retailers can (and do) take the retail value of their stocks (by category) and deduct the gross profit (by category) as an estimate of cost.

(i)   This stock should be valued at £5,000 (cost) as the stock is selling consistently.

(ii) This stock should not be in the balance sheet at any value, as it will not generate any cash in the future.

(iii) As in (i) above this stock can be valued at £1,000 (cost) for balance sheet purposes. As there are more risks associated with holding single artist CDs the stock levels should be continually reviewed.

(iv) In this situation the selling pattern has changed and the posters have stopped selling. The posters must not appear in the balance sheet as they will not generate any future cash.

E3.4 Partex

	1996	1997	1998
	£	£	£

(a) **Balance sheet as at 31 December – Debtors**

	1996	1997	1998
Debtors including debts to be written-off	88,000	110,000	94,000
Write-off of debts to profit and loss account (1)	(4,000)	(5,000)	(4,000)
	84,000	105,000	90,000
Bad debt provision at 4% of debtors (2)	–	3,360	4,200
	(3,360)	(4,200)	(3,600)
Debtors at end of year	80,640	104,160	90,600

(b) **Profit and loss account year ended 31 December – Bad debts**

	1996	1997	1998
Bad debts written-off (1)	4,000	5,000	4,000
Bad debt provision at 4% of debtors (2)	–	(3,360)	(4,200)
	3,360	4,200	3,600
Bad debts charge for year	7,360	5,840	3,400

E3.5 Tartantrips

(i) Sum of the digits depreciation

The company needs to decide the economic life of the asset (say ten years in this example) and its estimated residual value at the end of its life (£1m in this example).

Cost	£5,000,000
Residual value	£1,000,000
Amount to be written-off over ten years	£4,000,000

Over ten years the digits $10 + 9 + 8 \ldots 2 + 1$ add up to 55.

Depreciation in year 1 is $10/55 \times £4,000,000$	=	£727,272
Depreciation in year 2 is $9/55 \times £4,000,000$	=	£654,545
Depreciation in year 3 is $8/55 \times £4,000,000$	=	£581,818
and so on until		
Depreciation in year 9 is $2/55 \times £4,000,000$	=	£145,546
Depreciation in year 10 is $1/55 \times £4,000,000$	=	£72,727
Total depreciation for ten years		£4,000,000

(ii) Straight line depreciation

This method is very simple to operate. The company needs to decide on the economic life of the asset and its residual value at the end of its life (as above). The annual depreciation will be:

Depreciation per year is £4,000,000 divided by ten years = £400,000 per year

It can be seen that there is a constant charge to the annual profit and loss account for each of the ten years for 'wear and tear' of the fixed asset.

(iii) Reducing balance depreciation

This method is quite different to the straight line method because the depreciation charge is much higher in the earlier years of the life of the asset. The same sort of estimates are required: economic life, residual value, which are used in a reducing balance formula to calculate each year's depreciation.

The reducing balance formula where d is the percentage depreciation to charge on the written down value of the asset at the end of each year is

$$d = 1 - \sqrt[10]{1,000,000/5,000,000} = 14.9\% \text{ (which may also be calculated using the Excel DB function)}$$

Depreciation in year 1 is 14.9% of £5,000,000 = £745,000

Depreciation in year 2 is 14.9% of £4,255,000 = £633,995

Depreciation in year 3 is 14.9% of £3,621,005 = £539,530

and so on until year ten

The total depreciation for ten years is   £4,000,000

E3.8 Gremlins

Trial balance for Gremlins Ltd as at 31 March 2000

	Debit £000	Credit £000
Depreciation on office equipment and furnishings	156	
Bank overdraft		609
Accountancy and audit fees	30	
Electricity paid in advance	45	
Computer system (net book value)	441	
Advertising and promotion	135	
Share premium account		240
Interest received		15
Plant and equipment (net book value)	927	
Amount for final payment on factory machine due March 2002		252
Trade debtors	1,110	
Goodwill	204	
Twelve-year lease on factory	330	
Rents received		63
Prepaid expenses	885	
Interest paid	120	
Office electricity	66	
Retained earnings at 31 March 1999		513
Stocks of materials at 31 March 2002	585	
Telephone	87	
Distribution costs	162	
Other office utilities	72	
Cost of goods sold	1,659	
Administrative salaries	216	
Sales salaries	267	

Furniture and fixtures (net book value)	729	
Sales		3,267
Office rent	165	
Finished product at 31 March 2000	84	
Debenture		750
Trade creditors		1,257
Cash	51	
Share capital		1,560
	8,526	8,526

Gremlins plc
Profit and loss account for the year ended 31 March 2000

	£000	
Turnover	3,267	
Cost of sales	(1,659)	
Gross profit	1,608	
Distribution costs	(564)	[135 + 162 + 267]
Administrative expenses	(792)	[156 + 30 + 66 + 87 + 72 + 216 + 165]
Operating profit	252	
Other income	63	
Profit before interest and tax	315	
Net interest	(105)	[120 − 15]
Profit before tax	210	

Chapter 4

E4.1 Candyfloss

(a) **Candyfloss cash flow 6 months to 30 June 2000 using the direct method**

	£000	£000
Operating cash flow		76.0
Receipts from customers		
Payments		
Flowers suppliers	59.5	
Employees	5.0	
Other overheads		
Rent	4.0	
Operating expenses	7.0	75.5
Cash inflow from operations		0.5

Investing activities

Purchase of lease	15.0	
Lease fees	1.0	
	16.0	
Purchase of van	14.5	(30.5)
Net cash outflow before financing		(30.0)
Financing		
Loan	3.0	
Issue of shares	18.0	21.0
Net cash outflow for period		(9.0)

(b) **Candyfloss profit and loss account for 6 months to 30 June 2000**

	£000	£000	
Sales		84.0	
Cost of flowers	54.0		
Operating expenses	8.0		
Wages	5.0	(67.0)	
Gross profit		17.0	
Overheads			
Rent	2.0		
Depreciation	1.5		$[(14.5 - 2.5)/4 \times 50\%$ for the half year]
Bad debts	1.5	(5.0)	
Net profit for period		12.0	

(c) **The difference between the cash flow and profit for the period is**

$- £9,000 - £12,000 = - £21,000$

Both cash and profit give an indication of performance.
The profit of £12,000 may be compared with the cash inflow from operations of £500

	Profit	Operating cash	Differences
	£000	£000	
Sales/receipts	84.0	76.0	sales 8 not yet paid by customers
Bad debts	(1.5)		sales assumed will never be paid
Flowers	(54.0)	(59.5)	9.5 in stock and 4 not yet paid for
Wages	(5.0)	(5.0)	
Operating expenses	(8.0)	(7.0)	1 not yet paid
Rent	(2.0)	(4.0)	2 rent paid in advance
Depreciation	(1.5)		1.5 not cash
	12.0	0.5	

(d) A number of items in the profit and loss account are subjective and open to various different methods of valuation

Bad debts	1.5	different subjective views as to whether customers may pay or not
Stocks	9.5	different valuation methods
Depreciation	1.5	different bases may be used

- additionally cash flow shows how much was paid out for the lease and for the van and what financing was obtained
- cash flow gives a clear picture of the financial performance, looked at alongside the balance sheet which shows the financial position at a point in time
- looking at the profit and loss account from period to period it is difficult to compare performance and with that of similar businesses because of different approaches to asset valuation

E4.4 Medco

Medco Ltd
Cash flow statement for the year ended 31 December 2000

Reconciliation of operating profit to net cash flow from operating activities

	£
Operating profit	2,500
Depreciation charges	2,000
Loss on sale of fixed assets	500
Increase in stocks	(1,000)
Increase in debtors	(1,000)
Decrease in creditors	(2,000)
Net cash inflow from operating activities	1,000

Cash flow statement

	£
Net cash inflow from operating activities	1,000
Interest paid	(100)
Taxation paid	(400)
Capital expenditure	(10,500)
	(10,000)
Equity dividend paid	(750)
Management of liquid resources	(2,100)
Financing	6,000
Decrease in cash	(6,850)

Reconciliation of net cash flow to movement in net debt/funds

	£
Decrease in cash for the period	(6,850)
Cash inflow from increase in loans	(1,000)
Change in net debt	(7,850)
Net funds 1 January 2000	2,000
Net debt 31 December 2000	(5,850)

Note 1 to the cash flow statement – gross cash flows

	£	£
Returns on investments and servicing of finance		
Interest paid		(100)
Capital expenditure		
Payments to acquire tangible fixed assets	(12,500)	
Receipts from sales of tangible fixed assets	2,000	
		(10,500)
Financing		
Issue of ordinary shares	5,000	
Increase in loans	1,000	
		6,000

Note 2 to the cash flow statement – analysis of change in net debt

	At 1 Jan 2000 £	Cash flows £	At 31 Dec 2000 £
Cash and bank	5,000	(2,850)	2,150
Overdraft	(2,000)	(4,000)	(6,000)
Loans	(1,000)	(1,000)	(2,000)
Total	2,000	(7,850)	(5,850)

E4.6 Littleco

Littleco Ltd
Cash flow statement for the year ended 31 December 2000

Reconciliation of operating profit to net cash flow from operating activities

	£
Operating profit	2,100
Depreciation charges	2,000
Decrease in stocks	2,000
Increase in debtors	(2,000)
Decrease in creditors	(2,000)
Net cash inflow from operating activities	2,100

Cash flow statement

	£
Net cash inflow from operating activities	2,100
Interest paid	(100)
Taxation paid	(400)
Capital expenditure	(10,000)
	(8,400)

Equity dividend paid	(450)
Financing – new ordinary shares	5,000
Decrease in cash	(3,850)

Reconciliation of net cash flow to movement in net debt/funds

	£
Decrease in cash for the period	(3,850)
Change in net debt	(3,850)
Net funds 1 January 2000	–
Net debt 31 December 2000	(3,850)

E4.7 Sparklers

Sparklers plc
Cash flow statement for the year ended 31 October 2000

Reconciliation of operating profit to net cash flow from operating activities

	£m
Operating profit	41.28
Depreciation charges	10.10
Loss on sale of fixed assets	1.40
Increase in stocks	(20.00)
Increase in debtors	(36.40)
Increase in creditors	8.40
Net cash inflow from operating activities	4.78

Cash flow statement

	£m
Net cash inflow from operating activities	4.78
Returns on investments and servicing of finance (note 1)	(0.48)
Taxation – corporation tax paid	(6.40)
Capital expenditure (note 1)	(21.60)
	(23.70)
Dividends paid	(10.20)
	(33.90)
Financing (note 1)	0.30
Decrease in cash	(33.60)

Reconciliation of net cash flow to movement in net debt (note 2)

	£m
Decrease in cash for the period	(33.60)
Cash flow from increase in debenture	(0.30)
Change in net debt	(33.90)
Net debt 1 November 1999	–
Net debt 31 October 2000	(33.90)

Note 1 to the cash flow statement – gross cash flows

	£m	£m
Returns on investments and servicing of finance		
Interest received	0.08	
Interest paid	(0.56)	
		(0.48)
Capital expenditure		
Payments to acquire tangible fixed assets	(23.60)	
Receipts from sales of tangible fixed assets	2.00	
		(21.60)
Financing		
Increase in debentures		0.30

Note 2 to the cash flow statement – analysis of change in net debt

	At 1 Nov 1999 £m	Cash flows £m	At 31 Oct 2000 £m
Cash and bank	1.20	(1.20)	–
Overdraft	–	(32.40)	(32.40)
Debentures	(1.20)	(0.30)	(1.50)
Total	–	(33.90)	(33.90)

Working

	£m	£m
Depreciation		
Depreciation 31 October 2000		21.50
Depreciation at 31 October 1999	19.00	
Depreciation on assets sold in 2000	(7.60)	(11.40)
Charge for the year 2000		10.10
Loss on sale of assets		
Proceeds on sale		2.00
Net book value: cost	11.00	
Depreciation	(7.60)	(3.40)
Loss on sale		(1.40)
Dividends paid		
Dividends payable at 31 October 1999		6.00
Dividends declared for 2000: preference		0.20
ordinary interim		4.00
ordinary final		12.00
		22.20
Less dividends payable at 31 October 2000		12.00
Dividends paid during 2000		10.20

Purchase of fixed assets

Fixed assets balance 31 October 2000		47.80
Fixed assets balance 31 October 1999	35.20	
Cost of fixed assets sold	(11.00)	(24.20)
Fixed assets purchased		23.60

You should refer to the relevant sections in Chapter 4 to check your assessment of the reasons for the increased overdraft.

Chapter 5

E5.1 Freshco

Profitability ratios for Freshco plc for 2000 and the comparative ratios for 1999

Gross margin, GM

$$\text{Gross margin \% 2000} = \frac{\text{gross margin}}{\text{sales}} = \frac{£204 \times 100\%}{£894} = 22.8\%$$

$$\text{Gross margin \% 1999} = \frac{£166 \times 100\%}{£747} = 22.2\%$$

Profit before interest and tax, PBIT (or operating profit)

$$\text{PBIT \% 2000} = \frac{\text{operating profit}}{\text{sales}} = \frac{£103 \times 100\%}{£894} = 11.5\%$$

$$\text{PBIT \% 1999} = \frac{£87 \times 100\%}{£747} = 11.6\%$$

Net profit, PAT (return on sales, ROS)

$$\text{PAT\% 2000} = \frac{\text{net profit}}{\text{sales}} = \frac{£56 \times 100\%}{£894} = 6.3\%$$

$$\text{PAT\% 1999} = \frac{£54 \times 100\%}{£747} = 7.2\%$$

Return on capital employed, ROCE (return on investment, ROI)

$$\text{ROCE\% 2000} = \frac{\text{operating profit}}{\substack{\text{total assets} - \text{current liabilities} \\ \text{(average capital employed)}}} = \frac{£103 \times 100\%}{(£233 + £233)/2} = \frac{£103 \times 100\%}{£233}$$

$$= 44.2\%$$

$$\text{ROCE\% 1999} = \frac{£87 \times 100\%}{(£233 + £219)/2} = \frac{£87 \times 100\%}{£226} = 38.5\%$$

Return on equity, ROE

$$\text{ROE\% 2000} = \frac{\text{PAT}}{\text{equity}} = \frac{£56 \times 100\%}{£213} = 26.3\%$$

$$\text{ROE\% 1999} = \frac{£54 \times 100\%}{£166} = 32.5\%$$

Capital turnover

$$\text{Capital turnover 2000} = \frac{\text{sales}}{\text{average capital employed in year}} = \frac{£894}{£233} = 3.8 \text{ times}$$

$$\text{Capital turnover 1999} = \frac{£747}{£226} = 3.3 \text{ times}$$

Report on the profitability of Freshco plc

Sales for the year 2000 increased by 19.7% over the previous year, but it is not clear whether from increased volumes, new products, or higher selling prices.

Gross margin improved by 0.6% to 22.8% of sales, possibly from increased selling prices and/or from lower costs of production.

Operating profit dropped by 0.1% to 11.5% of sales despite the improvement in gross margin, because of higher levels of distribution costs and administrative expenses.

ROCE improved from 38.5% to 44.2%, indicating a more effective use of funds by Freshco.

Return on equity dropped by 6.2% to 26.3%. This was because profit after tax remained fairly static but equity was increased through an issue of shares and increases in general reserves and retained earnings.

Capital turnover for 2000 increased to 3.8 times from 3.3 in 1999, reflecting the significant increases in sales levels in 2000 over 1999.

E5.3 Freshco

Liquidity ratios for Freshco plc for 2000 and the comparative ratios for 1999

Current ratio

$$\text{Current ratio 2000} = \frac{\text{current assets}}{\text{current liabilities}} = \frac{£208}{£121} = 1.7 \text{ times}$$

$$\text{Current ratio 1999} = \frac{£191}{£107} = 1.8 \text{ times}$$

Acid test (quick ratio)

$$\text{Quick ratio 2000} = \frac{\text{current assets} - \text{stocks}}{\text{current liabilities}} = \frac{£208 - £124}{£121} = 0.7 \text{ times}$$

$$\text{Quick ratio 1999} = \frac{£191 - £100}{£107} = 0.8 \text{ times}$$

Defensive interval

$$\text{Defensive interval 2000} = \frac{\text{quick assets}}{\text{average daily cash from operations}} = \frac{£208 - £124}{(£80 + £894 - £70)/365}$$
$$= 34 \text{ days}$$

$$\text{Defensive interval 1999} = \frac{£191 - £100}{(£60 + £747 - £80)/365} = 46 \text{ days}$$

Report on the liquidity of Freshco plc

The current ratio and the quick ratio have both dropped slightly to 1.7 times and 0.7 times respectively. However, the defensive interval has dropped significantly from 46 days to 34 days at which level the company could potentially survive if there were no further cash inflows.

Net cash flow from operations improved from £7m in 1999 to £8.1m in 2000. Investments in fixed assets were at lower levels in 2000 and matched by a reduction in long-term financing (debentures).

E5.5 Laurel

(i)

Profitability ratios for Hardy plc for 2000 and the comparative ratios for 1999 and 1998

Gross margin, GM

$$\text{Gross margin \% 2000} = \frac{\text{gross margin}}{\text{sales}} = \frac{£161 \times 100\%}{£456} = 35.3\%$$

$$\text{Gross margin \% 1999} = \frac{£168 \times 100\%}{£491} = 34.2\%$$

$$\text{Gross margin \% 1998} = \frac{£143 \times 100\%}{£420} = 34.0\%$$

Profit before interest and tax, PBIT (or operating profit)

$$\text{PBIT \% 2000} = \frac{\text{operating profit}}{\text{sales}} = \frac{£52 \times 100\%}{£456} = 11.4\%$$

$$\text{PBIT \% 1999} = \frac{£61 \times 100\%}{£491} = 12.4\%$$

$$\text{PBIT \% 1998} = \frac{£50 \times 100\%}{£420} = 11.9\%$$

Net profit, PAT (return on sales, ROS)

$$\text{PAT\% 2000} = \frac{\text{net profit}}{\text{sales}} = \frac{£20 \times 100\%}{£456} = 4.4\%$$

$$\text{PAT\% 1999} = \frac{£28 \times 100\%}{£491} = 5.7\%$$

$$\text{PAT\% 1998} = \frac{£25 \times 100\%}{£420} = 6.0\%$$

Return on capital employed, ROCE (return on investment, ROI)

$$\text{ROCE\% 2000} = \frac{\text{operating profit}}{\substack{\text{total assets} - \text{current liabilities} \\ \text{(average capital employed)}}} = \frac{£52 \times 100\%}{(£284 + £292)/2} = \frac{£52 \times 100\%}{£288}$$

$$= 18.1\%$$

$$\text{ROCE\% 1999} = \frac{£61 \times 100\%}{(£237 + £284)/2} = \frac{£61 \times 100\%}{£260.5} = 23.4\%$$

ROCE% 1998 is not available because we do not have the capital employed figure for 31 March 1997.

Return on equity, ROE

$$\text{ROE\% 2000} = \frac{\text{PAT}}{\text{equity}} = \frac{£20 \times 100\%}{£223} = 9.0\%$$

$$\text{ROE\% 1999} = \frac{£28 \times 100\%}{£215} = 13.0\%$$

$$\text{ROE\% 1998} = \frac{£25 \times 100\%}{£200} = 12.5\%$$

Capital turnover

$$\text{Capital turnover 2000} = \frac{\text{sales}}{\text{average capital employed in year}} = \frac{£456}{£288} = 1.6 \text{ times}$$

Capital turnover 1999 $= \dfrac{£491}{£260.5} = 1.9$ times

Capital turnover 1998 is not available because we do not have the capital employed figure for 31 March 1997.

Report on the profitability of Hardy plc

Sales for the year 2000 were 7.1% lower than sales in 1999, which were 16.9% above 1998. It is not clear whether these sales reductions were from lower volumes, fewer products, or changes in selling prices.

Gross margin improved from 34.0% in 1998 to 34.2% in 1999 to 35.3% in 2000, possibly from increased selling prices and/or from lower costs of production.

Operating profit to sales increased from 11.9% in 1998 to 12.4% in 1999 but then fell to 11.4% in 2000, despite the improvement in gross margin, because of higher levels of distribution costs and administrative expenses.

ROCE dropped from 23.4% to 18.1%, reflecting the lower level of operating profit.

Return on equity increased from 12.5% in 1998 to 13.0% in 1999 but then fell sharply in 2000 to 9.0%. This was because of the large fall in profit after tax in 2000.

Capital turnover for 2000 was reduced from 1.9 times in 1999 to 1.6 in 2000, reflecting the fall in sales levels in 2000 over 1999.

Efficiency ratios for Hardy plc for 2000 and the comparative ratios for 1999 and 1998

Debtor days

Debtor days 2000 $= \dfrac{\text{trade debtors} \times 365}{\text{sales}} = \dfrac{£80 \times 365}{£456} = 64$ days

Debtor days 1999 $= \dfrac{£70 \times 365}{£491} = 52$ days

Debtor days 1998 $= \dfrac{£53 \times 365}{£420} = 46$ days

Creditor days

Creditor days 2000 $= \dfrac{\text{trade creditors} \times 365}{\text{cost of sales}} = \dfrac{£38 \times 365}{£295} = 47$ days

Creditor days 1999 $= \dfrac{£38 \times 365}{£323} = 43$ days

Creditor days 1998 $= \dfrac{£26 \times 365}{£277} = 34$ days

Stock days (stock turnover)

Stock days 2000 $= \dfrac{\text{stock value}}{\text{average daily cost of sales in period}} = \dfrac{£147}{£295/365}$
$= 182$ days (26.0 weeks)

Stock days 1999 $= \dfrac{£152}{£323/365} = 172$ days (24.5 weeks)

Stock days 1998 $= \dfrac{£118}{£277/365} = 155$ days (22.2 weeks)

Operating cycle days

Operating cycle 2000 = stock days + debtor days – creditor days = 182 + 64 − 47
$= 199$ days

Operating cycle 1999 = 172 + 52 − 43 = 181 days

Operating cycle 1998 = 155 + 46 − 34 = 167 days

Operating cycle %

$$\text{Operating cycle \% 2000} = \frac{\text{working capital requirement}}{\text{sales}} = \frac{(£147 + £80 - £38) \times 100\%}{£456}$$

$$= 41.4\%$$

$$\text{Operating cycle \% 1999} = \frac{(£152 + £70 - £38) \times 100\%}{£491} = 37.5\%$$

$$\text{Operating cycle \% 1998} = \frac{(£118 + £53 - £26) \times 100\%}{£420} = 34.5\%$$

Asset turnover

$$\text{Asset turnover 2000} = \frac{\text{sales}}{\text{total assets}} = \frac{£456}{£385} = 1.18 \text{ times}$$

$$\text{Asset turnover 1999} = \frac{£491}{£374} = 1.31 \text{ times}$$

$$\text{Asset turnover 1998} = \frac{£420}{£303} = 1.39 \text{ times}$$

Report on the working capital performance of Hardy plc

Average customer settlement days worsened successively over the years 1998, 1999 and 2000 from 46 to 52 to 64 days. This was partly mitigated by some improvement in the average creditors settlement period which increased from 34 to 43 to 47 days over the same period. The average stock turnover period worsened from 155 to 172 to 182 days over 1998, 1999, and 2000. Therefore, mainly because of the poor debt collection performance and increasingly high stock levels, the operating cycle worsened from 167 days in 1998 to 181 days in 1999 and to 199 days in 2000 (operating cycle 34.5% to 37.5% to 41.4%). Asset turnover reduced from 1.39 to 1.31 times from 1998 to 1999 and then to 1.18 in 2000, reflecting the degree to which sales had dropped despite increasing levels of total assets.

Liquidity ratios for Hardy plc for 2000 and the comparative ratios for 1999 and 1998

Current ratio

$$\text{Current ratio 2000} = \frac{\text{current assets}}{\text{current liabilities}} = \frac{£253}{£93} = 2.7 \text{ times}$$

$$\text{Current ratio 1999} = \frac{£251}{£90} = 2.8 \text{ times}$$

$$\text{Current ratio 1998} = \frac{£197}{£66} = 3.0 \text{ times}$$

Acid test (quick ratio)

$$\text{Quick ratio 2000} = \frac{\text{current assets} - \text{stocks}}{\text{current liabilities}} = \frac{£253 - £147}{£93} = 1.1 \text{ times}$$

$$\text{Quick ratio 1999} = \frac{£251 - £152}{£90} = 1.1 \text{ times}$$

$$\text{Quick ratio 1998} = \frac{£197 - £118}{£66} = 1.2 \text{ times}$$

Defensive interval

$$\text{Defensive interval 2000} = \frac{\text{quick assets}}{\text{average daily cash from operations}} = \frac{£253 - £147}{(£70 + £456 - £80)/365}$$

$$= 87 \text{ days}$$

$$\text{Defensive interval 1999} = \frac{£251 - £152}{(£53 + £491 - £70)/365} = 76 \text{ days}$$

Defensive interval 1998 is not available because we do not have the trade debtors figure for 31 March 1997.

Report on the liquidity of Hardy plc

The current ratio and the quick ratio have both dropped over the three years from 3.0 to 2.7 times, and 1.2 times to 1.1 times respectively. The defensive interval has increased from 76 days to 87 days at which level the company could potentially survive if there were no further cash inflows.

(ii)   There are a number of areas that require further investigation. The following five ratios may be particularly useful to assist this investigation:
    Return on capital employed, ROCE
    Debtor days
    Creditor days
    Stock days
    Current ratio.

(iii) The relevant information has not been provided to enable the following investment ratios to be calculated for Hardy plc, which would have improved the analysis of Hardy plc's performance:

Earnings per share, eps

Cannot be calculated because we do not have details of any preference share dividends and the number of ordinary shares in issue.

Dividend per share

Cannot be calculated because we do not have details of the number of ordinary shares in issue.

Dividend cover

Cannot be calculated because we have not been able to calculate earnings per share, eps, and dividend per share.

Dividend yield %

Cannot be calculated because we have not been able to calculate dividend per share, and we do not have the market prices of the company's shares.

Price/earnings ratio, P/E

Cannot be calculated because we have not been able to calculate earnings per share, and we do not have the market prices of the company's shares.

Capital expenditure to sales %

Cannot be calculated because we do not have details of capital expenditure.

Capital expenditure to gross fixed assets %

Cannot be calculated because we do not have details of capital expenditure.

Chapter 6

E6.1 Ace

1. UK plcs must disclose tangible fixed assets separately as a single figure in the balance sheet and they must be summarised in the notes to the accounts.

2. Since 1981 plcs have recorded their tangible fixed assets at either cost or at a carrying value.

3. The cost of tangible fixed assets may then be depreciated, according to company policy.

4. Under the old 1981 Companies Act, companies could revalue their tangible fixed assets as and when they thought fit.

5. Under the accounting standard FRS 15 Accounting for Fixed Assets companies must now revalue all assets within a category of tangible fixed assets or leave them all at cost.

6. Shareholders have not seen a marked improvement in information on tangible fixed assets reported in financial statements.

7. Where tangible fixed assets have been owned many years by a company, the historical cost is almost certainly out of date.

8. The balance sheet will frequently not reflect a market value of tangible fixed assets, because of material changes over the years to the ownership, of the company.

E6.10 Guinness

Guinness plc five-year profit and loss account

Horizontal analysis

	Year 5	Year 4	Year 3	Year 2	Year 1
Turnover	108.4	107.3	107.5	106.9	100.0
Gross profit	93.9	92.2	93.5	91.7	100.0
Other investment income	(470.8)	(195.8)	(370.8)	200.0	100.0
Profit before interest and tax (operating profit)	107.5	99.1	104.6	89.1	100.0
Net interest	48.5	55.9	63.7	92.2	100.0
Profit before tax	122.6	110.2	115.1	88.3	100.0
Tax on profit on ordinary activities	107.0	103.7	100.4	102.1	100.0
Profit on ordinary activities after tax	129.5	113.0	121.5	82.3	100.0
Minority interests	106.9	103.4	106.9	75.9	100.0
Profit for the financial year	130.7	113.5	122.3	82.6	100.0
Dividends	124.5	127.4	117.7	108.9	100.0
Retained profit	135.9	102.1	126.1	61.0	100.0
Earnings per share	124.9	104.6	113.2	81.5	100.0
Interest cover	220.4	177.6	163.3	95.9	100.0
Dividend cover	95.7	87.0	100.0	78.3	100.0

Guinness plc five-year profit and loss account

Vertical analysis	Year 5	Year 4	Year 3	Year 2	Year 1
Turnover	100.0	100.0	100.0	100.0	100.0
Gross profit	20.3	20.1	20.4	20.1	23.4
Other investment income	2.4	1.0	1.9	(1.0)	(0.6)
Profit before interest and tax (operating profit)	22.7	21.1	22.3	19.1	22.9
Net interest	(2.1)	(2.4)	(2.8)	(4.0)	(4.7)
Profit before tax	20.6	18.7	19.5	15.1	18.2
Tax on profit on ordinary activities	(5.5)	(5.4)	(5.2)	(5.3)	(5.5)
Profit on ordinary activities after tax	15.1	13.4	14.3	9.8	12.7
Minority interests	(0.7)	(0.6)	(0.7)	(0.5)	(0.7)
Profit for the financial year	14.5	12.7	13.7	9.3	12.0
Dividends	(6.2)	(6.5)	(5.9)	(5.5)	(5.4)
Retained profit	8.2	6.3	7.7	3.8	6.6

Sales
The horizontal analysis shows an increase in sales of 8.4% over the five years, most of which was gained from year two over year one. Since year two, sales have not increased materially.

Gross profit
The horizontal analysis shows a drop in gross profit of 6.1% of sales over the five years. The vertical analysis shows that gross profit at 23.4% of sales in year one has dropped to 20.3% of sales in year five. The group may have been suffering from increased competition as its brands failed to continue to maintain their profitability.

Operating profit
The horizontal analysis shows an increase in operating profit of 7.5% of sales over the five years, despite the drop in gross profit levels. This is due to the extremely large gains in investment income. The vertical analysis shows that operating profit has been maintained fairly level over the five years at 22.9% of sales in year one to 22.7% of sales in year five.

Interest payable
The horizontal analysis shows a drop in interest payable by year five to less than a half the level in year one. The vertical analysis bears this out, showing interest payable of 2.1% of sales in year five compared with 4.7% of sales in year one. The group's borrowings were probably significantly reduced as little expansion has taken place, indicated by a reliance on mature markets and a lack of new ideas. The increased interest cover confirms the loan repayments.

Profit for the financial year
The horizontal analysis reflects a small increase in profit levels from 12.0% of sales in year one to 14.5% of sales in year five. The vertical analysis shows a steady increase in profit over the years except for a drop in year two, because of the negative investment income and high interest payments in that year.

Dividends
The level of dividends has been up and down over the years but year five is slightly higher at 6.2% of sales than year one which was 5.4% of sales, as shown in the vertical analysis. Dividend cover has been maintained at around two times.

Earnings per share

The horizontal analysis shows an increase of almost 25% in earnings per share in year five compared with year one, having recovered from a dip in earnings in year four.

Chapter 7

E7.1 Share options

Past governments have made employer/employee share option schemes tax efficient and therefore schemes are now very common amongst plcs.

Many plcs have found that their share prices react to specific management policies and decisions, for example take-overs and disposals of businesses. Users of financial information can assess these decisions, knowing of the options awarded to the directors.

Many plcs have found that they can only keep/attract high calibre managers by including share options in their remuneration packages.

Investing institutions demand more and more information regarding directors' remuneration. This can influence their basic hold/buy/sell decisions. The financial press frequently includes criticism of specific companies.

E7.2 Perks

Directors do not necessarily own the company they work for; the shareholders do.

Any monies (expenses) that a director takes from the company will affect the annual profit.

Annual dividends are paid from the annual profits.

The shareholders approve the accounts at the AGM, which includes remuneration of the directors.

If the directors hide information regarding their remuneration and benefits from the shareholders, then that part of the accounts may not show a true and fair view of the situation.

E7.3 Contracts

Before the new corporate governance code was introduced, shareholders found that their directors had powers that were increasing, especially regarding length of contract and compensation for loss of office.

The Cadbury and Greenbury committees recommended that directors' contracts should be no longer than (first) three years (Cadbury) and then one year (Greenbury). These committees had looked at the evidence presented to them. Hampel (1998) provided that the contracts should be one year or less.

The financial press regularly comments on the compensation paid to a director, where company performance has been acknowledged to be poor. There is always reference to the length of outstanding directors' contracts.

Shareholders can decide whether to hold/buy/sell shares if they have advance information on the type of contracts being awarded to the executive directors of their company.

UK financial institutions have also become pro-active regarding the length of directors' contracts issue. They have noted that in the past too many highly paid directors were awarding themselves contracts in which compensation for loss of office was very expensive to pay. The situation in 2001 is that it often costs companies potentially over £1m to buy out a chief executive from just a one-year contract.

E7.7 Tomkins

Equity shareholders are the owners of the company, and the level of their dividends usually varies with levels of profits earned by the company.

Directors are appointed by the shareholders, and remunerated for their efforts.

Major multi-national companies are difficult to manage successfully over a long period of time. The remuneration of directors should reflect that difficulty.

The information that has been given about Tomkins plc shows that there is an executive director who earns a basic salary of just below £1 million a year, an amount which most shareholders would like to see disclosed in the accounts and discussed at the AGM.

The bonus of £443,000 will also generate some interest amongst the institutions and individual shareholders. Institutions (and the UK Government) are seen to put pressure on directors if they feel pay awards are excessive.

The consultancy agreement for a non-executive director may also be of interest to the various users of the notes to the accounts.

Chapter 8

E8.1 Bluebell Woods

(i) Absorption costing

$$\text{Overhead absorption rate} = \frac{\text{budgeted fixed production cost}}{\text{budgeted units of production}} = \frac{£3,526}{4,300} = £0.82 \text{ per unit}$$

		£
Selling price per unit		5.84

Total production costs per unit

		£	
Direct material	[£0.85 × 2kg]	1.70	
Direct labour	[42 × £4.20/60]	2.94	
Variable production overhead		0.12	
Variable production cost		4.76	
Fixed production overhead		0.82	see above
Full production cost per unit		5.58	

Four-week standard profit statement

		£
Sales	[4,300 × £5.84]	25,112
Cost of sales		
Direct material	[£4,300 × £1.70]	7,310
Direct labour	[£4,300 × £2.94]	12,642
Variable production overhead	[4,300 × £0.12]	516
Fixed production overhead		3,526
		23,994
Profit for the period		1,118

E9.3 Break-even and profit

Selling price = £15
Marginal cost = £9
Contribution = £6

Contribution to sales ratio % = $\dfrac{£6 \times 100\%}{£15}$ = 40%

£ sales value at break-even point = $\dfrac{\text{fixed costs}}{\text{contribution to sales ratio \%}}$

= £30,000/40%

= £75,000

Profit for January = contribution − fixed costs

= (40% × £120,000) − £30,000

= £48,000 − £30,000

= £18,000

E9.4 Magazines

The UK newspaper and magazine markets appear to be price sensitive and publishers frequently use the cover price as a marketing/selling tool.

It is almost certain that the publisher will look at existing magazine selling prices to establish the current marketplace situation.

A magazine business model will then be developed and the cover price and advertising revenue will be critical.

The forecast revenues influence the number of pages in the post-launch period.

In the review of weekly marketing campaigns target costing is likely to be a key management tool, which may be used to try and avoid major mistakes in certain consumer mass markets.

E9.8 Crispian Brown

(i) **Absorption costing**

Budget direct labour hours 50,000 hours for 2000

Overhead absorption rate per direct labour hour

= $\dfrac{\text{purchase order costs + scrap/rework costs + machine costs + shipment costs}}{\text{direct labour hours}}$

= $\dfrac{(£204,000 + £379,000 + £182,000 + £135,000)}{50,000 \text{ hours}}$ = £18 per direct labour hour

Full unit production costs of the Super and the Standard

		Super £		Standard £
Direct materials		40		25
Direct labour	(2 hours × £7)	14	(1 hour × £7)	7
Factory overhead	(2 hours × £18)	36	(1 hour × £18)	18
Unit production costs		90		50

(ii) ABC

Using an ABC costing approach the full production cost of each unit of the Super and the Standard may be calculated:

Planned for the year 2000

Number of purchase orders	= 600 orders for the year
Purchase order costs	= £204,000
Cost per order	= £340
Scrap/rework	= 2,000 jobs for the year
Scrap/rework costs	= £379,000
Scrap/rework costs per job	= £189.50
Machine hours	= 35,000 hour per year
Machine costs	= £182,000
Cost per machine hour	= £5.20
Shipments	= 900 for the year
Shipment costs	= £135,000
Cost per shipment	= £150

(iii) and (iv) Overhead costs per unit of the Super and the Standard on an ABC basis

		Super £		Standard £
Purchase orders	(200 × £340)	68,000	(400 × £340)	136,000
Scrap/rework	(1,000 × £189.50)	189,500	(1,000 × £189.50)	189,500
Machine hours	(20,000 × £5.20)	104,000	(15,000 × £5.20)	78,000
Shipments	(250 × £150)	37,500	(650 × £150)	97,500
Total overhead costs		399,000		501,000
Number of units		5,000		40,000
Unit overhead costs		£79.80		£12.525

(v) Unit production costs of the Super and the Standard

		Super £		Standard £
Direct materials		40		25
Direct labour	(2 hours × £7)	14	(1 hour × £7)	7
Factory overhead		79.80		12.525
Unit production costs		133.80		44.525

(vi) Summary of unit product costs

	Super £	Standard £
Full absorption cost per unit	90.00	50.00
ABC cost per unit	133.80	44.525
Difference	43.80	5.475

If we compare ABC unit costs with full absorption costs we can see that the profit reported on the Super model may be overstated by £43.80 per unit. The final profit is dependent on the selling price, but it seems likely that this product may actually be losing money.

Similarly, the profit on the Standard model may be understated by £5.475.

If the activities identified are truly related to the products and only incurred as a result of producing and selling the products then it would theoretically improve company performance by dropping the Super model.

In practice the costs may not be wholly attributable to the products, but even so savings may be made. Alternatively, the processes may be re-engineered to provide cheaper and more efficient activities, reducing costs and therefore making the Super product more profitable.

Chapter 10

E10.1 McPrentill

At the break-even point

Fixed cost = contribution

Or

Fixed cost per unit = contribution per unit

Contribution per unit = selling price − variable cost per unit

Therefore, at the break-even point

Fixed cost per unit = selling price − variable cost per unit

Or

Fixed cost per unit + variable cost per unit = selling price

(i) At a volume of 5,000 books

Break-even selling price

$$= \text{fixed cost per unit} + \text{variable cost per unit}$$

$$= \frac{£20,000}{5,000} + £12$$

$$= £16$$

plus 40% to cover fixed costs and profit $= £6.40$

Selling price to customers $= £22.40$

(ii) At a volume of 10,000 books

Break-even selling price

$$= \text{fixed cost per unit} + \text{variable cost per unit}$$

$$= \frac{£20,000}{10,000} + £12$$

$$= £14$$

plus 40% to cover fixed costs and profit $= £5.60$

Selling price to customers $= £19.60$ which is a discount of 12.5%

However, McPrentill may alternatively charge £22.40 for 5,000 books as in (i) above

Variable costs	10,000 × £12	£120,000
Fixed cost		£20,000
Total costs		£140,000

plus 40%	£56,000
	£196,000
5,000 × £22.40	£112,000
	£84,000

which divided by 5,000 is £16.80 (a discount of 25%) that may be charged to the large customer for 5,000 books.

(iii) At a volume of 20,000 books

Break-even selling price = fixed cost per unit + variable cost per unit

$$= \frac{£20,000}{20,000} + £12$$

$$= £13$$

plus 40% to cover fixed costs and profit = £5.20

Selling price to customers = £18.20 which is a discount of 18.75%

However, McPrentill may alternatively charge £22.40 for 5,000 books as in (i) above

Variable costs	20,000 × £12	£240,000
Fixed cost		£20,000
Total costs		£260,000
plus 40%		£104,000
		£364,000
5,000 × £22.40		£112,000
		£252,000

which divided by 15,000 is £16.80 (a discount of 25%) that may be charged to the large customer for 15,000 books.

E10.2 Calvin Williams

(i)
(a) We can draw a decision tree using

 as an outcome point, and

as a decision point

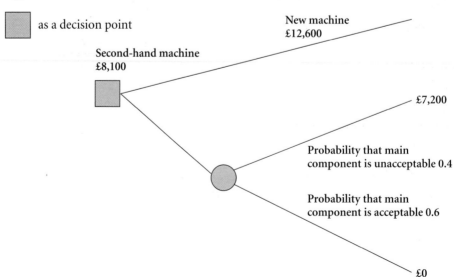

The expectation at the outcome point is

$(0.4 \times £7,200) + (0.6 \times £0) = £2,880$

At the decision point we can consider the two alternatives

Calvin may buy a new machine costing £12,600

or

Calvin may buy second-hand, the expected costs of which are

$£8,100 + £2,880 = £10,980$

On this basis Calvin should buy the second-hand machine.

(b) The second-hand machine may need a new central copying unit and so the total outlay would be $£8,100 + £7,200 = £15,300$. There is a 40% chance that the decision to buy second-hand may in fact turn out to be more expensive.

A new machine would be expected to break down less often than a second-hand machine. Also, servicing costs would be less and the time that Calvin would be non-operational with a broken-down machine should be less.

Therefore, Calvin needs to carefully consider the servicing contract offered with the new machine and the second-hand machine.

(ii) The effective cost of the second-hand machine now becomes $£8,100 + £600 = £8,700$

The options that may be considered are:

New machine   £12,600

Second-hand machine   £8,700 if the central copying unit is acceptable

Machine and test $£8,700 + £7,200 = £15,900$ if the central copying unit needs to be replaced

If the second-hand machine is tested and the central copying unit is not acceptable, buying the new machine would give a total cost of $£600 + £12,600 = £13,200$.

Calvin should have the second-hand machine tested. If the central copying unit is acceptable, he should buy it. If not, he should buy the new machine.

E10.3 Hurdle

(i) In view of the scarcity of labour, labour hours are obviously a key factor. Since any new work undertaken by the company will entail diverting labour from the standard product (for which there is a heavy demand) the first thing that must be done is to find a contribution per hour of the key factor.

Standard product

	£	£
Selling price		28
Marginal cost:		
Materials	10	
Labour 0.5 hours × £10 per hour	5	15
Contribution		13
Contribution per labour hour (£13 × 0.5 hours)		26

Make-versus-buy decision for the special component

Making the component

		£
Materials cost		100
Labour cost	4 hours at £10 per hour	40
Opportunity cost	4 hours at £26 per hour	104
Total cost to make special component		244

Since the component can be purchased for only £220 then it is cheaper for the company to buy it rather than make it.

The contract costs can now be calculated assuming that the special component may be purchased.

		£
Materials cost		600
Special component		220
Labour cost	100 hours at £10 per hour	1,000
Opportunity cost	100 hours at £26 per hour	2,600
Total cost of contract		4,420

(ii) The contract may be accepted by the company if the contract price is greater than £4,420.

(iii) If a 20% mark-up is required by the company then the contract price should be £4,410 plus 20%, which is £5,304.

Chapter 11

E11.1 Earextensions

Sales price £50

	Jan	Feb	Mar	Apr	May	Jun	Total
Sales budget							
Units	50,000	60,000	72,000	86,400	86,400	86,400	441,200
£	2,500,000	3,000,000	3,600,000	4,320,000	4,320,000	4,320,000	22,060,000

E11.2 Earextensions

	Jan	Feb	Mar	Apr	May	Jun	Total
Production budget (units)							
Opening stock	0	12,000	14,400	17,280	17,280	17,280	0
Production	62,000	62,400	74,880	86,400	86,400	86,400	458,480
Sales	50,000	60,000	72,000	86,400	86,400	86,400	441,200
Closing stock	12,000	14,400	17,280	17,280	17,280	17,280	17,280

E11.3 Earextensions

Production overheads

Direct labour hours

Assemblers	3.0 × 458,480	1,375,440 minutes =	22,924 hours
Operators	1.5 × 458,480	687,720 minutes =	11,462 hours
Total	4.5 × 458,480	2,063,160 minutes =	34,386 hours

Total production overheads   £4,100,000

Production overheads per direct labour hour $\dfrac{£4,100,000}{34,386}$ = £119.235 per hour = £1.987 per minute

Unit gross margin budget

			£	£	£
Sales price					50.000
Unit cost					
Direct labour	Assemblers	3 minutes @ £10 per hour	0.5000		
	Operators	1.5 minutes @ £8 per hour	0.2000		
				0.7000	
Materials	Electronic assembly		23.3000		
	Keypad		1.0000		
	Case		2.0000		
				26.3000	
Overheads	4.5 minutes @ £1.987 per minute			8.9426	
					35.9426
Unit gross margin					14.0574

	Jan	Feb	Mar	Apr	May	Jun	Total
Direct labour budget (£)							
Production units							
× £0.70 per unit	43,400	43,680	52,416	60,480	60,480	60,480	320,936

E11.4 Earextensions

	Jan	Feb	Mar	Apr	May	Jun	Total
Materials purchases and usage budget (units)							
Electronic assembly							
Opening stock	10,000	31,200	37,440	43,200	43,200	43,200	10,000
Purchases	83,200	68,640	80,640	86,400	86,400	86,400	491,680
Usage	62,000	62,400	74,880	86,400	86,400	86,400	458,480
Closing stock	31,200	37,440	43,200	43,200	43,200	43,200	43,200
Keypad							
Opening stock	30,000	31,200	37,440	43,200	43,200	43,200	30,000
Purchases	63,200	68,640	80,640	86,400	86,400	86,400	471,680
Usage	62,000	62,400	74,880	86,400	86,400	86,400	458,480
Closing stock	31,200	37,440	43,200	43,200	43,200	43,200	43,200

Case

Opening stock	20,000	31,200	37,440	43,200	43,200	43,200	20,000
Purchases	73,200	68,640	80,640	86,400	86,400	86,400	481,680
Usage	62,000	62,400	74,880	86,400	86,400	86,400	458,480
Closing stock	31,200	37,440	43,200	43,200	43,200	43,200	43,200

Materials purchases and usage budget (£)

Electronic assembly £23.30 per unit

Opening stock	233,000	726,960	872,352	1,006,560	1,006,560	1,006,560	233,000
Purchases	1,938,560	1,599,312	1,878,912	2,013,120	2,013,120	2,013,120	11,456,144
Usage	1,444,600	1,453,920	1,744,704	2,013,120	2,013,120	2,013,120	10,682,584
Closing stock	726,960	872,352	1,006,560	1,006,560	1,006,560	1,006,560	1,006,560

Keypad £1.00 per unit

Opening stock	30,000	31,200	37,440	43,200	43,200	43,200	30,000
Purchases	63,200	68,640	80,640	86,400	86,400	86,400	471,680
Usage	62,000	62,400	74,880	86,400	86,400	86,400	458,480
Closing stock	31,200	37,440	43,200	43,200	43,200	43,200	43,200

Case £2.00 per unit

Opening stock	40,000	62,400	74,880	86,400	86,400	86,400	40,000
Purchases	146,400	137,280	161,280	172,800	172,800	172,800	963,360
Usage	124,000	124,800	149,760	172,800	172,800	172,800	916,960
Closing stock	62,400	74,880	86,400	86,400	86,400	86,400	86,400

E11.5 Earextensions

	Jan	Feb	Mar	Apr	May	Jun	Total
Overheads, selling, administrative, financial costs budget (£)							
Production overheads (£4,100,000 less depreciation £50,000)	675,000	675,000	675,000	675,000	675,000	675,000	4,050,000
Selling and administrative costs	900,000	900,000	900,000	600,000	600,000	600,000	4,500,000
Interest (0.2% of sales)	5,000	6,000	7,200	8,640	8,640	8,640	44,120

Profit and loss account budget

	Jan	Feb	Mar	Apr	May	Jun	Total
Sales units	50,000	60,000	72,000	86,400	86,400	86,400	441,200
Figures in £							
Sales	2,500,000	3,000,000	3,600,000	4,320,000	4,320,000	4,320,000	22,060,000
Cost of sales	1,797,130	2,156,556	2,587,866	3,105,440	3,105,440	3,105,440	15,857,872
Gross margin	702,870	843,444	1,012,134	1,214,560	1,214,560	1,214,560	6,202,128
Selling/ administrative/ interest costs	905,000	906,000	907,200	608,640	608,640	608,640	4,544,120
Profit/(loss)	(202,130)	(62,556)	104,934	605,920	605,920	605,920	1,658,008
Cumulative profit and loss account	(202,130)	(264,686)	(159,752)	446,168	1,052,088	1,658,008	

E11.6 Earextensions

	Jan	Feb	Mar	Apr	May	Jun	Total
Finished product stock valuation budget @ £35.9426/unit	£431,311	£517,573	£621,088	£621,088	£621,088	£621,088	
Over (under) absorption of production overheads	76,413	76,413	76,413	76,413	76,413	76,413	458,480
units	62,000	62,400	74,880	86,400	86,400	86,400	458,480
	14,413	14,013	1,533	(9,987)	(9,987)	(9,987)	0
@ £8.9426/unit	£128,893	£125,316	£13,712	£(89,307)	£(89,307)	£(89,307)	£0
Cumulative stock adjustment	£128,893	£254,208	£267,920	£178,614	£89,307	£0	
Total finished goods stock	£560,204	£771,782	£889,008	£799,702	£710,395	£621,088	

E11.7 Earextensions

Trade debtors budget (£)

Sales		Jan	Feb	Mar	Apr	May	Jun
	2,500,000	2,500,000	2,500,000				
	3,000,000		3,000,000	3,000,000			
	4,320,000			3,600,000	3,600,000		
	4,320,000				4,320,000	4,320,000	
	4,320,000					4,320,000	4,320,000
	4,320,000						4,320,000
Total debtors		2,500,000	5,500,000	6,600,000	7,920,000	8,640,000	8,640,000

Trade creditors budget (£)

Materials purchases		Jan	Feb	Mar	Apr	May	Jun
	303,000	303,000	303,000				
	2,148,160	2,148,160	2,148,160	2,148,160			
	1,805,232		1,805,232	1,805,232	1,805,232		
	2,120,832			2,120,832	2,120,832	2,120,832	
	2,272,320				2,272,320	2,272,320	2,272,320
	2,272,320					2,272,320	2,272,320
	2,272,320						2,272,320
Total creditors		2,451,160	4,256,392	6,074,224	6,198,384	6,665,472	6,816,960

Cash flow budget (£)

Customer receipts	Jan	Feb	Mar	Apr	May	Jun	Total
	0	0	2,500,000	3,000,000	3,600,000	4,320,000	13,420,000
Supplier payments	0	0	303,000	2,148,160	1,805,232	2,120,832	6,377,224
Direct labour	43,400	43,680	52,416	60,480	60,480	60,480	320,936
Overheads	675,000	675,000	675,000	675,000	675,000	675,000	4,050,000
Selling and administrative costs	900,000	900,000	900,000	600,000	600,000	600,000	4,500,000
Interest	5,000	6,000	7,200	8,640	8,640	8,640	44,120
Total payments	1,623,400	1,624,680	1,937,616	3,492,280	3,149,352	3,464,952	15,292,280

Cash flow	(1,623,400)	(1,624,680)	562,384	(492,280)	450,648	855,048	(1,872,280)
Opening balance	355,000	(1,268,400)	(2,893,080)	(2,330,696)	(2,822,976)	(2,372,328)	355,000
Closing balance	(1,268,400)	(2,893,080)	(2,330,696)	(2,822,976)	(2,372,328)	(1,517,280)	(1,517,280)

E11.8 Earextensions

Balance sheet budget (£)

	Dec	Jan	Feb	Mar	Apr	May	Jun	Depreciation per month
Fixed assets	495,000	486,666	478,332	470,000	461,666	453,333	445,000	8,333
Stocks	303,000	1,380,764	1,756,454	2,025,168	1,935,862	1,846,555	1,757,248	
Trade debtors	0	2,500,000	5,500,000	6,600,000	7,920,000	8,640,000	8,640,000	
Cash and bank	355,000	(1,268,400)	(2,893,080)	(2,330,696)	(2,822,976)	(2,372,328)	(1,517,280)	
	1,153,000	3,099,030	4,841,706	6,764,472	7,494,552	8,567,560	9,324,968	
Trade creditors	303,000	2,451,160	4,256,392	6,074,224	6,198,384	6,665,472	6,816,960	
Loans	450,000	450,000	450,000	450,000	450,000	450,000	450,000	
Share capital	400,000	400,000	400,000	400,000	400,000	400,000	400,000	
Retained earnings	0	(202,130)	(264,686)	(159,752)	446,168	1,052,088	1,658,008	
	1,153,000	3,099,030	4,841,706	6,764,472	7,494,552	8,567,560	9,324,968	

Chapter 12

E12.1 Nilbog

Flexed budget

		Budget		Flexed		Actual	
Units (Fishermen)							
Opening stock finished goods		0		0		0	
Unit production		10,000		9,600		9,600	
Unit sales		10,000		9,000		9,000	
Closing stock finished goods		0		600		600	
Cubic yards (materials)							
Opening stock materials		0		0		0	
Materials purchases		30,000		30,800		30,000	
Materials usage		30,000		28,800		28,000	
Closing stock materials		0		2,000		2,000	

Figures in £							**Actual to Flexed Budget Variances**	
Sales	(10,000 × 48)	480,000	(9,000 × 48)	432,000	(9,000 × 48)	432,000	sales price	0
Opening stock:								
Finished goods		0		0		0		
Materials		0		0		0		
Materials purchased	(10,000 × 3 × 3.6)	(108,000)	((9,600 × 3 + 2,000) × 3.6)	(110,880)	(30,000 × 3.84)	(115,200)	materials price	(7,200) 30,000 × (3.6 − 3.84)
							materials quality	2,880 (30,800 − 30,000) × 3.6
Direct labour	(10,000 × 2 × 6.6)	(132,000)	(9,600 × 2 × 6.6)	(126,720)	(22,000 × 6.48)	(142,560)	labour rate	2,640 22,000 × (6.6 − 6.48)
							labour efficiency	(18,480) (19,200 − 22,000) × 6.6
Variable overhead	(10,000 × 2 × 2.4)	(48,000)	(9,600 × 2 × 2.4)	(46,080)	(22,000 × 2.0)	(44,000)	overhead spend	8,800 22,000 × (2.4 − 2.0)
							overhead efficiency	(6,720) (19,200 − 22,000) × 2.4
Fixed overhead	(10,000 × 2 × 4.8)	(96,000)		(96,000)		(100,000)	overhead spend	(4,000) 96,000 − 100,000
Closing stock:								
Finished goods		0	(600 × 38.4)	23,040	(600 × 38.4)	23,040		
Materials		0	(2,000 × 3.6)	7,200	(2,000 × 3.6)	7,200		
Net profit		96,000		82,560		60,480		(22,080)
Net profit £ per unit		9.60		9.17		6.72		

Flexed budget to budget variances

Sales volume   (9,600) (10,000 − 9,000) × 9.6

Fixed overhead volume

   (3,840) (10,000 × 2) × 4.8 − (9,600 × 2) × 4.8

Total variances   (35,520) actual minus budget profit

Operating statement for period 5 in 2001 (4 weeks)

		£
Budget sales	10,000 × £48	480,000
Standard cost of sales	10,000 × £38.4	384,000
Budgeted profit		96,000

Variances	Favourable £	Unfavourable £	
Sales volume		9,600	
Materials			
Price		7,200	
Quantity	2,880		
Direct labour			
Rate	2,640		
Efficiency		18,480	
Variable overhead			
Expenditure	8,800		
Efficiency		6,720	
Fixed overhead			
Expenditure		4,000	
Volume		3,840	
	14,320	49,840	(35,520)
Actual profit			60,480

Stock is valued at standard cost at each month end so that a true month activity is reported, not previous inadequacies.

Variances	Favourable £	Unfavourable £	Likely causes of variances
Sales volume		9,600	An extra 1,000 units had been planned for period 5 at £9.60/unit standard profit.
Materials			
Price		7,200	Factors may be economic, currency fluctuations or poor standards.
Quantity	2,880		Low defects, better quality, better stock control, different production methods, improved labour training.
Direct labour			
Rate	2,640		Lower grade, union negotiation, less overtime.
Efficiency		18,480	Machine breakdowns, rework (but not apparent from materials quantity).
Variable overhead			
Expenditure	8,800		Poor standard, tighter cost control.
Efficiency		6,720	Machine breakdowns, rework (but not apparent from materials quantity).

Fixed overhead

Expenditure	4,000	
Volume	3,840	Under-recoveries of fixed overhead because of low volumes.
	14,320	49,840

E12.3 White Heaven

(i) Ideal standard cost per Shell

		£	£
Direct materials			
Clay	5 kg × £2.00	10.00	
Glaze	3 kg × £4.00	12.00	
			22.00
Direct labour			
Grade A	1 hour × £7.20	7.20	
Grade B	0.75 hours × £6.00	4.50	
			11.70
Indirect labour	0.25 hours × £5.00	1.25	
Maintenance	0.05 hours × £10.00	0.50	
Variable overhead			
Direct materials	15% × £22.00	3.30	
Direct labour	10% × £11.70	1.17	
			6.22
Total variable costs			39.92
Fixed overhead cost			
Supervisors' salaries	£95,000/50,000	1.90	
Other	£109,000/50,000	2.18	
			4.08
Ideal standard cost per Shell			44.00

(ii)

Grade A direct labour

Originally 1 operator working for 1 hour made 1 Shell

Or, 10 operators each working for 1 hours made 10 Shells

Now 1 operator working for 1 hour makes 0.5 Shells
And 9 operators each working for 1 hour makes 9 Shells
So 10 operators each working for 1 hour makes 9.5 Shells

So 1 Shell takes $\frac{10}{9.5}$ hours = 1.053 hours

The rate is now £7.20 + £0.40 or £7.60 per hour
Therefore 1 Shell costs 1.053 hours × £7.60 = £8.00 direct labour

Grade B direct labour

Originally 1 operator working for 0.75 hours made 1 Shell

Or, 10 operators each working for 0.75 hours made 10 Shells

Now 1 operator working for 0.80 hours would ideally make 1 Shell

Or, 10 operators each working for 0.80 hours would ideally make 10 Shells

But 2.5 operators working for 0.80 hours only make 0.6 Shells each or 1.5 Shells

And 7.5 operators each working for 0.80 hours make 1 Shell each or 7.5 Shells

So 10 operators each working for 0.80 hours make 9 Shells

So 1 Shell takes $\frac{8}{9}$ hours $= 0.889$ hours

The rate is now £6.00 + £0.30 or £6.30 per hour

Therefore 1 Shell costs 0.889 hours $\times$ £6.30 = £5.60 direct labour

Attainable standard cost per Shell

		£	£
Direct materials			
Clay	£10.00 + 10%	11.00	
Glaze	£12.00 − 12.5%	10.50	
			21.50
Direct labour			
Grade A	see workings	8.00	
Grade B	see workings	5.60	
			13.60
Indirect labour	0.25 hours × £5.20	1.30	
Maintenance	0.05 hours × £10.20	0.51	
Variable overhead			
Direct material			
Clay	15% × £11.00	1.65	
Glaze	20% × £10.50	2.10	
Direct labour	10% × £13.6	1.36	
			6.92
Total variable costs			42.02
Fixed overhead cost			
Supervisors' salaries	£95,000/50,000	1.90	
Other	£109,000/50,000	2.18	
			4.08
Attainable standard cost per Shell			46.10

(iii)

Ideal standard cost per Shell	= £44.00 × 49,000 units	= £2,156,000
Attainable standard cost per Shell	= £46.10 × 49,000 units	= £2,258,900
Variance	= £2.10 × 49,000 units	= £102,900

E12.5 Millennium

	Budget	Flexed	Actual		Variances
Units	4,300	4,100	4,100		
	£	£	£		£
Sales	25,112	23,944	24,805	price	
	4,300 × £5.84	4,100 × £5.84	4,100 × £6.05	4,100 × (5.84 − 6.05)	861F
Materials	7,310	6,970	7,169	price	
	4,300 × 2 × £0.85	4,100 × 2 × £0.85	(6,600 × £0.83)	8,500 × (0.8434 − 0.85)	56F
			+(1,900 × £0.89)	quantity	
				0.85 × (8,500 − 8,200)	255A
Labour	12,642	12,054	13,387.50	rate	
	4,300 × 0.7 × £4.20	4,100 × 0.7 × £4.20	2,975 × £4.50	2,975 × (4.50 − 4.20)	892.50A
				efficiency	
				4.20 × (2,870 − 2,975)	441A
Contribution	5,160	4,920	4,248.50		
Fixed overhead	3,526	3,526	3,800	spend	
	4,300 × £0.82			3,526 − 3,800	274A
Profit	1,634	1,394	448.50		
Profit per unit	£0.38				
	£1,634/4,300				
Volume variance	1,634	1,394		sales	
	budget profit	− flexed budget		0.38 × (4,100 − 4,300)	76A
				fixed overhead	
				0.82 × (4,100 − 4,300)	164A
Total variances					1,185.50A

	£	£
Budget profit		1,634
Sales variances		
Price	861F	
Volume	76A	785F
Materials variances		
Price	56F	
Quantity	255A	199A
Labour variances		
Rate	892.50A	
Efficiency	441A	1,333.50A
Fixed overhead variances		
Spend	274A	
Volume	164A	438A
Actual profit		448.50

Chapter 13

E13.3 Lubosh

All the cash flows in the question apart from the initial investment are real cash flows.

Using the rates quoted calculate the money cash flows:

Cash inflows

Year	£m	Net £m
1	50	50
2	50×1.07	53.5
3	50×1.07^2	57.245

Cash outflows

Year	£m	Net £m
0	40	40
1	30	30
2	30×1.08	32.4
3	30×1.08^2	34.992

Calculate NPV

Year		Net cash flow in money terms £m	Discount factor @ 17%	DCF £m
0		−40	1.00	−40
1	[50 − 30]	20	0.85	17
2	[53.5 − 32.4]	21.1	0.73	15.403
3	[57.245 − 34.992]	22.253	0.62	13.79686
Total				6.19986

NPV is £6,199,860.

The Mondino project pays back in cash terms in less than two years but in more than 18 months, and pays back in discounted cash terms in less than three years but in more than two years. Neither comply with Lubosh plc's criteria. You should calculate the IRR of the Mondino project using the interpolation/extrapolation technique described in Chapter 13.

You should refer to the relevant sections in Chapter 13 to check your assessment of further considerations and your recommendation as to whether Lubosh should undertake the Mondino project.

E13.8 AAK

(i)

Year	Equipment £000	Running costs £000	Lighting, heating, etc. £000	Total outflow £000	10% discount rate £000	Present value £000
0	120			120	1.00	120.000
1		40	15	55	0.91	50.050
2		44	15	59	0.83	48.970
3		48	15	63	0.75	47.250
4		52	15	67	0.68	45.560
5		56	15	71	0.62	44.020
Present value						355.850

We can assume that the annual sales at the full level is S. We first need to calculate the present value of each year's expected sales.

Year	Sales	10% discount rate	Present value
1	0.4S	0.91	0.364S
2	0.7S	0.83	0.581S
3	1.0S	0.75	0.750S
4	1.0S	0.68	0.680S
5	1.0S	0.62	0.620S
Present value			2.995S

Contribution $=$ sales $-$ variable costs

Because the prices of drinks are to be set at double their direct (variable) costs then half of the total present value of sales 2.995S must represent direct costs and the other half must represent contribution.

Therefore contribution $= \dfrac{2.995S}{2}$

$= 1.4975S$ which is the present value of the contribution from the drinks

To break-even at an annual interest rate of 10% the present value of the contribution from drinks must equal the present value of the total outgoings, which is £355,850.

$$1.4975S = £355,850$$

$$S = £237,629$$

Therefore the required sales of drinks in each year are:

Year		£
1	£237,629 × 40%	95,052
2	£237,629 × 70%	166,341
3		237,629
4		237,629
5		237,629

(ii) Aspects of the proposals that require further investigation:

● Can the facilities be used outside normal opening hours for alternative uses in order to increase the contribution?

- Has market research been carried out to support the belief that there will be additional future benefits?
- Will the proposed cost plus drinks pricing methods result in competitive prices?
- Perhaps there is a better way for this project to utilise the space and the capital, and perhaps food may be an option.

E13.9 Lew Rolls

(i)

				Super			Superlux			Exec			Excel	
	10%	20%		10%	20%		10%	20%		10%	20%		10%	20%
Year	DF	DF	CF	DCF	DCF	CF	DCF	DCF	CF	DCF	DCF	CF	DCF	DCF
			£m	£m	£m	£m	£m	£m	£m	£m	£m	£m	£m	£m
0	1.00	1.00	−3	−3	−3	−7	−7	−7	−12	−12	−12	−15	−15	−15
1	0.91	0.83	1	0.91	0.83	2	1.82	1.66	0	0	0	10	9.10	8.30
2	0.83	0.69	1	0.83	0.69	2	1.66	1.38	0	0	0	10	8.30	6.90
3	0.75	0.58	1	0.75	0.58	2	1.50	1.16	7	5.25	4.06	0	0	0
4	0.68	0.48	1	0.68	0.48	2	1.36	0.96	7	4.76	3.36	0	0	0
5	0.62	0.40	1	0.62	0.40	2	1.24	0.80	7	4.34	2.80	0	0	0
Total			2	0.79	−0.02	3	0.58	−1.04	9	2.35	−1.78	5	2.40	0.20

(ii)
Calculation of IRR

From the table above calculate the IRR for each of the projects using interpolation/extrapolation as shown in Figs 13.3 and 13.4 in Chapter 13 to obtain:

	Super	Superlux	Exec	Excel
IRR	19.8%	13.6%	15.7%	20.9%
Ranking of projects (highest IRR ranked 1st)	2	4	3	1

(iii)
Net present value

	Super	Superlux	Exec	Excel
NPV of each project	£790,000	£580,000	£2,350,000	£2,400,000
NPV/£ invested	£0.263	£0.083	£0.196	£0.160
Ranking	1	4	2	3

NPV per £ invested is the more reliable evaluation method for appraisal of this project therefore, given the £24m total investment constraint the decision should be to invest:

	£m	NPV per £ invested	NPV £
Project A	3	£0.263	790,000
Project C	12	£0.196	2,350,000
Project D	9	£0.160	1,440,000
Project B	0	£0.083	0
Optimum total NPV			£4,580,000

If IRR rankings were used to make the investment decision:

Project D	15	£0.160	2,400,000
Project A	3	£0.263	790,000
Project C	6	£0.196	1,175,000
Project B	0	£0.083	0
Total NPV			£4,365,000

which is not optimal

(iv) and (v) You should refer to the relevent sections in Chapter 13 to check your solutions.

Chapter 14

E14.3 Priory

(i) Net debt to equity

Net debt	100	250	800
Equity	300	500	800
Gearing (%)	33%	50%	100%

(ii) Long-term loans to equity and long-term loans

Long-term loans	200	200	600
Equity/LTL	500	700	1,400
Gearing (%)	40%	29%	43%

E14.4 Lucky Jim

If shareholders' equity is E and the net financial debt D
then the relative proportions of equity and debt in the total financing are:

$$\frac{E}{E + D} \text{ and } \frac{D}{E + D}$$

$$\frac{E}{E + D} = 2/3$$

$$\frac{D}{E + D} = 1/3$$

Cost of equity $e = 18\%$

Return on financial debt $d = 12\%$

WACC = $(2/3 \times 18\%) + (1/3 \times 12\%) = 12\% + 4\% = 16\%$

The present value of future cash flows in perpetuity $= \dfrac{\text{annual cash flows}}{\text{annual discount rate}\%}$

$$= \frac{£35,000}{0.16} = £218,750$$

Net present value, NPV = £218,750 − £200,000 = £18,750

Using WACC to discount the cash flows of the project, the result is a positive NPV of £18,750 and therefore the project should be undertaken.

E14.5 Supermarket

	2001	**2000**	**1999**
Adjusted net assets	£5,000m	£4,769m	£4,377m
Market value	£17,808m	£11,531m	£11,995m
MVA	£12,808m	£6,762m	£7,618m

Chapter 15

E15.1 Oliver

Production costs

		£	
Raw materials	[40% × £5,300,000]	2,120,000	held in stock on average 4 days
Direct labour	[25% × £5,300,000]	1,325,000	finished goods held in stock
Overheads	[10% × £5,300,000]	530,000	on average 7 days
		3,975,000	

The production cycle is 14 days

Working capital requirement

			£		£
Raw materials	[£2,120,000 × 4/365]			=	23,233
Work in progress					
Raw materials	[£2,120,000 × 14/365]	=	81,315		
Direct labour	[£1,325,000 × 14/365 × 25%]	=	12,705		
Overheads	[£530,000 × 14/365 × 25%]	=	5,082		
					99,102
Finished goods	[£3,975,000 × 7/365]			=	76,233
Debtors	[£5,300,000 × 60/365]			=	871,223
Creditors	[£2,120,000 × 30/365]			=	(174,247)
Total working capital requirement					895,544

E15.5 Worrall

Cost of sales is 80% of sales

Variable cost of sales	80% × 90%	=	72% of sales
Therefore			
Contribution		=	28% of sales

Proposed debtors

Sales, increased by 20% are	120% × £8m = £9.6m		
Credit allowed increased to 90 days	£9.6m × 90/365	=	£2,367,123
Current debtors	£8m × 60/365	=	£1,315,068
Increase in debtors		=	£1,052,055

Gains

Increase in contribution	(£9.6m − £8.0m) × 28%	=	£448,000
Losses			
Increase in bad debts	(3% × £2,367,123) − (2% × £1,315,068)	=	£44,713
Increase in financing costs	£1,052,055 × 10%	=	£105,206
Total losses per annum			£149,919
Net gain			£298,081

The net gain to Worrall Ltd is £298,081 per annum and so an increase to 90 days' credit may be recommended.

Appendix 1

EA1.1 Hall

Hall Ltd
Profit and loss account for the year ended 31 December 2000

	2000 £	1999 £
Sales	12,000	11,000
Cost of sales	8,000	7,000
Gross profit	4,000	4,000
Expenses	3,000	2,500
Operating profit	1,000	1,500

Working
1999
Cost of sales: opening stock £600 + purchases £7,100 less closing stock £700
2000
Cost of sales: opening stock £700 + purchases £8,300 less closing stock £800 less the obsolete stock of £200
Cost of sales for 2000 must exclude obsolete stock as it has not been sold
Expenses £2,800 plus the obsolete stock £200

EA1.2 Accruals

(a) The invoices for the common utilities rarely coincide with accounting period ends. To ensure that costs up to the year end are appropriately included, an adjustment is required for the consumption between the invoice date and year end.

(b)

	Debit £	Credit £
Profit and loss account		
Electricity to 15 December 2000	10,000	
Accruals for charges 16 to 31 December 2000	300	
Total electricity costs for the year 2000	10,300	
Gas to 20 December 2000	5,000	
Accruals for charges 21 to 31 December 2000	150	
Total gas costs for the year 2000	5,150	
Balance sheet		
Electricity accrual at 31 December 2000		(300)
Gas accrual at 31 December 2000		(150)
Total accruals at 31 December 2000		(450)

EA1.7 Oblivion

Oblivion Ltd
Profit and loss account for March 2000

	Addition to profit £	Reduction to profit £	Profit £
Profit per draft accounts	41,000		41,000
Discounts allowed to customers		1,248	(1,248)
Sales invoice missed out	857		857
Transposition error (£540 entered as £450)		90	(90)
Missed bank charge		660	(660)
Discounts received from suppliers	1,200		1,200
Revised profit	43,057	1,998	41,059

EA1.8 Etcoakco

Capital

	Debit £	Credit £
Transaction 1		100,000
Balance c/f	100,000	
	100,000	100,000
Balance b/f @ 1/1/01		100,000

Cash

	Debit £	Credit £
Transaction 1	100,000	
Transaction 2		50,000
Transaction 3		7,000
Transaction 5		400
Transaction 11	27,600	
Balance c/f		70,200
	127,600	127,600
Balance b/f @ 1/1/01	70,200	

Fixed assets – shop

	Debit £	Credit £
Transaction 2	50,000	
Balance c/f		50,000
	50,000	50,000
Balance b/f @ 1/1/01	50,000	

Fixed assets – fittings/equipment

	Debit £	Credit £
Transaction 3	7,000	
Transaction 4	20,000	
Balance c/f		27,000
	27,000	27,000
Balance b/f @ 1/1/01	27,000	

Printing/stationery expenses

	Debit £	Credit £
Transaction 5	400	
Balance c/f		400
	400	400
Balance b/f @ 1/1/01	400	

Payables

	Debit £	Credit £
Transaction 4		20,000
Transaction 6		31,250
Balance c/f	51,250	
	51,250	51,250
Balance b/f @ 1/1/01		51,250

Stock

	Debit £	Credit £
Transaction 6	31,250	
Transaction 10		27,500
Balance c/f		3,750
	31,250	31,250
Balance b/f @ 1/1/01	3,750	

Sales

	Debit £	Credit £
Transaction 7		23,000
Transaction 8		27,600
Balance c/f	50,600	
	50,600	50,600
Balance b/f @ 1/1/01		50,600

Receivables

Transaction 7	23,000	
Transaction 8	27,600	
Transaction 11		27,600
Balance c/f		23,000
	50,600	50,600
Balance b/f @ 1/1/01	23,000	

Cost of sales

Transaction 10	27,500	
Balance c/f		27,500
	27,500	27,500
Balance b/f @ 1/1/01	27,500	

Index

The names of companies mentioned in the book are in **bold** type.
Definitions of key terms may be found on the pages that are highlighted in colour.

Tomkins 159, 174, 251–2, 265
top-down process 176, 180
total productive maintenance (TPM)
    335, 341
total quality control (TQC) 335, 341
total quality management (TQM) 340,
    342
trade creditors (or accounts payable or
    purchase ledger) 4, 25, 47, 49,
    580, 582, 597, 598
trade debtors (or accounts receivable
    or sales ledger) 4, 25, 37, 51,
    62, 65, 580, 583, 597, 599
TransTec 253
Travelodge 297, 350
treasury management 3, 27
trend analysis 210–11, 538
trial balance 53, 65, 579, 585, 599
true and fair view 14, 27
turnover 80, 107
TVR 542

under-absorption of overhead 291,
    300
unit cost 288, 300
unsystematic risk (or market risk)
    509, 520
Urgent Issues Task Force (UITF) 19
users of financial information 10–11

valuation
    of debtors 62–3

of fixed assets 58–61
of stocks 61–2
value
    analysis 334, 342
    engineering 334, 342
    expected 374, 378
value added statement 226–9, 231
    advantages 226
    classification of items 228
    disadvantages 228
variable cost (marginal cost) 283, 300,
    359
variable production overhead
    289–91
variance 390, 414
    adverse 428
    direct labour efficiency 431,
        435
    direct labour rate 431, 435
    direct materials price 431, 435
    direct material usage 431, 435
    favourable 428
    operational 443, 445
    overhead 431, 436
    planning 443, 445
    sales price 432–9
    sales volume 432–9
variance analysis 390, 414, 428–32
    flexed budget 425–8
    operating statement 434
    percentage rule 443
    reasons for variances 442–3

statistical control charts 443
statistical significance rule 443
Vauxhall 351, 392, 534
vendor managed inventory (VMI)
    540, 563
Versailles 253
vertical analysis 150, 180, 211–12
vertical format balance sheet 52–3
Virgin Air 28
Volkswagen (VW) 358
voluntary winding up 255, 262

waste 534–7
weighted average cost of capital
    (WACC) 159, 180,
    504–6
window dressing 44, 66
working capital (WC) 37, 66, 526,
    527–33
    cycle 528–9
    policy 533–4
working capital management 526
    bank overdrafts 556
    cash, see cash management
    debtors, see debtor management
    stocks, see stocks management
    trade creditors, see creditor
        management
working capital requirement (WCR)
    115, 138, 527–33
work-in-progress 95, 107
wrongful trading 256, 262